MASTERPLOTS II

POETRY SERIES

MASTERPLOTS II

POETRY
SERIES

4

Luk-Pre

Edited by
FRANK N. MAGILL

SALEM PRESS

Pasadena, California   Englewood Cliffs, New Jersey

Library of Congress Cataloging-in-Publication Data
Masterplots II: Poetry series/edited by Frank N. Magill
   p. cm.
   Includes bibliographical references and index.
      1. Poetry—Themes, motives. I. Magill, Frank
   Northen, 1907-
   PN1110.5.M37 1992   91-44341
   809.1—dc20   CIP
   ISBN 0-89356-584-9 (set)
   ISBN 0-89356-588-1 (volume 4)

PRINTED IN THE UNITED STATES OF AMERICA

LIST OF TITLES IN VOLUME 4

MASTERPLOTS II

POETRY SERIES

LUKE HAVERGAL

Author: Edwin Arlington Robinson (1869-1935)
Type of poem: Lyric
First published: 1897, in *The Children of the Night*

The Poem

"Luke Havergal" is a haunting poem of thirty-two lines about a desperately be-reaved man being tempted by a voice from the grave to commit suicide in order to reunite with a beloved woman who is dead.

One of Edwin Arlington Robinson's finest performances, "Luke Havergal" was a favorite of President Theodore Roosevelt, who, even though he promoted the poem and the poet's career, found the contents of the poem to be obscure in meaning. Although Robinson by his own admission aimed "to put a little mysticism" in his verses, the morbid death-prone mysticism of "Luke Havergal" is not all that diffi-cult to decipher. The poem conveys, through sound and image, a compelling emo-tion of a half-crazed longing for love that entices a man grieving over the death of his beloved woman to take his own life.

Reared in Gardiner, Maine, Edwin Arlington Robinson created a mythical "Til-bury Town" out of his New England birthplace and populated the fictional place with eccentrics, such as this desolate lover, who lead wasted, blighted, or impoverished lives. The poet was an American exemplar of the realism permeating European liter-ature, especially novels and short stories, in the second half of the nineteenth cen-tury. Appropriately, "Luke Havergal" reads like a revealing and realistic short story in verse, providing readers with a snapshot portrait of a lonely main character; its "plot" is a sad case of grief-stricken abandonment of the desire to live, and the pursuit of a beloved woman in death.

The first stanza is an exhortation by a voice from the grave tempting Luke Haver-gal to reunite with a departed woman through a journey into death in a place of falling leaves, twilight, and setting sun.

The second and third stanzas repeat the call for Luke Havergal to seek darkness and death in the gloomy west on a bitter, suicidal walk lit, not by the dawn of the rising sun in the east, but by the fire of his unrequited, desperate passion flashing from his eyes and reflecting on his forehead. The falling leaves are but a reminder of a dying nature and a dying Creator of nature (lines 13-14) that seem in sympathy with Luke Havergal's suicidal thoughts. Death is good, and to be in hell beside the departed woman will almost be a heaven for Luke Havergal.

The final stanza practically repeats the first stanza as it presents the voice's cli-mactic, and possibly successful, effort to seduce lonely and lovestricken Luke Hav-ergal to trade his wretched life for a promise of romance in the grave.

Forms and Devices

"Luke Havergal" is a lyric poem consisting of four stanzas whose prevailing meter is iambic pentameter with variations. The eighth line of each stanza is an iambic dimeter beat echoing the sound and sense of the previous line in its closing words ("In eastern skies," "To tell you this," "Luke Havergal").

Of particular interest in each eight-line stanza is the unusual and intricate rhyme scheme (*aabbaaaa*), which repeats final sounds so as to convey a powerfully cumulative insistence in the voice's seduction of poor Luke Havergal. This repetition of final sounds combines with the repetitious last two lines of each stanza to provide Luke with an almost unavoidable compulsion to commit a romantic suicide.

The images and allusions all stress darkness and death—the destination and terrible outcome of Luke Havergal's romantic desolation and desperation. In contrast to the rising sun of "eastern skies" is Luke's wild "twilight" time for a walk to the gloomy "western gate" of the setting sun, under which vines bloom to a terminal blood-red ripeness and where leaves fall like fleeting and fading words that are ultimately indecipherable. Luke's eyes are fiery red, and his forehead is flushed crimson. It provides him with an unnatural light for his way into the dark on his topsy-turvy pilgrimage into hell, activated by his misplaced fidelity to the memory of his beloved dead lady. Like a God who slays Himself—possibly like a Christ-Creator who allows Himself to be crucified—Luke finds himself tempted to harrow hell, through suicide, in an attempt to recover the object of his desire.

Most important, this suicidal pilgrimage may well be Robinson's modern version of the classical journey into Hades by a Roman hero such as Aeneas. Aeneas was similarly drawn into a dark rendezvous with his dead lover, Queen Dido, under the guidance of the Sibyl, the Roman prophetess at Cumae in Vergil's great epic poem, the *Aeneid* (c. 29-19 B.C.). In fact, the ruling motif of Robinson's entire poem seems to be this classical allusion to the Sibyl at Cumae by the gates of Hades. The motif of the Vergilian journey into Hades acts as an implicit underlying contrast for the desperate romantic plight of a modern antihero, Luke Havergal.

Themes and Meanings

"Luke Havergal" is an address to a lovelorn man, spoken by a seductive voice from beyond the grave to encourage him to rejoin a dead lover by taking his own life. He is told that he may find her through suicide. Although the poem might appear to display a faith in life after death, the intense desolation of his experience points, rather, to an expression of longing for death and an inability to endure more life in such grief-stricken loneliness.

Readers coming to terms with the poem should have in mind the famous classical tale of Aeneas' walk into Hades, led by the Sibyl at Cumae (who communicated prophecies on torn leaves blown into the wind). They were on their way to meet his former lover, the dead Queen Dido, who had committed suicide; the story appears in book 2 of Vergil's *Aeneid*. If Luke Havergal is reminded that sacrifice is necessary for his descent into the dark and his reunion with his beloved ("God slays Himself with every leaf that flies,/ And hell is more than half of paradise"), analogously the Roman hero Aeneas must wait until the Sibyl sacrifices to the goddess of the night for his entrance into the underworld where his suicidal lover Dido passes her melancholy existence.

What follows is a paraphrase of pertinent passages from book 2 of the *Aeneid* for comparison with "Luke Havergal." Aeneas had been told by the prophet Helenus to seek, upon his arrival at Italy, the cave of the Sibyl at Cumae, a woman of deep wisdom, who could foretell the future and give Aeneas proper advice for founding the great Roman empire. Aeneas found her, and she warned him that the descent to the underworld was easy but that the return was perilous. Aenas and the Sibyl found themselves in the Fields of Mourning, where unhappy lovers dwelled who had been driven to suicide. There Aeneas caught sight of Dido and, weeping, addressed her: "Was I the cause of your death? I left you against my will." She, like a piece of marble, was silent and averted her gaze. He was shaken and wept long after he lost sight of her.

Thomas M. Curley

LULLABY

Author: W. H. Auden (1907-1973)
Type of poem: Lyric
First published: 1937; collected in *Another Time*, 1940

The Poem

W. H. Auden's "Lullaby," his most famous love lyric, perhaps is better known by its famous first line, "Lay your sleeping head, my love." In musical and rhetorical lines of mostly trochaic tetrameter verse, the narrator watches his sleeping lover through the night and, in four ten-line stanzas, reflects upon the value and necessity of both passionate love and beauty and their brevity.

The speaker gazes upon his lover beside him and sings this philosophical "lullaby" about love, beauty, and time's ruthless pull. The speaker realizes that time eventually will erode his lover's beauty, as it some day will suck children down into their graves. He prays to be allowed to hold his beloved in his admittedly "faithless arm" until dawn, because at this enchanted moment the beloved seems to him to be "entirely beautiful." The speaker asks for a temporary reprieve from time for this one exquisite night to prolong the beauty of the moment and of his lover.

In the next stanza, the narrator reflects on the timeless and boundless feelings people experience when they are ardently in love and feel united in body and soul. Lovers seem to "swoon" into an enchanted union in which their bodies and spirits merge—it is as if Venus, the goddess of love, suffused them with feelings of sympathy, "Universal love," and "hope" so that the mortals feel unity and timelessness. Into this idyllic feeling of timeless passion, Auden inserts another form of intense "carnal ecstasy," which is experienced through the mind. Ascetic hermits through abstract thought find a mystical passion that also leads to feelings of unity and timelessness. Auden equates these two different modes of finding passionate and timeless unity—one through the body with a mortal lover, and one through the mind with a spiritual entity.

As in many Auden poems, there is a sudden reversal in the third stanza. The speaker makes an ironic shift in attitude away from the timeless feelings of ecstasy associated with passionate love to the more realistic view that this moment of tenderness and ecstasy may vanish at the stroke of midnight. Even though he realizes that nothing is certain and his lover's faithfulness may evaporate, even though this moment of passion may be as short-lived as the latest fashionable madman's ranting, and even though this night may cost him dearly, the speaker is ready to pay the costs and to suffer whatever pains the cards of fortune may heap upon him. At any cost, he wants nothing to be lost from this one magical, fleeting night— "Not a whisper, not a thought,/ Not a kiss nor look." He wants to seize this night of passionate ecstasy from time and make it eternal.

In the last stanza, the magical night ends, the vision of beauty and love fades, but the speaker prays for a benevolent day that will bless his still dreaming lover. Apparently, the speaker has been contemplating the beauty of his lover and their passion the entire night. The speaker hopes that the dawn brings his beloved a day so beautiful that this lovely mortal world will obliterate the need for supernatural worlds — the day should be a veritable heaven on earth. He invokes the "involuntary powers" of love, beauty, and poetry, and hopes they will feed the lover so that he may survive all the times of dryness and times of insults that life may bring. The speaker wishes his lover will be blessed and soothed by this lullaby and will be watched over by a benevolent godlike human love.

Forms and Devices

Auden was fond of rhetorical patterns of repetition, especially complex forms of parallelism leading to paradoxes. He also juxtaposed surprising ideas to create unique metaphors. For example, grammatically parallel phrases begin two of the last four lines of the poem. Line 37 begins with "Noons of dryness," and line 39 with "Nights of insult," which are ways Auden metaphorically depicts difficult time periods in life. "Noons of dryness" metaphorically links the hottest time of day to the tactile image of "dryness" to imply a kind sterile desert. "Noons" and "nights" are linked by parallelism, which implies that the speaker wants his beloved not only to wake up that day to joy and beauty, but also to be protected by his human love every day for his whole life. It is paradoxical that Auden uses specific times, noon and night, metaphorically to imply a wish for timeless love and joy.

The meditations on love, beauty, and passion in "Lullaby" take place over a single night which the speaker wishes to preserve. Auden makes this one night partially appear "timeless" by using present-tense verb forms in all stanzas of the poem: He uses "Lay" and "let" in stanza 1; tries "have," "lie," and "wakes" in stanza 2; employs "pass," "raise," and foretell in stanza 3; and ends with "Let," "bless," and "Find" in the final stanza. He makes this magical night consistently "present" so that subliminally one may participate in the speaker's meditation.

Auden favors speakers who seemingly are present, but also to some degree are detached from the action, contemplating it. His speaker in "Lullaby" has a complex vision of human love and sees the contradictory impulses and feelings implied. By asking a sleeping beloved, who cannot answer, to rest on his "faithless arm," the speaker implies that he wants love (but not necessarily undying fidelity) and that all human love is transient. Auden's speaker seems to be conscious of his own contrary impulses; he wants passion and wants it never to end, but knows it must end. He seems to observe himself thinking; the poem's readers look over his shoulder.

Themes and Meanings

Auden, who wrote many different forms of poetry, here blends two traditions — the nursery-rhyme lullaby and the *carpe diem* motif. Since the poem begins by addressing an adult lover, not a child as is usual in a lullaby, it is a non-traditional form of the lullaby. Yet the poem is also very musical; it ends by being soothing and wishing eternal love for the lover just as a parent might wish for eternal happiness for an innocent child in a traditional lullaby.

Auden also includes variations of the *carpe diem* theme in this lyric. In a traditional *carpe diem* poem, such as Andrew Marvell's "To His Coy Mistress," a male speaker, usually promising undying devotion and love, tries to persuade a reluctant or coy female beloved to make love to him now while they are still young and passionate rather than old and gray. He claims if they love each other they are, in a way, "married" and should consumate their passion. In "Lullaby," the gender of the beloved is ambiguous; since Auden was homosexual, both lover and beloved could be males. The speaker in "Lullaby," instead of promising eternal love, says that his arm is "faithless" and questions the whole notion of fidelity. Most *carpe diem* poems are attempts to establish a carnal affair, but Auden's poem seems to be set after the lovers have made love—a kind of post-coitus meditation. In both traditional *carpe diem* poems and Auden's "Lullaby," passionate love is primary and necessary. The goal of this poem and of more traditional *carpe diem* poems is to preserve a fleeting moment of carnal ecstasy and intense beauty and thereby temporarily to defeat time. In "Lullaby," therefore, Auden playfully and artistically weaves together non-traditional elements from both the *carpe diem* and lullaby traditions to create his own new hybrid form of poetry.

"Lullaby" also is about the power of poetry to accomplish the impossible—to freeze time temporarily. To make a magical night of love immortal and timeless, the poet writes a poem about it that captures the contrary pulls between passion, beauty, time, and human awareness of all three and relays it to readers in the present tense. By writing the poem, Auden attempts to preserve the feelings and attitudes evoked by one of the most powerful emotions humans ever experience: passionate love.

David J. Amante

LYCIDAS

Author: John Milton (1608-1674)
Type of poem: Elegy
First published: 1638, in *Justa Edouardo King*; collected in *Poems of Mr. John Milton*, 1645

The Poem

"Lycidas" is a pastoral elegy in which John Milton laments the drowning of his friend and schoolmate, Edward King, at the University of Cambridge. Mainly iambic pentameter, with irregularly appearing short lines of six syllables, the poem's 193 lines are divided into verse paragraphs of irregular length and changing rhyme schemes. In the convention of the pastoral poem, the first-person persona of the poem is a shepherd, who speaks of King as the lost shepherd Lycidas; in the convention of the elegy, "Lycidas" progresses through sadness over an individual's death and reflection on human mortality to a final consolation—not only in the redemptive message of Christianity, but in recognition of the social value of the poet's art. Milton uses these two forms not primarily to express personal grief over King's death, but to engage the dominant political and religious issues of his age.

"Lycidas" opens by addressing the laurels and myrtles, symbols of poetic fame; as their berries are not yet ripe, the poet is not yet ready to take up his pen. Yet the untimely death of young Lycidas requires equally untimely verses from the poet. Invoking the muses of poetic inspiration, the shepherd-poet takes up the task, partly, he says, in hope that his own death will not go unlamented.

The poet recalls his and Lycidas' life together in the "pastures" of Cambridge, and notes the "heavy change" suffered by nature now that Lycidas is gone—a "pathetic fallacy" in which the willows, hazel groves, woods, and caves lament Lycidas' death. Milton concludes this passage, however, by suggesting that nature's apparent sympathy is, in fact, the subjective perception of the mourning shepherds: "Such, Lycidas, thy loss to shepherd's ear" (line 49).

The shepherd-poet reflects in the following verse paragraph that thoughts of how Lycidas might have been saved are futile. The poet turns from lamenting Lycidas' death to lamenting the futility of all human labor: What meaning can work have when all life comes to this? Why not give oneself over to physical pleasures, the poet asks, when life may be cut short before one can attain the rewards of a moral life?

At this point, another voice asserts itself in response to the poet's questions; Phoebus, the sun-god, an image drawn out of the mythology of classical Roman poetry, replies that fame is not mortal but eternal, witnessed by Jove (God) himself on judgment day.

Milton then turns "Lycidas" to one of pastoral poetry's chief functions in the Renaissance, as commentary on ecclesiastical abuses. Following a procession of mythical nautical figures, "the pilot of the Galilean lake" (either Saint Peter or Christ) derides those shepherds (clergymen) who, unlike Lycidas, care more for their own well-being than for their sheep. Such shepherds neglect their flocks, "rot inwardly," and spread only disease. In a couplet that is clearly apocalyptic, the poet stresses the fate of such clergymen at the hands of God's avenging angel: "But that two-handed engine"—apparently a double-edged sword—"at the door,/ Stands ready to smite once, and smite no more" (lines 129-130).

The poem's pastoral landscape and elegiac tone then reassert themselves. The poet calls for flowers to deck the hearse of Lycidas but then recognizes that this is a foolish and simply rhetorical plea: Lycidas has no hearse since his body remains adrift in the sea. Such expressions are merely "false surmise" to comfort frail minds reticent to confront the awfulness of Lycidas' death and the dispiriting reflections to which it gives rise. The poet then invokes an explicitly Christian angel rather than a pagan, pastoral deity to "look homeward" (line 163) and pity those who grieve over the loss of Lycidas.

The last two verse paragraphs establish the elegy's Christian consolation and the poet's readiness now to embark on his poetic career. Lycidas is not dead but resurrected in Christ (lines 172-73). Shifting into third-person narrative, the poem concludes with the "uncouth swain," the shepherd-poet himself, rising and, in a gesture of hope, preparing to leave the pastures he shared with Lycidas for "fresh woods, and pastures new" (line 193).

Forms and Devices

The first function of the language of the poem is to create a sense of the pastoral environment, and Milton does this by continual reference to the natural elements of the countryside and to the pagan deities that haunt the pastoral landscapes of classical Greek and Roman poetry. The poet also needs to establish the allegorical reference of this pastoral to an English setting and to the issues that concerned King and himself as divinity students at Cambridge. Milton thus adds some specifically English and Christian figures to his cast of mythological characters: for example, Camus, the god of the River Cam that runs past Cambridge, and "the pilot of the Galilean lake."

The shifting rhyme scheme of the poem (and some lines have no rhymes at all) suggests the disorder created by Lycidas' death and, perhaps, the shepherd-poet's admitted inadequacies as a poet, although one recognizes it as the creation of Milton's own exceptional poetic talent. The irregular lengths of the verse paragraphs, ranging from eight to thirty-three lines long, also contribute to this atmosphere of disorder. The shepherds' sense of disorder in nature is reflected in the rhythm (the sound) of the poem: "Such, Lycidas, thy loss to shepherd's ear" (line 49).

The upset emotions that are themselves the true source of disorder are expressed also through the expletive repetition of key words and phrases: "once more" in line 1, "dead" in line 8, the name of Lycidas used three times in the first verse paragraph and continually throughout the poem, and "now thou art gone" in lines 38-39. Repetition also serves to introduce the final consolation of the poem, with "weep no more" repeated twice in line 165; here, however, the repetition is not an emotional expletive but a forceful imperative. This closing sense of consolation must then, in some way, dispel the psychological disorder of the shepherds and reestablish harmony in the poem. Indeed, the final verse paragraph, the shortest and most concise in the poem, contains the simplest rhyme scheme—*abababcc*—rhyming words that refer again to the beauties of the pastoral setting. Order can once again be found in nature and heard in the ears of the poem's readers.

Themes and Meanings

John Milton was an intensely religious writer, which is to say, a political writer, since in the seventeenth century, politics and religion were inseparable elements of English society. Milton's greatest work, *Paradise Lost* (1667), retells the story of Genesis in the form of an epic in order to "justify the ways of God to men" (*Paradise Lost*, line 26). The great political conflicts of the age, that led ultimately to the English Civil War in the 1640's, involved questions about the doctrinal and administrative nature of the Church of England. In the eyes of many of Milton's contemporaries, episcopacy (church administration by a hierarchy of bishoprics) left control of church doctrine in the hands of a few when people needed to be free to encounter scripture in light of their own rational understanding. Such a hierarchy of clergy also opened the church to abuse by individual clergymen whose motives were personal gain and political ambition, rather than the moral and spiritual instruction of their parishioners, their "flocks." Milton did not separate these political and religious concerns from his poetic interests. In fact, as one can judge from "Lycidas," these concerns constitute the motivation and foundation for his career as a poet.

Although the occasion of "Lycidas" is the death of Edward King, Milton's reflections on this loss lead to the central moral and political questions of the poem and of his own life: What is the meaning of a moral life when death can cut it off at any time? The rewards of the greedy and self-indulgent are evident in the physical pleasure they take from life; but what are the rewards of the good? What is the good of a religion administered by a corrupt clergy? What help is it to be a good man and, for Milton, a good poet?

Pastoral poetry was thought of by Renaissance writers as the poet's apprenticeship; poets must hone their skills in this form before attempting the greater achievement of epic. Milton's two chief models for this conception of the poet's career were Vergil (70-19 B.C.), the classical Roman poet who composed his pastoral *Eclogues* (43-37 B.C.) before writing his great epic, the *Aeneid* (c. 29-19 B.C.); and in English poetry, Edmund Spenser (c. 1552-1599), who began his career with the pastoral *Sheapheardes Calender* (1579) before writing his greatest work, the epic *The Faerie Queene* (1590, 1596). In this pastoral, Milton gives this progression from pastoral to epic, from apprenticeship to full acceptance of the poet's task in mature society, a psychological dimension. As the poem moves from allegorical pastoral deities to more explicit references to the figures of Christianity itself, without the mask of the pastoral, so the pleasures of youth, including indulgence in "false surmise," give way to recognition of the truth, however awesome it may be, and to mature acceptance of life's responsibilities. For Milton, that maturity required the responsibility of the poet to confront the imperative political issues of his age. Milton did not, as Edward King had done before his untimely death, choose a career in the clergy. Instead, he chose to find a wider audience as a poet. The restoration of order at the end of the poem announces Milton's control over his craft and his acceptance of responsibility for a literary career committed to an unflinching engagement with the political and religious conflicts that shaped English society in the mid-seventeenth century.

James Hale

MAC FLECKNOE

Author: John Dryden (1631-1700)
Type of poem: Satire
First published: 1682; revised in *Miscellany Poems*, 1684

The Poem

Mac Flecknoe is a satiric poem of 217 lines, written in heroic couplets (pairs of rhyming lines of iambic pentameter). The poem has been commonly adjudged the best short satiric poem in the English language. In it, John Dryden seeks to lampoon Thomas Shadwell, a well-known playwright and indifferent poet, by placing him in an incredible and wholly invented fictional world. He is portrayed as "Mac" (or the son of) Flecknoe—Richard Flecknoe having been an even less accomplished poet than Shadwell. Both of them, the poem implies, are of Irish (and hence of outlandish, remote, and barbarian) stock.

The poem unfolds in a mock-heroic scene; all the machinery of the epic is utilized to exalt the "form" of the poem—high diction, lengthy similes, heroic and kingly actions, archaic vocabulary and spelling—while the content is debased, low, and farcical.

In the fictional setting, Flecknoe is presented as being the exalted king of the realm of Nonsense, which extends all up and down the empty Atlantic Ocean; he dwells in the pompous city of Augusta (in fact, synonymous with London). At the outset, the king determines to relinquish his crown and to choose at once the dullest of his children to assume the throne. In a trice, he determines upon "*Sh—,*" a corpulent and stupid oaf whose writings are wonderfully bad enough to render him properly deserving of this regal selection. Crowds of third-rate poets and hack authors throng to his ceremonial inauguration. There, the father, like an ancient priest, becomes dazed, inspired, and oracular, proceeding to give a vast seventy-one-line speech, prophesying that his son's reign will be as distended as his body is oversized and predicting, under his aegis and tutelage, the virtual triumph of inept and monstrous art throughout the land of Nonsense.

The fond father is never permitted to complete this mantic oration, for a trapdoor mechanism drops open, and the still-declaiming father, the would-be seer, drops down into a pit and disappears, leaving only his mantle as garment and emblem to the aspirant and expectant son. Thus the poem jolts and jostles to a sudden disruptive halt by the introduction of an underground *deus ex machina*. The new king has never received a proper coronation and is appropriately left speechless by this ill omen that abruptly silences the sanctimonious forecasting of his future successes in the land of high witlessness and ineptitude.

Forms and Devices

Mock-epic and mock-heroic strategies in *Mac Flecknoe* abound everywhere. Nowhere are the satire's subjects Richard Flecknoe and Thomas Shadwell overtly impugned or assaulted. Instead, they are enveloped and eventually suffocated by the poem's intentionally overblown language and imagery. They are virtually hymned to death in a witty "praise of folly." As in panegyric poems on great figures and famous men, *Mac Flecknoe* does nothing throughout but exalt and applaud its protagonists for the mature and magnificent qualities of their ignorance and artistic incompetence. No one, it is piously intoned, can compare in nullity with them.

Indeed, these pathetic human creatures are praised and puffed up like blowfish: The town Augusta suggests Augustus and the Augustan Age in Rome, a period of high culture and monumental achievement, and the solemn preparations for the appearance of Mac Flecknoe echo William Shakespeare's presentation of Cleopatra. The two rulers, father and son, are at various times compared to Augustus, to Arion, to Romulus, to Ascanius, to Hannibal, to Elijah, to John the Baptist, and by implication to Christ Himself. This absurd hyperbole is counteracted by an opposing system of analogies that compare the king and his son to little, insignificant people: to earlier minor poets and playwrights such as Thomas Heywood, James Shirley, Thomas Dekker, and John Ogilby; to a dim-witted character named Simkin; and to an oxymoronic Maximin. In the same fashion, the imperial city Augusta is exalted by heroic verse but is simultaneously brought low by the poem's focusing on the city's worst locales—Grub Street, the theater district, Pissing Alley, and a precinct of whorehouses.

Similarly, Shadwell's gravity and import are offset by clusters of imagery through the poem that accentuate his obesity and his supposed pregnancy, and, above all, by scatological analogies (as in lines 100-103) that reduce him to fecal matter:

> From dusty shops neglected Authors come,
> Martyrs of Pies, and Reliques of the Bum.
> Much *Heywood*, *Shirly*, *Ogleby* there lay,
> But loads of *Sh*—almost choakt the way.

Suitably, as his grossness and size become enlarged, so does his intellect continue to shrivel and shrink, until he is "but a kilderkin [a very small cask] of wit."

The apex of this double rhythm, which urges the poem upward while tearing it down, is to be found in the constant organization of anticlimaxes. Wherever a sentence commences with high diction, it is destined at its close to topple into low; whenever a thought is elevated, it is certain to tumble. Monarch oaks are introduced, only to lie supine. Effort is exerted, only to produce negligent results; pregnancy is repeatedly announced, only to be aborted.

The poem's overall plot is itself a masterpiece of uncreativity; Dryden's verse imitates bad poetry. It is shaped with a series of ludicrous events, none of which ever mature to fruition or climax. Indeed, the poem's sole action is the early selection of a successor, quickly and easily achieved. Thereafter, the new king never manages to be crowned, nor the old seer ever to complete his prophetic harangue. All is anticlimax and ineptitude.

Themes and Meanings

Scholars have been unable to trace the exact causes of the quarrel between Dryden and Shadwell, but Dryden certainly disliked Shadwell's reliance upon low farce and what he considered Shadwell's rather too-simplistic rendering of playwright Ben Jonson's comedy of humors. In any event, the poem is not to be remembered as a mere lampoon against Tom Shadwell.

At the least, Dryden's satire debunks the crafting of cheap, imitative dramas, filled with clenches and clichés, with commonplaces and the usual tricks and trap-doors of everyday farce. (Many characters and scenes from Shadwell's plays are alluded to or parodied in this poem.) Similarly, Dryden's poem mimics a seventeenth century "sessions" poem, in which a convocation is held to crown a new poet laureate.

Beyond these imitations, *Mac Flecknoe* branches out wittily to inculpate much of English society in the period—a society in quest of quick and easy jests and enter-tainments, a society representative of the newly emerging urban mass culture inter-ested in light, popular art. Such an art debases the past; it excludes major authors (such as John Fletcher and Ben Jonson) and their traditions, or cheapens and pros-titutes them. Such a world displays, Dryden demonstrates, neither nature nor art, but it does curry favor with a new tide of egotism and self-indulgence. The charac-ters in the poem seem to be preeminently self-indulgent, destroying older traditions and replacing them with tawdry "issue" of their own making. This has been, to be sure, a frequent complaint about modern urbanized civilizations in general since the early seventeenth century. In Dryden's poem, major literary traditions are degraded or dismissed, replaced by nugatory amusements and games, such as the trifling mak-ing of acrostics and anagrams.

What Dryden is in a sense decrying—as does much satire—is the steady deterio-ration of venerable and customary values. It is noteworthy that the once-stately para-pets, walls, and watchtowers of the fictive metropolis Augusta in the poem have become ruins, their neighborhoods now chockful of fledgling actors and common strumpets. Any glories from the immemorial past have all but vanished. Further, even this poem itself can no longer partake of the grand heroic and epical mode; the best that can be mustered in the now-fallen world of Dryden's satire is a defective and broken piece of poetry, a mock-epic. The result is certainly amusing, but it is saddening, too, when one recollects all the culture of the days of yore that has been bent and broken until it has crumbled and fallen away.

John R. Clark

A MAGUS

Author: John Ciardi (1916-1986)
Type of poem: Lyric
First published: 1966, in *This Strangest Everything*

The Poem

John Ciardi's "A Magus" is composed of forty-seven lines forming four stanzas of unequal length. The title, which can mean a wise man, an astrologer, a magician, or a priest, apparently refers to the "missionary from the Mau Mau" mentioned in the first line. As the narrator relates in the opening stanza, this missionary has come to testify to "an amazing botany" apparently caused by "spores blowing from space." This metamorphosis of plants into incredible hybrids provokes the cryptic observation, "The Jungle has come loose,/ is changing purpose."

The latter part of the first stanza is in italics to indicate the missionary's own words. The strange new qualities of transformed "Jungle" are apparently only part of a larger event, for the missionary declares, "Nor are the vegetations/ of the new continuum the only sign." He then claims that "New eyes" now regard the world and note its change, spreading the propaganda to form "new verbs" from its seed. "Set watches on your gardens," he ambiguously advises.

The second stanza opens with the narrator's cautious reaction to this incredible communication: "I repeat it as he spoke it. I do not interpret/ what I do not understand." Although claiming no comprehension of the message, he nevertheless intuits the nature of the messenger, for the religious overtones of his words—especially, "But he does come,/ signs do appear"—clearly link the missionary-magus to the supernatural events he describes.

In the following division of the stanza, the narrator goes on to relate other, equally strange phenomena, such as "poisoned islands," fish that "glow in the dark," and "unknown air." All of these contrast with the signs of the new organic "continuum," for they are the inorganic marvels of modern technology, as the references "lectern," "radar," "phone," and "planes" indicate.

As the preceding stanza did, the third begins with the narrator's own reactions. His opening question— "How many megatons of idea is a man?"—links humanity and technology, metaphysics and physics. His words are the same as before, with one significant exception: "I have heard, and say/ what I heard said and believe." His belief, although clearly centered on the natural world and its odd new order, is focused on the magus himself. Twice, the narrator asserts that he has witnessed miracles and portents—such as the transmutation of "water to blood" and the curiously faithful "cloud" formed by the birds—that surround the magus. Although the narrator sees these things with his own eyes, he remains mystified: "these things I believe whose meaning I cannot say."

Consisting only of a one-line statement ("Then he closes his fist and there is nothing there"), the final stanza abruptly ends both the poem and its miraculous vision. Both the unsettling question at the end of stanza 2 ("Is a fact true?"), and the sudden nothing in the magus' hand provoke readers to pose their own questions and make their own judgments.

Forms and Devices

"A Magus" contains many elements that are associated with clearly defined religious traditions. The poem's cryptic language, its references to the four elements (earth, air, fire, and water) and symbolic colors (black, white, and red), its presentation of inexplicable signs and occurrences, and its focus on a messianic herald of a new order all indicate that it belongs to the time-honored form of mystic revelation. The poet updates this tradition, however, by inserting concrete, quintessentially modern issues and attitudes into this framework.

Ciardi creates a complex, often suggestive, and mystifying poem by using such devices as eclectic imagery, unusual juxtapositions: and an almost regular rhyme scheme. Images of conflict and change are especially abundant throughout the poem. For example, the first stanza is dominated by images of strange, nightmarish transformations in the vegetable kingdom, such as fruit "with a bearded face that howls" and "Mushrooms that bleed." Through the common theme of change, colonialism and racism also provide images that become curiously linked to this "amazing botany." For example, the reference to the Mau Mau (a secret terrorist organization in Kenya) alludes to Kenya's transformation from colonial docility to militant independence, a new order that is surreally mirrored in the organic world's "new continuum." This implicit analogy is made more explicit by the missionary's metaphor "A root is a tongue," in which the idea of native land and native tongue become firmly united.

Images of technological conflict predominate in the second stanza. Certain scientific images— "radar," "[Geiger] counters," "red phone"— contribute global ecological and political associations to the poem's millenarianist vision. Yet others present modern technology within a context of violence, as when the planes "howl to the edge of sound" and "crash through" the world.

Ciardi even uses science's chronic interrogation of the universe as a symbolic image, for questions embody the insatiable, inquisitive hunger of the scientific method itself. For example, by asking, "Is a fact true?" the poet uses the assumptions and logic of scientific inquiry to highlight the values science implicitly asserts. When "Israeli teams" allegedly find "the body" of Christ, the question arises whether Christianity and Easter automatically are "false," or "not true." By posing the important question closing stanza 2, the narrator reminds the reader that the "fact" of science does not preserve an accurate, integrated picture of truth, although it may believe it does; actually, it only presents particular fragments of that truth.

This observation provides the context for the third stanza, in which the poet brings together many of the eclectically gathered images so as to convey a series of significant juxtapositions. Science and humanism, faith and reason, African and European, black and white— all converge in the irrational scene the narrator witnesses. Incredible, inexplicable "facts"—the British "Lion" who renounces his "Empire," the magus' spontaneously combustible hand, the supernatural "ray" that shoots "to the top of the air" from the magus' head—intermingle in the incomprehensible realms of magic and miracles.

The last stanza presents a final, critical, juxtaposition: When the magus "closes his fist and there is nothing there," illusion and reality, truth and lie, confront each other. Using the ultimate device of an open-ended ending, the poet deftly completes the poem's form and meaning by obscuring its own mystical vision and devices.

Themes and Meanings

It is no coincidence that "A Magus" first appeared in a poetry collection entitled *This Strangest Everything* (1966). A remarkable hodgepodge that contains abundant evidence of the social, political, and ecological crises of the Cold War years in which it was written, the poem encompasses a wide variety of themes. By employing unnatural images and irrational shifts of subject, however, the poet draws attention to the fact that its meaning cannot easily be reduced to some simple moral, religious, or sociopolitical statement.

By confronting readers with vivid devices, provocative questions, and a mystifyingly abrupt and not very satisfying ending, the poet forces them to acknowledge the fact that they are indeed reading a poem and not a history book or a newspaper. Poetry, acutely aware of its forms and devices, is the form that traditionally conveys in a highly memorable manner the bewildering complexity of the world.

At the center of this world is the mystery of life, "this strangest everything," which poets since time immemorial have been praising and celebrating in their poems. Ciardi's poetry is no exception, a fact emphasized both by this particular poem and by the poet's own advice to his readers: "To read a poem, come prepared for delight."

Ciardi provokes delight in a variety of ways throughout "A Magus," as its own unique surprises, mystifications, and evocations attest. Reveling in the myriad wonders of the real world, the poet also revels in the strange wonders of his own creation—of space-spores giving rise to howling fruit and upside-down trees, of planes that crash through time and space, of missionaries to Kenya who command birds to enter the fire of their hand, where they "glow like metal."

According to Ciardi, true poetry "insists on battering at life, and on making the poem capture the thing seen and felt in its own unique complex. It does not repeat; it creates." The rhyme and rhythm of the language in "A Magus," its strange premise and skewed vision, and its unsettling images and juxtapositions all combine to form a memorable experience, something "seen and felt," not merely read and summarized.

The multilayered complexity and dynamic depths of imagination displayed by the poem echo the richness of human experience itself. For significant human experience, as poet and narrator alike urge the reader to remember, is not rooted exclusively in the rational and explicable; as the narrator so insistently points out, the world is full of "things I believe whose meaning I cannot say."

The inability to formulate and express meaning of experience, especially poetic experience, or even to understand fully what one hears and sees, is a central concept of the poem. It is also, as Ciardi would no doubt point out, one of the most common aspects of the indescribable, ever-changing reality of being human.

Terri Frongia

THE MAN-MOTH

Author: Elizabeth Bishop (1911-1979)
Type of poem: Lyric
First published: 1936; collected in *North & South*, 1946

The Poem

"The Man-Moth," by Pulitzer prize-winning poet Elizabeth Bishop, is an early work; it was written when she first lived in New York City in 1935. The idea for this poem came to her from a misprinting of the word "mammoth" as "manmoth" in a newspaper. She was inspired to imagine what sort of creature this might be. The Man-Moth of the poem is a mysterious nocturnal inhabitant of the city — half man, half moth — whose fearful, obsessive actions represent the city's interior, imaginative life. The poem is a dreamlike fantasy that works as a fable or allegory of modern city life. It is interesting to put this poem into its historical context and to imagine the world in which the young Elizabeth Bishop, recently graduated from Vassar College, was writing, for this was during the Depression; moreover, events in Europe were already leading to World War II. Both the hopes and the darkness of the time seem reflected in the poem, which is tragic in tone.

"The Man-Moth" is a free-verse poem divided into six stanzas of eight lines each, with the short first line of each stanza indented. Each of these indented lines announces a different stage in the Man-Moth's story. In the first stanza, Bishop depicts not the Man-Moth but a man, seen from above, "battered moonlight" shining on the worn surfaces of city buildings and on the self-engrossed man himself. Images of light and shadow, the man as "an inverted pin," and the palpable sensation of moonlight, "neither warm nor cold," create a strange, lonely setting for events to follow.

The man pays little attention to the moon, in comparison to the Man-Moth, who emerges unseen in the second stanza, crawling from under the city sidewalk and beginning his climb toward the moon that he imagines "is a small hole" in the night sky. The Man-Moth is fearful and nervous but determined to "investigate."

His brave but naïve effort to crawl through the moon is doomed, however; there is no hole in the sky, and he cannot escape the city. He falls back down to it, where he must try to cope with the frightening apparatus of city life, particularly embodied in the subway train and the dangerous electrified third rail.

Images of the Man-Moth struggling to deal with the subway doors, riding backward so that he cannot see where he is going, and worrying that if he does not sit still and keep his hands in his pockets he will do something to hurt himself are easily recognized by anyone who has tried to get around in a large, modern city and has not found it easy. The Man-Moth is almost childlike in his vulnerability. These are all images of a loss of control, and like a sensitive child who must navigate the world of adults, the Man-Moth fears losing that control.

At this point in the poem when the Man-Moth seems most human, Bishop slightly adjusts the viewpoint by speaking to "you," distancing the Man-Moth from the reader. Casually, as a naturalist telling someone where to find bird's eggs or edible mushrooms, she describes the process for using a flashlight to get the Man-Moth to surrender his "only possession." The eye of the Man-Moth is mysterious, dark, and nonhuman—the eye of an insect. Fixed by the light, it closes and secretes a tear. Like a magician or street performer, he will try to palm or hide it, but Bishop tells the reader to pay close attention and "he'll hand it over" —a prize of cool water "pure enough to drink."

Forms and Devices

Bishop uses a regular number of lines in each stanza so that the poem has a formal appearance on the page, though it is in free verse. She does make use of irregularly placed consonant rhymes for emphasis and musical effect, such as the *t* sound at the end of "moonlight" and "hat," and the *s* sound at the end of "properties" and "thermometers" in the first stanza. She also uses consonant sounds within lines for musical resonance, such as "on," "pin," "moon," and "Man," also in the first stanza. Reading the poem aloud, one becomes aware of the musical interweaving of repeated vowel and consonant sounds throughout the poem. Although the sound patterns in the poem are irregular, these sounds give a fullness to the language and help pace the reading of the poem, which is slow and sonorous.

Strong visual imagery is extremely important in this poem. Images of light and dark create a sense of heightened drama and suggest the gritty realism of early black-and-white films set in city landscapes or black-and-white photography of the period. She describes the Man-Moth's shadow at one point as being like "a photographer's cloth," referring to the cloth photographers use to shut out light when using old-style view cameras. The photographer, with his head under a black cloth, looking through the round lens of the camera, is somewhat like the Man-Moth under the black sky looking at the round moon overhead or like the person who catches the Man-Moth and stares into his black eye with a flashlight to see the elusive tear.

Bishop also uses irony as a dramatic device. The first example is the title itself, which is customarily printed with an asterisk, leading the reader to a footnote explaining that the title was based on a mistake in a newspaper. The powerful original word "mammoth" provides ironic contrast with the trembling vulnerability of the Man-Moth. There is also dramatic irony in the lack of awareness in the man presented in the first stanza. Though he stands in his own small shadow, a shadow cast by the moon, he is only slightly aware of the moon's mystery and its effect on him, and he is not at all aware of the mysterious Man-Moth whose life parallels his own. Finally, the Man-Moth's attempt to escape through the hole in the sky, which is the moon, is ironic because it is both brave and foolish, an act doomed to failure. Elizabeth Bishop's view of the individual in the modern world clearly seems ironic.

The poet also uses Surrealist imagery for strong emotional impact. The Man-Moth is an irrational dreamlike figure acting out an existential dilemma that is difficult to express. Bishop mentions "recurrent dreams" in the poem, making a connection with Surrealist and Symbolist work that incorporate dreamlike images and evoke the subconscious.

Themes and Meanings

At one level, Elizabeth Bishop's poem is simply a strange and wonderful story, a fairy-tale fantasy about a character caught between two worlds like the Beast in "Beauty and the Beast" or some other transformation tale. There is no Beauty, however, to save the Man-Moth, who is the epitome of alienation in a modern, urban setting.

Like a moth, the Man-Moth spends his life in two opposite states, one as an obsessed creature pursuing the moon as a moth flies toward a street lamp, and the other as the subterranean larval being who lives in the earth-tunnels of the subway. Like a human, the Man-Moth strives for something better than what he knows, but all too often he falls back into fear and confusion and lives a life of unfulfillment.

The meaning of the moon is ambiguous, but clearly it is something lofty and impossible to reach. Typically, the moon is an emblem of madness and obsession, but it is also a romantic image of lovers and artists—a feminine power—reflective, cool, attractive, mysterious. Visually, the moon can look like a hole in the sky. Probably the young Bishop projected her own efforts to deal with the artist's life in the city into the poem. If the poem depicts the loneliness and frustration of the artist's struggle to create, however, it also has broader meaning: It seems to present the human struggle to escape earthly trials into some higher state of enlightenment. Some readers see the Man-Moth's struggle as a religious quest, but others are more likely to see it as an existential drama in which it is impossible to answer the universal "why?"

In any case, the quest is a lonely one. Although the poem is set in a city landscape, that landscape is almost empty of life. Even when the Man-Moth rides the subway, there is no feeling of crowdedness. The trains are "silent" and start moving at "full, terrible speed" as if no one were at the controls. When the Man-Moth thinks of the dangerous "third rail" of the train, it is his own impulse to touch it that he fears, not some outside threat.

Finally, the poet tells the reader, if the Man-Moth is forced to surrender his tear, like the bee losing its stinger, he will die. The tear, representing emotion, is "his only possession." Read literally, the poem tells the reader that it is death to give up feeling, however uncomfortable feeling can be. In strange and beautiful images, the poem depicts mysteries of human life.

Barbara Drake

THE MAN WITH THE BLUE GUITAR

Author: Wallace Stevens (1879-1955)
Type of poem: Lyric
First published: 1937, in *The Man with the Blue Guitar and Other Poems*

The Poem

"The Man with the Blue Guitar" is a long poem consisting of thirty-three rather short sections in four-beat couplets, most of them unrhymed. The title, which reminds the reader of a Pablo Picasso painting by the same title, suggests a musical piece, though more in the sense of an improvisation than a formal musical composition (something that Wallace Stevens imitates effectively in "Peter Quince at the Clavier").

The poem starts out in the third person but switches to the first person, so the piece becomes a dialogue between the guitarist and his audience, which acts as a kind of chorus. The chorus seems to pose certain idealized questions about its own place in poetry. Rejecting those overtures, the guitarist says that he plays things "as they are," although things "Are changed upon the blue guitar." He then goes on to improvise in various ways about how this might be done—in essence, about how poetry is related to the audience or to the world in general.

Stevens himself was an insurance executive, so he knew the world in a practical sense; yet he was also a poet, a creator. Though he did not confuse the two worlds, he saw them as coextensive. In "The Man with the Blue Guitar" he takes the reader into the world of the poet and asks the reader to see, feel, or improvise about the world from the poet's perspective.

Sections I-VI set the stage for the musical drama. Stevens tests out various interrelationships between the blue of the guitar, or the poet's imagination, and the green world, "things exactly as they are." The poet/guitarist depends upon the world he changes — shears, patches, tries to "bring . . . round" — but is never able to remake perfectly.

In section VII, the improvisation changes; the guitarist becomes more metaphysical. He begins to play with various ideas about reality and what the fictive person can do with it. Thinking becomes a metaphor or stage for the guitarist's, or poet's, activity as creator. It is as if the poet takes over the role of the godhead and in the process, now wholly secular, tests out the possibilities as well as the limits of a poet's abilities relative to the world.

The guitarist also sets himself a task: to "evolve a man" (section XXX). He speaks of the poet as singing "a hero's head,/ large eye," or creating man in a mythic or symbolic sense. He hopes to do more than this, and he uses certain metaphors for man, such as the clown on the stage (XXV) or the notion of "the old fantoche" (XXX), reminiscent of the "walking shadow" in William Shakespeare's *Macbeth* (1606).

In the final sections of the poem, however, the poet returns to the original thesis — the relationship between poet and audience. In the closing couplet, which is rhymed, suggesting a certain finality, the "imagined pine, the imagined jay" — the world and the imagination — are still in juxtaposition, as if to say the guitarist still needs to balance outer and inner worlds in the ever-changing drama called life.

Forms and Devices

As the title suggests, "The Man with the Blue Guitar" is similar to a musical piece, specifically an improvisation. There is no poetic precedent for this form, so the poet employs a loosely knit structure to fit his theme. The use of thirty-three (an odd number) parts suggests that there is nothing set about the overall composition. Similarly, in each part the number of couplets, usually five or six, varies from as few as four to as many as seven. Nor is the rhyming consistent, though certain sections do rhyme, giving the illusion of finality.

The poem is filled with musical terms to reinforce the aesthetic nature of the exercise; it is "a tune," a "serenade." At the same time, the musician is a creator, so Stevens employs images more appropriate to a carpenter. The guitarist's "bang" suggests violent action, where things may be "destroyed," but at the same time the guitarist (or builder) is "a mould" to shape things — ultimately "to evolve," or re-create, man himself. This is a mammoth task, involving "mountainous music," but it is still music and, therefore, temporary — always "passing away." While the "leaden twang" continues, however, it is like "reason in a storm," suggesting that all reality, including the listener, is caught up in the rhythms of the improvisation.

In addition to being musical, the poet is an artist. Like Pablo Picasso, the guitarist becomes an abstract expressionist, rearranging fragments of reality into a unified whole. One way the artist works is through color, changing the world so that what one sees is the "sun's green" and "cloud's red" — unnatural but imaginative realities. Sometimes colors are used to dismiss transcendent realities, the "gold self aloft," or to show the limits of the imagination, "enraged by gold antagonists in air." Stevens always returns to the blue imagination in balance with the green world; in fact, they are so close that occasionally the artist speaks of the "overcast blue of the air," as though mind and object often intermingle in the process of imagining, or creating.

The artist is a master of imagery — he works in visual representations; Stevens uses animals, for example, to fill in his canvas. Many might see the poet as "angelic," but for Stevens he is always of this world, "a worm composing on a straw." Sometimes he must deal with fluctuating subjects in the world, such as "liquid cats," but he never resorts to romantic or idealized visions, "the lark fixed . . . in the museum of the sky." He rather tires to maintain a balance between the guitarist, "the lion in the lute," and external reality, "the lion lock in stone."

Finally, the guitarist is also part dramatist. Sections I-VI are a virtual stage, after which the poem moves toward a climax in section XXII, where Stevens tells the reader directly: "Poetry is the subject of the poem." In XXV, the poet-dramatist imagines the mind itself as a stage, where the poet is a clown, and his "nose" and "fat thumb" are properties that help one to experience the dramatic and comic process of re-creating reality through imagination. Here the clown's nose is primary, for it enables the poet to give a center of gravity, or stability, to the poet vis-à-vis the world as he educates, entertains, indeed re-creates the world for his audience.

Themes and Meanings

Wallace Stevens was not a particularly philosophical poet, but he was an idea poet, for ideas always lurk behind his aesthetics. Unlike E. E. Cummings, who in poems such as "a man who had fallen among thieves" often centers on relationships, community, and love, thereby challenging Christians to live up to their biblical roots, Stevens is more concerned with immediate reality and how one perceives it. He dismisses belief systems in order to focus on the present as a poet. His challenge is to people in their immediate context, to their imaginative capability, and to this end he takes the reader inside the man with the blue guitar.

In the background of Stevens' poem are key thinkers of all times and places, notes Joseph Riddle in *The Clairvoyant Eye* (1965). Stevens assumes with Heraclitus that the world is in flux, and as a student of Georg Hegel he sees reality as moving forward creatively. Stevens also must have admired James Joyce's young Steven Dedalus as Steven pursues new worlds as poet and thinker in *A Portrait of the Artist as a Young Man* (1916). At the same time, he rejects the idea of God or the divinity of Christ, even undercutting Ralph Waldo Emerson's notion of transcendence, as he does T. S. Eliot's "still point," in favor of an immediate and changing world.

Where Stevens is most original is in his creative images, according to William York Tindall, through which he makes his reader ponder important subjects. He takes Paul Verlaine's marionette, for example, and puts him in the brutal world, "Oxidia" — violent and toxic, unlike the mythological Olympia. Here the marionette figure sees three crosses: Christ on the cross, a telephone pole, and the cross stick of the marionette. Rejecting transcendent answers, and located in the real world (the world of the telephone pole), the artist is able to entertain his audience, something that metaphysically may be both comic and tragic. That is the poet's (Stevens') idea of what is real.

Perhaps one of the strongest statements about the potential value of the imagination comes in section XIV, in which Stevens compares the imagination to a candle, which he says is "enough to light the world." In contrast to the German chandelier (which represents scientific knowledge, reason), the candle provides clear insight at any time of day:

> At night, it lights the fruit and wine,
> The book and bread, things as they are.

The fruit and wine and book and bread have no symbolic or sacramental value, but are simply "things as they are." Here, Thomas J. Hines has said, the blue guitar, which has been used throughout the poem, defines itself and its potential (the candle), and so proves that it can generate a definition of itself within its own constructs.

Hines also notes that philosophically, in the mid 1930's, Stevens was closest to Edmund Husserl's phenomenological method; in "The Man with the Blue Guitar," the poet organizes his world around a single intuition, with which he then works in a fictive or imaginative manner. He did not evolve a new notion of man's essence or being, but his improvisions on the blue guitar present a wide variety of options for looking at reality and at humankind's place in it.

Thomas Matchie

MANHATTAN, 1975

Author: Carl Rakosi (1903-   )
Type of poem: Narrative
First published: 1983, as "Manhattan"; collected as "Manhattan, 1975," in
  The Collected Poems of Carl Rakosi, 1986

The Poem

"Manhattan, 1975," a narrative poem in free verse, deals with various aspects of city life. The nature of New York life is reflected in the form of the poem; half-lines that begin at the left margin alternate with headless lines that begin where the half-lines that precede them end, giving the poem a broken, fragmented appearance. The traditional stanza form is replaced by five syntactical and semantic units. The title refers to Manhattan in particular, but in its criticism "Manhattan, 1975" describes any city experience.

The poem alternates between the description of street scenes and reflective passages. The first of the five units begins with a hypothetical dialogue, indicated by the conjunction "if" in the first line, between an imaginary female "you" and a male "I." The topic of the conversation is sexual. The youth of the woman is implied by the freshness of the earth and the upcoming buds, symbolizing the breasts of the young woman. Once fully matured, she will lose her virginity in the city. This thought is expressed by mentioning her hymen and by associating purity, which is her presexual but also pre-Manhattan stage, with the whiteness of buds. While the female "you" is introduced by the mention of her hymen, the first unit of the poem ends with the male "I," stating his sex in the double entendre of the line "P. S. Nuts to reason."

Summer is coming, and nature is awakening; so is the girl's sexuality. The male "I" is excited by her sexual awakening, as is indicated in the line "the tiniest nerve-endings trembling." At the same time, his feeling is repressed because it is "within its chest-walls" — a comparison of his feelings to people living within city walls. Dodo, the man's nickname, both suggests his puckish spirit and alludes to the dodo bird, or a fool, making fun of his feelings.

Beginning with the question "Who's that in the light/ cotton dress," the second unit deals with a grown-up woman who, driven by the desire for sex, follows a call from the earth, waiting for a lover. This idea is expressed by her dress, her behavior, and the biblical quotation from the book of Ruth (1:16). The part ends with a promise that the man reads in a smile and with his "down to earth" sexual failure.

The third unit is introduced by a song praising summer and implying opportunities for men to have sex. Suddenly, the poem shifts, and the joyful, lusty tone of the sexual allusions in the first unit is now replaced by references to death. Whereas the male repressed his emotions in the first part of the poem, now his feelings seem to be dead, "close, mortal musk," and intercourse becomes a mechanical act without love— "sexual, befuddling . . ./ a whiff of dead breaths/ intermittently crossing."

The lyrical "I" at the beginning of the fourth unit is a reflection of Carl Rakosi himself: "I could imagine lion cubs." The male-female relationship, expressed by the pronoun pair "I-you" in the first part of the poem, is connected to the fourth part by the word "progenitor"; both words suggest reproduction. The "progenitor" can also be associated with God through the references to the Old Testament in this passage, such as "And irrelevance, where was its sting" (a revision of 1 Corinthians 15:55-56). The anonymity of the city leads to a disillusioned confession by the poet: "O my radical past,/ I am not embarrassed,/ but is this all that remains?"

The poem closes with street scenes, expressing the negative influence of the city by means of the fading colors of the parrot's feathers. The anonymity of the city leads to a reduction of the human being to particular parts. Thus all one sees or hears from the woman at the opening of this fifth unit is her voice; furthermore, making love becomes a lucrative business, and the hustler is "cast in sandstone" like the saints of European cathedrals. The city experience has created a new species, the "hominid Americanus." The poem ends on a note of hope—"Lady, be comforted!"—despite all the misunderstandings and disputes.

Forms and Devices

"Manhattan, 1975" is written in the tradition of a group of poets, including Carl Rakosi, who called themselves "Objectivists." Objectivism claims that the poem is an object and has to be dealt with as such, apart from its meaning. Therefore, special consideration is given to form.

The form of the poem is eye-catching, because the lines are broken up. Each half-line, beginning at the left margin, is continued in the following line by a headless line that is set off from the left margin. "Manhattan, 1975" is a dialogue in which voices are separated by the half-lines and headless lines.

The form of this poem is a new, American one, appropriate for depicting American life. The traditional poetic devices of European literatures—such as rhyme, meter, even line and stanza—have been abandoned and replaced by dialogues. The poem has become narrative.

The dialogues that take place in this poem include the imaginary dialogue between a man and a woman in the first part of the poem, the actual dialogue between a woman and the parrot man, and the failure of dialogue between the two senators from North and South Carolina.

A further device of this poetic form is the use of quotations and intertextuality; that is, different parts of other texts are interwoven into the poem, such as references to the Old Testament. Rakosi uses biblical imagery, direct quotations from the Old Testament, and allusions to the Bible, in which a biblical quotation is changed: "And irrelevance,/ where was its sting?" Furthermore, he chooses biblical names, such as Ruth and Noah, reflecting his own Jewish heritage.

Themes and Meanings

Isolation and anonymity, as part of the city experience, are the central issues in

"Manhattan, 1975." Rakosi, who was a dedicated social worker, shows a great concern for the well-being of others, and at one point in the poem he questions his own personal accomplishments. As Diane Wakoski has said, Rakosi reminds the reader "that to live intelligently is never to relax or to leave unnoticed any slightly foolish thing."

"Manhattan, 1975" contrasts the American reality, of which Manhattan is the quintessential experience, with medieval and Renaissance England. The language of the poem and its form, reminiscent of Ezra Pound's headless lines, are American. Rakosi undoubtedly stands in the American tradition, as he points out in the poem himself: "I among them/ (impossible to keep Whitman out of this)." Walt Whitman (1819-1892) is the American poet par excellence, and he also lived in New York. Therefore, the poem portrays an American experience in an American narrative style.

In addition, Rakosi pays tribute to the American novelist Ernest Hemingway. The quotation "(I could imagine lion cubs at play/ bumping awkwardly against each other)" comes from Hemingway's novel *The Old Man and the Sea* (1952).

An allusion to T. S. Eliot, an American who became a British subject, bridging British and American elements, is given by the parrot that speaks Sanskrit, a language used in T. S. Eliot's poem *The Waste Land* (1922). The line "And irrelevance,/ where was its sting," which is essentially a Biblical quotation, also alludes to the poetry of John Donne.

The sensual character of "Manhattan, 1975," combined with its fondness for rituals, reminds one of the poet Robert Herrick. While in Herrick's May poems the Queen of May is in the center of the fertility rites, "insouciance is King/ of the May" in the city experience of America, where intercourse, as an expression of love leading to fertility, has become a mechanical act to be purchased on any corner.

The message of Puck, a spirit in English folklore, along with images from nature, becomes a paradox in Manhattan. Reality and ideal are separated like Ireland and Britain, as indicated by the line "From outside the pale," which is the dividing line between Catholic Ireland and Protestant Northern Ireland.

Rakosi's frustration with the city is also illustrated in the anonymous English "Cuckoo Song" (c. 1250). Rakosi adds to the Middle English "sumer is i-cumin in/ lhude sing cuckoo" an American "Yay." Furthermore, he changes the word "cuckoo," with which spring is associated, to the word "city." The city has replaced nature, as the alliteration of city and cuckoo indicates. Yet the poem offers comfort, implying that there is salvation after death, "He is safe with Noah now"; and the ending of the poem moves away from the anonymous, impersonal treatment of people living in New York to a more respectful and hopeful "Lady, be comforted!"

Hartmut Heep

THE MAP

Author: Elizabeth Bishop (1911-1979)
Type of poem: Lyric
First published: 1935; collected in *North & South*, 1946

The Poem

"The Map" is a descriptive poem divided into three stanzas. The first and last are eight-line stanzas with repeated Petrarchan rhyme schemes (*abbacddc*), while the longer central stanza is written in free verse.

In "The Map," Elizabeth Bishop records her thoughts on the nature of a map's relationship to the real world. Implicitly, the poem asks why maps fascinate people so much. The poet suggests that the human fascination with small-scale representations of land and water has to do with the imagined worlds maps can offer, the images of far-off people and places that maps can bring to mind. More precisely, maps excite the viewer's imagination. "The Map" celebrates the mapmaker's (or poet's) power to create illusion and fantasy as well as new ways of looking at what is real.

The poem begins with shapes and colors—what most people first notice about maps. For example, land is "shadowed green," and it "lies in water," which is blue. Here, however, all certainty ends, and a series of provocative but unanswered questions begins. The poet sees "Shadows," not sure if they are "shallows." Also uncertain is whether the line on the paper indicates the land's edges or "long sea-weeded ledges."

On first looking at the map, the poet sees water surrounding and supporting land. The second half of the first stanza, however, suggests a relationship between the land and the sea that is mysterious and unexpected. The land is active—it seems to lean, lift, and draw the water around itself. The poet asks, "is the land tugging at the sea from under?" Because these questions go unanswered, the reader begins to understand that not everyone interprets a map the same way.

In the long central stanza, the map receives the close inspection for which Bishop's poetry is well known. Newfoundland (perhaps "new found land") suggests that the imagination can create new territory, new realities. In Labrador, "yellow, where the moony Eskimo/ has oiled it," the dreamer, the "moony" imaginer, paints the land to suit her vision of it. Stroking the lovely bays "under a glass as if they were expected to blossom" suggests the map's magical quality as well as its aesthetic beauty. Perhaps "blossom" suggests how one's expectations grow while studying a map.

The poet also inspects the carefully printed names, which "run out to sea" and "cross the neighboring mountains." The juxtaposition of the artificial (printed names) with the "real" (sea and mountains) reminds the reader that the map is a man-made object. For the poet, it is a representation by which to compare reality with perception. Stanza 2 ends with a playful image: The peninsulas are "thumb and finger/ . . . feeling for the smoothness of yard-goods." The poet seems to prefer her fanciful perception to the real places the map represents. This image also looks again at the relationship of land to water.

Examining that relationship further, the poet suggests in stanza 3 that the "waves' own conformation" is what determines the shape of the land, rather than the land's outlines determining how far the water lies. The poet sees Norway running south in the shape of a hare, and then, getting back to the art of cartography, casually wonders, "Are they assigned, or can the countries pick their colors?" These three observations suggest questions of perspective. For example, how one sees an object—such as this map—is a very personal experience. The poet's (unrevealed) conclusions are her own; there are not definitive answers, no "favorites."

That is why the cartographer's representations and use of tools, records, and perceptions are "More delicate than the historians'." The historian attempts to deal with facts, and chronologies of events, objectively. Although she dares not distort truth, the mapmaker, unlike the historian, deals with possibilities imaginatively, for the artist celebrates the notion that to be completely objective is impossible.

Forms and Devices

Like many of Bishop's poems, "The Map" exemplifies her mastery of organic form. The poem's structure grows out of and also contributes to its expression. The rhymed stanzas (1 and 3) reflect precision, balance, and elegance—they have a life of their own, exactly as the map lives its life "unperturbed," existing "under a glass," independent of the viewer's scrutiny. The controlled pace of these stanzas helps to create the tone of careful exploration and tentative suggestion that the poet's observations convey, especially in the first stanza.

The map is, furthermore, an inanimate object made animate by the personification of land and sea. For example, "the land lean[s] down" and lifts and tugs, the waters "lend," and the profiles of land investigate. The rhymed stanzas are also the question stanzas, in which the poet asks (and never answers) questions about what she sees and imagines in the map. These unanswered questions shape the poem, propel it forward, and frame it with a tone of uncertain yet determined speculation.

The long, unrhymed stanza is a close description that seems to start at the top and move southward, as if the poet were running her fingers down along the map's colored lines. A running commentary of metaphors animates and finally personifies the peninsulas as women. Bishop uses a very natural word order, the same order of words one would use in a good sentence. This technique welcomes the reader into the poem, which reads as if the narrator were wondering aloud. The long, central stanza also uses first-person plural ("we"), as if to draw the reader further and more intimately into the poet's speculation on what a map really is and on its ultimate purpose.

In the first stanza, the verbs are very active; the land leans, lifts, and tugs. In contrast, stanza 2 begins with land that "lies flat and still." The following verbs in the same stanza reflect determined, if cautious, motion: "oiled," "blossom," "run," "cross," and "take." These verbs indicate that the poet's exploration in this stanza is painstaking and precise; she is well aware that details risk being overlooked "when emotion too far exceeds its cause."

Stanza 3 gathers together what the poet has learned about the map. She looks once more at the relationship of land to water (a recurring puzzle), and she notes other details: hare-shaped Norway and the "profiles" of land that investigate the sea. Yet this final stanza's main effect is to turn the viewer's attention away from the map and inward, for reflection. The final question—"can the countries pick their colors?"—accomplishes this shift in perspective because it reminds the reader that whoever drew the map made artistic (imaginative) decisions in its execution. It also introduces the final thematic statement, the poem's puzzling last line.

Themes and Meanings

The simplicity of the title promises a straightforward description of an object—a real map—which the poet delivers with fine-tuned and surprising nuances. One is soon aware, however, that the description is both objective and emblematic. That is, a real map is very carefully and faithfully described, but the map is also a symbol capable of suggesting meanings or connections beyond itself.

For one thing, the map is an emblem of imaginative promise. It might show its reader how to get to a specific place, or it might lead to hidden treasure. Because the images on maps are by definition constructions of the mind, perhaps the map represents the mind attempting to plot a landscape so that it can find its way.

By placing "The Map" first in both *North & South* (1946) and *The Complete Poems* (1969), Bishop also suggested that "The Map" may lead to a way of understanding her work, especially her sense of how an "objective" work of art may embody an artist's subjective experience. As early as the second line of the poem, for example, Bishop's subjective kind of seeing becomes apparent. Her fanciful images—the "clean cage for invisible fish" and "Norway's hare"—suggest that what one sees depends on how one looks or uses her imagination.

As with the ever-changing relationship between land and water, the concept of subjective perception arises often. The poet's unique and often whimsical account of the map reveals her uniqueness of vision—her way of experiencing the world and of expressing that experience. While the questions in stanza 1 first introduce the idea that individual perspectives can differ, the lines in stanza 2 suggest that individual perspectives—and not the external world itself—may in fact determine what is real.

In "The Map," Bishop is in fact exploring the imagination rather than the landscape. The poem might even be read as a rumination on the value or status of poetry. "The Map" is not about actual geography but about refusing to standardize the images each person projects onto a place. Bishop is trying to revive and renew sight, to make images new.

Expressing the imagination's own way of seeing, while retaining one's sense of the real world, is the challenge the artist accepts and struggles with. The question of whether empirical truth or imaginative truth is more valuable in humankind's efforts to chart the world around it is unanswerable. Probably, both perceptions are required. The poet, however, uses more delicate, more powerful colors to paint the facts with a sharper and subtler stroke; they give reality a beauty and form that the historians' literal black-and-white representations cannot approach. The map-maker's images are fragile, yet keen and subtle, the results of a particular imagination shaping the real. That expression—the delicate "map-makers' colors"—comprises the poet's varied, rich, and peculiar ways of seeing.

JoAnn Balingit

A MAP OF MONTANA IN ITALY

Author: Richard Hugo (1923-1982)
Type of poem: Lyric
First published: 1973, in *The Lady in Kicking Horse Reservoir*

The Poem

"A Map of Montana in Italy" is a lyric poem in free verse, arranged into a single stanza of thirty-four lines. It is the opening poem in Richard Hugo's fourth book of poems, *The Lady in Kicking Horse Reservoir*, and it is dedicated to Marjorie Carrier.

The poem is written in the first person, in the present tense, the voice distinctively Hugo's. It is rather flat in tone, with subdued emotions. Although the syntax is simple and rather prosaic, the poem's style is tight, direct, and without extraneous words. The situation of the poem is that Hugo (who lived in Missoula, where he taught at the University of Montana from 1963 until his death in 1982) has come upon a map of Montana while he is touring in Italy. Perhaps the map has been tacked up on a wall, or maybe it is in an atlas open upon Hugo's lap.

The poem begins with two descriptive, though incomplete, sentences: "On this map white. A state thick as a fist/ or blunt instrument." The third sentence is complete but brief, straightforward, metaphoric, and declarative: "Long roads weave and cross/ red veins full of rage." The long and often undeveloped gravel or dirt roads of Montana are printed in red, symbolizing to Hugo that anger is a statewide characteristic. The introductory style of these sentences suggests that the speaker wishes to impress the reader with tough talk, as though he is in a pugnacious mood. Not until the poem's fourth sentence does the speaker identify himself as a Montanan. "Big Canada," he says, "map maker's/ pink, squats on our backs."

Next Hugo recalls the imagery of two of Montana's unique animals. He makes a witty connection between one of the map's colors, "Glacier Park's green," and his "envy" of the reclusive grizzly bears that live there, then he describes how "antelope sail/ between strands of barbed wire and never/ get hurt" on the eastern Montana prairie. Subsequently, over the next fifteen lines, he turns his attention to the people who live within the state's borders.

First, Hugo alludes to Billings and Great Falls, the state's "two biggest towns," describing them as "dull deposits/ of men getting along," who never miss church and censor "movies and books." Second, he calls Helena and Butte the state's "two most interesting towns," claiming they "have the good sense to fail." Then he turns to charging Montana's population with alcoholic immaturity ("There's too much/ schoolboy in bars") and with greed ("too much talk about money.") There follows an oblique comparison of Montana with a Kafkaesque Poland, and suggestion that with "so few Negroes and Jews," the usual scapegoats of urban America, Montanans have been "reduced/ to hating each other, dumping our crud/ in our rivers, mistreating the Indians."

Returning to the map, Hugo notes how its color, white, aptly connotes "winter, ice." The description is used as a transition to Italy, where the snow is more distant and less threatening ("It's white here too/ but back of me, up in the mountains) and the wild animals of Italy, "obsequious wolves," are not as ferocious as Montana's grizzly bears.

Finally, as if pining for Montana's roughneck violence, Hugo tweaks the Italians, saying, "No one fights/ in the bars filled with pastry." Then he concludes with a general quizzical observation on the romance of the West: how, on the night before, "the Italians/ cheered the violence in one of our westerns."

Forms and Devices

The style of "A Map of Montana in Italy" is in many ways typical of the whole body of Hugo's poetry. Although Hugo studied with Theodore Roethke at the University of Washington in Seattle, the younger poet never adopted Roethke's broad interests in rhymed, formal verse, such as the villanelle, kyriel, and limerick, each of which Roethke employed quite successfully. Instead, Hugo seems to have discovered his own voice early and stayed with that voice throughout his life.

Hugo's voice is one of little modulation and tightly controlled pitch, a uniquely characteristic drone. Writing in "Richard Hugo: Getting Right," from a book-length collection of essays entitled *Local Assays: On Contemporary Poetry* (1985), Dave Smith says that Hugo's "music has always been insistent and derived from Anglo-Saxon sonic practices. He loves a strongly stressed line, usually three to five stresses, whose density and intensity is always willing to risk overwhelming the ear."

"A Map of Montana in Italy" aptly fits Smith's description. The poem's rhythm is irregular, a good example of free verse; however, while the lines seem to be measured in length predominantly by the eye, the poem still generally scans into five hard stresses per line, or an irregular pentameter.

Also typical of Hugo's style is this poem's use of alliteration, the repetition of consonant sounds at the beginning of words, and assonance, the repetition of vowel sounds. In his excellent collection of lectures and essays on poetry and writing, *The Triggering Town* (1979), Hugo writes of his interest in repetitive sounds. "When I was a young poet," he says, "I set an arbitrary rule that when I made a sound I felt was strong, a sound I liked specially, I'd make a similar sound three to eight syllables later. Of course it would often be a slant rhyme. Why three to eight? Don't ask. You have to be silly to write poems at all."

Note, how in the following lines Hugo adheres to his rule of sound, stitching words together based in large part upon the repetition of the consonants *b*, *m*, *p*, and *g*, and the vowel sounds short *i*, short *a*, and long *e*:

> Big Canada, map maker's
> pink, squats on our backs, planning bad winters
> for years, and Glacier Park's green with my envy
> of Grizzly Bears.

Later in the poem, Hugo gets away from sweet-sounding lines and speaks in a voice that is more matter-of-fact and prosaic. Lines 24 and 25 read: "Each year, 4000 move, most to the west/ where ocean currents keep winter in check." There is much less music in that line. And the concluding three-and-a-half lines of the poem read:

> No one fights
> in the bars filled with pastry. There's no
> prison for miles. But last night the Italians
> cheered the violence in one of our westerns.

Except for a repetition of the *f* in fights and filled, and the *p* in pastry and prison, this section of the poem is much less alliterative. It is also less condensed; in those last three sentences Hugo uses the definite article (the) three times, when he only needed it once. The sentences are short, declarative, and rather dry. The poet's voice seems to have fallen completely away from its beginning high lyrical tone to a flatter, prosaic depression.

Themes and Meanings

Maps and references to towns on maps appear in many of Richard Hugo's poems. Hugo uses maps as anyone may use them: to dream about, move toward, and discover new territory. Thus, many of his poems become word maps for places themselves. Hugo's poems display psychological and social landscapes, as this poem does for Montana. It is the feel of Montana's size and natural beauty, its isolation from the rest of the world, its sense of abandonment, and its frontier violence and restlessness that Hugo hopes to survey in "A Map of Montana in Italy," especially as these are seen from a perspective of relative serenity in the Old World.

Hugo made three important trips to Italy. The first came during World War II, when he served as a bombadier in the Air Force. On the second, in 1963, he obsessively returned to the places he had known during the war. In an essay entitled "Ci Vediamo," Hugo relates how, centering on the war and the places he had known during the war, he meets an Italian soul mate named Vincenzo, who tells him, "Of all the Americans here during the war, you're the only one who ever returned." First Vincenzo bursts into tears, sobbing. Then Hugo responds, matching Vincenzo "sob for strangulated sob." On his third trip to Italy, from 1967-1968, funded by a Rockefeller Foundation Creative Writing Fellowship, Hugo wrote "A Map of Montana in Italy" and many other poems that went into *The Lady in Kicking Horse Reservoir*. As a result, Hugo wrote of Montana in this poem from the perspective of a returning American serviceman, scholar-poet, and tourist.

The poet's tone seems to be colored by several conflicting emotions: nostalgia for home; pride in Montana's physical beauty, wildness, and vigor; disgust for its juvenile bluster; anger over its restrictive behavior; and an underlying cynicism about the modern frontier state and the way its history is viewed by Hollywood. The poem's theme hinges not only on how Hugo views the wild, cold, tough, isolated, and de-populated map of Montana, but also on how it contrasts with Italy.

Hugo portrays Italy as a nonviolent place, entertained nevertheless by Hollywood's myth of violence in the West. He claims that Italy's "most ferocious animals" are "obsequious wolves," meaning that they are submissive, obedient, or servile. Italians themselves are not merely peaceful and civilized; saying that their bars are "filled with pastry" is like calling them cream puffs. Hugo's statement that "There's no/ prison for miles" seems ironic, as though he were disappointed that Italians are law-abiding citizens.

The final sentence of the poem serves to focus the double edge of Hugo's senti-ment. He is as saddened by the reality of Western life as he is by those gullible enough to enjoy a romanticized version of its violence. Furthermore, the safety of civilized life in Italy strangely mirrors the pathos Hugo sees in contemporary West-ern life, where crimes, such as polluting rivers and mistreating Indians, are not at all like the bold outlines of good and evil pictured in Hollywood Westerns. Hugo's poetic persona is often one of the tough guy, reminiscent, as Hugo himself noted, of Humphrey Bogart's film image. In "A Map of Montana in Italy," Hugo's tough per-sona never flinches from exposing Montana's nihilism and abuse, characteristics that create a parallel toughness in the poet's voice.

William Hoagland

MARIANA

Author: Alfred, Lord Tennyson (1809-1892)
Type of poem: Lyric
First published: 1830, in *Poems, Chiefly Lyrical*

The Poem

"Mariana" is a lyric poem of seven twelve-line stanzas, each ending in a refrain. The epigraph, "Mariana in the moated grange," is from William Shakespeare's *Measure for Measure* (1604), in which Mariana has been deserted by her lover, Angelo. The poem is also indebted to John Keats's *Isabella* (1820).

"Mariana" begins with a vivid depiction of setting and mood. The grange and its garden have fallen into disrepair. The flower plots are clogged with "blackest moss." Like Mariana, they are fertile but bereft of human care; they remain fallow. The house, too, is neglected. The roof's "ancient thatch" is worn and full of weeds; "rusted nails" allow the pear tree to fall from the gable wall; the gate's "clinking latch," moved only by the wind, remains "unlifted." This description of physical decay is emphasized by the obsessive lament of Mariana's refrain. Her life is "dreary"; she is "aweary, aweary" because "He cometh not," and she wishes that she were dead. Hers is the only human voice to break the silence.

The still-life effect of stanza 1 is followed by the slow passage of time in the remaining stanzas. She weeps morning and evening, so preoccupied with her earthly longing for Angelo (the unnamed "he" who haunts the poem) that she cannot "look on the sweet heaven." She hears only the sinister "flitting of the bats." When she does look out her window, all she sees are "the glooming flats." When she is able to sleep, "she seemed to walk forlorn," but whether sleepwalking or dreaming, she is "without hope of change."

Natural elements only emphasize her isolation. She hears "the night-fowl crow" and "the oxen's low," but not Angelo, whose name echoes these rhymes. The vegetation surrounding the grange, where "blackened waters slept" and "clustered marish-mosses crept," is lushly cloying, the claustrophobia heightened by the tongue-tying syntax.

The poplar tree is symbolic of Mariana herself, its shadow falling "Upon her bed, across her brow." Standing alone in the landscape, it trembles in the wind, and its "gnarled bark" shows signs of age, while "the wooing wind aloof" plays on its limbs. The wind is symbolic of Angelo, invisible yet felt in the desire of Mariana's limbs.

In stanza 6, Mariana reaches her emotional crisis. Each sensory detail in "the dreamy house" is magnified and amplified, her senses reaching a hallucinatory lucidity. Doors creak, flies buzz, and mice shriek with maddening volume. The house seems haunted with "Old faces," "Old footsteps," and "Old voices."

In the final stanza, the poem's imagery comes together to "confound her sense" in both meanings of sense. Both perception and sanity are overthrown. She dreads the setting of the sun when "the day/ Was sloping toward his western bower." The use of the masculine "his" is important. Just as Mariana's name rhymes with that of the virgin goddess of the moon, Diana, so Angelo's name rhymes with that of the sun god, Apollo. (Ironically, Apollo pursued Daphne, the nymph who was metamorphosed into a tree.) Both the sun and Angelo have passed Mariana by. Since Apollo is also the god of rationality and order, his disappearance over the horizon also foreshadows the beginning of yet another haunting night.

Forms and Devices

"Mariana" appeared to universal critical acclaim for its pictorial qualities. It has been said that Alfred, Lord Tennyson's poem prefigured the practices of the Pre-Raphaelite painters and poets, for whom an accumulation of vivid detail and an emphasis on feeling over idea were major tenets. John Everett Millais' painting of "Mariana" is one of the centerpieces of Pre-Raphaelite painting.

John Stuart Mill praised Tennyson's excellence in "scene-painting, in the higher sense"—that is, in "the power of *creating* scenery, in keeping with some state of human feeling; so fitted to it as to be the embodied symbol of it." The emotions in the poem are suggested by the accumulation of precise details, the layering of which acquire symbolic force, before being stated directly in the refrain.

The poem's point of view encourages the reader to identify with Mariana's state of mind. In *Tennyson: The Unquiet Heart* (1983), Robert Martin has said that the poem "foreshadows Tennyson's success in later works that were in all but name dramatic monologues." Mariana's perceptions and emotions become those of the reader's.

Distorted imagery reflects Mariana's hypersensitivity, a result of being deprived of human companionship. At the height of her crisis, she animates her environment with hallucinations. Her vision is magnified ("The blue fly sung in the pane"); her hearing is amplified ("the mouse/ Behind the wainscot shrieked"). Tennyson's own myopia may account for his tightly focused, close-up imagery, but the effect creates almost cinematic distortions of space and time, as in the slow-motion or time-lapse vision of the rusted nails falling from the knots.

Personification is another way Tennyson lends human emotion to inanimate objects. Used tritely, it can result in what John Ruskin called "the pathetic fallacy." Used properly and with purpose, however, personification can be a powerful projection of psychological reality. Nature is so embued with Mariana's psychological state as to become a projection of her own emotion. Mariana has only the inanimate world with which to converse, so it is no wonder that she sees the broken sheds as "sad," the grange as "lonely," or the morning as "gray-eyed" at the end of a sleepless night. The morning reflects her own lusterless eyes because she needs the empathy of her surroundings.

Several devices of repetition mimic the monotony that Mariana feels. Rhyme, assonance, and alliteration heighten the static quality of her vigil. Chief among these devices is the refrain itself, with its feminine rhymes of "dreary/aweary." Tennyson well knew, however, that the depiction of monotony should not itself become monotonous, so he takes care to vary the end of the refrain slightly in each stanza.

No analysis of a Tennyson poem would be complete without noting its musicality. The importance of sound in evoking Mariana's mood cannot be overemphasized. Soft vowels and consonants dominate, especially those of her and Angelo's names, to express the oh's and ah's of languishing desire. That Angelo's name is never uttered, only evoked in echo-like rhymes and in the implied comparison to Apollo, shows a deft psychological touch: Mariana is unable to speak her obsession.

Themes and Meanings

"Mariana" is a good poem with which to begin the study of Tennyson. It shows his technical strengths of pictorial and musical qualities, as well as his greatest weakness: a lack of philosophical depth. What Tennyson lacks in ideas, he makes up for in psychological acuity and emotional accuracy. Still, "Mariana" is more than a lyrical portrait of monotony in the manner of Keats, with its sensuous evocation of melancholy; it also reflects the Victorian search—or wait—for a subject and style of its own. Published in 1830 at the end of the Romantic period, "Mariana" begins to show the problem with the Romantic lyric stance in the face of emerging Victorian concerns.

A major Victorian concern was the crisis of doubt brought on by apocalyptic social and intellectual changes. While the Industrial Revolution was laying waste to a way of life close to nature, the explosion of scientific discoveries was similarly laying waste to traditional ideas about religion. The result was a general feeling of abandonment. In "Dover Beach," Matthew Arnold proposed that even in the absence of worldly or religious hope, couples could at least "be true to one another." Yet Mariana is deprived of even this consolation. Seen in this light, her abandonment by Angelo reflects this larger crisis in faith, and her inability to act is analogous to stalled Victorian energies.

In later poems, such as "Lucretius" and "Despair," Tennyson explores what happens when, in the absence of a transcendent faith, the material world is a person's only reality. He concludes that such a view can end only in despair. Under the weight of her desire for Angelo, Mariana cannot "look on the sweet heaven," and she sinks into the sensuous experience of her surroundings. Desire turns to despair. Only in the final refrain does Mariana invoke a higher power for the first time: "Oh God, that I were dead!" (In the poem's sequel, "Mariana in the South," Mariana joins a convent, forsaking worldly desire in order to focus her attention on the otherworldly.)

"Mariana" is the first of several early Tennyson poems, such as "The Lady of Shallot" and "The Palace of Art," to employ an isolated feminine alter ego to express Tennyson's conflict between passive escape and active engagement. "The Lotos-Eaters" choose reverie and sensation over worldly duties. Not until "Ulysses" does Tennyson resolve the conflict by opting for active engagement in the world. Significantly for the reading of "Mariana," "Ulysses" was Tennyson's way of dealing with his grief over the death of his friend Arthur Henry Hallam. Like Mariana, he felt abandoned by the friend he loved, and he wanted to die—if only to be able to join Hallam in death. In his elegy to Hallam, *In Memoriam* (1850), Tennyson's acknowledged masterpiece and a poem that has been called the single most representative work of the Victorian period, Tennyson compares himself to a widow awaiting her lover's return—a situation very similar to the one that he first explored in "Mariana."

Richard Collins

MARRIAGE

Author: Gregory Corso (1930-   )
Type of poem: Meditation
First published: 1960, in *The Happy Birthday of Death*

The Poem

"Marriage" is a lengthy comic meditation in free verse on the topic announced by the poem's title. More specifically, the opening line poses two questions: "Should I get married? Should I be good?" The male speaker considers these questions, though he has no intended companion in mind. Rather, the meditation considers the various social archetypes of married life and whether they suit the speaker, who seems to see himself as a subversive of sorts. The poem is divided into seven verse paragraphs of varying length, and it is organized by a variety of scenarios the speaker imagines.

The longest of these scenarios imagines a conventional marriage to "the girl next door." This fantasy envisions a courtship that mixes the odd ("Don't take her to movies but to cemeteries") with the romantically orthodox ("she going just so far and I understanding why"). A familiarly comic scene of meeting the fiancée's parents follows, as does a description of the wedding and the honeymoon. At the imagined Niagara Falls honeymoon, the speaker is so horrified by the corny lasciviousness of the honeymoon ritual that he chooses not to consummate the marriage. He will, he imagines, stay up all night staring at the hotel clerk and "Screaming: I deny honeymoon! I deny honeymoon!" Eventually, he will abandon his marriage and live beneath Niagara Falls itself as "a saint of divorce," a crazed spirit bent on disrupting the marriage consummations in the thousands of "almost climactic suites."

All the scenarios similarly end in rejections of marriage. He next imagines a more blissful domestic scene with his wife "aproned young and lovely and wanting my baby." Here, his subversive tendencies play out as practical jokes aimed at suburban orthodoxy: He will cover the neighbor's golf clubs with old Norwegian books; he will speak insanely to local canvassers for charities; he will order "penguin dust" from the milkman. This fantasy gives way to a more serious scenario in which, motivated by love for his wife, he strives to be the ideal cultivated father, giving the child a rattle made from "broken Bach records" and sewing "the Greek alphabet on its bib."

Reality intrudes, however, and the speaker imagines that he is more likely to live in a rat- and roach-infested walk-up apartment in New York City than in such a blissful Connecticut farmhouse. There his wife will be yelling at him to get a job while his "five nose running brats in love with Batman" charge about the overcrowded apartment. As that fantasy ends in a rejection of marriage, he imagines one more scenario: a sophisticated Manhattan penthouse with an elegant wife in evening dress sipping a cocktail. Even that idyll is rejected: "No, can't imagine myself married to that pleasant prison dream."

Having concluded that marriage is impossible for him, the speaker muses briefly about love, but dismisses it as being "as odd as wearing shoes." Finally, he sees a fearful vision of himself alone and unmarried: "all alone in a furnished room with pee stains on my underwear/ and everybody else is married!" The knowledge that loneliness may well await those who reject the conventions of matrimony influences the melancholy tone of the concluding lines. He imagines that just as his own sensibility exists, so must it be possible for a woman whom he could marry to exist. She could exist anywhere, however—even in ancient Egypt—and both the speaker and the idealized lover wait alone.

Forms and Devices

Tone is a central issue in interpreting this monologue. By invoking and exaggerating orthodox images of matrimony, Gregory Corso comically burlesques the social order. The use of hyperbole and stereotypical images interspersed with absurdist proclamations ("yelling Radio belly! Cat shovel!") creates a humorous incongruity. Indeed, ironic or surprising juxtaposition accounts for much of the poem's originality and comedy. The image of hanging a picture of Arthur Rimbaud on the lawn mower juxtaposes the romantic decadence of the youthful French poet with the most conventional tool of suburban lawn maintenance. Such an incongruity, Corso implies, parallels the incongruity of the speaker's free spirit entering into orthodox matrimony. That Rimbaud abandoned his poetic vocation at a very young age and became a conventional businessman heightens the irony of the juxtaposition.

The poem progresses through a series of such tensions in which idyllic visions of marriage are quickly countered by nightmarish ones. Similarly, the conventional is repeatedly subverted by the unorthodox. The alternations of this poetic dialectic are reflected in the use of "but" and "yet" to mark the shifts in thought that lead to the rejection of traditional marriage and "goodness" in response to the questions of the opening line. The comic exaggeration and manic intensity of the frequent exclamations—the poem has thirty-five exclamation points—is balanced by certain seriousness. That human companionship must take the form of a surrender to social orthodoxy is a serious problem that Corso wishes to expose.

Both Corso's theme and technique are typical of the Beat movement in literature with which he is associated. The combination of deliberate anticonventionality with language charged with intensity and free association characterizes the work of Corso's contemporaries—Jack Kerouac, Allen Ginsberg, and William Burroughs. Like these writers, Corso reached his maturity in the highly conventional decade of the 1950's and reacted vehemently against the American dream. The reader sees some of the stylistic consequences of this reaction in the speaker's penchant for disruptive absurdism. Saying "Pie Glue" instead of "I do" at the wedding ceremony, thinking "Flash Gordon soap" in the midst of his interview with his lover's parents, trying to dream of "Telephone snow"—all these forms of linguistic disruption of the expected reflect the Beat desire to shock the reader out of complacency.

The use of free verse and prosaic syntax (even while the content reaches for the bizarre) is also characteristic of Beat poetry. Similarly, the heavy use of allusion and proper nouns works to put the stuff of contemporary culture into the poem. This culture is itself a hodgepodge of old and new: Thus Ingrid Bergman can appear beside Tacitus, Blue Cross beside Bach, the Knights of Columbus beside the Parthenon. Weaving the items of a cultural mishmash into an extended diatribe, Corso taps the energy of his position as a self-appointed subversive in a highly conventional society.

Themes and Meanings

The poem's title and opening questions leave little doubt about the issues central to the work. Corso's approach, though, of considering a social institution in light of competing stereotypes is provocative. The poem implicitly argues that marriage can be more effectively understood through cultural images of it than through abstract considerations of love: "O but what about love! I forget love."

Corso deliberately focuses on rituals and the clichés that surround them, such as meeting the parents ("we're losing a daughter/ but we're gaining a son"), the wedding itself ("And the priest! he looking at me as if I masturbated/ asking me Do you take this woman for your lawful wedded wife?"), and the honeymoon ("all those corny men slapping me on the back/ She's all yours, boy! Ha-ha-ha!"). One may be tempted to dismiss these rituals and cultural clichés as formalities that are finally unimportant to the real issue of two individuals forming a lifelong bond. In "Marriage," however, Corso insists that the clichés reveal much about this culture. The form of the poem argues that clichés and stereotypes shape the actual life choices available to people.

One cannot help but notice how minor a role the wife plays in these imagined scenarios. Indeed, the poem has an egotistical and male bias that is not uncommon in Beat literature and American literature as a whole. The tendency in classic American literature for the male hero to flee from women and marital domesticity into the heroic wilderness runs from Mark Twain's *The Adventures of Huckleberry Finn* (1884) and Herman Melville's *Moby Dick* (1851) to Kerouac's *On the Road* (1957). While "Marriage" is hardly a quest romance as those novels are, it participates in the male rejection of home and marriage as imprisoning. Corso even uses the phrase "pleasant prison dream" to dismiss his final marriage fantasy. The surprising absence of feminist sensibility in a literary movement that celebrates the outsider and values difference is one of the characteristics that makes much of Beat literature seem dated.

Though one may find Corso's comic dismissal of marriage as oppressive conventionality to be a little glib, the poem nevertheless bespeaks a significant anxiety of modern society—that growing up involves a continual sacrifice of individuality and freedom, and that the price of insisting on those qualities is isolation and alienation. As a young man, Corso spent time in prison and (like Ginsberg) in the psychiatric wards of Bellevue Hospital. As "Marriage" shows in its concluding lines, Corso has a keen awareness of the price of not participating in social conventions. "All the universe married but me!" the poet hyperbolically exclaims, and the reader senses the seriousness of human aloneness lurking beneath the lively comic images: "so I wait—bereft of 2,000 years and the bath of life."

Christopher Ames

MARRIAGE

Author: Marianne Moore (1887-1972)
Type of poem: Satire
First published: 1923; collected in *The Complete Poems of Mariane Moore*, 1967

The Poem

   Marriage is relatively long for a non-narrative poem, nearly three hundred lines. The unidentified speaker retains distance from the subject, offering comments as a neutral "one" and as a more personal "I," but depending throughout on a technique characteristic of Marianne Moore: the interpolation of quotations as part of the poem's statement. The general tone is of detached, wry observation.

   The poem opens with a characterization of marriage as either an institution or an enterprise, followed by a query as to what Adam and Eve would think about it. The speaker then extends the Adam and Eve allusion to describe a generic bride and groom. The Eve-bride is characterized by beauty, accomplishment, and contradiction; she upsets the careful rationality of ordered creation with the disturbance of passion. The story of the snake in the garden of paradise is referred to as a convenient exoneration of Adam. The lengthy description of the Adam-groom begins with a vision of Adam in paradise as if depicted in a highly detailed Persian miniature. The speaker goes on to enumerate the man's assertive qualities, which can lead him to overlook the potential dangers of women as he maintains a formal pose, speaking with a specious sense of ownership of public accomplishments and external qualities; eventually, he foolishly begins to believe in his own image, satisfied that he has become an "idol." In the next several lines, he is described as being overcome with passion, against which his rational qualities are helpless, eventually "stumbling" over marriage, which will prove his (literal) downfall.

   At this point, the speaker intervenes with a commentary on "Unhelpfuwl Hymen," the classical god of marriage, characterizing the social institution as a lavish, artificial attempt to re-create lost paradisiacal bliss. The following fifty lines of the poem offer comments on the superficial outward forms of marriage in polite society, with teas, banquets, and social rituals, contrasted with the passionate and even violent reality underneath, in which assault may be called affection and male power may be asserted arbitrarily and destructively.

   The next fifty lines offer alternating commentary from the two partners. The man criticizes women for disappointing men by not always being beautiful; the woman accuses men of being obsessed with trivia. He retorts with a characterization of woman as nothing but a deceptive vessel (a coffin at that), and she replies that men's affections are shallow and inconstant. She accuses him of knowing "so many artists who are fools"; he shoots back that she surrounds herself with "so many fools/ who are not artists." Both individuals are absorbed in self-love: He is oblivious to the existence of other people, and she focuses narcissistically on her appearance. The speaker of the poem then intervenes with another question, asking what can be done for these "savages," and continues the commentary on the mystery of love and commitment, so impenetrable as to seem unreal. A successful marriage as a true union of opposites is rare, the speaker goes on to say; it is a matter of deceptive simplicity and a profound enigma. In the closing lines of the poem, the speaker tries to sum up the essential paradox of a successful marriage in the lines of Daniel Webster, "Liberty and union, now and forever," and offers an emblem of this union in a cryptic allusion to the cliché of the wedding portrait.

Forms and Devices

Marianne Moore's most characteristic poetic device was quotation of passages taken from her wide reading. *Marriage* makes liberal use of this device, drawing upon many sources for its far-flung allusions. An article in *Scientific American*, for example, provides an account of a young woman who writes simultaneously in three languages; *Marriage* incorporates the description into a characterization of the ideal bride as formidably and aggressively accomplished. Anthony Trollope's *Barchester Towers* (1857) provides the quotation commending the age of forty-five to seventy as the best time for a man to marry, sentiments ascribed to the fatuous groom in Moore's poem.

While the sources for her citations are disparate, ranging from scientific reports to women's magazines to the classics, a significant few recur in this poem. Richard Baxter's treatise on Christian doctrine and piety, *The Saints Everlasting Rest* (1649), is the source for four of the passages in *Marriage*. Baxter was an eighteenth century Puritan, and although she respected him as an authoritative spiritual voice, Moore's displacement of his words to an alien context might be seen as satirizing her sources. Thus, she makes Baxter's enumeration of the comprehensiveness of God's interest in humans ("past states, the present state," and so forth) into the pompous speech of her self-absorbed, immature Adam-groom. Along with Baxter, the Bible is quoted more than once (Ecclesiastes and Amos), which with the pervasive allusion to the biblical myth of Adam and Eve sets the poet's meditation on marriage firmly within the western Judeo-Christian tradition. The tradition itself, however, forms an object of satire as the poem's speaker pokes fun at this central institution. Also, Moore draws on more varied and secular sources, which counterpoint the religious sources: William Godwin (agnostic philosopher) and M. Carey Thomas (feminist educator) also provide citations, as do William Hazlitt and Francis Bacon.

Moore's method of developing her argument in *Marriage* is highly allusive and associational. The reader is expected to absorb allusions to Adam and Eve, Hymen, Ahasuerus (the so-called Wandering Jew of European folklore), the garden of the Hesperides (where the golden apples of Greek myth grew), William Shakespeare and a quotation from his play *The Tempest* (1611), and the nineteenth century American senator Daniel Webster. The associations surrounding these allusions, like the focus on a wedding masque in *The Tempest* in which the goddess Hymen appears, are expected to become part of the radiating meanings of the poem. The method also combines extremely abstract and analytic language with an intense pictorial sense. The narcissistic bride, for example, sees herself as "a statuette of ivory on ivory," a highly vivid image conveying the illusive fragility, purity, subtlety, and value of the art object. The icon of bride-as-statuette is followed by a sententiously precise abstract motto: "one is not rich but poor/ when one can always seem so right."

Themes and Meanings

While *Marriage* is a satirical poem, the object of its satire is elusive and ambiguous. At some points, marriage itself seems to be satirized as a romantic delusion. Given the author's orthodox and conservative Christian belief, however, such an interpretation has limited persuasiveness. Rather, her witty barbs seem aimed more at the incrustations of artificial forms and manners that have obscured the elemental passionate union, and equally at the deceptions and misrepresentations made in the name of marriage. When love comes into the discussion, it is either as infatuate fixation, as in the passage from Trollope on "love that will gaze an eagle blind," or the mutual narcissism of the self-absorbed couple. Finally, the speaker admits to an inadequacy of rational explanation in, characteristically, another cited passage, this one from French fabulist Jean de La Fontaine: "Everything to do with love is a mystery." The true paradox is the institution of marriage as a combination of public contractual obligation and intimate, emotional experience.

The contrast between the public, social façade of marriage and the internal emotional dynamics of a love relationship emerges most forcefully in the dialogue between man and woman that the speaker reports in the last half of the poem. This exchange is actually a series of alternating pronouncements rather than a true dialogue, as the two principals actually speak to each other only at one point. The promiscuity ascribed to males is imagined in the butterfly proposing, in a pun within a pun, to "settle on the hand" of the young woman. The natural freedom of the insect is associated with the libertinism of artists and contrasted with the boring philistinism of so-called polite society, which was earlier defined in the religious dedication to the superficial social ritual of afternoon tea (in a quotation from an aristocratic Frenchwoman writing in a women's magazine).

As with most social satire, *Marriage* is in many respects a topical poem. Besides understanding the literary, historical, and mythological allusions, the reader should have some acquaintance with the customs and forms of the society being depicted, and even with the personal lives of some of the sources cited. The butterfly quotation alludes to the marriage proposal made by Ezra Pound to Hilda Doolittle (better known as H. D.), which was reportedly opposed by her father in the words quoted. Similarly, the milieu of the drawing room and the afternoon "at home," no less than the formal studio portrait of the wedding couple, are integral to the poem's statement. Understanding these elements, like those of the poem's social context, enriches the reader's experience of the poem's philosophical statement.

Helen Jaskoski

THE MASK OF ANARCHY

Author: Percy Bysshe Shelley (1792-1822)
Type of poem: Ballad
First published: 1832

The Poem

The Mask of Anarchy, a ballad of ninety-one stanzas, was inspired by the "Peterloo Massacre" in Manchester, England. On August 16, 1819, several thousand people gathered in St. Peter's Fields to hear the orator Henry Hunt speak in favor of reform in the English government. The assembly was broken up violently by militia and cavalry, who attempted to arrest Hunt. At least ten people were killed and hundreds injured.

The first stanza tells how news of the massacre led the sleeping Percy Bysshe Shelley "To walk in the visions of Poesy"; the images he envisions within his poetic imagination are essentially a reenactment of "Peterloo," with a happy ending. The first twenty stanzas offer a hideous parade in which the sins of government hide behind the likenesses of individual politicians of the day. The poem's title is therefore a pun both on "mask," to conceal one's identity, and on "masque," a dramatic form of entertainment based on an allegorical theme. Murder "had a mask like Castlereagh," Robert Stewart Castlereagh, the Foreign Secretary who often introduced unpopular repressive measures in Parliament. Fraud bears the mask of Lord Chancellor John Scott Eldon, the judge who took two of Shelley's children away from him. Hypocrisy bears the likeness of Lord Sidmouth (Henry Addington), Home Secretary in the Tory Government. Other horrible beings follow, "All disguised, . . ./ Like Bishops, lawyers, peers, and spies."

Last in the procession is Anarchy himself, a symbol for the English government. He claims: "I am God, and King, and Law!" Anarchy's "white horse" is "splashed with blood," reminiscent of the Death that rode a pale horse in Revelation. He is followed by "hired murderers," loyal bloodthirsty soldiers whom Shelley associates with those who took part in the killings at "Peterloo."

The macabre masquerade spells doom for the oppressed. Thus, Hope is described as a "maniac maid" resembling "Despair." She rushes by the procession, proclaims her "Misery, oh, Misery!" and lies on the ground before Anarchy, resigned to a dismal fate. Then an ambiguous "Shape" emerges, causing Anarchy to flee and to trample his followers to death. This entity brings with it "A sense awakening and yet tender" that brings the people hope. A mysterious voice is heard, like the cry of the "indignant Earth," nature itself.

The impassioned speech made by this voice takes up the final stanzas of the poem. The speech is a cry from freedom, urging the oppressed to "Rise like Lions . . ." and to "Shake your chains to earth like dew." The first part of the speech paints a poignant picture of the dismal plight of the working class caused by despotism. Next the concept of freedom is discussed. To the common laborer, freedom means simply the food and shelter that are denied under tyranny. Freedom is synonymous with justice, wisdom, peace, and love. In the name of freedom, the oppressed from all across the country are urged to unite in a great "Assembly" to demand reform. Shelley suggests a nonviolent struggle: "Stand ye calm and resolute." The great potential within the united numbers of the oppressed is expressed in the final words of the speech: "Ye are many—they are few."

Forms and Devices

Shelley wrote *The Mask of Anarchy* to appeal to the working class. He avoided any overly sophisticated or difficult poetic techniques that might have made the poem inaccessible to an uneducated audience. This lack of sophisticated technique should not be viewed as a weakness. The poem's relatively simple language, structure, rhythm, and metaphors enhance its direct and vigorous message of liberty.

Structurally, the poem follows standard convention in the use and arrangement of stanzas. Each of the ninety-one stanzas has four lines, except for eight five-line stanzas scattered throughout, used in times of particular emphasis (for example, when the voice calls for those assembled to "Rise like Lions . . ." in stanza 38). The stanzas are arranged in an uncomplicated plot structure. The first twenty-one stanzas describe the procession. The next fifteen stanzas include Hope's desperate act, which provides the conflict and makes way for the entrance of the "Shape" and the voice. The remaining fifty-five stanzas make up the speech of freedom. Within this plot structure, the tendency is toward symmetry. After the introductory stanza establishing Shelley's dream, the descriptions of Murder, Fraud, Hypocrisy, and Anarchy receive two stanzas each. The following twelve stanzas that describe the horrible masquerade are balanced by the twelve stanzas (excluding the two on Hope) devoted to the mysterious, yet hopeful, "Shape." Within the final speech, thirteen stanzas portraying the slave-like conditions of the working class are balanced by thirteen stanzas describing freedom.

The poem's rhythm and rhyme are that of street balladry, a form accessible and familiar to the working class. The poem's prosody makes various stanzas easy to remember, like a well-worn song. Most of the stanzas consist of seven syllables per line of trochaic rhythm, a heavy stress followed by a light stress: "*I* met *Mur*der *on* the *way*— " (stressed syllables in italics). At times this meter varies to include lines of eight or ten syllables, but this rarely jars the rhythmic ease of the poem.

The simple rhyme scheme facilitates the rhythm's smooth beat. The four-line stanzas usually follow an *aabb* pattern, while the five-line stanzas follow *aabbb*. Frequently the scheme is even simpler in that all line-ending words within the stanza rhyme (for example, stanza 42 with "weak," "peak," "bleak," "speak"). Most of the rhymes are one syllable ("fly," "sky") with an occasional two-syllable rhyming couplet ("waken," "shaken") to make the poem even more musical.

Shelley is known for his elaborate metaphors and obscure allusions, but in *The Mask of Anarchy* he rejects such complex artifice and offers simpler, more familiar images and references to suit his poor, uneducated audience. Most of Shelley's readers would have recognized the allusion to Revelation in describing Anarchy as "Like Death in the Apocalypse." Similarly, the "Shape" who is "Brighter than the viper's scale" alludes to the snake, a well-known symbol of resistance to oppression. Throughout the poem, Shelley uses symbols and metaphors of oppression and liberty familiar to the common people of the day.

Themes and Meanings

Shelley's emotionally polemic poem is intended to further the cause of governmental reform, an issue that was dividing England at the time. Some of the reform efforts Shelley advocated were expanded suffrage and greater freedom of speech, press, and assembly. The poem supports these causes by metaphorically elaborating on the concepts of tyranny and liberty, describing the effects of each in concrete, poignant images. In simple yet searing language the poem vehemently denounces tyranny as exploitative and as going against the very laws of nature. Liberty, however, is a God-given right of every person. Living by the precepts of liberty will ensure a happier, more fruitful existence.

Liberty is seen in concrete and practical terms. The poem avoids any abstraction that would make freedom seem unrealistic and overly idealistic, a "superstition" doomed "soon to pass away." On the contrary, freedom is ". . . bread,/ and a comely table spread." It provides for the very necessities of life, clothing and food, things denied under tyranny.

Freedom is also associated with justice, providing for "righteous laws" that would forbid the kind of exploitation allowed by tyranny. Here one can see that Shelley did not advocate lawless revolution. Liberty does not mean the freedom to ignore law, but the establishment of equitable law. Lawlessness would be no improvement over tyranny. In fact, the masquerade of tyrants and the poem's title itself show that Shelley equates tyranny with anarchy. Tyranny creates gross inequities that will inevitably cause revolution and anarchy. Shelley warns of this by reminding the reader of France ("Gaul" in stanza 59), where injustice led to bloody revolution and to a more malevolent tyranny under Napoleon. Thus, as the poem states, liberty "Thou art Peace . . ." Blood would never be shed if governments functioned based on the true precepts of liberty.

This adherence to law is seen in Shelley's concept of the assembly and what they should do. This assembly, made up of the oppressed throughout England, is symbolic of the power of numbers against a lesser foe: "Ye are many—they are few." Shelley advocates a kind of passive resistance. The members of the assembly are to stand strong and resolute, "With folded arms and steady eyes," in the face of the enemy. They should allow the tyrants to "Slash, and stab, and maim, and hew, —" without retaliating or making any attempt to defend themselves. This should shame the enemy into defeat; some ("true warriors") will even join the protesters in their resistance. This is not a call for violent revolution or bloody revenge, but a plea for "righteous law" as suits the wisdom and reason of liberty.

In contrast, the consequences of tyranny are violence and suffering. This is seen in the bloodthirsty characters of the masquerade who knock out the brains of children and trample their subjects into a "mire of blood." The effect of tyranny on the working class is slavery, poignantly described in the first section of liberty's speech. Shelley created such a horrifying vision of tyranny that its antithesis—liberty—seems society's only legitimate haven.

Heidi Kelchner

MASKS

Author: Sonia Sanchez (1934-　　)
Type of poem: Lyric
First published: 1984, in *Homegirls and Handgrenades*

The Poem

"Masks" is a poem of forty mostly short, free-verse lines about the struggle African Americans face in defining themselves. The masks to which the title refers are not only those that blacks in America have adopted to protect themselves but also those that have been forced upon them.

The critic Houston Baker, Jr., sees two primary voices present in Sonia Sanchez's poetry. She has what he calls a "Greenwich Village/e. e. cummings" voice, marked by a personal tone and a loud, confrontational voice that seems to explore the revolutionary edges of what a black aesthetic might be. "Masks" integrates these two sides of the poet and comes up with something new: It has the reflective nature of some of Sanchez's quieter poetry, but it also has a directly confrontational stance. Further, its images have an almost mystical quality distinct from the very direct quality of the images of many of her earlier poems.

The poem shows a willingness to be confrontational in its epigraph: "Blacks don't have the intellectual capacity to succeed," Sanchez quotes William Coors, chairman of Coors Brewing Company, which, in the early 1980's, when the poem was written, had been accused of unfair hiring and labor practices by the American Federation of Labor-Congress of Industrial Organizations. The implication is that such racist beliefs are both the cause and effect of living behind socially stereotyped masks.

The first stanza begins with images of rivers and lakes, imagery which by itself might suggest life and renewal. The lakes, however, are patrolled "by one-eyed pimps/ who wash their feet in our blue whoredom." This line suggests the images of African Americans as pimps and hookers that were popular in action films and television shows when Sanchez wrote this poem. Following the epigraph, the "pimps" in question might also be industrialists who are willing to hire blacks only for low-paying jobs, in effect making black people who work for them into "whores."

The second stanza talks about black people waiting for the right season "to change our masks" — not to take off masks, but simply to change them. Later in the poem, the narrator mentions hearing an "unhurried speaker" in a temple talk of "unveiled eyes." The need to "unveil" eyes speaks of the need to take the masks off completely. That the speaker is "unhurried" may suggest a lack of urgency. The message makes the narrator of the poem sit up straight and tall, but this spirit of rejoicing slowly sinks into a "twilight of/ distant smells," perhaps the smell of the drying blood on the masks mentioned in the unrhyming couplet which follows.

The "fee, fie, fo, fum" quote from the story "Jack the Giant Killer" has at least a double meaning. On one hand, the poetic narrator identifies with the trickster, Jack, whose blood is threatened by a ruling giant and who, in some versions of the story, hides from the giant in a cloak of darkness. On the other hand, Jack eventually defeats the giant. As quoted in this poem, these lines seem to offer a possible hope that those who consider themselves ruling "giants" will one day be toppled. Within the context of the poem, however, this hope might be read by some as having a hollow ring to it, and the implied threat may be seen as simply another mask.

The next stanza returns to pessimism. "O my people/ wear the white masks," the poem says, meaning that blacks live out roles defined by white society. The reference to speaking "without speaking" indicates the impotence of language spoken from behind such masks, and the "words of forgetfulness" blacks hear are the words that do not acknowledge the damages caused by the ongoing history of racial oppression. The final line, "o my people," is a statement of love and connection, but also of lament and sorrow.

Forms and Devices

The imagery that begins the poem—of water running, of a river flooding, of days growing short (as in the autumn), and of waiting for days to grow warm again—are images of natural life in motion. Sanchez uses this imagery to call attention to the stasis of waiting for the right season "to change our masks" and never finding the right one to abandon the masks.

"Our days are edifice," she says, conjuring a powerful metaphor of days that are like imposing, unchanging buildings. The poem goes inside such a building, a temple, where the narrator hears hopeful words of the possibility of change—specifically of the possibility of taking off the masks that blacks have to wear to adapt to white society. The spirit of change sinks, however, as if into a twilight.

The appearance of the story of "Jack the Giant Killer" has a certain connection to the "one-eyed pimps" mentioned near the beginning. The "one-eye" suggests a Cyclops, perhaps the Cyclops who patrolled an island on which Odysseus and his crew landed in Homer's *Odyssey* (c. 800 B.C.). The story is relevant in that the Cyclops spills the blood of, and eats, many members of Odysseus' crew. Odysseus and his remaining crew escape by disguising (or masking) themselves as sheep, after having bloodied and blinded, but not killed, the giant Cyclops. Like the story of Jack and the beanstalk, this poem contains the possibility that a tricky, less powerful person can overcome a larger, more powerful one.

This poem, however, has a pessimistic view of the ultimate consequences of relying on such masking. The danger, the poem warns is that it is hard to take off a mask that one has used for protection. This comes through especially in the three short, unrhyming couplets. The calls in each case to bring the mask have an almost ritualistic feel, as if donning this mask, which is associated with whiteness and blood, is part of a regularly recurring rite. That these three couplets are set aside on the page, interrupting several stanzas about a speaker in a temple, also contributes the impression that donning this mask is a distorted and unfortunate ritual.

Themes and Meanings

The story of Odysseus and the Cyclops bears an interesting relationship to this poem. What Sanchez sees happening to African Americans is analogous to the plight of Odysseus and his men, who are never able to take off their sheep's clothing.

"Masks" invites direct comparison to Paul Laurence Dunbar's "We Wear the Mask," written eighty-eight years earlier. Dunbar's poem talks of wearing the mask "that grins and lies" and "hides our cheeks and shades our eyes." Dunbar sees wearing a mask as an essentially effective defensive strategy, but one with a cost.

Sanchez's poem focuses on the cost. Once masks are worn, they stay on. As she implies at the beginning of the poem, seasons change, but the time for taking off the masks never arrives. The need to look at the world directly is understood, but still the masks are donned. The mask changes not only the way one is seen but also the way one sees.

Such masks are ultimately ways for people who are black to live in a white society. As such, they are "white" masks, "chalk" masks, masks that draw the blood of the wearer because they do not let even the wearer of the mask see himself or herself clearly. The result is that people "speak without speaking," meaning that they let the mask do the speaking for them.

The final cost is seen in statements such as the racist statement made by William Coors that Sanchez uses to begin the poem. Masks are used as Dunbar's poem makes clear, to hide one's true thoughts from such a potentially antagonistic person. It is easy for such a person to see only what he or she wants to see or is willing to see of the people behind the masks.

It would not have been out of character for Sonia Sanchez to write an angry and compelling diatribe in response to the statement by William Coors. What she wrote instead is a meditative, and to an extent mournful, account of the pain of living behind masks and the need, but also the difficulty, of removing such masks.

Thomas J. Cassidy

THE MAXIMUS POEMS

Author: Charles Olson (1910-1970)
Type of poem: Poetic sequence
First published: The Maximus Poems, 1960; *Maximus Poems IV, V, VI,* 1968; *The Maximus Poems, Volume Three,* 1975; collected as *The Maximus Poems,* 1983

The Poem

The Maximus Poems, comprising more than six hundred pages of free verse, was written between the years 1950 and 1969, the last entry being composed less than two months before Charles Olson's death. During this time, Olson published various parts as works in progress. The first ten poems, for example, were printed in 1953, and the next twelve in 1956. These twenty-two poems were combined with another sixteen to make up the first volume of the Maximus sequence, *The Maximus Poems.* By 1963, Olson had completed *Maximus Poems IV, V, VI,* although they were not published until 1968. By explicitly dividing this second volume into three books, Olson implied, after the fact, that the first volume should be considered similarly divided. The final volume, published posthumously, was compiled from the disordered mass of Olson's papers by Charles Boer and George Butterick. This last volume, though not divided into books, can be considered, as Olson himself put it, "Books VII and After."

Because of the wide scope of Olson's attention and his constant shifts of focus, reading *The Maximus Poems* can prove to be a frustrating experience to a student accustomed to more conventionally "meaningful" poetry. *The Maximus Poems* seem to provide little footing for interpretation; as soon as the reader thinks he or she has latched onto a piece of something, immediately the poem launches in a new direction, and the reader loses balance again. (To the reader approaching the work for the first time, *A Guide to The Maximus Poems of Charles Olson,* 1978, by George F. Butterick is helpful; Butterick provides a footnote to virtually every reference, obscure and not so obscure, that Olson makes.)

The Maximus of the title was a philosopher of the second century A.D. who lived in Tyre, an ancient city which, in being a major port, parallels the Gloucester, Massachusetts, of Olson's poem. Tyre was also one of the few cities that resisted Alexander the Great's unification of what was then the known world into one state. Olson begins by assuming the persona of Maximus in the title of the first poem: "*I, Maximus of Gloucester, to You.*" Assuming this bardic voice (in the tradition of Walt Whitman's *Leaves of Grass* (1855), Olson/Maximus begins addressing the people of Gloucester. The persona of Maximus of Tyre emblematizes one of Olson's principal concerns: that the citizens of Gloucester resist the homogenizing influences of the state and of commercialization and remain true to the particular concerns of their own community with its particular locale.

Many of the poems in *The Maximus Poems,* especially in volume 1, take the form of letters addressed to Gloucester and are often explicitly indicated as such (as in

"Letter 3" or "Letter, May 2, 1959"). As the work grows, the epistles become infrequent, replaced by meditations on subjects ranging from poetics to Gloucester history. In volume 2, fragments of one or two lines appear — quick insights into various meaningful connections within the material thus far arranged. Maximus begins *The Maximus Poems* by chiding the citizens of Gloucester for giving in to the forces of commercialization and by comparing the work upon which he is about to embark to the building of a nest, a kind of protective wall built from discarded fragments. Much of the rest of the first book is directed at Vincent Ferrini, a friend of Olson and the editor of *Four Winds*, a local literary quarterly. Maximus criticizes Ferrini for publishing poetry espousing abstract idealizations rather than focusing on the particularities of Gloucester. Had Ferrini done the latter, he would have brought forth literature from the Gloucester locale as the fishermen bring forth fish from its shoals.

With "Letter 10," the last of the first book, Maximus begins the excavation of historical detail that will occupy him throughout the rest of the poems. One of his principal concerns is to determine that Gloucester was first a fishing village, founded upon an interaction between its settlers and its environs, rather than a Pilgrim settlement established with an abstract purpose in mind. In "Letter 23," he suggests that the establishment of Gloucester was part of the fight against mercantilism and the Chambers of Commerce, the attempt of a community to live naturally in its locale, "merely sowing,/ reaping, building/ houses & out houses," as he later puts it in the poem "Stiffening, in the Master Founders' Wills." Nevertheless, the Gloucester of the 1950's has fallen. Men such as Nathaniel Bowditch and Stephen Higginson ("Letter 16") had, in the past, exploited Gloucester for their own ends; others, such as John Burke ("John Burke") did the same in the twentieth century; now "the Deisels/ shake the sky" ("Letter, May 2, 1959") and the citizens trivialize the fishermen who have died at sea ("Maximus, to Gloucester, Sunday, July 19").

In *Maximus Poems IV, V, VI*, Maximus (Olson) widens his scope to include mythology, geology, and human migration. For example, in "Maximus, From Dogtown—I," he raises to mythological stature the goring by a bull of a Gloucester sailor named Merry in 1892. In "*Maximus Letter # Whatever*," he tells the story of a man who acquired a house that he could carry on his head. Principally, the speaker seems intent, especially in book IV, to present as many details as possible, without drawing connections. A fragment from a merchant's account book, a notation regarding the particular flowers growing at a certain address, entries from an almanac — anything seems to merit inclusion. By the end of the volume, an intricate web of cross-references has been built, which both look back to the first volume and forward to the next, yet no explicit inferences are drawn, as was done in *The Maximus Poems*.

The final volume, probably because it was not arranged by Olson, lacks both the coherence of the first and the intricate design of the second. The persona of Maximus begins to drop; many poems are signed with the poet's real name. A personal tone enters more frequently, and there are fewer dazzling intellectual leaps. Often, an undercurrent of grief pervades, from the loss of his wife and from his failure to rewrite the conscience of his beloved city. Because of these factors, this last volume is perhaps more approachable than the previous two.

Forms and Devices

Charles Olson was a proponent of what he called "projective verse." Though his twentieth century predecessors had already abandoned fixed meters for the loose flow of free verse, Olson believed that they had not gone far enough; the arbitrary authority of syntax must also be broken. Olson suggested that syntax abstracts words from their essential relation to the objects for which they stand and from their myriad possible relations to one another. In bowing to the rules of syntax, a poet risks falling into the same trap inherent in the use of metrical schemes: trying to make things work out correctly according to arbitrary rules, playing a mere game with the content of his or her poetry instead of attempting to place the represented objects in their true relations to one another.

The first poem provides an excellent example of Olson's method in the lines "flight/ (of the bird/ o kylix, o/ Antony of Padua/ sweep low, o bless/ the roofs." Abandoning syntax allows each perception to follow quickly one after another, allowing an increase in vigor and scope similar to the increase that free verse earlier had allowed. Specifically abandoning the ordinary syntax of verb tenses allows a mythologizing of time—an entry into an eternal present—as in the poem "Maximus, from Dogtown—I," which describes the bull that kills the sailor Merry waiting for Merry to arrive, "not even knowing/ death/ was in his power over/ this man who lay/ in the Sunday morning sun." The bull waits for Merry, who is yet to arrive, while standing over Merry's already "fly-blown" body. Finally, sudden shifts in voice, which adherence to syntax makes difficult, become a simple matter of juxtaposition. Widely varying material—historical, mythological, scientific data—can all be brought into immediate relation with a consequent increase in the layers of significance.

Olson also broke from the use of a justified left margin, not to create a formal arrangement as is found in John Keat's "Ode to a Nightingale," but rather to indicate digressions and shifts in thought, as William Carlos Williams had begun to do in *Paterson* (1946-1958). Thus, for example, in "Letter 23," Maximus breaks off in mid-thought with "*muthologos* has lost such ground since Pindar," indents, and picks up with a digression concerning Pindar, "the odish man." Sometimes, as in the poem beginning "I have been an ability" in *The Maximus Poems, Volume Three*, he abandons the margin altogether and allows the lines to loop and circle about the page. Elsewhere, words spot the page like the names of cities on a map in which the terrain has been excised. Though often his poems look nontraditional and difficult, Olson uses the page as a field with particular effects and suggestions in mind.

Themes and Meanings

Parallel to his abandonment of syntax was Olson's rejection of what he called flowing narrative, or stories which carry the reader along and allow an effortless merging with an apparently natural flow of events. "Experience," he wrote,

> like matter, is discontinuous, and the act of writing is the act of object. . . . It is an essential act, to align experience, and by words alone to create such space around the words that they become a thing as solid in the mind, or the ear, as a stone or cowslip in the hand.

Instead, he sought what he called a narrative of resistance, in which each poetic object stands separate from those around it, without being linked into some systematized narrative that creates a false hierarchy of events by forcing them to bend to the necessities of the narrative structure. Events should be presented with equal emphasis throughout, not highlighted or glossed over according to the whims of the story line; however, flowing narrative has such a strong hold on the imagination that it proves difficult to represent experience in its actual discontinuity.

Indeed, Olson realized that in the first volume of *The Maximus Poems* he had fallen into the trap. He had attempted to create a flowing narrative from the myriad events recorded of Gloucester's history. The attempt to center the later development of Gloucester on a battle over a fishing stage discounted the innumerable hidden events, those that went unnoted in historical accounts but had as much influence upon Gloucester as the more notable events. One sees him fighting against the hold of flowing narrative in his dredging up of oral history—stories told by old sailors in "1st Letter on Georges" and "[2nd Letter on Georges]"—and in his pacing off of the property lines around Gloucester ("Letter, May 2, 1959"), attempting to uncover the crucial, unrecorded struggles for power.

In *Maximus IV, V, VI*, he succeeds in throwing off the fixated search for a flowing narrative, which accounts for much of the apparent difficulty of the volume. In the opening poem, he leaps from the security of his porch into a blizzard. The last word, left dangling, is Gondwana, the name of the massive continent that eventually broke up to form the smaller continents in existence today. The idea, then, of rifts, divisions between the various contents and objects of his poem, is immediately presented; it is picked up throughout the volume, as in the poem composed of the two words *tesserae*/commisure. *Tesserae* are the pieces of stone or glass used in making a mosaic. Commisure refers to the seam or juncture at which two things are joined. Similarly, the poems of this volume are separate objects which, though placed side by side, remain discrete. The emphasis is on the seam, not seamlessness. Nevertheless, things do fit together, as is suggested in the poem beginning "All night long," though the work of joining is a sleeping act, performed in the unconscious. As with *tesserae*, the poems can fit together to create many different patterns.

One such pattern might be made from the references to mapping, as in the poem beginning "Peloria   the dog's upper lip," with its avowel that the poet is "making a mappemunde. It is to include my being." This can be fit to the various conjunctions of body parts with places in Gloucester as well as to the mythological references to the earth to create a sense of what such a world map might comprise. Although it is important to realize that not all interpretations will fit, it is perhaps more important to refrain from all-embracing interpretations. The former merely demonstrate poor seeing, the latter, blindness—not simply to *The Maximus Poems* but very likely to that which they, in their complexity, strive to imitate—life itself.

Peter Crawford

MEETING THE BRITISH

Author: Paul Muldoon (1951-   )
Type of poem: Lyric
First published: 1987, in *Meeting the British*

The Poem

The nine slant-rhymed couplets of "Meeting the British" tell a brief and simple story that encapsulates many elements in the history of the discovery and conquest of America by Europeans. The title sets up the situation of the poem, an encounter between Native Americans and British explorers in the eighteenth century. It is not until the last couplet, however, that one is entirely sure who is speaking and thus who is "meeting the British." This openness requires readers to complete the implications of the poem's details, implications not explicitly discussed in the text.

The speaker of the poem first notes the season and weather when he and his group "met the British": the "dead of winter," with snow-covered earth and sky the same "lavender" color. He remembers being able to hear the convergence of two frozen-over streams and recalls his own surprise at himself "calling out in French" to the European strangers. He then notes not a dramatic confrontation or the details of a high-level encounter but the fact that neither of the two British officers could "stomach" the tobacco used by the speaker's group. The speaker also, however, experienced a new sensation: the "unusual scent" from the handkerchief of the colonel, who explains (in French) that *"C'est la lavande,/ une fleur mauve comme le ciel"* (it is lavender, a flower purple as the sky). The last couplet notes the gifts of the British to the speaker and his people: "six fishhooks/ and two blankets embroidered with smallpox."

Forms and Devices

"Meeting the British" uses motifs and imagery carefully chosen to appeal to several senses to establish the complex web of relationship and difference, communication and missed communication, that the poem asserts is the essence of the encounter between the three cultures (British, French, and Native American) represented in the story. Even the form—couplets, but without regular meter and with only slant rhymes—suggests an order at best tentative, relationships at best problematic. The reader of the poem must supply much of what is not said directly, however, to complete the text.

The unusual word "lavender"—the color of the snow-covered earth and the sky, and the scent from the colonel's handkerchief—in itself carries one such motif. When it first appears in couplets 1 and 2, it emphasizes the speaker's sensitive appreciation of the natural world and the unity among earth, sky, and speaker. When it reappears, not in its English form but in the colonel's French, that reappearance emphasizes the distance between the main speaker, who knows "lavender" as a color in nature and an emblem of unity, and the colonel, whose *"lavande"* is first of all a perfume and only secondarily derived from the "flower purple as the sky." The mere image of the English gentleman-explorer carrying a perfumed handkerchief in the wilds of the new world further distances him from the speaker.

Just as "lavender" encompasses the complex relationships between British and Native American in appeals to the senses of sight and smell, so the "two streams coming together" which the speaker can hear despite their being frozen appeals to the sense of hearing and reminds readers of the incompatibility of the cultures. The speaker's own voice is "no less strange" to him than those muted water sounds when he remembers himself "calling out in French," not his own language; when the colonel is directly quoted in French, not English, readers are invited to hear strange and unexpected sounds incompatible with their habitual ways of communicating.

Even the sense of taste proves to be a point of difference: When the speaker recalls that neither British explorer "could stomach our willow-tobacco," the "our" places the Europeans' tastes outside the normal range for the speaker. The gifts offered to the speaker are similarly problematic: The fishhooks can only invite greater exploitation of the natural world, and the attractive blankets whose embroidery in reality is smallpox spell doom for the speaker and his people, doom much more profound than differing tastes in tobacco.

The speaker emphasizes that this encounter is with the incompatible by characterizing three elements in the story as "strange" or "unusual": first, his being able to hear the natural phenomenon of the two streams converging beneath the ice; second, his own use of French to hail the explorers; third, the aroma of the colonel's perfume. This progression, from the relatively familiar natural world through the speaker's own self-consciousness of linguistic alienation to a wholly different world of behavior and value, demonstrates the speaker's ultimate loss of control over his fate.

Themes and Meanings

"Meeting the British" above all concerns conflicts between cultures, especially those occurring when Europeans first conquered North America. The poem asks the reader, an English-speaker more than two hundred years after the encounter presented, to step inside the consciousness of the conquered culture. It lets a reader experience what it might have been like to have met the British for the first time.

Because the events in the poem happened long ago and the horrendous effects of European conquest on Native American populations are part of history, Paul Muldoon can give the imagined memories of the speaker melancholy resonance. Even the simple, almost hackneyed phrase "the dead of winter" in the first line implies, by the end of the poem, the deaths of many individuals and of an entire culture. The image of the "frozen" streams suggests not only the rigid, encrusted cultural elements that will prevent an amicable relationship but also death itself in the encounter of their "coming together." European influences had alienated the speaker from his language even before the events of this poem—he is able to speak French and knows enough to "call out" to the English officers in French.

The deepest and subtlest effect of the meeting between Native American and European here is the automatic assumption of the Englishmen that their culture is superior, and the ways in which the Native Americans acquiesce in this view. That the explorers do not speak a native language, but instead rely on the speaker's previous knowledge of French, demonstrates their desire to dominate and exploit, not to understand. Similarly, the movement from lavender in nature to lavender as an artificial perfume, part of a hyper-civilized affectation of one of the explorers, demonstrates in miniature the shift in values experienced by the speaker. Furthermore, since the speaker is remembering the encounter as an event in the past, and since the only words he quotes directly from the explorers is the description of the scent, his use of "lavender" to describe snow and sky may signify that he has adopted the colonel's very vocabulary, taking the linguistic infection as if it were a case of European-borne smallpox. Muldoon here gives a voice to the forgotten natives who bore the brunt of European expansion into the Americas.

Julia Whitsitt

MEMORIAL FOR THE CITY

Author: W. H. Auden (1907-1973)
Type of poem: Elegy/meditation
First published: 1949; collected in *Nones*, 1951

The Poem

"Memorial for the City" is a four-part meditation of 147 lines dedicated to the memory of Charles Williams, the English Christian theologian who died in 1945. The "City" of the title is all cities as they aspire to become "the City of God," as in the epigram quoted from Juliana of Norwich (c. 1342-1420).

Part 1 takes the view of a crow alternating with the lens of a camera; neither the animal nor the machine recognizes a spiritual dimension. Their view is that of Homer (c. eighth century B.C.), who narrated a world without the "meaning" of history since Christ. A crow can sit atop a crematorium and not care what is burning, in the same way that a camera can cover a battle without passion. Events of destruction and despair simply happen, from burning towns to weeping town officials. Natural beauty is the continuing, indifferent landscape for human suffering— the result is a deceptive picture of reality.

The Roman poet Vergil (70-19 B.C.) marked the period of transition from pre-Christian to Christian Rome. That city is in ruins after the devastation of World War II, but its destruction does not produce in us the grief of ancient Greeks. Pagan and Classical culture is history as "a chaos of graves"; the present state of postwar Europe suggests a future of "barbed-wire" stretching ahead without end. In concentration camps for prisoners of war and displaced persons, we bury the dead and bear misfortunes with a fortitude that we do not understand.

The second part catalogs Christian history to explain the present refusal to despair. Emperors and popes struggled with one another and produced a new kind of city: a center of civilization, a city-state in which people lived without fear of one another. Religious and spiritual values replaced secular and carnal ones; merchants and scholars helped to build "the Sane City," which welcomed learning and spiritual love, which placed public order before private desires. Then Martin Luther attacked the Roman Church as corrupted by material wealth, so Rome became "the Sinful City" during Europe's Protestant Reformation.

Then people began to look into the workings of nature and politics. What they found, to begin the Renaissance, was a nature without a soul, and those princes who took nature as their guide became ruthlessly ironic and efficient as machines. One consequence was the French Revolution, when Mirabeau (Honoré-Gabriel Riqueti) "attacked mystery" in Paris. He and his followers aimed to build "a Rational City," but Paris turned against the Revolution, "used up Napoleon and threw him away." "Heroes" of Reason inspired searches for perfection, for noble savages uncorrupted by civilization: "the prelapsarian man." Europeans searched for "the Glittering City," braving danger and despair. They found, instead of unfallen humanity in a golden city, a New World as a place for "the Conscious City."

Part 3 examines the ruins of a city bombed during the war. Barbed wire runs through the city, into the countryside. Images of the barbed wire run through one's dreams. It is the symbol of the human predicament, the inhumanity and corruption over which people trip and make fools of themselves. If the wire is a mirror of our spiritual condition, however, there is something behind the mirror: an "Image" which does not change as people change. It is an image of indifference. This "Image" is the "flesh" of "Adam waiting for His City." It is also "our weakness," which speaks the words of Part 4.

The poem ends with a dramatic monologue by "Our Weakness" — the voice of Adam, our human flesh. In human weakness is divine strength, for weakness is the fracture of pride. Therefore Adam did not become Lucifer and fall into absolute evil, because Adam was too "weak." Even classical gods and heroes were used by human weakness. Saints and lovers were fulfilled by weakness, and characters of great literary and musical imagination were products of saving weakness. These are the figures of mistakes and errors, vices and illusions, but they are the evidence of limitation and need; weakness causes people to discover their sinful selves, and that may rescue people from pride.

Forms and Devices

Each part of "Memorial for the City" is composed of a different verse form: first is an irregular, measured verse in three stanzas rhyming only on concluding couplets; second are nine regular, unrhymed stanzas of seven lines each; third are five regular, rhymed stanzas of six lines each; fourth are eighteen long, unrhymed lines, each line a completed sentence, most beginning with "I."

This variety of verse forms reinforces variation history, a main subject of the poem. Yet the primary device for developing the poem is an ironic use of metaphorical images of sight: from the balancing of crow and camera, with their cold, two-dimensional views of a static nature, to the mocking mirror between viewer and the Image of Adam, to the mirrors and photographers of Metropolis. One must break through the animal view, the mechanical vision; one must look past the mirror that reflects, to find the constant Image of impersonal Adam shared by all humanity.

The central symbolic image examined through the eyes of the crow, the lens of the camera, and in the reflection of history's mirror is the City. The poem marks the changing character of cities by abstracting a representative feature of the city at each significant phase of its development, turning that feature into an epithet, and capitalizing both epithet and city to suggest a personified entity: thus, European history is a movement of changing characters, from the "Post-Vergilian City," to the "Sinful City," "Rational City," "abolished City," and, beckoning all, the city Adam awaits, "the City of God."

An effective way to identify each city with its special historical era is to cite a person whose life contributed a particular quality to mark the city. Pope Gregory identifies the city in the sixth century; Martin Luther names it in the sixteenth century; and Mirabeau transforms it in the eighteenth century. Persons of history, however, become mixed with characters of myth, legend, and literature in the last section of the poem: from Prometheus to Captain Ahab. Such devices shape a poem of dense allusion to a history more product than producer of imagination.

Themes and Meanings

There are two dominant themes in "Memorial for the City": History can be flat and meaningless fact, or it can be substantial and meaningful fiction. The first theme is introduced in the first part of the poem, to mark the unchanging nature of a classical world before the advent of Christianity, but that theme does not disappear in the time of the "Post-Vergilian City." Flat and meaningless history as "eternal fact" always threatens to return, to emerge from the domain of substantial, meaningful history, because the foundation of human reality is a nature which is always the same. As a hard exterior, seen with crow's eyes or camera's lens, that nature knows no time and has an unchanging history. It returns to threaten repossession of modern humanity, but it never can, because there too much has been added by the Christian era.

Even when people "know without knowing," when people cannot see where the "barbed-wire" ends, they still know that they "are not to despair" because of history as substantial and meaningful fiction. The point about the fiction, made largely in the last section of the poem, is that it is what imagination makes of the raw material of nature and experience; cities are as much fictions as are the myths about Prometheus or the novels of Herman Melville. Cities express human character, in spirit as well as in body. Since Adam is the constant image behind the mirror, Adam is also the image of the continuing City. Until the heavenly City is reached, Adam's image, in all mankind, builds and rebuilds its city, waiting to be made perfect.

Finally, the "memorial" made here is a looking back into history to find a source of explanation for present circumstances, in which people suffer from miseries of war; but the "memorial" is also a sign of hope for the future, which may beckon with its promise of another city still to be built. Pride of accomplishment, of monumental buildings, and glittering glass skyscrapers will be undermined by essential human weakness, as all such cities have been in history. The "memorial" is for the death of pride and for the power of frailty to keep human history from becoming "a meaningless moment" of "eternal fact."

Richard D. McGhee

MEMORY

Author: Arthur Rimbaud (1854-1891)
Type of poem: Lyric
First published: 1895, as "Mémoire," in *Poésies complètes*; collected in *Rimbaud: Complete Works, Selected Letters*, 1966

The Poem

"Memory" is a poem of ten quatrains, divided into five sections. The lines in French are twelve syllables, cut with pauses and run on at unpredictable intervals. The stanzas rhyme in a regular *abba* pattern. "Memory" does not capitalize the initial letter of each line. Most probably composed in the spring of 1872, it remained unpublished until the posthumous *Poésies complètes*.

Formed around a riverside scene, perhaps drawn from memory of the August day in 1870 when Arthur Rimbaud first ran away to Paris, "Memory" is precise in its reference yet vague and fluidly suggestive in its language and imagery. The first line invokes "Clear water," an opening followed by two distinct sets of images. The first set gathers around concepts of purity, as in children's tears, white flesh, silk, and exalted emotion, with references to the old French monarchy and angels. An abrupt "No" cuts this thread and introduces a series of less abstract images: impressions of the river, moving gold, with cool, heavy plant arms; and a bed canopy of blue sky and bed curtains of shadow.

In the second section, the river frames little girls in green, who act the part of willow trees from which birds spring. A marsh marigold, qualified as a coin, an eyelid, and a mirror, rivals the heat-hazy sun. The exclamation — "Your conjugal vow, o Spouse!" — is tied to the next quatrain and the figure of Madame. It compromises the glowing flower image.

Section 3 presents Madame as well as He, the man. Madame was prefigured in the "Spouse" of the fourth stanza. She is rigid; threads of handwork fall about her like snow. She holds a parasol and proudly crushes a flower underfoot. Nearby, children are reading, red books set on flowery green, but this scene is cut by "Alas!" It is a background for the man's escape. "He" joins earlier images of purity, since his flight is "like a thousand white angels." "She" is "all cold and black." She runs after Him, leaving the riverside scene.

The poem plunges into the emotions of Section 4, regret for the arms of pure plants and April's moons in the river bed, joy in riverside wanderings on August evenings with their seeds of decay. "She" weeps under the city walls; poplars breathe from above. The poem returns to water, a dull, gray sheet with an old man dredging in an immobile boat.

A first-person narrator in the last section speaks of himself as a toy, with arms too short to reach flowers. Like the dredger, he is in an unmoving boat on dark water. As the poem ends, the voice laments willows and roses of the past and his own impotence, fixed as he is in place on a boundless eye of water. The last phrase, ". . . to what mud?" sounds a note of seeming hopelessness. The poet stresses emotional immediacy; the poem is written in the present tense.

Forms and Devices

"Memory" came late in Rimbaud's poetic career as one of the last of his verse poems. One of the usual identifying marks of verse is missing, as Rimbaud uses lower case initial letters in all but sixteen of the poem's forty lines, contrary to his usual practice. Another suggestive point is that all of the rhyming words of the poem end in a mute *e*, what the French call "feminine" rhymes. Standard French verse form decreed the alternation of "feminine" with "masculine" rhymes. Rimbaud's "Drunken Boat" (1871) follows this rule scrupulously. This distinction is lost in translation, but it is unlikely to be a random variation in verse form. These are examples of deliberate formal experiment.

By far the most interesting formal variation in "Memory" is Rimbaud's off-beat use of the twelve-syllable verse line. An Alexandrine contains twelve syllables and pauses between the sixth and seventh syllables (the caesura). In orthodox French poetry, Alexandrine verse is chosen for serious and exalted subjects. Use of enjambment, the running on of a sentence from one line to the next without a pause, was a striking variation in form. In "Memory," the verses flow one into another with no respect for syntactical unities. They are broken by exclamations and interjections. The measured flow of classic Alexandrines is absent. In its place is a seemingly random ripple of language. The images of "Memory" also run one into another with the same disregard for formal structures.

Not only do the original French verses use end rhymes, they use interior rhymes, for example in stanza 2, "sombre—ombre," and in stanza 5, "ombrelle—ombelle." Assonances are used, as in stanza 3, "saules—sautent—oiseaux"; stanza 5, "prairie prochaine"; and stanza 10, "roses des roseaux." In their close sound relation, these words knit a structure within the compromised formal framework of "Memory," a doubled system of end and internal rhymes and assonance uniting the whole text.

The rapid succession of images and their juxtaposition in clear pictures are also distinctive. In the first stanza, clear water evokes a set of ideas tied with purity, and follows them to the Maid of Orleans and angels at play. The associations are linked through silk, which is like women's skin and lilies, and is also the stuff of the oriflamme, the red silk banner symbol of French kings. The pure lily is also a symbol of the Virgin Mary and of the French monarchy. Joan of Arc, who led an army to relieve Orleans in defense of the French monarchy, is a virgin and an exalted figure of religious nationalism. These links do not exhaust the images, but rather may be expanded until the river running through sun and shadow is the nucleus of a starburst of connections. "Memory" is formally dense; its many images, its complex pattern of rhyme and rhythm, and its breaking of traditional rules all contribute to its final richness.

Themes and Meanings

"Memory" paints an idyllic river landscape and then abandons it, glorifies escape, and ends in regret. It may refer specifically to the August afternoon of Rimbaud's first escape from his stern mother and younger sisters, left behind in their riverside city as he went to Paris; there were, however, many abandonments in Rimbaud's life. His father left when the poet was a young child. When Rimbaud wrote "Memory," he believed his father to be dead. (The older man died in 1878.) His older brother ran away shortly before Arthur did. When Rimbaud wrote "Memory," he had left Paris and poet Paul Verlaine to return home. He was contemplating another escape, both from France and from verse. (His flight to Belgium with Verlaine took place in July, 1872.) The composition of prose poems, later entitled *Les Illuminations* (1886; *Illuminations*, 1932), soon consumed his attention. *Une Saison en enfer* (1873; *A Season in Hell*, 1932), also prose, was his last literary composition and the only book he ever saw into print.

If abandonment and loss, abundant in the poet's life, are central in "Memory," so are the themes of joy and liberation. There is joy in the elaboration of the riverside scene, all purity, golden light, and flowers, with flashes of mythical, angelic figures. Rivers have their tutelary nymphs; Rimbaud's river has the brilliant, white flesh of women in the first stanza and the young girls, who are almost willow trees by the water, in the second section. The revels of angels, the gaily flashing banners of the warrior maiden, are positive, powerful images. The willow-girls allow birds to spring from them. The last stanza laments the dust shaken from willows by a wing; escape has a price, regret for the "April moons." Yet the escape, in a flurry of white wings, a bound over the mountain, is also part of the same energy and joy. The birds were already unbridled.

The cold, black, rigid figure of Madame, not only the poet's mother but also the force of structure, of rules of initials, of Alexandrine rhythm, of alternating rhymes, intrudes in the idyll, standing between the sun and the marsh marigold, crushing flowers, and scattering snowy threads over the prairie. On one side of her there is innocence, motion, warmth, children reading red books in green grass. On the other there are tears, a sheet of dark water, and an old man dredging from an unmoving boat. It is "her" rigidity that forces abandonment and loss, rather than the joy-filled flight for freedom.

The identification between "he," the man who escapes, and the first person of the last section centers around this old man. He is both the father whom Rimbaud believed dead and the poet himself, returning to dredge the dark waters of memory, repeating a pattern of loss. For Rimbaud, to speak of boats and water must recall his earlier "Le Bateau ivre" ("The Drunken Boat"), a wild journey of discovery ending in yearning for "a black, cold puddle where . . . a stooping child full of sorrows releases a boat frail as a May butterfly." Longer and more regular in verse form than "Memory," the "Drunken Boat" sketches the same pattern of intoxicating escape and eventual regret. The boat of "Memory," anchored to a boundless gray eye, is not identical to the waterlogged "Drunken Boat." The speaker in the last stanzas of

"Memory" laments the past, yet he questions the chain which holds him to the mud beneath those boundless waters. At the heart of "Memory," in spite of its regrets of lost delight, lies the germ of another attempt at escape.

Anne W. Sienkewicz

MEMORY

Author: Christina Rossetti (1830-1894)
Type of poem: Lyric
First published: 1866, in *The Prince's Progress and Other Poems*

The Poem

"Memory" is a poem of thirty-six lines expressing a woman's voluntary renunciation of love, which, remembered with wrenching self-abnegation in life, will be consummated with her beloved in an afterlife of perfect fulfillment.

Part 1 of the poem was written in 1857, and part 2 came into being in 1865, when Christina Rossetti was at the height of her creative powers. The sister of the two Pre-Raphaelite writer-artists, Dante Gabriel and William Michael Rossetti, Christina gave expression to some of the escapist Pre-Raphaelite tendencies in her own poetry. She had, however, a uniquely religious sensibility, influenced by her intense involvement with the Anglo-Catholic movement within the Victorian Church of England. One of the greatest English religious poets of the nineteenth century, she strove for a disciplined purity in her daily life, giving up not only theater, opera, and chess, but even two suitors for her hand in marriage because of her scruples about the beliefs of one man and the lukewarm piety of the other.

"Memory" is a striking testimony to a woman's conscious rejection of love in her life, a courageous choice alleviated only by remembrance of her love and by the hope that the relationship will be renewed in paradise. The five stanzas of part 1 stress the woman's loneliness and courage in her choice to renounce love and yet to hide it in her hollow heart where it once gave joy. She has always kept her love a secret, and its renunciation required a stoically cool objectivity in the wrenching process of her rigorous self-examination and exorcism of love in this life. Nevertheless, her chilling choice to forgo romance in life has broken her heart, which gradually dies within her and causes her to age prematurely.

The four stanzas of part 2 examine the aftermath of her choice and elaborate on the single optimistic note of part 1—that love survived in the woman's memory despite the decision to reject romance: "I hid it within my heart when it was dead" (line 2). Part 2 affirms the enduring vitality of her supposedly dead love in the hiding place of her heart, where romantic memories reign over her existence through cold winters and splendid summers. Although she no longer worships a love that is "buried yet not dead" to her (line 30), in the autumn of her life, she indulges in romantic memories and dreams of a consummation of her love-longing in a paradise of love.

Forms and Devices

"Memory," a lyric poem consisting of nine four-line stanzas termed quatrains, has a rhyme scheme of *abab* in part 1 and *abba* in part 2. It is noteworthy that in part 2 the initial and final lines of each stanza end with the same feminine (or weak) rhyme, in keeping with the sense of the poem's conclusion that the woman's stoic renunciation of love has softened into tender remembrance and a fond hope of eventual reunion beyond the grave.

In part 1, the prevailing meter is iambic pentameter ("Ĭ nŭŕsed ĭt ín my̆ bósŏm whíle ĭt líved"), although the last line of each stanza employs iambic trimeter ("Ălóne ănd nóthĭng sáid"). In part 2, the metrical system in each stanza alternates between iambic pentameter (with an extra short sound on the feminine end rhyme in the first line of each stanza) and iambic dimeter (with an extra short sound on the feminine end rhyme in the last line of each stanza):

> I have a room whereinto no one enters
> Save I myself alone:
> There sits a blessed memory on a throne,
> There my life centres.

Cooperating with this appropriately controlled but fluctuating sound system is an abundance of assonance and consonance in the poem ("I nursed it in my bosom while it lived").

To underscore the contrast between experienced love and deferred love, the poem employs the earthier metaphor of having formerly "nursed" a vital love in the "bosom" in contrast to the chaster, more literal equivalent of having now "hid" a dead love in the "heart" (line 2). There are other metaphors, such as "the perfect balances" to convey the cold objectivity of the woman's judgment in renouncing earthly love (lines 9-12), such as "the bloodless lily and warm rose" to suggest the seasons and her lingering love (lines 27-28), or such as "life's autumn weather" to indicate her aging process (line 33).

The poem verges on allegory, a literary form that tells a story strong on meaning rather than on narrative, capitalizing on personified abstractions rather than on concrete symbols, characters, and events. Thus, the woman must contend with the personified abstractions of "truth" (lines 5-6), the "idol" love (lines 15, 17), and "a blessed memory on a throne" in her heart (line 23), where her life centers—without sinful idolatry—and where her buried love still lives (lines 24, 29-32). All this is a semiallegorical dramatization of the woman's inner psychology of love deferred through self-discipline.

The poem is terse and elliptically understated in its severe language. The diction is monosyllabic and bare-boned in its simplicity to convey the stoic determination to withhold love in life for a perfect consummation of romance in the hereafter.

Themes and Meanings

"Memory" is a poem about a woman's voluntary renunciation of love, although still cherished in memory in this life, with the hope for a perfect consummation of romance in a paradise of eros beyond the grave. What William Rossetti noted about his sister is relevant to the theme of self-abnegation in "Memory": "She was replete with the spirit of self-postponement." She created a poetry of deferral, deflection, and negation in which these denials and constraints gave her a powerful way to articulate a poetic self in critical relationship to the little that the world offers and to help her become one of the most moving religious poets of the Victorian era.

Antony H. Harrison, in *Christina Rossetti in Context* (1988), asserts a direct relationship between her strong religious sense of the emptiness of all worldly things and her portrayal of self-abnegation in a passionate romance: "As is clear to any student of Christina Rossetti's poetry, *vanitas mundi* is her most frequent theme, and . . . this theme is as pervasive in her secular love poetry, as it is in her devotional poems, where a wholesale rejection of worldly values and experiences would be expected."

Particularly arresting in "Memory" is the unusually honest and graphic description in part 1 of the woman's courageous decision that leads her to relinquish and yet cherish in memory her deferred love of another. The arduous psychological process of delaying the consummation of romantic passion as a matter of coolly deliberate, even ascetic, choice is an uncommon theme for love poetry, and Christina Rossetti handles her unusual subject matter with a compelling excellence.

Although this is not really a Pre-Raphaelite poem, "Memory" does exhibit some traits of her brothers' artistic preoccupations, such as an interest in a lover's passionate devotion for a departed lover, as in Dante Gabriel Rossetti's "The Blessed Damozel," where an escapist hope of reunion in an afterlife also cheers a disconsolate female speaker overcome with a comparable longing for love.

Thomas M. Curley

MENDING WALL

Author: Robert Frost (1874-1963)
Type of poem: Narrative
First published: 1914, in *North of Boston*

The Poem

"Mending Wall" is a dramatic narrative poem cast in forty-five lines of blank verse. Its title is revealingly ambiguous, in that "mending" can be taken either as a verb or an adjective. Considered with "mending" as a verb, the title refers to the activity that the poem's speaker and his neighbor perform in repairing the wall between their two farms. With "mending" considered as an adjective, the title suggests that the wall serves a more subtle function: as a "mending" wall, it keeps the relationship between the two neighbors in good condition.

In a number of ways, the first-person speaker of the poem seems to resemble the author, Robert Frost. Both the speaker and Frost own New England farms, and both show a penchant for humor, mischief, and philosophical speculation about nature, relationships, and language. Nevertheless, as analysis of the poem will show, Frost maintains an ironic distance between himself and the speaker, for the poem conveys a wider understanding of the issues involved than the speaker seems to comprehend.

As is the case with most of his poems, Frost writes "Mending Wall" in the idiom of New England speech: a laconic, sometimes clipped vernacular that can seem awkward and slightly puzzling until the reader gets the knack of mentally adding or substituting words to aid understanding. For example, Frost's lines "they have left not one stone on a stone,/ But they would have the rabbit out of hiding" could be clarified as "they would not leave a single stone on top of another if they were trying to drive a rabbit out of hiding."

In addition to using New England idiom, Frost enhances the informal, conversational manner of "Mending Wall" by casting it in continuous form. That is, rather than dividing the poem into stanzas or other formal sections, Frost presents an unbroken sequence of lines. Nevertheless, Frost's shifts of focus and tone reveal five main sections in the poem.

In the first section (lines 1-4), the speaker expresses wonder at a phenomenon he has observed in nature: Each spring, the thawing ground swells and topples sections of a stone wall on the boundary of his property. In the second section (lines 5-11), he contrasts this natural destruction with the human destruction wrought on the wall by careless hunters.

The last sections of the poem focus on the speaker's relationship with his neighbor. In the third section (lines 12-24), the speaker describes how he and his neighbor mend the wall; he portrays this activity humorously as an "outdoor game." The fourth section (lines 25-38) introduces a contrast between the two men: The speaker wants to discuss whether there is actually a need for the wall, while the neighbor will only say, "Good fences make good neighbors." The fifth section (lines 38-45) concludes the poem in a mood of mild frustration: The speaker sees his uncommunicative neighbor as "an old-stone savage" who "moves in darkness" and seems incapable of thinking beyond the clichéd maxim, which the neighbor repeats, "Good fences make good neighbors."

Forms and Devices

In his essay "Education by Poetry" (1931), Robert Frost offers a definition of poetry as "the one permissible way of saying one thing and meaning another." "Mending Wall" is a vivid example of how Frost carries out this definition in two ways—one familiar, one more subtle. As is often the case in poetry, the speaker in "Mending Wall" uses metaphors and similes (tropes which say one thing in terms of another) to animate the perceptions and feelings that he wants to communicate to the reader. A more subtle dimension of the poem is that Frost uses these tropes ironically, "saying one thing and meaning another" to reveal more about the speaker's character than the speaker seems to understand about himself.

When the speaker uses metaphor in the first four sections of "Mending Wall," he does it to convey excitement and humor—the sense of wonder, energy, and "mischief" that spring inspires in him. Through metaphor, he turns the natural process of the spring thaw into a mysterious "something" that is cognitive and active: "something . . . that doesn't love a wall," that "sends" ground swells, that "spills" boulders, and that "makes gaps." He playfully characterizes some of the boulders as "loaves" and others as "balls," and he facetiously tries to place the latter under a magical "spell" so that they will not roll off the wall. He also uses metaphor to joke with his neighbor, claiming that "My apple trees will never get across/ And eat the cones under his pines."

In the last section of the poem, however, the speaker's use of simile and metaphor turns more serious. When he is unable to draw his neighbor into a discussion, the speaker begins to see him as threatening and sinister—as carrying boulders by the top "like an old-stone savage armed," as "mov[ing] in darkness" of ignorance and evil. Through this shift in the tone of the speaker's tropes, Frost is ironically saying as much about the speaker as the speaker is saying about the neighbor. The eagerness of the speaker's imagination, which before was vivacious and humorous, now seems defensive and distrustful. By the end of the poem, the speaker's over-responsiveness to the activity of mending the wall seems ironically to have backfired. His imagination seems ultimately to contribute as much to the emotional barriers between the speaker and his neighbor as does the latter's under-responsiveness.

Themes and Meanings

"Mending Wall" is about two kinds of barriers—physical and emotional. More subtly, the poem explores an ironic underlying question: Is the speaker's attitude toward those two kinds of walls any more enlightened than the neighbor's?

Each character has a line summing up his philosophy about walls that is repeated in the poem. The speaker proclaims, "Something there is that doesn't love a wall."

He wants to believe that there is a "something," a conscious force or entity in nature, that deliberately breaks down the stone wall on his property. He also wants to believe that a similar "something" exists in human nature, and he sees the spring season both as the source of the ground swells that unsettle the stone wall and as the justification for "the mischief in me" that he hopes will enable him to unsettle his neighbor's stolid, stonelike personality. From the speaker's perspective, however, when the neighbor shies away from discussing whether they need the wall, the speaker then sees him as a menacing "savage," moving in moral "darkness," who mindlessly repeats the cliché "Good fences make good neighbors."

The speaker does not seem to realize that he is just as ominously territorial and walled in as his neighbor, if not more so. The speaker scorns the neighbor for repeating his maxim about "good fences" and for being unwilling to "go behind" and question it, yet the speaker also clings to a formulation that he repeats ("Something there is that doesn't love a wall") and seems unwilling to think clearly about his belief in it. For example, the speaker celebrates the way that spring ground swells topple sections of the stone wall. Why, then, does he resent the destruction that the hunters bring to it, and why does he bother to repair those man-made gaps? Similarly, if the speaker truly believes that there is no need for the wall, why is it he who contacts his neighbor and initiates the joint rebuilding effort each spring? Finally, if the speaker is sincerely committed to the "something" in human nature that "doesn't love" emotional barriers (and that, by implication, does love human connectedness), why does he allow his imagination to intensify the menacing otherness of his neighbor to the point of seeing him as "an old-stone savage armed" who "moves in darkness"? To consider these questions, the speaker would have to realize that there is something in him that *does* love walls, but the walls within him seem to block understanding of his own contradictory nature.

Frost ends the poem with the neighbor's line, "Good fences make good neighbors," perhaps because this cliché actually suggests a wiser perspective on the boundary wall than the speaker realizes. This stone "fence" seems "good" partly because it sets a clear boundary between two very different neighbors — one laconic and seemingly unsociable, the other excitable, fanciful, and self-contradictory. On the other hand, this fence is also good in that it binds the two men together, providing them with at least one annual social event in which they can both participate with some comfort and amiability. To recall the two meanings of the title, the activity of mending the wall enables it to be a "mending wall" that keeps the relationship of these two neighbors stable and peaceful.

Terry L. Andrews

THE MENTAL TRAVELLER

Author: William Blake (1757-1827)
Type of poem: Lyric
First published: 1863, in *Life of William Blake*, by William Gilchrist

The Poem

"The Mental Traveller," written in 1803 but not published until 1863, consists of twenty-six long-measure quatrains, a stanza form commonly used in ballads. Since each line has four beats, the measure is considered longer than that found in more traditional ballad stanzas, in which every other line has only three beats. The poem's title refers to its narrator, a traveler from another mental realm who observes and describes the cycle of suffering in the "Land of Men & Women."

Perspective is an important element in William Blake's poetry, and it is important to realize that the traveler's perspective on human experience differs from the experience of the men and women themselves: The "dreadful things" the traveler hears and sees are things that "cold Earth wanderers never knew." Thus, rather than narrating the life stories of individuals, the mental traveler describes male and female archetypes that exemplify, in general terms, the nature of existence in the material world.

The narrator begins his description of the cyle of life with a grim recounting of the birth of a baby, "begotten in dire woe," who, if it is a boy, is nailed to a rock, crucified, and cut open by an old woman. As the boy becomes older, however, the woman grows younger, and their violent relationship is reversed: The male tears off his chains and "binds her down for his delight." Even at this early stage in the poem, the narrator makes it clear that the male-female relationship in the land of men and women is characterized by inequality and struggle rather than by harmony. Moreover, since the female is associated with nature (she is the male's "Garden fruitful Seventy fold"), this discord also exists between man and nature.

As the man grows older, he piles up wealth in a vampirelike way, feeding on "The martyrs groan & the lovers sigh." The female, however, becomes a baby, and in time she and her lover drive the man from his house. As a beggar, the male character wanders until he can find a maiden to embrace "to Allay his freezing Age." His embrace of the maiden leads to the contraction of his senses ("For the Eye altering alters all"), and he begins to grow younger. "By various arts of Love beguild," he pursues the maiden into a wasteland. Ultimately, he becomes the "wayward Babe" and she turns into the "Woman Old" described in the beginning of the poem. This frowning baby strikes terror into shepherds and wild animals, and none can touch him until the old woman nails him to a rock and begins the cycle all over again.

From the mental traveler's point of view, then, human life is an endless cycle of conflict between male and female, man and nature, rich and poor. Because men and women are not aware of this cycle, they are condemned to repeat all of the "dreadful things" the poem describes.

Forms and Devices

The structure of "The Mental Traveller" can be represented by a circle, and since the poem ends as it begins, the circle can be seen as constantly revolving. Among other things, this circle reflects the cycle of the seasons, the periods of life, and recurrent myths. Since the circle is never broken, no permanent change can take place in the land of men and women—everything must be repeated. Not even death interrupts the cycle. After growing old, the male character embraces a maiden and reverses the aging process.

Nature is symbolized by the female figure in the poem, and the male character uses nature both as a garden and as a source of rejuvenation. When the female is "a Virgin bright," he "plants himself" in her—a phrase that suggests both sexual intercourse and agriculture—and gains riches from her. Then, however, the female figure disappears and the male loses his vitality—his connection with nature and life seems to be severed as he grows older. While she reappears as fire, he experiences winter, and his "freezing Age" is reversed only when he can embrace a maiden. Thus, while the female archetype in the poem represents nature, vitality, and life, the male tends to fade, freeze, and create, through his altering vision, a vast desert. Toward the end of the poem, the male character takes the form of a baby who has the power to wither arms, drive animals off the land, and make fruit fall off trees. Thus the poem moves through the planting of spring, the harvesting of summer and fall (stanzas 8-9), and the freezing of winter (stanza 15), and then retraces the natural cycle so that the process is repeated. Throughout this process, the male lives off the female like a parasite; she, in her turn, beguiles and then nails down the male. In "The Mental Traveller," the natural cycle is seen as a battleground between the male and female archetypes: No progression is possible, since progression cannot exist without some kind of cooperation.

In keeping with the "dreadful" nature of the cycle in "The Mental Traveller," Blake uses sadomasochistic imagery to describe the relationship between the male and female archetypes in the poem. The baby boy is given to an old woman who commits a series of violent acts against him: She nails him on a rock, "binds iron thorns around his head," "pierces both his hands & feet," and "cuts his heart out at his side/ To make it feel both cold & heat." She lives, sadistically, for his shrieks. When the boy grows older, however, the violence is reversed, and he binds her down. As the fingers of the old woman "number every Nerve" of the male character, so the male character "plants himself in all [the] nerves" of the female figure. Human relationships, the poem suggests, are predicated on bondage and torture, and one of the most important cycles of "The Mental Traveller" is the tragic cycle of violence begetting violence.

Themes and Meanings

In any analysis of "The Mental Traveller," the narrator is one of the main puzzles. He tells the reader next to nothing about himself, yet the poem cannot be fully understood unless the speaker's perspective is somehow identified. There is a clue to his viewpoint, however, in the first two lines, in which the mental traveler says he has traveled through "a Land of Men/ A Land of Men & Women too." These lines are not redundant: The narrator suggests by the clarification in the second line that he is from a world in which the sexes are not separated, an androgynous realm that in Blake's myth is called Eternity. Thus he sees this land of men and women from the perspective of an eternal and presents it, not as some "cold Earth wanderer" might, but in his own visionary terms. According to Blake's myth, in Eternity or Eden the male and female principles are combined: There is none of the discord described in "The Mental Traveller" because men and women are united in a harmonious whole. From the point of view of the mental traveler, then, the idea of separate men and women is very troubling — it can only lead to conflict and suffering.

If the mental traveler is an eternal, the land he describes is Earth, shaped in the poem by the narrator's eternal perspective. In Blake's myth, this land would most likely be identified as generation, or the state of experience, a vision of life that is described in his *Songs of Innocence and of Experience* (1794). As several of Blake's other works make clear, in experience men and women are trapped in cycles. In some of these cycles, a revolutionary youth (often called Orc) rises up against the tyrant lawgiver (named Urizen) and defeats him, only to turn into a tyrant himself. Ultimately, another revolutionary youth appears, and the cycle is repeated. Violence begets violence, with no end in sight.

In terms of male versus female, the same process can be observed. Love turns into competition, and wiles and manipulation replace sincerity and innocence. The male and female archetypes in "The Mental Traveller" can never meet each other as equals: One is either older or younger than the other, and the relationship as a whole is characterized by bondage and submission, not cooperation and progress. The visionary presentation of the human condition presented in the poem is thus a fearful judgment on human life, which the traveler views as an endless cycle of violence and futility. The only way out of this cycle is for the men and women trapped in it to see themselves as the traveler sees them, to expand their mental vision and achieve a state of enlightenment in which separation would be replaced by unity, repetition by progress. In other words, the people of this fallen world need to know the nature of their existence and their power to transform it, for, as the narrator says, "the Eye altering alters all."

William D. Brewer

METAMORPHOSIS

Author: Louise Glück (1943-   )
Type of poem: Poetic sequence
First published: 1985, in *The Triumph of Achilles*

The Poem

"Metamorphosis" is a forty-nine-line lyric sequence divided into three numbered sections: "Night," "Metamorphosis," and "For My Father." It is written in free verse. Louise Glück has written a number of poems about her father; in this one, like the others, she seems to identify closely with her first-person narrator. She describes the metamorphosis of her powerful father into a childlike, dying man and her own development from fearful daughter into resilient adult.

"Night," the first section of the sequence, is a double portrait of the poet's parents. It begins by envisioning the couple at night in the father's sickroom. The father will die soon—as evidenced by the "angel of death" hovering over the scene—but only the mother perceives that death is in the room. The second stanza describes the mother ministering to the father. Gently touching his hand and forehead, she treats him as if he were a child instead of her husband. The poet says that her mother touches the sick man's body "as she would the other children's,/ first gently, then/ inured to suffering." While the dying man is portrayed as a vulnerable child, his wife is seen as a full-time mother who is used to suffering along with those in her care.

In the last stanza, the poet announces ambiguously, "Nothing is any different," possibly implying that her parents have always had a child-mother relationship. Then she identifies the cause of the father's dying: "Even the spot on the lung/ was always there." These lines end the first section on a despairing note; death is an omnipresent force in everyone's life.

The second section, "Metamorphosis," focuses on the relationship between the poet and her dying father. Again she describes him as childlike: "Like a child who will not eat,/ he takes no notice of anything." The poet, unlike her depiction of her mother in the first section, does not envision herself as a benevolent figure tending to his needs.

In the section's opening lines, she feels neglected by him, and then she compares his unseeing gaze at her to a blind man staring at the sun. Now that he is dying, he is beyond her power to affect him. In the last stanza, the sick father turns his face away from his daughter. She sees that his metamorphosis is complete: He is physically incapable of making any responsible, meaningful connection—or "contract"—with her.

The third section, "For My Father," shows the poet undergoing a metamorphosis of her own. Instead of describing her father in the third person, as she does in the poem's first two sections, she addresses him directly. She tells him that she will be able to live without him and that she is no longer afraid of death—his or her own. She also tells him, indirectly, that she loves him and will miss him after he dies: "I know/ intense love always leads to mourning."

The poet concludes by saying that she is no longer afraid of her father's body, thus hinting that he was a threatening figure in her childhood. Like her mother in the first section, she can now touch her father's face. She can acknowledge feelings of rejection and fear ("I feel/ no coldness that can't be explained,") and treat her father with benevolence. She has metamorphosed into a kind parent figure, while he has metamorphosed into the helpless child she once was.

Forms and Devices

The poem exemplifies Louise Glück's penchant for combining the personal with the abstract. As in most of her poems, the language is stark, the ideas are briefly stated, and the overall effect resonates with significance far greater than the actual scene described. In "Metamorphosis," a relatively short poem, she mentions or alludes to the following: death, dying, excitement, suffering, solitude, love, mourning, fear, shock, and tenderness. These abstract words heighten the emotional impact of the sequence's three brief scenes: the mother tending to the father, the daughter observing the sick father, and the daughter tending to the father.

The abstractions occur in lines that are otherwise understated and conversational, such as the beginning of the second section: "My father has forgotten me/ in the excitement of dying." Glück's poems often reflect this overlapping of the ordinary with the extraordinary. A line that begins with a seemingly simple declaration suddenly evolves into a powerful observation or ephiphany. This pattern is also seen in whole poems. In each section of "Metamorphosis," the concluding lines cast a new light on the images and emotions sketched in the preceding lines.

The first section's abrupt conclusion has a pained, almost hostile feeling to it. The poet refuses to sentimentalize the mutually dependent relationship between her parents. In the second section, the ending succinctly portrays a lifelong communication gap between father and daughter. Again, the last lines suggest that Glück refuses to soften her perceptions of her father even as he is dying. The last section ends on a more forgiving note. The poet seems to be moving toward an understanding of her father and his significance in her life. The concluding image of her hand against his cheek contrasts surprisingly with the blunt, aggressive statements she makes earlier in the section.

"For My Father" reverses the surprising course of the first two sections. Instead of moving away from potential sentimentality toward startling objectivity, the last section moves from objectivity toward a subtle expression of love. The poem's division into three parts contributes to the overall effect of a metamorphosis. Each section functions as a freeze-frame, portraying the poet's attitude toward her father.

In the first, she seems to feel removed from both of her parents; she is even not present in the scene she imagines. In the second, she is actively involved in the scene, but she is still unable to make contact with her father. In the third, she is finally able to address him directly—at least directly within the poem—and express a gentleness which seems meant as much for herself as for him.

Themes and Meanings

"Metamorphosis" is both a dry-eyed look at a dying man and a tightly controlled expression of self-preservation. The poet is trying to resolve her feelings toward her father, understand her family's past, and plan for her own future. Her terse, often oblique statements suggest that these related processes are difficult for her and not easily put into words.

Characteristically, Glück relies as much on the absence of detail as on specific information to convey the import of her message. Even the space between the separate sections has a weight to it; the poem moves stoically toward its resolution. "Metamorphosis" precedes by five years Glück's fifth collection of poems, *Ararat* (1990), which is a sequence of thirty-two poems about her family. In the later collection, Glück's father has died, and many of the poems deal with her continuing efforts to resolve her feelings for him.

The last poem in *Ararat* suggests that Glück has gone beyond the conflicting emotions and tentative reconciliation of "Metamorphosis." In "First Memory," she writes: "I lived/ to revenge myself/ against my father, not/ for what he was—/ for what I was." She concludes that the emotional pain she felt while growing up did not mean that she was unloved, but rather, "It meant I loved." The ending of "Metamorphosis" hints at such a resolution but does not state it outright. It is a poem about the process of overcoming pain and grief and moving on toward a new life; it is not about the fulfillment of that process.

"Metamorphosis" and the autobiographical poems in *Ararat* represent Glück's obsessive desire to plumb the depths of personal relationships. Many of her other poems (such as the nine-part sequence, "Marathon," in *The Triumph of Achilles*) deal with romantic love relationships. In those poems, as in those about her family, Glück wields tight control over the emotions she displays in print. She refuses to give in to the obvious, the sentimental, or the overly ornamental figure of speech.

Glück is often an unsettling poet to read, because she is so willing to grapple with conflicting emotions that many people would rather not recognize in themselves. Although her poems are often rooted in her own life, the sketchy details, the reliance on abstractions, and frequent allusions to mythology give them broader application. Despite her seeming coldness at times, Glück's poems often return to the theme of love. In "Metamorphosis," a complex psychological portrait, she recognizes implicitly at the poem's end that the seemingly inappropriate emotions she has felt— hostility, neglect, and fear—may coexist with, and even heighten, her strong feelings of love for her father.

"Metamorphosis" is an example of Glück's continuing effort to look at herself and the world with a clear, unstinting gaze. Never one to sugarcoat a scene or ignore the drama of a small gesture, she captures in "Metamorphosis" the story of her own growth, which ironically, but perhaps inevitably, parallels the story of her father's decline.

Hilary Holladay

MICHAEL

Author: William Wordsworth (1770-1850)
Type of poem: Pastoral
First published: 1800, in *Lyrical Ballads*

The Poem

Michael is a long poem in blank verse, its 490 lines divided into sixteen stanzas. The *Michael* of the title is the poem's protagonist. The subtitle, "A Pastoral Poem," seems to challenge the traditional conception of pastoral poetry as a form for the idyllic and the bucolic, and to prepare the reader to accept the "low and rustic life" as the ideal pastoral.

The poem is written in the third person. The poet himself assumes the role of narrator, guiding the reader to a tragic scene. There, he relates the tale of Michael with intense love and pure passions. In spite of some homely conversations, the poet speaks in his own character. From the viewer of a tragic scene to the listener of a tragic tale, the narrator emerges as the creator of a tragic poem in new style and new spirit.

The poem begins with a two-stanza prelude. The poet, almost like a tour guide, introduces to the reader a hidden valley in pastoral mountains and advises the reader to struggle courageously in order to reach it. There, through "a straggling heap of unhewn stones," the poet thinks "On man, the heart of man, and human life." He decides to dignify the aged Michael for the delight of men with natural hearts and for the sake of youthful poets.

The main body of the poem can be divided into three parts. Part one (stanzas 3 to 5) extolls the unusual qualities of Michael, an eighty-year-old shepherd—his gains from nature and his love for nature. Together with his wife Isabel and son Luke, Michael's household presents a picture of endless industry. Through the images of an ancient lamp and the evening star, the poet depicts that archetypal family as "a public symbol."

The second part (stanzas 6-12) reveals the conflict between Michael's love for his inherited property and his love for his son. It vividly portrays Michael's care and love for his son from cradle to the age of eighteen. When he is summoned to discharge a forfeiture, however, Michael eventually chooses to send Luke to the city to earn money rather than sell a portion of his patrimonial land. Before Luke leaves, Michael takes him to the deep valley where he has gathered up a heap of stone for building a sheepfold. He not only educates Luke with two histories—the history of Luke's upbringing and the history of their land—but also asks Luke to lay the cornerstone of the sheepfold as a covenant between the father and the son.

The last part contains only three short stanzas. It briefly recounts Luke's good beginning and eventual corruption in the city. Luke is driven overseas by ignominy and shame. Despite his grief over the loss of his son, the strength of love enables old Michael to perform all kinds of labor and to work at building the sheepfold from time to time as before. He lives another seven years, then dies with the sheepfold unfinished. Three years later, at his wife's death, their estate goes into a stranger's hand. All is gone except the oak tree, which embodies both nature and Michael's indestructible spirit.

Forms and Devices

In September, 1800, William Wordsworth put forth his new poetics in his "Preface to *Lyrical Ballads*." Wordsworth opposed sentimentalism that resorted to violent stimulants and gaudy and inane phraseology to gratify certain stereotypes of imaginative association. *Michael* is one of the experimental poems Wordsworth wrote to demonstrate the strength of his new poetics. The success of *Michael* is characterized by the freshness of its subject, the naturalness of its diction, and the vividness of its rural picturesque imagery. Along with *The Ruined Cottage* (wr. 1797-1798) and *The Brothers* (1800), *Michael* establishes the common and rural life as a legitimate subject matter for Romantic poetry. By exploring elemental affections in a domestic world, the poem displays the beauty and dignity of lowly life and extracts cathartic pleasure from the pathos of humanity.

Wordsworth's efforts at experimenting with a new poetic language in *Michael* are obvious. For example, in lines 178-179, one reads "Thence in our rustic dialect was called/ The Clipping Tree — a name which it bears," and in lines 91-92, "To deem that he was old — in shepherd's phrase,/ With one foot in the grave." Apart from such declarative lines, in many places the reader can feel the poet's imitation of the language of the common people. For example, "Well, Isabel, this scheme/ These two days has been meat and drink to me" (283-284); "else I think that thou/ Hadst been brought up upon thy father's knee" (360-361). It is not the simple adoption of the language of ordinary men but Wordsworth's skillful metrical arrangement of the plain, simple diction that makes a new poetic language. The resilient, vigorous musical cadences of lines 40-52 are set in a basic iambic pentameter, which is pleasing to the English ear. The rhythm of the phrase "stout of heart and strong of limb" resembles the beating pulse of rustic people. The phrase "the meaning of all winds,/ Of blasts of every tone" gives symmetrical beauty to its syntactical visual form. The lines "he heard the South/ Make subterraneous music, like the noise/ Of bagpipers on distant Highland hills" link the inaudible subterranean sound to the sound of the noise. Yet because of the vastness of the pastoral landscape, the distance turns the noise into a music so subtle that it almost fades into the inaudible. Such peculiar aural sensitivity enables Wordsworth to convey the rustic people's intimacy with nature.

Wordsworth emphasizes that the story of Michael is "a history/ Homely and rude." The phrase "Homely and rude" expresses the peculiar beauty of the poem; in its tone, the poem is affectionate and homely. As shown in the lines "he to himself would say, 'The winds are now devising work for me!' " and "why should I relate/ That objects which the shepherd loved before/ Were dearer now?" the conversational style is exactly right for a tale to be told by "the fireside" or in "the summer shade."

This "homely and rude" beauty is effectively conveyed by the rustic symbols and images. By using the never-ceasing spinning wheels to represent "endless industry" and the humble lamp to stand for a modest but inextinguishable spirit as well as for frugality, Wordsworth gives the poem a rare freshness, simplicity, and profundity. Wordsworth typically employs a common rustic object such as a cottage to convey his extraordinary thematic ideas. In *The Ruined Cottage*, he uses the decaying of the cottage into a hut to depict the decline of Margaret's mind; in *Michael*, he uses the cottage on a rising ground with a large prospect and the lofty name "The Evening Star" to elevate Michael to a public symbol. The images in the second part of the poem are centered on the themes of education and protection. The old oak, the Clipping Tree (Michael), is opposed to a fettered sheep and a hooped sapling (Luke). As the central symbol of the poem, the sheepfold, an image of protection, evokes multiple meanings: It is the covenant between the father and son, the link of love, the anchor and the shield. At the end of the poem, the unfinished sheepfold, eternally fragmentary and incomplete, suggests the hope for human continuity. The oak, which carries the "inherent and indestructible qualities of the human mind" represented by Michael is permanent, while all human gains and losses are mere passing shows of being.

Themes and Meanings

Coming to terms with human loss and the power of love to support an otherwise unbearable situation are the poem's basic themes. The rich meanings of the poem, however, depend on how one interprets the character of Michael.

Michael, as an archetype, represents the collective entity of humanity. He is the shepherd or patriarch for humankind and the mother who rocks the cradle. He manages material loss with a cheerful hope, and he remedies and accepts the loss of his son in silent grief and stubborn perseverance. Throughout his life, he functions as the guide for a public life, the educator of youth, and the guardian of nature. Under Wordsworth's Romantic exaltation, Michael, an archetypal hero of unusual strength at an incredibly great age, embodies a natural paradigm, an inextinguishable spirit crystallized out of the good qualities bequeathed from generation to generation.

Michael can also be seen as a man of his time. As social history, *Michael* is relatively accurate; it records the infiltration of new capitalism into rural areas and the encroachment of trade upon the land. The prototype of Michael is that small independent proprietor of land called a "statesman." If one regards *Michael* as a lamentation over the rapid disappearance of this class of men, one may find Wordsworth politically quite conservative. In fact, Wordsworth does instill the spirit of his age into his imaginary character. To some extent, Michael is a rustic version of a self-made man; through his own efforts, he doubles his inheritance and wins the freedom of the land. He cherishes the freedom of the land as a sign of his individualist independence. Yet he is also tempted by the rags-to-riches story and by the opportunities of getting rich in the cities. Michael's pragmatic judgment of gain and loss eventually leads to his choice of property over his son. Michael's tragedy reveals the demoralization of domestic affections in the face of commercial realities. Luke's corruption is very much an extensive projection of Michael's inner corruption. At the loss of Luke, the individualist Michael, purged of the contamination of the material age, merges into the collective entity of the archetypal Michael.

Michael, above all, is Wordsworth's vision of Natural Man. Being a shepherd of nature, he merges his whole life with nature. Nature is the test of his courage, the fruit of his labor, and his ever-faithful companion. His blood and sweat nourish nature, and nature repays him with pleasure (lines 65-79). The covenant between him and nature is stronger than the covenant between him and his son, because nature is the anchor of human integrity and purity.

In his creation of Michael as a man of nature, Wordsworth not only expresses the "passions that were not my own" and his concern with the bond between nature and man, but also identifies himself with Michael to explore the bond between the rustic life and the poet. He shares Michael's sensitivity to nature, his experience and wisdom gained from nature, his singularity, and his solitude. Wordsworth's description of Michael as having breathed "the common air" and "learned the meaning of all winds,/ Of blasts of every tone" pictures an ideal natural poet who has gained freedom in the poetic representation of nature and human life. To create a new poetic path, Wordsworth needs Michael's indestructible spirit and must refuse to cater to the depravity of the age. Michael's stubbornness in not giving an inch of the free land expresses Wordsworth's determination to strike ahead, by himself, even when other poets fail to follow.

Although Wordsworth was only thirty when he wrote *Michael*, he seemed to imagine himself as an old poet of natural heart, using the tale to show "youthful Poets" his experience in composing poems. He notices what others might "see and notice not." From "a straggling heap of unhewn stones," the shapeless material of nature, he spins endlessly, as with Isabel's two wheels of "antique form." The natural objects, like "dumb animals," and the characters, like restless "summer flies," come and go in his murmuring imagination until his senses are blurred. Then he recollects the eternal truth in tranquil solitude. With this heap of rough stones, he hews and builds a sheepfold—a tombstone for Michael and an eternal monument for the poet. It is unfinished, for the old poet expects continuity. It turns back into its original material, "a straggling heap of unhewn stones," for the old poet hopes that the youthful poets can start anew.

Qingyun Wu

MIDDLE PASSAGE

Author: Robert Hayden (1913-1980)
Type of poem: Narrative
First published: 1945; revised in *Collected Poems*, 1985

The Poem

"Middle Passage" is a three-part narrative poem that uses various personae to depict in the Symbolist style—using suggestion rather than direct statement—the trans-Atlantic slave trade. Resembling T. S. Eliot's *The Waste Land* (1922), the poem is a synthesis of historical voices, an assemblage of brief dramas unified by both a poetic consciousness—"Middle Passage: voyage through death/ to life upon these shores"—and an invisible, ethereal consciousness in the guise of a spiritual voice: "*Deep in the festering hold thy father lies.*" The poet uses these two voices to manipulate the perspective on events that are related to slavery.

The title "Middle Passage" refers to the middle journey of the triangular slave trade that began in the fifteenth century. The first leg of the journey entailed leaving the home port and sailing to the African coast to pick up Africans who would be sold as slaves in the New World. The middle passage is the portion of the journey in which Africans were transported to the New World, particularly the Caribbean, "Hispaniola," or the American South, the "barracoons of Florida." The third part of the trip was the return to the home port.

The major voices in section 1 are from a sailor's diary and a court deposition. The diary conveys the uneasiness, fear, and anxiety of the crew: "misfortune follows in our wake like sharks." It also describes the ways in which captured Africans committed suicide to avoid enslavement: "some try to starve themselves . . . [some] leaped with crazy laughter to the waiting sharks, sang as they went under." The sailor's voice also questions why he and his crewmates are cursed— "Which one of us has killed an albatross?"—referring to Samuel Taylor Coleridge's *The Rime of the Ancient Mariner* (1798).

The voice of the court transcript contrasts a public account of the slave trade— "cargo of five hundred blacks . . . stowed spoon-fashion"—with the previous private account of the middle passage. The deposition describes the nature of the "plague among our blacks"—physical diseases, madness, and thirst arising from "sweltering" conditions—and a shipwreck. The lasciviousness and immorality of the "Crew and Captain" are indirectly introduced as a "curse" upon the captured Africans: "the negroes howling and their chains entangled with the flames," "the comeliest of the savage girls kept naked in the cabins," and the Captain perishing "drunken with the wenches." The slave trade itself may be the albatross. Another voice in this section offers a religious justification for slavery and, indirectly, the inhumane middle passage: to bring "heathen souls unto Thy [God's] chastening." Implicitly, part 1 asks how physical cruelty can be used to bring about spiritual salvation.

The second section is the self-glorifying recollection of an old slave trader, "twenty years a trader," who describes how the vanity and greed of "nigger kings" was used to initiate war "wherein the victor and vanquished/ Were caught as prizes for our barracoons." The old sailor's remembrance indicates that greed among both whites and Africans is the primary justification for the slave trade. He does not regret his inhumane activities, and he would still be involved in the suffering and cruelty described in part 1 "but for the fevers melting down my bones." The "old salt's" voice also provides stereotypical descriptions of Africans as heathens: childlike in their love of cloth and "trinkets," savage in that they drink from cups made out of the "skulls of enemies" and are willing to burn villages and murder "the sick and old" for profit. These negative descriptions, combined with racist epithets, buttress the earlier religious justification for slavery. The attitude underlying the justification of the material exploitation and religious conversion of Africans is that they are beastlike and uncivilized.

Part 3 begins with the voice of the narrative consciousness which was established in section 1. With this voice, the poem moves from a literal and historical re-creation of events to a symbolic re-creation. This voice echoes the implied fate reflected in the image of the shipwreck in part 1 — "where the living and the dead, the horribly dying lie interlocked." It also provides a simple but multifaceted assessment of the origins of the middle passage. Further, it clarifies the inherent irony of the previous sections: "the jests of kindness" or "bright ironical names" of the ships. It establishes the middle passage as one of the "shuttles in the rocking loom of history." The image of the loom and the metaphor of weaving are implicit in the interwoven narrative voices that appear throughout the poem.

The second voice, which appears in italicized passages here and in section 1, is that of an invisible spirit. A re-creation of the essence of the angelic spirit Ariel in William Shakespeare's *The Tempest* (1611), this voice symbolizes the irrepressible spirit of humanity: the "deep immortal human wish, the timeless will." It is also the voice of accusation, reflecting the spirit of those "with human eyes whose suffering accuses you, whose hatred reaches you." The essence of this elusive, ethereal, and elemental consciousness is absorbed and is reiterated later in this section by the "narrative consciousness."

The third voice in this part provides an account of a Spanish sailor who was one of the two surviving white slavers on the ship *Amistad* (Friendship). The speech, intended by the Spanish speaker to elicit sympathy for him by detailing the brutalities of the mutineers— "how these apes threw overboard the butchered bodies of our men, true Christians all" — is filled with irony. His tale of "unspeakable misery" contrasts with the earlier descriptions of slaves who "went mad of thirst and tore their flesh and sucked the blood." Unintentionally, he indicates that the "murderous Africans" enacted the timeless will to be free. This voice also explains, indirectly, how slavery can exist in a land in which all men are thought to be created equal and endowed with inalienable rights to life, liberty, and the pursuit of happiness.

The poem ends with the universal spirit of life and "timeless will," which are symbolically linked to the "black gold, black ivory, black seed" of part 1.

Forms and Devices

The poet Michael S. Harper refers to Robert Hayden as a Symbolist poet struggling with the facts of history. "Middle Passage" reflects that view. It is both a historically based dramatic narrative and a Symbolist poem. The narratives, interspersed voices, and names, which are derived from a variety of historical sources, are intended to serve as symbols. Little-known and well-known "objective correlatives," historical and literary rather than personal, are used throughout the poem. For example, the poem begins with "*Jesus, Estrella* [Star], *Esperanza* [Hope], *Mercy*," which are later referred to as "bright ironical names" of "dark ships." The ship *Jesus* was sailed in 1562 by Captain John Hawkins from England to Guinea. He loaded his ship with Africans, sailed to the islands in Hispaniola, sold his human "cattle stowed spoon-fashion" to planters, and returned with a rich cargo of ginger, hides, and pearls. The large profits Hawkins made encouraged English involvement in the slave trade.

Section 3 refers to a well-known event. In 1839, a group of Africans led by Cinquez mutinied against being transported to Cuba. Gaining control of the ship, they sailed to Montauk, Long Island, and sought freedom. John Quincy Adams defended the fifty-four Africans before the Supreme Court and gained their freedom.

In addition to direct historical references, the poem utilizes literary references. One example is a variation on Ariel's song in Shakespeare's *The Tempest* (act 1, scene 2)—the voice of the invisible consciousness: "Deep in the festering hold [Full fathom five] thy father lies;/ of his bones New England pews [coral] are made/ those are altar lights [pearls] that were his eyes."

Hayden avoids the traditional use of rhyme, meter, and stanza; instead, he uses narrative structure—form and content—to achieve unity of effect. "Middle Passage" also utilizes intertextual verbal complexities, ambiguities, irony, paradox, imagery, metaphor, and symbolism, as advocated by the New Critics. The multiple voices overlap and interweave these devices while the speakers act as participants—and symbols—in the drama. The poet's historical memory and imagination achieve a unity of effect with the whole drama rather than merely a memorable line or phrase.

The intertextual relationships of words—through irony, as with the plague or with slavers as "Christians, all"; paradox, as in "you cannot stare that hatred down or chain the fear that stalks the watches"; ambiguity, as in the multiple meanings of "blindness"; or symbol, as in "bringing home/ black gold, black ivory, black seed"—add unity to the poem. Yet the seemingly disparate elements are unified into a coherent whole by means of structure, voice, and historical theme, and "organic unity"—natural facts corresponding with spiritual facts, in Ralph Waldo Emerson's sense—is achieved. Although some of Robert Hayden's poetry has been regarded as elusive and obscure, an understanding of "Middle Passage" is not dependent upon a knowledge of historical or literary allusions, since the poem's universal symbols and interrelated voices provide the "historical moment and context" from which the reader can understand an event in history.

Themes and Meanings

The central purpose of "Middle Passage" is to record, poetically and objectively, the process of change and the paradox of permanence among all humans: "immortal human wish, the timeless will." The poem does so by using images to illustrate conflicting claims and viewpoints about the slave trade. The nature of exploiters— private, public, religious, and legal—is contrasted with the voices of their victims. "Jests of kindness on a murderer's mouth" assault the concept of moral "human progress" for which the voices are praying.

A protest against man's inhumanity to man and the presence of evil is implicit in the description of the realities of the slave trade. Figuratively, the middle passage can also be regarded as a middle part of the evolving human consciousness— "Shuttles in the rocking loom of history"—a consciousness that requires evolving from a deathlike spiritual condition to a new life, a new beginning.

Another theme, which appears in the symbol of the invisible voice and the image of Cinquez, is the universal and ageless desire for freedom. Ariel, in his angelic whiteness, and Cinquez, in his "murderous" blackness, represent the primeval in the poem. They are also related, historically and metaphorically, to all those who seek justice and liberty. Invisibility caused by various forms of internal and external blindness is a metaphor for African Americans, as in Ralph Ellison's novel, *Invisible Man* (1952).

Although the time period of the poem begins in the sixteenth century and its final event occurs in the nineteenth century, "Middle Passage" also reflects a transitory stage in the development of America and African Americans: "weaving toward New World littorals that are mirage and myth and actual shore." The universal quest to arrive safely, in a religious, commercial, private, or public sense, is a recurrent theme in "Middle Passage." By means of this theme, Hayden projects death as an intensification of life. All of humanity is in a middle passage, traveling toward mental, social, physical, and spiritual salvation.

Norris B. Clark

MILTON

Author: William Blake (1757-1827)
Type of poem: Epic
First published: 1804-1808

The Poem

William Blake's *Milton: A Poem in 2 Books*, like John Milton's *Paradise Regained* (1671), is a short epic poem. Instead of using the more traditional pentameter, Blake wrote *Milton* in "fourteeners," a long seven-beat line that he patterned after biblical verse. *Milton* is named for John Milton (1608-1674), Blake's great seventeenth century precursor, and Blake makes Milton (or his vision of Milton) the poem's protagonist.

The first book of *Milton* describes the Bard's song and Milton's descent from Eternity to earth. Milton has been walking in Eternity since his death, unhappy because his "Sixfold Emanation" is "scatter'd thro' the deep/ In torment." This sixfold emanation may represent Milton's three wives and three daughters, but critics have suggested that it could also symbolize Milton's writings or Milton's hopes for social reform in England. It takes, however, the Bard's song to motivate Milton to redeem his sixfold emanation.

The first part of the Bard's song summarizes Blake's myth of the Fall, a myth that is more fully developed in Blake's *The Book of Urizen* (1794). This Fall is presented as a fragmentation of the original unified man (Albion) into various entities (Zoas), who are further fragmented into emanations and specters. With each division comes a corresponding contraction of the senses, and the Zoas are plunged into torment and perceptual confusion. In the midst of the chaos that is the material world, Los (the Zoa who represents the imagination) begins to build Golgonooza, the city of art.

After giving this brief account of the Fall, the Bard tells a story which appears to be patterned after Blake's quarrel with one of his patrons, William Hayley. This traumatic episode in Blake's life is represented in *Milton* by the conflict between two sons of Los, Palamabron (Blake) and Satan (Hayley), who exchange jobs: Palamabron takes over Satan's mills, and Satan takes over Palamabron's "Harrow of the Almighty." This arrangement leads to disaster—Palamabron's horses go wild, and Satan's mills are put in a state of confusion. Satan's effort to make Palamabron do a job for which Palamabron is not suited resembles, in Blake's mind, Hayley's practice of giving Blake the wrong artistic tasks. Satan, like Hayley, appears polite and mild but finally shows his true nature and departs in rage, setting himself up as God over Earth.

After hearing the Bard's song, Milton decides to return to the natural world, a level of existence which he refers to as eternal death. He descends to hasten the final redemption of humankind, which has not learned from his writings that heroic martyrdom is superior to the warfare described in Homer's epics, and also to ensure that he himself will be prepared for the Last Judgment. According to Milton, he in his selfhood (or without his emanations) is the Satan described in the Bard's song, and in order to save himself and humanity he will have to come to terms with his emanations and his poetic legacy on Earth.

Milton then falls, as his own Satan does in *Paradise Lost* (1667, 1674), and confronts the God he created in that same poem, called Urizen by Blake. He struggles with Urizen in order to correct his own past religious errors, trying to humanize Urizen with red clay while Urizen attempts to baptize Milton with icy water. At the same time, in another manifestation, Milton enters Blake through Blake's left foot, inspiring his poetic successor to help in the work of poetic redemption.

The second book of *Milton* describes the descent of Milton's sixfold emanation, Ololon, to join Milton on Earth. She comes to Blake's cottage in Felpham and asks the poet about Milton, who, she says, fell from eternity for her sake. In Blake's view, Milton did not understand women: His first marriage led to a volume on divorce, his daughters were said to have been irritated by his demands on them, and in Milton's *Paradise Lost*, the influence of Eve leads to the Fall. Thus, in order to prepare fully for the Last Judgment, Milton must come to terms with Ololon, or his female counterpart; when he and she are reunited, Milton's transformation is complete. The poem ends with Blake's vision of the twenty-four cities of Albion and the final preparations for the redemption of the world.

Forms and Devices

The first copies of *Milton* were printed and illustrated by Blake himself, and these copies still can be consulted by scholars of the poem. Although the poem itself is of primary importance, it seems likely that Blake wanted the readers of *Milton* to consider the illustrations along with the verse. The title page of Blake's illuminated edition shows the figure of Milton, well-muscled and with his back to the viewer. He is striding forward with his right arm thrust in front of him, dividing the flames facing him and separating the syllables of his own name, which is printed "MIL/TON." Without the benefit of this illustration, the reader of the poem would miss Blake's visualization of his protagonist as a strong, naked man moving forward aggressively to accomplish his quest.

In a later plate of Blake's edition, Milton is again shown, striding across the river Jordan to grapple with Urizen. Urizen, who represents the lawgiver God of *Paradise Lost*, holds the stone tablets of the law in both his hands, but Milton's struggle with him seems to be breaking Urizen's grip on them. Milton also divides the word "Selfhood" in half with his right foot, just as he separated his own name in the title page with his right arm—the idea that Milton must annihilate his selfhood is thus emphasized in both illustrations. Other illustrations include a picture of Milton entering Blake (falling backward, with a foot thrust forward) in the form of a star and a sketch of Blake meeting Ololon in front of his cottage in Felpham. Although many students of *Milton* encounter the poem as a poetic text, the illuminated version enables readers to see the work in the way Blake intended it to be seen: as a series of plates in which the texts and the illustrations complement and clarify one another.

Although *Milton* has been called a brief epic, it differs from earlier epics in its abandonment of linear progression. In *Milton*, everything essentially happens in the same instant: Milton simultaneously struggles with Urizen, enters Blake's left foot, lies down in a coma, and walks in Heaven. This is partially attributable to Blake's radical reconfiguration of the concept of time: From the perspective of Eternity, "Every time less than a pulsation of the artery/ Is equal in its period & value to Six Thousand Years." It is only man's fallen conception of time that regards it as a linear progression—in Eternity, chronological time is abolished, and everything exists in the eternal present. Yet there is another reason for the confusing simultaneity of the poem: Milton's movements are not through time and space but through different perspectives, from the fourfold vision of Eden to the single vision of Ulro. Because *Milton* has so many layers, it sometimes seems sequential when it is really describing a single instant seen from a variety of viewpoints. This simultaneity is shown in the "movements" of the characters: Milton descends in the first book, and Ololon does not leave Beulah until the second book, yet Ololon seems to get to Felpham before Milton does. According to the rules of chronological time, that would make no sense, but the poem does not reflect a linear progression. Milton and Ololon leave Eternity and are reunited in Felpham in the same instant.

Further complicating *Milton* is Blake's extensive use of symbolism. Like his other prophetic poems, *Milton* contains many allusions to Blake's mythic figures and perceptual states. Moreover, Blake employs natural symbols in *Milton*, such as the lark and wild thyme. Both the lark and wild thyme are extremely important in *Milton* because they are Los's messengers and, as such, herald the coming apocalypse. Blake also compares the lark to an angel (a messenger of God) and uses this bird to represent the new idea that corrects the religious errors of the past. When Blake recovers from his vision at the end of *Milton*, the lark and the purple-flowered wild thyme are the first things he sees—they symbolize both an actual moment in Blake's garden in Felpham and the Last Judgment that is about to come, thus bringing together the natural and visionary realms presented in the poem.

Themes and Meanings

Milton is sprinkled with allusions to Milton's works, although Blake does not hesitate to rework Miltonic symbols and concepts to suit his own vision. For example, Blake describes Milton in Eternity as "pondring the intricate mazes of Providence," a phrase that recalls the mazy reasoning of the fallen angels in *Paradise Lost* (Book II, lines 555-561). Moreover, when Milton leaves Eternity, his cometlike descent to earth recalls the description in *Paradise Lost* of Satan's fall. The comparisons between Milton and his devils are not, of course, accidental: Part of what Milton does in the poem is repudiate his former Puritanism. In terms of the three classes of men described in the poem, the Elect, the Redeemed, and the Reprobate, Milton begins the poem as the Elect and becomes a Reprobate.

Traditionally, the Elect are considered saints, the Redeemed are repentant sinners who are saved, and the Reprobate are sinners who are ultimately damned. Blake employs but reworks these classes: The Satan of *Milton* is a member of the Elect, and Blake presents him as a hypocritical pharisee; Blake's Redeemed live in doubts and fears and are tortured by the Elect; his Reprobates (or Transgressors) are the geniuses who act from inspiration, and they include Jesus and the prophets. According to Blake's *The Marriage of Heaven and Hell* (1790), the biblical Jesus has more in common with Milton's Satan than with Milton's Messiah, and the figure Milton presents as God in *Paradise Lost* is, from Blake's perspective, a tyrannical lawgiver who favors reason over the imagination. This God becomes Satan in *Milton*, and Milton must struggle against him and eliminate the Satan (Miltonic God) within himself in order to be purified. Once this purification takes place and Milton joins Jesus in the ranks of the Reprobates, he can become one with his sixfold emanation, Ololon, and annihilate his selfhood.

Nevertheless, *Milton* is clearly not only concerned with correcting Milton's errors but also appears to have been inspired by a crisis in Blake's own life; one of Milton's roles in the poem is to enter Blake and inspire Blake to follow his poetic vocation. When he wrote the poem, Blake was living in Felpham near his patron, William Hayley, a minor poet and biographer who sought to make Blake into a painter of miniatures and illustrator. Although grateful for Hayley's help, Blake was frustrated because his work for Hayley prevented him from writing his epics, and Hayley evidently had no interest in Blake's poetic efforts. In this situation, Blake must have thought often about Milton, who had postponed his own great epic in order to help in the Puritan cause. Blake and Hayley inevitably quarreled, and Blake began to realize that Hayley, although generous in a material sense, was a destructive influence on his art. As Blake writes in *Milton*, "Corporeal Friends are Spiritual Enemies."

After hearing the story of conflict between Palamabron and Satan, Milton decides to come down to Earth—the immediate cause of his descent is, in a sense, Blake's crisis and his lack of confidence in his poetic vocation. Yet when Milton enters Blake's foot, and Los, the imaginative Zoa, enters Blake's soul, Blake regains his powers as a poet-prophet. Milton's struggle against Urizen, who turns into Satan, parallels Blake's own struggle against Satan/Hayley, and in both cases the forces which would suppress or pervert the poetic imagination are defeated. Milton corrects the errors of his works, Blake writes *Milton*, and the universe draws nearer to final redemption, or "the Great Harvest & Vintage of the Nations."

William D. Brewer

MILTON BY FIRELIGHT

Author: Gary Snyder (1930-   )
Type of poem: Lyric
First published: 1958; collected in *Riprap*, 1959

The Poem

"Milton by Firelight" is a short poem with four stanzas, which vary in length from seven to twelve lines. As its title suggests, the poem reviews the vision of John Milton from the perspective of one who is camping "by firelight." Place and date of composition are provided by the author as "Piute Creek, August 1955." High in the Sierra Nevada, Piute Creek defines an arid, mountainous terrain where during the summer of 1955 Gary Snyder was employed as a laborer. His work was to build "riprap," which, according to his poem "Riprap," is "a cobble of stone laid on steep, slick rock to make a trail for horses in the mountains."

The poem opens with a stanza introduced by a line from Book IV of John Milton's *Paradise Lost* (1667, 1674): " 'O hell, what do mine eyes/ with grief behold?' " The well-known and still revered Christian myth "of our lost general parents" is brought into Snyder's poem by this intertextual reference to the great English epic. The line quoted expresses Satan's self-pity and resentment on first viewing Adam and Eve in the Garden of Eden.

The first stanza continues with a statement and a question. The statement, in the form of a long participle phrase, reveals that the speaker of the poem (Snyder himself at age twenty-five) has deep appreciation for "an old/ Singlejack miner" with whom he has been working. The miner is a master at riprapping and is completely at home in the Sierra Nevada: He "can sense . . . the very guts of rock" and can "build/ Switchbacks that last for years" under hard use by both humans and weather. In the face of such wise and skillful interaction with reality, Snyder somewhat testily questions the worth of Milton's "silly story" about humankind's supposed blessed state and subsequent fall from bliss.

The "Indian," or "chainsaw boy," of the second stanza is, like Adam and Eve, an "eater of fruit": He and the mules came down to camp "Hungry for tomatoes and green apples." The Indian, however, like the miner, is not a hero from Christian or Miltonian mythology but a nonfictional contemporary of Snyder who is also a worker. As an American Indian, he has no need to worry about Milton; he has his own indigenous culture, one that goes back thousands of years. The "green apples" for which he hungers are real apples, not symbols of knowledge of good and evil. Like the miner, this boy preserves a certain innocence: He lives with the diurnal cycle of nature, sleeping under night skies and seeing the river by morning, hearing the jays squall and the coffee boil.

Shifting perspective in the third stanza, the speaker flatly states that in ten thousand years "the Sierras" will be "dry and dead," home only to the scorpion. Such is the effect on the mountains caused by "weathering" and the expanses of geologic time. From this ecological perspective, there seems to be no excuse for human sentimentality; there is "No paradise, no fall." There is only nature and humankind, although the speaker cannot refrain from voicing his frustration with regard to "Man, with his Satan/ Scouring the chaos of the mind." He erupts: "Oh Hell!"

A mood of peaceful acceptance overcomes the speaker in the concluding stanza, as the camp fire fades and reading is no longer possible. "Miles from a road" now, work too is no longer possible; Snyder and the "bell-mare" relax into the promise of a summer's night.

Forms and Devices

To some extent, "Milton by Firelight" is a critique of an outmoded symbolic way of developing a poetic argument. Snyder makes little use of rhetorical or metaphoric flourish, compared with other writers of the late 1950's; instead, he creates by more direct, simple, and "natural" (organic) means. His use of words tends to stress their referentiality (apple as a fruit) rather than their rhetorical effect or symbolism (apple as an emblem of supernatural knowledge). Snyder's poetic stance is both dramatic in its direct presentation of the speaker's total situation and ironic in its treatment of Milton's traditional mythology.

The stanzas may be read as a sequence of dramatic scenes (arranged in a chronological order) that delineates the progression of the speaker's thoughts from his initial disturbed reaction to Milton's myth to his concluding attitude of repose and reconciliation: "Fire down." The dramatic perspective of the poem is centered on the speaker's consciousness and is enhanced by the detailed presentation of the physical setting. The reader seems to know when and why the speaker thinks and feels what he does. The device of omitting the first-person pronoun from the text encourages the reader to enter into the speaker's experience. Mental associations and opinions, as though just then entering the speaker's (and the reader's) consciousness, are encountered with the same immediacy as the jay's squall or the clang of the "bell-mare." In fact, the use of "bell" and "mare" as a single, hyphenated word more accurately names an experience rather than an object: The "clanging" comes from neither the mare nor the bell alone but from both moving together. Thus, the reader encounters a poetry of experience, a meditation rooted in place.

Embedding Milton's myth in Snyder's poem makes possible an ironic framework within which Snyder can evaluate the relevance of Milton's mythology. Snyder is attempting to set up Milton for a fall of his own. In identifying with the miner, the American Indian, and the horse, the speaker of the poem assumes a role analogous to that of the *eiron* in Greek comedy. The *eiron* is a deliberately understated but clever character who typically makes a fool of the self-deceiving and loudmouthed *alazon*. Milton is not really a braggart, but Snyder has necessarily adopted this ironic stance toward this Christian mythology to guard himself (and his reader) from its potentially negative effects.

The stable irony of the speaker's position allows him several times to undercut the authority of Milton's myth, at least for himself in his wilderness situation. The "story/ Of our lost general parents,/ eaters of fruit?" may indeed seem "silly" in the high Sierra, where a miner or an American Indian boy has a real hunger for nonsymbolic "tomatoes and green apples." The Christian myth means nothing to these innocents, who have their own stories by which to live. Eden, with its thornless roses and idealized human nature, is an anthropocentric fiction; it never existed nor will exist—not even when "In ten thousand years the Sierras/ Will be dry and dead, home of the scorpion." As the green apples ironically mock the forbidden fruit of Eden, so the dry and dead Sierra Nevada mountains mock the garden itself and the scorpion image mocks Satan. The reality of the scene seems to send the message that from the ecological perspective, as from the innocent perspective of a primary culture, there is "No paradise, no fall."

Themes and Meanings

"Milton by Firelight" is part of what Snyder was later to call his "de-education." The poem demonstrates the importance of a mythology—that system of inherited stories that shapes a given culture—and the importance of revising it to stay in touch with the total, ever-changing environment. Snyder's stance toward *Paradise Lost* must be skeptically ironic because Milton's system attempts to justify human beings' authority over the natural world, whereas his own beliefs require that humans accept their rootedness—that is, their proper place in the ecological web of life. A false or outmoded mythology not only damages the planet but also gets in the way of fully living one's personal life. The questioning of Milton's story, the narrative of the American Indian boy, the ecological vision of the Sierra Nevada mountains, and the speaker's concluding empathy with the "bell-mare" are all part of Snyder's moral effort to free himself from what he considers the potentially oppressive mythology of American and European culture.

Snyder's wisdom is a complex blend of ecological, Buddhist, and Native American lore. His goal is joyful hard work—with a clear mind—in a healthy wilderness environment; for example, there is the "Singlejack miner, who can sense/ The vein and cleavage/ In the very guts of rock." At one with the land, this miner is in effect married to it. The "rock," no longer apart from the man, is perceived as having "guts," "vein[s]," and "cleavage"—features that, appropriately, are both human and mineral. Both the miner and the American Indian boy are in place, at home, rooted. Their thinking, like the poet's, is concrete—not abstracted from reality. Moreover, the work of the miner in particular is effective: He builds "Switchbacks that last for years." The miner's sensitivity and productivity make him an archetypal embodiment of Snyder's personal vision.

In contrast to the miner's clarity is the self-pitying egotism of Satan, who beholds "with grief" even the idealized Eden. Satan is alienated from the natural world because he selfishly wishes to use it for revenge against God. He is a victim of his own chaotic feelings, " 'O hell, what do mine eyes/ with grief behold?' " He projects his inner chaos onto nature, so that chaos is all he can see. He is the archetype of self-conscious humankind: "Man, with his Satan/ Scouring the chaos of the mind." Where "man" and his Satan are, there will be the mental tendency to exploit nature by projecting a heaven or a hell. All too human and sentimental, this tendency clouds the human vision of what is and separates humankind from the world.

Yet, by entering fully into the rhythm of work with the miner, or into the rhythm of nature with the American Indian, one can hope to avoid this tendency to distort reality. As Snyder writes in "Piute Creek," "All the junk that goes with being human/ Drops away," even "Words and books . . . Gone in the dry air." For Snyder, when the self-centeredness drops away, clarity is possible. This sentiment reflects Snyder's respect for the Oriental traditions of meditation.

The final stanza's "Scrambling through loose rocks/ On an old trail" is a phrase that, while overtly referring to the mare, provides the reader with a possible analogue to Snyder's meditative action of reading and reconstructing the "old trails," the mythic life roads of the past. Although Snyder seems to reject the Christian myth of the Fall, he does make use of "Satan" as a metaphor for humankind in its alienated, self-conscious mode, "Scouring the chaos of the mind." Milton's myth was right for his own age, but myths should change as cultural and natural environments change. Snyder's response to his environment has been to help reinvent an adequate mythology for his era.

Gerard Bowers

THE MIND IS AN ENCHANTING THING

Author: Marianne Moore (1887-1972)
Type of poem: Meditation
First published: 1944, in *Nevertheless*

The Poem

"The Mind Is an Enchanting Thing" is a poem of six six-line stanzas. As in most of Marianne Moore's verse, the line length varies in a regular pattern repeated in each stanza. Here the syllable counts vary as follows: 6, 5, 4, 6, 7, 9. That is, the first line of each stanza is six syllables, the second five, and so forth. A subtle rhyme scheme typical of Moore is also repeated in each stanza: *abaccd*. Moore's use of indentation further gives this poem a distinctive shape on the page. Lines 1, 3, and 6 of each stanza appear flush left; line 2 is indented somewhat, and lines 4 and 5 are indented equally but a bit more than line 2. In spite of these typographic variations, the poem is composed of eight complete and grammatical sentences (with Moore using the capital letter only at the beginning of a sentence).

As the title announces, this brief poem is an exploration of the mind, perhaps an attempt at definition. The poem presents a variety of similes and metaphors for the mind and its functions of observation, memory, and emotional balance. Forms of the title word "enchantment" appear three times, revealing different senses in which Moore relates the mind to magical attraction and delight. In the title, the mind itself is "enchanting," that is, capable of enchanting others. In the opening line of the poem, however, the mind has become "an enchanted thing," a subtle shift that indicates the mind's susceptibility to the powers of things outside it that it observes. In the fourth stanza, the mind is described as "a power of strong enchantment," because it is "truly unequivocal." It is clear that we are operating in a difficult and abstract linguistic environment in reading this poetic attempt to fix in words the shifting experiences of consciousness and memory.

Moore's abstractions, however, are almost always combined with closely observed details of the concrete world, and this is true of the metaphors of this poem. The mind is variously compared to the "glaze on a/ katydid-wing," a German pianist performing a work by Domenico Scarlatti, the beak and the feathers of the kiwi (a flightless New Zealand bird), a gyroscope, and the shining of an iridescent dove's neck in the sunlight. None of these are obvious metaphors, to put it mildly. They all point to Moore's penchant for precision: her interest in the details and quirks of specific animals, or the particularities of an individual musician's rendering of a composer's work. That the fall of a gyroscope serves as an image for the abstract quality of being "unequivocal" epitomizes Moore's desire to link the abstract to physical detail.

The various metaphors suggest the mind's power of observation as it notes the minute subdivisions upon the katydid's wing or the shining of a dove's neck feathers in the sunlight. The poem also specifically points to other qualities of the mind. The mind has a certain clumsiness, "feeling its way as though blind,/ [it] walks along with its eyes on the ground." Memory gives mind both hearing and sight, here revealed through the direct metonomies of "ear" and "eye." The mind is capable of correcting for the heart's excessive emotion: "It tears off the veil . . ./ the mist the heart wears." Above all, perhaps, the mind is gloriously inconsistent (a word Moore remarkably works twice into her brief lines). Through all these qualities, Moore celebrates the quirkiness and particularity of the mind engaged in perception, memory, and thought. Unlike the tyrannical Herod, who kept true to his oath and beheaded John the Baptist, the mind can change, and that metamorphic quality is celebrated by Moore in the poem's final lines: "it's/ not a Herod's oath that cannot change."

Forms and Devices

Moore's talent for the unusual but illuminating metaphor is apparent in the metaphoric range of this poem, and the very abstractness of the central subject, the mind, forces the poet into figurative language. "Mind" is as much a process as a concrete entity, but Moore's insistent use of the pronoun "it" (ten times) and the very word "thing" in the title works against this abstraction. The tension of the poem lies in this effort to pin down abstraction with precision.

A consideration of mind is perforce a consideration of language, which shapes thought, memory, and emotion. Moore's poems are always fascinating explorations of sound and diction within her distinctive poetic form. The reference to "Gieseking playing Scarlatti" is probably as appealing to Moore for its sound as for the actual concert she recalls (which, she reports elsewhere, she attended at the Brooklyn Academy in the 1930's). Similarly, Moore uses both "Apteryx" and "kiwi" as synonyms for the same New Zealand bird. The hard p, t, r, and x sounds of the word resonate nicely with Gieseking and Scarlatti of the previous line, while the exotic "kiwi" is paired with the sounds of w, f, and h in a stanza including "rain-shawl," "haired feathers," "feeling," "way," "though," "walks," and "with."

Moore's orchestration of sounds is apparent in her often surprising rhymes as well: sun/legion, the/Scarlatti, submits/it's. Some of the rhymes specifically reinforce the poem's themes: most notably, mind/blind which suggests the limitations of perception, but also heart/apart, which points to the tension between thought and emotion, and unequivocal/fall which ironically defines trueness and certainty in terms of the inevitable "fall" of the turning gyroscope. Moore's skill in manipulating her strict syllabic line lengths also lends to the subtle brilliance of the poem. One five-syllable line is filled simply by the key word, "inconsistencies," while that word makes up one of three terms in a tongue-twisting nine-syllable line: "it's conscientious inconsistencies." The look of the poem on the page (as well as its syllabic formality) reminds one that this is a work from the age of the typewriter. Like her contemporary William Carlos Williams, Moore composed and revised on a typewriter, and the machine shapes the look of her "manuscripts" — appropriately enough for the machine age in which Moore and Williams grew to adulthood.

The particular surviving manuscript of this poem (part of the Rosenbach collection) is notable for the drawing of a shoe-polish container lid upon it. It is Kiwi brand polish, and the lid reproduces the odd little animal replete with his "rain-shawl/ of haired feathers." This drawing should remind the reader of the care Moore took in gathering her materials from a variety of sources, bestiaries, atlases, anthropological studies, illustrated magazines, accounts of baseball games, and advertisements. As much as Moore's poems are elaborate organizations of words and sounds, they also reveal her fascination with accurately observed particularities. "Apteryx" appeals not only because of its sound, but because of its origin in the Greek word for wing (thus echoing the katydid-wing of the previous stanza). The image of the "apteryx-awl" comments on the kiwi's odd beak—long, narrow, and pointed. Its eyes are on the ground, one suspects, in search of food, but it is important to Moore that that posture should be natural for the bird if the comparison is to work.

Themes and Meanings

"The Mind Is an Enchanting Thing" might well serve as a theme for all Moore's poetry: the celebration of the active intelligence engaged with the things of the world in the complex play of language and meaning. The poem's difficulties are of a piece with what it celebrates, a changeable struggling consciousness. The ability to alter and to grapple with confusion are the mind's strengths, as is its perception of detail, both observed and remembered. The virtues of the mind, Moore suggests, lie not in traditional power but in its ability to complicate and question. Thus the mind pleasurably engages "the inconsistencies of Scarlatti," while it rends the veil of the hyperbolic heart. The mind resists the tyrannical, as the contrast with Herod suggests.

The poem was written and published during World War II, and the sense that the mind is more complex than a bold Herod would countenance is relevant to the time. Gieseking, who enchanted Moore with his brilliant musicianship, was a German pianist whose continued performances in Nazi Germany led to his being banned from the United States for many years. The "inconsistency" that allows the poet to relish the music while deploring the political regime it came to be associated with is appropriately lauded in the poem. It is only when humans cease to be thought of as intricate finely tuned intellects that tyranny and atrocity become possible. The enchantment of the mind works against such dehumanization.

The poem is finally both an example of and a celebration of the mind's activity. The intricate nettings of the insect wing, the fine feathers of the odd bird, the rainbow of colors reflected off the fragile neck of the bird of peace are all images for the almost infinite complexities of human thought in action.

Christopher Ames

MINIATURE

Author: Yánnis Rítsos (1909-1990)
Type of poem: Lyric
First published: 1961, as "Mikrographia," in *Parentheses, 1946-47*; collected in
   Rítsos in Parentheses, 1979

The Poem

"Miniature" is a free-verse poem of fourteen lines. The title, especially in Greek, denotes a small-scale drawing of the type that Yánnis Rítsos is known to have drawn on hundreds of stones and on the backs of Greek cigarette boxes. While the title self-consciously limits the size of the poem, it is deceptive in that it does not indicate its scope.

The poem captures an awkward moment in time in which two people who are about to have tea are unable to connect. A woman of indeterminate age stands at a table, slicing lemons for tea. The round slices, with sections like spokes, are compared to the wheels of a carriage in a fairy tale. A young officer is sitting nearby, "buried" in his armchair. A tangible distance separates them. Instead of looking at her, he lights a cigarette with a trembling hand.

Time stands still, in the "heartbeat" of a clock. The moment passes, and it is "too late" to act upon the unspecified "something" that has been "postponed." The chance for the two to connect has been lost. Instead of facing each other, they escape into a mundane activity: "Let's drink our tea."

The poem concludes with a series of rhetorical questions. At first glance, these seem unrelated to what has happened, or rather to what has not happened, since the focus of the poem is on the absence of action. "Is it possible, then, for death to come in that kind of carriage?" Evidently, there has been a death, as though life not seized, a desire not acted upon, is not merely the absence of life, but death.

The exact nature of the desire, like the exact relationship between the woman and man, is unspecified. Perhaps she is his mother, wife, sister, or lover. Perhaps he is returning from or going to war. (The date of the poem's composition coincides with a terrible era of Greek history, immediately after the Nazi occupation and during the civil war.) The urgency of life, like the presence of death, stymies them.

In the end, all that remains of the moment is the metaphor of the carriage, created by the woman only to be left behind "for so many years on a side street with unlit lamps." Perhaps the lamps are "unlit" because they missed connecting with the officer's match. Finally, after many years, the moment reappears in "a small song, a little mist, and then nothing." Perhaps the memory of the carriage has inspired the small song of the poem itself, which is followed by an obscure melancholy before it disappears again into the nothingness of forgetfulness or death.

Forms and Devices

Rítsos' strength is in the simplicity of his language, so his work suffers relatively little in translation. He is a prolific and popular poet—his more than ninety volumes have been widely translated, and many of his poems have been successfully put to music—whose work speaks simply to human experience and emotion.

Relatively unconcerned with complexities of form, syntax, or allusion, Rítsos depends on the emotional impact of ordinary objects lovingly observed. In a 1966 poem called "Insignificant Details," Rítsos suggests that common objects are the poet's sacred text: "their secret meaning (beyond gods and myths,/ beyond symbols and concepts) only poets understand." It is the poet's job to cast them in such a light that anyone can be made to understand by feeling their significance.

Rítsos' populist realism is suffused with a magical quality, a result in part of the influence of Surrealism, but his poetry owes its dreamlike effects not to the psychic automatism or the unconscious, but to experiences grounded in the everyday life of the body. In "Miniature," for example, he appeals to the childlike free play of the imagination, in which semblances instantaneously become similes. The thin slices of lemon are "like yellow wheels for a very small carriage/ made for a child's fairy tale," and the clock "holds its heartbeat."

Rítsos' poems are more visual (and visceral) than intellectual. Motifs from sculpture and painting are common. Often, he creates a sort of optical illusion in which metaphor replaces reality. In "Abstracted Painter," a poem that recalls the optical illusions of the artist M. C. Escher, a painter draws a train, and one of the carriages cuts away from the paper to return to the carbarn, with the painter inside. Something similar occurs in "Miniature" when the reader is left not with the human situation, but with the metaphor of the carriage, with death inside. Imaginative symbol replaces experience.

Rítsos gives his poem a dramatic context, as though implying that the magic of metaphor erupts in the midst of the most mundane human activities. The reader is given only a parenthetical scene in a larger drama and is invited to speculate about the nature of the tension of desire and restraint between the woman and the man, the "something . . . postponed" that is unspoken and unenacted. The dramatic conflict is not overtly expressed in their actions; the conflict must be discerned beneath their actions.

Within the two adults are two children who are illuminated by the yellow of lemon slices and match flame. The woman performs her household chores while dreaming of escape, like Cinderella, in a magic carriage (here made of a lemon rather than a pumpkin). The officer is a boy afraid of love, romantic or maternal. His nervous hand holds the match, its warm glow highlighting his "tender chin and the teacup's handle," which connects him with the woman.

It is difficult to say whether "Miniature" is a sonnet or merely a lyric that happens to contain fourteen lines. Rítsos' early work used all the conventions of rhyme and meter, but later he abandoned them for free verse. "Miniature" can, however, be read as an ironic twist on the tradition of the sonnet, with all the trappings of missed connection and imaginative consolation.

Themes and Meanings

"Miniature" appeared in the first of two collections called *Parentheses* (1946-1947 and 1950-1961). In terms of mathematics and symbolic logic, these short poems are "parenthetical" in that they contain unified propositions, symbolic or psychological. In terms of human relationship, writes Edmund Keeley in *Rítsos in Parentheses* (1979), "the two signs of the parenthesis are like cupped hands facing each other across a distance, hands that are straining to come together, to achieve a meeting that would serve to reaffirm human contact between isolated presences."

This is certainly the human theme of "Miniature," but this is also a poem about the dual nature of experience, the ways in which imagination informs and enriches reality. Lemon slices may spice a cup of tea or inspire a fairy tale; both are necessary. It is the poetic moment that connects the real world with the imaginary. In such moments one makes one's meanings. As Rítsos says in another poem, "an endless interchange shaped/ the meaning of things."

The poetic moment also unites time and timelessness. The chatter and business of everyday life, like preparing tea, is ruled by the clock, but the imagination exists between moments, when "The clock/ holds its heartbeat." At these moments, all such sound and fury are suspended, but the stilled "heartbeat" of the clock is also associated with death, which is brought in the fairy tale's carriage.

Yet death and life is another duality that the poetic moment unifies, for it is when one is closest to death that one most appreciates life. One's perception of mortality quickens one's pulse, makes more urgent one's joy in the particulars of life, the smell of lemon peel, for example, and makes one want to live. Lemons always symbolize a desire for life for Rítsos, who, while a political prisoner in 1950, wrote: "[w]e have not come into this world/ simply to die./ Not when at dawn/ there is the smell of lemon peel" ("Chronicle of Exile III," February 15, 1950). Rítsos celebrates poetry's ability to discern the interpenetration of life and death, reality and illusion, for the one always makes one yearn for the other. To alter William Wordsworth's famous claim, in moments of imagination, one sees into the "death" of things.

Rítsos' vision is tragic, not pessimistic or nihilistic. As a Marxist, he sees "nothing" at the end of life to justify existence; as an existentialist, he believes that one makes one's meaning along the way. The nothingness of death is preceded by "a small song, a little mist." The tragic undertone is caught better in the connotations of the Greek: The word for mist also means melancholy, although the homonym for mist (missed) may convey something of what is lost in translation; the word for song (*tragoudi*) echoes its root in Greek tragedy. Thus the little song (*mikro tragoudi*) is only a minor tragedy, resulting in this miniature portrait (*Mikrographia*) of missed connection.

Out of the little tragedies of missed connections, Rítsos suggests, come the consolations of the small songs of memory, those parenthetical miniatures of the imagination called poems. Like the spray of the cut lemon, the song of the poem captures the imaginative moment in a melancholy mist, before the onset of nothingness. It is the smell of lemon peel, however, cut by one's hands and shaped by one's desire, that makes one want to live, and by living create meaning—and connection—in one's life.

Richard Collins

MINIVER CHEEVY

Author: Edwin Arlington Robinson (1869-1935)
Type of poem: Satire
First published: 1910, in *The Town Down the River*

The Poem

"Miniver Cheevy" is a short poem of thirty-two lines satirizing an embittered town drunkard who bemoans the difference between a romantic heroic past and a mundane modernity and yet does nothing to improve his squalid lot in life. The satire is a double-edged blade, undercutting both the illusions of the do-nothing dreamer and his complaints about the triteness of his modern environment. The weight of the ridicule, however, is leveled primarily against the speaker.

Reared in Gardiner, Maine, Edwin Arlington Robinson created a mythical "Tilbury Town" out of his New England birthplace and populated the fictional place with eccentrics, such as Miniver Cheevy, who lead wasted, blighted, or impoverished lives. Robinson's work was an American exemplar of the realism permeating European literature, especially novels and short stories, in the second half of the nineteenth century. Appropriately, "Miniver Cheevy" reads like a revealing and realistic short story in verse, providing readers with a snapshot portrait of a main character whose story is a sad case of inaction and arrested development lost in futile reverie.

The poem opens with Miniver Cheevy so wrapped up in dreams of the past that he loses weight and weeps in self-pity. His frustration stems from idealized visions of medieval glory and classical heroism set in Camelot (King Arthur's legendary castle), Thebes (the realm of Sophocles' Oedipus), and Troy (King Priam's doomed city in the *Iliad*). Sadly, any romance or artistry that once gave rise to epic poetry and grand tragedy seems to him to have dwindled in the present to the stature of a bum on local welfare ("now on the town").

So it is that Miniver daydreams about legendary personages, such as the Medici rulers of Renaissance Florence, whose wickedness would incite him to perform his own evil deeds, if only he could escape into the past and be a member of that infamous family. He would gladly trade his commonplace clothing for medieval armor, although he still holds on to some modern corruptions, such as his love of money, which otherwise he scorns in his escapist imagination.

Poor Miniver, "born too late," wastes his life in intense, useless contemplation that leads to confusion of mind. He blames his futility, not on himself, but on the unlucky timing of his existence, as alcohol fuels his irresponsible dreams.

Forms and Devices

"Miniver Cheevy" is a satire consisting of eight quatrains, each with alternating feminine (weak) end rhymes conveying the futility of the speaker's escapism through sound effects. Assonance and consonance permeate the poem.

The prevailing meter in the first three lines of each quatrain is iambic tetrameter with variations ("Hĕ wépt thăt hé wăs évĕr bórn"). The metrical regularity lends a singsong effect that seems to lull Miniver into his romantic dreaming, until the illusion evaporates in the ironic dissonance of the short fourth line of every quatrain, with its abrupt two iambic beats and a fluttering unaccented sound of the feminine end rhyme ("Aňd hé hăd réasŏns"). Thus, readers can almost hear the dreams float away into a vapid realm of comic nonsense ("Ŏf írŏn clóthĭng") or reality ("Aňd képt ŏn drínkĭng").

The poem is a satire, ridiculing the folly of the speaker for the moral instruction of readers. Instances of burlesque—making what is high appear to be ridiculously low—occur in the descriptions of Priam's heroic compatriots (line 12), romance and art (lines 15-16), the Medicis (lines 17-18), and the wished-for armor (lines 23-24). The medieval and classical allusions to places, figures, and objects create an inappropriate romantic backdrop for modern, mundane Miniver.

The poem is a fine example of ironic compression, with a maximum reduction of the number of words to create a bluntness necessary to annihilate the dreamer's illusions in the minds of readers. The very name "Miniver" suggests, elliptically, both his minimalness and an antiquated medieval knight's name. Moreover, to call Miniver simply "a child of scorn" engenders a double meaning: that he is an object of scorn to others, and that he is the very personification of one who is scornful of his environment. Again, abrupt phrases, such as "And he had reasons" or "And kept on drinking," add to the many ironies reverberating throughout the poem.

Robinson characteristically uses diction that mixes the elegant and the mundane ("He mourned Romance, now on the town,/ And Art, a vagrant"), the abstract and the concrete ("He missed a mediæval grace/ Of iron clothing"), as well as the exotic and the flat ("Miniver loved the Medici,/ Albeit he had never seen one") to achieve the maximum satiric effect, deflating both the dreamer and the dream.

Finally, the repetition of "and thought" in lines 27 and 28, is a brilliant stroke, capturing Miniver's stupid dedication to fantasy. Speaking volumes about Miniver's mental dullness and irresponsibility, the repetition appealed to Robert Frost, Robinson's greater disciple, another twentieth century poet of the New England scene. As Frost noted in his introduction to *King Jasper* (1935), "The first poet I ever sat down with to talk about poetry was Ezra Pound. It was in London in 1913. . . . I remember the pleasure with which Pound and I laughed over the fourth 'thought' in 'Miniver thought, and thought, and thought,/ And thought about it.'. . . [Robinson's] theme was about unhappiness itself, but his skill was as happy as it was playful."

Themes and Meanings

"Miniver Cheevy" is about a small-town drunkard living in the mundane present and wasting his life away in futile fantasies about a medieval and classical antiquity. It is a verse portrait of an irresponsible and idle dreamer who expends his energy in reverie and who will never face up to the truth of himself as a self-created failure.

The poem is built on ironic contrasts between the unheroic Miniver as he is, and his dreams of adventure, romance, and art associated with heroic figures of the legendary Trojan War in ancient Greece, King Arthur's knights of the Round Table in the Middle Ages, and the dazzling brilliance and corruption of the Medici in the Renaissance. What a great figure he might have been, Miniver reasons, had he been born at the right time. That he has not succeeded is not his fault; he uses the classic excuse that the rest of the world is wrong.

Miniver escapes from the world of reality into a world of dreams induced by alcohol. Each stanza's final short line with its feminine ending provides an appropriately tipsy rythm. The name Miniver, with its suggestion of the Middle Ages, patchwork royalty, and minuteness, coupled with the diminutive-sounding Cheevy, sums up his failure. The tone of the poem is one of humor, pathos, and sympathetic understanding, but there is a mocking note also, an intimation that Miniver's unfortunate situation is not the result of any cosmic flaw in a nonexistent high tragedy; Miniver is a clown prince of his own tragicomedy of life.

Thomas M. Curley

MR. EDWARDS AND THE SPIDER

Author: Robert Lowell (1917-1977)
Type of poem: Meditation
First published: 1946, in *Lord Weary's Castle*

The Poem

Early in his literary career, Robert Lowell researched the life of the eminent eighteenth century American preacher Jonathan Edwards with the aim of writing his biography. He never wrote the life, but two of his best-known poems derive from this purported venture. "Mr. Edwards and the Spider" is a poem of five nine-line stanzas that fuses several experiences of the Northampton, Massachusetts, minister having to do with spiders, either literally or metaphorically. Lowell adopts the voice of Edwards in meditation.

The first stanza summarizes the content of a remarkable letter that Edwards wrote, probably at the age of ten or eleven, to an English correspondent of his father. In it, he recorded his observations of the habits of flying spiders and drew some unusually mature inferences, for example, that since their journeys were always seaward, the spiders were in effect seeking their own death. Written in a decidedly scientific spirit, the letter discloses a gifted naturalist in the making.

In his second stanza, Lowell shifts his attention to Edwards' most famous (though hardly most representative) work, the sermon that he delivered as a guest preacher in Enfield, Connecticut, at the height of the religious revival called "The Great Awakening" in 1741. "Sinners in the Hands of an Angry God" compares the individual members of that congregation to "a loathsome spider" that God dangles over hell. In a dramatic presentation of the intransigent Calvinist version of Original Sin, Edwards assured his listeners that God would be justified in dropping them into hell at any moment. "What are we," Lowell asks, after Edwards, "in the hands of the great God?"

Next, Lowell introduces the black widow, whose bite is poisonous and can be deadly, and reiterates the appropriateness of God's wrath. In the fourth stanza, the poet invents an incident in which Edwards, as a small boy, sees a spider being cast into fire and offering little resistance to it. The final stanza draws in Josiah Hawley, an uncle of Jonathan Edwards, who early in the Great Awakening committed suicide by cutting his own throat. Here and in another poem, "After the Surprising Conversions," Lowell makes use of letters Edwards had written to Benjamin Colman, a fellow minister in Boston, describing Hawley as having fallen into "a deep melancholy, a distemper that the family are very prone to," and attributing his death to the Satanic incursion that the Great Awakening was designed to combat. A few days after the bloody incident, Edwards saw evidence of "a considerable revival of religion," but he later reported to Colman that the temptation to suicide was spreading alarmingly among the townspeople.

Finally, the black widow is death itself, "infinite" and "eternal." To Edwards and no doubt to Hawley, death could be the prelude to an everlasting damnation, although Lowell couches his speaker's concluding words in terms ambiguous enough to accommodate the possibility of different interpretations by successive readers.

Forms and Devices

Lowell works the meditation into an elaborate stanza in an iambic meter ranging from three to six poetic feet long with a demanding rhyme scheme of *abbacccdd*. Having set this restrictive and regularly recurring form for himself, the poet runs the speaking voice across it in such a way as to create felicitous variations of rhythm, pace, and emphasis.

About half the lines as well as the transition between two of the stanzas show enjambment, and half the sentences begin within lines. There is great variety, also, in the length, arrangement, and function of the sentences. The first stanza, for example, is composed of two descriptive sentences of twenty-seven and thirty-five words, while the hexameter line at the end of the second stanza consists of two balanced questions: "How will the hands be strong? How will the heart endure?" Longer, often-periodic sentences combine with abrupt questions such as these and snappy assertions such as the concluding "This is the Black Widow, death" to give the impression of an agile mind at work.

In this and other early poems, Lowell shared the practice of poets such as Dylan Thomas and Marianne Moore, contrivers of intricate patterns who muted the rhymes and disguised the rhythmic schemes, thus artfully concealing art. The sound effects of this poem enhance the movement of the meditating mind without calling attention to themselves—which is why the analysis of such poems must do so.

"Mr. Edwards and the Spider" also illustrates Lowell's penchant for merging seemingly disparate elements into a surprising unity. Edwards' youthful admiration for flying spiders and his heavy-handed appropriation of them twenty-five years later, playing as it does on his congregation's theologically induced loathing of spiders for the sake of frightening them into the straight and narrow path, reveal two totally different aspects of a many-sided man. The modern reader, coming upon these two works of Edwards, are likely to lament the disappearance of the budding naturalist into the fire-and-brimstone preacher, but Lowell teases them imagistically into coexistence in this poem, adding also the poisonous black widow. Edwards' listeners would naturally tend to associate this type of spider with the Devil. In fact, Edwards' fellow Massachusetts minister Edward Taylor (who ended his long pastorate in Westfield about the time Edwards began his in nearby Northampton) had portrayed "Hell's spider" memorably in a poem and had doubtless also done so in his sermons. By amalgamating these spiders, Lowell suggests the complexities and contradictions of Edwards' character in one relatively short poem.

Lowell accomplishes this feat by collapsing time in the consciousness of his speaker. As a result, he could combine several elements, one of which is the early keen interest in nature's ways that surely continued in the preacher. Another is Edwards' painful recollection of an unbalanced parishioner harried by religious emotion into a desperate act. Lowell also infuses his subject's powerful rhetorical gift and, in acknowledgment of Edwards' philosophical bent, his predisposition to meditate on death. The result of Lowell's compression is no doubt a "Lowellized" Edwards but nevertheless a more comprehensive portrait of the man than one is likely to glean from any one of his surviving works.

Themes and Meanings

Lowell is a twentieth century writer whose preoccupation with the dark side of human nature and of modern culture led him to a study of the American colonial mind. No more an apologist for Puritanism than was Nathaniel Hawthorne in the nineteenth century, he could not on the other hand accept the optimistic tradition in American letters that, beginning with Edwards' contemporary Benjamin Franklin and proceeding through the transcendentalists of Lowell's New England and Walt Whitman, discounted or minimized the effects of what Puritans had generally identified as original sin.

Edwards, born only three years before Franklin, exemplifies a religious commitment about to yield to a rationalist, humanist, and increasingly secular outlook. Edwards was a brilliant conservative fighting a rearguard action against irresistible change. Although destined to fail, Edwards unflinchingly faced the reality of powers that defy and belie purely rationalist accounts of human nature. In doing away with an angry God, the generations after Edwards were banishing the most plausible available explanation for many of the afflictions that have since become likely to be summed up in an expression such as "the human condition."

Beginning in his second stanza, Lowell has Edwards address a "you" who remains unspecified until the fifth stanza, when the addressee becomes Hawley, for Edwards as well as for his readers a disturbing example of deviant human behavior. It is easy enough — too easy, in fact — to see Hawley as the victim of ministerial mischief, a precarious temperament driven into psychosis by a kind of religious reign of terror. Such a characterization, however, ignores the fact that the modern world has its Josiah Hawleys, too.

Edwards himself would not have characterized death as "the Black Widow," as Lowell does, but death was nevertheless a terrible prospect to one who could not be sure whether he was destined for heaven or hell. Compounding that dilemma, Lowell's Edwards asks, "How will the heart endure?" and wonders what a life is worth. The poem seems to seek an explanation for the guilt that so many people feel (including rejectors of Calvinism). It questions the disappearance in recent times of the majestic calm that leading intellectuals such as Ralph Waldo Emerson and Henry David Thoreau displayed while upholding self-reliance as an antidote to the mind troubled by a legacy of sin and corruption.

For many readers, "To die and know it" means something different from what it would mean to Edwards. Lowell's black widow has no anger to appease, and no appeal is possible. Lowell has Edwards ask the question, "But who can plumb the sinking of that soul?" For Lowell, it is less a moral question than a psychological one. His Edwards continues to be a kindred spirit despite the death of his theology, for even if his answers are not sufficient, at least he knew how to ask the right questions.

Robert P. Ellis

MONT BLANC

Author: Percy Bysshe Shelley (1792-1822)
Type of poem: Meditation
First published: 1817, in *History of a Six Weeks' Tour*

The Poem

Mont Blanc is a meditative and descriptive poem in five unequal stanzas of irregularly rhymed iambic pentameter. As with several of Percy Bysshe Shelley's poems, scholars still dispute important details regarding its text. An early title specifies that the poem was conceived "at the extremity of the vale of Servoz"; a later subtitle has it "written in the vale of Chamouni," which is a trough-like valley at the base of Mont Blanc. Mont Blanc itself is a stupendous sight as one comes upon it suddenly around a bend of the ravine through which the river Arve (originating in one of the glaciers of Mont Blanc) runs. Shelley probably stood on a bridge (the Pont de Pellisier) crossing the ravine to contemplate the scene. In his day, Mont Blanc was thought to be the highest mountain in Europe. From the bridge, it looms before the observer as one of the most dramatic views anywhere in the Alps; it is noted for its height, its formidably jagged rocks, its unforgettable glaciers, and the eerie whiteness from which it derives its name.

The first stanza of *Mont Blanc* reflects on the human mind itself, comparing it to the ravine of the Arve over which the poet is standing. The Arve flows through the ravine as influences from the material world flow through the mind, like a stream of consciousness. The river and the ravine have shaped each other, but the extent to which each has shaped the other is unclear. The second stanza is a more tangible demonstration of the thought process described in the first. The Arve now is specifically described as Power, meaning not only the material power of matter in motion, but also the power of nature to influence the mind, even to the extent of creating poetry.

In the third stanza, the poet/narrator turns his attention from the ravine below him to the domineering mountain directly ahead of and above him. Like everyone else, he is awestruck, almost hypnotized, as he contemplates its impersonal command of the entire scene. Dominating even the lesser mountains by which it is flanked, Mont Blanc appears to transcend all the limits of earthly existence, especially the short-lived mortality of mankind. Despite attempts by the intellectualizing poet to find some kind of beginning for the mountain (through earthquakes or volcanic eruptions), it seems virtually eternal.

Stanza 4 then pointedly contrasts the mortality of man and his works with the timelessness of the material world and its "primeval" (existing from the beginning) mountains. Most of the stanza is devoted to a vivid description of Mont Blanc's glaciers, which are inexorably destructive of anything human placed in their paths to oppose them. The closing lines paradoxically affirm the hydrological cycle, in which snow, ice, glaciers, the Arve (a river derived from the glaciers but bringing fertility to man), the ocean, and the water evaporated from it are all seen to be one.

Finally, stanza 5 sums up Shelley's profound meditation upon Mont Blanc, power, and human existence by first acknowledging the power of nature and then surprisingly but effectively disputing it by championing the primacy of the human mind over any manifestation of the material world.

Forms and Devices

Mont Blanc is a difficult poem, in part because Shelley attempted to capture within it the very rapid workings of his own mind. At several points, the poem seems unfinished, abandoned rather than perfected. For this reason, one's reading of it should probably depend more upon the major images it evokes than upon the precision of its sometimes uncertain language.

The poem abounds with symbolic landforms, some of which cannot be precisely identified or related altogether coherently with others. In stanza 1, for example, lines 6-11 constitute an elaborate simile based upon some landscape not immediately at hand (though perhaps a version of the same scenery that is developed later on). Both the "feeble brook" of line 7 and the "vast river" of line 10 are products of "secret springs" (line 4) and have something to do with human thought; none of this, however, is very clear. The most usual reading is that the "vast river" is the same as the "universe of things" flowing through the mind in lines 1 to 4. If so, then the human mind is dominated by passively received sense impressions (as in the philosophy of John Locke) rather than by its own autonomous creations. Throughout the poem, however, one sees the mind regularly allegorizing the world of nature and thereby giving it a significance that it would not otherwise possess.

In his gripping natural descriptions throughout the poem, Shelley utilizes a category of landscape aesthetics already denominated in the eighteenth century as the sublime. Its complementary opposite is the picturesque, in which (like a modern tourist) one was invited to stand in precisely the right spot so as to see before one a natural scene resembling a landscape painting, with foreground, background, side curtains, and a center of interest all in order, as if arranged by a master artist. Such views commonly celebrated God's creative talent, reaffirmed traditional religious belief, and consequently spared the observer any troublesome awareness that his outlook may have become obsolete. It was different with the sublime, which emphasized the amoral power of nature and its heedlessness of mankind. Far from reassuring and safeguarding the observer, the sublime tended instead to emphasize his helplessness, destabilizing him both physically and intellectually.

One sees the contrast between these two modes of landscape perception most obviously in stanza 3, lines 76 to 83. They too are puzzling, in part because of a major crux (textual difficulty) in line 79, where Shelley wrote "In such a faith" in one version and "But for such faith" in the later and generally accepted one. Do they mean the same thing, or did Shelley change his mind? The kind of faith involved is undoubtedly William Wordsworth's rather than that of Christian orthodoxy; in any case, the stanza's last lines refer to the Mountain's "voice." Shelley apparently wavered here between accepting a benign, Wordsworthian view of nature and the harsher, perhaps more realistic one that he then affirms so impressively in stanza 4.

Themes and Meanings

Shelley's *Mont Blanc* is one of the most philosophical of all landscape poems; it is also among the greatest. It is partly a reply to William Wordsworth's "Lines Composed a Few Miles Above Tintern Abbey" (1798), in which both the type of landscape described and the implications suggested by it are much cozier. Both poems deal with the human mind, but Shelley (unlike Wordsworth) is not concerned with its development through childhood to maturity. Instead, he takes for granted a richly endowed adult mind that simultaneously perceives and abstracts. Unlike Wordsworth, he is not fundamentally concerned with memory. Thus, one not only sees the poet's mind at work, creating the very poem one is reading, but one also sees his mind analyzing itself. It is clear that the mind in question is both rational and creative.

Besides analyzing itself, the poet's mind also analyzes nature, particularly in its relations to humankind. That nature strongly influences human thought is both implied and assumed; for one thing, nature is often beautiful and therefore attracts one's attention. Shelley records no evidence to suggest that natural beauty is in any way purposeful, however; for him, no divine being deliberately created an aesthetically pleasing world for the enjoyment of its human inhabitants. Nor is nature a moral teacher (as Wordsworth held), except in ways that typical nature-lovers had never recognized.

The world of Mont Blanc—which, for Shelley, encompasses the entire earth—is fundamentally indifferent to either the survival or the happiness of humankind. Any benefits it bestows upon humans are therefore not divine favors but mere accidents. The outstanding difference between nature and man, for Shelley, is that nature endures throughout time whereas man does not. This is the real lesson to be learned from nature (lines 92-100).

Yet Shelley does not ultimately concede. In the final stanza, he confronts Mont Blanc straightforwardly, both as a fact and as a symbol. He sees the height, the power, the coldness, and the isolation of Mont Blanc and celebrates them (in lines 139-141). The material universe, already seen to be eternal, is infinite as well (lines 60, 140). Yet in a strikingly abrupt conclusion—three lines that ultimately outweigh all the rest of the poem—a shocking reversal takes place, as Shelley taunts the gigantic mountain by pointing out that its only significance (indeed, nature's only significance) is that given to it by the human mind. In this sense, then, the eternal universe in which humans live is constantly being re-created according to human dictates.

Dennis R. Dean

MOONLIGHT

Author: Paul Verlaine (1844-1896)
Type of poem: Narrative
First published: 1867, as "Fêtes galantes"; as "Clair de lune" in *Fêtes galantes*,
 1869; collected in *Paul Verlaine: Selected Verse*, 1970

The Poem

Composed of twelve ten-syllable lines, "Moonlight" is divided into three stanzas, each of which possesses its own regularly alternating rhyme scheme (*abab, cdcd, efef*). The title of the collection in which the poem originally appeared, *Fêtes galantes*, bears considerable importance on a visual level to the interpretation of this piece. Antoine Watteau (1684-1721) was renowned as the painter of "fêtes galantes," jewel-like renderings of men and women dressed in satins, lounging gracefully in nature's lushness. In the same way that Watteau, in *A Pilgrimage to Cythera*, invites the eye to take in the golden splendor of love in paradise, Paul Verlaine invites the reader to discover a world colored by moonlight and enlightened by strolling musicians.

In the first stanza, Verlaine compares the soul of an unknown person — "your soul" — to a landscape, which is personified as being gladdened by masked musicians, who play the flute and dance, dressed in gaudy colors. Contrasting with the happy countryside, the musicians exhibit traits of sadness, scarcely concealed by their colorful disguises.

The second stanza focuses on the musicians, now singing huskily of love that conquers and the fullness of life. Seemingly doubtful of the happiness that they depict in song, they offer music that blends with the softness of the moon's rays. The personification of the landscape in the first stanza continues in the final stanza; the moonlight rays are sad, birds dream, fountains sob in ecstasy. The coldness of marble statues contrasts with the subdued spirituality of personified elements in this concluding stanza.

Through the musicians' "gaudy colours of disguise," Verlaine evokes the timeless opposition between "l'être et le paraître," between reality and illusion. It is ironic that the initial tone of joy and joviality in the first stanza should yield to one of pronounced sadness, permeating nature as well as mankind. The fact that Verlaine chose this poem to be the collection's *pièce luminaire* reveals that, as the introductory poem, it was likely meant to set the stage for further development of similar scenes. Both time and place — night and countryside — lend themselves to a meditative state, one that belies the gaiety conveyed by the strolling musicians.

Verlaine's sensibility is revealed effectively through the painterly aspect of his poetry. The association between the collection's title and Watteau's work is, therefore, all the more fitting, since Verlaine brings into play with precision and wistfulness particular scenes found in eighteenth century French painting. It is, however, the irony in "Moonlight" that goes beyond a simple romanticized landscape, since the main point of this poem is the metaphorical depiction of a person's soul. The development of the poem's focus from the comparison between soul and landscape in the first stanza to the portrayal in the second of the musicians' sadness, and finally to the climax in the third stanza underlining the moon's sad beauty differs markedly from the aesthetics of those plastic arts that evoke a similar scene. Verlaine's skill as a writer enables him, therefore, to illuminate gracefully an aspect of the human condition that is perhaps imperceptible to the casual observer.

Forms and Devices

Verlaine's poetry is extremely mellifluous. It is not surprising that "Moonlight" has been set to music by Claude Debussy (in 1881), Gabriel Fauré (1887), and Gustave Charpentier (1896). The musical qualities of the original text result largely from the resonance of *b*'s, *f*'s and *v*'s combined with the proliferation of *a*'s. Curiously, the smooth flow of the English version is strengthened by the repetition of *s*'s, a somewhat dissonant sound that succeeds, nevertheless, in creating an ethereal quality ("soft moonlight rays—so beautiful to see," line 9) that elevates the scene to a dreamlike level of existence. Generally speaking, Verlaine utilizes simplicity of form and musicality to encapsulate a commonplace of eighteenth century plastic arts, but at the same time, he offers on a visual level a new dimension to this cliché. By penetrating the façade of the country idyll, he underscores a hidden anguish that seizes the reader's attention in the penultimate line of the final stanza.

The microcosm depicted by the poet serves as an obvious point of comparison with the soul that is mentioned in the first line of the first stanza. At the opening of the text, Verlaine establishes the metaphor evoking "your soul" as a landscape that progressively reveals itself to be less than joyous, although it is initially presented as a "chosen landscape glad." The irony of this metaphor is that the reader assumes incorrectly from the poem's first line that the remainder of the text will blindly follow a pattern like that of Watteau's paintings, which depict images of pleasure and revelry in a setting of natural perfection. The subtlety with which Verlaine visually guides the reader is the key to his use of irony. Given the often romanticized symbolism associated with moonlight, the image of which is present in the title as well as in the second and third stanzas, the reader's expectations that the text will fashion yet another superficial rendering of love and tranquillity under the moonlight seem to be confirmed. Gradually, however, there appear indications that "Moonlight" will rebel against romantic conventions. The musicians "strum the lute and dance and are half sad" (line 3); "They seem to doubt that they can happy be/ And blend their song with soft rays of the moon" (lines 7 and 8). The minstrels' song tells of the power of love and the fullness of life, and it intermingles with the moonlight, oddly described in line 9 as "sad moonlight rays." This shift from the gladness of the landscape in the first stanza to the sadness skillfully rendered in the second and third stanzas culminates in a curious paroxysm of emotion in the poem's final lines: "And sparkling fountains sob in ecstasy/ Amid the marble statues in the glade." The strangeness of this personification creates an eerie atmosphere, given the odd combination of tears and profound happiness suggested by this image. It is to be noted, however, that the marble statues evoke a permanent physical state, and that they exist in isolation. This final image completes the metaphor by drawing the reader's eye to the permanence of physical existence, anchored in solitude, and contrasts sharply with the soul mentioned at the beginning of the text. The opposition between the heaviness of physical existence and the ethereal quality of spirituality is, therefore, effectively rendered by means of the ironic development of the text's central metaphor.

Themes and Meanings

Painting a metaphorical picture of a person's soul, "Moonlight" evokes simple desires for beauty, love, and tranquillity. The atmosphere of increasing disillusionment that emanates from the poem lends itself to a meditative and introspective tone. The reader inevitably wonders whether love and happiness can be found in reality. The central metaphor suggests that everyone carries an "interior landscape" within, and in this particular case, the elements that form it are, paradoxically, both beautiful and forlorn. The dichotomy between *l'être* (being) and *le paraître* (appearance) is one of the most important themes of "Moonlight." In addition to this perhaps surprising combination of physical beauty and sadness, Verlaine communicates to the reader the impossibility of attaining complete happiness. In doing so, the poet suggests that in life, as in the afterlife—the latter symbolized by the soul—man's desires for perfection, be it for overly romanticized love or a perfect life, will inevitably remain unfulfilled. In this way, Verlaine guides one through a self-examination that poses various questions concerning one's expectations in life as well as one's appreciation of the ambient world. The true essence of existence is, therefore, not visible on the surface.

There is, however, some ambiguity in the concluding lines of the poem, for although "sparkling fountains sob in ecstasy," "even birds dream in the leafy shade." Sadness is seen not as a stultifying force, but as one that leads to introspection and contemplation. One important aspect of "Moonlight" is Verlaine's obvious love of natural beauty; the poet endeavors to encourage the appreciation of a beauty that is neither gaudy nor artificial. "Moonlight" puts into perspective hopes and desires in order that the individual might have a more balanced conception of existence, one that is unencumbered by the physical, which is symbolized by the marble statues anchored in their own permanence. They are to be admired for what they offer, but one must remember to appreciate them for what they are: objects created by man that render his creativity immortal.

"Moonlight," a deceptively simple narrative poem, addresses philosophical and aesthetic preoccupations that have long fascinated writers and artists. Why does it seem that sad songs are the most beautiful? What special aesthetic attraction does sadness exert? Verlaine does not provide the answers. The poet does, however, endeavor to challenge the reader's beliefs by creating with words a scene that does not conform to the aesthetics of eighteenth century plastic arts. Crossing boundaries and provoking unexpected reactions, Verlaine demonstrates a particular perception of existence through his mastery of irony.

Kenneth W. Meadwell

MOONLIT NIGHT

Author: Tu Fu (Du Fu, 712-770)
Type of poem: Lyric
First published: wr. 756, as "*Yüeh yeh*"; collected in *Ch'uan T'ang Shih*, early
  eighteenth century; collected in *The Selected Poems of Tu Fu*, 1989

The Poem

"Moonlit Night" is one of Tu Fu's most frequently translated short lyrics. Because love poems are relatively rare in Chinese poetry, "Moonlit Night" is a rather precious gem.

As the poem opens, the poet imagines that his wife must be by herself in her boudoir, gazing at the moon in Fu-chou (Fuxian county, Shaanxi province). He feels sorrowful because his children, so small and so far away from him, will not understand why they should remember Ch'ang-an (Xi'an, Shaanxi province). At this point, half of the poem is already over, and it seems that nothing extraordinary has been said. Suddenly, however, what could very well be a prosaic poetic idea gathers momentum and becomes vitalized when the focus shifts back to the wife in the next two lines, here translated literally:

> [In the] fragrant mist, [her] cloud-hair [gets] wet;
> [In the] limpid light, [her] jade-arm [gets] cold.

In this couplet, the poet invokes the presence of the absent wife with complex sensory experiences, suggesting that the wife, losing sleep over the absent husband, must be pondering deep in the night. Unexpectedly, this suggestion turns around the relationship between the subject and object of the longing, making the separation between the couple unbearably poignant. In the conclusion, the poet wonders when he and his wife will be together again, so that, leaning against the open casement, both of them could have their "trails of tears" dried at the same time by the moonshine.

"Moonlit Night," though apparently a brief and simple poem, was actually composed under circumstances of epic proportions. In 755, a civil war known as the "An-Shih Rebellion" broke out in China. The revolt was led by the border Commander-Governor An Lu-shan and his lieutenant Shih Si-ming. An Lu-shan, whose military and political influence had been accumulating since 742, turned his troops toward the capital Ch'ang-an, which soon succumbed to the rebel forces. Shortly before the capital fell, the Emperor Hsüan-tsung and his family, as well as Prime Minister Yang Kuo-chung, had already set out for Ch'eng-tu in flight. On their way, at a place called Ma-wei-p'o, the imperial guards mutinied and killed the prime minister. Blaming Yang Kui-fei, the emperor's *femme fatale*, for the insurrection, the guards demanded her death. The emperor had no choice but to comply. Li Heng, the crown prince, was also persuaded to leave the emperor and go north; after reaching Ling-wu (in Gansu province), upon the abdication of his father, he succeeded to the throne as Emperor Su-tsung. Meanwhile, Tu Fu, who had been granted a position before the siege of Ch'ang-an, set out from his home in Fu-chou in an attempt to join the new emperor. On his way, he was captured by the rebels and taken to the fallen capital, where he was detained for eight months. The poem "Moonlit Night" was written in these circumstances in the autumn of 766, probably on the occasion of the Mid-Autumn Festival, when family reunion is a general custom.

Forms and Devices

"Moonlit Night" is a poem written in the "recent style," as opposed to the "ancient style." The "recent style," which matured in the T'ang dynasty, requires a poem to follow regular tonal patterns and also to observe the rule of semantic and syntactic parallelism for its couplets. There are two kinds of recent-style poems. One is known as the *lü-shih*, or "regulated verse." It consists of eight lines, usually with two couplets in the middle. The other is known as the *chüeh-chü*, or "truncated verse." A "truncated" poem, which has only four lines, almost seems to be half of a regulated poem. Whether "regulated" or "truncated," a recent-style poem has either five or seven characters per line.

"Moonlit Night" is a regulated poem with five-character lines. Although most regulated poems have two couplets in the middle, "Moonlit Night" has only one. In fact, this poem is rendered extraordinary by its sparing use of a single couplet, which occurs in lines 5 and 6. Because the language of the entire poem is rather plain except for these two skillfully crafted lines, the couplet, which deals with the imagined sleeplessness of the wife, in effect achieves a kind of poetic climax or stasis by arresting the reader's attention.

The beauty of the couplet can be analyzed on two levels. On the rhetorical level, although in fact it is the poet who is saddened by the absence of his spouse, the two lines make the wife grieve over the husband's absence. This is a mimetic or mutual projection in which the interplay between presence and absence is designed to dramatize the separation between the couple. By reversing the subject-object relationship, this couplet allows the poem to elevate itself from prose to poetry. On the semantic-syntactic level, the couplet is also remarkable for its use of two conventional synecdoches— "cloud-hair" and "jade-arm"—to stand for the wife. Furthermore, each of these synecdoches also interacts with the elements of the environment: Just as the "cloud-hair" gets wet in the "fragrant mist," the "jade-arm" also gets cold in the "limpid light." These interactions not only achieve interesting synesthetic effects, but also produce the precise psychological condition that is desired by the poet. Finally, the words "wet" and "cold," which in Chinese can be verbs as well as adjectives, are placed at the strategic endings of the lines in a kind of climatic apposition to the environmental elements and synecdoches, thus suggesting that "wet" could refer to either the "fragrant mist" or the "cloud-hair" (or both), and "cold" to either the "limpid light" or the "jade-arm" (or both). This appositional syntax further reinforces the sensorial synaesthesia as well as the psychological yearning; indeed, the culmination of the couplet in the word "cold" seems to blend the sensory with the psychological by confusing the two levels of feeling.

Themes and Meanings

Family reunion is an important theme in Chinese poetry, and many poems are based upon the "reunion *topos* [topic]." In a poem employing this *topos*, the full moon—especially that of the Mid-Autumn Festival, when the moon is roundest and brightest—takes on symbolic meanings because it reminds the poet of his or a family member's separation from the home. "Moonlit Night" certainly belongs to the genre of poetry built around the "reunion *topos*."

What sets "Moonlit Night" apart from other poems dealing with separation and reunion, however, is its ingenious treatment of the object of longing. Traditionally, it is usually a man who yearns for a reunion with a friend or a brother. Tu Fu has, in fact, written another "Moonlit Night" poem about his brother using the reunion *topos*. The yearning for one's wife in this poem subtly adds to the general theme of separation and reunion the somewhat more novel theme of love. In addition, as far as the tradition of Chinese love poetry is concerned, it is usually the wife who yearns for the return of the traveling husband, whereas here it is the husband who yearns to return to his wife, who he believes is also yearning at the same time for his return. In its layering of yearning upon yearning, "Moonlit Night" may be described as a love poem in which the relationship between subject and object is obscured. The ending of the poem, which must have shocked its readers because of its rather direct proclamation of passionate feelings, in effect inaugurates a new sensibility that Chinese male poets will feel comfortable to exploit thereafter.

From a larger perspective, it can be said that a political theme is also intertwined with the reunion theme and the love theme of the poem. In "Moonlit Night," as lines 1, 2, 5, and 6 make clear, one of the basic situations is that of a woman who is saddened by the absence of her husband. This allows the reader to see the poem from the perspective of the "boudoir plaint" convention that has been popular since the Han dynasty. In a "boudoir plaint" poem, a wife usually laments the absence of her heartless husband, who is traveling as a merchant, fooling around with courtesans in the city, serving in the capital as a bureaucrat, or stationed at the frontier to fight against barbarians. In a subtle sense, "boudoir plaint" poems are not simply love poems but also, more importantly, allusive critiques of government policies such as war and social evils such as the practice of concubinage that have led to the desolation or desertion of the woman. T'ang poetry is in fact replete with examples of "boudoir plaint" poems that raise serious questions about the tragic dimensions of war. In Tu Fu's poem, a political theme along the lines of the "boudoir plaint" tradition thus lurks behind the mention of place names such as Fu-chou and Ch'ang-an. Considering Tu Fu's reputation as a patriotic poet, the hardships involving him, his family, the people, and the nation as a whole could very well be part of the cause for tears to be shed upon the reunion of husband and wife.

Balance Chow

THE MOOSE

Author: Elizabeth Bishop (1911-1979)
Type of poem: Narrative
First published: 1976, in *Geography III*

The Poem

Elizabeth Bishop's "The Moose" is a narrative poem of 168 lines. Its twenty-eight six-line stanzas are not rigidly structured. Lines vary in length from four to eight syllables, but those of five or six syllables predominate. The pattern of stresses is lax enough almost to blur the distinction between verse and prose; the rhythm is that of a low-keyed speaking voice hovering over the descriptive details. The eyewitness account is meticulous and restrained.

The poem concerns a bus traveling to Boston through the landscape and towns of New Brunswick. While driving through the woods, the bus stops because a moose has wandered onto the road. The appearance of the animal interrupts the peaceful hum of elderly passengers' voices. Their talk — resignedly revolving itself round such topics as recurrent human failure, sickness, and death — is silenced by the unexpected advent of the beast, which redirects their thoughts and imparts a "sweet sensation of joy" to their quite ordinary, provincial lives.

The poem is launched by a protracted introduction during which the speaker indulges in descriptions of landscape and local color, deferring until the fifth stanza the substantive statement regarding what is happening to whom: "a bus journeys west." This initial postponement and the leisurely accumulation of apparently trivial but realistic detail contribute to the atmospheric build-up heralding the unique occurrence of the journey. That event will take place as late as the middle of the twenty-second stanza, in the last third of the text. It is only in retrospect that one realizes the full import of that happening, and it is only with the last line of the final stanza that the reader gains the necessary distance to grasp entirely the functional role of the earlier descriptive parts.

Now the reader will be ready to tackle the poem again in order to notice and drink in its subtle nuances. Bishop's artistry will lie plain, particularly her capacity to impart life to a rather unnerving redundancy of objects and to project a lofty poetic vision from a humble, prosaic incident.

Forms and Devices

Description and narrative are the chief modes of this poem. Nevertheless, at critical moments the actual utterance of the anonymous characters is invited in ("Yes, sir,/ all the way to Boston"). The binder of these varied procedures is the speaker's tone of voice: calm, subdued, concerned with detail and nuance, capable of a quiet humor, in sovereign, though unassuming, control.

The thirty-six-line introduction is the most sustained piece of writing in the poem. It forms a sequence of red-leaved and purple Canadian landscapes through which the blue bus journeys. Then, in smaller units, for another thirty-six lines the bus route is reviewed, main stops mentioned, and further details concerning the passengers, the weather, and the scenic sights duly recorded. Day is replaced by evening, and light gives way to darkness. The eleventh stanza brings in a climactic moment of equilibrium and economy of design. Beginning with the thirteenth stanza, the first quotes are used, as they will again be in the twentieth, twenty-fourth and twenty-fifth, and, finally, in the twenty-seventh stanza. Stanza 14—the moonlight episode—is the very center of the poem. This section is rhymeless, though this is amply compensated for by the triple epithets in the third line, and it marks the transition from the outer, natural world to the inner, human concerns of the second part of the work, which includes lines 85-129. Usually unchronicled and unheroic human tragedy receives an indirect presentation, culminating with the moving and dramatically rendered twentieth stanza. The third part of the poem begins, appropriately, in mid-stanza with line 130. The encounter with the moose—the climax of the entire poem—is allotted two descriptive stanzas (the twenty-fourth and the twenty-sixth). The remaining two stanzas form a kind of a coda, bringing the poem to an end with a powerfully ironical twist obtained by juxtaposing the "dim smell of the moose" to the "acrid smell of gasoline."

The diction of the poem modulates in accordance with the needs of its plot. Thus the first part, devoted to the landscape, is richly descriptive, replete with qualifying epithets that, toward the end (in line 75 and in line 81), come in by threes, like beads on a string. In the second part, dealing with the passengers' plight, learned, latinate words such as "divagation," "auditory," "hallucination," "eternity," and "acceptance" signal the presence of the narrator-commentator. In the third part—the one reserved for the moose—epithets return. In the climactic twenty-fourth stanza, the most distinctly poetic devices—explicit comparisons—are bestowed on the protagonist: "high as a church,/ homely as a house." Moreover, the four additional epithets lavished on the moose contribute to the grandeur of its appearance: "towering, antlerless," and "grand, otherworldly."

By careful calibration and timing of her tropes, Bishop succeeds superbly in achieving her ends. Contrast is attained by her control over all compartments of language, and her austere, restrained tone and strategy of deferral and understatement are dramatically effective.

Themes and Meanings

"The Moose" is ultimately about the human need to be purged and, if possible, cured of selfhood. Self-absorption or narcissism is not only a passing malaise afflicting teenagers. Older people regard themselves in the mirror of their memories; they often run the risk of becoming trapped in despair or self-pity. Hence, the need to forget one's obsessions and delusions is a pressing one.

The moose miraculously appears in Bishop's poem to offer the passengers of the bus, the narrator included, a remedy for their solipsism. Curiosity is stirred in them, and a sweet, joyful sensation supervenes. The author invests her wildlife messenger with an otherworldly or religious awesomeness. The female moose becomes for the nonce Mother Nature—grand, fearless, and unselfconscious. Both like a church and like a house, the moose cow is a prehistoric reminder that humans are not stranded in this world, that there are dignified creatures that seem to be freer and more self-sufficient than humans are, and that human lives are richer because they exist. It is this almost mystical sense of fellowship that pervades the last third of Bishop's poem.

Humans need the moose as a friendly "other" capable of dispelling the anxiety induced by their inability to communicate significantly across the ghetto of the human species. Civilization has ruined nature and has alienated humankind from it. The man-made environment of highways, bridges, and buses cuts across the wildlife habitat in order to reach the Boston of human discontent. At the end of the poem, the clash between the "dim smell" of the moose and the "acrid" smell of gasoline poignantly dramatizes the incompatibility between nature and culture. This disharmony has been foreshadowed in the poem by the subtle overlapping between the reds and purples of sunsets and maple leaves and the "blue, beat up enamel" of the bus, whose hot hood the moose finally gave a welcome sniff. Even though the encounter is brief, its effects will reverberate in the readers' wakened consciousness.

There is a distinguished tradition of poetry writing to which Bishop's "The Moose" belongs. It can be traced back, as poet John Hollander has noted, to William Wordsworth's *The Prelude* (1850), whose so-called episode of the Winander Boy (book V, lines 389-413) deals with the ancestral impulse to talk to nature's creatures. The Winander Boy initiated such a dialogue by mocking the hooting of owls. To his delight, the birds responded in kind. In between the mystic silences, nature's deeper secret motions flooded the boy's heart and soul. For the British Romantic, such a communion with nature could still be available to a few elected spirits whose purity and innocence had already marked them for intense experiences and an early death.

Hollander also noted a connection between Robert Frost's poem "The Most of It" and "The Moose." Frost had his male protagonist proudly call out to nature for something more than the "copy speech" that the Winander Boy had elicited from his owls. His wish for "counter-love, original response" was finally granted by the sheer chance appearance of a powerful buck that, lordlike, tore his way through tarn and wilderness without bothering at all to acknowledge the presence of the human intruder.

By contrast, Bishop's female moose has the curiosity to approach the trespassing bus in order to look it over and assess it in her mute, non-aggressive way. Finally, it is the bus that, pressed for time, leaves the spot—her territory—while the moose remains on the moonlit macadam road without budging.

Stefan Stoenescu

MORRO ROCK

Author: Garrett Kaoru Hongo (1951-   )
Type of poem: Meditation
First published: 1985; collected in *The River of Heaven*, 1988

The Poem

"Morro Rock" is a long poem in free verse, its eleven stanzas varying in length from three to twenty-eight lines. The rock of the title is a landmark offshore in Morro Bay, California; it serves as a focus for memory and meditation as the narrative moves from various descriptions of the rock to events and images suggested by its form, location, and environs. Ultimately, the rock becomes a symbol for the play and importance of the imagination and for the uncertainty of reality.

Although Garrett Kaoru Hongo's poem is autobiographical, it ultimately moves beyond the personal voice to make a statement about perception and about the act of writing poetry. In this sense, it can be termed metapoetic.

The poem begins in mid-line with a dash, as if the first description offered of the rock is simply another in a series of possibilities. In the fog, the rock resembles a fedora; in the sun, it invokes the choppy yet unified movement of a modern sculpture. No matter how it is described, the rock is perceived as an intrusion, something out of place and unnatural as it violates the smoothness of the ocean surface and the regularity of the surf. The second stanza is interpretive. The narrator indicates the importance of the perceiver in giving Morro Rock its identity. He imagines its omnipresence in various situations, such as a tuna run, the franticness and carnage of which reminds him of the war. In stanza 3, a day at the beach with one's father encompasses an attempt to capture the perfect photograph, to render the rock as an artistic artifact. Finally, in stanza 4, the rock plays a part in a love story gone awry.

The last line of stanza 4 offers an important comment on the role of the rock. When the lovers feel the emptiness of the death of their affair, "The Rock filled the space behind us." Morro Rock is simultaneously an absence and a plenitude, or a fullness of presence. It offers a hinge for the attachment of meaning, a mass that can occupy the blank spaces of knowing and reading reality in one's life.

In stanza 5, the "true" affair of the author's teens becomes mythicized, material at once for sordid retellings at youthful gatherings and archetypal accounts among the aged for all time, like the biblical narrative of Abraham and Sarah. The love story is carried forth in stanza 6, the center of the poem. Here are the homely and superficial details of a typical courtship, its innocuous beginnings. No one can object, just as no one can truly understand the nature of Morro Rock, until the surface is scratched. When the lovers merge physically to offer a unit in opposition to or rivalry with the agreed-on truths and morals of the community, they become scapegoats and martyrs to their new vision: After "finding the gods/ in each other, . . . the lovers were killed with stones, . . . and a quick, purging fire of hate." They are the victims of racial prejudice, but their love becomes generalized with the use of words with mythological resonances: the riders "hooded like hanged men," the women "keening in the night . . . crowlike," the lovers' death "smeared with bruises/ and the beach tar and twigs of ritual."

Stanza 8 restates the indifference of nature and its enduring, cyclical processes, but now the writing is imbued with the magic of human interpretation. The ruined building stands for the rival "religion" established by the lovers, which the society annihilated ritualistically as representing an order that they could not accept. Cranes here can be seen as birds of beauty and sadness, purity of vision, an unattainable ideal, as in Yasunari Kawabata's novel *Sembazuru* (1952; *Thousand Cranes*, 1958). The pair of cranes is real, but they are also symbolic, natural gods that cleanse the area of the sacrifice of the lovers as the amorous birds themselves dance "a curious rite of celebration." The paradoxical images of love and death, of union and destruction, of order and chaos, and of clarity and obscurity merge when the cranes settle on Morro Rock. Their presence of whiteness, naturalness, and fertility contrasts starkly with the "Rock's dark brow." Its status as a proper noun, along with its personification, reveals its somber omnipresence—black, intrusive, and barren— and its paradoxical absence—of color and of meaning.

The parallel three-line stanzas with which the poem ends move away from description, narration, and memory to philosophical reflection about Morro Rock and its agency in this poem. Stanza 9 is a statement reaffirming the merging of opposites in the action witnessed within the poem, which began in love and ended in death but proved them not to be opposites in that process. The poem emphasizes that the truth of the autobiographical experience lies in fact, in memory, and in any similar retelling. Literature and poetry even help to render it more clearly, more true in spirit, like a rock that becomes smoother and more lovely with the erosion of the tide. Finally, one is left with the rock, the initial object of definition in the poem. The entire poem has rotated on its centrality, yet here the narrator releases it to its own independent existence. People fashion reality from the materials at hand, filtered through memory, emotion, sensation, and knowledge of other stories, poems, and myths. The poet captures the truth here, yet Morro Rock remains the enigmatic matter that is only itself, "this chunk of continent equal to nothing."

Forms and Devices

The poem achieves momentum primarily through capturing complex images: moments in time now remembered in their particulars from a distance and therefore crystallized and essentialized. The poet uses the images connected with Morro Rock to show how its meaning and existence change according to the imagination of the perceiver. The rock can be a hat or a horse, but more important it can be a major figure in the formation of art, which symbolizes differing personal realities.

The images ultimately move toward a contrast of opposites, which the poem contrives to merge paradoxically: Two opposing actualities can both be true at once. Morro Rock itself is the principal embodiment of the paradox, for it is the ostensible subject of the poem, present in some form in every vignette, yet it really is not pertinent to the human actions portrayed, except as a pivot for interpreting events. The oppositions are apparent in contrasts of colors (black/white), of textures (fluffiness/hardness), of time (personal/communal past), of emotions (love/hate), of events (sexual union/death), and of diction (specific/mythological).

At the end of each major stanza, the rock has metamorphosed into something symbolic that carries the tenor of the poem. In stanza 1, it is a junked car engine, the churning of its pistons alien to the natural churning of the surf. In stanza 2, it becomes the spokesman for the margin between sea and land, a "black bead . . . eloquent on the horizon." In stanza 3, it is a clipper or messenger ship. In stanza 6, the rock becomes a tacit agent of the murder of the lovers, for they "were killed with stones," perhaps even pieces broken off Morro Rock by the surf.

The poem seems most cryptic in its final three stanzas: The first and last of the trio are philosophical and poetic statements that turn on the metaphor offered in the central tercet. Here, Morro Rock is transformed into a jewel (that is, the artistic rendering of its presence) and a Platonic reality separate from its earthly form, a reality indicated by its starry truth (like a jewel) spelled forth in a human making of meaning (which is art).

Themes and Meanings

"Morro Rock" is dedicated to the poet Mark Jarman. Hongo fashioned the poem in the Chinese tradition of poetic debate. He means to answer Jarman's belief in the necessity of poetic narrative. Hongo's poem reveals the impossibility of certainty in experience and in art. When narrative is attempted, it cannot escape the image and intrusion of the imagination. According to Hongo, "The world exceeds the word" and "Creation itself is the first language." Poems, then, can only be language about a preexistent language, which is the world of experience.

Hongo began the poem while daydreaming about his father, who had recently died, and the particulars of what he enjoyed about the California shore: "how much he loved humble things like a breakfast out, a drive along the coast, a gesture of friendliness between strangers." The memory of his father merged with a yearning for the pier ("the ocean, the gulls screeching, the salty air, the perfumed chill of a winter sea pitching under the pilings") and the repressed memory of his own first sexual experience, a love affair that was deemed interracial and was violently punished. All this description, however, is after the fact. Hongo was not entirely conscious of the poem's genesis as he created it:

> I wrote the poem not knowing I'd fabulize an erotic myth about social outrage and the persecution of sexual splendor. I got something in about violence and love and regret. I got California into it, my father and my mourning for him into it, and I disguised my own memory of a bad time with two big encounters with racism. I remembered the rhythms of those times and caught, for a moment, the scent of a girl's skin under a bronze satin blouse.

Sandra K. Fischer

THE MOST OF IT

Author: Robert Frost (1874-1963)
Type of poem: Lyric
First published: 1942, in *A Witness Tree*

The Poem

"The Most of It" is a lyric poem cast in twenty lines of rhymed iambic pentamer. The title contains a dual meaning that reflects an important contrast between the attitudes of the male character in the poem and of Robert Frost himself.

The man in the poem wants "the most of it": He wants more out of life than it ordinarily provides. Thus he spends time alone in nature, seeking a certain kind of response from "the universe," but he feels disappointed when nature does not provide that kind of response.

On the other hand, the title also ironically alludes to the common phrase, "make the most of it." Through this allusion, Frost implies that the man expects the world to do too much for him and that he should participate more energetically in perceiving and creating satisfaction for himself. The poem suggests that the man has not "made the most" of his experience in this sense; Frost, through a powerful display of his poetic prowess, definitely has.

Though Frost does not separate the lines into stanzas, the action of the poem falls into two distinct sections. The first eight lines present the man and his situation, while the last twelve describe his sighting of "a great buck," a large male deer. The first section introduces a man with an exalted—perhaps too exalted—conception of himself: "He thought he kept the universe alone." As another person might think of "keeping" house, this man thinks of himself in a domestic relationship with the "universe," and he seeks a response from nature to reassure him that he does not keep it alone. He is frustrated when all he hears is a "mocking echo" of his own voice, though he is crying out for "counter-love, original response."

In the second section of the poem, the man sights "a great buck," but he seems strangely unmoved by the experience. Disappointed by his quest in nature, the man feels that "nothing ever came of what he cried/ Unless it was the embodiment that" he saw across the lake. He believes that his pleas have produced either no response, or perhaps—merely perhaps—one encounter, which is then described in detail. A being, which the man would like to believe is the "embodiment" of the "counter-love" or "original response" that he seeks, crashes through the talus (loose rock below a cliff) on the other side of the lake and swims toward him. As it moves closer, however, the man realizes that it is not another human, but a large male deer. With great power, the buck moves quickly out of the lake, across the rock-strewn beach, and into the underbrush. The poem ends with a curiously abrupt coda: "—and that was all." This flat statement might be taken to mean that neither the buck nor anything like it ever appeared to the man again; more likely, it expresses the man's rueful sense of letdown at this incident and perhaps his entire quest.

Forms and Devices

Through the vivid imagery and powerful form of "The Most of It," Frost draws a vivid contrast between the man's naïvely sentimental expectations of nature and the harsh but awe-inspiring reality that he does encounter but seems to be too narrow-minded to appreciate.

The first section of the poem presents a situation in which the man's sentimental view of nature seems ironically out of synch with the details of the natural world around him. As noted earlier, in his rather domestic scenario, he thinks of himself "[keeping] the universe" as if it were a house. What he wants from nature sounds more like what one would want from another person, perhaps a wife: "counter-love, original response." What he faces in the scene around him, however, is a "tree-hidden cliff across the lake" and a "boulder-broken beach." Frost's images suggest that nature in this situation is too obscure, remote, and harsh to provide the man with the human kind of response that he is convinced he needs to find there.

Similarly, in the second section, Frost's images show how nature provides the man with an experience that is ironically so "original," so "counter" to his own expectations, that it is difficult for him to respond to it. The verbs that Frost chooses for the buck's first appearance clearly associate the animal with the wild and harsh natural scene of the first section: He "crashed" in the talus and "splashed" into the water. On the other hand, by mentioning twice what the man wants to see, Frost emphasizes the way the man's preconceptions obstruct his responsiveness to the buck: "Instead of proving human when it neared/ And someone else additional to him." In contrast to the human response the man had hoped for, the images of the buck's actions present a thrilling spectacle of wild, inhuman nature:

> As a great buck it powerfully appeared,
> Pushing the crumpled water up ahead,
> And landed pouring like a waterfall,
> And stumbled through the rocks with horny tread,
> And forced the underbrush—and that was all.

The abrupt tag-line to this spectacular description, "—and that was all," provides one final indication that the man finds little, if any, satisfaction in the sighting of the powerful deer. Frost, on the other hand, reinforces the impression that as a poet he does "make the most" of the buck's appearance through a virtuoso display of poetic form. He heightens the impact of his narrative by providing a strong underlying rhythm of iambic pentameter. Further, Frost casts his twenty lines into five quatrains with a rhyming pattern of *abab*, and he contrasts the limited perspective of the man with the expansive power of the buck by the way he manages syntax within these quatrains. For example, the two quatrains in the first section are both complete sentences, in consonance with the man's self-enclosed view of his situation. Frost describes the encounter with the buck in one long sentence of twelve lines. It is as if the expansive power of the buck, which gains momentum as Frost adds phrases in an accumulative parallel structure ("And landed," "And stumbled," "And forced"), is trying to burst out of the limited perspective of the man who witnesses it. The beginning and end of the long sentence ("And nothing ever came of what he cried// . . . — and that was all") create a frame that dramatizes the sense that the man cannot let go of his limiting preconceptions.

Themes and Meanings

The central theme in "The Most of It" is the human attempt to commune with nature — to connect with some spirit or presence and lose the sense of isolation and alienation. Frost's poem shares this theme with a long tradition of earlier Western literature, stretching from the classical myth of Narcissus and Echo in Ovid's *Metamorphoses* (c. A.D. 8) through pastoral, romantic, and transcendentalist literature in the centuries since the Renaissance.

Much of this earlier literature would suggest that the reader might bring to "The Most of It" a sympathetic and supportive view of the man's spiritual quest. In particular, New England Transcendentalists such as Ralph Waldo Emerson and Henry David Thoreau, whose writings Frost admired, posited a pantheistic Oversoul (Emerson's term) that would nourish the spirit of people who sought it in nature. Also, Frost would have been aware of the close correspondence between the man in his poem and a similar character to whom nature's voices do respond in "There was a boy," a famous section in the 1805 version of William Wordsworth's *The Prelude* (Book V, lines 364-388).

On the other hand, Frost's presentation of his character suggests a more ironic sense of the man's similarities to Narcissus, the archetypally self-centered character in the classical myth. Like Narcissus, Frost's man seems to suffer in an echo chamber largely of his own making. He acts on the naïve belief that all he should need to do is call or "cry out" (the phrase conveys passionate desire, but it also connotes a baby crying as if for its bottle), and nature should then respond with some form of "counter-love" or "original response." When nature does provide a startling encounter with a powerful animal, the man seems to consider briefly the possibility that this experience might be significant. Yet the abrupt ending of the poem (" — and that was all") suggests that the man's response is hardly adequate to the spectacle that Frost's powerful imagery and syntax have dramatized.

"The Most of It" indicates that those who would commune with nature would do well not to blind themselves with limiting expectations or preconceptions. Rather, such seekers should be as open, aware, and responsive as they can be to whatever experiences nature provides. Such encounters may not always be warmly reassuring, as Frost's man had hoped; however, to those seekers willing to "make the most" of such experiences through open-minded responsiveness (and perhaps through the work of forming those experiences into art, as Frost and many others have done), the results are often richly satisfying.

Terry L. Andrews

THE MOTHER

Author: Gwendolyn Brooks (1917-   )
Type of poem: Lyric
First published: 1945, in *A Street in Bronzeville*

The Poem

"The mother" is a short poem in free verse, written mostly in the first person. In her narrator, Gwendolyn Brooks adopts the persona of an impoverished mother. In the tradition of the lyric, this narrator addresses the reader directly and personally to convey her feelings. The poem contains thirty-five lines, which are separated into three stanzas. The title, "the mother," is ironic, for this mother is a woman who has lost her children because of very difficult and painful decisions — decisions that she believes were for the best.

Brooks's "the mother" implicitly explores the impact of abject poverty on the life of a female character. The poem depicts the struggles and regrets of a poor woman who has had many abortions. The mother has continuing anxiety and anguish because of her difficult decisions. The very first line of the first stanza, "Abortions will not let you forget," immediately draws attention to the title, "the mother," and to the importance of the word love — what it has meant to the narrator to love her children or, rather, the children she might have had.

The narrator of the poem, the mother of the lost children, ultimately accepts responsibility for her acts, although she seems to alternate between evading and admitting that responsibility. Throughout the poem, the narrator refers to her decisions with concrete adverbs and adjectives.

The brief final stanza is climactic. The narrator confronts her familiarity with her lost children and, despite her decision to abort them, proclaims her love for them. The final line, consisting of only one word, "All," is particularly effective in that it stands in stark contrast to the apparent harshness of both her decision and her own attitude toward that decision.

The city is an important and recurring symbol in Brooks's work. She has created a series of portraits of women inhabiting Bronzeville, a setting for many of her poems, which may be taken symbolically as the African-American community. In a way similar to that of Richard Wright, Gwendolyn Brooks's work expresses the tragic and dehumanizing aspects of the ghetto experience. Brooks also ventures deep beneath the surface of the ghetto experience to uncover areas of a poor person's life that frequently go unnoticed and should not necessarily be considered terrible or ugly.

Forms and Devices

A sharp contrast is created in "the mother" between potential — what could have been — and reality, what has been. This contrast establishes a dialectic of dreams versus reality, since, in the mother's imagination, the lost babies still exist and grow even though she knows that the babies are dead. Throughout the poem the mother drifts between the imaginative and the real, finally revealing her need to believe in an existence after death.

In stanza 2, she imagines giving birth, suckling babies at her breast, and hearing them cry and play games; she even thinks of their "loves" and marriages. Yet these thoughts are bluntly followed by the words, "anyhow you are dead."

The speaker cannot quite bear the word "dead," however, and immediately follows it with "Or rather, . . ./ You were never made." The alternation of accepting and evading responsibility, of plainly saying "my dim killed children," then denying that terrible picture, gives the poem its complexity and its deep emotion. The speaker begins, in the first stanza, by using a second-person address— "the children you got that you did not get"—then switches, in the second stanza, to the painfully personal first-person meditation: "I have heard . . . the voices of my dim killed children." Her attempt to keep a distance between herself and the experience she describes fails. In stanza 2, she addresses the children who were never born with a series of clauses beginning with "if," attempting to apologize or explain herself to them: "If I sinned," "If I stole your births." She can conclude these thoughts only with the contradictory statement, "Believe that even in my deliberateness I was not deliberate."

An important unifying device in the poem is memory. Memory is constantly functioning in "the mother." The narrator is in a fluid and changing relationship with the past, and specifically with her decisions that have drastically affected the present. These decisions keep intruding into the present, and her recollections move between her dreams of what might have been and the harshness of her memory of what caused her to decide as she did.

Themes and Meanings

"The mother" mourns the loss of children aborted because of the poverty of the mother. By extension, it also mourns the loss of things that do not reach their potential, such as the loss experienced by a race of people whose growth has been interrupted or altered. One contrast and conflict that emerges in the poem is that between the desire of the mother to do what was best for her children and the finality of her decisions. The depiction of the narrator—honest, reflective, and self-aware—prevents an immediate positive or negative characterization. Instead, like the decisions she has made, the narrator is complicated—full of conflicting emotions regarding both herself and her lost children. Ironically, it was the mother's moving concern for her children as well as her own circumstances which caused her to decide to have the abortions.

Throughout the poem, a strategic use is made by the narrator to the fate she knows would have been her lost children. Because of the harsh honesty which she refers to her decisions to have abortions, this reflection upon what the live's of the children would have been like is made more believable. Her reliability as a narrator is established by the time she gets to an accounting for the reasons she made her decisions.

An important difference between Gwendolyn Brooks and contemporary writers Richard Wright and Ralph Ellison, who also use poor urban settings in their writing, is that she devotes much more attention to the experiences of women. Women may not be lacking in Wright's and Ellison's writing, but they are typically in the background and are of secondary importance to the male characters. Like the work of Ann Petry, Brooks's work concentrates on the importance and implications of the poor urban experience on women as well as men.

Brooks's poems offer a realistic view of the diversity of poor urban women. This view is in sharp contrast to the stereotypes which have grown up around such women (whore and matriarch, for example) and have made their way into literature. Brooks intentionally fails to provide some sort of unifying, uniform characterization of poor urban women. The narrator depicted in "the mother" remains one of many possibilities, not the only possibility. There are also women in Brooks's poems who are sexually repressive, ordinary, exploited, protected, despairing, or aggressive. The only common characteristic these women share is a similar environment and heritage; throughout Brooks's poems, women emerge as individuals. The women have different goals, priorities, and values, and have varying levels of misery, tolerance, and talents. This variety points to the recurring theme in Brooks's work of individual identity and individual problems.

David Lawrence Erben

THE MOWER, AGAINST GARDENS

Author: Andrew Marvell (1621-1678)
Type of poem: Pastoral
First published: 1681, in *Miscellaneous Poems*

The Poem

In the *Miscellaneous Poems* of Andrew Marvell, published posthumously, "The Mower, Against Gardens" stands first in a set of four pastoral poems centering on the figure of the mower. A significant proportion of Marvell's poetry is pastoral by nature, but, as here, Marvell uses the pastoral convention in a most original way to ask fundamental questions about man's fall, his passions, and the possibility of (re)gaining lost innocence within nature. Traditionally, pastoralism has opposed the innocence of country life (typified by the shepherd) to the corruption of civilization and the culture of the city. Marvell replaces the figure of the shepherd with a more ambiguous one, the mower, and he suggests that country life itself may be invaded by the corruption of the city. In other words, there is a moral and spiritual threat that mere place, or state, by itself, is insufficient to prevent. In the three other "mower" poems, the mower himself is seen losing his peace of mind through his passionate sexual feelings for a shepherdess, Juliana. He "falls" in love and in the ensuing despair and moral confusion thinks of death. As a mower, he sees himself as bringing death to the grass; he, too, has been cut down by passion.

In this poem, however, the mower is much more unambiguously denouncing the corruption typified by the ornate enclosed garden that was coming into vogue in the seventeenth century. The references to horticultural innovations point clearly to this as well as to the enormous prices paid for certain tulip bulbs, and the great effort made to discover new plant species for decorative purposes (lines 15-18; 24-25). The mower believes that this is where man's luxuriousness is most in evidence at the present time (rather than in clothes, jewelry, or houses). "Luxuria" was considered one of the seven deadly sins, covering what is meant by sensuality, hedonism, and excessive appetite. The garden of luxurious man's making is thus the opposite of the original garden, Eden; yet both gardens stand corrupted by man and are prime evidence of his Fall.

The first part of the poem covers evidence of man's ostentatious consumerism, his misapplication of the simplicities of nature. This, by itself, the mower would be willing to forgive. What makes the display insupportable is man's cross-breeding, grafting kind on kind, in a way forbidden biblically (in the books of Leviticus and Deuteronomy). He is thus causing a sort of incest: identity, kind, and species become confused. Even birth becomes unnatural in a new sterility (line 30).

The mower's final figure of this sterility is one of the "fauns and fairies" that exist as spirits in nature, but that have now become reduced to material ornaments in the garden. His final act of defiance is to suggest the continuing presence of such spiritual forces in that nature which remains.

Forms and Devices

The forty-line poem is written in a non-stanzaic form. Yet there is a hidden stanza structure: The first part of the poem in reality consists of four quatrains and a couplet to round off the first eighteen lines; the second part is similar, leaving a final quatrain as conclusion.

This careful balancing is reflected in the paired rhyming scheme, so that each quatrain is basically two balancing or parallel couplets. Each couplet has as its first line an iambic pentameter line and as its second an iambic tetrameter line — an unusual form for Marvell. The shorter second lines thus avoid the full heroic couplet developed by John Dryden in the next generation of British poets and retain the terseness and epigrammatic quality typical of much of Marvell's poetry. The form also suggests a directness and simplicity that matches the poem's opposition to ornateness.

The imagery is also noteworthy, as might be expected of a Metaphysical poet. The recurring train is sexual, manifesting itself in a series of vivid conceits. "Seduce" (line 2) suggests that the vice mentioned in the first line is of sexual appetite and reminds one of Satan's seduction of Adam and Eve — a motif that his contemporary, John Milton, was to weave into the language of *Paradise Lost* (1667, 1674). Sexual fallenness is suggested by the cosmetic conceit (lines 11-14) used of the flowers, with the biblical subtext of Christ's words "Consider the lilies of the field" producing other resonances. "Dealt with" (line 21) suggests sexual traffic; the biblical conceit of "forbidden mixtures" suggests incest and miscegenation. There is sexual immorality in "adult'rate" (line 25), sexual luxury in "Seraglio" and "Eunuchs" (line 27), and unnaturalness in the sexless cherry (lines 29-30) — which has been taken to refer either to the stoneless cherry (with "stones" being a contemporary colloquialism for testicles) or to a cherry fruited through grafting. Sexual purity is only suggested by "pure" (line 4) and "Innocence" (line 34).

Thus the new Fall of Man is still seen in sexual terms. Marvell, however, does fill this out with other striking conceits — the enclosed garden as "a dead and standing pool of Air" (line 6) is particularly forceful, in that water and air both normally connote freedom of spirit and movement. Enclosure thus brings restraint, and the garden becomes a prison where the innocent plants are raped ("enforc'd") and corrupted into double-mindedness (line 9).

Themes and Meanings

Taken by itself, the poem remains fairly unambiguous in its meaning. Humankind, in its economic and cultural development, has generated more wealth than it knows what to do with. In a false sophistication, man has replaced nature with an art that is merely tasteless display. While this is serious enough, what he has really done is to corrupt nature itself. The purity of natural innocence is replaced by a seduced nature, which is then reduced further in its moral and spiritual power by becoming merely a taste, a vogue. Moral and spiritual categories are lost, as is, ultimately, man's identity as a created being. Man's hubris is to take over God's creation, rather than steward it, for his own exploitative pleasures. Such a reading would accord with the Puritan ethos of the seventeenth century as expressed, for example, in Milton's *Comus* (1637); it would also accord with the ecological morality of the late twentieth century.

Such a straightforward reading can be questioned, however, in two ways—first, by linking this poem with the other mower poems, second, by linking it to "The Garden," one of Marvell's best-known poems. If the figure of the mower in all the poems is considered, then he is not, perhaps, the upright Puritan he appears to be here. Ultimately, he is overtaken by passion; he falls himself. Nature's innocence, then, seems either illusory or too fragile for man to hold. Perhaps the mower himself is overly proud or is biased; he may not be the mouthpiece for Marvell that the first reading suggests.

Alternatively, if "The Garden" is placed alongside the poem, the garden there is portrayed as Eden restored, even if not permanently. There the garden retains its luxuriousness—"the luscious clusters of the vine" press themselves on the poet ("The Garden" line 35), for example—but in this luxury the poet is able to meditate imaginatively and enter into a Platonic quietude of spirit. Perhaps Marvell is presenting again to the reader Edmund Spenser's two gardens of *The Faerie Queene* (1590, 1596)—that of Acrasia ("the bowre of Blisse"), which is seductive and dangerous, and of Adonis, which is the Platonic paradise where souls are regenerated.

If this is so, then juxtaposing these two poems actually brings one back to the original reading. "The Garden" can then represent the rediscovery of the true garden, as against the false garden portrayed in this poem. Even if the figure of the mower is to be seen ambiguously, the point that Marvell is making is still that man, cut off from nature, loses being; any passion, be it lust or luxury, can cause this severance. What must matter for man is spiritual presence, not technical skill or material control.

David Barratt

MUSÉE DES BEAUX ARTS

Author: W. H. Auden (1907-1973)
Type of poem: Meditation
First published: 1939, as "Palais des Beaux Arts"; collected in *Another Time*, 1940

The Poem

"Musée des Beaux Arts," which is French for "museum of fine arts," is a poem about the universal indifference to human misfortune. Following a series of reflections on how inattentive most people are to the sufferings of others, the poet focuses on a particular rendition of his theme: a sixteenth century painting by the Flemish master Pieter Bruegel, the Elder, called *The Fall of Icarus*.

W. H. Auden spent the winter of 1938 in Brussels, where he visited the Bruegel alcove of the city's Musées Royaux des Beaux-Arts. "Musée des Beaux Arts" was inspired by the poet's fascination with the Icarus painting, as well as by two other canvases by Bruegel: *The Numbering at Bethlehem* and *The Massacre of the Innocents*. It was written in 1939, when Auden was distressed over the defeat of the Loyalists in the Spanish Civil War and the acquiescence of Europeans to the ascendancy of Fascism.

The poem consists of two sections, the first a series of general statements and the second a specific application of those generalizations. Like the great Flemish Renaissance artists, the poet observes how very marginal is individual calamity to the rest of the world. Most others continue with their mundane activities without paying any attention to the kinds of extraordinary events that poets and painters usually dramatize. In particular, instead of highlighting the magnitude of that mythical catastrophe, Bruegel depicts the bizarre disaster of Icarus falling from the sky as if it were peripheral and utterly inconsequential to anything else. Oblivious to what is happening to hapless Icarus, no one and nothing—neither a farmer nor the sun nor a ship—are distracted from proceeding with business as usual.

The second section of "Musée des Beaux Arts" is an abbreviated analysis of the Bruegel work, in which the poet emphasizes how the painter composes his pastoral scene in such a way as to minimalize the significance of a boy suddenly plopping into the sea. Except for the obscure background detail of individual death, the landscape might seem idyllic. Auden's point is a simple one, and, by expressing it simply, succinctly, and nonchalantly, he intensifies the horror of universal apathy.

Forms and Devices

The first noun in "Musée des Beaux Arts" is "suffering," yet the poem is constructed to demonstrate that it is only in its own first line and nowhere else in the world that human agony receives any emphasis. Elsewhere in his writing, Auden often employs recondite and archaic words, but in this poem he deliberately restricts himself to a very plain vocabulary. The effect of commonplace phrases is to emphasize the banality of suffering. The poet's tone is nonchalant, as if to echo the carefree way in which most people ignore the tribulations of others. Passion and reverence are out of place in the kingdom of the blasé.

The reader is told that, at the time of "the miraculous birth" (an allusion to the momentous arrival of Jesus), children were most concerned with ice skating and "did not specially want it to happen." The use of "specially" rather than "especially" suggests a child's vocabulary; it projects an air of innocence ominously at odds with the horror the poet feels. Even the reference to ice skating in ancient Palestine is an obvious anachronism, and its flippancy, too, is a deliberate incongruity, designed to call attention to something very wrong: the fact that indeed no one pays attention.

At the end of the first section, the "dreadful martyrdom" of the Crucifixion is undercut by the neighborhood dogs' "doggy life." The adjective "doggy" again suggests a childlike vocabulary, and the deliberately sloppy use of "life" rather than the more grammatically appropriate "lives" embodies the offhanded attitude that repulses the poet. While Jesus is being tortured to death, the executioner's horse calmly scratches his rump; the childish euphemism "behind" reinforces the air of innocence at the same time that it taints it with the reader's knowledge of the utter incongruity of such terminology in the face of blatant evil.

The second stanza reduces the entire catastrophe of Icarus' descent to the ingenuous phrase "a boy falling out of the sky," thereby dismissing it as effectively as the ploughman, the sun, and the ship do. Mockingly, Auden end-rhymes "green" and "seen," though those words are less important than others around them and they are not the ends of syntactical units of thought.

"Musée des Beaux Arts" is written as free verse, in lines so irregular and discursive that the poem might seem indistinguishable from prose. It is an appropriate form for a work that deals with the prosaic, with a breezy refusal to recognize drama, so preoccupied are people with unexceptional happenings. The wandering line "While someone else is eating or opening a window or just walking dully along" is a perfect marriage of form and content; a litany of trite activities, the line itself walks dully along the page and seems to end as arbitrarily as a shorter line such as "They never forgot," which appears to break at random. The poem is art disguised as artlessness, depicting a world in which artlessness is a failure of attention and hence of ethics.

The poem is an elaborate exercise in anticlimax, in the effort to undercut any serious, sustained attention to what is significant. Although formal sentences are not supposed to conclude with a preposition, "Musée des Beaux Arts" trails off more than concludes, with the preposition "on." One is left with the specious tranquillity of the foolish half-rhyme "calmly on" — the verbal equivalent of exactly the kind of amoral insouciance that the poem, camouflaging itself as part of the problem, depicts and condemns.

Themes and Meanings

Auden's poem is an example of ekphrasis, the embedding of one kind of art form inside another—in this case, a famous painting summarized in a poem. If art, as traditionally conceived, is the deliberate, labored product of human attentiveness to detail, "Musée des Beaux Arts" is centrally concerned with the temptations of artlessness. It is itself artful in its own guise of criminal artlessness.

Bruegel's *The Fall of Icarus* captures the final moment of an elaborate and portentous Greek myth. Icarus was imprisoned with his father Daedalus, the master craftsman, in the labyrinth that the latter had constructed on the island of Crete. In order to escape, Dedalus devises wax wings that will enable father and son to fly free of the island. He cautions Icarus not to soar too close to the sun, lest it melt the wings' wax. With the arrogance of youth, Icarus ignores his father's warning and, after his wings melt, plummets into the sea and drowns. In Bruegel's rendition, as though the event were indeed marginal to the course of human affairs, Icarus' leg is the only part of him still—barely—visible above the water, in the lower right-hand corner of the canvas. The disappearance of the imprudent boy is not the center of the viewer's attention, just as it passes unnoticed by everyone else within the frame. Like Bruegel, Auden would force one to take notice of universal disregard.

James Joyce chose Stephen Dedalus as the name of his aspiring novelist in *A Portrait of the Artist as a Young Man* (1916), and Dedalus, an ingenious architect and inventor, is often appropriated from Greek mythology as a prototype of the artist. Beginning with its title, an elegant French phrase that seems blatantly out of place with the poem's homely style and its rustic landscape, "Musée des Beaux Arts" questions the ability of art to matter in a world of intractable apathy. Not only is Dedalus rendered powerless, but the horrendous death of his son Icarus passes unheeded and unmourned. Even the sun, which, by melting the wax wings, is most directly responsible for the catastrophe, shines without pause or compunction.

Written in a conversational, vernacular style, Auden's poem is much more accessible than many of the other major poems of the modern period. Disarmingly direct, it is all the more stunning in its indictment of evasiveness. The "expensive delicate ship" that sails blithely away from an amazing event seems more intent on commercial operations than on concern for an individual human being, as if money mattered more than life. Despite and because of its apparent disingenuousness, "Musée des Beaux Arts" is one of the most haunting English poems to have emerged from the middle of the twentieth century, when millions of human beings were being uprooted, imprisoned, or slaughtered while the rest of the world went calmly about its business. Sociologists have documented the increasing desensitization and alienation of the modern, industrial, urban citizen, but it is probably the museum of fine arts and the anthology of poetry that provide the clearest diagnosis of twentieth century anomie. Readers of poetry are, by definition, attentive. For any reader appalled by widespread failure of attention, "Musée des Beaux Arts" is, like the plop of young Icarus into the green water, indelibly etched in the mind.

Steven G. Kellman

MY FATHER IN THE NIGHT COMMANDING NO

Author: Louis Simpson (1923-   )
Type of poem: Meditation
First published: 1963, in *At the End of the Open Road*

The Poem

"My Father in the Night Commanding No" is a meditation on the permanence of childhood experiences and impressions. One of the poet's earliest recollections is of evenings at home when his father would order him to stop whatever he was doing. The father, depicted as silently reading and smoking, is a forbidding figure. Even in the evening he has no time for amusement; he "Has work to do." The phrase "Smoke issues from his lips" suggests something more sinister than the smoking of a cigarette or pipe, something almost demoniacal.

The mother, on the other hand, provides the child with entertainment. She plays a record on the phonograph, perhaps an aria from an opera, which the boy finds jarring. She may also read to him—heroic tales that enable his imagination to stretch to encompass heroic deeds and strange sights. He may even be transported, through these tales, to the mythical island of Thule.

In adulthood the speaker has, in fact, traveled far and seen many things. He lists the cities to which he has gone: Paris, Venice, Rome. He has experienced, he says, "The journey and the danger of the world,/ All that there is/ To bear and to enjoy, endure and do." The language suggests that the journey has not been entirely safe or pleasant, but he has experienced what he had hoped, as a boy, to experience. He is now grown, with children of his own. They play in his presence, not fearing him as he had feared his father: "they were expecting me." Strangely, however, his father is still present in his mind, sitting and reading silently. His mother cries in his memory, presumably for something that happens in an opera or a tale; there is a sense that the past never changes. The speaker has moved beyond them, has avoided the rigidity which marked his father's behavior, but this does not alter their stance.

These figures are fixed and are rigid like puppets. The fact that he cannot change their relationship to him frustrates the speaker. He tries, still, to understand them, to see the reasons his father always seemed to be working, and the cause of his mother's tears, but they are gone and there are no answers. The conclusion of the poem suggests that children, whether his remembered self or his own children, do not realize what role memory will play in their lives.

Forms and Devices

"My Father in the Night Commanding No" consists of eleven four-line stanzas. In each stanza, the first, second, and fourth lines are written in iambic pentameter, and the third line, containing four or five syllables, is in irregular meter. The first and fourth lines rhyme, although the rhyme is not always emphatic or exact. Thus, in the third stanza, "hill" is rhymed with "still," but in the eighth the rhyme words are "move" and "love," in the ninth "sit" and "puppet."

The early part of the poem relies on imagery more than figurative devices for its effects. Some of the images are homely, as when the mother winds the old-fashioned record player (the "gramophone"). Others romantically evoke the stories that aroused the boy's imagination: "a prince, a castle and a dragon." In memory he stands "before the gateposts of the King . . . of Thule, at midnight when the mice are still."

The second part of the poem, dealing with his adult life, finds the speaker moving to more general images and more use of figures of speech: "Landscapes, seascapes" suggest the places he has been but also paintings that depict places he has seen only in works of art. The cities he visited "held out their arms." His imagination lured him on: "A feathered god, seductive, went ahead." When he returns to the memory of his parents, he sees them metaphorically as figures in a puppet show. He speaks of "the stage of terror and of love" on which actors sit, but these actors have wooden heads, and their positions never vary.

The tone of the poem is ironic. The speaker, until the end of the poem, directs the irony at himself rather than at his parents. He is almost sarcastic about what he has done in life and the places he has seen. The flat tone in which he describes the events of his adult life is in sharp contrast to the romantic language about the castle and the prince: "All that there is/ To bear and to enjoy, endure and do." The stronger irony comes when he sees himself in relation to his parents as if they were all mere puppets with no volition of their own. What they felt and why they did what they did is no longer important. Their roles have been fixed by the action of memory. The irony changes in the final stanza; it is made more general, so as to include all memories of childhood and the fact that people do not recognize what is happening while it is going on.

Themes and Meanings

"My Father in the Night Commanding No" is a meditation on the strange role of memory in human life. In Louis Simpson's view, memory establishes permanent images that a person, later in life, does not necessarily understand and cannot change. As an adult, the speaker in the poem wonders about his parents: Why did his father's work make him seem harsh and distant; what was there in the music (which the boy found grating) that made his mother cry? Did the mother have more personal reasons for crying? Why has his adult experience not made him capable of knowing what they felt? The answer to some of these questions may be carried by the wind. The first mention of this conventional symbol of change comes in the pivotal paragraph in which memory brings back the images of the father reading and the mother crying. That stanza ends, "And the dark wind/ Is murmuring that nothing ever happens," a paradoxical notion, given the wind's usual symbolic role.

In the final stanza, the wind is referred to once more: " '*Listen!*' the wind/ Said to the children, and they fell asleep." The wind here seems to be saying that some things, specifically those things of childhood which are held in the memory, are not subject to change. People change, as the speaker's boyhood fantasies have become a kind of adult reality, even though what is recalled from youth remains; but this is adult knowledge. When the memories are being formed, one is unaware of the process that is taking place, ignorant that what one learns then will stay with one for the rest of one's life.

"My Father in the Night Commanding No" is a gentle poem. It contains no images of violence, and other than the early sense of the father as a menacing figure there is little of an overtly sinister nature. There is sorrow in the poem, however, as well as a sense of the mystery of human memory. A dark undercurrent suggests that in some ways people's characters and attitudes are fixed at an early age, without their knowledge. Finally, there is regret that while the speaker's memories will never change, he will never fully understand them.

John M. Muste

MY FATHER MOVED THROUGH DOOMS OF LOVE

Author: E. E. Cummings (1894-1962)
Type of poem: Elegy
First published: 1940, in *50 Poems*

The Poem

E. E. Cummings' "my father moved through dooms of love" is an elegy in seventeen four-line stanzas. The poem commemorates Cummings' own father, the Reverend Edward Cummings, a Unitarian minister and Harvard University professor.

The poem is written in the first person. Unlike much of Cummings' love poetry, in which the speaker addresses his beloved while the reader overhears, in this poem the speaker addresses the reader directly. Cummings offers the example of his father's life for the reader to consider and closes the poem with the moral of the story.

The first four stanzas make up the first section of the poem, which introduces the speaker's father as a man of tremendous capacity for love. His father, Cummings makes clear, understood the complexities and dangers of loving. The repeated pattern "my father moved through *this* of *that*" may be understood to mean "my father experienced *this* before he achieved *that*" or "my father opened himself to the risk of *this* in order finally to achieve *that*." The first stanza gives a picture of a man who realized the danger of being rejected ("dooms"), the risk of losing one's identity in a love relationship ("sames"), and the potential of a lover to become possessive or possessed ("haves"). He faced these dangers squarely and finally emerged as a whole man, capable of loving and being loved. He used this great power to enrich the lives of those close to him. Those wondering "where" found that the answer was "here"; those weeping over "why" were comforted to sleep. No one, "no smallest voice," called to him in vain.

The next section begins with a capital letter (one of only three in the poem), moves through stanzas 5 through 8, and concludes with a period. Here, Cummings celebrates his father's movement through "griefs" into "joy."

The third section, stanzas 9 through 12, again begins with a capital letter and ends with a period. This time, the father moves through "dooms of feel"; that is, he learns to accept and express the full range of human emotion. Stanza 13 speaks briefly of one more quality of Cummings' father: He knew his place in the universe. That is, he knew that the relationship between humans and the natural world was not one of "they" but of "we." The last four stanzas of the poem take a dramatic turn. After the affirmative tone of the description of his father, Cummings now shifts to a harsh description of the society in which his father lived. Now the language is not of joy and singing but of "mud" and "scheming," "fear" and "hate." Stanzas 14 through 16 list the many ways in which people can harm themselves and one another. The language here is simpler; evils exist right at the surface, while goodness may be harder to understand. The final stanza contains the moral: However great or small the evils of the world might be, the fact that one person—Cummings' father—was able to embrace his humanity fully shows that the power of love is greater than the evils of the world. The love that exists as an active force in the world, exerted by individuals, is "more than all."

Forms and Devices

Many of Cummings' most famous poems, including "in Just-" and "r-p-o-p-h-e-s-s-a-g-r," rely on the poet's play with typography and space on the page to convey his message. "My father moved through dooms of love" belongs to the body of Cummings' work that uses more conventional imagery and stanzaic form. Although each of the sections describing his father is self-contained, Cummings unifies them and underscores their common theme of humanity's connectedness to the natural world, by threading through them imagery of the passing of time and the cycle of birth, growth, death, and rebirth.

The imagery in the first section is of awakening and birth, and here Cummings deals with different levels of time. The life cycle is played out with each sunset and sunrise. The father operates at the renewal phase of the cycle in line 3: "singing each morning out of each night." The immediacy of the night-into-day cycle is important to the poem, because Cummings emphasizes the role of the individual within the universe. Stanza 4 reminds the reader that what is at stake is not only tiny roots but also mountains; Cummings is concerned not only with the passing of a day but also with the time it takes for a mountain to grow.

The most important example of the life cycle in this poem is the changing of the seasons. Stanza 3 describes his father's love as an "April touch" that, like spring, awakens "sleeping selves." Stanza 7 picks up the cycle of the year with a reference to midsummer, and the cycle continues in stanza 10 with the "septembering arms of year" and in stanza 11 with "octobering flame." In most poems, the movement from spring through summer into autumn would also be a movement from happiness into sorrow, but in these stanzas the tone is still affirming. The imagery of the changing seasons reinforces the father's role in the natural world, but Cummings is emphatic that the darker seasons are to be embraced, not feared or avoided. Thus, when the poem finally comes to an image of winter, in stanza 12, it is a positive image: "if every friend became his foe/ he'd laugh and build a world with snow." Stanza 13, the last stanza dedicated to the father, is the most explicit, and shows the cycle completed. The imagery here is of spring come again.

There is no imagery of light or darkness, no mention of time, in the description of the evils men can bring. Stanzas 14 through 16 present a list of horrors, but there is no sense here of a cycle—no sense of relief (or re-leaf). There is only "dumb death," with no regeneration to follow. The imagery of the life cycle belongs only to the father, for it is only he who has learned the paradox that in order to escape death one must first encounter and accept it.

Themes and Meanings

"My father moved through dooms of love" is a tribute to Cummings' dead father, but it lacks many of the elements one might expect in an elegy. There is no physical description of the deceased, no mention of mourning or refusal to mourn, and, in fact, no mention of the father's death beyond the use of the past tense. In a very real sense, the poem is not about the poet's father at all, but about a philosophy of love and of life. Cummings raises the poem to this level by avoiding any specific references to his father. There are no details or anecdotes in the poem that point to one particular man, no clues to the identities of those around him. Beginning with his genuine respect for his father, Cummings exaggerates his father's capacities to delineate his own ideals. The poem's father is not a man, but an idealized representation of what an individual could be, of how love can operate in the world.

For Cummings, the individual is of great importance. Love as Cummings believes in it is not an ethereal gift of the spirit world, but a force that exists in the natural world that people inhabit. There is no call to a higher power to solve the world's ills; only the individual, battling evil with the power of love, can redeem the world. Through the example of the life of one person—not a divine savior, but a man as human as the poet's own father—the poem demonstrates the effect that one individual can have on other people. Through his love, he can bring them peace, joy, and nobility. Those who wield this kind of love find it a powerful force, but it does not come easily. Embracing the world means embracing all of it, and there are risks. Love everyone, and some will not love you back. Speak the truth, and some will turn against you. Develop your capacity to feel, and you will feel sorrow as well as happiness. Not many people are willing to try this kind of love, but one individual can give another hope and the courage to try, and then there are two.

"My father moved through dooms of love" is not simply a poem about feeling better. Moving beyond the example of his father, Cummings presents a very specific list of what is wrong with the world. The individual who can confront his own fears and failings can also confront the world's—and must, if the world is to be redeemed. In the last two lines, the poem returns to its key words: "father" and "love." "Father" is the individual person, who has the power to change the world. "Love" is the name of that power.

Cynthia A. Bily

MY LAST AFTERNOON WITH
UNCLE DEVEREUX WINSLOW

Author: Robert Lowell (1917-1977)
Type of poem: Narrative
First published: 1959, in *Life Studies*

The Poem

"My Last Afternoon with Uncle Devereux Winslow" is a richly autobiographical poem of 152 lines, divided into four parts. The shortest part is an eleven-line description of the poet at only five-and-a-half, dressed in a sailor blouse; the longest parts (I and IV) are about fifty lines each and narrate an account of Robert Lowell's memory of a young uncle, who was shortly to die of Hodgkin's disease. Lowell's *Life Studies* volume (1959), to which this poem makes a significant contribution, contains many clearly rendered portraits of the poet and his extended, old-moneyed family. These poems mark a turning away from the well-wrought, high modernist poems of Lowell's youth to personal, unguarded, and even "confessional" poems, as they were called by early critics. The later poems came out of Lowell's battles with mental illness, his brief imprisonment as a conscientious objector, his difficulties in love and marriage, and his rich memories of the Bostonian Lowells and Winslows. In this poem, the portrait of three Winslow generations—grandparents, parents, and child—is wonderfully restrained, at times charming, and finally disturbing.

After the title there stands a caption: "1922: the stone porch of my Grandfather's summer house." Part I has several verse paragraphs devoted to this setting. The small child, Robert, is sitting on his grandfather Winslow's porch; nearby, a tenant farmer has placed a pile of earth and lime in preparation for mixing cement for a root-house. This is a working farm, but it is also a Winslow family retreat. The child came here often, and the adult narrator remembers almost every collected item on his grandfather's porch. There is an alley of poplars, a rose garden, a stand of pine beyond the house. Lowell remembers huge sunflowers, as big as pumpkins, and two maids bringing out iced tea and other cold drinks on this particular afternoon.

In part II, Lowell recalls that he was wearing new pearl-gray shorts from the finest children's store in Boston. The poem moves "up" in part III, as a camera might, to show the windows of the billiards room, behind which the child could see his "Great Aunt Sarah" practicing on a keyboard. Lowell's grandmother could barely tolerate Sarah's practicing; she would rather play cards. In the second paragraph of this section, Lowell shares some old family gossip: Aunt Sarah not only tried and failed to become a concert pianist, but she also broke off an important engagement—she "jilted an Astor."

The long last section (part IV) returns briefly to the vantage point of young Robert, now imagining himself taken up high above the farm; he can look down on the small ponds and see his uncle Devereux's duck blind and, beyond that, his hunting cabin, which is already boarded up—either because it is the end of summer or because of the uncle's illness. He describes many of the collected items inside the cabin, which suggest much about the uncle's coming of age before World War I. Lowell, in the long closing paragraph of this section and the poem itself, thinks of how terrified he was to be the child caught between the emotions he felt for both his beloved, overbearing grandfather and his handsome, doomed uncle, who suddenly comes to stand immediately behind the small boy. Devereux, ridiculously over-dressed, is reflected in the same mirror used to give the boy an image of himself. Suddenly the young Lowell seems to have a vision of his uncle's bright colors gone. The child has been sitting on the porch with his hands in black dirt and white lime, and the narrative ends abruptly in a portent of death: "Come winter,/ Uncle Devereux would blend to the one color."

Forms and Devices

The most common beat in spoken English is the iamb (a weak syllable followed by a strong syllable). The English language generally alternates its weak-strong stresses with great regularity. For this reason, modern poets such as Lowell can still be highly rhythmic even when they give up the conventions of regular meter. The term free verse, which is not to be mistaken for a total disregard for beats and counts, is fittingly applied to this poem. Free verse allows Lowell a conversational or intimate tone when he wishes and a freedom to make line breaks that group words more or less at will. In lines 24-33, for example, he gives each item on his grand-father's porch its individual line. Then, in drastically shortening his conclusion (lines 34-35), he is able to drive home forcefully four telling adjectives to describe grandfather Winslow. The well-chosen words form a little stack which the eye takes in at once:

> was manly, comfortable,
> overbearing, disproportioned.

Later, Lowell will use the same freedom to create surprises in rhyme and juxtapositioning. The effect is comic:

> tilted her archaic Athenian nose
> and jilted an Astor.

The "archaic" modifies Athenian, but lands on top of the Astors. Much playfulness can come into the decisions that free verse demands and allows. Another example from the poem illustrates the decision-making typical of Lowell's inventive line breaks:

> A fluff of the west wind puffing
> my blouse, kiting me over our seven chimneys,
> troubling the waters . . . .

Lowell could have kept "my blouse" up with the previous line, but he would have lost some of the comic positioning of the fluff/ puff opening and closing of that line. Now "blouse," by its closer proximity to its metaphor (kite), works quite independently of the previous line. Clearly the line about troubled waters, biblical in its nature, gathers strength by standing alone.

This loosely organized poem achieves a formal tightness by establishing early images that reappear in various ways. The child's early reflection in a mirror later gives way to Devereux's; the two images are inextricably tied to each other. The boy ("a stuffed toucan") is overlayed with Devereux (as a brushed "riding horse," "a blue jay," "a ginger snap man," a creamy layer "in the top of the bottle"). Reinforcing this notion of absurd, oppressive clothing are the moments in the poem which glimpse the Victorian poses and hair styles in Devereux's "almost life-size" posters.

The materials for the poem are mostly generated from the setting, and Lowell uses few allusions. The most important one is the allusion to the dissolution of Rome. Perhaps the fall of empires begins at home: "I was Agrippina/ in the Golden House of Nero. . . ." (The mother of Nero was put to death for her open opposition to her son's personal decisions regarding divorce and remarriage.)

The Lowell family's period pieces, their domestic quirks and habits—their card games, novels, hobbies, souvenirs, and mementos—provide the narrative material and the strong images for much of the poem. Lowell shows much more than he tells, but by so doing he tells much.

Themes and Meanings

This afternoon in 1922 was an important moment for the poet. With him, the reader looks back on such moments and realizes that much of one's personal histories can be compressed into such spots of time. The passing of time is certainly a major theme of the poem.

The stakes do not seem very high in the opening scenes. A petulant child prefers the solid "Norman" (as in architecture) stodginess of his grandfather to the longings of his martini-drinking parents, who wish to escape to yet another family mansion. For a time he delays in letting readers know that the family is coming apart; he takes them safely back to great-aunt Sarah's escapades, for example. No one can see what is coming. The reader is cushioned from it within the pastoral setting. By the time Lowell actually claims that he was terrified and "all-seeing" (as was Agrippina), however, some readers may realize how many hints he has given. Through the untimely death of his uncle, which is something of a portent, this larger family is seen to be standing at the end of the times they have known. The family force is spent; grandfather Winslow and his generation have run their course. An era has passed, and there is a strong suggestion that Lowell's parents, aunts, and uncles are not empowered to bring about the new era. Most telling are the young Devereux's Edwardian trappings. He may have rushed to join the European campaign by volunteering through Canada, but Devereux is a throwback—a romantic who came of age looking at imperial images dating back to the Boer Wars—men bravely dying for country on the African veldt. The horrors of World War I, which caused young men to question the Western world order in poems such as T. S. Eliot's *The Waste Land* (1922), never touched these blue-blooded Brahmans. They will die from lack of change; history will remember them as childish. The grandfather says, with dramatic irony, of his grown son and daughter-in-law, "You are behaving like children."

Much of the poem's meaning is implied in its gradual unfolding not as memoir but an elegy of sorts. Its tones of lament are realized through hindsight on the part of the reader. Details that seemed merely close observation on Lowell's part—the pencil marks on the door proving that Devereux stopped growing in 1911—are not innocent. Time stopped for these people in 1911. A rereading of the poem causes all the autobiographical details to jump out with a resonance that Lowell intends—those "bullrushes" (one now thinks of the baby Moses entering the house of Pharaoh); the "deathlike" silence of Boston's Symphony Hall, where Aunt Sarah used to practice; the hopelessly dated coils like "rooster tails" in the hair of the music-hall belles in the posters; the comic sentimentality in the pastel of Huckleberry Finn, the "fools'-gold nuggets" and reference to silver mines, which in the United States were long defunct by 1922. Winslow had called his silver mine the *Liberty Bell* in his chronic failure to imagine anything beyond his old-world Boston or his virgin pines "forever pioneering."

Beverly Coyle

MY LAST DUCHESS

Author: Robert Browning (1812-1889)
Type of poem: Dramatic monologue
First published: 1842, in *Dramatic Lyrics*

The Poem

Underneath the title "My Last Duchess" is the name Ferrara, and the poem's sole speaker is the Duke of Ferrara, a character based in part on Alfonso II, Duke of Ferrara (in Italy) in the sixteenth century. Alfonso's wife, a young girl, died in 1561, and Alfonso used an agent to negotiate a second marriage to the niece of the Count of Tyrol.

In Robert Browning's poem, the Duke of Ferrara speaks to an agent representing the count. The duke begins by referring to "my last Duchess," his first wife, as he draws open a curtain to display a portrait of her which is hanging on the wall. She looks "alive," and the duke attributes this to the skill of the painter, Frà Pandolf. After saying that he alone opens the curtain, the duke promptly begins a catalog of complaints about the way his wife had acted.

The joyous blush on her cheek that can be seen in the portrait was a result, the duke says, of her reaction to Frà Pandolf's compliments about her beauty. The duke blames his late wife for smiling back at Frà Pandolf, for being courteous to everyone she encountered, for enjoying life too much. She failed to appreciate his name, which can be traced back nine hundred years, and she failed to see him as superior to others. The duke would not condescend to correct her attitude. She should have known better, he says, and "I choose/ Never to stoop."

The final characterization the duke gives of his former duchess reveals his obsessive possessiveness and jealousy. He acknowledges that she smiled when she saw him, but complains that she gave much the same smile to anyone else she saw. His next statement reveals that he caused her to be killed: "I gave commands;/ Then all smiles stopped together." He does not elaborate further. There is her portrait, he says, looking as if alive. The duke tells the agent that they will next go downstairs to meet others. Then, in less than five lines, the duke refers directly to the proposed marriage arrangement. In the same suave tones he has used throughout, he suggests that because the count is so wealthy there should be no question about his providing an "ample" dowry for his daughter to bring to the marriage. The duke adds, however, that it is "his fair daughter's self" that he wants.

As the duke and the count's agent start down the stairs, the duke points out a bronze statue of Neptune taming a seahorse and notes that it was made especially for him by Claus of Innsbruck. Although this appears to be a change in subject, it summarizes the duke's clear message to the agent. In addition to the wealth she must bring, the second wife, like the seahorse, must be "tamed" to her role as his duchess. The clear implication is that if she does not meet his requirements, she may well end up like the last duchess, "alive" only in a portrait.

Forms and Devices

The poem is a dramatic monologue, a form that Browning used and perfected in many of his works. In a monologue, one person is the sole speaker, and often there is a specific listener or listeners; here, the listener is the count's agent, through whom the Duke of Ferrara is arranging the proposed marriage to a second duchess. The reader must work through the words of the speaker to discover his true character and the attitude of the poet toward the character. The poem is "dramatic" in the sense that it is like a drama, a play, in which one character speaks to another, and there is a sense of action and movement as on stage.

The duke claims that he does not have skill in speech, but his monologue is a masterpiece of subtle rhetoric. While supposedly entertaining the count's agent as his guest by showing him the portrait, the duke by implication explains his requirements for his new wife. His last duchess, according to his version of her, had a heart "too soon made glad" by such things as watching a sunset or riding her white mule around the terrace, and she should not have responded with pleasure to anything or anyone but the duke himself. Browning allows the reader to infer what kind of man the duke is by piecing together the past and present situation. A basic device used throughout the poem is irony. Instead of seeing an unfaithful wife as the duke pictures her, the reader sees the jealous and egotistical mind of the duke himself. The duke seems to assume that the agent will follow the logic of why he commanded that his duchess be eliminated, and he lets the agent know how easily it is within the duke's power to issue such commands.

The poem is written in rhymed iambic pentameter lines. A striking aspect of form in the poem is the repeated use of enjambment, in which a line's sense and meaning runs on into the following line, so that the rhymed couplets are "open" rather than closed. This technique, in which the syntactical pauses rarely coincide with line endings, creates a tension in the rhythm and places emphasis on the horrors the duke reveals as the sentences end in mid-line (caesura). The lines thus often appear irregular, an informalizing of a formal pattern, as though the duke is relaxing his proud formality and speaking casually.

The lines are extremely concentrated. Not a single word is wasted. Throughout the poem there is a chilling meiosis, the words imparting much more than they express. The apparent pauses, shown by dashes, purportedly indicate a hesitation as the duke considers what to say, but actually they suggest his consummate arrogance and manipulative control of the situation. Twice the agent starts to question or interrupt, but the duke smoothly deflects the interruptions and continues speaking. He is in total control of the situation, however casual he may pretend to be.

When the duke finally refers to the marriage arrangement directly, he summarizes the situation succinctly. He first mentions the money he will expect, then mentions the count's daughter. At first this seems merely to confirm the duke's emphasis on money. Yet since he had clearly stated his solution for ending his first marriage, the words "his fair daughter's self . . . is my object" become particularly sinister. Unless he can possess his next duchess as he possesses the portrait and the bronze statue, she too may become only an artifact on the wall, as nameless as the first duchess.

The pace of the poem builds toward the revelation that the duke ordered his wife killed, then to the quick summation of his terms for the marriage arrangement. The matter-of-fact tone that he uses throughout the poem shows that the duke considers himself totally justified, and he remains unrepentant and secure in his sense of power over others.

Themes and Meanings

"My Last Duchess" shows the corrupt power of a domestic tyrant. Browning uses this theme again in his longest poem, *The Ring and the Book* (1868-1869), in which the sadistic Count Guido kills his wife after falsely accusing her of adultery.

Spoken monologues often reveal more to the listener (and reader) than the speaker intends, but this arrogant aristocrat has no hesitation. The Duke of Ferrara obviously considers himself superior to others and above laws and morality. He clearly states that he gave the commands that stopped his wife's smiles altogether. After all, he tells the agent, "she liked whate'er/ She looked on, and her looks went everywhere." The duke was irritated by such behavior and had it eliminated. He uses his power to get others to do his will, including, presumably, the agent. As he had others eliminate his wife, and as he had a painter and a sculptor create objects of art to his specifications, he assumes that the agent will provide the kind of duchess he wants. He seems unconcerned about any hesitations a potential second wife might have about how his first marriage ended. He appears confident his demands will be met, both the ample dowry and the subservient wife.

The jealousy and possessiveness that seem to accompany the duke's assertion of power suggest that he will be equally suspicious of any living wife, and indeed the portrait of his last duchess is more satisfactory to him than was the duchess herself. He can open or close the curtain as he pleases; he can exert complete control.

Browning's genius created a character whose own words condemn him and show him as a ruthless, corrupt man who misuses his power. What makes the Duke of Ferrara especially horrifying is that he feels no repentance and no need for repentance. There have been no checks on his abuses of power thus far, and there is nothing to suggest that he will not continue his egotistical and tyrannical ways.

Lois A. Marchino

MY LIFE HAD STOOD—A LOADED GUN—

Author: Emily Dickinson (1830-1886)
Type of poem: Lyric
First published: 1929, in *Further Poems of Emily Dickinson*

The Poem

"My Life had stood—a Loaded Gun—" (the title is not Emily Dickinson's, since she did not title her poems) is a short poem of twenty-four lines divided into six stanzas. The poem is written in the first person from the point of view of a speaker who compares her life to "a Loaded Gun." In fact, the voice of the speaker and the voice of the gun are identical throughout the poem.

In the opening stanza of the poem, the speaker tells how her life—of which she speaks as if it were "a Loaded Gun"—had been full of potential power yet unused and inactive ("a Loaded Gun—/ In Corners") until its "Owner" came by, "identified" it, and carried it away. The speaker (as gun) then contrasts, beginning in the second stanza, what her life is like now that she has been claimed and put into use by her "Owner." Together, the speaker (gun) and her owner are free to wander anywhere they like ("We roam in Sovreign Woods") and have the power and authority to pursue even the prized game of royal reserves ("And now We hunt the Doe").

Halfway through the second stanza, however, the speaker begins to turn away from the power of the royal "We" and to focus instead on her own sense of emerging individual power: "And every time I speak for Him—/ The Mountains straight reply." In these lines, the speaker usurps the owner's right to speak for himself. Moreover, whereas in the past the speaker's life has stood "In corners," unnoticed, like a wallflower, the speaker gleefully reports that now as soon as she speaks, nature immediately takes notice of her ("The Mountains straight reply"). In other words, the gun is fired and the mountains immediately echo the sound.

The third through the fifth stanzas continue to develop—in the voice of the gun—the speaker's growing realization and enjoyment of her own power. The third stanza compares the burst of light when the gun is fired to a "smile" from a volcano ("a Vesuvian face") as it releases its pleasure, and the fourth stanza celebrates the "good Day" that is "shared" by gun and owner. By the fifth stanza, the speaker revels in her power as a "deadly foe," and the speaker's sense of her own volition and power reaches a climax. Her actions are now characterized as completely autonomous, and the poem focuses in detail on delineating the specifics of her power: No one survives "On whom I lay a Yellow Eye—/ Or an emphatic Thumb."

A sharp break occurs, however, between the fifth and the final stanza. As if the speaker—at the height of her power—suddenly realizes that the "Owner" who brought her to life can disappear just as abruptly as he appeared, her ecstatic revel in power halts, and the speaker's voice falters in a frantic attempt to devise some rationale that might enable her to retain her power. For "He longer must [live] than I," she muses, because "I have but the power to kill" but not "the power to die."

Forms and Devices

The most important poetic device in the poem is the metaphor, a figure of speech used to denote an idea (or an object) by suggesting an analogy or likeness between them. The metaphor of the speaker's life as a gun, in fact, occurs in three stages, structuring the poem in terms of the speaker's past, present, and future life. The speaker first reveals that in the past her life was like a passive, "Loaded Gun." She then—for the greater part of the poem (the central four stanzas)—moves into a narration of her life in the present by comparing her life to a gun that is actively engaged in firing. By the final stanza, the speaker contemplates the future of her life as if it were an empty gun, devoid of its bullet, its "emphatic Thumb."

The metaphoric qualities of the poem become increasingly complex as the speaker develops additional metaphors to characterize the primary metaphor, the gun. The gun's fire is spoken of as if it were a "smile," a volcanic ("Vesuvian") eruption, and a "Yellow Eye," and the gun's bullet becomes an "emphatic Thumb." This layering of metaphor upon metaphor functions to underscore—within the language and experience of the poem itself—those qualities of repression and masking that are central to the poem's theme regarding the expression of will and power.

This sense of repression and disguise with respect to power is further enhanced in the poem by the speaker's tone or attitude toward the subject being described. The speaker's simple, matter-of-fact narrative style together with her "cordial" choice of words—"roam," "speak," "smile," "light," "glow," "pleasure," "shared"—to depict the act of erupting, exploding, or killing build into the reader's experience of the poem the work's underlying explosive tensions. The reader is lulled, too, by the perfectly regular, hypnotic metrical rhythm of the language until at the final stanza the reader is jarred by the speaker's desperate rationalization of her existence. This focus in the poem on creating an experience in which the reader participates is one of the qualities that defines modern poetry and is a technique that Dickinson characteristically employed in her poems.

Dickinson's effective manipulation of language to construct the poem can be seen in her exploitation of certain grammatical structures. The repetition in the first two lines of the second stanza—"And now," "And now"—conveys the eager, excited, and expectant voice of a newly empowered being. Similarly, the juxtaposition at the end of the poem of repeated grammatical structures containing different words effectively embodies and reveals both the speaker's sense of fragmentation and her desperate attempt to resolve her conflict. The juxtaposed clauses "He—may longer" and "He longer must" followed by the phrases "the power to kill" versus "the power to die" simultaneously contain and convey the speaker's effort to scramble and rearrange the elements of language itself in order to maintain her will and her power.

Themes and Meanings

In this poem, Dickinson begins with a familiar American scene—a gun, a hunter, and a hunting trip in the woods—and transforms it into a poem about a divided self—a self filled with the potential for pleasure and power but without the means to express pleasure and power for herself. The central concerns of the poem are the separation within the speaker of her "Life" from the means to express it autonomously and the consequences for her in the expression of power and pleasure.

The structure of the poem underscores these concerns. The poem's most obvious structure—moving from past to present to future—makes possible the thematic progression of the poem from impotence to power to impotence or, in other terms, from repression to eruption to fear of repression. As the poem develops, the unleashing of the speaker's pleasure and power builds to a climax as the speaker's awareness of her ability to act and enjoy increases. The speaker's interaction with her own autonomous power, in fact, leads her to either the realization or the illusion (the poem never makes clear which one it is) that she can be the author of her own pleasure and power.

At the final stanza, the speaker (as gun) is pulled from her reverie of power by her sudden recollection of her dependence on her "Owner." It is he, after all, who must pull the trigger. Her realization corresponds metaphorically to her emptiness after her powerful bullet has been fired. In response to this threat of static emptiness (reminiscent of her condition at the beginning of the poem), the speaker now makes desperate attempts to puzzle out some rationale that might enable her to perpetuate her ecstasy of autonomous power. The speaker's train of thought proceeds in this way: Although the gun may "live"—in the sense of existing only as an unused object leaning in corners—longer than the "Owner" will, the owner must "live"—in the sense of having the human will and power to lead an autonomous life—longer than the gun will because the gun has only the kind of power that consists of being the means to effect something (death) but not the kind to do something on its own, of its own accord (to die).

At this point, one of the most significant questions posed by the poem becomes clear: For whom in the nineteenth century would pleasure and power be problematic should they be expressed? If one asserts that the speaker of the poem is female, another dimension is added to the poem. The poem then depicts not merely the plight of a speaker who is dependent on the actions of another for the release of its power but the plight of a female speaker who must—because will and power have traditionally been characterized as masculine qualities—identify extensive portions of her female self as masculine. Thus, to acknowledge and act on those aspects of her self, she must split herself irrevocably. The speaker's own will, pleasure, and power come to be perceived in the poem, therefore, as dangerous forces that give pleasure but that also threaten to destroy the identity and integrity of the female self: In metaphoric terms, for the speaker to express her power is for her to "hunt the Doe." In this way, Dickinson's poem questions society's notions both of power and of the appropriate means for its expression, specifically the way in which ideas concerning power are constructed with respect to males and females.

Angela M. Estes

MY MOTHER WOULD BE A FALCONRESS

Author: Robert Duncan (1919-1988)
Type of poem: Lyric
First published: 1968, in *Bending the Bow*

The Poem

"My Mother Would Be a Falconress" is a seventy-one-line lyric divided into fourteen verse paragraphs of varying lengths. The poem looks and sounds traditional by Robert Duncan's mid-career (1956-1968) standards. The medium length of the work developed out of its underlying compositional law; the text has been generated concentrically from a core statement that stresses again and again the indestructible relation between the speaker—the poet's alter ego—and his mother's will. There is an unwavering acknowledgment on the speaker's part of his mother's unquestionable authority. Her will to power is expressed by the verbal component of the nominal predicate "*would be* a falconress," which, given the present-tense context of the whole poem, expresses her desire, determination, and single-mindedness of purpose. The complying speaker responds with total submission: "And I . . ./ would fly." An experiment in pedagogy or coaching is taking place. Apparently, it is working smoothly and to the satisfaction of both trainer and trainee.

Imperceptibly, however, two correlative developments gather momentum. With every paragraph, the falconress lets her falcon fly a little farther beyond the circumference or horizon of the previous venture. In this way, she expands the territory of her hunting and at the same time strengthens her falcon's range. A symbiosis of sorts more and more characterizes their relationship, but in spite of that there grows in him a desire to be on his own. Eventually, their antagonism becomes fierce and the falcon behaves ruthlessly toward his mistress. He never achieves complete autonomy, however, and years after her death the pull of her will still tyrannically restrains and directs him.

The progress through these stages is minutely charted by the poet. The relatively few constitutive elements of the story are permanently reshuffled, reiterated, and only gradually and incrementally modified. With each additional verse paragraph, the reader edges forward toward some dimly guessed resolution. This movement could be described as a slow meandering. Certain statements or phrases are obsessively repeated as in a ballad. The speaker seems to be hypnotized by his own tale. Past, present, and future seem at times indistinguishably blended, and the verbal "would be" becomes a marker of habitual or recurrent action. As in any traditional text, the reader experiences a mixture of linear progression and concentric recurrence with a dramatic sense of impending resolution and closure.

Forms and Devices

In a prose piece entitled "A Lammas Tiding," Duncan gives the following account of the circumstances attending the composition of this poem: "I wakened in the night with the lines '*My mother would be a falconress—And I a falcon at her wrist*' being repeated in my mind. Was the word *falconress* or *falconness*?—the troubled insistence of the lines would not let go of me, and I got up and took my notebook into the kitchen to write it out at the kitchen table. Turning to the calendar to write the date, I saw it was Lammas: 2 AM, August 1, 1964" (*Bending the Bow*, page 51; Lammas commemorates Saint Peter's deliverance from prison).

This extraordinary confession—which is similar to Samuel Taylor Coleridge's famous account of the production of his "Kubla Khan"—goes on to inform the reader about other genetic details. Thus astrologically, Saturn, Duncan's birth planet, was most brilliant between one-thirty and two, the very half-hour during which the poem was put on paper. Then, Duncan muses, William Blake's *Visions of the Daughters of Albion* (1793), which he had been reading for several nights before going to sleep, most likely provided him with the key image of "the ravenous hawk," which in turn triggered a comment from Duncan's life companion, the painter Jess Collins. On and on, the train of associations or dream logic of the poem is disentangled thread by thread.

"Dreams ever betray our minds," Duncan remarks on the same page, thereby suggesting that the remembered dream is a conscious fragment of the unconscious. Hence as Freud indicated, it is possible to learn much about oneself and one's mind from the verbal accounts of one's own dreams.

This poem was communicated or "received." The poet transcribed it in a state of trancelike wakefulness. There remained very little room for revision or rewriting. The text emerged like Athena from the head of Zeus, helmeted and with breastplate buckled on; or, more accurately perhaps, the poem's body took its shape from the tenebrae of the poet's reservoir of intuitions, archetypes, and recondite knowledge. Duncan was a visionary poet, a great integrator of religious myths and hermetic insights.

The poem was in a way a tribute to his foster mother, Minnehaha Symmes, who had adopted him when he was barely six months old. The affective link between them was so powerful that after Minnie's death Robert continued to write letters and poems to her. It was in his adopted family that the future poet came into contact with esoteric, occult, and theosophical lore, thereby gaining access to the tradition of romantic mystics and mythmakers such as William Blake, Percy Bysshe Shelley, Gérard de Nerval, and William Butler Yeats. As a matter of fact, in spite of his strong ties with experimental postmodern groups such as the Bay Area poets (Jack Spicer, Kenneth Rexroth, Philip Whalen, Michael McClure) and the Black Mountain poets (Charles Olson, Robert Creeley, Denise Levertov), Duncan came to regard his modernity more and more as an offshoot of the nineteenth century mind and sensibility.

"My Mother Would Be a Falconress" is a poem that fits the transcendentalism of this tradition in both rhetoric and sound.

The blood imagery, central to any initiatory myth or rite of passage, lends a lurid coherence to the poem, reinforcing its sense of medieval hierarchy and allegiance with its correlative patterns of obsessively repeated dominance and submission. On a more local scale, the "·" sign—larger than an ordinary full stop and placed at some distance from the end of a statement (after the eleventh and the thirteenth sections)—designates, in the poet's own words, "a beat syncopating the time at rest; as if there were a stress. He the artist strives not for a disintegration of syntax but for a complication within syntax, overlapping structures, so that the words are freed, having bounds out of bound" (*Bending the Bow*).

The formal structure of the poem is determined by a moment of inspiration and grace. Both the relationship between the protagonists and the rhythmical phrasing have been communicated to the poem at once. The primary musical feeling about the fittingness of the verbal utterance is, in Duncan's own words, "the criterion of truth in a poem."

The poem's circular restatements and its dialectical progress are compatible, and between them they create the singular complex beauty of the poetic field.

Themes and Meanings

"I am strongly, strongly persuaded that the entire area of poetry is consciousness," Duncan has said. Such a statement offers a reliable vantage point from which to consider Duncan's project as a whole. For beyond rhetoric and incantation, beyond manic insistence, there is a pointed effort to understand the complex give and take of the situation, and there is a genuine striving to grasp, analyze, and discriminate among degrees of involvement, to define the inner tensions and their outcome. There results a clearer picture of the transformations undergone by the original input, or given data, of the remembered dream. What is all this about if not an enhanced state of consciousness?

Now, viewed from a restricted angle, the theme of the poem is the precarious balance between the mutual attraction of dominance and dependency on the one hand, and, in a less conspicuous manner, between the gradual disenchantment and eventual separation on the other. In the words of Duncan's biographer, "Already at the time Robert realized that his mother was to embody the other, restrictive and destructive pole of womanhood in his life and work. . . . According to one account, the difficulties began with Robert's emerging homosexuality" (Ekbert Faas, *Young Robert Duncan*, 1983).

This speculation supports a sexual reading of the poem that undoubtedly has been on Duncan's mind. The symbolism generated by such elements of the text as the treading of the mother's wrist, the bleeding involved, the dreaming within the little hood with many bells, the falling, or such elaborations of these elements as the hooded silence, the muffled dreams, the jangling bells, the tearing with his beak, the curb of his heart, or the still more refined degrees of complication in formulations such as "as if I were her own pride, as if her pride knew no limits" or "it seemed my human soul went down in flames," and, finally, that climactic talking with himself—in addition to its clusters of associations, the symbolism shows also a progression from the merely descriptive to more oblique formulations and thence to the final solipsism of the speaker-narrator. Underlying all this as a common denominator is the ubiquitous blood imagery, a major presence throughout Duncan's poetry, both emblem and binder of his constitutive mysticism.

As the "hood" or sheath image might arguably evoke details of both female and male sexual anatomy, so could it suggest—because of the bells attached to it—the kind of protection, seclusion, and even blindness of the artist who needs remoteness and purity so that his or her imagination can freely spin out its alternative vision of reality. Duncan seemed to have such a possibility in view when, at the very end of his explicatory prose piece "A Lammas Tiding," he pointed out that "there is another curious displacement upward, for the bell which is actually attached to a falcon's leg by a bewit just above the jess, in the dream becomes a set of bells sewn round the hood, a ringing of sound in the childhood of the poet's head."

The punning on "hood" and "childhood" should be read against the eye-injury accident that occurred in Duncan's early childhood, which put his vision out of focus. That kind of protective ringing in his childhood ears would become a compensatory habit of sound or an inner sense of cadence. A poet's discanting is based on that, and Duncan was a poet who relied on the musical possibilities of words.

Another startling disclosure of this quotation is that the whole fabric of the poem, with all its details (one of which at least flies in the face of practical reality; that is, in the sport of falconry the bird is used as killer, never as a retriever), has been a dream. The poem's power and unique attraction are comparable to those of such imagistically related masterpieces as Hopkins' "The Windhover" and Yeats's "The Second Coming."

Duncan's dangerous relationship to his muse, his arduous experimenting to expand the circumference of his domain (an Emersonian and Dickinsonian concern), and his battling against society's distortions, pressures, or demands may equally challenge one's appetite for allegorical readings.

Stefan Stoenescu

MY PAPA'S WALTZ

Author: Theodore Roethke (1908-1963)
Type of poem: Lyric
First published: 1942; collected in *The Lost Son and Other Poems*, 1948

The Poem

In "My Papa's Waltz," Theodore Roethke imaginatively re-creates a childhood encounter with his father but also begins to attempt to understand the meaning of the relationship between them. The poem may be read as a warm memory of happy play, but when one is familiar with the rest of Roethke's work, a darker view of the event emerges. Although the poem is only sixteen short lines, it is one of Roethke's most moving and most frequently anthologized poems.

Theodore Roethke was born and grew up in Saginaw, Michigan, where his father and uncle operated a large and successful greenhouse. Sometimes Roethke's father would stay up late into the night watering and otherwise tending to his plants. After a drink to relax, he would swing his son Theodore around the kitchen in a bearlike dance and then carry him off to bed. Roethke stated in an interview that his father would hook his son's feet through the father's rubber bootstraps and, with Theodore's feet thus trapped, haul the youngster about.

Roethke's poetic description of this scene conveys both the father's love for the son and the son's fear of this overpowering event, a combination which explains why the poem has haunted so many readers. At first the child finds merely the smell of the alcohol on his father's breath overwhelming, but he endures the experience and hangs on to his father's shirt: "Such waltzing was not easy." The "waltz" is so violent that pots and pans begin to fall to the floor, and the audience of this intended hilarity is not amused: "My mother's countenance/ Could not unfrown itself."

This activity comes as a release after the father's hard work in the greenhouse: "The hand that held my wrist/ Was battered on one knuckle;" and "You beat time on my head/ With a palm caked hard by dirt." What is fun for the adult is an ordeal for the child. When his father misses a step in his wild dance, the child's ear scrapes against his father's belt buckle. This detail also indicates that the child is quite small, since, while standing on his father's boots, his head reaches barely past his father's waist; this account must be a recollection of very early childhood.

The entire experience acts as a sort of dramatic lullaby, as it is the last event of the day before bedtime. The child, however, is hardly relaxed and ready for sleep, since to survive the "waltz," he has had to "cling" to his father's shirt; he continues to do so as he is carried away to bed.

Forms and Devices

Roethke uses a number of poetic devices that reinforce the meaning of the poem; the meter, although it is iambic, sometimes adds an extra feminine syllable at the end of the second or fourth lines, such as "Could make a small boy dizzy" and

"Such waltzing was not easy." The additional foot produces a stumbling effect that adds to the poem's description of a clumsy waltz.

The poem's short lines also reinforce the fact that this experience is happening to a child. In his later poetry, Roethke uses nursery rhymes, jingles, and playground taunts to suggest the world of children to which he was trying to return in imagination and spirit. In "My Papa's Waltz," however, there is nothing to imagine, since the incident really happened—apparently more than once. Roethke wants the reader to identify with the child, not the adults in the poem, so he not only writes the poem from the viewpoint of a child but also uses the short lines common in poetry written for children (Roethke himself wrote two such volumes) and in the verses that children themselves write. "Papa" is a child's term for a father; nevertheless, the reader is not allowed to forget that this poem is an adult remembrance of an event from childhood. "Countenance," for example, is not a word that a child would be likely to use to describe someone's face.

The diction of the poem also underscores the child's sense of fright at the experience. Although at first reading the poem may seem funny, with utensils falling in slapstick fashion as the father and child bang around the kitchen, it is clearly not amusing to the child who has to hold on tightly to his father to avoid falling like the pots and pans. Dazed by the whiskey on his father's breath, he must hang on "like death." At the end of the dance, he is still "clinging" to his father's shirt, not embracing his father's body with warmth. From the child's perspective, the "waltz" has been something to endure, not to enjoy.

Themes and Meanings

In "My Papa's Waltz," Roethke unites two of his more important themes—his attempt to understand his relationship with his father and his use of the dance as a metaphor for life itself.

Roethke's father, Otto, was a person who enjoyed the outdoors and the pursuits usually associated with masculinity: sports, hunting, and fishing. Like most fathers, he wanted his son to be like him, but it was clear very early in Theodore's life that he could not and would not follow in his father's footsteps. For example, Theodore subscribed to a poetry journal when he was in the seventh grade. In a pattern common in many families, Otto Roethke loved his son but could not approve of his path in life; Theodore loved his father but was unable to demonstrate that love in ways that his father could understand. Worse, Otto died while Theodore was still a teenager, so the father never learned what a leading role in his chosen field the son would play—nor did Theodore have a chance during his father's lifetime to resolve the differences between them.

Much of Roethke's mature work embodies his attempt to sort through this relationship and, ultimately, end it, so that the poet could be free to become not merely the son of his father but himself. "The Lost Son," which many critics regard as Roethke's breakthrough work (in which he first asserts himself most forcefully in his own poetic manner), concerns his attempts to come to grips with the death of his father. Although the father has died, it is the son, unsure of his identity, who is lost. Ironically, in trying to become free of the memory of his judging father, Roethke discovers how much like the older man he is.

The point of connection between the two is the greenhouse and the world of plants that Roethke's father nurtured. Here the tender side of Otto's nature asserted itself, for it takes patience and loving care to raise plants; they will not grow at the point of a gun or as a result of threats. "My Papa's Waltz" significantly occurs after a long day's work at the greenhouse, where the father has developed a "hand . . . battered on one knuckle" and "a palm caked hard by dirt."

The father has fulfilled himself in his work and wants to show his love for his son, but only after taking a drink (or three) to unwind. Like many men, he finds it difficult to express love, even in a physical way, without first becoming someone else through the aid of drink. Men must still be men, so the manner of expression of that love is a roughhouse "romp," not a hug or a kiss. Theodore, who later failed during the hunting and fishing trips in which his father made him participate, does not make a very good dancing partner, either. He is not a willing dancer, but is dragged along; a child, he has no choice but to acquiesce.

The poem also suggests that the "waltz" may be the father's unconscious way of punishing his son, of demonstrating that, even in the feminine and romantic world of the dance, a man must be tough. Is it really necessary to beat time on the boy's head? Does he understand that he may be hurting his child with the scraping buckle? Whatever his intentions, the waltz becomes a seal on the day's activities, a last bit of interaction before the boy is put to bed.

In Roethke's later poetry, he develops the metaphor of the dance as a symbol for life lived to the fullest. To Roethke, a beautiful dance most of all symbolizes love, fulfillment, and union with the rest of life, as in "I Knew a Woman," "The Waking," and "Four for Sir John Davies." The first appearance of a dance in Roethke's poetry is "My Papa's Waltz," and, significantly, because the dance is between the poet and his father, the dance itself is unlovely and, to the child, frightening, and its meaning is ultimately ambiguous. The ambiguity extends to the rest of the poem. Does the child's mother frown because of the father's tipsiness, the destruction wreaked by the dance, the violence of the dance itself, or the fact that it is imposed upon the child? The welter of meanings and associations means that each reader must judge the poem for himself or herself, perhaps drawing on memories of adult expressions of love that were too strong for a child. This confusion also keeps the poem fresh and contributes to its continued life.

Jim Baird

MY SWEETEST LESBIA

Author: Thomas Campion (1567-1620)
Type of poem: Lyric
First published: 1601, in *A Booke of Ayres*

The Poem

"My Sweetest Lesbia" is a song composed of three stanzas, each six lines long, rhymed *aabbcc*. It is the first of Thomas Campion's twenty-one songs in a collection shared equally with lutenist Philip Rosseter. Other songbooks of Campion's era (those by John Dowland, for example) present arrangements for four-part singing, but Campion and Rosseter require a solo voice and a simple accompaniment in their works: a "naked ayre without guide, or prop, or color but his own." As the first song in a group that primarily examines kinds of love (unrequited, bawdy) and contrasts high and low society, strict and loose morals, and age and youth, "My Sweetest Lesbia" stands as an overview, an entryway, an opening statement.

The first stanza is a translation and condensation of the Roman poet Catullus' poem 5 (*Vivamus, me Lesbia, atque amemus*). Addressing Lesbia, which is the *nom à clef* of Catullus' "beloved," Campion's singer makes a proposition that they "live and love," even though wiser people may censure them. (The name, incidentally, does not have any particular lesbian sexual implications.) The reason the singer offers is metaphorical: Sun and moon may set and quickly revive, but as soon as the much weaker light of love sets, he and his lover will sleep "one ever-during night."

Stanza 2 diverges from the Catullus poem. The subject is warfare, and the point of view shifts from the embracing "we" of the first stanza to a distancing "they." If all would live in love, like the singer, war would end and no alarms would disturb peaceful sleep—unless they came from the camp of love. Fools waste their "little light," however, and actively pursue, through pain, their "ever-during night." Love is not merely a consolation for individual lovers; it could be a universal peacemaker, a means of disarmament ("bloody swords and armor should not be"), and a sleep enhancer ("No drum nor trumpet"). Campion seems more disturbed by excess noise than by weaponry, but the languorous "peaceful sleeps" and the "camps of love" are more a matter of aphrodisiacs than of soporifics.

The last stanza switches to "I," then to "you," underscoring the separation to come through death. When I die, the singer declares, I do not want my friends mourning for me, but lovers gracing my "happy" tomb with sweet pastimes. The singer ends by designating Lesbia as his amatory executor: *You* close up my eyes and "crown" with your love my "ever-during night."

Forms and Devices

The poem is written in rhymed couplets of iambic pentameter, the heroic couplets familiar in English from Campion's predecessor Geoffrey Chaucer to his successor Alexander Pope. In the work of these others, however, the form is used for narrative, expository, or satirical purposes. It is not the usual form for a song, although one other piece in *A Booke of Ayres*, "Follow Thy Saint," is written in heroic couplets and several songs are iambic pentameter. Shorter lines of varying lengths, as in William Shakespeare's "Under the Greenwood Tree," are more likely to be set to music. Most of the songs in this collection employ these shorter lines.

Heroic couplets are certainly not what one would expect from a slightly older Campion, who experimented with quantitative meters, in which the length of syllables, how long or short they are to say aloud, is measured instead of the accents. In his preface, he praises the Greek and Latin poets (such as Catullus) who wrote quantitative verse and were the "first inventors of ayres," while denigrating the "fashion of the time, ear-pleasing rhymes without art." "My Sweetest Lesbia" follows the fashion of 1600 but is extremely artful. Part of Campion's concern with meter is literary, as he looks back admiringly at classical models while sneering at his contemporaries and even at himself, but part of his concern is strictly musical. As a composer, he works with quarter notes and the three-quarter time in which most of the song is written.

Campion himself composed the beautiful music for this song, so the question of detaching the words from their setting is more difficult than usual to resolve. Readers can enjoy the poem on the page for its neat three-part structure, its antithetical repetitions ("light" versus "night"), its graceful rhetorical power, and its extension of Catullus' witty, hyperbolic gambit into something profoundly human and moving. The text alone should not, however, be considered as anything more than an excerpt of the work as a whole.

The last two lines of each stanza represent a partial refrain. The first halves of these lines vary, but the second halves are repeated throughout the song and contrast with each other, one's "little light" versus an "ever-during night." The music stipulates that the phrase "ever-during night" be repeated at the end of each stanza. It is the only phrase so singled out, an emphasis intended to deepen the sense of mortality, the dark alternative to the love proposed by the singer. This effect is not present in the text alone. Furthermore, when the song is performed, the last two lines of each stanza are repeated, emphasizing the theme and its urgency.

The rhyming is simple and conventional, making use of thematically important words such as "dive" and "revive." The language is formal but clear, uncluttered and economical, a good illustration of Campion's remark that "What epigrams are in poetry, the same are ayres in music, . . . short and well seasoned." The alliteration of *l* dominates the song's first line, "My sweetest Lesbia, let us live and love," and is used through all three stanzas to emphasize important words: Lesbia, live, love, lamps, "little light," "lead their lives," life, lovers, and the imperative verb "let," which appears four times. The liquid *l* sound is also embedded in several important words: "sleep," "alarm," "fools," "timely." An important function of this alliteration is purely musical: repeated *l* sounds are melodious in themselves.

Themes and Meanings

The most insistent images in the song deal with light and dark. Day and night lengthen into life and death. The "little light" of human beings seems frail, weak, and no match for the "great lamps" of heaven, but if that light is used lovingly, it can be enough to make mortality something to celebrate, rather than something to mourn. By implication, the "sager sort" who disapprove of lovemaking, the lovers' "deeds," ally themselves with the military "fools" who "waste their little light." Those kinds of worldliness deprive men and women of the illumination that might make living worthwhile.

The poem is a declaration of *carpe diem*, "seize the day," a common theme of this period. It takes the rhetorical form of a lover's plea and belongs with the "amorous songs" Campion mentions in his preface. Acting against the passage of time, the warring of nations, and mortality itself, lovers can at least avoid wasting their lives and their light. The modesty is audacious. Love is sufficient in itself to offset the enormities of the world. This love is one that is earthly and enduring, one that makes even the prospect of death almost cheerful, a "triumph." In other words, people love because death looms, but that love makes death an occasion for revelry. Love, the song says, makes living worthwhile.

To what extent, is the song really a love poem in the usual sense? Does the reader imagine that the "you" of the poem is a real person, someone being wooed and seduced? Or is Campion's mistress more an idea than an individual woman? It may be significant that the song is addressed to Catullus' Lesbia. In another song based on the same original, Ben Jonson changes the name to the more euphonious Celia, a character in his play *Volpone* (1605). At least in dramatic terms, a real woman is represented there.

Campion's beloved, however, seems to live not in his own London but in the Rome of Catullus or out of the mortal world altogether. Her name comes to him secondhand. It is strictly literary and allusive, a means of paying homage to Catullus and thereby to the Greek poet Sappho of Lesbos, who is Catullus' real honoree.

The stately tone and epigrammatic neatness of the song make the love it espouses seem reserved, respectful, and even lofty. This is a hymn to love in the abstract. Campion seems to fret more about impersonal warfare than about personal love, yet his fervor is true and overwhelming. It is tempting to see Lesbia as love itself, or as an earthly goddess who will perform the singer's last rites. She is, in fact, the muse, the generative spirit of poetry and music. As the first piece of a whole collection of songs, "My Sweetest Lesbia" serves as an invocation to the muse. It is a love song to art, to its endurance and enduring beauty.

John Drury

MYRIS: ALEXANDRIA, 340 A.D.

Author: Constantine P. Cavafy (Kōnstantionos Petrou Kabaphēs, 1863-1933)
Type of poem: Dramatic monologue
First published: 1929, as "Myris: Alexandria tou 340 M.X."; in *Poiēmata*, 1935; collected in *Poems*, 1951

The Poem

The speaker of this rather long dramatic monologue is a pagan Greek in the city of Alexandria, Egypt, in the year A.D. 340, lamenting the death of his Christian lover. The speaker tells of his visit to the house of the dead man and, of there watching the Christian rites, and becoming aware not only that has he lost his lover to death, but that perhaps never knew him at all. The poem does not quite fit the usual definition of a dramatic monologue, though, in that one cannot be sure whom the speaker is addressing. He may, indeed, be talking half to himself, even as he is reporting what has happened to someone else, someone who may have known the dead man, Myris, but not very well.

The conversational, almost colloquial, intensely felt tone of the poem is expressed in its language, in its lines, and in its word choices. Although the lines have varying numbers of syllables, usually between eleven and fifteen, Constantine P. Cavafy's basic metrical pattern is a deliberately loose iambic. He uses no rhyme, although, since modern Greek has a rather limited vowel pattern as well as being a relatively inflected language, there are always sound echoes made by the repeated vowels and by those inflections. The poem is divided into stanzas or, rather, verse paragraphs, of varying length; the first three paragraphs are each four lines each, but the next four are ten, eight, twenty-three, and seventeen lines.

The speaker begins by describing how, the moment he learned of the "calamity," he went to Myris' house but did not enter it, since he "avoids" going into Christian houses, especially at times of sorrow or celebrations. The statement itself indicates the distance between the speaker and the beloved. The speaker stands in the hall, outside the room where the dead body lies; he can see a little of the large, rich room, suggesting that this Christian family is well-to-do.

The speaker, saying, "I stood and wept in a corner of the hall," regrets that his and his friends' future parties will no longer be worth much without Myris. Beside him, some old women talk about Myris' pious end, of his holding a cross and having the name of Christ on his lips. Four Christian priests enter, praying "to Jesus/ or to Mary (I don't know their religion very well)."

Here the speaker remarks that he and his friends had known that Myris was a Christian but that Myris had taken a more than active part in their wild parties, although now the speaker remembers a few moments when casual references to religion had been made and the young man had drawn away.

The priests continue to pray, and the speaker becomes aware of how intense they are. At last he begins to realize that he is truly losing, has lost, his love, that Myris has become one with the Christians and is now a stranger or, perhaps, has always been a stranger. Overcome, the speaker runs from their "horrible house" before his memory of Myris can be changed by their Christianity.

Forms and Devices

This is the longest of the poems that Cavafy printed while he was alive. Its very length allows a kind of exploration that shorter poems do not. The gradual lengthening of the stanzas also suggests an intensifying of emotion, a longer explosion of feeling; however, as in most of his later poems, Cavafy makes little use of figures of speech here, no similes, no metaphors, no rhymes except for the partial rhymes given (in the Greek) by the inflected endings of words. Indeed, the first part of this poem seems almost a flat report. As noted above, Cavafy's language, at least in translation, is conversational and colloquial.

It is structure and language then, not figures, which carry the poem's meanings; there is a kind of dialectic at play, a gradual revelation of the speaker's growing awareness. This revelation is given, first, through structure, a shifting between emotional expression and seemingly straight description, and between the past and the present. Second, the revelation is given through language and its "silence," that is, through statement by implication rather than by direct words.

The only word in the first twelve lines that reveals emotion is the word "calamity," in the first line: "When I heard of the calamity, that Myris had died." The next eleven lines are an almost emotionless description of the speaker going to the house and, standing there, observing the displeasure of the relatives of Myris. Although the emotion is there, it is expressed by the silence, the lack of words, rather than by their presence.

Now, however, direct expression of feeling takes over: "I stood and cried," the speaker says. Immediately afterward, he repeats the words "I thought upon" three times in the next seven lines (in Greek this is one word, suggesting "reflecting" upon something). That is, he moves back to the past, remembering aspects of Myris and so attempting to recover the past.

Then he returns once more to description, to the external, presenting the old women and the priests, at the same time emphasizing his alienation from Myris by his admission that he knows very little about Christianity.

Returning to the past, he remarks that he and his friends had known Myris was a Christian, but that Myris had lived as though that fact did not matter, not even speaking of his religion. Still, the speaker begins to reveal how little he had known Myris, since only now does he seem to remember the times that Myris pulled back from their pagan words or acts.

The last section mixes description and emotion. It exists almost entirely in the speaker's present, for the past has been lost. As the priests pray, the speaker is seized with the awareness that Myris has left him, has become one with his own people, the Christians. The speaker, fearing that he has been deluded by his own passion into believing that he knew Myris, flees, hoping to hang onto some positive memory before it is changed by the Christian funeral service. The last line of the poem, with its fear of loss, is a significantly Cavafian line, since loss of love, of home, of culture, is a major theme in his work.

Themes and Meanings

Cavafy is a poet of the city, of civilization, of social and personal relations, of humans relating to humans. He is not, at least not directly, concerned with the natural—not even with humankind's relation with the natural. Unlike nature, the individual's life is not cyclic; it does not repeat itself. Loss, losses of all kinds, are therefore inevitable. Moreover, one must note that Cavafy's people are confined within themselves; they live in a world of enclosure with the self as all-consuming, since belief in a greater order than oneself has been lost. Writing about characters in history, as well as about the moments of history that give rise to the characters, allows Cavafy to dramatize all of his themes, but especially that of how one person relates to another.

Alexandria in A.D. 340 was a unique historical moment—a high, dramatic moment. The city was still one of the great centers of Greek civilization, a civilization not yet Christianized. Christianity, although it had been made legal by the Roman emperor Constantine some twenty-five or so years earlier, was still years away from being the prevailing religion of the empire. The sons of Constantine were battling for the throne; there was great conflict over what Christianity itself believed.

If one had eyes, however, the end of the old religion was in sight. There is a willful blindness on the part of the speaker. He is concerned only with his pleasures, with his love for Myris, not with the stir of ideas, the immense changes in civilization going on about him.

Cavafy presents him both affectionately and with some distance. The speaker as egoist, locked within himself, is incapable of seeing others as human beings in themselves. At the same moment, he is a lover who has lost his beloved, a sad figure at any time. At the end he may have learned something, but not in time truly to change. Moreover, he reflects Cavafy's own ambivalence toward Christianity, the religion in which he was reared but into which he never quite fit. The final thematic matters, even teachings, of the poem, then, are that history can and does destroy individuals and individual relationships, that humans live in a world of loss, and that egoism can blind a person.

L. L. Lee

THE MYSTERY OF THE CHARITY OF CHARLES PÉGUY

Author: Geoffrey Hill (1932-   )
Type of poem: Elegy
First published: 1983; collected in *Collected Poems*, 1985

The Poem

The Mystery of the Charity of Charles Péguy is an elegy in ten parts, consisting of as little as seven and as many as eighteen four-line, irregularly rhymed verses. An elegy — a poetic lament on the death of a person who may or may not be known intimately by the poet — sometimes requires special knowledge of the life of the deceased. Geoffrey Hill has a formidable reputation for being difficult to understand at the best of times, but *The Mystery of the Charity of Charles Péguy* has the added density of reference to the life of this somewhat minor figure in late nineteenth and early twentieth century French intellectual and political circles. Who Charles Péguy was and what he did should be known or the poem may make no sense to the reader.

Charles-Pierre Péguy, born in France in 1873, was a brilliant scholar who became a journalist, poet, political philosopher, and the founder and editor of *Cahier de la Quinzaine* magazine, which Péguy used to support young writers and to propound his own ideas about French politics, society, and religion. He was a leader in the fight to prove the innocence of Captain Alfred Dreyfus (1859-1935), a French-born Jew who, in 1894, was accused of selling military secrets to the Germans, and whose guilt seemed to be confirmed by the fact that he was Jewish. The Socialists supported the fight to clear the innocent Dreyfus, but during the fight, Péguy became increasingly dissatisfied with the manner in which the Socialists had pursued the matter. He eventually broke with the Socialists in 1900, repudiating his former support of France's Socialist leader, Jean-Joseph-Marie-Auguste Jaurès (1859-1914), and carrying on a running battle in print and in public against what he saw as a debasement of Socialist principles. In 1910, Péguy emerged as a major literary figure with the publication of his book on Joan of Arc, *Le Mystère de la charité de Jeanne d'Arc* (*The Mystery of the Charity of Joan of Arc*, 1950). The title of his book provides the basis for the title of Hill's poem.

Péguy eventually returned to the religion he renounced as a young man, Catholicism, and began writing religious poems and developing philosophical ideas. Péguy claimed that he was always a Socialist, despite his return to religion and his repudiation of official French Socialism, but his rigorous refusal to compromise, his moral absolutism, and his support of French military solutions to the growing German problem made him a "man in the middle." He was despised by former friends and colleagues in the Dreyfus and Socialist movement and taken up by and admired by conservatives. He was one of the first to enlist at the outbreak of World War I; he was one of the first to die in the Battle of the Marne.

In the first section of "The Mystery of the Charity of Charles Péguy," the question of Péguy's responsibility for the untimely death of Socialist leader Jaurès is put in two contexts: the death itself and the more general question of the role of thinkers in moments of history in action. This rhetorical musing leads to an examination of Péguy's character in the second section and his role as a defender of truth in the face of political and social compromise. Unlike his adversary, he is like a child, unaffected by triviality. Near the end of section 2, the place of his death is shown, and it is suggested that in his death his character was confirmed, even if he has become simply one of the innumerable statues in Paris.

In the third section, Péguy is remembered after death in a kind of piling up of the idealities of his life. He had, for example, made two pilgrimages to the cathedral at Chartres on behalf of his children. The other places have either direct or indirect connections with his life or hide allusions to his dreams for France: For example, Domrémy is the birthplace of Joan of Arc and the Colombey-les-deux-Eglises may be a reference to General Charles de Gaulle (1890-1970), who is buried there and who also had a fearsome reputation for defending France. Saint Cyr is the home of the French military academy.

In the fourth section, the real world of compromise, self-interest, and class interest is examined, and Péguy's failure to win over those forces is expressed in terms of his work as a publisher in his little shop in Paris. In the end of the section, the death of Jaurès is rationalized, seen as inevitable, and juxtaposed against Péguy's own death. That death is explored in section 5 in concert with his love of the land and his connection with the simple people of the land; there is a rightness in the death taking place on the land, in a field of beetroot, where flesh quite properly is absorbed and courage is played out with dignity, as the recondite reference to "English Gordon" implies. (General Charles Gordon, beseiged at Khartoum, Africa, by a Moslem force, was reputed to have walked sedately down a staircase to his death without attempting to avoid the thrust of the spears.)

In section 6, the question of French justice comes up. It is considered in the light of the stripping of Dreyfus of his military trappings, which leads to a suggestion of wider martrydom, including that of Christ at the hands of societies that have become morally debased and where all are, at the least, time servers or cowards. The seventh section continues listing those betrayed and those who have served and sacrificed themselves for the native lands. Section 8 examines, with a graphic vigor, the soldiers pushing themselves on in thuggish battle to their deaths. There is little suggestion of glamor or glory in this passage, but there is an aura of admiration for the courage and determination of those poilus, ready to give their lives in defense of their native soil.

Section 9 presents an idealized French landscape for which Péguy, in a sense, was always fighting in letters, in politics, and in war, but it ends with somber anticipations of the battle that must be fought and that will be won by men such as Péguy. Section 10 begins on the battlefield, as the dead bodies are collected. The question arises, as in the second verse of the first section, of how humankind is to take such actions — are they tragedy or farce? Whatever the case, there is no question that it is a time both for praise and lament.

The poem is a somewhat rambling, maundering contemplation of Péguy's life, character, and historical importance. As a result, Hill shuffles ideas in and out of the various sections in repetitive waves.

Forms and Devices

The elegy has taken many adjustments through the centuries, but the twentieth century in particular has manipulated it with considerable enthusiasm and not much respect. It has lost much of its romantic oversimplification at the hands of twentieth century poets, and the idea that one should not speak disrespectfully of the dead is often ignored. T. S. Eliot has something to do with the technique of this poem, but W. H. Auden is equally helpful in terms of the way Hill thinks about Péguy's life and death. Auden wrote several elegies, often about famous people, and he was not loath to reveal the weakenesses as well as the strengths of his subjects.

The elegy, as a rule, praised exclusively, although there are intimations of some reservation in how Andrew Marvell contemplates historical figures in his poems of lament. Auden, however, can be frank about flaws in great men; in contemplating the death of the poet William Butler Yeats in his poem "In Memory of W. B. Yeats," Auden openly admits that "You were silly like us." It has something to do with the twentieth century zeal for frankness and suspicion of an idealized version of life; it also may have something to do with an inability to be certain about what is right or wrong, which is an aspect of the twentieth century Western sensibility.

Clearly, frankness is a strong influence on Hill's poem, because Péguy is revealed in an antiromantic way—stubborn, narrow-minded, and sometimes bloody-minded in his attitude toward others, which manifested itself in his attack on Jaurès. So, in a sense, what the poem is, ultimately, is a peculiar mix of admiration and wry reservation that does not resolve itself one way or another, but still allows for an ultimate sadness; it is best described as a kind of antielegy in which excessive admiration is severely curtailed.

The Hill canon, in general, is often the source of critical quarrel because he can be difficult to understand. Often, his lines cannot be turned into prose, a common practice of most poetry readers, although there is a kind of aesthetic "rightness" about them that is unexplainable rationally. This is not a failure on Hill's part, unless it is presumed that poetry must always make intellectual sense. Hill, in fact, is deliberately ambiguous. His debt to Eliot intensifies this problem because he tends to pile up images as Eliot did, without providing the linkages that one expects of ordinary metaphors and similes. Hill's images merely appear, often out of a loose association of ideas.

The last verse in the first section is an example of how this occurs. The problem posed earlier of how to take history, either as tragedy or farce, is now put into the specific context of the troops marching off to battle in World War I. It is seen in the context of early newsreel films, put succinctly in the second-to-last verse as "juddery bombardment of a silent film." What Hill has in mind is the way in which those early films jumped about, made a clanking noise as the film ran through the projector, giving even the military procession a kind of comic inconsequentiality that is reinforced further by his punning on the word "reeling."

This practice of slapping one image on top of another, one thing leading to another without the help of such linking phrases as "as if" or "it was like," can best be understood not as a linguistic device but as a visual one in which one image is often, as in motion pictures, laid on top of another or in which one image melts into another. If the reader thinks of the lines as linguistic attempts to affect visual (or musical) fusions of continual changing images, much of the problem will be solved, as it will be if Eliot or Auden is read in a similar manner.

This inclination to sophisticated imagistic trickery, however, should not be seen as Hill's only strength. He often can be densely lyrical, as in his evocations of the French countryside in sections 5 and 9, and he is much admired for the thick, bruising descriptions of battle that are in many of his poems. For all of his basic tonal seriousness, however, there is a playfulness about his use of blatant clichés, which he often refreshes or, as one critic put it, "rinses and restores." Perhaps the most daring is at the end of section 4, where he joins two clichés to describe the death of Péguy: "So, you have risen/ above all that and fallen flat on your face."

Themes and Meanings

The intention of an elegy is to praise the deceased, provide a kind of solemn listing of the accomplishments of the dead. This poem, given its source in Auden's antielegies and the desire of Hill not simply to idealize Péguy, opens to a wider consideration of Péguy's successes and his failures. In a way, the poem suggests, Péguy's life was a failure, but that does not, ultimately, preclude the poet from admiring his subject. The poem takes a further turn past the antielegy to pick up aspects of the "dramatic monologue" in which a problem is solved, in a sense, in the very act of being discussed poetically. Hill fuses the elegy to the dramatic monologue in which the problem is not the subject's (as it usually is in that form), but the poet's. How is he to praise a man with whose conduct he does not entirely feel easy, particularly if that man's work is so clearly a public failure and that man may have been responsible, even inadvertently, for the death of another man of political and moral importance. How does one praise a person of such mixed accomplishments?

The original *Times Literary Supplement* publication of the poem was preceded by a quotation from Péguy, which has not been reprinted in Hill's *Collected Poems*, but which gives some idea of why Hill admires him. In French, the quotation roughly translates as follows: "We are the last, almost beyond the last. Besides, after us, begins another age, quite a different world, the world of those who don't know anything." In the notes following the poem in *Collected Poems*, Hill has a short biographical note on Péguy that ends, "Péguy's stubborn rancours and mishaps and all, is one of the great souls, one of the great prophetic intelligences, of our century. I offer *The Mystery of the Charity of Charles Péguy* as my homage to the triumph of his 'defeat.' "

The poem is also an indictment of those people, such as the Socialists, who would compromise their principles, even if such compromise was made to further the the process of social and political improvement. Even more to the point, the poem is a swinging attack upon the unprincipled, "the lords of limit and of contumely," even if, as is stated in section 4, "This world is different, belongs to them— ." The poem does not suggest that the time servers and the incumbents of compromise are defeated, nor that Péguy was always right, but it attempts to bring the spectrum of human endeavour at its worst and at its best into some kind of humane perspective, much in the way that Yeats attempted to deal with the Irish political problem in his poems. Hill concedes in that second-to-last verse of the poem that "Low tragedy, high farce, fight for command," but it still remains that there is room for praise and for mourning ("éloge and elegy") in considering the life of Péguy, a man of such principle that he, in a sense, became a victim of his own character.

Charles Pullen

MYTHISTOREMA

Author: George Seferis (Giorgos Stylianou Seferiades, 1900-1971)
Type of poem: Poetic sequence
First published: 1935, as *Mythistorima*; collected in *George Seferis: Collected Poems, 1924-1955*, 1967

The Poem

Mythistorema is a sequence of twenty-four lyric and dramatic poems in free verse. The title is a colloquial word for "novel" that combines the ideas of myth and history. The author's note states: "MYTHISTOREMA—it is its two components that made me choose the title of this work: MYTHOS, because I have used, clearly enough, a certain mythology; ISTORIA [both "history" and "story"], because I have tried to express, with some coherence, circumstances that are as independent from myself as the characters in a novel."

The poem's narrator, like that of a novel, moves freely among various points of view and identities, yet his voice is always distinctive. This voice, linking past and present in a tone of tragic nostalgia, is the coherent center of the poem.

The sequence begins with a kind of preface to the poems that follow. The narrator and his fellows have been on a journey "to rediscover the first seed," to renew "the ancient drama." They have waited in vain for "the angel" (also translated as "herald" or "messenger") to show them the way. Bodies and spirits broken, they returned with "these carved reliefs of a humble art."

Their "limbs incapable, mouths cracked," they can no longer draw water from the source of inspiration, the "well inside a cave." The seekers are like cave dwellers whose reality is an illusion, as in Plato's myth of the cave. The ropes of the well "have broken; only grooves on the well's lip" remind them of their "past happiness," when it was "easy for us to draw up idols and ornaments." Now, however, "the cave stakes its soul and loses it" in the oppressive "silence, without a drop of water."

The narrator describes waking from a dream with a "marble head in my hands." It has become part of him, though he cannot tell what it is trying to say to him. It has exhausted him and mutilated his hands. Poem 4 begins by quoting Socrates: The way a soul "is to know itself" is to look into a soul. This suggests that the marble head, "stranger and enemy," is to be identified with the narrator. Similarly, the singing and seeking of Jason and his Argonauts are identified with the narrator; all will die unremembered, and in this there is an ironic "Justice."

Poem 5 questions the ability of memory and imagination to give present substance to one's personal (and cultural) past. We try to recall "our friends," but it is only hope that deceives us into thinking "we'd known them since early childhood," before they "took to the ships." In art, one tries to depict the ships, but only in sleep does one approach them and "the breathing wave"; what one actually seeks is "the other life" of imagination wedded to experience that the friends stand for, "beyond the statues."

One who found the ancient "rhythm of the other life" in his art was the "old Friend," French composer Joseph-Maurice Ravel. Far from the Greek landscape, in a room "lit only by the flames from the fireplace" but radiant with the "distant lightning" of imagination, he animated the broken statues and "tragic columns" into "a dance among the oleanders/ beside new quarries." Though the artist will die, hope and light "will spring" from his art.

Modern humanity exists in a parched and stagnant period of alienation and exile, writing letters to fill "the gap of our separation," unable to speak to one another, though bound by a hope that the "Star of dawn" (Venus) offers love, joy, and peace. Feeding on "the bitter bread of exile," the wanderers pay for their "decision to forget" their homeland, as they wonder: "Who will accept our offering, at this close of autumn?"

The exiles ask what their souls seek in wandering "from harbor to harbor." They cannot forget who they are long enough to enjoy earthly or heavenly beauties, flying fish or stars. They find work moving "broken stones," but cannot express their "broken thoughts" in foreign tongues. They breathe the memory of home "with greater difficulty each day" and swim in new seas with no sense of community, alienated from their own bodies. Yet they continue "non-existent pilgrimages unwillingly" to find the beautiful islands "somewhere round about here where we are groping."

A sense of urgency impels the narrator to continue the journey without waiting for his friends to return from known islands or "the open sea." To renew his purpose and power, he strokes rusted cannons and oars "so that my body may revive and decide." Like "Odysseus waiting for the dead among the asphodels," he had hoped to make contact with Adonis and gather his own soul, "shattered on the horizon," but found only enervating silence.

Poems 11 through 14 shed a "little light from our childhood years" in the present darkness before moving to an island one might see in any Greek harbor today, for "the same landscape recurs level after level/ to the horizon." Here Odysseus and his men land to mend their oars, yet they forget that the sea "unfolds a boundless calm" and set out with "broken oars." The sea, "once so bitter," is "now full of colors in the sun." The radiance of the "red pigeons in the light," which are like Homeric birds of omen, inscribes "our fate" in "the colors and gestures of people/ we have loved."

The narrator recalls a lover sleeping, her shadow lost in "the other shadows" of dreams. Living the sensual life the gods "gave us to live," he pities the solipsists who speak to cisterns and wells and drown in the echo of "the voice's circles."

In the voice of Orestes, the exile describes life, this "time of trial," as a chariot race, circling endlessly, observed by "the black, bored Eumenides," who are unforgiving. He longs for the race's end, but goes on because "the gods so will it." He despairs: "there's no point in being strong" because "no one can escape" to the sea. A premonition of battle and death warns that the boy who saw the light must also "study the trees" that bear the wrinkles of the fathers so that he will know all of life.

Poems 18 through 22 bear the heaviness of grief. The speaker is "sinking into the stone"; all he had loved has vanished and collapsed; he laments having let life pass through his fingers "without drinking a single drop." All is uphill, and friends "who no longer know how to die" are "a burden to us" (poem 19). Bound to a rock, a wound in his breast for the vulture and the hawk, he asks how far the stones sinking into time will drag him. He is troubled by death, unlike the trees that breathe "the black serenity of the dead" or the statues with their static smiles (poem 20). Setting out, the travelers saw the broken statues but refused to believe that life could be so "easily lost." Now they are more like statues every day, "brothers in stone," though they have not "escaped the circle" as have the ancient dead, who, risen again, "smile in strange silence" (poem 21). Wandering among the "broken stones" for "three or six thousand years," the travelers try to remember "dates and heroic deeds." What they seek, however, is to know how "to die properly" (poem 22). Unlike the friends who "no longer know how to die," they hunger for a heroic death.

The last two poems offer first a glimmer of hope in the almond blossoms and the gleaming marble, which seem just "a little farther," "a little higher" — then tragic resignation as the travelers admit the failure of their struggle. In death, these "weak souls among the asphodels" cannot offer hope to the future "victims," but they can offer the serenity of death: "We who had nothing will teach them peace."

Forms and Devices

"Mythistorema" was a turning point in modern Greek poetry, largely because of its language. For a hundred years, Greek poets had been divided between the literary (*katharevousa*) idiom and the spoken (*demotiki*) idiom. The purists tended to see ancient Greece through the eyes of post-Renaissance Europe, while the demotic poets concentrated on modern Greece. George Seferis aimed for a vision of ancient Greece as experienced in the contemporary Greek landscape, and this is reflected in his elegant demotic idiom. In *Modern Greek Poetry* (1973), Kimon Friar writes that Seferis "has used only those words in the living demotic tongue which have his own touch and weight and has honed them into what perhaps may be the purest and leanest of modern Greek idioms."

This is reflected in Seferis' use of the mythical method, legendary figures appearing in modern harbors, to show the connection, as well as the distance, between then and now. In the years before writing *Mythistorema*, Seferis was taken with T. S. Eliot's essay on James Joyce's 1922 novel *Ulysses*, which argued that the mythical method could be used instead of narrative to show "a continuous parallel between contemporaneity and antiquity."

The use of metaphor in the poem underscores this parallel between the ancient and the modern. The extended or "epic" metaphor of the odyssey to the beautiful islands, or Orestes' chariot race, combines with the mythical method to form a modern allegory.

As Walter Kaiser writes in his introduction to *Three Secret Poems* (1969), "For Seferis, the Greek sun is this ultimate paradox, both life-giver and death-bringer, desired and feared, 'angelic' and 'black.'" "You stare into the sun," says Seferis in another poem, "then you are lost in the darkness." This use of chiaroscuro (light and dark imagery) is essential to Seferis' poetry, a device that is both metaphorical and thematic.

The controlling tone is a tragic nostalgia (a good Greek word for the "ache to return home"). This tone was what first drew Seferis to Eliot, whose *The Waste Land* (1922) Seferis was translating while writing *Mythistorema*. In *On the Greek Style* (1966), Seferis comments that Eliot's poetry gave him something "inevitably moving to a Greek: the elements of tragedy."

The tragic element, combined with a use of dramatic monologue that is similar to Eliot's, gives Seferis' narrator his distinctive voice, freeing him to move from first to third person or to become Jason, Orestes, or Odysseus as the poetic occasion demands. Yet the voice remains consistent, linking the personal with the universal, the historical with the mythical. As Philip Sherrard has pointed out in *The Marble Threshing Floor: Studies in Modern Greek Poetry* (1956), however, "The human person is the centre of the scene, it is he who as a concrete, living, suffering and perplexed being, speaks. He is not simply a device."

Themes and Meanings

Mythistorema is a poem about the continuity of past and present as it is preserved in personal experience and cultural memory. More specifically, it is about the attempt to discover the heroic past of ancient Greece in the modern landscape. For Seferis, this attempt is a contemporary odyssey, an imaginative journey through the Greek experience, both ancient and modern, which consists of a shared spiritual and historical experience of suffering and disaster. Kimon Friar's translation of the title of this work "The Myth of Our History," suggests that the poem is the story of this shared experience, part myth and part history.

Memory and imagination are the vehicles of this journey, which is really an act of understanding. The narrator's quest in search of the origins of his Greek identity unifies the poem's imagery of the sea, which can be, like life, both embittering and soothing. Seferis has commented that "the bows of ships have a special place in the imagery of our childhood, as perhaps do the shapes of footballs or the photos of deceased relatives for other people." When the narrator tries to recall friends who have sailed away, both memory and imagination fail him; only while sleeping in cellars that smell of tar, like the hold of a ship, does he come close to them and "the breathing wave." His true search, however, is for the life of imagination wedded to experience, which the friends represent: "we search for them because we search for the other life,/ beyond the statues."

The broken stones and statues of Greece, the landscape and cultural artifacts that come down to the present, remind one that one's suffering is neither unique nor uniquely modern, and stir memory and imagination to link one's tragedy with the eternally recurring tragedy of myth and history.

The broken statues that appear throughout the poem—first as an ambiguous inspiration and burden in the form of a marble head found in a dream, and finally as the "brothers in stone" who "smile in strange silence" — communicate with one, though one does not always know what they are saying. Once one has grasped them, however, they become part of one, difficult "to disunite again." Like Ravel's music, they say that it is possible to recapture "a rhythm of the other life, beyond the broken/ statues." They are mirrors of the soul in which it is possible to see "the stranger and enemy"; they break down the barrier between present and past, erasing such illusory oppositions as waking and dreaming, weird and familiar, I and thou. The marble head — the narrator — is a modern Odysseus, Jason, or Orestes. The only difference is that "the ancient dead have escaped the circle and risen again/ and smile in strange silence" to teach serenity. It is this silence that is invoked at the end of the poem, for like them, those who are here will teach "peace" to those who come after.

Water imagery is always associated with the imaginative journey. Modern life is a life of exile. Like refugees caught up in disaster, one is unable to appreciate the beauties along the way, "sorry" to "let a broad river pass through [one's] fingers/ without drinking a single drop." Life itself offers abundance, but in this exile most people are too concerned with searching and suffering to appreciate it. Once, waters "left on the hands/ the memory of great happiness" when human "souls became one with the oars and the oarlocks"; now, one hopes only to be remembered, like Elpenor, by an oar marking one's grave.

The modern landscape is parched; the rivers, wells, and springs of inspiration have dried up: "only a few cisterns — and these empty — that echo, and that we worship." The cistern, a personal and cultural resevoir of faith and inspiration, is an important symbol that Seferis developed in "The Cistern." Modern Greeks, says Seferis, tend to worship echoes of the past instead of creating anew, like Ravel, "a rhythm of the other life." To quench its spiritual thirst, to get rid of "the 'Waste Land' feeling," as Seferis called it, modern humanity journeys in self-imposed exile toward the beautiful islands "somewhere about here where we are groping."

Given modern inertia, the narrator wonders how anyone ever had faith in the future. To marry and to have children now seem "enigmas inexplicable to our souls." Nowadays, going to "the harbors on Sunday to breathe," one sees "the broken planks from voyages that never ended,/ bodies that no longer know how to love." Some know of the cisterns, like the poet, but "drown in the voice's circles" without enjoying the reward of simply living. Only the serenity of death awaits them, and on this tragic note of failure, the poem ends.

It has been said that poetry is the art of delineating the limits of human failure. If the quest for the seed of the ancient drama has failed, the poem has not. For just as the past is inherited in fragments, so the poem passes "the myth of our history" to posterity. Given that all souls are seekers by nature, it is inevitable that the journey will be repeated, but our failure, like that of those who came before us, can be instructive: "We who had nothing will teach them peace."

Richard Collins

A NARROW FELLOW IN THE GRASS

Author: Emily Dickinson (1830-1886)
Type of poem: Lyric
First published: 1866, as "The Snake"; collected in *Poems: Second Series*, 1891

The Poem

"A narrow Fellow in the Grass" (the title is not Emily Dickinson's, since she did not title her poems) is a short poem of thirty-two lines divided into five stanzas. The poem begins and ends with two balanced stanzas of four lines each, which surround a central stanza of eight lines. Dickinson's poems appear to many readers to be written in free verse; the underlying metrical structure of her poetry, however, incorporates the traditional pattern of English hymnody: alternating lines of eight syllables and six syllables. Although Dickinson employs this traditional metrical pattern as a model in her verse, she frequently violates and strains against its conventions.

The poem is written in the first person from the point of view of an adult male ("Yet when a Boy, and Barefoot—/ I"). The poem thus uses the voice of a persona—a speaker other than the poet—who initiates a cordial relationship with the audience, addressing the reader directly: "You may have met Him—did you not."

The poem is structured to relate the speaker's experience in encountering nature, specifically in the form of a snake. The speaker begins by characterizing the snake in friendly, civilized terms: The snake is a "Fellow" who "rides" in the grass, a familiar presence that even the reader has encountered. Again, in the second stanza, the snake appears to act in a civilized manner as it "divides" the grass "as with a comb." Despite the snake's cultured appearance, the first two stanzas introduce the snake's ability to appear and disappear suddenly.

In the third stanza—the central and longest of the poem—the snake's actions become increasingly unpredictable and inexplicable. The speaker notes the snake's preference for "a Boggy Acre," a place "too cool" even for "Corn," let alone human beings, then recounts a childhood incident in which he bent down and attempted to "secure" a snake but it escaped him: "It wrinkled, and was gone." What first appears to be some tool or toy ("a Whip lash") for the child to use or play with eludes not only human control but also human perception and attainment.

The fourth stanza of the poem finds the speaker abruptly back in the present, asserting—again in the polite language of refined society—his connections with the realm of nature: "Several of Nature's People/ I know, and they know me." The speaker insists that his feelings for these inhabitants of nature are ones characterized by "cordiality." This assertion, however, is contradicted in the final stanza by the speaker's depiction of the effect on him each time he encounters the snake: chilling terror ("a tighter breathing/ And Zero at the Bone"). What begins as a poem ostensibly about a snake becomes, in this way, a poem about the effect of an encounter with a snake—and perhaps by extension with nature itself—on an individual human being.

Forms and Devices

One of the most important poetic devices at work in the poem is the tone: the speaker's attitude toward the subject being described, the snake. The tone is deceptively simple and light, referring to the snake as a "Fellow." As the speaker introduces the reader to the snake in the same way that one might introduce an acquaintance, he constructs a metaphor, a way of talking about the snake as if it were a jaunty "Fellow" who "rides" about, a friendly sort whom one surely has "met" in the course of ordinary, everyday life.

The effect of this light, off-handed tone together with the matter-of-fact narration and the metaphorical construction of the snake as an ordinary, civilized "Fellow" is to lead the reader into a situation in which he or she can be taken off guard just as the speaker is unnerved by his encounter with the snake. Indeed, immediately following the initial three-line, polite introduction to the snake, Dickinson jars the reader with one of her characteristic transformations of language: "You may have met Him—did you not/ His notice sudden is." At first glance, one reads these lines as a question followed by a statement about the snake's abrupt appearance: it gives "sudden notice." Dickinson herself insisted, however, that the third and fourth lines of this first stanza were to be read as one statement. Reading as Dickinson intended, then, the verb "is" becomes transformed into a noun with "sudden" as its adjective, and when the speaker apparently asks the reader, "Did you not notice his sudden is?" he assaults the reader's sense of ease and familiarity with language just as the snake has assaulted his sense of being at home in nature. This wrenching of language from its ordinary functions and the emphasis on the poem as an experience for the reader rather than as a preached message are two important characteristics of Dickinson's poetic technique which make her one of the first modern poets.

The progression of metaphors and images which the speaker constructs to describe the snake reflects the speaker's attempts to deal with his encounters with the snake. Beginning as a civilized "Fellow" who neatly divides the grass "as with a Comb," the snake, by the end of the second stanza and the beginning of the third, has become a "spotted shaft." The speaker relates that this ominously threatening object—far from being a civilized companion—prefers to reside in "a Boggy Acre," a place which resists human cultivation.

The narration in the central stanza of a childhood encounter completes the transformation of the snake from the personified "Fellow" to an object. Now the snake is perceived to be first a "Whip lash" and then some ungraspable "it" which engages in a game of hide-and-seek with the speaker.

At the beginning of the fifth stanza, the speaker retreats to his personification of nature's inhabitants, asserting knowledge of and connections with "Nature's People" and the "cordiality" he feels for them. The sixth and final stanza, however, contrasts his sense of ease in nature with his feelings of terror upon meeting the snake: "tighter breathing/ And Zero at the Bone."

Even as the repeated *s* sounds and the serpentine long and short line lengths in the poem's opening seven lines usher the reader into an encounter with the snake, so the varied *o* sounds of the central stanza—boggy, floor, too, cool, corn, boy, barefoot, noon, gone—give way to the full force of the repeated *o* rhymes which arrive at the end of the poem, blow by blow, with the horror of the snake: fellow, alone, zero, bone.

Themes and Meanings

This is a poem about making a journey into nature, one of the characteristic themes of American literature. According to Ralph Waldo Emerson and Henry David Thoreau—two members of the Transcendental movement in American literature with whom Dickinson has frequently been compared—such an excursion into nature could put human beings in contact with the higher laws of the universe. Dickinson's poem offers both an exploration and a critique of this view. Hers is a poem about coming into contact with nature—moving from a distance to proximity with nature—but more important, it is a poem which contrasts the perceptions of nature from a distance with the reality of nature experienced at first hand.

Although the poem begins with an Emersonian view of nature as accessible to human understanding, it moves from the perception of the snake as a familiar acquaintance to the snake as something which can freeze the speaker with terror. The poem recounts the dissolution of the speaker's sense of ease and familiarity while in nature. The startling encounter with the snake, in fact, evokes his need to assert and reaffirm a sense of connection to the natural world. His assertion of a knowledge of "Nature's People" indicates his desire for a personified nature that he can know. In short, the speaker needs to believe that nature can still function for him—as it did for other Transcendentalists—as the means for "transport" to some higher yet friendly realm: "I feel for them a transport/ of cordiality."

This statement stands in the poem, however, only as the speaker's attempt to reassure himself because nothing else in the encounter with the snake supports the assertion. On the contrary, the central incident in the poem—the bewildering and frightening meeting with the snake—reaffirms with terrifying certainty nature's true relation to the speaker. Rather than a familiar "Fellow" whose recurrent presence can calm, reassure, and keep one company, nature in some of its manifestations plays an alarming game with human beings, often "Unbraiding" or unraveling their grip on reality. Nature's inhabitants appear and disappear suddenly—leaving the observer both terrified ("tighter breathing") and chillingly empty ("Zero at the Bone") of whatever comforting notions about nature he is able to sustain when nature remains at a distance. By the end of the poem, the implications of the "Whip lash" metaphor become clear: the snake as whiplash represents finally both something in nature capable of violence and pain and the scar left on human consciousness by nature's sudden, violent act.

Angela M. Estes

A NAVAJO BLANKET

Author: May Swenson (1919-1989)
Type of poem: Meditation
First published: 1977; collected in *New and Selected Things Taking Place*, 1978

The Poem

"A Navajo Blanket" is a fourteen-line poem in two stanzas of equal length. In the poem, May Swenson is describing the dazzling colors and distinctive designs of a traditional blanket made by the Navajos of the American Southwest. The colors and shapes of the blanket make her think of what the blanket represents—the Navajo people, their culture, landscape, and ceremonies. In this meditation on the blanket, however, she is also writing about an experience in which the individual undergoes a transformation of consciousness through the experience of a work of art.

The appearance of the two stanzas of the poem on the page suggests the shape and design of the blanket. The lines of words across the page are like the rows of thread in a weaving, and the shape of the whole poem is generally rectangular with a zone of space like a band of white across the center. The words "paths" and "maze" describe what the blanket's design looks like and announce that the poet is going to draw the reader into a complex experience, simply as the pattern and color of the blanket draw the eye into its complex design. The first stanza leads the reader into the maze pattern of the blanket, and the second stanza leads the reader out, a movement that seems to imitate the balanced pattern of the blanket itself. She moves through the various associations and states of mind evoked by the blanket, from being dazzled and disturbed by its brightness, to being calmed at its center, and finally, leaving the blanket and its design with a refreshed mind, described in a striking simile as being like "a white cup." The poem is written in the second person ("you"), which draws the reader into the experience and vision. The poet wants the poem to be more than her own personal response to experience.

When Swenson describes the Blue, Red, and Black lines as paths that pull the reader into the "maze," she seems to be saying that there are different ways by which one can enter into the design, simply as there are different ways to approach a work of art or an experience. She uses the word "field" to describe a flat plane, such as the surface of the geometrically patterned blanket, but she also uses the word to suggest an actual field or open space in a landscape. When she says "Alight," there is a change in what is going on in the poem. No longer is this simply a blanket; it is also a place with "gates" and "a hawk" sitting on "the forearm of a Chief." She asks "you" to undergo a transformation, to become something like a hunting hawk in repose. That the hawk is hooded means that one surrenders to the experience blindly as if going into a trance.

At this point, the poem pauses. Consciousness is suspended between day and night, Sun and Moon; there is no sense of time passing. Then the direction of the poem shifts, and the dreamer in the poem follows "the spirit trail, a faint Green thread," an exit that is part of the traditional design of the weaving, and finds a way out of the maze.

At the end of the poem, the mind is described as a white cup that has been washed like a dish. The white cup makes one think of the skull itself, which is now clean and ready to reuse, as the person in the poem returns refreshed to the everyday world. Thus, looking at the blanket has become a spiritual exercise that restores a sense of balance and calm.

Forms and Devices

May Swenson is well known for her ingenious use of language, giving her the ability to re-create a subject visually and aurally. Here the lines of words, the two blocks of words that make up the two stanzas, and the space between the stanzas imitate the appearance of the blanket. Her use of strong colors re-creates the dazzling effect of the blanket. The colors also may be symbolic, although there is no specific explanation of that symbolism in the poem. Perhaps blue and red suggest the sky and red earth of the Southwest. Black may be death, trance, night, or dry vegetation in summer, among other possibilities. Green leads back to life, like something growing or a life-giving river, and white seems to represent enlightenment, calmness, or emptiness. She capitalizes the colors found in the blanket, as she capitalizes Sun and Moon, which gives these words particular importance, whereas "white" is not capitalized and thus seems to be simply a description of something, not a powerful object in itself.

Besides using the visual effect of the poem on the page and visual images in the language, Swenson makes sound an important part of the poem. Although "A Navajo Blanket" does not have a conventional rhyme scheme, she uses the repetition of various sounds to create mood and meaning throughout. In the second line, she uses the alliterative "paths," "pull," and "pin" to emphasize the connection between these words, and the *i* sound in "Brightness" and "eyes" in the third line similarly helps the reader hear the connection in sense between these two words, both of which have to do with seeing. "Hooded" and "hawk," "fasten" and "forearm," and "sleep" and "center" are other alliterative word pairs that give the poem a musical quality and emphasize important words.

The idea of entering into the design of the blanket and then leaving it is also reinforced by some mirroring in the two stanzas, so that, for example, the first and last lines of the poem both involve color, the second lines from top and bottom have to do with movement from one stage to another, the fourth lines from top and bottom have to do with entering and leaving, and so on.

Metaphor is important in Swenson's poetry, and she often develops a comparison that surprises and delights readers once they recognize it, like a riddle that seems obvious after one knows the answer but that is mysterious until one does. At first, the blanket in the poem is simply an object with a bright, hypnotic design, but words such as "paths" and "field" make the reader begin to see the blanket as a landscape. Looking at the blanket becomes a journey into that landscape.

The poetic devices in the poem are never simply decorations of an idea but are an integral part of the poem itself, creating a concrete experience on the page, in the ear, and in the mind's eye.

Themes and Meanings

May Swenson often writes about things in such a way as to transform common objects and experience into something mysterious and new. She is also interested in states of consciousness—sleep, dreams, meditation, trance, life, and death—awareness and the loss of it. In this poem, she is writing about a transformation in consciousness brought about by a work of art. "A Navajo Blanket" combines several subjects. It is a poem celebrating the beauty of a particular kind of Native American craft. It is also about a mystical experience in which the design of the blanket draws the observer into an altered state of awareness. Finally, the poem is about the experience of art itself, which might include poetry as well as weaving and any other art form. She says that art takes one out of oneself and gives renewal and refreshment.

The nature of art and its effect on human life is a subject that is bound to intrigue an artist, particularly a meditative poet such as Swenson who often finds her inspiration in common things, an eye blinking, a wave rolling up on the beach, a skunk cabbage, or some other object that is so familiar one has stopped really seeing it. In her poems, Swenson restores a sense of awe to the world. The blink of an eyelid becomes a slow series of monstrous events; the movement of waves becomes a perpetual motion machine. So, too, does "A Navajo Blanket" become a key to past and present, the story of a culture, a mysterious maze into which one is compelled to enter and where one undergoes a strange out-of-time experience, and an allegory about the effects of art on the individual. The poem is also about a blanket, a work of art, that is, artifice, something made by human hand and shaped by human imagination.

Swenson's poems often have a strong sense of closure. This one is no exception. In the last line, the cycle is complete, and, like a chalice or a bone china cup, "your mind/ is rinsed and returned to you." Refreshed, one is free to exit the maze of the blanket and the poem itself.

Barbara Drake

THE NEGRO SPEAKS OF RIVERS

Author: Langston Hughes (1902-1967)
Type of poem: Lyric
First published: 1921; collected in *The Weary Blues*, 1926

The Poem

"The Negro Speaks of Rivers" is Langston Hughes's most anthologized poem. Hughes wrote this brief poem in fifteen minutes in July, 1920, while crossing the Mississippi on a train ride to visit his father in Mexico. It is one of Hughes's earliest poems, and its subject established the emphasis of much of his subsequent poetry. Hughes's poetry may be divided into several categories: protest poems, social commentary, Harlem poems, folk poems, poems on African and Negritude themes, and miscellaneous poetry on various other nonracial subjects and themes. "The Negro Speaks of Rivers" centers on African and Negritude themes. Hughes's writing always shows an identification with Africa, and his later poetry on African subjects and African themes demonstrates his growing sophistication and knowledge of the history and problems of Africa. Along with its emphasis on African themes, this poem so poignantly and dramatically expresses what it means to be a black American that it helps to assure Hughes's continuing fame.

Through the images of the river, Hughes traces the history of the African American from Africa to America. The muddy Mississippi makes Hughes consider the roles that rivers have played in human history. The first three lines introduce the subject of the poem. The primary image of water symbolically represents the history of humanity, acknowledging the fact that rivers are more ancient in the history of the earth:

> I've known rivers:
> I've known rivers ancient as the world and older than the flow of
>   human blood in human veins.

The next line connects the poet with the river and acknowledges the influence of waterways on the history of the African American: "My soul has grown deep like the rivers." This line is repeated at the end of the poem, re-establishing the connection between the human essence and the river as well as the river's role in African-American life.

The middle section reveals the connections between the history of the African American and four important rivers of the world: the Euphrates, the Congo, the Nile, and the Mississippi. The three African rivers are a part of the ancient history of black people when they were free, living in majestic kingdoms and forming the great civilizations of Africa. The poem more specifically relates to the African American, who is the victim of slavery and discrimination in the New World, where rivers were used to transport black slaves.

The last section of the poem, "I've known rivers:/ Ancient, dusky, rivers// My soul has grown deep like the rivers," re-emphasizes the beginning section by restating the influence of rivers on the soul and life of black people from antiquity to the twentieth century. The final line of the poem repeats the statement that connects the human soul to the rivers of the world.

Forms and Devices

"The Negro Speaks of Rivers" is a lyric poem. Lyric poetry is rooted in song and establishes the ritual of the human condition, in this case the condition of black people. In this poem, Hughes is both a teller (poet) and participant (African American) in the drama being described. Through the intense images of this poem, the reader is able to participate in the emotion and poignancy of the history of black people. Since Hughes discusses this history beyond that in America, he transcends localism and projects upon his reader a world experience.

The diction of the poem is simple and unaffected by rhetorical excess. It is eloquent in its simplicity, allowing readers of all ages and sophistication to enjoy a first reading; however, as one reads this poem, the deeper meaning reveals itself.

The primary image of "The Negro Speaks of Rivers" is water; its function as the river of time is to trace the heritage and past of the African American. The flowing, lyrical lines, like water, are charged with meaning, describing what the river has meant to black people in America. Hughes's poetic ability and technical virtuosity are nowhere as evident as in this short poem, which formed the basis for his early acceptance as a brilliant poet. Hughes uses the repeated line "My soul has grown deep like the rivers" to emphasize the way rivers symbolize not only the physical history of the African American but spiritual history ("my soul") as well. The river is also a symbol of the strength of black people as survivors who move through history. Finally, the rivers reflect the direct path of blacks to America.

The entire poem is based on an extended metaphor comparing the heritage of the African American to the great rivers of the world. The poet reveals the relationship between the river and the lives of black people, starting with a river known to be important during the earliest great civilizations and ending with a river on which slaves were transported, to be bought and sold in the slave markets of America.

Themes and Meanings

Langston Hughes was deeply concerned with the history and social condition of his people. "The Negro Speaks of Rivers" reflects the poet's interest in both topics. This poem also speaks of a mystic union of blacks throughout the world, for it traces their history back to the creation of the world, giving them credit for spanning time and for founding the greatest civilizations that humanity has ever known.

Hughes received the inspiration for this poem as he crossed the Mississippi River by train, feeling melancholy yet drawing pride from thoughts of the rivers that played a part in the history of his race. The images of beauty and death, and of hope and despair, all fused in his adolescent sensibility, causing him to create one of his most beautiful poems. The use of words such as "soul" and "rivers" allows Hughes to touch the deepest feelings and spiritual longings of his own soul and the souls of his people. With the use of the words "deep," "flow," "dusky," and "ancient," Hughes describes the actual rivers that were involved in black history, all the while emphasizing the long and glorious history of his race. With this poem, Hughes, often called "the poet of his people," plunges into the deep well of African-American history, uniting it with global African history.

The poem, with its allusions to the setting sun, human blood, and deep, dusky rivers, suffuses the images of death as it speaks of the immortality of the soul. Hughes celebrates the life of black people by acknowledging death, but the images of death presented in the poem are overshadowed by emphasis on the life of the soul—in this case, a racial soul which runs throughout time like a river. As the muddy water of the Mississippi turns golden in the sunset, so does the poet turn the memory of the history and survival of his people into brilliance. With images of water and pyramid, the verse suggests the endurance of the black physical presence and spirit from ancient Egypt to the nineteenth and twentieth centuries. The muddy Mississippi caused Hughes to think about the roles in human history played by the Congo, the Niger, and the Nile, as slaves were passed down these waters to be sold; once sold, these same slaves may have ended up being sold again on the Mississippi. The Mississippi also caused Hughes to think about Abraham Lincoln and the role he played in the abolition of slavery in America.

Pride in one's history is a constant theme in the poem. Hughes views the history of black people, even in slavery, with a sense of pride as he points out the ability of his people to survive their harsh and violent treatment in America. Hughes's confidence in the strength of blackness is a major part of his theme of pride; this confidence and pride is his legacy to African Americans. Black culture is still embattled, but Hughes provides a device for countering the argument that black people are without a vital and universal history.

Betty Taylor-Thompson

NEITHER OUT FAR NOR IN DEEP

Author: Robert Frost (1874-1963)
Type of poem: Lyric
First published: 1934; collected in *A Further Range*, 1936

The Poem

"Neither Out Far nor In Deep" is a lyric poem consisting of four four-line stanzas, making use of a regular rhyme scheme (*abab*). The meter is for the most part regular iambic trimeter, although several lines include one or two extra syllables. Only in the second stanza does Robert Frost provide precise imagery; for the most part, he relies on general description.

The setting of the poem is the seaside. The poet's original observation is that the people, out for a day's recreation at the beach, always look toward the water; "They turn their back on the land." What they can see are a ship out on the ocean, passing to an unknown destination, and a gull standing on the wet sand near the water.

This is apparently a puzzle, since there is more variety and presumably more of interest on the land than on the ocean, which does nothing but come to the beach and then retreat. The Line "Wherever the truth may be" in the third stanza suggests that the people are searching for the truth and hope to find it by watching the unchanging ocean, with its endless repetitions of the same movements, rather than on the land, which presumably is more subject to change.

The people being described, like everyone else, have limited vision: "They cannot look out far./ They cannot look in deep." Yet they keep on looking, presumably because there is nothing else for them to do. They cannot help searching for answers, even from such an unlikely source as the inscrutable ocean.

Forms and Devices

The regularity of the form and the abruptness of the lines reinforce the ironic tone of "Neither Out Far nor In Deep." The form implies a rigidity in the minds of the people being described, a lack of imagination which leads them always to look in one direction, however unrewarding their study may be. The poet distances himself from them with the occasional extra syllables which prevent the rhythm of the poem from taking on a sing-song quality.

The language and imagery are unusually generalized for Frost, who preferred to employ specific imagery. The poet does use the word "sand" to represent the entire shoreline, and the second stanza does contain relatively precise visual images of the ship, hull down out at sea, and the "standing gull," but all the other imagery in the poem is deliberately general. Those being described are not individualized in any way; they are simply "The people." That they lack individuality is emphasized by the fact that they turn a singular "back" to the land, instead of individual "backs." They all behave in the same way.

This generalized imagery continues in the third stanza. "The land" is given no specific qualities or dimensions; it only "may vary more." The ocean reaching the shore is not described in terms of breaking waves, foam, or swirling surf; it is only "the water." This seems to suggest that the people in their looking fail to see anything in detail, which can only be one more obstacle to their understanding.

What has seemed to be simple and general description of a common scene has become increasingly ironic through the first three stanzas, and the ironic tone becomes even more forceful in the final stanza, where the poet's scorn for those he describes becomes almost overwhelming. His scorn is not for the question they seem to ask, but for their approach to it. Their vision is extremely limited; they are neither far-sighted nor able to look deeply into the questions of existence. They hope that the ocean will give them answers to the ultimate questions, but they are looking at an aspect of the world which is simply there, unchanging in its nature, providing no answers at all. They continue to look, however, since the limitations on their ability to see has never prevented them from continuing their search. The heavy emphasis on the three final words accents the irony. The final irony, available to the reader, is that the poet is no better than they are; he cannot see any deeper or farther than they can.

Themes and Meanings

Frost's poems describing relatively ordinary scenes or events often conclude by raising much larger issues about the meaning of life and death and the nature of reality. Some of these poems, including the popular early poems "The Tuft of Flowers," "Two Look at Two," "The Onset," or the excellent but little-known late lyric, "On the Heart's Beginning to Cloud the Mind," conclude by suggesting a positive answer—that all will somehow be well, and that man's deepest fears are unjustified.

Yet as the critic Lionel Trilling pointed out in a famous speech, given at a dinner celebrating Frost's eighty-fifth birthday, there is another side to Frost's work which belies the easy confidence of those poems in which he assumes the guise of a kindly, reassuring old Yankee. "Neither Out Far nor In Deep," like such other poems as "Design," "Once by the Pacific," "Home Burial," and "Desert Places," evokes the grimness and eventual emptiness of human existence without offering any consolation or grounds for hope. This kind of poem represents an entirely different side of Frost, an entirely different way of responding to those ultimate questions.

"Neither Out Far nor In Deep" was one of the poems cited by Trilling. At first glance its inclusion among the author's grimmer works seems questionable. On the surface, the poem is little more than an amusing observation about an ordinary scene—people at beaches, after all, do always look toward the ocean, and what they see might well include a ship passing out at sea and at least one gull standing where a wave has left water on the sand.

The poem turns around with the second line of stanza 3, "But wherever the truth may be —." Frost here introduces the idea that the people looking toward the ocean are (or ought to be) doing more than casually staring; they hope that the ocean can somehow bring them the truth. As the final line makes clear, their looking is not casual, for they are keeping "watch." This suggests both alertness and danger, since those who keep watch, like soldiers, ordinarily do so because they fear what might be out there.

As the poem clearly suggests, however, their watch is futile. On the one hand, the ocean does not divulge its secrets; nothing happens except that "The water comes ashore" ceaselessly, an endless repetition of wave on wave, the ebb and flow of the tides, reflected in the rhythm of the short, insistent lines. On the other hand, their watch is futile because of the limitations imposed on human vision—these anonymous people are simply not equipped for the task of finding answers to the deeper questions of life.

Frost seems to have been unable to ignore questions of final meaning. Such questions crop up in a high percentage of his poems. The closest he came to resolving them was to say, in "On the Heart's Beginning to Cloud the Mind," "I knew a tale of a better kind" and to choose to believe that tale. In "Neither Out Far nor In Deep," however, he makes no such choice. Rather, he is both observer and participant in a search for meaning in which the searchers fear what they cannot see; the search for meaning is doomed to fail.

John M. Muste

NEW YEAR LETTER

Author: W. H. Auden (1907-1973)
Type of poem: Epistle/letter in verse
First published: 1941, as "Letter to Elizabeth Mayer"; collected in *The Double Man*, 1941

The Poem

"New Year Letter" is an occasional poem written to commemorate the beginning of 1940. Although it is a letter to W. H. Auden's friend Elizabeth Mayer, its scope greatly exceeds the parameters of most personal letters, as it reflects upon an incredible range of subjects. It can be considered primarily a meditation on World War II and a tribute to Auden's friend. The poem's three parts develop by association rather than by logic.

Part 1 focuses on the disorder of the world in 1940, the human desire for order, and the order that art creates. It begins with a depiction of Americans filing along the streets on January 1, 1940. Auden captures the mixed atmosphere of "singing," "sighing," "doubt," and anticipation in the United States; which had not yet entered the war but was acutely aware of it. The Americans' preoccupation with "Retrenchment, Sacrifice, Reform" reminds Auden of the atmosphere of anticipation and fear in Brussels "twelve months ago"—before the war had begun.

Vague about the cause of contemporary social problems, Auden describes Europe as a "haunted house" threatened by "the presence of The Thing." His concluding statements compare the worldwide dilemma to a crime in a conventional mystery novel: "The situation of our time/ Surrounds us like a baffling crime./ There lies the body half-undressed// And under lock and key the cause/ That makes a nonsense of our laws." The poet wants to warn against too easily blaming or accusing others. All are responsible for the crises of 1940: "our equipment all the time/ Extends the area of the crime/ Until the guilt is everywhere." The principles that underlie civilization have failed.

A discussion of art and a catalog of "great masters" of literature follow. Auden celebrates art because of its harmonious order, which can enlighten and inspire: "For art had set in order sense/ And feeling and intelligence,/ And from its ideal order grew/ Our local understanding." This tribute to art and artists, however, ranging from Dante through Rainer Maria Rilke, is confused by constant disclaimers. The impulse to impose art's order upon life willfully results in fascism. In this poem, he "would disown,/ The preacher's loose inmodest tone." "No words men write," Auden claims at the end of part 1, "can stop the war." Yet, art—the "greatest of vocations"—can give orders to be imitated and general parables that can be applied to the particulars of human lives: Just as it is necessary to search in order to understand the parables behind art, one must search to understand one's personal and political lives.

The danger inherent in art's order and the too fervent desire for order or "preacherly" truths is developed in part 2's discussion of the preference for absolutes, for "*idées fixes* to be/ True of a fixed Reality." Part 2 examines evil but always returns to the heresy of the search for absolutes. It begins with a portrait of an Inferno-like landscape, the world of World War II. The entire section maintains an allegorical atmosphere by personifying evil as the devil.

The fear of change and the desire for personal and social perfection lead to the monism that Auden decries in his criticisms of "vague idealistic art" and the "Simon-pure Utopian." Good and bad people alike have been guilty of fixed commitments to inflexible ideals. Auden demonstrates the inevitable error of such a devotion in his description of characters as disparate as the devil ("Prince of Lies"), Sarah Whitehead, William Wordsworth, and Karl Marx.

Although Auden believes in an eternity which transcends the imperfect human condition, he does not believe that humans can apprehend this perfection. The devil is the "Prince of Lies" because he pretends to be the "Spirit-that-denies" this imperfection. Ironically, Original Sin underlies the duality that the devil would disprove. Change is inevitable and, because of humanity's fallen nature, the truth cannot be known. Auden's discussions of Marx, Christ, and Charles Darwin praise them for the falsehoods that they betrayed. The inevitable duality of human beings and the impossibility of absolutes lead Auden to the paradox of the essential human condition. The ability to live with this paradox and to accept the multiplicity of human lives results in the "gift of double focus."

Part 3 develops the poem's recurring topics and specifically blames industrialism and the Enlightenment for World War II. It begins with a description of the disorder of New Year debauches in New York City, which Auden juxtaposes to the order and harmony of Mayer's house a week earlier. This order created by art and love is a model of the "real republic" for which all should strive. Yet, such order cannot be imposed. Humans live in an imperfect world of "Becoming" rather than a perfect world of "Being," which results in choice and freedom. Freely accepting the inevitable imperfection of the world can allow for moments of "perfect Being."

Auden next turns to the chaos and anxiety around him and contrasts the catastrophes of 1940 with the fall of Roman civilization. Whereas "Rome's hugger-mugger unity" was destroyed by the animal forces of barbarians, modern civilization has been destroyed by the intellectual powers of industry. Hitler—whom he describes as a "theologian" and a self-created "choice"—is a direct result of the selfishness that drives modern culture.

Auden insists that humans recognize that they live in both private and public worlds, explains the importance of history in the formation of human character, and reminisces about his childhood in England. England differs from the United States, which as a "fully alienated land" epitomizes the modern condition. These reflections on alienation lead to a description of the war in Europe, which he explicitly blames on the Renaissance and the Enlightment. The religious (Martin Luther, Councils, translations), philosophical (Michel de Montaigne, scholars), political ("Prince" Niccolo Machiavelli, cavalry), and scientific (navigation) changes of the

Renaissance resulted in "Empiric Economic Man." The rationality, selfishness, and free will of this new culture were responsible for isolation and loss of community.

Auden admits that the material conditions of human existence have improved and that this cultural revolution has never completely dominated: Jean-Jacques Rousseau, Søren Kierkegaard, William Blake, and Charles Baudelaire all protested its philosophy. The freedom that humans have given themselves has turned on them. They blame politicians and governments for failures, but a harmonic community necessitates an acceptance of personal responsibility for contemporary crises.

The rest of the poem indicts the selfishness, materialism, free will, and isolation of Empiric Economic Man, especially as realized in American culture. New York's skyscrapers are condemned as "secular cathedrals" and machines are blamed for revealing that "aloneness is man's real condition." Auden argues that the only way to create a unified community is to recognize failings and to accept others' weaknesses and differences: "true democracy begins/ With free confessions of our sins" and "all real unity commences/ In consciousness of differences."

The poet invokes a series of beneficent and loving powers (Unicorn, white childhood, Dove, Ichthus, Wind, Clock). He then addresses his "dear friend Elizabeth," whose loving kindness brings peace and "a warmth throughout the universe." He ends by admitting human imperfections and thanking Mayer for "forgiving, helping," and illuminating the world with love.

Forms and Devices

"New Year Letter" is a verse epistle in rhyming tetrameter couplets. It was the second poem in Auden's collection of poems entitled *The Double Man* (1941; entitled *New Year Letter* in England). Its fifty-six pages of rhymed couplets were followed by eighty-seven pages of notes to the poem. These notes include citations that explain particular lines, sections from works whose meanings bear on the poem, and additional poems by Auden. The poem is most fully understood with its explanatory notes and in the context of this volume.

Long and carefully contoured verse epistles and verse essays reached their height during the Augustan Period of English Literature with Alexander Pope and Jonathan Swift. Auden reverts to a decorous and social poetic form used by poets who lived in a more socially coherent time. His verse is formal; its rhythm and rhymes are exact. He uses this conventional, traditional verse to suggest the unity and coherence to which lives and art, and the world, should aspire.

Although he observes such traditional conventions, however, Auden uses many technical devices that call this order into question. Auden's shorter line gives his epistle a momentum and urgency that iambic pentameter couplets lack. His heavy use of enjambment also pressures the pace of his lines and prevents his couplets from becoming predictable or monotonous.

One of Auden's main arguments is the impossibility of absolute or "preacherly" truths. It is a great feat, however, to use a metaphysical and rational discourse while denying the validity of such a discourse. Auden undoes his primary discourse in several ways, especially in his notes to the text. Beneath the apparently smooth surface of tetrameter couplets lies an array of fragmented poems, notes, and excerpts which constantly suggests chaos. Auden's description of the "snarl of the abyss/ That always lies just underneath/ Our jolly picnic on the heath" could apply to the relationship between the poem and its notes.

The self-consciousness of Auden's use of traditional form, apparent in the omnipresent comedy and humor, destabilizes the text. Comic rhymes—such as "links and thinks"—present specific examples of the humor that pervades this text: The devil knows "that he's lost if someone ask him/ To come the hell in off the links/ And say exactly what he thinks." Comic rhyme and diction constantly undermine the authority of the poem, even as it speaks wisdom. Humorous and irreverent diction, such as "through the Janus of a joke/ The candid psychopompos spoke," seems to trivialize Auden's insights. They exist, however, in order to avoid the egotism and self-importance that he deplores.

Another prominent formal device is the use of periphrasis or euphemism. Auden rarely names his subjects: He does not say, "We are at war," but rather mentions "the situation of our time." His description of war or fascism as "the presence of The Thing" that hangs over Europe is vague and unspecific. He does not name Rousseau, Marx, Christ, or Darwin, but rather refers elliptically to "a liberal fellow-traveler," "the German who,/ Obscure in gaslit London," "the ascetic farmer's son," and the "naturalist, who fought/ Pituitary headaches." The United States is "that other world" in which I stand/ Of fully alienated land." Auden's refusal to name is a denial of authority and is a way of involving the reader in his text. The poem insists that literature be used as parables to help unravel the mystery novels of history. Auden's evasion compels the reader to probe and search his poem as he would have one probe and search the world for understanding.

Themes and Meanings

Auden surveys the world around him in 1940 and finds isolated individuals at war with one another. He wants a plural, loving community which he describes at various points in the poem: "The seamless live continuum/ Of supple and coherent stuff,/ Whose form is truth, whose content love,/ Its pluralistic interstices/ The homes of happiness and peace,/ Where in a unity of praise/ The largest *publicum*'s a *res*,/ And the least *res* a *publicum*. The importance of a genuine, unselfish love touches almost every aspect of Auden's discussion. Great art, for example, is praised because of its ability for "charity, delight, increase." The tribunal of former artists who oversee contemporary artists do not judge them, but rather "love" them. Marx is praised because of his charity and because of his discovery that "none shall receive unless they give;/ All must co-operate to live."

In order to undo the isolating and alienating tendencies of civilization, Auden suggests humble acceptance of one's own limitations and living a life which contributes to others. Auden's letter itself acts out many of the aspects central to his message. As both a letter and a tribute to his friend Elizabeth Mayer, it is a loving and unselfish act which gestures outside himself and ends in humble recognition of his own inadequacies. It is also important to Auden's themes that both he and Mayer are exiles—aliens in the most alienated of countries—and that she is German. Auden cautions against too quickly casting blame for "the situation of our time" on one nation, people, or political party. Adolf Hitler is a product of a civilization for which all are responsible. By hating or dismissing all Germans, the Allies would be no better than he.

The description of Auden's loving community—"the seamless live continuum"— ends with *res* and *publicum* united. Personal responsibility for civilization's founderings means that a thing cannot be separated meaningfully from its society. Part 3 explains the fallacy of presuming that public and private lives can be separated. "New Year Letter," however, highlights the importance of the private life by continually recurring to the little worlds of order that Mayer creates. Preoccupations with political problems were causing Auden's contemporaries to shun the private life and to disdain the personal as a subject of poetry. "New Year Letter" makes clear that personal gardens must be cultivated if the public situation is to be salvaged. The poet's frequent turning from general description to personal address highlights this fact.

The importance of both public and private lives is implicated in the title of this volume, *The Double Man*. The title embraces the multiple aspects of human beings and underlines the most important operative principle in the poem: paradox. This paradox resulted from the Fall and has governed the human existence of mixed uncertainty and faith ever since. The inevitability of human imperfections accounts for the mixed tone that describes life as a "reverent frivolity" and that underlies the confusing, tortured play with words and contradictions. The omnipresence of paradox discredits linear, rational thought.

Laura Cowan

NEW YEAR LETTER

Author: Marina Tsvetayeva (1892-1941)
Type of poem: Epistle/letter in verse
First published: 1928; as "Novogodnee"; in *Versty III*; collected in *Selected Poems*, 1987

The Poem

One of the greatest friendships in the life of the Russian poet Marina Tsvetayeva was conducted wholly by letter during a few months of 1926 with the Austrian writer Rainer Maria Rilke. Rilke, the most important German-language poet of the twentieth century, represented for Tsvetayeva the ideal poet. After Rilke died unexpectedly on December 29, 1926, Tsvetayeva's shock and grief took the form of several works in prose and verse that reacted to his death. "New Year Letter," written in February, 1927, is an attempt to come to terms with Rilke's death. It also represents one side of a companionable conversation between two poets about their craft and constitutes a statement about Tsvetayeva's philosophy of poetry.

The poem, written in the first person and addressed to Rilke, opens with the traditional Russian New Year's greeting, *S novym godom*, "Happy New Year." Tsvetayeva calls the poem "my first epistle to you in your new/ . . . place"—that is, in the afterworld—thus implying that the poem is a continuation of their previous correspondence and denying the power of death. The poem then describes how Tsvetayeva learned of Rilke's death when an acquaintance dropped by to ask if she would write a memorial piece about him for a newspaper. Tsvetayeva, who cannot conceive that the great poet is dead, and who regards an acknowledgment of his death as a kind of betrayal, refuses; most of the remaining part of the poem is concerned with her ideas about writing as an act of immortality, and about the life of the poet as both eternal and full of sacrifice. It is couched in the form of a letter to Rilke, who, as a newcomer in heaven, is still getting accustomed to the working conditions there.

The poem alludes to a number of things that appear in the two poets' letters to each another (such as Rilke's questions about specific Russian words) or in Rilke's poetry (such as the famous Orlov trotting horses, which appear in his poem "Nächtliche Fahrt. St. Petersburg" [1908, Night Ride, St. Petersburg]). Throughout the poem, Tsvetayeva asks Rilke questions about his new state of being, assuming almost the role of an interviewer. She wants to know what the journey was like, and asks about his first impressions of the universe and his last ones of the planet Earth. Tsvetayeva implicitly compares the human world to a sad farce when she portrays Rilke leaning over the "scarlet rim" of his theater box and looking down on humanity from his position beyond death.

In the next section, the focus shifts from Rilke's new situation to Tsvetayeva's, as she recalls that New Year's Eve is almost upon her, and wonders with whom and to what she can drink a toast. Rilke's death has made her pensive, and she does not wish to celebrate in the usual boisterous fashion. Instead, she says, she will drink a quiet toast with Rilke to his new, third state of being, which is neither life nor death, but, she implies, a kind of place outside time where poetry is created. Tsvetayeva ponders the many obstacles that life throws in the path of a poet and concludes that Rilke has achieved this new state, where he will create with a "new sound," "new echo," "new hand-position."

The last section presents Tsvetayeva's wishful vision of the afterlife: a succession of Heavens ascending like terraces; a succession of growing, mutable Gods (referring to a central image in Rilke's works); and finally, a ladder rising into the sky above Rarogne, the Swiss village where Rilke is buried. The poem ends with the poet's hopes of someday meeting Rilke after all, and with the image of Tsvetayeva herself climbing up the ladder, her hands filled with gifts for him—the gifts of her poems.

Forms and Devices

"New Year Letter" is a poem of some 195 lines of varying length that uses a variety of metrical patterns. Rather than being organized into regular stanzas, the poem is divided into sections, ranging from four to thirty-two lines long, according to subject matter and to the rhythm of the poet's thought processes. Sections sometimes contrast with the sections that precede them in tone or lexical level, as, for example, when an emotionally charged passage is followed by a laconic, colloquial one. One device that serves as a kind of structural leitmotif is the formula "Happy . . . ," which is used in the first line to wish Rilke a happy New Year. This phrase, with other objects substituted for "New Year"—such as "Happy break of day," "Happy whole me," "Happy new world"—appears throughout the poem. The phrase underscores the sense of new beginnings associated both with the day and with Tsvetayeva's conception of the "third state" in which Rilke now finds himself. It also bears with it the theme of generosity and giving, which was important to both poets and figured in their correspondence.

It is difficult to explain the linguistic innovations of a poem written in one language to an audience who will read it in another. This is especially true of Tsvetayeva, whose uniqueness lies at least in part in her bold, fresh treatment of Russian. Her poetry is technically challenging even for a Russian reader. She is known for her strong, rapidly changing rhythms, which can resemble anything from jazz to a religious chant.

Equally characteristic is her unusual approach to rhyme. "New Year Letter" is a good example of this, and the David McDuff translation does a good job of reproducing the effect, though the specific rhymes cannot be carried over. Except for one short section, the poem is written in rhymed couplets. Tsvetayeva uses a variety of rhyme types, from true rhyme, sometimes several syllables deep, to mere assonance (repetition of vowel sounds) or consonance (repetition of consonant sounds). The fact that many of these rhymes are only approximate makes the overall effect subtle and unobtrusive. It is only on second reading that one realizes the unusual juxtapositions. The pattern of rhymed couplets is sustained except for a four-line section in which Tsvetayeva, realizing that Rilke has been freed by death to devote himself totally to poetry, reverts to the formula of the New Year's greeting and wishes him a "Happy new sound," a "Happy new echo." Here Tsvetayeva uses an alternating rhyme in an *abab* pattern, and rhymes the words *drug* and *zvuk* (friend and sound). In life, she says, everything was a hindrance to Rilke's work, even passion and friendship. Now he will be able to work unhindered, and his words will harmonize with his world, as *sound* and *friend* are now allowed to harmonize in rhyme.

Another peculiarity of Tsvetayeva is her habit of inserting foreign words into the Russian line, even in the rhyming position. There are several examples of macaronic (multilingual) rhyming in this poem, such as *krajnyj* (extreme) and *Rainer*, Rilke's first name, or *ladon'ju* (with my palm) with *Rarogn'a*, the site of Rilke's grave. Tsvetayeva was fluent in German and French, and as she made clear in numerous poems, essays, and letters, she felt a profound kinship with Germanic culture. Acutely aware of language, she apologizes to her friend for writing to him in her native Russian instead of German, the tongue in which she had written to him in life. She seems to feel that using Russian creates a greater distance between them than has Rilke's death itself. Then, however, Tsvetayeva makes a point that she had already made in her letters to Rilke and elsewhere: The specific language in which one writes is immaterial, since all poets write in the same "angelic" language that transcends nationality. Her mixing of languages is a symbol of her belief that the boundaries between languages, between nations, are evanescent.

Themes and Meanings

It has been suggested that any poem written as a lament for the dead has a strong autobiographical component. In other words, the poem tells the reader as much about the living poet as it does about the dead person. This is true on several levels in "New Year Letter," and each level illustrates a major theme of the poem. Tsvetayeva is the first-person heroine of her own poem, addressing Rilke from a number of points of view. First, she writes as a person deprived of a friend whom she never met. She and her fellow Russian poet Boris Pasternak had planned to visit Rilke in Switzerland, but the latter's sudden death destroyed those plans. In the poem, Tsvetayeva muses on what it would have been like to have had a rendezvous and a chat with Rilke in a poor Paris suburb like the one in which she lives.

Second, "New Year Letter" is a kind of love poem. Always impulsive, Tsvetayeva in her letters to Rilke had quickly assumed the personal *du* form of address, and her tone of intimacy and longing had nearly frightened Rilke away. Now, with no chance that a relationship can ever develop between them, Tsvetayeva laments as if for a dead lover, while at the same time admitting poignantly but accurately that "nothing has worked out for us at all." They were never lovers—indeed, they never even met—but Tsvetayeva feels she knows Rilke so well through his words, and through the things they have in common, that she claims the right to address him as if they had been.

Finally, Tsvetayeva writes as a poet whose main concern is her craft, and who regards Rilke as an inspiration, a symbol, and her own ideal audience—for who but a master poet can fully understand another? In their correspondence and in the poems he wrote for her, Rilke had helped Tsvetayeva through a crisis of insecurity about her work. Living in poverty in Parisian exile, she was often faced with problems of literal survival for herself and her family. Her poetry was constantly threatened by lack of time, energy, solitude, and even an audience, since the Russian political situation had virtually deprived her of readers. Rilke himself had been forced to make difficult decisions concerning the role of poetry in his life; painfully but firmly, he had chosen his art, to the exclusion of family and a life as a normal social being. By his friendship, his example, and the literary fruits of his sacrifice, Rilke had encouraged Tsvetayeva to go on.

For Tsvetayeva, Rilke was also a symbol of all poets. Elsewhere she refers to him as Orpheus, the greatest singer in Greek mythology, and in "New Year Letter" she says of the heaven she imagines for him, "If you're there, so is verse, in any case," thus equating him with poetry itself! By writing this "letter" to Rilke, engaging him in a dialogue about his writing and hers, it must have seemed to Tsvetayeva that she was somehow keeping him alive, postponing the time when she must admit his physical death, and therefore both the possibility of mortality and the death of poetry. Throughout the poem, Tsvetayeva echoes themes and images that play a central role in Rilke's writing: death, love, the angels, God, childhood, poetry. In "New Year Letter," she has created both a tribute to a loved fellow poet and a promise to go on writing herself, in the face of all obstacles.

Patricia Pollock Brodsky

NIGHT

Author: Robert Bly (1926-   )
Type of poem: Lyric
First published: 1962, in *Silence in the Snowy Fields*

The Poem

"Night," written in free verse, is a short poem divided into four sections, each of which is four lines long. Like many of Robert Bly's titles, "Night" appears to be a title without pretense or philosophical complexity; the poem is, however, richer in meaning than the title indicates. Night is a time for dreamlike thought, unmoored from the world of daylight's reason and logic. Bly's four sections offer four visions of night's mysteries.

The poem is written in the first person, but it moves from a particular first-person-singular speaker—Bly himself—to a more generalized first-person plural. By writing in the first-person plural—"we"—the poet takes an enormous risk, because he appears to be speaking for all humanity. When a poet says "I," the reader must believe the speaker. When a poet says "we," thereby including the reader in his or her pronouncement, the reader may object to the statement or worldview.

The poem begins with what appears to be an extremely logical "if/then" proposition: "If I think of a horse," then "I feel a joy." Bly complicates the logic, however, by appending what appears to be an odd metaphor: If he thinks of a horse he feels joyful, as if he had thought of a pirate ship. The circular movement from thought to joy and then back to thought again is counteracted by the centrifugal force in the logic of the poem that jumps from the horse in a field to a pirate ship surrounded by flowers. The mood of the poem is immediately set by the dreamlike logic of the metaphors and the poem's eccentric movement.

The second section is typical of Bly's work: He anthropomorphizes the natural world. The happiness Bly felt in section 1 becomes so contagious that even the box elder trees "are full of joy." The magic of night leads to the melting together of normally separate objects: The horse becomes like a ship, and the joy passes from Bly the observer to the observed trees. Because it is night, Bly tries to convince the reader that the lilacs and the plants are sleeping, once again blurring the boundaries between things by anthropomorphizing. The final image is loaded: "Even the wood made into a casket is asleep." The wood still participates in the natural order, being able to sleep as well as the lilacs, even though it has undergone the transformation from nature's tree to humans' wood. Of course, the casket is also the final resting place for someone lodging in the realm of eternal sleep.

The third stanza once again melds disparate realms. The butterfly joins earth with air by carrying "loam on his wings," while the amphibian toad—the bridge between two worlds—joins earth with water by "bearing tiny bits of granite in his skin." The zone of sleep in section 2 is revisited in the final image of section 3, in which the tree leaves and "bits of earth at its root" are asleep.

The concluding section wakes up the poem with copious movement. If the trees and plants can sleep like humans, why cannot a person be like a "sleek black water beetle./ Skating across still water"? In a "night poem," the possible metamorphoses are endless. The final change in the poem is perhaps the most startling. In a poem that has been silent, devoid of voices and animal sounds, the final image of a mouth opening, not to speak but to swallow, is arresting. The poem is stopped by death.

Forms and Devices

"Night" is so deceptively simple that a reader might miss the careful structuring in the poem. Generally, there is a falling away or a downward movement in each of the four sections. The first three prepare the reader for the jolt of the final macabre image of death swallowing its victim.

In the first stanza, a scene filled only with moonlight is transformed when Bly imagines a horse "wandering about sleeplessly." The thought of this horse is immediately replaced by that of the pirate ship, and the horse's sleeplessness gives way to the sleep-coated trees and plants and flowers in the rest of the poem. The poet proffers one thing, then takes it away. The second stanza drops from the heights of the box elder tree to the lilacs and plants and, finally, into the casket, which might already be in the ground. The third stanza recapitulates this downward movement twice: It begins with a loamy butterfly on the wing and moves downward to a granite-infested toad; it observes the crown of a tree and ends with the "earth at its root."

This downward movement echoes the thematic transformation from joy to the eeriness of death. The concluding death of the beetle is everyone's death, which should not come as a complete surprise. Each section tries to warn the reader by establishing this pattern of presence and disappearance, of flight and a final resting place in the earth. Each person is like the beetle skating across the water in seemingly perfect freedom, only to discover that will means nothing in the end. Each person moves from life to death as easily as this night poem shifts from the crowns of trees to the earth around their roots.

Each section of the poem enacts the death of the beetle. The poet's imagination apparently skates along in any direction it wills, but the form of the poem belies this haphazardness. Each time the poet tries a flight of fancy, the world of death pulls him down. Night is a time when the imagination runs wild, but finally, at least in this poem, the imagination runs back to the ultimate form of night, which is death.

Themes and Meanings

The form of the poem as discussed earlier, leads the reader to its meaning. The poem suggests the obvious truth that human beings often want to ignore: Life leads to death as inevitably as day leads to night. Despite the downward movement within each stanza, however, Bly also seems to suggest that joy need not be forgotten simply because decline is inevitable.

Bly risks using the pathetic fallacy—providing nature with human traits—in order to remove the boundaries that normally exist between the natural world and the human one. The risk lies in the believability of the image: Do plants really sleep? Can trees feel joy? Do trees actually obey anything, since obedience implies will? Bly would like to remove this world of reason because he sees in it the basis for human alienation from the environment. In Bly's world, one enters a mythic landscape before the fall, in which the human and the natural elements are one.

The poem resists a totally depressing reading as a result of this use of the pathetic fallacy. If the trees and plants are like humans, why cannot humans be like them? The trees are full of joy, at least in Bly's eyes, even though their death is inevitable. The earth that gives them life is also the earth that will accept them in death. The butterflies, emblematic of the spirit world, contain bits of earth or loam in their wings; their flight joins spirit and flesh, life and death. If the poem suggests that death is contained in life, the other side of the argument is also put forth: Life is contained in death. In another poem in *Silence in the Snowy Fields*, "Summer, 1960, Minnesota," Bly creates an image that is very similar to the closing one in "Night":

> Yet, we are falling,
> Falling into the open mouths of darkness,
> Into the Congo as into a river,
> Or as wheat into open mills.

The image of falling into a dark mouth is bleaker in "Night" only because one is not given a clear picture of what happens on the other side. In "Summer, 1960, Minnesota," the transformation of wheat into bread in the open mouths of the mill suggests that there is no such thing as death; in "Night," the final image of the skating beetle being sucked under can have positive resonances only if one remembers previous poems in the collection or the hints of metamorphosis given earlier in the poem. If things are constantly changing places inside a poem, then there can be no final, gruesome image: Death must lead to something else, even if that something else is present only in the white space at the end of the poem.

In Bly's world, tragedy comes from a willful struggle to deny what is inevitable; comedy, or true joy, derives, as in the case of the box elders, from "obeying what is beneath them." Death is always lying beneath one, no matter how easily or comfortably one is skating along. In order to achieve the type of joy that Bly thinks is possible, one has to become one with the animals and all created things and say yes to life, a life that has death as its final word. The trick seems to be that, in order to become like leaves or loam, one must dispense with the kind of self-consciousness that makes art possible. Bly, by writing in unrhymed free verse that is extremely associative in its organization, seems to suggest that an unfettered imagination can be the key to a healthy mind and soul. The very care with which he organizes his poem's structure, however, points to the paradox at the center of his poem: Death is in life, and life is in death; pain is in joy, and joy is in pain.

Kevin Boyle

NIGHT AND MORNING

Author: Austin Clarke (1896-1974)
Type of poem: Lyric
First published: 1938, in *Night and Morning*

The Poem

"Night and Morning" is a short poem of thirty-six lines, divided into four stanzas with nine lines each. The title indicates the direction the poem moves—from night to morning—but also the division of feeling expressed by the speaker, who has thoughts at night that subvert his feelings in the morning.

The first stanza opens with a statement of certain knowledge, as the speaker expresses his personal identification with those who have suffered misery for hundreds of years. As in a dream, in his sleep he feels the injury of pride, the shame of mockery, and the humiliation of insult. These are elements of the suffering narrated in the Passion of Christ, as suggested by the reference to "the house of Caesar." This identification is only partial, however, since the speaker's thoughts are divided by doubts. The result is that he is tormented into a despair that must borrow clothing to disguise his doubts.

When morning comes, in the second stanza, the speaker goes to Mass, where he arrives with others at the appointed hour. He observes the celebration of Holy Eucharist (Holy Communion) as a ritual of mere appearances: There is no awesome transformation of the wafer and wine into the body and blood of Christ. The priest turns his back on his congregation when he adores his God. The speaker still feels his spiritual torment, even after Mass, even after the saints have all been celebrated.

In his continuing torment, the speaker recalls in the third stanza how humble acts of faith in the past have annihilated the complications of thought and deliberation. He recalls that many have labored, in great intellectual discourses, from rostrums, in early morning hours of composition, to lift simple life into heights of significance. All those labors, however, are now as forgotten as are the many intellectual martyrs who sought to restore truths of dead languages (including Latin) into living ideas.

Finally, in the last stanza, the speaker celebrates the time when, long ago, Europe was alive with intellectual debate and followed the lead of logic. Then the reality of heaven united with the reality of earth; human beings felt whole, proud, and united in their communion with one another. In that time, faith was a product of intellectual commitment, as divinity shared its being with humanity: "God was made man once more."

Forms and Devices

"Night and Morning" is both a form of confession and an internal debate. It uses metaphors and allusion within a framework of irony to make its meaning rich and complex. As a confession, it may be spoken to a priest, or a psychoanalyst, but it is confessional mainly in an ironic sense: What ought to be confessed, loss of faith, cannot be confessed to those with faith. It can only be expressed, or confessed, to one's self. In this respect, the poem has the form of a debate between body and soul, with a translation of the disputants into "thought" and "belief."

Biblical and church (Roman Catholic) allusions give the poem context and orientation. "The house of Caesar" of stanza 1 is countered by "the nave," "the altar," "adoring priest," and "the congregation" of the second stanza. Kneeling and Holy Communion (Eucharist) allude to church ritual in the third stanza, continued into the final stanza with its "choir" and making of God into man. The poem alludes to specific biblical events from the New Testament and the church calendar, beginning with the Passion of Christ in the first stanza, All Saints' Day in the second, "cockrise" and "miracle that raised . . . the dead" in the third (as references to the Resurrection and the raising of Lazarus). Historical allusions are broadened in the third stanza, with "councils and decrees" (such as the Council of Trent) and scholastic debates of the Middle Ages and Renaissance in the last stanza's "learned controversy" and "holy rage of argument."

Metaphors join abstractions with concrete images to dramatize the pain of intellectual doubt: "the tormented soul . . . must wear a borrowed robe," "minds that bled," and "logic led the choir." Metaphors also unite logical contraries in conceits of paradox: "every moment that can hold . . . the miserable act/ Of centuries," and "God was made man." When these are expressed from within a framework of irony, they acquire an additional feeling of pain. Their very expression becomes subject to doubt, as if to say, it is not church figures who have bled in body for humankind — rather, it is the intellectual skeptics, the doubters themselves, who have bled and sacrificed to make possible a religious history of doubtful substance.

Irony unfolds at the center of the poem, when the speaker observes that the priest turns "his back/ Of gold upon the congregation." Literally, this occurs in the celebration of the Mass; figuratively, it exposes the sterile and hypocritical relationship of priests (church/religion/faith) to people. Irony here develops from the device of punning, continued into the final couplet of the second stanza: "All saints have had their day at last,/ But thought still lives in pain." Besides echoing the expression "Every dog has its day," this couplet turns upon the celebration of "All Saints' Day" to show how ineffective it is in relieving the speaker's spiritual pain.

Themes and Meanings

"Night and Morning" has three main themes. Modern individuals of thought and education find it difficult to hold on to traditional religious beliefs; moreover, the modern Church has failed to keep alive the faith of the past, because the modern Church does not foster intellectual inquiry. Finally, modern individuals suffer from internal conflicts of self-division, hidden under the same cloak of hypocrisy that afflicts the institution of the Church itself.

These themes are developed in ironic and self-critical ways. Intellect should be laid to rest during the sleep of night, but instead it asserts itself to challenge faith. Ironically, at night the speaker can most fully identify with the suffering Christ, because the speaker suffers most at night from his pain of doubt. The Church, like the priest, turns its back not only on the people of the congregation, but also on its own history; its "many councils and decrees/ Have perished," partly because they did not address individual needs, partly because they did not educate simple minds, and partly because they were merely abstractions without force to survive uncomprehending persons who submitted without thought—"gave obedience to the knee." Instead of keeping Europe "astir/ With echo of learned controversy," the Church has acquiesced to a passive authoritarianism.

The consequence of that acquiescence, for a person of thought, is unbearable agony. Unable to believe in miracles and mysteries entirely, yet unable to refuse belief entirely, the speaker resigns himself to sharp self-division: He goes through the motions, like other "appointed shadows," gives "obedience to the knee," and observes "the miracle" in which "God was made man once more." At night, however, after the "dreadful candle" is snuffed, he will know once again "the injured pride of sleep."

The meaning produced by this mixture of themes is that the modern mind suffers beneath the appearance of conformity to public ritual. It goes on with the appearance, wearing "a borrowed robe," because it does not have a more certain answer to spiritual questions. It yearns for the vitality of a past when thought and belief were one, but in the present that yearning is felt as a burden, not a relief, of history. Read again after one has finished the final stanza, "Night and Morning" grows in power and complication. The first stanza reads with more pain, more even than the pain of the suffering body of Christ, because the speaker cannot be relieved by the Passion and sacrifice—he can only be tormented, like Christ himself. Night brings more suffering, with confession of unbelief, to the morning, with its confession of belief. Darkness of night produces enlightenment within the speaker; light of morning conceals an interior darkness of soul.

These themes are elaborated with variations by the ten lyrics that follow "Night and Morning" in Austin Clarke's *Night and Morning* collection of 1938: from the ironies of celebrating Holy Week as the shadows of "Tenebrae," through the thoughtless, almost inhuman ritual observances of "Martha Blake," to the unholy madness exhibited when the "heavens opened" to reveal deep darkness in "Summer Lightning." Such themes and such poems represented a significant turn in the career of Clarke; he pressed more of his painful emotions more often into such bitter and ironic lyrics as those introduced by "Night and Morning."

Richard D. McGhee

NIKKI-ROSA

Author: Nikki Giovanni (1943-   )
Type of poem: Lyric
First published: 1968, in *Black Judgement*

The Poem

"Nikki-Rosa," a short, introspective poem of thirty lines, dispenses with the conventional marks of written poetry—punctuation and capitalization—creating the effect of the narrator speaking directly to her audience. The title, "Nikki-Rosa," suggests the merging of the personal life with the public or political one and indicates the evolution of a radical, from the girl Nikki to the militant Rosa, the name alluding to Rosa Parks, a Civil Rights activist.

In the poem, a black narrator addresses a black audience, assuming a store of shared experiences, experiences that would be foreign to a white middle-class audience. The narrator—a woman, as indicated by the title—realizes that her childhood contained a mixture of good and bad events. Nevertheless, the negative memories, caused by poverty, are outweighed by the positive, provided by a strong, close family. Unfortunately, "they," the critics and biographers, will record the lack of an "inside toilet" but will fail to mention the warm baths given in "one of those/ big tubs that folk in Chicago barbecue in." The critics will "never talk about how happy you were to have your mother/ all to yourself." The narrator fears that the simple pleasures of her childhood will be overlooked.

The poem juxtaposes the events of the narrator's youth with future biographers' misreading or misinterpretation. The biographers will mention her father's drinking and her parents' fighting but miss the closeness of the extended family. They will not see "that everybody is together and you/ and your sister have happy birthdays and very good christmasses." The biographer will notice the poverty but not the richness of the strong, supportive family. They will not understand that "Black love is Black wealth." Because of this blindness, the narrator hopes that "no white person ever has cause to write about me." The white critics would note the hardships but miss the love: "they'll/ probably talk about my hard childhood and never understand that/ all the while I was quite happy."

Forms and Devices

The poem "Nikki-Rosa," void of any punctuation, appears as one long thought. The memories of childhood are jumbled together, much the way someone would remember his or her youth. This seemingly formless nature of the poem thus mimics the thought processes of the narrator. The particular events merge, leaving the feel of a happy childhood that presumably would elude the biographer or critic.

Nikki Giovanni's poems, including "Nikki-Rosa," are accessible to a wide and diverse audience primarily because the images are drawn from everyday life and the language is simple and direct. This accessibility has made her a very popular poet;

her public readings have large audiences and her books and sound recordings enjoy good sales. In "Nikki-Rosa," as well as in many other of Giovanni's poems, the commonplace images are taken specifically from a working-class setting. The narrator describes family meetings, birthdays, and a large tub used for bathing. Thus the poem presents a realistic portrayal of day-to-day family life.

Rooted in an oral tradition, Giovanni in "Nikki-Rosa" combines ordinary language with the natural rhythms of speech. She avoids dense vocabulary and obscure symbols and allusions, relying instead on simple words, a conversational tone, and the clarity of the lines to convey her meaning.

Themes and Meanings

"Nikki-Rosa" introduces several themes that are important to the poem, to Giovanni's other poems, and to her development as a poet. "Nikki-Rosa" first appeared in *Black Judgement* (1968), which contains both revolutionary poems and brief, introspective lyrics. The political poems from the volume received the most critical attention and earned for Giovanni the reputation of a radical militant. Her work was discussed as part of the "new Black poetry of hate." These poems were the result of anger caused by the continued oppression of blacks, and the poems urged violence, black assertiveness, aggression, and black pride. Nevertheless, the lyrics, with their emphasis on the individual and on relationships, prefigure her later work.

"Nikki-Rosa" contains both elements and therefore bridges the gap between the two styles. The poem, written on April 12, 1968, a few days after the funeral of Martin Luther King, Jr., hints at the division between whites and blacks: "I really hope no white person ever has cause to write about me." Whites cannot understand the black experience. In addition, because of the power structure in America, whites should be held accountable for the poverty that is experienced by many blacks, poverty caused by an inferior education, lack of social services, and discrimination.

"Nikki-Rosa" presents the childhood of a girl from an impoverished family who later will become a black activist. Nikki, the young girl, will grow up to be the radical Rosa. The name Rosa recalls Rosa Parks, who, in 1955, refused to give up her bus seat to a white rider, precipitating the year-long Montgomery, Alabama, bus boycott that brought national recognition to Martin Luther King, Jr.

While it is tempting to see the Nikki of the poem as Nikki Giovanni, it is best not to. Giovanni, from a middle-class family, did not experience directly the poverty of the narrator, although as a child she learned about urban poverty from her parents, who were social workers. As a college freshman, she considered herself a Goldwater Republican. Nevertheless, through the example of her outspoken, militant grandmother and because of the events of the 1960's—the antiwar demonstrations; the Civil Rights Movement; the assassinations of Malcolm X, John F. Kennedy, Martin Luther King, Jr., and Robert Kennedy; and the riots in various urban centers throughout the nation—she became radicalized. Thus, while the poem is not strictly autobiographical, it does suggest the development of a radical consciousness that parallels the development of Giovanni's.

The poem hints at the anger that is found in the other poems in the volume and in *Black Feeling, Black Talk* (1968), but primarily "Nikki-Rosa" emphasizes the importance of the love and support that is often found in the black family, a theme that becomes important in her later volumes, such as *The Women and the Men* (1975). As seen in "Nikki-Rosa," the love of the immediate and extended family can overcome the problems that poverty engenders. It is the family that will enable its members to survive the racism that is prevalent in the society. A strong black family will lead to a strong black community, which in turn leads to a strong black nation. This evolution is Giovanni's hope: As she writes in the autobiographical work *Gemini* (1971), "I really like to think a Black, beautiful, loving world is possible." The wealth of the black community is not measured in stocks, savings accounts, and possessions but in something more intangible, love. Outside the black community, however, "they never understand Black love is Black wealth."

"Nikki-Rosa" hints at the radical nature of Giovanni's early poems. Yet, more importantly, it points to the direction that her later poems would take, a shift to a more humanistic view which encompasses all races.

Barbara Wiedemann

THE NINE MONSTERS

Author: César Vallejo (1892-1938)
Type of poem: Meditation
First published: 1939, as "Los neuve monstruos," in *Poemas humanos*; collected
   in *The Complete Posthumous Poems*, 1978

The Poem

"The Nine Monsters" is a seventy-line poem, divided into four stanzas of varying
lengths. The poem is written loosely in the form of an address, perhaps a speech, in
which the poet discourses on the subjects of pain and misfortune to an audience of
"human men" and "brother men." It would appear that the poem begins somewhere
in the middle of the speech, since the opening line of the poem implies continued
speech.

After the outbreak of the Spanish Civil War in 1936, César Vallejo was active as a
vocal defender of the Spanish Republic. In Paris, where he had lived since 1923, he
attended meetings and assemblies and helped in the effort to raise money for the
Republican cause. While autobiographical information is not necessary to study
"The Nine Monsters," it is helpful to know that at the time Vallejo wrote the poem
(it is dated November 3, 1937), he was out canvassing the streets and speaking to
crowds about the war. The speechlike nature of the poem is more apparent in this
context.

In the first stanza, the poet or speaker notes the rapid and ceaseless spread of pain
in the world. Pain has become the dominant fact of life, so much so that those who
suffer are virtually martyrs to it. Pain is so great that it constantly redoubles itself.

The speaker then turns his attention, in the second stanza, to the historical moment. It is the age of pain, he says. There has never been a time more vulnerable to
its debilitating attack. Even affection has been marred by pain. Health, paradoxically, means death. Everything conceals pain, and the speaker wishes to draw everyone's attention to the fact—even the government (the secretary of health) must hear
his appeal.

The third stanza shifts attention to pain's cousins: misfortune, evil, and suffering;
they, too, are spreading rapidly, flooding the world and overturning the established
order. At this point, the speaker elaborates on the "nine monsters" of the title. Six
times in six lines he repeats the number nine, each time using it to enumerate another aspect of what, presumably, constitutes the monsters mentioned in the title.
One thing is sure: The "monsters" are closely connected to sound, primarily apocalyptic sound.

The fourth stanza is the poem's longest. Whereas in the previous stanzas the
speaker has commented on the extent of pain in the world and on the places where it
is active, in stanza 4, the reader's attention is directed to the activity of pain. Pain is
seen as an active force. It grabs people, drives them wild, nails them, denails them.
In effect, pain is personified; it comes alive and stalks human beings. It is associated

with creative and destructive principles: Life and death occur "as a result/ of the pain."

The poem ends with the speaker's personal agony, the sadness he feels at witnessing this enormous suffering. It is all too much for him; there is nothing to be done about it; the extent of the suffering is too vast.

Forms and Devices

The distinguishing characteristic of Vallejo's poetic technique is his extraordinary ability to shatter language—the very thing poetry depends on—and through its deconstruction, to create a new (albeit esoteric and unnatural) medium to communicate the chaos he sees all around. In essence, Vallejo conveys his message by destroying the traditional means by which a message can be communicated. Syntax, grammar, and even vocabulary come apart in his poetry. From the rubble, he re-creates the text, in completely new combinations, so that meaning is reconstituted in a way never before possible. Vallejo uses words the way a Cubist such as Pablo Picasso or Georges Braque uses shape. Cubism forces one to view an image simultaneously from a multiplicity of new angles, so that "normal" perception of that image is no longer valid. Similarly, Vallejo requires language to be read in an entirely new way: The traditional logic of grammar is discarded, and readers are forced to reconstruct it themselves so that the "normal" interpretation of the words is no longer valid. As the syntax is wrenched apart in a Vallejo poem, so, too, is meaning wrenched apart. Readers are often left with irrational, private, and ultimately ambiguous images that parallel the ambiguous nature of contemporary experience.

The first stanza of "The Nine Monsters" is a good example of this technique. The stanza appears to be a single, medium-length sentence—at least it is punctuated that way—however, this sentence has no beginning and no conclusion. Although a subject and a verb are provided ("pain grows"), the sentence soon loses all grammatical sense. The phrase "the pain twice" is repeated several times as though the speaker has lost the train of thought and must return to what he has already said. The broken syntax of the first stanza is reminiscent of other modernist poems, such as T. S. Eliot's "The Hollow Men," in which a sequence of fragments is spliced together. The resulting jumble falls short of effective communication. This device may baffle the reader, but there is a point to the confusion: Many of Vallejo's poems are meditations on the modern human's inability to discover meaning in his or her experiences. In "The Nine Monsters," moreover, the broken phrasing gives the impression that someone in excruciating pain is trying to speak. The manner of the speech thus reflects the theme of the speech. The poet finds the pain of life so unbearable that his ability to deliver coherent discourse is impaired.

Vallejo is also a great poet of swift association, a device that allows the poet to leap from one image to another, thus bringing together ideas and images that superficially seem to have little in common. He is willing to take risks in these associations. For example, few other poets would dare to associate cabinet drawers with the heart and wall lizards. Such seemingly implausable connections are jarring and disturbing. The reader is forced to account for the contradictions in these connections. Perhaps in doing so, the reader can glimpse deeper, hidden realities.

Themes and Meanings

The greatest difficulty in discussing the meaning of this poem lies in deciding what to do with the title. The title appears to be significant. There is, therefore, a temptation with a title such as this—a title that names something—to determine its symbolic intention. Vallejo refers to "nine monsters." The reader's job, it would seem, is to figure out what those monsters represent. There is, however, a danger in approaching the imagery of a poem as a set of hieroglyphics that must be deciphered. It is not always the case that symbolism can be neatly solved, as though it were a code. In poetry, the ideational bias is especially problematic. This bias overemphasizes the interpretation of meaning in a work of art, when in fact a complete aesthetics focuses on numerous aspects of that work in order to discover its effectiveness. Meaning, then, is not something hidden to be solved like a riddle. Rather, meaning is derived from the total aesthetic experience.

In lines 33 through 37, Vallejo repeats the number "nine" several times, clearly echoing the title. Although the monsters are not named, it is apparent that these monsters have something to do with sounds heard in the inner ear. This ear creates the sounds itself; and it creates them in response to moments of suffering and pain— "the hour of crying," or "the hour of hunger," for example. So the monsters might be related to the intensification of pain at certain moments, such as throbs or jolts or anything that aggravates maladies. Beyond that, their significance is esoteric.

One thing is clear in the poem: Pain itself is monstrous; it grows phenomenally; it attacks humans; it causes upheaval in the world. In several instances, the speaker makes some curious assertions about pain. There has never been so much pain, he says in the second stanza, but why does the speaker locate pain in the lapel or in arithmetic? Through swift associations, the poet connects some rather mundane items, thereby drawing attention to the extent of pain's infiltration into daily life. Everything, he wants to say, contributes in some measure to our suffering. He particularly associates pain with modern gadgetry and entertainment. Even those things normally thought of as comforts or diversions, such as movies and music, are in fact sources of pain.

The poem ends with a question for the Secretary of Health: What can be done about this rampant pain? This is a rhetorical question, not a demand. The speaker knows all too well that political or governmental solutions to the problem are ineffectual or nonexistent. Anything humankind attempts will be overwhelmed by suffering.

Stephen Benz

NOCTURNE

Author: Tomas Tranströmer (1931-   )
Type of poem: Lyric
First published: 1962, as "Nocturne," in *Den halvfärdiga himlen*; collected in
   Twenty Poems, 1970

The Poem

"Nocturne" is a short poem in free verse, its sixteen lines divided into four stanzas. The title, suggesting a musical composition, establishes the mood of the poem. The night, in one of its traditional aspects, is a time for reverie, permitting the free play of thought and emotion expressed, for example, in the nocturnes of Frédéric Chopin. The poem is written in the first person. Sometimes poets use the first person to speak through a persona, whose outlook and experience may be quite different from their own. Here, however, no distinction is implied between Tomas Tranströmer the poet and the speaker of the poem. In the classic tradition of lyric poetry, the poet addresses the reader directly, with the authority of personal experience.

"Nocturne" takes as its point of departure an experience that will be familiar to most readers. When one is driving at night, objects that are caught in the beam of the headlights loom out of the darkness, almost as if they were moving forward. Instead of ignoring this trick of perception as one normally does, Tranströmer accepts it at face value. The scene is transformed, as in a folktale or dream. There is a childlike quality to this vision, too; the magically animate houses, which "step out/ into the headlights" as deer or cattle might, "want a drink."

When the poet turns his attention to sleeping humanity, there is an important shift in perspective. In the second stanza, instead of speaking from immediate personal experience, the poet adopts the generalizing manner of the sage. The last two lines of the stanza in particular recall the voice of the Preacher in Ecclesiastes. (In Swedish, the quasi-biblical parallelism of these lines is even more pronounced.) Like the Preacher, but more gently, he records human folly.

In the third stanza, there is a shift back to immediate personal experience as the nighttime drive described in stanza 1 continues. Again the lyric vision is triggered by precise observation of familiar details: the "melodramatic color" of the trees caught in the headlights and the uncanny clarity of leaves illumined against the night. The metaphorical transformation enacted in stanza 1 continues here as well: The trees are granted sentience and mobility.

The fourth stanza concludes the poem yet leaves it open-ended. In stanzas 1 and 3, the poet has been seeing in the dark, thanks to the headlights of his car; now, in bed and on the verge of sleep, he is seeing in the dark in another sense. Tranströmer notes how the images one sometimes "sees" immediately before sleep seem to come from outside one's consciousness, of their own volition.

Something from outside wants to get in—not to force entry, but to give a message. The poem concludes with another image that is rooted in a familiar sensation: the tantalizing experience of a revelation that cannot quite be grasped before sleep takes over.

Forms and Devices

References to music abound in Tranströmer's poems. (By profession a psychologist, he is said to be an accomplished pianist as well.) Readers who know his work in Swedish lament the loss in translation of the music of his verse. A recording of Tranströmer reading his poems (*The Blue House*, Watershed C-214) is very helpful in this respect; "Nocturne" is one of several poems that he reads in Swedish as well as in English. Inevitably much is lost in transit between languages. Still, if it is true, as Robert Hass writes in his introduction to *Tomas Tranströmer: Selected Poems, 1954-1986* (1987), that Tranströmer "has been translated into English more regularly than any European poet of the postwar generation," much in his poetry must survive and even flourish in translation.

One reason that Tranströmer translates so well is that he is above all a poet of metaphor. "My poems are meeting places," he has said. "Their intent is to make a sudden connection between aspects of reality that conventional languages and outlooks ordinarily keep apart." What is particularly interesting about this credo is that it could serve equally well as a definition of metaphor.

"Nocturne" consists of a series of images in which one thing is seen in terms of something else. Most of the metaphors are implicit at least to some degree; the comparisons are not completely spelled out. For example, the poet never explicitly compares the houses that "step out" to animals, but his description unmistakably suggests the comparison. Some of the metaphors require a bold leap (it is surprising to think of houses transformed into living creatures), while others delight by their simple rightness (the flickering light on the trees from the passing car resembles firelight).

In "Nocturne," many of the metaphors follow a common pattern, reinforcing one another. The pattern is established in the first stanza with the "Houses, barns, nameposts, deserted trailers" that "take on life." In stanza 1, inanimate objects come alive; in stanza 3, trees are described in terms normally reserved for the animal kingdom: They are said to be "silent in a pact with each other," as if they could talk if they wished, and they follow the poet home. In stanza 4, "unknown images and signs," instead of being drawn by the poet, sketch themselves.

This pattern of transformation, which suggests a magical spell cast by the night, culminates in the image that concludes the poem: "In the slot between waking and sleep/ a large letter tries to get in without quite succeeding." A letter is normally a passive object, but here the poet attributes will, intention, purpose to it. Not every metaphor in the poem, however, fits the pattern of passive-into-active. The "slot between waking and sleep," for example, is a marvelous metaphor in which a unit of time—the brief interval of heightened receptivity before sleep—is described in terms of a unit of space.

It is characteristic of Tranströmer to end a poem with an enigmatic image which, like the last line of a haiku, requires the reader to make a connection with what has gone before. "After a Death," "Out in the Open," and "Going with the Current" are other good examples of Tranströmer poems with this kind of ending.

Themes and Meanings

"Nocturne" is a poem about vision. What makes a poet a poet? In one of their guises, poets are visionaries or seers; they see things that many people do not see, or they see familiar things in an unfamiliar way. Countless lyric poems since the Romantic period have centered on this visionary faculty; to a greater or lesser degree, they are poems about the very power of vision that they exemplify.

Addressing this theme, many poets have employed a paradox: Darkness, normally a time when vision is limited at best, heightens their perception. For Octavio Paz, for example, in poems such as "Same Time," "Clear Night," and "San Ildefonso Nocturne," night is the realm of interior vision, yielding poetic revelation. This is a favorite motif of Tranströmer as well; one of his books of poems published after "Nocturne" is entitled *Mörkerseende* (1970), variously translated as *Night Vision* (1971) and *Seeing in the Dark* (1970).

Why should night be conducive to poetic vision? By day, people are preoccupied with their jobs, families, and all the business of everyday life. (For the purposes of the poem, one must ignore the fact that many people in modern societies have to work at night. "Nocturne" implies not a literal contrast between day and night but a contrast between attitudes.) Even while they sleep, they remain in the grip of those preoccupations; meanwhile, "the mystery rolls past." The poem's primary focus, however, is not negative (the lack of vision); rather, the poem shows how a contrasting attitude — receptiveness to mystery — opens one to unsuspected wonders.

There are two ways in which "Nocturne" differs from many poems on the same theme. The first is the modesty of its claims. The poem ends with a failure: The revelation that seems to be right at the edge of the poet's consciousness, within reach, is not after all vouchsafed to him. Moreover, this whimsical, domesticated image invites the reader to identify with the poet ("I too have had such intimations") rather than regard him as one possessing special powers. Nevertheless — here is the second distinction — it is important to note that the poet's visionary power entails receptiveness to something that is trying to get through to him. He is not essentially alone in the universe; he is not arbitrarily imposing meaning on a meaningless world.

Beyond that, to drag the poem into a philosophical debate would be silly; it does not pretend to bear that kind of weight. One version of the poet-seer is the poet-as-child. "Nocturne" resembles one of those children's stories in which, after everyone is thought to be asleep, the dolls and the stuffed animals and the toy soldiers begin to frolic, unaware of the spellbound child who is watching them through the not-quite-shut nursery door.

John Wilson

A NOISELESS PATIENT SPIDER

Author: Walt Whitman (1819-1892)
Type of poem: Lyric
First published: 1868; collected in *Leaves of Grass*, 1871

The Poem

"A Noiseless Patient Spider" is a short poem, its ten uneven lines divided into two stanzas of five lines each. The initial focus of the poem is a spider that is being observed by the speaker. The use of the indefinite article "a" in the title and the first line individualizes this arachnid, separating it from the representative mass and emphasizing the personal nature of its efforts. The adjectives "noiseless" and "patient" anticipate the poem's tone of pathos.

This poem is written in the first person, which is typical of lyric poetry; less common, however, is that the speaker directly addresses and converses with his own soul, which occurs in the second stanza. The reader observes the one observing (the speaker), the one observed (the spider), and the one addressed (the soul).

"A Noiseless Patient Spider" begins with a description of a common and relatively insignificant incident: A spider, all alone on a little promontory, quietly and tirelessly casts out web-threads from its spinnerets into an illimitable, inestimable emptiness that is all it can see; quickly, untiringly, continuously, it attempts to examine and define this significant, palpable unknown that binds it. In this first stanza, the speaker, a seemingly dispassionate viewer of this scene in nature, is almost indiscernible, the only reference to his presence being the words "I marked."

The designation that the spider "stood isolated" makes clear that its continued launching of filaments is a personal endeavor, its location on a promontory, as opposed to the plain, adding a dimension of precariousness. The description of the filaments emanating "out of" the spider "itself" makes clear that the process is innately creative; the metaphor of the web intensifies the action by conveying ambiguity concerning success.

In the second stanza, the poet transfers his focus from nature to humanity: In the pantheistic tradition, the experience of the spider becomes a metaphor symbolizing the soul's quest for the unification of earthly and heavenly existence. Directly addressing his own soul, the persona visualizes in the spider's action a reflection of the pathetic yet heroic struggle he is waging to find immortality. The sense of human insignificance is monstrous. The speaker is imprisoned, "surrounded" by the barrenness, yet alienated, "detached." The unknown vastness is palpable: "oceans of space." Intimidated by the gulf between life and what follows, the soul stands "Ceaselessly musing, venturing, throwing, seeking the spheres to connect them."

The instability of the situation is confirmed by the soul's attempts to "anchor," and the improbability of success is made explicit with the confessed ignorance of the destination, which is identified only as "somewhere." The means available to effect a connection is also less than encouraging: A silken thread seems much too fragile to form an eternal bridge. The poem concludes without resolution, leaving only the lingering image of the soul casting forth its gossamer threads, with the persona's final "O my soul" sounding like a cry.

Forms and Devices

In another poem, "Had I the Choice," Walt Whitman expresses a special preference for the ability to convey the "undulation of one wave" and asks the sea to "breathe one breath . . . upon my verse,/ And leave its odor there." "A Noiseless Patient Spider" (like numerous other poems) communicates indirectly this sound and sense of the sea. In the lines "And you O my soul where you stand,/ Surrounded, detached, in measureless oceans of space," the poet simulates the flux and reflux of the ocean, simultaneously communicating the motion of the action that is occurring: the soul perpetually casting forth, anticipating a connection with heaven.

In this instance, much of this sensation of waves laving the shore is achieved by the poet's use of alliteration of the sibilant *s*, making up 28 of the total 140 syllable sounds in the poem. This marriage of sense and sound occurs often in Whitman; equally effective in this poem is his simulation of casting: "Forth filament, filament, filament."

In a letter to Ralph Waldo Emerson (August, 1856), Whitman spoke of poets "walking freely out from the old traditions"; he became the forerunner of such innovation through his rejection of conventional subjects, language, rhythm, and rhyme. Yet his preference for open verse, although unorthodox, provides, surprisingly, plentiful evidence of his frequent reliance on traditional uses of repetition.

One such reiterative device is epanaphora (initial repetition), which is used effectively in the conclusion of "A Noiseless Patient Spider": "Till the bridge you will need be form'd, till the ductile anchor hold,/ Till the gossamer thread you fling catch somewhere, O my soul."

Epanalepsis (internal repetition), however, contributes more than epanaphora to this particular work. For example, the word "marked" refers first to the persona— "I marked"— then to the spider, who "mark'd how to explore," providing an essential transitional link between the two. Other examples of the use of internal reiteration of words (or their variant forms) to provide coherence in this short, ten-line poem follow: "you," "stood and stand," "surrounding" and "surrounded," "them," and "ever." Whitman's use of the interjection "O" affords yet another example of epanalepsis, and the sense of awe imparted by the usage is sustained indirectly by means of assonance in "Soul," "oceans," "form'd," and "anchor hold."

In his 1876 preface to *Leaves of Grass*, the poet referred to his verses as his "recitatives" (the recitative is a musical style in which the text is presented rhetorically in the rhythm of natural speech with some melodic variations), and Whitman's poetry exudes a sense of music throughout, not in the traditional manner, but in a new vein, much of it emanating from his expertise in using the repetition of sounds, words, and phrases to create expressive rhythms.

Whitman's handling of the centrifugal metaphor of the spider affords an excellent example of the Romantic concept of nature as wayseer for human truth; as he wrote in "Song of Myself," "The nearest gnat is an explanation, and a drop or motion of waves a key." The spider throwing out webs and the soul thrusting toward eternity afford a singular analogy that can be extended logically even beyond the poem. If the actions are successful, the processes will end with a miracle in the beautiful symmetry of an intricate web for the spider, and the achievement of the fusion of the carnal and the spirit for the soul.

Themes and Meanings

"A Noiseless Patient Spider" is a poem about loneliness, a common theme in verse. This loneliness, however, cannot be relieved by a pensive memory as in William Wordsworth's "I Wandered Lonely as a Cloud," nor is it an emotion emanating from a lost relationship as in Robert Frost's "Reluctance." This is a loneliness that grows out of an inherent tendency of the body and soul to attempt to unite with an elusive divine entity in order to gain immortality.

It is significant that loneliness arising from separation from one's kind is self-generated and voluntary—the spider "stood isolated." Ironically, "detachment," which is related to the soul, connotes instead a severing of ties by some force on a higher level; such an unnatural separation generates a compelling inner urgency to reattach and thereby restore access to the immortal circuit. The absence of color in the poetic description intensifies the pathos of the plight of the soul, infusing a feeling that is almost despair.

The sense of skewed proportion is frightening. A minuscule spider, attempting to chart a boundless vacuity with grossly inadequate equipment, becomes a living symbol of the pathetic plight of mortal humanity. The human soul, too, must deal with the unknown. Unlike the spider's day-by-day spinning, however, the soul's reaching out is not part of the daily routine: It is an essential, extraordinary phenomenon. The impending premonition of a continued moral crisis is disturbingly inherent in the effort: Everything (immortality) is hanging on a silken thread, which is being tossed tentatively and figuratively into an unidentified, undefined "somewhere."

In "Song of Myself" (stanza 50), Whitman affirmed: "There is in me—I do not know what it is . . ./ It is not chaos or death—it is form, union, plan—it is eternal life—it is Happiness." In "A Noiseless Patient Spider," the poet focuses on this conundrum of death and immortality. Neither the persona nor his soul realizes the euphoria suggested by the title of the group of poems in which they first took breath, "Whispers of Heavenly Death," for the poem ends without closure. In keeping with his concept of life and death as ongoing and evolutionary, Whitman chose neither to present the beauty of the symmetry of the finished web nor to record the necessary order imposed upon earthly chaos. Instead, he paused to expose the trauma of the soul's desperate search for meaning, and in the untiring throwing out of gossamer threads, he revealed the infinite beauty of the heroic dignity of the human soul.

Phyllis J. Scherle

THE NORTH SEA

Author: Heinrich Heine (1797-1856)
Type of poem: Poetic sequence
First published: 1826-1827, as *Die Nordsee*, in *Reisebilder*; collected in *Heine's Poem, The North Sea*, 1916

The Poem

The North Sea is the last section of the collected poems in Heinrich Heine's *Buch der Lieder* (1827; *Book of Songs*, 1856) and consists of two cycles of poems in free verse. In the final version, authorized by Heine, the first, optimistic cycle contains twelve poems and the second, less cheerful one has ten.

The title indicates how important the sea is for Heine as a setting. Despite predecessors such as Johann Wolfgang von Goethe and Rahel Varnhagen von Ense, Heine is credited with having established the sea as a topic in German literature and with being the foremost poet of the sea.

The poems of *The North Sea* are among Heine's most important works. They are unique among his works: Only in 1825 and 1826, when he wrote these poems, did he use free verse. In his mastery of the new form, Heine achieves a beauty of style in verses with well-chosen words, striking contrasts, and mythical imagery. *The North Sea* proves Heine's strength and independence as a poet.

Heine's own love for the sea enters directly into the poems. Visits to the North Sea in the summers of 1825 and 1826 supplied motivation and material for the first and second cycles, respectively. Heine felt the sea was invigorating and good for his health. His personal experience is subtly reflected in the poems and in the cycles' moods. Since he felt less relaxed in 1826, the second cycle is less cheerful.

The first person in the poems is largely Heine himself. He took his impressions of the sea and transformed them into great poetry about nature, which in turn is the point of departure for philosophical and mythological reflections. With such a combination of nature and reflection, he adds new energy and new irony to the Romantic tradition that influences his sensitivity. These poems were perceived as turbulent and restless by the contemporary audience, explaining why their reception was initially slow. Nevertheless *The North Sea* was, in Heine's lifetime, translated into many languages and contributed to his world fame.

Each individual poem of *The North Sea* can stand by itself. The "Evening Twilight" at sea brings back pleasant childhood memories, while in "Sunset" the poet feels comfort only compared to Heine's own myth of the sun's and moon's eternal separation. In "A Night by the Sea," the love encounter between a woman and the godlike poet undergoes an ironic reversal because he is afraid of an "undying cough." In yet another reversal, the poet is told in "Poseidon" that he is not worth divine wrath.

"The Avowal" is a key poem of the first cycle because the poet expresses an optimistic view of love in the grandiose metaphor of writing his proclamation of love in the sky with a burning tree. This poem is as much about love as about poetry itself.

"Night in the Cabin" consists of six songs professing love to woman, while in "Storm," the poet imagines a far-away woman's loving thoughts reaching out to him. "Peace at Sea" is contrasted with the ship's boy stealing and with a seagull catching fish. The following two poems reflect one another directly: in "A Wraith in the Sea," the underwater apparition of a city and the poet's love invite him to leap into the sea. In "Purification," the poet understands this apparition as his own madness and wishes to ban it.

"Peace" praises Jesus Christ, who walks "over the land and the sea," bringing peace to the world. Heine had converted from Judaism to Lutheranism in June of 1825, and the version of the poem in *Book of Songs* does not contain earlier satirical elements. Some critics contend it is a weak ending for the first cycle.

The less cheerful second cycle begins with "Ocean Greeting," which celebrates the sea's liberating force. The next poems evoke threatening forces, with Greek gods as forces behind the "Tempest," and also mourn the loss of love with the imagery of being "Shipwrecked."

"The Setting of the Sun" varies Heine's myth of the unhappy marriage of gods. As the second cycle's key poem, "The Song of the Okeanides" reveals the reality of separation hidden behind the poet's illusion of love. The next poems vary the theme and then give way to more optimistic ones.

Even "The Gods of Greece" are dead and replaced by Christianity. Only a fool waits for the answer to the "Questions" about the meaning of life. Changing the thematic flow, "The Phoenix" asserts new hope for love. The poet's increasing intoxification in "In Haven" ultimately extends to the whole drunken world, and is thus both pessimistic and humorous.

"Epilog" ends the collection of *Book of Songs*. It gently asserts love in a comparison that alludes to the powerful Romantic image for yearning: the blue flower.

Forms and Devices

Heine paid close attention to questions of form, so the interpretation of form is particularly important in regard to the author's intentions. Three major formal devices shape the structure of the poems in *The North Sea*: free verse, compound adjectives, and ironic reversal.

Heine wrote free verse only during the years he worked on *The North Sea*. The verses are without rhyme, fixed meter, or set length; they are flexible according to the poet's needs. Free verse was introduced to German poetry by Friedrich Gottlieb Klopstock and was used by major poets such as Johann Wolfgang von Goethe, Friedrich Schiller, and Novalis. Heine is a master of the form and uses it to create various effects—for example, the motion of the waves: "more wild than wind and waters."

This example uses alliteration to help echo the rhythmic and musical effect of the sea. Alliteration is often lost in translation, just as is the second major formal device, compound adjectives. Heine invents words, such as "happiness-blinded" and "Olympus-shaking," to describe persons or events in a new and precise way. Depending on the translations, sometimes only one out of five compound adjectives in German is translated by an English compound adjective. Yet, since such word formations are even more extraordinary in English, the effect of the translation is comparable to that of the German original.

Heine's rhetoric and, in particular, his compound adjectives make his poems sound like epics by Homer. In fact, part of Heine's experience of the North Sea was the reading of Homer, whose German translation is reflected in Heine's poems. Especially in those poems with Greek themes, it becomes obvious that Heine is both part of a long-standing tradition and independent because of his awareness of history. The latter enables Heine to use traditional elements for his own purposes — for example, to express the theme of love and separation.

A third major device in Heine's poetry affects the structure of the poems. It is the ironic reversal for which Heine is famous. Typically, this device takes the mood of a poem and turns it around: Suddenly and unexpectedly, the sentimental tone shifts to bitterness, as in "The Song of the Okeanides," or to mockery, as in "A Wraith in the Sea" with its abrupt ending, and as in the first poem of *The North Sea*, in which celebration of his new love surprisingly ends in the poet relinquishing his reason. This aspect of structure leads to questions of themes and meanings.

Themes and Meanings

Although the sea is ever-present as the setting of the poems, the three major themes in *The North Sea* are mythology, love and separation, and poetry itself. Heine's use of mythology is threefold. First, he uses myth as a form of expression; second, Heine creates his own myths; and finally, he mocks antique myths.

In Heine's day it was common to use mythological references to talk about something else. In Heine's case, myths expressed his existential theme: love and separation. In the "Song of the Okeanides," the poet first indulges in reveries of love and is then interrupted by the "compassionate water-maids" who, calling him a fool, show him the reality of separation and desperation.

The myths that Heine invents about the unhappy marriages of gods have this same function in "Sunset" and "The Setting of the Sun." On one hand, both poems intensify the feeling of separation by showing that the gods suffer eternally. On the other hand, this adds a humorous tone when the poet feels blessed because he is mortal and, thus, will not suffer forever.

Heine extends the humorous tone to mockery when, in "A Night by the Sea," the godlike poet is afraid of catching colds that are as eternal as divine existence. Particularly in "The Gods of Greece," Heine shows his irreverence: The poet confesses that he has never liked the Greek and Roman gods who have degenerated and now merely "drift slowly like monstrous ghosts" in the night sky.

This poem demonstrates a considerable distance from the serious role Greek mythology played for German classicists such as Johann Wolfgang von Goethe and

Friedrich Schiller. Schiller mourns the death of the old gods in one poem; Heine borrows its title and writes a new poem mocking the gods. Heine embeds his ideas about Greek mythology in description of nature and understands the gods' decline as part of the eternal struggle of being.

"The Gods of Greece" have been replaced by Christianity. The latter, however, appears to be both positive ("Wonder-worker") and negative ("doleful"). In connection with the poem's description of Venus Libitina, the "corpse-like goddess," Heine seems to attack the tendencies in Christianity that deny sensual pleasures. It is important here that the old (sensual) gods have only been pushed aside and are still present. Like most of his other poems, this one varies Heine's basic assumption of the world's incoherence, which is the source of his second major theme: love and separation. Even in the positive poems, the poet is typically away from his love, either preparing to meet her or simply thinking about her. These situations are very delicate. In "Coronation" the poet states that love robs him of his reason, and in "The Song of the Okeanides" his positive feelings are transformed into depression.

"The Avowal," probably the most positive poem of *The North Sea*, can be understood as strangely removed from real love. It presents Heine's third major theme: poetry about itself. The poet professes his love, but the poem is more about his power to do so than about a woman. He uses a tree that he dipped into a volcano as his "colossal flame-soaked pen" in order to make his words stay in the sky forever. Thus Heine celebrates both the power of poetry and his own stature.

Ingo Roland Stoehr

NOW SLEEPS THE CRIMSON PETAL

Author: Alfred, Lord Tennyson (1809-1892)
Type of poem: Lyric
First published: 1847, in *The Princess*

The Poem

"Now Sleeps the Crimson Petal" is a short lyric of fourteen lines. It begins with two stanzas of four lines each. Next comes a couplet, and the poem concludes with another four-line stanza. The reader of the poem will at once note that it has no title but is known by its first line. The reason for this is that the lyric forms part of a large epic, *The Princess*. The epic includes several famous lyrics, including "Tears, Idle tears" and "Come Down, O Maid."

"Now Sleeps the Crimson Petal" is read by Princess Ida to the prince, who is recovering from wounds incurred in battle. The prince loves Ida; she, although well-disposed to him, has yet to reveal her own feelings. In the lyric, she at last does so; its content makes it clear that she reciprocates his love.

Alfred, Lord Tennyson faced a difficult problem in writing about love. The Victorians held extremely strong views about what might properly be discussed in public. Sexual love was definitely not on the acceptable list: Much that might appear in a modern motion picture rated acceptable for family audiences would by the Victorians have been classed as beyond the pale.

Tennyson fully shared the values of his time. The task that thus faced him in "Now Sleeps the Crimson Petal" was to suggest the circumstances of a romantic encounter while shunning any direct description that violated propriety. Tennyson accomplished this feat through the use of appeals to nature and references to mythology.

Although the poem is read by the princess, the speaker in it is a man appealing to a woman. The scene is a palace garden at night. The flowers personify sleep, and the trees are quiet: "Nor waves the cypress in the palace walk." In a striking image, a fish is represented as sleeping: "Nor winks the gold fin in the porphyry font" (porphyry is an igneous rock, often used in Persian palaces). The speaker invites the lady he addresses to wake up.

The purpose for which he wishes her to do so becomes quickly apparent in the next stanza. He refers to the Greek myth in which Zeus, disguised as a shower of meteors, ravished the maiden Danaë. He suggests that the lady is willing to receive him: "And all thy heart lies open unto me." The couplet, which now follows, suggests that the encounter has ended. The speaker, continuing to identify himself with Zeus, departs: "Now slides the silent meteor on." As the woman bears physical evidence of the encounter, so does he have her thoughts imprinted in him.

The intermingling of thoughts implies that the encounter has been of deep significance. This is confirmed in the concluding stanza, in which it transpires that the speaker and the lady have by no means finished their romance. Drawing an analogy with the lily, which folds itself up and "slips into the bosom of the lake," he invites the lady to follow suit: "So fold thyself, my dearest, thou, and slip/ Into my bosom and be lost in me." The poem then concludes with an image of the total unity of lover and beloved.

Forms and Devices

The lyric is written in an unusual form. It is a ghazal, a Persian love poem, in which a single word or phrase is repeated at short intervals. Each stanza ends with "me": "with me," "to me," "unto me," "in me," and again "in me." The repeated phrase acts as a substitute for rhyme. A number of images in the lyric are standard in the Persian love poem: roses, lilies, peacocks, cypresses, and stars.

By using this exotic form, Tennyson suggests a situation and a mood out of the ordinary. The normal conventions are suspended for the duration of the romantic encounter.

To speak of a romantic encounter is often to suggest a difficulty: How can the man overcome the woman's resistance? The speaker solves the problem by avoiding it altogether. The result of the encounter between him and the lady is, in his mind, inevitable. Tennyson's choice of words, along with the extraordinary circumstances suggested by the poem's strange form, aid in creating the illusion of inevitability. Each stanza begins with "Now," suggesting a continuous movement. The effect is enhanced in the first stanza, in which the second and third lines begin with "Nor." This word is so similar to "now" that the reader must pay close attention to avoid a misreading. Given the progression of "Nows," resistance on the woman's part becomes next to impossible.

Tennyson also uses words that suggest peace and drowsiness rather than violence. The poem scrupulously avoids the slightest hint of struggle. The flowers sleep: The activities from which the cypresses and goldfish rest are waving and winking, both rather mild affairs. The humorous "winks" suggest a lighthearted mood. A similar effect occurs in each stanza. The peacock "droops" and "glimmers." The "silent" meteor "slides"; the lily "folds" and "slips." All these verbs hint at peace and repose.

Tennyson's most serious problem in conveying a mood of peace stems from his use of the legend of Danaë, in Greek mythology a story of rape. He solves the difficulty with characteristic ingenuity. He turns the name Danaë into an adjective: "Now lies the earth all Danaë to the stars." The separate existence of the woman is thus elided: She fails to resist because she cannot. She has been emptied of her substance and transformed into a modifier.

The poem also reverses standard male and female attributes, adding even further to the motif of unity. Traditionally, males are active and females are passive. Thus, the feminine peacock "droops," and the lady's heart "lies open." The male, personified as a meteor, "slides on" and "leaves." The final stanza, however, executes a *volte-face*. Now it is the feminine lily that "folds" and "slips" into the lake. It is the lady whom the speaker calls upon to take the initiative by "folding herself." The poem's careful combination of figures is unified to achieve a common effect—the two lovers cannot be parted.

Themes and Meanings

"Now Sleeps the Crimson Petal" exemplifies a peculiar feature of the Victorian attitude toward love. Although by convention writers were supposed to exercise extreme reticence, in fact they did not do so. Tennyson cannot give a direct description of physical love, but his suggestions make his meaning unmistakable. When the speaker says, "And all thy heart lies open unto me," the reader cannot help but wonder what really "lies open."

The use of indirect allusion rather than direct description enhances the erotic effect. The reader cannot take in the scene passively but must use imagination in order to grasp the poem's meaning. Because of the beauty of the words, the reader is in danger of missing the fundamental occurrence represented by the lyric's appearance in *The Princess*. A woman reads an erotic poem in the presence of a man who has earlier professed his love for her. Nothing could be more alien to the notion of feminine modesty, but unless the reader portrays the scene in his own mind, the radical challenge to customary behavior will be missed.

The analysis just given might appear to fit a conventional picture of Victorian hypocrisy. In this view, the Victorians avoided certain words and aspired to a high-minded righteousness. In fact, they failed to practice what they preached: So long as the correct forms were observed, behavior was much less restricted than might appear. Many were reluctant to use the phrase "breast of chicken"; yet, at the same time, prostitution flourished.

There is no reason to accuse Tennyson of hypocrisy, whatever may be true of others among his contemporaries. He believed that love was a spiritual experience of great value. A romantic couple in their behavior reflect the movement of nature toward unity. The key to Tennyson's attitude to love lies in the final stanza, in which the lily slips into the lake. If the lady follows the behest of the speaker and, imitating the lily that is self-absorbed into the lake, becomes lost in the lover, an advance toward the unity of nature has taken place.

One can thus see why Tennyson is the reverse of hypocritical in the poem. He does not use poetic conventions in order to suggest pruriently what law and custom will not permit him to state directly. Instead, he sincerely believes in a philosophy of unity that nature and human loves illustrate. The theme of organic unity in nature was a near constant in Tennyson's work. A famous line of *In Memoriam* (1850) states: "I doubt not thro' the ages, one increasing purpose runs." The theme was common to many of Tennyson's contemporaries, including Thomas Carlyle and Francis Thompson.

Bill Delaney

NUTTING

Author: William Wordsworth (1770-1850)
Type of poem: Narrative/pastoral
First published: 1800, in *Lyrical Ballads, with a Few Poems*, second edition

The Poem

"Nutting" is a short autobiographical poem of fifty-six lines. It describes a youthful encounter with nature that helped to chasten William Wordsworth's moral sense and heighten his poetic sensitivity to the life shared between himself and the outer world. In remarks dictated to Isabella Fenwick in 1843, Wordsworth said that the verses, written in Germany in 1798, started out as part of his great autobiographical poem on the growth of the poet's mind, *The Prelude* (1850), but were "struck out as not being wanted there. . . . These verses arose out of the remembrance of feelings I had often had when a boy, and particularly in the extensive woods that still stretch from the side of Esthwaite Lake towards Graythwaite."

The geography of the poem is the magnificent English Lake District, for which Wordsworth's life and art as a poet of nature are famous. Wordsworth was born in Cockermouth, West Cumberland. After his mother's death, the eight-year-old Wordsworth went to Hawkshead Grammar School, near the scene of "Nutting," in the remote rural region that he and collaborator Samuel Taylor Coleridge made the poetic center of a literary revolution in England. Wordsworth and his three brothers boarded in the cottage of Ann Tyson, "the frugal Dame" rearing the boy of "Nutting," who gave to young Wordsworth simple comfort, ample affection, and freedom to roam the countryside on free days and some nights. These wanderings produced the traumatic experiences of poetic development amid nature documented in this poem and throughout *The Prelude*.

"Nutting" opens by noting a double consciousness: a speaker's mature mind discovering the "heavenly" impact of an early encounter with nature on his youthful mind (lines 1-4). It begins very abruptly to narrate one of those watershed experiences in Wordsworth's poetic growth. He set out to gather hazelnuts, suitably attired with pack, stick, and secondhand clothes that he had saved at the bidding of Ann Tyson for protection against nature on the way (lines 5-15).

His walk into the woods ends at a solitary bower, the scene of his impending spiritual revelation in nature, where the hazel trees symbolize a sexual and unspoiled life force in their resemblance to male genitals: "Tall and erect, with tempting clusters hung,/ A virgin scene" (lines 16-21). The boy gazes at the hazel trees with a gluttonous, self-satisfied appetite of hunger and sex, as if he were an explorer who had at last discovered an exotic treasure all for himself (lines 21-29).

Refusing to rush into the actual nut-gathering in order to savor his conquest, he rests his cheek against a fleecelike mossy stone. He hears a murmuring stream and seems to begin achieving a joyous communication with nature that is, however, undercut by the mature speaker's harsh comment on his remembrance of his youthful heart's response to mere "stock and stones/ And . . . vacant air" (lines 30-43). The harshness is perhaps explained by an intervening memory in the mature speaker's mind about the boy's subsequent cruelty to a virginal nature. The boy proceeds to unleash rape and riot ("merciless ravage") on the "mutilated bower" of hazel trees and to violate the innocent sexuality of the universal life force that inheres in nature (lines 43-51). As a consequence, guilt rushes into his youthful mind to teach him at that moment and in later years (in the company of his "dearest Maiden") that "there is a spirit in the woods" at one with individuals who have gentle, sensitive souls (lines 52-56).

Forms and Devices

The apparent simplicity of "Nutting" should not blind readers to the subtleties of its rhetoric and meaning. The poem might be designated a pastoral narrative, because it is a seemingly straightforward story of a rural protagonist in a country setting, pursuing pastoral pleasures that touch on love and sex, despite the absence of conventional items such as shepherds, lutes, and love laments found in ancient bucolic poetry.

Yet "Nutting" is new, revolutionary poetry in form and meaning, created by Wordsworth as a conscious challenge to classical norms of literature. For example, it is an autobiography of unprecedented intimacy and such deceptive simplicity that traditionalists might have considered its unpretentious tale about a boy's walk into the woods too commonplace to be dignified enough for elevated poetry. Such a detailed narration of an ordinary person's spiritual crisis struck a daringly confessional note. Wordsworth spearheaded the innovations that would help to democratize modern poetry with an unrestricted range of subject matter and with a vernacular speaking voice.

Wordsworth's mastery of an elegant yet flexible blank verse is part of the remarkable intimacy of "Nutting." Blank verse is unrhymed iambic pentameter that Wordsworth inherited from John Milton's much more solemn *Paradise Lost* (1667, 1674) and transformed into a supple sound system capturing the speaking voice of a common man who is sensitive, simple, and yet cultivated enough to reflect on the larger meaning of his unthinking youthful adventures in nature.

Although "Nutting" seems straightforward and ordinary, it is a mythic narrative of everyman's pilgrimage of life elevated beyond an uneventful walk into the woods by two interrelated metaphors of a knight's quest and an explorer's journey of discovery. As M. H. Abrams remarked in *Natural Supernaturalism* (second edition, 1973), the pilgrimage motif was central to Wordsworth's poetry: "It is time to notice that Wordsworth's account of unity achieved, lost, and regained is held together . . . by the recurrent image of a journey: . . . Wordsworth's 'poem on my own poetical education' converts the wayfaring Christian of the Augustinian spiritual journey into the self-formative traveler of the Romantic educational journey."

So it is in "Nutting." The little boy is first depicted as an overdressed and raggedy knight-errant of yore "sallying forth" with a "motley" armament for nut-gathering that ominously distances him from nature and, even worse, will be used to destroy nature in the bower of pristine sexual bliss (lines 5-21). Allied with this motif of a knight's dubious quest is the complementary motif of an explorer's exploitative journey of discovery on which, like cruel *conquistadores* in the New World, the boy invades the *terra incognita* of unspoiled nature and guiltily pillages the new-found treasures of the primitive environment (lines 22-53).

Themes and Meanings

"Nutting" is a poem about the possibilities and problems of a communion between humans and nature; it involves the irony that the boy's revelation of a communication between himself and nature occurs by means of his violation of nature. Wordsworth's *The Prelude*, arguably the greatest nineteenth century poem in the Western world, terms such revelations of nature's presence "spots of time" and narrates similar moments of the poet's spiritual development through youthful violations of nature in episodes of boat stealing and woodcock snaring. "Nutting" was originally designed to be part of these traumatic experiences of poetic growth in Book I of *The Prelude*.

Excerpted from the longer poem, "Nutting" is a beautifully complete poem in its own right that was published in the second 1800 edition of the groundbreaking *Lyrical Ballads*, which contains an influential literary manifesto in the preface authored by Wordsworth under Coleridge's inspiration. The poetic principles of the preface find embodiment in "Nutting." The typically Wordsworthian theme of the poem focuses on a semimystical experience of a young man's joyous, if fitful, apprehension of the spirit of life in the universe, the meaning of which is probed in the mature mind of the narrator remembering an early time of mindless pleasure in nature. The poem shows that moments of spiritual apprehension are not easy to come by, to preserve with the same initial pleasure, or to interpret clearly. At the outset, the mature narrator has to point out the special significance of his boyhood adventure in nature ("One of those heavenly days that cannot die"), because the ensuing narrative begins stressing a contrary message of civilized resistance to, rather than communion with, the countryside. The boy's overdressing and weapon-wielding are a defensive posture, almost a gesture of belligerence against the pristine bower of hazel trees that in his insensitive mind represents only a feast to devour and, implicitly, a male sex organ to rape and mutilate.

Not until line 33, where he pauses from undertaking the nut gathering, does he first hear the sounds of nature and let his imagination transform surface reality into deeper fantastic insights of oneness with the woods ("fairy" water-breaks of a flowing stream murmuring to the boy; mossy stones that are not simply rocks but, through simile in the creative imagination, become "like a flock of sheep"). These insights cause momentary "pleasure" and "joy" within the communing heart of the boy and create later recollection and spiritual solace in the mind of the mature narrator who must combat the inevitable disillusionments of life springing from the aging process. An intervening memory of the boy's ensuing rape of the bower, however, sullies the remembrance of those joyous insights for the mature narrator (lines 41-48). The narrator ends by recollecting the boy's second communication with nature that is no longer a heartfelt enjoyment of the rural scene but becomes the guilt-ridden recognition of being discovered in wrongdoing under "the intruding sky" for having devastated the now "silent" hazel trees (lines 48-53).

In the company of an unspecified "dearest Maiden," the mature narrator affirms the lesson he has learned—that, despite all human devastation, there is an unconquerable spirit in the woods ready to be in sympathy with a humanity of humble and open hearts. So ends a poem that is beautifully representative of the Romantic movement in European literature.

Thomas M. Curley

O THE CHIMNEYS

Author: Nelly Sachs (1891-1970)
Type of poem: Meditation
First published: 1946, as "O die Schornsteine," in *In den Wohnungen des Todes*;
 collected in *O the Chimneys*, 1967

The Poem

A free-verse poem of twenty lines originally in German and divided into four stanzas, "O the Chimneys" is a meditation on the Nazi death machine that destroyed six million Jewish people in the Holocaust. The chimneys of the title refer to those ovens built to incinerate the bodies of concentration camp victims killed in gas chambers.

Throughout the poem, the Nazi death camps are called "abodes of death" that are "devised." That is, they are technologically planned and scientifically administered for destruction. This statement conveys with chilling horror the clinical efficiency, the numbing methodicalness and appearance of business-as-usual that filmmakers such as Claude Lanzmann and philosophers such as Hannah Arendt have associated with the implementation of the Final Solution.

The smoke of the furnaces in which the Jewish people are burned, in the first stanza, becomes dust, which the poet associates with Jeremiah and Job, both martyrs to stubborn, defiant faithfulness to God. In the Hebrew Scriptures, Jeremiah becomes a political outcast, Job a social one, as each resists easy presumptions about God's justice.

Similarly, the poet raises questions about her people's suffering: Who or what receives it? Who devised it? These questions hang in the air with their tangible evidence: ashes, dust, smoke. Such suspension freezes the event, in history and consciousness. The event is moreover a cosmic one, blackening stars or sunbeams. The poet—and the reader, both now witnesses to the crime—find themselves on the border, the "threshold," between life and death.

Quoted beneath the poem's title is a verse from Job (19:26): "And when this my skin has been destroyed, from my flesh shall I see God," which some interpreters have understood as an affirmation of resurrection. Rather than a sense of discontinuity, however, the poet's revelation conveys a sense of metamorphosis, in which Israel's body and the smoke rising through the air are "dissolved" into each other, ever present in the atmosphere.

Forms and Devices

With its emphasis on imagery—on metaphor, juxtaposition, and ellipsis—rather than on complex rhythmic texture or intricate rhyme scheme, Nelly Sachs's poetry can be readily appreciated in translation.

The poem images the Jewish victims of the Holocaust as a single human body; thus particularized, their suffering is made more concrete, more immediate, more identifiable. Unlike the Nazi administration of the Final Solution, the fate of the victims cannot be abstracted into numbers, into statistics. The poet further concretizes the Holocaust by embodying the Nazi genocide in its death camps. The controlling image of the camps resonates in specific references to "chimneys," "abodes," "stone upon stone," "house," and "threshold."

The dynamic imagery of transmutation is evident throughout the poem, as flesh is dissolved in smoke and roads materialize from dust. As in Sachs's other work, biblical imagery submerges the poem in the depths of myth. The casualties of the Holocaust are associated with Jeremiah and Job, linking their suffering with that of the prophets and wise men. The simultaneity of Jewish existence, transcending time and space, confounding life and death, is thereby grasped in the poet's vision.

The poet asks rhetorical questions regarding the sufferings of the Holocaust, conscious of the inadequacy of any conventional explanation. Such questions echo the series of rhetorical questions with which God reveals himself to Job out of the whirlwind. The reader is thus drawn into the eternal dialogue engaging God and humanity.

Themes and Meanings

By alluding to Job in the poem, Sachs connects the Holocaust to the thorny question of innocent suffering, so scandalous to moral certitude. Her conjuring of natural and cosmic imagery, her parable of smoke and dust and air, suggests that the scandal of the Holocaust can best be comprehended by metaphysical or mystical insight. Such comprehension is not explanation; rather, it is an encounter with the mystery of existence. This encounter occurs at the nexus of flesh and dust, spirit and matter, life and death. Thus, on the verge of extinction, the enduring presence of the Jewish people is revealed.

Sachs herself was a survivor of Nazi Germany, emigrating to Sweden in 1940. Her major work, which established a reputation that eventually led to a Nobel Prize in Literature in 1966, was written during and after World War II. Her body of poetry forms a witness to the Holocaust. This witness, like that of other Holocaust writers, especially Elie Wiesel, is unflinching and resistant to moralizing. The spirit of Job, who affirmed his integrity in the face of doubt and suffering, informs the work of these authors.

Sachs, in addition, demonstrates sympathy with the Jewish mystics, the Kabbalists, who relentlessly pursued *tikkun*, or the reconciliation of a shattered creation. Her poetic vision unites body and spirit, nature and the cosmos, death and life, in a ceremony of metamorphosis.

Amy Adelstein

THE OCCIDENT

Author: Georg Trakl (1887-1914)
Type of poem: Lyric
First published: 1915, as "Abendland," in *Sebastian im Traum*; collected in
   Selected Poems, 1968

The Poem

The poem's German title, "Abendland," usually translated as "The Occident,"
names the West as the land of evening (*Abend*), the land where the sun sets. In Georg
Trakl's time, the word referred primarily to the Western European nations. In haunting imagery of evening and approaching night, the poet found a perfect metaphor for
what he saw as the late hour in the decline of Western culture, a powerful tool for
expressing his sense of foreboding about the depth of night to which that decline
might lead. The poem was written in the last months before the outbreak of World
War I. The very name the Occident (*Abendland*) invoked for Trakl this imagery of
evening and this sense of lateness.

"The Occident" is divided into three sections. In the first, the central tension of
the poem is established in the contrast between two stanzas. The first contains remarkable images of death and decline, and the second centers on the image of Elis, a
boy who seems to be unaffected by decline and to await a time of rebirth or springtime. Elis, a subject of two other poems by Trakl in the same volume, represents the
original world from which the real world has declined, as well as the rebirth that
will come after decline reaches its nadir.

The second section of the poem evokes a quiet tone of lament for the heartbreak-
ing beauty and peace of late evening. The world of evening is lovely and restful, but
it is fragile and is only a distant echo of its pure source and beginnings. Its beauty is
always about to be lost in night. Uneasiness about what will come surfaces as singers
wander with hesitant steps near thorns and people are said to have wept in their
sleep. The peace seems to be an ominous quiet before the storm.

The final section turns to the cities on the plain, above which angry clouds are
forming. By the end of the section, and the poem, the apocalyptic storm is breaking,
and even the stars are falling from the sky. This last image echoes the book of
Revelation, in which the world at the end of time descends into increasing darkness
until the stars themselves fall before the resurrection. (Trakl used this allusion and
the theme of a decline to absolute darkness earlier in his poem "Helian.")

When one considers the title again after reading the poem, "Abendland" or "The
Occident" seems a land filled with portentous evening light, about to lose itself in
the depths of darkness, with lightning bursting in the sky above its dying people.
The poem seems to invest decline with an uncanny force, as if the West, the land of
evening, were being carried to its fate by the irresistible forces of spiritual history.

Forms and Devices

Trakl, like Else Lasker-Schüler, to whom this poem is dedicated, is a poet of the German expressionist movement. The expressionists, who viewed the image as the basic unit of poetry, sought to intensify the vividness and expressive power of their images. They composed their poems of intense images much as one might compose music of notes or musical phrases. The coherence of a sequence of images is thus often thematic or emotional instead of logical, temporal, or spatial.

In "The Occident," Trakl's images are not connected with spatial transitions, as one might expect in the realistic description of a landscape, and one cannot piece together a story that the poem might tell. His sentence structures are also often incomplete or interrupted, so the images do not fall into a logical pattern of explanation. The first word of the poem, for example, the noun "Moon," appears in isolation, and serves no identifiable grammatical function in a sentence. A dependent clause compares the moon to something indefinite but pale, a "dead thing" as it would look if it were to step from a blue cave, but here the sentence breaks off and is never completed. As a result, the moon seems to loom symbolically. The reader can see this moon, with a patch of the sky lit up to a shade of blue around it, and has a sense of its eerie, deathlike presence. It stays before the mind, and a strong tone is established. Rather than subduing the image by means of description or a logical context, Trakl instead presents the reader with a series of other images, of petals falling across a stone path, a "sick thing" that is silver weeping by the "evening pond," and lovers who "died over" on a black boat.

In most poems by Trakl, one can reconnect the isolated images in a stanza by imagining them to be fragments of a landscape, but not without first sensing a strong undercurrent, a unity of tone and theme that makes the images and the landscape seem symbolic. Here the tone is uncanny and eerie, as if the strange moon were inscrutably related to the petals falling and the sick thing weeping. Thematically, the images all seem connected to decay, decline, and death.

Similarly, in each of the remaining stanzas, a symbolic landscape must be pieced together out of fragmentary images and the discovery of the unifying sense of tone and theme. In the second stanza of the first section, Elis walks in a grove full of hyacinths, seemingly free of the decline of the first stanza. In the second section, a quiet evening landscape is troubled by uneasiness and seems to be only a reprieve before a storm. In the last, cities on a plain are surrounded by a storm and dying peoples fall into apocalyptic darkness.

Trakl's apparently disjointed images present a series of symbolic landscapes that are not necessarily related spatially, or in the context of a narrative, or in a framework of logical development of ideas. Once one observes how these landscapes change color and tone and mood, however, one begins to grasp the feelings of lamentation and foreboding that Trakl sought to express. One accepts his vision of things to the extent that one finds his tone and imagery emotionally compelling.

Trakl also often reuses elements of images that he has developed in other poems. The moon, the pond, the cave, and the boat of the first stanza, for example, and later the grove, the footsteps, the hillside, the thunder, the wall, the hedge, and the thunderclouds, are all elements used in other poems in the same volume. Trakl constantly shifts color words in combinations with these elements, so that there is a red pond in another poem, a black hill in another, and a golden boat in a third.

Trakl also reuses symbolic figures he has created and developed elsewhere. The boy Elis and the lovers who may be spared decline by early death appear in several poems. The wanderer in the third section is the figure of the alienated artist that is familiar in Trakl's work.

For the reader of Trakl's poetry, these recurring figures and elements of imagery seem familiar, even though they appear in new contexts and combinations and their meanings change. Trakl seems to work with a basic set of symbolic elements and a kind of underlying grammar for their combinations in the symbolic landscapes of his poetry. The shifting combinations and variations make the vocabulary and grammar he has created seem flexible enough to express powerfully the truth of different types of spiritual climates.

Themes and Meanings

Trakl's poem was completed in June, 1914, a few months before the outbreak of World War I. In August, 1914, Trakl was drafted into the Austrian army as a pharmacist-lieutenant, and after three months of service in which he witnessed scenes of horrible carnage, resulting in his being placed under observation for psychological trauma, Trakl died of a cocaine overdose in November, 1914. As a result, the tone and subject of the poem seem eerily prophetic, and the disjointed syntactical arrangement of images is often thought to reflect the pressure of the time and the unraveling of logic in a world on its last legs, about to collapse into war.

"The Occident," then, is a marvelous expressionistic portrait of an era in which a civilization was carried irresistibly toward destruction. In his search for the expressive potential of the image, Trakl managed to reach a level of expression that is beyond the expression of personal feelings. He captured the anxiety of a period of history. In a language that is, in its repetition of elements and its portentous symbolic tone, so reminiscent of the language of prophecy, Trakl managed to anticipate the calamity in which the entire world would be involved.

The poem, however, is not concerned solely with decline. Trakl's poetry, prior to his last military assignments, is never a poetry of ultimate pessimism. The wanderer, the figure of the poet, turns aside from the materialistic current of the times to seek, uncertainly, a new idealism. The boy Elis, developed in several poems in Trakl's last volume, does not undergo the prevailing decline but awaits a time that will come after the decline has reached its lowest point. Such figures in Georg Trakl's poetry represent hope for the reawakening of spiritual values after the magnificent and terrifying sunset of the first decades of the new century, and after the night that would follow. They represent the hope of a new dawn.

Von E. Underwood

AN OCTOPUS

Author: Marianne Moore (1887-1972)
Type of poem: Meditation
First published: 1924; collected in *Selected Poems*, 1935

The Poem

"An Octopus" is a long, meditative, free-verse poem of 193 lines of varying length. Though meditative, it is not a reflective poem but one of active processes. Like many of Marianne Moore's poems, the title runs immediately into the first line of the poem, thereby limiting any sense of positioning the poem or preparing the reader. The reader confronts a series of shifting possibilities as suggested by the first sentence: "An Octopus/ of ice." This incomplete opening sentence establishes a metaphoric comparison that will be explored—but not fully or completely—in the poem.

The poem is a continuous shifting of perspectives, not on a single subject, but on the movement of analogies. Thus, after the poem's description of Mount Rainier and its surrounding ice fields as an octopus and its tentacles, it quickly compounds the activity of description with questions of travel, of perception, the difficulty of art, and the appropriation of nature as an aesthetic object.

"An Octopus" resists division into component parts of a whole argument; however, there are implicit shifts of focus. These shifts may be briefly outlined in the following manner: The first thirteen lines displace the reader because the metaphoric comparison of the mountain to the octopus is suspended. Lines 14 to 22 counterbalance the first section, for they become increasingly descriptive. At line 23, Moore self-reflexively shifts, stating: "Completing a circle,/ you have been deceived into thinking that you have progressed." The poem offers both descriptions and challenges to making the mountain, nature, or the other familiar and thus reduced to merely the scenic and clichéd.

The poem continues in this long section offering descriptions and suggesting that such descriptions are inadequate in various ways—grottoes that "make you wonder why you came" (line 62) or a beauty never fully spoken of "at home/ for fear of being stoned as an impostor" (lines 73-74). At line 75, the poem shifts from these questions of travel—that is, descriptions of the mountain in relation to a "you"—to a larger human presence among the various wild creatures, who themselves have become anthropomorphized. It is at line 75 that Moore names the site of this meditation, Big Snow Mountain; this is Mount Rainier, which she visited in 1922. Thus far, the poem's focus has been the mountain, with varying layers of particularized description. The poem nevertheless poses the paradoxical condition of knowing the other that is always difficult to apprehend: "conspicuously spotted little horses are peculiar;/ hard to discern among the birch-trees, ferns, and lily-pads" (lines 117-118).

The poem's single break follows line 127, which marks the poem's shift from the descriptive to the conceptual. Moore derides any pastoralism or appropriation of the landscape for moral purposes in the opening lines of this section. The Aristotelian ideals of attaining knowledge and propriety are contrasted to the "odd oracles of cool official sarcasm" (line 154); Moore shares with the Greeks the desire for accuracy, and also the understanding that knowledge will never be complete. This meditation continues with her linking Henry James's writing to the mountain, in that both have a "Neatness of finish! Neatness of finish!" (line 172). The Greeks' love of "smoothness, distrusting what was back/ of what could not be clearly seen" (lines 140-141), serves to draw Moore's sensibility into agreement with James and the Greeks.

The poem, however, closes with a long meditation on the ability of a word to signify an object: "Is 'tree' the word for these things" (line 180). The full understanding or perceiving of the mountain, or anything, can never be concluded. Moore's "Relentless accuracy" (line 173), like that of the Greeks or James, prohibits full closure.

Forms and Devices

"An Octopus" can be viewed as a collage; it contains citations from various sources, as indicated in the notes Moore provided to accompany the poem. These citations, set apart by quotation marks, introduce a sense of an assemblage of multiple perspectives or multiple voices other than the conventional lyrical "I." The quotation marks also create a tension between the apparent author and the cited words. Nevertheless, the various citations are seamlessly incorporated into the flow of the poem's descriptions. As a collage, the poem fits into a modernist aesthetic that sought to both create poems that were objects and to draw into poetry the daily and mundane and transform it into art.

"An Octopus" contains numerous examples of various tropes. Paradox is perhaps the striking trope outside of Moore's use of images. Again, the opening line provides an example of what is prevalent throughout the poem: The octopus is of ice—though significantly Moore omits the verb "is" so as to draw the juxtaposition of living creature and a lifeless elemental into a new thing. What she views—or how she views the mountain—is highly mutable, for "its clearly defined pseudo-podia/ [are] made of glass that will bend—a much needed invention" (line 4). The metaphor of the glacier as an octopus is further complicated by the metaphoric comparison of it as having the "crushing rigor of the python" and then further shifting the comparison to "'spider fashion/ on its arms' misleadingly like lace" (lines 9-11).

The poem celebrates the mountain through extraordinary images. Moore accumulates images through the use of catalogs, including catalogs of colors, "indigo, pea-green, blue-green, and turquoise" (line 34), of animals, "bears, elk, deer, wolves, goats, and ducks" (line 40), of gems, "calcium gems and alabaster pillars,/ topaz, tourmaline crystals and amethyst quartz" (lines 49-50). Her use of images often fuses with the paradoxical, as in "cliffs the color of the clouds, of petrified white vapor" (line 64). Here, as throughout the poem, the paradox is alchemical in that it transforms and fuses the opposing elements of stone and vapor. Indeed, she points to this idea of drawing together disparate elements "moisture works its alchemy,/ transmuting verdure into onyx" (lines 126-127). The full landscape is always in the process of transformation.

It is also characteristic of this poem, and of many of Moore's works, that the syntax cannot be simplified. Sentences are often complex, compound structures that depend upon momentum and the moment. Their form and logic is associative and accumulative, often carrying the reader away from the subject. Though Moore also includes short, direct sentences, none are statements of truth. The unfolding structure of Moore's sentences is thus also an aspect of the verbal collage's juxtapositions and the transformative processes of metaphor and image. Moore's sentences, however, do not lead to obscurity, rather they attempt a precision of observation and a desire for fact. The weaving of various citations with the observer's voice reinforces the drive for "Relentless accuracy."

Themes and Meanings

Among Moore's concerns in "An Octopus" is the view that writing is a phenomenon or an otherness analogous to the mountain. The reader's approach to the poem would entail similar dilemmas to that of viewing the mountain. Moore explores to what extent one can avoid objectifying an object—that is, turning away from its complexities and changing it into something identifiable. The demand for identity must be resisted, Moore implies through the poem's use of paradox, shifting perspectives, citations, and other devices. To resist identity, however, is not to give up "Relentless accuracy." The unresolved and incomplete quality of the poem suggests that neither the mountain nor the poem can be seen fully. Moore does not consider this as failure, but rather a sign of the necessity for a relentless pursuit of accuracy as well as a demand for active curiosity.

"An Octopus" exemplifies Moore's genius as an observer and a collector of observations. The naturalist's desire for details is demonstrated with her use of citations about the environment of the mountain. Yet, importantly, Moore does not settle for simply a descriptive poem. Like her protégé, the poet Elizabeth Bishop, Moore was concerned with such metaphysical and aesthetic issues as uncertainty, provisionality, voice, the definition of self, and the processes of seeing. "An Octopus" explores each of these concerns while offering a meditation on writing. Moore offers a continually shifting range of emotions in her descriptions of the mountain; the poem suggests the capacity writing has to contain these emotions while simultaneously not limiting them or fusing them into a unity. The analogy of the octopus never becomes symbolic, an identity, or a solitary truth. Moore, instead, assembles possibilities, all of which accumulate but never reach a summation.

The resistance to completion occurs in various ways. It should be noted that the poem underwent several substantial revisions after its original publication in *The Dial* magazine. In Moore's view, the poem as object was never a static piece, but always a process. And certainly a poem such as "An Octopus," concerned as it is with observation and description, questions the possibility of a full vision of an object. Perception hinges upon the position of the observer; in "An Octopus" the observer is essentially a tourist and not a native of the place. Notably about America's western landscape, "An Octopus" questions the definition of self and of an American or native self. Like the painter Georgia O'Keeffe or the poet William Carlos Williams, Moore was not an expatriate. Like Williams or O'Keeffe, Moore develops an idiosyncratic vision and reveals peculiarly American idioms. The self, construed as both personal and social, is portrayed as always in process, always appropriating perspectives and shedding them. Neither the self nor the object perceived can be captured in completeness or static essence.

James McCorkle

ODE: INTIMATIONS OF IMMORTALITY

Author: William Wordsworth (1770-1850)
Type of poem: Ode
First published: 1807, in *Poems in Two Volumes*

The Poem

In "Ode: Intimations of Immortality" William Wordsworth writes in the complicated stanza forms and irregular rhythms that are typical of the ode form. The 205
lines are divided into eleven stanzas of varying lengths and rhyme schemes. In the
title, Wordsworth attempts to summarize and simplify the rich philosophical content
of the poem.

The poem begins with an epigraph taken from an earlier poem by Wordsworth:
"The Child is father of the Man;/ And I could wish my days to be/ Bound each to
each by natural piety." In this section of "My Heart Leaps Up," the speaker hopes
that, in his maturity, he can maintain an intimate connection to the world, similar to
the bond that he had in his own childhood. Since the "Child is father of the Man,"
people should respect the child in them as much as they are bound to their own
fathers.

The first two stanzas of the poem quickly establish the problem that Wordsworth,
the first-person speaker, faces: "There was a time" when the earth was charged with
magnificence in the poet's eyes, when every common element "did seem/ Appareled
in celestial light," but that time has gone. The ode begins in elegiac fashion, with the
poet mourning because "there hath passed away a glory from the earth."

Oddly enough, this problem seems almost resolved in stanza 3 when Wordsworth
announces that "a timely utterance" (which is never revealed) relieves his grief.
Critics have never decided definitively what that "timely utterance" could be, but all
agree that Wordsworth seems tremendously healed by it. He boldly predicts that
"No more shall grief of mine the season wrong." The poem, which began in generalizations, becomes focused on a particular day in May, the heart of which makes
"every Beast keep holiday." Stanza 4 continues this celebratory mode for another
fifteen lines. The formerly sullen Wordsworth now senses "the fullness of [the]
bliss" of the "blessèd Creatures" and the joy of the "happy Shepherd-boy," the children culling flowers, or the infant "on his Mother's arm."

The poem shifts suddenly, however, with the simple connective "But" in line 52.
Despite the spring revelry of which Wordsworth says, "I hear, I hear, with joy I
hear!" the poem shifts into a melancholy mode: " — But there's a Tree, of many, one/
A single Field which I have looked upon,/ Both of them speak of something that is
gone." Wordsworth returns to the elegiac tone of the first two stanzas when he asks,
"Whither is fled the visionary gleam?" The poem leaves the joyful sounds of May
and tries to answer this question by turning to philosophical issues. Stanzas 5
through 9 track the complex musings of Wordsworth as he tries to explain what
happens in adulthood to "the glory and the dream" of youth.

Stanzas 10 and 11 return to the natural world and the "gladness of the May," but in them the reader can see that Wordsworth has been changed by his meditation. He acknowledges that "nothing can bring back the hour/ Of splendor in the grass, of glory in the flower" which belongs to the young only. Yet he suggests stoically that "We will grieve not, rather find/ Strength in what remains behind." Wordsworth finally salutes the power of the human heart, "its tenderness, its joys, and fears," and the poem ends not with the giddy and transient happiness of stanza 3 but with a mature, chastened poet accepting both the pleasures and the pains of "man's mortality."

Forms and Devices

Although, in some senses, "Ode: Intimations of Immortality" is an extremely abstract, difficult poem, Wordsworth does aid the reader by providing visual images for his philosophical ideas. Figurative language functions in the same way as a parable in the Bible: Concrete images help the reader *see* the point.

The fifth stanza, which begins the highly abstract and philosophical section of the poem, presents three metaphors that are repeated in later stanzas: God "is our home," heaven is filled with light, and as an individual grows up "shades of the prison-house begin to close" upon the child. The celestial light, which represents the spiritual realm, eventually fades and dies away as the "Youth . . . farther from the east/ Must travel." Literally, the youth, as he grows older, does not travel westward or move into a shady prison-house; Wordsworth uses metaphorical language to help the reader see the change from the liberty of pure spirituality to the gradual imprisonment by matter or the flesh.

In stanzas 6 and 7, Wordsworth adds to the philosophical picture. Nature, or the material world, "with something of a Mother's mind," makes "her foster child, her Inmate Man/ Forget . . . that imperial palace whence he came." Nature is figuratively represented as a foster mother, in opposition to God as the true father. The "imperial palace," or celestial home, is gradually forgotten by the "Inmate Man," who is Everyman, as he grows accustomed to the "prison-house" of earth.

Another attempt is made in stanza 8 to explain, through figurative language, the journey of the soul. The "heaven-born freedom" that is the infant's birthright becomes, in time, the "inevitable yoke" of mortal life, an "earthly freight," or "a weight,/ Heavy as frost."

This poem does not offer a sustained conceit or extended metaphor but moves somewhat quickly from one image to the next. The relationship between the foster mother and God the Father is pursued for two stanzas and then dropped. The image of the youth moving from east to west appears only once. The contrast between the "prison-house" that holds the "Inmate Man" and the "imperial palace" that lodges the soul, although it is central to the poem, is stated explicitly in only three lines. The home of the soul becomes the "immortal sea" in stanza 9, and what was formerly described as westward movement or a prison-house is visualized as distance from the sea: "Though inland far we be,/ Our Souls have sight of that immortal sea/

Which brought us hither." One of the joys of the poem lies in this constant shifting as the poet, in a meditative mode, tries to approximate in physical terms the complexity of his philosophy. With its rhythmical irregularities and stanza variations, the ode is particularly well suited to this discursive, expansive style.

Themes and Meanings

Between the third and the ninth stanza, "Ode: Intimations of Immortality" seems extremely bleak. Wordsworth suggests that human growth leads downward from the splendor of youth to the emptiness and grief of "palsied Age." He accepts Plato's notion that souls exist before as well as after they are joined with bodies. Unlike Plato, however, Wordsworth believes that little children and infants inhabit a world which is full of "visionary gleam" because they have only recently left the "imperial palace" in the spiritual realm and, "trailing clouds of glory," have entered the fallen world of matter. In childhood, according to Wordsworth, one's own immortality is intuited and so young people are perpetually joyful; they have a "heart of May" not because their bodies are strong and capable but because of their spiritual health. The bleakness comes when the "years . . . bring the inevitable yoke" of customary actions and "endless imitation." When the "celestial light,/ The glory and the freshness" of youth disappear, what is left?

The final three stanzas answer this question in a hopeful fashion. Memory serves as an important key for a kind of hard-earned happiness, "all that is at enmity with joy" cannot "utterly abolish or destroy" as long as one can recall the "delight and liberty" of childhood when God's light was all around. As the title explicitly states, in maturity, one garners "intimations of immortality from recollections of early childhood."

Wordsworth finds strength not only in memory but also in "the philosophic mind" that develops over time. In his poem "Lines: Composed a Few Miles Above Tintern Abbey," he claims that he need not mourn the loss of youth because he has received "abundant recompense" in his more mature vision of the world and his appreciation of the "still, sad music of humanity." The same idea is reshaped in "Ode: Intimations of Immortality." Speaking for all of humanity, Wordsworth admits that "nothing can bring back the hour/ Of splendor in the grass, of glory in the flower," but he insists that "We will grieve not, rather find/ Strength in what remains behind." What remains are not only those memories of early childhood but also the "primal sympathy . . . the soothing thoughts that spring/ Out of human suffering." Wordsworth powerfully suggests that it is sensitivity to others' suffering and compassion that distinguish the mature person from the youthful one and that provides a "recompense" for falling into the "prison-house" of consciousness. He finally suggests that the mature mind develops, over time, a "faith that looks through death."

The poet is able to conclude, in stanza 11, that he loves the "Brooks which down their channels fret,/ Even more than when I tripped lightly as they." There is a sense of reconciliation in these final lines; time is no longer the enemy because Wordsworth recognizes that the "philosophic mind" can develop only as one moves toward death. He loves nature even more than in youth because he has earned a sober appreciation of the human heart, "its tenderness, its joys, and fears." The false, transient euphoria of stanzas 3 and 4 is gone. Instead, the poem ends with a powerful, if somewhat muted, joy. Through suffering, a "philosophic mind" develops which allows one to endure and keep "watch o'er man's mortality."

Kevin Boyle

ODE, INSCRIBED TO W. H. CHANNING

Author: Ralph Waldo Emerson (1803-1882)
Type of poem: Ode
First published: 1847, in *Poems*

The Poem

"Ode, Inscribed to W. H. Channing" alludes frequently to historical people and events. The William Henry Channing to whom the ode is inscribed was a nineteenth century author and Unitarian minister, like his more famous uncle, William Ellery Channing. The younger Channing, a vigorous opponent of slavery, apparently occasioned this ode by urging his friend Ralph Waldo Emerson to join the cause in some formal or active way. The abolition issue was dividing increasing numbers of people. Daniel Webster, whom Emerson once greatly admired and probably had in mind all the while he wrote the ode, had turned against the Abolitionists in an effort to preserve the Union. Also, the Mexican War had just begun. This ode is Emerson's explanation of his reasons for remaining aloof, and a proclamation of his strong feelings regarding the issues.

Addressing Channing as the "evil time's sole patriot," the poet begins with an explanation of why he cannot leave his "honied thought" and study: "The angry Muse/ Puts confusion in my brain (lines 10 through 11). The "evil time" is riven by "the priest's cant" and "statesman's rant" and by politics ("politique") that are at best fraudulent. Anyone who chatters ("prates") about improved "arts and life" (line 14) should behold his country's raids into Mexico. Anyone who praises the "freedom-loving mountaineer" of the North should know that the poet has found, by the banks and in the valleys of its rivers, the agents ("jackals") of the slave owners (in search of fugitive slaves).

The fifth stanza cites New Hampshire as an example (or source) of the "evil," for it is "taunted" by little men— "bat" and "wren." The list of ills is long: If the disturbed earth should "bury the folk,/ the southern crocodile would grieve" (lines 30-31). "Virtue" babbles or equivocates ("palters"), and "Right" has disappeared; "Freedom" is hidden, and funeral eloquence disturbs those buried heroes it purports to put to rest; these two lines, and the earlier reference to "little men" (line 26), may allude to Daniel Webster, a native of New Hampshire, and to his funeral oration at Bunker Hill, which Emerson heard.

Stanza 6 addresses Channing again ("O glowing friend"), alluding to his apparent support of dividing the North from the South over the slavery issue. The poet asks rhetorically what good separation would do, since commerce and other affairs (represented by Boston Bay and Bunker Hill) would continue as the evil is everywhere ("Things are of the snake"). Further examples (stanza 7) show how affairs are topsyturvy: They serve who should be served. Deference to things rules the day (line 48), and the consequence is that mankind is ridden like a beast of burden by the very things it worships.

Stanza 8 returns to the causes of this travesty: People have confused the laws governing man and thing (line 55). Men should not be governed by physical law, which is good for building "town and fleet," but runs wild and destroys man's supremacy ("doth the man unking"). The next two stanzas develop the idea that different laws apply to different spheres. Physical laws fittingly fell trees, build, grade, till, and so on. Humans should make laws themselves for friendship and love, to benefit truth and harmony. The state should adjust to these laws "how it may" (line 69), as Olympus is ruled by Jove.

The longest stanza, 11, continues the idea that a proper order should obtain in human affairs. People have their fit realms of activity (line 75); when one is forced out of one's proper sphere, things go awry. The poet implies that man should trust the "over-god," who rules human affairs with a knowledge and power beyond man's, for he "Knows to bring honey/ Out of the lion" (lines 86-87). The final stanza turns again to conditions as they are—in Europe, aggression has reduced Poland—but the ode ends with a promise: The victors divide into two camps, half fighting for freedom, and the "astonished" Muse finds thousands defending her.

Forms and Devices

The poem is an irregular ode composed of twelve stanzas of unequal length, ranging from five to nineteen lines each, totalling ninety-seven in all. The lines have a range of two to five stresses (only lines 20, 21, 74, and the last line of the poem have five stresses). No consistent pattern is apparent in the use of stresses, though the seven lines in the third stanza all have three stresses each, and often lines with an equal number of stresses are grouped together. Most of the metric feet are iambs, and most of the lines end on a stressed syllable.

Freedom of form is also evident in the use of rhyme, which displays no consistent pattern from stanza to stanza. Most of the stanzas have only four rhymes, many of them paired (*aa* or *bb*, for example) and many alternated (*abab*). Though structurally diverse, the poem is also unified by a number of structural features. The individual stanzas are knit together by the rhymes, which are usually metrically stressed; by grouping together lines of equal number of stresses; and, often, by repetition. In stanza 7, for example, the first four lines repeat the same structure and verb: "The horseman serves . . ./ The neatherd serves . . ./ The merchant serves," and so on. Stanza 9 repeats the same sentence structure through a series of seven lines, each with two stresses.

The poet uses other means to unify the ode and elevate its tone. The apostrophe is used ("O rushing Contoocook!") along with personification ("Virtue palters; Right is hence") and allusions to classical figures, using the "Muse" at the beginning and end to represent the arts in general and poetry in particular, and citing classical mythology: "As Olympus follows Jove." These "learned" reminders of the formal nature of the ode are interwoven with indigenous material, place names (Boston Bay, Bunker Hill) and local topography (forest, mountain, orchard, glebe) to demonstrate the breadth and nature of the poet's vision, and to give much of the poem considerable symbolic power. The odic structure itself and references to classical figures place the poem in one tradition, while place names would be expected to arouse powerful associations in the minds of readers all too familiar with the importance of geography.

Themes and Meanings

The principal argument of the poem is that the times are clearly out of joint. Its strongest sentiments relate to the failure of men (such as Webster) to stand on the side of freedom and humanity, and against slavery and military aggression, whether in Mexico or in Poland. Though the poem is not a call to arms, its lofty stanzas accuse the "little men" who have betrayed Virtue and Right and give only lip service to Freedom. Instead, men force things and people out of their proper spheres and thereby "mix and mar," confusing things with human values. This idea is expressed sardonically in the use of "chattel" (line 48)—placed appropriately at the center of the ode—which means "movable possessions"; here, it refers to both livestock and slaves. In their passion to aggrandize themselves, men have reduced humanity to a thing, and elevated things to a place of eminence. The poet suggests a remedy: One should live for "friendship," for "love," and for "truth's and harmony's behoof" (lines 67-68). One must not be too zealous and get taken in by the "priest's cant" and "statesman's rant" or drawn into their "politique."

The poet is centrally concerned with the arena in which the issues are bruited and the battle waged. He depicts this concern by using geographical references (New Hampshire, Boston Bay, and the "southern crocodile," for example) and by instancing local figures and activities (the horseman, neatherd, merchant, and so on). In this way, the poem asserts that though one must be cognizant of the revered past, the present has a place and importance equal to the other, if not superior to it, and the issues addressed are endemic to the setting.

A strong faith permeates the ode and explains in part the poet's attack on the "little men" and those who have lost sight of Virtue and Freedom; it is a faith in order ("Every one to his chosen work"), in the issues, in the "over-god," and in man himself. Despite the destructive nature of man, the "over-god" will find "thousands" who will defend freedom and the arts. Meanwhile, the poet does not turn away from the evils—he is no "blindworm," for he has beheld the transgressions of "the famous States" (line 16) and has himself found, by the rivers of the North, the "jackals of the negro-holder." Perhaps the poet's "honied thoughts" are akin to the "honey" that the over-god "Knows to bring . . ./ Out of the lion" (lines 86-87). If so, the lion remains for the moment in his den ("My study"), naming the evils and their causes and cautioning his countrymen to proceed with a clear understanding of the distinction between men and things. The poet is optimistic that freedom and poetry will be defended even when a state is devastated, and the soldiers shall come from the ranks of the invaders themselves.

Bernard E. Morris

ODE ON A GRECIAN URN

Author: John Keats (1795-1821)
Type of poem: Ode
First published: 1820, in *Lamia, Isabella, The Eve of St. Agnes, and Other Poems*

The Poem

It is important to apprehend the dramatic situation in "Ode on a Grecian Urn" both to understand the poem on a literal level and to glean any larger meaning from it. A narrator looks at the pictures that decorate the outside of an urn; between the "leaf-fringed legend[s]" (line 5)—literally, the decorated borders on top and beneath the painted figures on the vase—the narrator sees two distinct scenes, consisting primarily of figures engaged in two activities common to Greek life: raucous sexual play and religious celebration.

The speaker in the poem addresses the urn directly, as if it were a living object. Viewing the first scene, which consists of a collection of young people engaging in some form of revelry, the narrator asks about the identity of the people and about their motives: Are the women escaping from the men, or is this a courting match? Why is there music (represented by a figure on the urn who is playing an instrument)? The scene makes the narrator realize that he can only imagine his own answers—but in a sense, the "unheard" melodies that he imagines are "sweeter" than those he might actually hear (lines 11-12). Gazing at what he believes to be two lovers about to embrace, he observes that, though they can never consummate their relationship, they will never change, either; instead, they will be forever in that heightened state of anticipation that precedes the climax of a love affair.

At the beginning of the fourth stanza, the narrator shifts his gaze to the second scene on the urn; in it, some townspeople are leading a calf to an altar for sacrifice. Once more the narrator asks questions: Who are these people? Where do they come from? Again he realizes that he cannot get the answers from viewing the urn; the questions will be forever unanswered, because the urn is not capable of providing such information. Rather, it sits silently, provoking his curiosity.

In the final stanza, the narrator recognizes the futility of his questioning and acknowledges that the urn is simply capable of teasing him "out of thought" (line 44)—leaving him unable to come to some logical conclusion about the stories depicted on the urn, and hence about the value of the urn itself. The narrator concludes by calling it a "Cold Pastoral" (line 45) whose ultimate worth lies in its beauty, not in its message.

Forms and Devices

John Keats's meditation on the significance of the pictures on this piece of classical pottery shares many of the characteristics of the Horatian ode. It consists of five stanzas of equal length (ten lines), with a consistent rhyme scheme in each: The first four lines are rhymed *abab*, and the final six lines contain three rhymes, arranged in various patterns (*cdecde* or *cdeced*). The limited number of rhymes, coupled with the many end-stopped lines, give the poem a restrained quality; readers are forced to pause often and are constantly, if subtly, brought back to previous lines by the rhymes. As with any rhymed composition, the reader comes to develop a sense of expectation at the end of a line; that expectation is fulfilled when the rhyming pattern is fulfilled. The regularity of stanzaic pattern and rhyme scheme is further reinforced by the poet's use of iambic pentameter as his basic meter. The slow cadence of this conversation-like line gives the poem a quality of meditation and seriousness. All these techniques work together to achieve Keats's aim: to get readers to pause, as his narrator does, to contemplate the significance of the two scenes on the urn.

The regularity of these formal devices is undercut, however, by Keats's use of ambiguity in his language. He makes extensive use of double entendre and paradox in describing both the urn itself and the scenes displayed upon it. For example, in the opening line, the narrator refers to the urn as a "still unravished bride." The word "still" can be read as an adjective meaning "unmoving" or "at rest," or it can be an adverb modifying "unravished," in which case it means "not yet." The urn is the "bride of quietness" and the foster-child of "silence" and "slow time," yet the narrator calls it a "Sylvan historian" — suggesting that it has a story to tell. Certainly such ambiguities create a tension within the poem; the reader is not really sure what kind of story can emerge from such a storyteller. That tension is reinforced by the pictures themselves, in which people seem to be arrested in the midst of activity. In the first one, the narrator sees a figure playing an instrument; no sound comes forth, however, and the only melody possible is that which the narrator imagines. Similarly, in the same scene two lovers are about to kiss, yet they remain as if in suspended animation. That situation is seen as both good and bad — "never, never canst thou kiss" (line 17), the narrator observes sadly to the young man pictured on the urn, but he immediately follows with the admonition, "yet, do not grieve," because the youth's beloved "cannot fade, though thou hast not thy bliss." These lovers are "For ever panting and for ever young" (line 27); they will never suffer the tribulations of real passion, which leave "A burning forehead, and a parching tongue" (line 30). This may be true, but the possibility lingers that they will never feel the joy of consummated passion either.

Similar tensions are present in the narrator's discussion of the second scene. Though the group taking the heifer to sacrifice appears happy, the narrator realizes that the "little town" from which these people have come will "forever" be "silent" and "desolate" (lines 38, 40). The implication is that, despite the joy depicted in the scene, there will remain an unexplained loss to counterbalance the apparent euphoria this work of art exhibits.

Themes and Meanings

The central theme of "Ode on a Grecian Urn" is the complex nature of art. The dramatic situation—the narrator's puzzling one-way exchange with the urn as he views the scenes painted upon it—is intended to provoke in the reader an awareness of the paradoxes inherent in all art, but especially visual art. The central question raised by the narrator is: What good is art? What purpose does it serve? The urn is beautiful, to be sure, but as a vehicle for conveying information it is woefully inadequate. No story on the urn is ever finished and communicated; all action is arrested at a single instant. Only through imagination is the narrator able to come to some human understanding of the "message" on the urn; hence, the work of art does not really have a message for its viewers at all, but only serves as a stimulus for engaging the imaginations of those who look upon it.

Perhaps Keats is suggesting that the "message" of art is always achieved through a participatory act. If there is a "truth" to be gleaned from the appreciation of art, it is a truth found only when the viewer serves as a co-creator with the artist in developing meaning. Such an interpretation helps to make sense of the final enigmatic lines of the poem: "Beauty is Truth, Truth Beauty—That is all/ Ye know of earth, and all ye need to know" (lines 49-50). Even that interpretation is subject to question, however, since readers cannot be certain exactly what the urn actually "says" to the narrator. In most publications, some or all of the words in the final lines are placed in quotation marks; in Keats's manuscripts, no quotation marks are used. The shift from "thou" (used by the narrator to address the urn) to "ye" (used in the final lines only) suggests that the entire sentence in the final lines are to be read as the urn's "message" to viewers. If that is the case, then the lesson of the poem is that one can never arrive at logical truth through an apprehension of art, since art does not work in the same way that logical thought does. The narrator's observation that the urn seems to "tease us out of thought" (line 44) supports such an interpretation. Nevertheless, art—here personified by the urn—has great value to serve as a form of pleasure and solace; it "remain[s]" a "friend to man" in the "midst of other woe" (lines 47-48). Keats is making a case for art on its own terms; he wants readers to see that appreciation of art for its own sake is as valuable as—perhaps even more valuable than—the extraction of meaning from works intended primarily to uplift the spirit of man simply by conveying a sense of the beautiful.

Laurence W. Mazzeno

ODE ON MELANCHOLY

Author: John Keats (1795-1821)
Type of poem: Ode
First published: 1820, in *Lamia, Isabella, The Eve of St. Agnes, and Other Poems*

The Poem

"Ode on Melancholy" is a three-stanza poem addressed to people who are susceptible to fits of melancholy, and it offers a prescription for coping with "the blues." John Keats says that the melancholy mood is full of beauty and potential spiritual instruction. Therefore, instead of seeking escape through intoxication or even suicide, the melancholy individual should savor the mood because it has divine properties. Lethe, referred to in the opening line, was one of the rivers of Hades in Greek and Roman mythology; drinking from it was supposed to cause forgetfulness. Proserpine was the goddess of Hades. Psyche was a nymph who represented the human soul. Wolfsbane, nightshade, and yew are all plants which have poisonous properties, and yew trees are commonly planted around cemeteries.

In the second stanza, the words "glut thy sorrow" encapsulate the poet's prescription. Do not be afraid of melancholy: enjoy it. Look at all the beauty of nature, including the beauty in a beautiful woman's eyes, and reflect upon the sad truth that none of it can last. Similar thoughts are expressed in Keats's "Ode on a Grecian Urn" and "Ode to a Nightingale." The fragility and perishability of beauty evoke melancholy but make the beautiful object more precious.

Pleasure and pain, joy and sorrow, delight and melancholy are opposite sides of the same coin: It is impossible to have one without the other. Anyone who is particularly sensible to beauty and pleasure is bound to be painfully susceptible to melancholy. Only the aesthetically sensitive person can appreciate the beauty of melancholy; melancholy adds dignity and spiritual significance to beauty. Vulgar, insensitive people will be afraid of it as of some threatening aberration and will try to escape from it with drugs or in extreme cases even in suicide.

Keats suggests throughout the poem that the way things look depends upon the emotional state of the observer. When one is in a melancholy state, things can look particularly vivid and beautiful. This impressionistic approach to artistic subjects became an enormously important movement throughout Europe and America later in the nineteenth century, and Keats may be regarded as one of its forerunners. It is not until almost the end of the poem that Keats uses the word Melancholy, with a capital "M," personifying or reifying melancholy and turning it into a goddess. There was no goddess of melancholy in Greek or Roman mythology; Keats is creating his own mythology. By doing this, he is suggesting that melancholy can be more than an aesthetic experience—it is actually akin to a religious experience— and implying that the numinous quality of the experience frightens unworthy people into seeking escape through oblivion.

Forms and Devices

One of the most striking devices of this poem is the use of *o* sounds to evoke a mood of melancholy. The first five words of the poem all contain the letter *o* and, in contrast to the dominant iambic rhythm of the remaining lines, these first five words, "No, no, go not to," are all heavily stressed. As well as setting the overall mood, the stress on the first five vowels serves notice that the poem is intended to be read slowly. What is being done here is similar to what a composer does with a musical composition when he marks his score *largo*: The performer is advised that the piece is to be played in a slow and solemn manner.

The *o* sounds are so densely crowded into the first two stanzas that scarcely a line does not contain at least one. The word "nor" is used four times in the first stanza, echoed by the word "or" which is used three times in the second stanza. In one line in the first stanza, there are five *o* sounds: "Your mournful Psyche, nor the downy owl." These sounds mimic the moans and groans of a person suffering from acute melancholy and help produce a mood of sorrow and despair.

A poet can convey feelings through the manipulation of the sounds of words just as a composer can with musical notes; modern poets, beginning notably with the French in the time of Charles Baudelaire, Prosper Mérimée, Arthur Rimbaud, and Paul Verlaine, experimented extensively with the use of such purely mechanical devices to create emotional effects. It is impossible to say who invented the idea, because it goes back at least as far as ancient Greece, when poets accompanied their recitations by strumming on musical instruments. William Shakespeare was certainly well aware of the power of the mere sounds of words to create moods, and Keats revered Shakespeare to the point of idolatry. Keats also seems to have been influenced in this area (as well as in his interest in the subject of melancholy) by the senior Romantic poet, Samuel Taylor Coleridge, who was a bold experimenter with the technical aspects of poetic composition, as demonstrated in his strange and wonderful fragment, "Kubla Khan."

In "Ode on Melancholy," the *o* sounds are so densely crowded into the first two stanzas that scarcely a line does not contain at least one. The word "nor" is used four times in the first stanza, echoed by the word "or" which is used three times in the second stanza. In one line in the first stanza, there are five *o* sounds: "Your mournful Psyche, nor the downy owl." These sounds mimic the moans and groans of a person suffering from acute melancholy and help produce a mood of sorrow and despair.

As in all of Keats's best poetry, there is extensive employment of visual imagery in "Ode on Melancholy." The many references to drugs and poisons reflect Keats's early training as an apothecary. He was developing a dangerous fondness for alcohol, and some of his poems, including "Ode to a Nightingale," suggest that he may have done some experimenting with drugs as well. The unusual images are what admirers of Keats admire most about him. Some examples in "Ode on Melancholy" are the twisting of wolfsbane until the roots are tightly wound around each other like the strands of a rope; making a rosary from poisonous yew berries; the downy owl; the weeping cloud; the bee-mouth sipping nectar from flowers. All these images demonstrate Keats's unusually vivid visual imagination, the faculty he exploited to write his greatest poems. An image worthy of Shakespeare himself, and reminiscent of his play *The Tempest* (1611), is "the rainbow of the salt sand-wave": that is, the rainbows that can be seen hovering just above the crests of breaking waves on bright, sunny days. This is the kind of natural beauty that people see but are not usually aware of seeing until an artist takes the image out of nature and uses it in a painting or a poem.

Themes and Meanings

It was because Keats took such intense delight in all the visual beauty of nature that he was also subject to melancholy. He had to reflect that he was going have to leave all this beauty when he died, and he was already suffering from premonitions of death at the time he wrote his "Ode on Melancholy" and the other great odes of his *annus mirabilis*, 1819. His brother had recently died of tuberculosis, and Keats had apparently become infected with the disease while nursing him. Keats was only twenty-five years old when he died in 1821. During his short career as a poet, he managed to secure a permanent place among the foremost English poets; however, one of the great tragedies of literary history is the loss of all the works this genius might have produced if he had been permitted to live out a normal lifespan.

Since Keats was subject to fits of melancholy, he took a strong interest in it. He lived long before the days of Sigmund Freud, or he would have been fascinated by psychoanalysis. One of Keats's favorite books was Robert Burton's *The Anatomy of Melancholy* (1621), which might be described as a primitive study of psychoneurosis. Like Burton, Keats realized that melancholy was a complex state that could be the source of intellectual as well as artistic inspiration, and that it was an ailment to which artists were particularly susceptible. As another great Romantic poet, Percy Bysshe Shelley, expressed it: "Our sweetest songs are those that tell of saddest thought."

What Keats is doing in "Ode on Melancholy" is exactly what twentieth century musical artists such as "Blind Lemon" Jefferson, Huddie ("Leadbelly") Ledbetter, Louis Armstrong, Charley Parker, Eleanor ("Billie") Holiday, and other jazz greats did with the blues. Melancholy can be defined as "the blues," and the word "melancholy" is invariably used in defining the blues.

In his "Ode on Melancholy," which by definition is a piece written in praise of melancholy, Keats is saying that the mood is something to be relished rather than something from which a sensitive person should seek to escape. His thesis is summed up in the following lines of the concluding stanza: "Ay, in the very temple of Delight/ Veil'd Melancholy has her sovran shrine." The fact that he was able to use his melancholy moods to create this masterpiece is proof in itself of his thesis.

Bill Delaney

ODE TO A NIGHTINGALE

Author: John Keats (1795-1821)
Type of poem: Ode
First published: 1819; collected in *Lamia, Isabella, The Eve of St. Agnes, and Other Poems*, 1820

The Poem

"Ode to a Nightingale" is a poem in eight numbered stanzas; as the title suggests, it takes the form of a direct address to a nightingale. The speaker, evidently the poet John Keats himself, hears a nightingale singing. This beautiful but melancholy sound, which has inspired legends since the time of ancient Greece, fills him with complex and conflicting emotions. It makes him happy because he can empathize with the bird's zest for living and procreating at the height of the spring season; at the same time, it makes him sad because he is alone and has been preoccupied with morbid thoughts.

In stanza 2, Keats wishes he had a whole "beaker full" of wine so that he could get intoxicated and lose consciousness. He describes the red wine in loving detail, then goes on to specify the mortal woes from which he would like to escape — primarily those associated with old age, sickness and death. "Where youth grows pale and spectre-thin and dies" refers to his brother Tom, who had recently died of tuberculosis, the disease which was to claim Keats's own life in less than three years.

Since Keats has no wine, in stanza 4 he decides to escape by creating poetry. He makes his poem engrossing by seeming to take the reader along with him in the process of creating it. He will become a wild bird in his imagination and share in the nightingale's view of the world. This notion represents the essence of the Romantic spirit: the attempt to achieve what is known to be impossible.

Nightingales are rather small, retiring birds that live in forests, thickets, and hedgerows. Consequently, in stanza 5 Keats imagines the nightingale's world as being dark and mysterious but at that time of year full of the scents of blossoming plants. This is the high point of the poem, but he is unable to sustain his illusion. Thoughts of death intrude. In stanza 6, he confesses sometimes to "have been half in love with easeful Death." He feels comforted by his experience of sharing in the nightingale's immortal consciousness, however; he realizes that life goes on, and his own death is a small matter in the overall scheme of things. The idea of death even seems "rich." In line 1 of the seventh stanza, Keats addresses the nightingale as "immortal Bird" and traces the nightingale's song through historical and magical settings.

Then his near-religious experience comes to an end. He is inexorably drawn back into the world of reality, with all its mortal concerns. The bird's plaintive song fades into the distance, and the poet is left wondering about the validity and nature of his experience.

Forms and Devices

This entire poem is based on a single poetic conceit that is so matter-of-factly taken for granted that it is easy to overlook: The poem tacitly assumes that the bird to whom Keats is addressing his ode is immortal—that in fact only one nightingale exists and has ever existed. It looks exactly the same and sounds exactly the same as birds of that species have looked and sounded for countless centuries. Furthermore, the nightingale is immortal because it has no conception of death. Only human beings suffer from the fear of death and the feeling of futility with which death taints all human endeavor. Finally, the bird can be considered immortal because of the familiar Greek legend that the nightingale is the metamorphized soul of the ravished princess Philomela.

The bird that Keats hears singing can only be a few years old at most, yet the subtle assumption of its immortality is perfectly natural because the nightingale looks the same and sounds the same as its ancestors, which were heard "in ancient days by emperor and clown" and even further back by Ruth, whose story is told in the Book of Ruth in the Old Testament. Keats was an ardent admirer of William Shakespeare, and the naturalness of the poetic conceit in "Ode to a Nightingale" shows that Keats appreciated and understood the essence of Shakespeare's greatness, which lay in his use of simple, natural imagery—rather than imagery employed by some of his better-educated contemporaries that was pretentious, bookish, and artificial.

Keats's outstanding poetic gift was his ability to evoke vivid images in the mind of his reader. "Ode to a Nightingale" is full of such vivid images, the most famous of which is his "magic casements, opening on the foam/ Of perilous seas, in faery lands forlorn." Because of the spell that Keats has created up to this point, the sensitive reader is given a glimpse of those bright, blue, foam-crested seas through those magic casements—but only a glimpse of that magical world is ever allowed to any mortal, and then both Keats and his reader must return to reality, with its troubles, fears, and disappointments.

Another example of Keats's inspired imagery is contained in the lines, "The coming musk-rose, full of dewy wine,/ The murmurous haunt of flies on summer eves." With one stroke, Keats creates a large half-open flower glowing with soft interior lighting like a comfortable pub where the flies like to gather with their elbows on the tables to sip wine and talk about whatever flies might talk about on long summer eves.

Other striking images in "Ode to a Nightingale" are the beaker "full of the warm South" that has "beaded bubbles winking at the brim," the syncopated effect of "fast fading violets covered up in leaves," and poor Ruth standing in tears in a land so alien and unsympathetic that even the very grain in the fields looks strange and unappetizing.

Keats soon discovered that his forte lay in his vivid visual imagination, and his greatest poems are so crowded with visual imagery that they seem like beautiful murals.

Themes and Meanings

In "Ode to a Nightingale," Keats is really only talking about the beauty of nature and how painful it is to think of dying and having to leave it. These are thoughts with which every reader can identify. What makes Keats a great poet is that the feelings he expresses are common to all humanity. This feature, found in all of his greatest poetry, is called universality, and it is generally regarded as the distinguishing feature of all great art. An aspiring writer can learn from Keats that the secret of creating important work is to deal with basic human emotions.

Keats was going through considerable mental anguish when he wrote this poem. His brother Tom had just died of tuberculosis. He himself had premonitions of his own death from the same disease, which turned out to be true. He was in love with young Fanny Brawne but found it impossible to marry her because he had rejected the career in medicine for which he had been trained; he was finding it impossible to make a living as a writer. Like many present-day poets, he was tortured by the fact that he had chosen an impractical vocation; yet, it was the vocation for which he believed he was born, and it was the only thing he wanted to do.

The ode has a piquant, bittersweet flavor, not unlike the flavor of a good red wine, because it deliberately blends thoughts of beauty and decay, joy and suffering, love and death. Keats had rejected the teachings of the established church, as can be seen in his posthumously published sonnet entitled "Written in Disgust of Vulgar Superstition," in which he describes Christian church dogma as a "black spell." This left him in the position of having to find his own answers to questions that the church had automatically answered for centuries. Keats thought that all religions consisted of stories made up by imaginative individuals to mask the real truth about life. Borrowing from Greek mythology and other sources, he tried to create new stories; however, as a modern man with a modern scientific education, he knew that his stories were inventions, whereas the poets and prophets of the past really believed in the gods about which they talked; they were not using them as mere poetic metaphors. This is why Keats cannot stay with his nightingale. The elusive bird might even be seen as a metaphor for the alienated condition of modern man.

Bill Delaney

ODE TO EVENING

Author: William Collins (1721-1759)
Type of poem: Ode
First published: 1746, in *Odes on Several Descriptive and Allegorical Subjects*

The Poem

"Ode to Evening," a single stanza of fifty-two lines, is addressed to a goddess figure representing the time of day in the title. This "nymph," or "maid," who personifies dusk, is "chaste," "reserv'd," and meek, in contrast to the "bright-hair'd sun," a male figure who withdraws into his tent, making way for night. Thus "Eve," or evening, is presented as the transition between light and darkness.

William Collins further stresses a female identity in his appellation "calm vot'ress." With this feminine form of "votary" he designates a nun, or one who vows to follow the religious life. This combination of modesty, devotion, and "pensive Pleasures" alludes to the dominating figure of John Milton's "Il Penseroso."

The poem has three parts: the opening salutation, locating Eve in sequence and in the countryside; the center, a plea for guidance in achieving a calm stoicism, with a qualification, showing the reason for the request, and a shift to a personal viewpoint; and a grand finale with a roll call of the seasons and a return to a universal dimension.

Throughout most of the poem, Collins acknowledges Eve's authority and twilight's pleasures, combining pastoral imagery with classical allusions. These give the poem a Miltonic overtone, familiar to readers of Collins' day, and a close connection to his contemporaries, such as James Thomson and Joseph Warton.

After the opening apostrophe to Eve, nature takes over the first section (lines 3-14), with images of water in references to "solemn springs" plus the sun's "cloudy skirts" and "wavy bed." The wind plays a small part in setting the scene with only the one reference to "dying gales" subsiding to the point where "air is hush'd." An allusion to John Milton's "Lycidas" appears in the auditory image which invades the stillness in these lines: "Now air is hush'd, save where the weak-ey'd bat,/ With short, shrill shriek flits by on leathern wing" (lines 9-10). Other noises, less ominous, come from the beetle and the bee, a "pilgrim born in heedless hum."

The second part of the poem starts with a request to the "maid compos'd," who is worthy of emulation. "Now teach me," Collins says, to write lines in keeping with the atmosphere Eve creates. The term "numbers" here stands not only for versification and metrics but also for poetry in general. This section splits into the prayer itself, the details of evening's "genial, lov'd return," and an ominous dimension that makes the depiction more realistic than the classical allusions do. The signal for return is the appearance of Hesperus, the evening star. At this point, place deities, termed "Hours," "elves," and nymphs, become servants preparing evening's chariot for her entrance.

The poet takes center stage here, injecting a view of nature with "chill blustering

winds" and "driving rain" that make him reluctant to follow Eve. A scene reminiscent of William Shakespeare's *King Lear* being exposed to violent weather on the
heath is softened with the sound of a church bell.

Finally, the poem presents the cyclical pageant of nature. Starting with a series of
images befitting "meekest Eve" and sharply summarizing each season, the ending
brings together the benefits possibly resulting from devotion to the goddess.

Forms and Devices

Written in imitation of the Roman poet Horace, this poem is considered a Horatian rather than a pastoral ode, although it contains rural imagery and some conventions associated with pastoral poetry. The verse is unrhymed, with a metrical pattern
developing as follows: alternating sets of two iambic pentameter lines and two
shorter lines of iambic trimeter.

The sequence of longer and shorter couplets is more important for purposes of
unity here than it would have been had the lines been rhyming couplets. Collins' use
of couplets follows the neoclassical tradition, but his introduction of the short trimeter lines and the last of rhyme are viewed, in that context, as an aberration. His
balancing of long and short couplets helps to structure a poem considered too short
for the verse paragraphs of blank verse and too long for one stanza. If each four-line
set is viewed as a unit, the poem could be divided into thirteen stanzas. Ultimately,
the metrical balance reflects the alternation of day and night, although only a transitional part of this cycle is the focus of the content and the imagery.

Collins uses conventional neoclassical poetic diction without resorting to extreme
or ridiculous phraseology. One possible exception is the "pilgrim born in heedless
hum," a metaphor for a bee. Primarily, however, Collins' metaphors stand on their
own merits, sometimes coming close to clichés but not overcome by them. Language depicting pastoral images, such as "oaten stop," "yon western tent" of the
sun, the "folding star" of Hesperus, and the mountain and valley landscapes, establish the general tone of the poem and reflect Collins' neoclassicism. The Miltonic
overlay created by these images, by the imitations of Miltonic style, and by lines
alluding to others by Milton cannot be ignored.

Nature imagery serves to depict how darkness begins to take over the atmosphere
without fanfare and develops a personality for Eve. The combination of these details
and the adjectives used to describe Eve, such as modest, chaste, and meek, creates a
comfortable feeling.

The comforts of tone and quiet devotion are driven off, however, by personal
references to the poet, who, in spite of "willing feet," is hiding inside the "hut,/
That, from the mountain's side,/ Views wilds, and swelling floods" (lines 34-36)
because of the cold and rainy winds on a suggestively Shakespearean heath. The
image of spring would be overpowered by this picture, despite the sound of the
church bell, were it not for the compelling pictures created for the other seasons in
the ending.

Themes and Meanings

Ostensibly, "Ode to Evening" is a nature poem, one of those often considered a prelude to the Romantic movement or a deliberate and intentional antidote to the heroic genres most prominent in the earlier part of the Augustan age. The poem looks forward to the Age of Sensibility, a label which poems such as Thomson's *The Seasons* (1730) and Warton's *The Enthusiast: Or, The Love of Nature* (1744) helped to create. Collins' ode promotes scenic nature, as do these poems, in contrast to the neoclassical emphasis upon human nature. Similarly, it even hints at the sublime in the section describing the mountain storm and the view from the hut as well as in the images of winter at the end. Nevertheless, just as evening is neither day nor night, this poem is neither fully pre-Romantic nor conventionally neoclassical. It is transitional, subtle, and generally quiet, like its subject.

Even though Collins follows convention in imagery, diction, and verse form, he demonstrates that he is not a slave to it. The ode exerts the "gentlest" of influences, as its subject does. Even the superlatives Collins uses are not exaggerations, but the superlative forms of adjectives such as "gentle" and "meek."

The striking passages are, first, those depicting the prospect of a violent mountain storm as well as attack by winter on Eve's entourage and her flowing garments; and second, the images which are more sharply focused in the pageant of seasons which ends the poem. These seem to establish the grounds for the earlier prayer in hopes of adopting evening's calm demeanor and reserved behavior. Especially poignant are the lines describing how the wind and rain of the storm keep the poet's "willing feet" from obeying their desire to follow Eve. These lines seem highly personal in light of Samuel Johnson's famous phrase describing the poet, "poor dear Collins." Contemporaries' accounts of Collins' life, including those by his friends, record mental breakdowns which are entirely relevant if one notes the poet's own signals in this and other poems. The allusion to Lear on the heath is not the poet's personal equation of himself with Shakespeare's egotistical king; other characters who join the scene in the hut would be more suitable for comparison with Collins' presentation of himself. This passage is a faint echo of feelings expressed in the "Ode to Fear" from the same volume (1746). Although "Ode to Fear" is generated by Aristotle's discussion of pity and fear in his concept of catharsis, the personal element is a noticeable dimension and reinforces a biographical interpretation for both poems.

The final section ventures into a more vivid style of natural depiction. The fragrances of spring, the length of summer days, the effect engendered by autumn colors and temperatures are just as compelling as the violence of winter and are not overpowered by it. The apparent timidity of the earliest passages and the passion tapped in the heath scene have a purpose within the poem itself: a careful buildup to a final celebration. Collins' skillful manipulation of imagery and versification, along with the consequent modulations in tone and atmosphere, have created a poem representative of both the era and the inventive genius of the individual poet.

Emma Coburn Norris

ODE TO PSYCHE

Author: John Keats (1795-1821)
Type of poem: Ode
First published: 1820, in *Lamia, Isabella, The Eve of St. Agnes, and Other Poems*

The Poem

"Ode to Psyche," made up of sixty-seven lines, is divided into four stanzas of varying lengths. Although iambic pentameter is the dominant meter of the poem, John Keats often includes lines of iambic trimeter as well. The rhyme scheme is generally in a quatrain form of *abab*, but rhyming couplets are also employed. This technical complexity is typical of the ode form.

The poem begins with a direct address to the goddess Psyche, the personification of the human soul, and this one-sided conversation continues thoughout the poem. Keats himself is the first-person speaker, and "thou" is always the silent Psyche.

The first stanza, the longest in the poem, describes a vision or a dream Keats has of Psyche and her lover Eros lying "In deepest grass, beneath the whisp'ring roof/ Of leaves and trembled blossoms," beside a brook and "cool-rooted flowers": The soul—Psyche—and the body—Eros—lie together in the heart of nature. Keats imagines them not in a passionate embrace, but in a static, restful pose, as if he has come upon them after their lovemaking has ended. In another poem, "Ode on a Grecian Urn," he witnesses an eternal moment before any physical activity takes place between lovers and examines the difficulty in this position: Although "the maiden" will always remain beautiful and the man's love will last forever, the couple, frozen in the marble of the urn, will never share a kiss. "Ode to Psyche," in its peaceful description of Eros and Psyche, offers no such disquieting picture of love or art.

In the second stanza, the shortest in the poem, Keats disturbs the idyllic setting. He once again begins with an address to Psyche, describing her as the "loveliest vision far" of all Olympus' goddesses, more beautiful than Phoebe or Vesper, the moon or the evening star. The difficulty enters the poem, however, in Keats's description of the Greek gods as "Olympus' faded hierarchy!" He acknowledges their displacement in the West by Christianity and mourns it. Psyche, the "latest born" of all the Greek gods, was not embodied as a goddess until the second century A.D., so she was never properly worshiped, in Keats's mind. Although she is "fairer than" all the other goddesses, she has no temple in her honor, "nor altar heap'd with flowers;/ Nor virgin-choir to make delicious moan." In his poem, Keats attempts to remedy Psyche's abandonment. She may have "no shrine, no grove, no oracle" or prophet associated with her, but the poet, through the power of the human imagination, offers her recompense.

Keats admits in the third stanza that Psyche was born "too late for antique vows," and he realizes that the blessed time has passed when "the haunted forest boughs" were holy, when "the air, the water, and fire" were holy; reason and science have displaced the power of myth. The poem, however, does not give in to despair. The poet, once again addressing Psyche directly, asks permission to serve her: Let me be "Thy voice, thy lute, thy pipe . . . Thy shrine, thy grove, thy oracle."

Stanza 4 resolves the problem wonderfully. Keats will build a fane, or temple, "in some untrodden region of [his] mind." The poet will become the soul's priest, using his "working brain" to create a world filled with "soft delight" for the goddess. The mind of the poet will re-create the scene pictured in the first stanza; after the goddess is pleasantly seated in his brain, Keats will leave a "casement ope at night,/ To let the warm Love in!" Eros and Psyche will be reunited.

Forms and Devices

Part of Keats's reputation as a great poet derives from the appeal of his sensual, opulent phrasing. In "Ode to Psyche," however, the lush language is perhaps overshadowed by an atypical technique: Keats risks a monotonous sound in the poem by repeating certain key words. In order to make a point about the mind's ability to compensate for loss, Keats first describes what has been lost and then, by using the same wording, replaces it completely. For example, in stanza 2, Keats despairs because Psyche never had a "virgin-choir to make delicious moan/ Upon the midnight hours." In stanza 3, he offers himself to Psyche, saying "let me be thy choir, and make a moan/ Upon the midnight hours." In stanza 2, he mourns because Psyche, in the classical world, had

> No voice, no lute, no pipe, no incense sweet
> From chain-swung censer teeming;
> No shrine, no grove, no oracle, no heat
> Of pale-mouth'd prophet dreaming.

In stanza 3, he once again speaks to Psyche, saying, let me be

> Thy voice, thy lute, thy pipe, thy incense sweet
> From swinged censer teeming;
> Thy shrine, thy grove, thy oracle, thy heat
> Of pale-mouth'd prophet dreaming.

In the same way that the abundance of stanza 3 contradicts the emptiness of stanza 2, the fourth stanza contradicts the first. Keats concludes the poem by returning to the opening site, that forest in which he came upon the two lovers. Stanza 4 re-creates that pristine scene, but the new location is changed into a "fane," or temple, inside the poet's mind. Whereas the first stanza talks about a natural scene with fragrant flowers in blossom and the wind in the trees, the fourth stanza has a gardener named Fancy, or imagination, "breeding flowers" that are never the same and the "branched thoughts" of the poet's mind, "instead of pines," murmuring "in the wind." The original forest and its wildness are transmuted by Keats into a "rosy sanctuary" dressed "With the wreath'd trellis of a working brain." This extended metaphor, or conceit, of the final stanza concludes by joining the two lovers, or at least allowing Eros an entranceway into the sacred fane: "a casement ope at night" is an odd and metaphorical window in the brain through which Eros can pass to be with his love.

This dialogue between the stanzas, in which the first is joined with the last and the second with the third, is balanced by another device: The poem moves forward powerfully from start to finish simply because it is driven by the initial phrases of each stanza. The first three stanzas all begin with a similar technique. The goddess is invoked or praised in an exclamatory phrase that begins with an interjection: "O Goddess!" "O latest born and loveliest vision far/ Of all Olympus' faded hierarchy!" "O brightest!" The reader must wait until the final stanza to find an alteration of the form; after the first three stanzas address the goddess, the fourth stanza records the poet's resolve: "Yes, I will be thy priest!" Keats creates tension in the poem by combining these two techniques, which forces the reader to look at the relationships between stanzas in two different ways.

Themes and Meanings

One of the chief concerns of "Ode to Psyche" is the poet's role in a modern society. Like the other major poets of the early part of the nineteenth century, Keats found himself in a world that was beginning to be denuded of myth and ritual, a world in which reason and progress had started to strip "the air, the water, and the fire" of their holiness. The Christian ceremonies and rituals did not seem to have the same power, according to Keats, that the ancient, classical rites of worship had. In "Ode to Psyche," Keats attempts to reopen the door to mystery and holiness using the human imagination.

Keats's cure for the problem, however, is extremely self-absorbed. It is as if the poet can have an effect only on the level of the individual. The poem does not offer a recipe for a great awakening among the people of England or the world; instead, the poem traces a single poet's attempts to save a portion of the ancient mysteries for himself.

Apparently, this type of spiritual rebirth was not available to the "average" man or woman; Keats accentuates his special gift when he announces that "even in these days so far retir'd/ From happy pieties" of the past, he is able to see Psyche and sing about her "by [his] own eyes inspired." The poet is in no way a lowly creature; he creates his own inspiration, and his mind serves as the sacred temple in which the goddess will find her "soft delight." This ode has never been regarded by most readers as equal to "Ode on a Grecian Urn" or "Ode to a Nightingale," perhaps because of this poetic self-assuredness. Keats triumphs too easily in the poem; he rectifies the problem of a desacralized world by retreating into the mind of the poet alone.

The strengths of the poem, however, lie in the sheer power of Keats's imagination, his attempt to conjoin Eros and Psyche, the body and the spirit, in one being. He wants his mind, his own imagination, to be the place where the lovemaking takes place. The priest has become a poet who encourages the dalliances between the sexes. Although the reader never actually sees Eros and Psyche enter the "untrodden regions" of Keats's mind, the poem suggests that the union is possible. It ends with tremendous hopefulness, since it is in fact a hymn of praise not only to the goddess Psyche but also to the human soul and imagination, unaided by divine intervention.

Kevin Boyle

ODE TO THE CONFEDERATE DEAD

Author: Allen Tate (1899-1979)
Type of poem: Ode
First published: 1928, in *Mr. Pope and Other Poems*

The Poem

This ninety-two-line stream-of-consciousness meditation contrasts modern man with the heroes of the Civil War. Originally called an elegy, the poem's form suggests John Milton's "Lycidas" (1637), which is at once a lament for the dead Edward King and an examination of life in the 1630's. Similarly, Allan Tate both eulogizes the fallen Confederate soldiers and analyzes the plight of those living in the twentieth century. Written largely in iambic pentameter, the poem also employs hexameter, tetrameter, and trimeter. The poem oscillates between the regularity and formality associated with the sections portraying antique heroism and irregular rhythms reflecting the collapse of that world. Like the rhythm, the rhyme scheme varies. The second stanza, for example, begins with a quatrain, and the third with a couplet; rhymes recur at unpredictable intervals. Thus, "tomorrow" in the third stanza echoes "grow," "row," and "below" in the second.

In his essay "Narcissus as Narcissus" (1938), Tate remarks of the poem, "Figure to yourself a man stopping at the gate of a Confederate graveyard on a late autumn afternoon." Standing outside the cemetery, he sees the ordered rows of tombstones being worn away by time; the regular iambs of the first line break down before the elements in the second. The wind blows leaves about the neglected graveyard, and the fallen foliage impresses the onlooker with "the rumor of mortality." As he thinks about the soldiers who fell like leaves, he tries to derive consolation from the thought that the memory of those men endures, but he can summon only the cycle of nature. Tate describes the stanzas as "a baroque meditation on the ravages of time."

In the third stanza, the spectator addresses the soldiers directly as "you." Those men understood heroism; theirs was the complete vision of the Greek philosophers who could distinguish reality from illusion. Wanting to fuse himself with that world, the onlooker momentarily imagines that the leaves are soldiers, but he cannot sustain the illusion. Historical evocation of Confederate general "Stonewall" Jackson and of notable battles also fails to remove him from his own time; he is left with only the wind and death.

The image of the dying hound ends the first part of the ode, the strophe. The antistrophe begins in midline, posing the question of what remains for the spectator, representative of modern man, to do. How can he even speak of the dead, let alone become part of the past? The penultimate stanza suggests that he cannot, that creativity is impossible. All that remains is silent speculation culminating in self-destruction. The last lines offer another, only slightly more promising alternative— the worship of death—setting "up the grave/ In the house," implying a backward-looking poetic that imitates antebellum literature. "The ravenous grave" suggests not only death but also Edgar Allan Poe's "The Raven," representative of older versification and, because of its refrain, of doom.

The question of creativity remains unresolved. The spectator departs, and in his place Tate leaves "the gentle serpent" to guard the graves. Even here the ambiguity endures. The green color and the mulberry bush implying the silkworm (as Tate himself noted) suggest life, especially since the snake reminds the reader of Tate's "Mr. Pope," also published in 1928. In that poem Pope is likened to a snake, a symbol of creativity. Yet, as Tate remarks, the serpent "is the ancient symbol of time, and . . . time is also death."

Forms and Devices

The poem abounds in animal imagery that comments on the spectator. The first animal, "the blind crab," appears at the end of the second stanza. Again Tate's gloss clarifies the symbol: The crab "has mobility but no direction, energy but from the human point of view, no purposeful world to use it in." Moreover, with its hard exoskeleton, the crab is walled within itself. The Confederate soldiers also lie within a wall, but one that unites them in a common frame. The spectator, like the crab, is trapped in his own world. The crab also lacks vision, being blind, just as the spectator is cut off from the heroic image of the past.

The onlooker also resembles the hound bitch waiting for death. He has lost his vigor and his purpose. The hunt, like battle, is deadly but ritualistic, unifying and purposeful. The hound, a hunting dog, no longer engages in the activity for which it was born; instead, it lies motionless, as the onlooker remains stationary at the cemetery gate.

Tate next introduces the spider and owl, both associated with death. The former suggests as well the thin Confederate soldiers in their gray uniforms, and their heroic if doomed struggle resembles that of Arachne, who challenged Athena to a fatal spinning contest. The spider is like the onlooker, too, for like the crab it has an exoskeleton, and it lives within its own web. The jaguar and serpent conclude the catalog of animals. The jaguar that leaps into the pool represents Narcissus, yet another figure locked within himself. Like the crab, this jaguar has energy that lacks proper direction and so destroys itself.

The myths of Narcissus and Arachne are the most obvious classical allusions in the poem but not the only ones. Twice Tate suggests the paralyzing gaze of Medusa. The first reference appears in the second stanza when the stare of the stone angels on the tombstones petrifies the viewer. This image recurs in the penultimate stanza; Tate writes of "mute speculation, the patient curse/ That stones the eyes." This latter allusion links Narcissus and Medusa, for in the root of speculation is the Latin *speculum*, mirror. The means of slaying the Gorgon becomes the instrument of self-destruction as the inward searching of modern man deprives him of feeling and isolates him from the heroism of a Perseus.

Yet another series of references derives from Christianity. The cemetery is a walled garden with a serpent, suggesting that the old world of the Confederacy is an

Eden, but a decaying one because no one tends it in this fallen world. Even the angels charged with guarding paradise are crumbling. The word "election" in the first stanza carries religious weight: The soldiers, unlike the observer, were among the chosen, the blessed, who have been absolved through the "shrift of death." Whereas those men had vision, for the spectator night (darkness) rather than the divine (light) "is the beginning and the end," the alpha and the omega. Hence the wind, the spirit, fails to move him and is outside him, not within.

Themes and Meanings

Tate's own comments provide a good place to begin to understand his intent. The poem, he writes in "Narcissus as Narcissus," deals with solipsism—with modernity's lack of cohesion and the isolation of the individual. The world of the Confederate dead was unified. The soldiers knew "midnight restitutions," rage, heroism, the entire range of emotions that the spectator unsuccessfully attempts to evoke; the older society understood and believed what the twentieth century can only analyze. The soldiers acted, but moderns are merely onlookers. In the third stanza, the man at the gate assumes the guise of a sociologist, and later he becomes a historian recalling the old battles, but the tradition he seeks is dead. He can mummify it and so preserve the memory, but he cannot revitalize the heritage. Just as modernity has lost the unified vision of Parmenides and Zeno, so it has lost their heroism. Zeno's voice is muted in the present, but Tate also alludes to the philosopher biting off his tongue so that he could give no information to his captors.

Tate's confrontation with modernity is at once universal and personal. Everyone living in the twentieth century, Tate says in the poem, is a Narcissus, but for the Southerner this problem is particularly acute. Shortly after Tate completed the first version of this poem, he sent copies to various other writers for comments. His fellow Fugitive writer Donald Davidson wrote back,

> The Confederate dead become a peg on which you hang an argument whose lines, however sonorous and beautiful in a strict proud way, leave me wondering why you wrote a poem on the subject at all, since in effect you say . . . that no poem can be written on such a subject.

Divorced from his past, Tate was asking how the Southerner, how Tate himself, could continue to create. The Fugitives rejected modernity, but Davidson sensed that Tate was abandoning the effort to link himself with the agrarian world of the Old South. However desirable that fusion, Tate believed that it no longer was possible.

The poem is an elegy not only for the Confederate dead but also for the unusable past and for Tate's former belief in the viability of the Confederate tradition. Tate wrestled with the poem for a decade, and his ability to complete it marks a triumph. The Southerner could write about his heritage, could draw on the past, but he had to do so as a person of his own time. Tate proved Davidson wrong: A poem could be written on the subject, but it could not be a nineteenth century poem. Tate had come to recognize that by living in the past one creates rhetoric; by wrestling with it in the present, one produces poetry.

Joseph Rosenblum

ODE TO THE MOST HOLY EUCHARIST:
EXPOSITION AND WORLD

Author: Federico García Lorca (1898-1936)
Type of poem: Ode
First published: 1928, as "Oda al Santísimo Sacrament o del Altar"; in *Obras completas*, 1938; collected in *Collected Works*, 1991

The Poem

"Ode to the Most Holy Eucharist: Exposition and World," a relatively short poem in classic hexameters, is divided into three overall sections of four-line stanzas ("Exposition," "World," and "The Devil"), which are thirty-six, forty, and sixteen lines long. The title indicates the serious nature of the poem, but also suggests the possibility of an ironic reading by emphasizing the superlative degree in "Most Holy." This blending of high seriousness and ironic detachment is one of the hallmarks of the poem. When its first two sections were published in 1928, the poem carried the subtitle "Fragment" above the dedication, indicating that Federico García Lorca intended to add to the poem. The poem was completed during García Lorca's visit to the United States in 1929.

The poem's original dedication to the Spanish composer Manuel de Falla (1876-1946), a devout Catholic and friend of García Lorca, irritated de Falla; the composer agreed to accept García Lorca's friendly homage only because he hoped that the unfinished sections of the poem would reverse the evidently sacrilegious direction of the first two. De Falla's reaction has been typical of many readers of the poem in predominantly Catholic Spain; the poem is infrequently translated into English and is rarely included in anthologies of García Lorca's work.

The poem is written in the first person, and the speaker might easily be seen as García Lorca himself. In 1928, following the critical success of his "Gypsy Ballads," García Lorca experienced extreme emotional difficulty in adapting to sudden fame and the possibility that his homosexuality might become widely known. In a letter to Jorge Zalamea in the autumn of 1928, García Lorca noted: "By sheer will power, I've *resolved* these past few days, one of the most painful periods I've experienced in my life." Many critics have argued that "Ode to the Most Holy Eucharist" marks a brief return to the security of his Catholic upbringing in an effort to combat the emotional turmoil brought upon him by the increased scrutiny of the public. In essence, García Lorca was searching here for a way to come to terms with a *Dios anclado* (a God "anchored" in human terms). While he is clearly longing for the security of such a God, he cannot conceive of such a God in other than somewhat shocking human terms.

In the letter to Zalamea mentioned above, García Lorca referred to the composition of the rigorous hexameters of "Ode to the Most Holy Eucharist" as an exercise: "for discipline, I'm doing these precise *academic* things now and opening my soul before the symbol of the Sacrament." García Lorca's longing for control over the fragments of his life is reflected in the last line of the "World" section: "Immutable Sacrament of love and discipline." García Lorca also referred to "Ode to the Most Holy Eucharist" as "probably the greatest poem I've done."

The three sections of the poem might best be considered as three panels of a stained-glass window viewed in a large cathedral. "Exposition" focuses on the moment during the Catholic Mass when the wafer of bread is transformed into the body of Christ. "World" contrasts the nature of the divine with the nature of man and offers images of mankind's tawdry existence. The final section, "The Devil," presents a sensuous incarnation of evil in a manifestation of beauty. In order to understand García Lorca's method here, however, it might help to imagine that the stained-glass window had at one time been broken; what one sees now in the poem is a reconstruction, an assembling of fragments. In other words, much of the difficulty in reading this poem stems from the fact that there is no real narrative pattern or story to follow; García Lorca chooses to present an array of compelling images for contemplation rather than a series of methodical points for understanding. In this respect, the use of regular hexameters (frequently employed for heroic subjects, and therefore appropriate to the "Most Holy Sacrament") contrasts with the decidedly nonheroic images that the hexameters convey. The final effect is one of unease, of not knowing whether García Lorca is celebrating or mocking the "Most Holy Sacrament" of the Eucharist.

Forms and Devices

"Exposition" uses the setting of the Catholic Mass as its basic motif and specifically focuses upon the elevation of the wafer at the moment of consecration. As the elevation of the wafer within the monstrance (*ostensorio*, display frame) is accomplished, the speaker marks its comparison to, of all things, a frog's heart: "Live there, my God, inside the monstrance./ Pierced by your Father with a ray of light./ Trembling like the poor heart of the frog/ that the doctors put in a glass bottle." García Lorca is emphasizing a double transformation. The first transformation, depicted in the symbology of the mass itself, is devout, reflecting the transubstantiation of God into man: the mass commemorates the moment when God became man. The second, in the construction of the poem, is ironic and appears to devalue divinity by comparing the beating of the divine heart with that of a frog in a dissecting bottle. García Lorca also indicates, however, that the God in the monstrance is "trembling," having been pierced by a ray of light from his Father. Several traditions are blending here. First, García Lorca alludes to the Catholic belief that Jesus Christ was the son of God the Father. Second, he identifies that Father as a source of light (of enlightenment, or salvation to medieval Catholics). Finally, however, he emphasizes that God the Son, inside the monstrance, is trembling like the heart of a dissected frog. This last comparison emphasizes the contamination that the Son of God encountered as a result of his connection with humanity, and perhaps suggests that the Son of God made the transformation into the human with some fear. In any case, García Lorca's God here is a "God in infant's dress, diminutive, eternal Christ,/ a thousand times pronounced dead, crucified/ by the impure word of sweaty man."

In "World," García Lorca focuses on the human environment that divinity has chosen to enter. He presents this environment with a type of fragmented-image technique that is closely akin to T. S. Eliot's style in *The Waste Land* (1922). Most of the images are taken from the seamier side of life: "The razorblades lay on the dressing tables/ waiting impatiently to sever the heads"; "Clerks asleep on the fourteenth floor./ Prostitute with breasts of scratched glass"; "To assassinate the nightingale came three thousand men armed with shining knives." In each of these clusters of images, the meaning depends more upon the compelling quality of the image itself than upon its reference to a known story. In other words, unlike Eliot's *The Waste Land*, which ultimately rewards the reader who examines the sources used in the poem's composition, "Ode to the Most Holy Eucharist" relies solely on the arresting power of the images themselves to convey a picture of the dangerous nature of the world that the incarnating (recall that the poem focuses on the moment that God enters the flesh of man) God will inhabit. The entrance of God into such a world provides the antidote, or relief, for such danger, but García Lorca is aware that such relief requires a nonrational standard of belief. In two of his favorite lines, "The unicorn seeks what the rose forgets/ and the bird attempts what the waters impede," García Lorca emphasizes that belief in the impossible (the unicorn or the incarnation of Christ) makes possible what was hitherto thought to be out of the question (roses remembering or birds flying, or the salvation of man). Only the sacrament of the Eucharist is capable of soothing the heart of the frog in the glass bottle and the hearts of twentieth century humankind: "Only your balanced Sacrament of light/ soothes the anguish of unloosed love./ Only you, Sacrament, manometer that saves/ hearts flung at five hundred per hour." Finally, the sacrament is compared to a measuring device that would recognize an excessive speed and warn the operator against exceeding his own limitations.

Themes and Meanings

"Ode to the Most Holy Eucharist" is a poem about the nature of divine-human transformation. In it, García Lorca wonders whether humankind can be redeemed from essentially squalorous surroundings by faith in a deity that has entered into the form of man. García Lorca is challenging the notion that gods need to be resplendent in their divine powers—superhuman, larger than life, elevated in a monstrance for all to see. He wonders if the reverse is not more true: Instead of emphasizing the grandiose nature of the divine transformation, he instead emphasizes the "love and discipline" required for salvation. That is, "Ode to the Most Holy Eucharist" commemorates a ritual that is the enactment of a discipline; García Lorca's choice of regular hexameters echoes that discipline.

At the heart of that discipline lies simple love, a love that defies understanding, in the way that García Lorca's images of tawdry street scenes defy rational understanding but readily enable and reward contemplation. The last line of the "World" section captures this paradox beautifully: "Immutable Sacrament of love and discipline!" In "Ode to the Most Holy Eucharist," García Lorca strove to discover a way out of his own increasing agitation with the world around him, feeling the condemnation of his society and his childhood religion for his homosexuality, but yearning for the peace of that "God in infant's dress, diminutive, eternal Christ." "Ode to the Most Holy Eucharist" is a demonstration of García Lorca's own dedication to love and discipline.

Peter D. Olson

ODE TO THE WEST WIND

Author: Percy Bysshe Shelley (1792-1882)
Type of poem: Ode
First published: 1820, in *Prometheus Unbound*

The Poem

Like many of Percy Bysshe Shelley's poems, "Ode to the West Wind" was inspired by a natural phenomenon, an autumn storm that prompted the poet to contemplate the links between the outer world of nature and the realm of the intellect. In five stanzas directly addressed to the powerful wind that Shelley paradoxically calls both "destroyer" and "preserver" (line 14), the poet explores the impact of the regenerative process that he sees occurring in the world around him and compares it to the impact of his own poetry, which he believes can have similar influence in regenerating mankind.

In each stanza, Shelley speaks to the West Wind as if it is an animate power. The first three stanzas form a logical unit; in them the poet looks at how the wind influences the natural terrain over which it moves. The opening lines describe the way the wind sweeps away the autumn leaves and carries off seeds of vegetation, which will lie dormant through winter until the spring comes to give them new life as plants. In the second stanza, the poet describes the clouds that whisk across the autumn sky, driven by the same fierce wind and twisted into shapes that remind him of Maenads, Greek maidens known for their wild behavior. Shelley calls the wind the harbinger of the dying year, a visible sign that a cycle of nature's life is coming to a close. The poet uses the third stanza to describe the impact of the wind on the Mediterranean coast line and the Atlantic ocean; the wind, Shelley says, moves the waters and the undersea vegetation in much the same way it shifts the landscape.

In the final two stanzas, the speaker muses about the possibilities that his transformation by the wind would have on his ability as a poet. If he could be a leaf, a cloud, or a wave, he would be able to participate directly in the regenerative process he sees taking place in the natural world. His words—that is, his poetry—would become like these natural objects, which are scattered about the world and which serve as elements to help bring about new life. He wishes that, much like the seeds he has seen scattered about, his "leaves" (line 58), his "dead thoughts" (line 63)—his poems—could be carried across the world by the West Wind so that they could "quicken to a new birth" (line 64) at a later time, when others might take heed of their message. The final question with which the poet ends this poem is actually a note of hope: The "death" that occurs in winter is habitually followed by a "new life" every spring. The cycle of the seasons that he sees occurring around him gives Shelley hope that his works might share the fate of other objects in nature; they may be unheeded for a time, but one day they will have great impact on humankind.

Forms and Devices

The structure of "Ode to the West Wind" is exceptionally complex. Each of the five stanzas is itself a terza rima sonnet, consisting of fourteen lines divided into four triplets and a concluding couplet. Through the complex, interlocking rhyme scheme of terza rima, Shelley gives the poem a strong sense of rhythm. The form also gives emphasis to the concluding couplet in each stanza, thereby focusing the reader's attention on the final line or lines. The effect Shelley achieves is important, for he wishes to emphasize, in the first three stanzas, the speaker's plea that the West Wind heed his call, and in the final stanza he wants to highlight the significant rhetorical question with which the poem ends.

The primary literary trope in the poem is personification. Shelley repeatedly addresses the West Wind as if it were an animate, intelligent being; one might be reminded of the way elements of nature are represented in classical Greek or Latin literature, or in American Indian writings. Shelley wants readers to consider the Wind a living force that helps shape the landscape—literally, the physical landscape, and metaphorically, the landscape of human minds and attitudes.

Shelley uses three major images of the poem—the wave, the leaf, and the cloud—to demonstrate the ways in which the West Wind treats elements of the physical landscape. The poet's scene-painting is especially noteworthy; in a few short lines in each of the first three stanzas he depicts the effects of the fierce autumn wind on the ocean, the earth, and the sky. In the fourth stanza, he applies these descriptions to himself, calling on the West Wind to work its magic on him in the same way it has on the natural world, so he too will "die" only to rise again and give life—intellectual life.

One of the most striking images in the poem is used in the fourth stanza to describe the poet's present plight: "I fall upon the thorns of life! I bleed!" (line 54) he cries out to the West Wind. In that single line, following his plea that he be made like the wave, the leaf, or the cloud so he can be transformed by the powers of the wind, Shelley expresses the problem of the Romantic poet: He would soar to new heights of understanding and deliver insight into life to all humanity if he could, but his human nature keeps him affixed to the earth, with all its troubles and stumbling blocks. Life itself is seen as a painful rosebush whose thorns afflict one who wishes to rise above the day-to-day humdrum of human existence. Shelley realizes that he cannot do so. Nevertheless, he has hopes that his works may be like those natural objects that seem to die in winter only to rise to new life in spring. He compares his verse to "ashes and sparks" from an unextinguished fire (line 67), which he hopes the wind will scatter so they may flare up in other places, thereby widening his impact on others.

Themes and Meanings

In "Ode to the West Wind," Shelley examines and compares two phenomena that are particularly potent: the power of nature and the power of poetry. Like most Romantic poets, he sees a clear link between these two, believing that the poet's power arises from nature, inspired by it and akin to it in many respects. Many similes in this poem, and in others by Shelley, focus readers' attention on the comparisons. Donald Reiman has described the themes of this poem as "the Poet's personal despair and his hopes for social renewal" expressed "in images drawn from the seasonal cycle" (*Percy Bysshe Shelley*, 1969). Hence, the destructive power of the West Wind parallels Shelley's fear that the beauty of the natural world, and metaphorically the beauty of his own works, is doomed to oblivion by a hostile and insensitive force. At the same time, however, he recognizes that the destructive power of the West Wind is but a part of a larger cycle in which what seems like death is merely a necessary stage in the process of regeneration that perpetuates life itself. In the final stanzas of the poem he offers some hope that, despite his being constricted by his humanity and possibly being ignored by those whom he wishes to enlighten, he may one day be able to speak to others. Like the new life that comes inevitably every spring, his works may be "reborn" when people (perhaps those other than his contemporaries) discover them and listen to Shelley's calls for social and moral reform.

The specifics of Shelley's plan for reforming the world do not appear in "Ode to the West Wind." Rather, this poem focuses on the process by which his other works may one day achieve their purpose in the world. Those familar with classical or Renaissance poetry may notice a similarity between this poem and those by Horace or by Ben Jonson, whose "Go, Little Book" verses appeal in a similar way for the continued life of their poetry. Like those poets who preceded him, Shelley hopes that his work will one day be read and appreciated by an audience that can understand his deep concern for the improvement of humankind, one that will be willing to listen to his plan for bringing about such improvement.

Laurence W. Mazzeno

OF MODERN POETRY

Author: Wallace Stevens (1879-1955)
Type of poem: Lyric
First published: 1940; collected in *Parts of a World*, 1942

The Poem

"Of Modern Poetry" attempts to redefine poetry for a world with no stable structures or values. Its form approaches blank verse, but it is not close enough to that form to be so labeled. The form is flexible, with five stresses in most lines but six or four in others. The loose form is appropriate for this poem, as a part of its argument is that modern poetry refuses labels, designations, and categories of all kinds.

The poem begins with its basic definition: Modern poetry is "The poem of the mind in the act of finding/ What will suffice." Contemporary poetry must be self-descriptive; it must look at itself searching and must observe its own invention. Thus, poetry is not so much a product as an act or activity. In the past, the speaker continues, the "scene was set": Poetry was formerly a matter of following the conventions. Everyone knew what was considered poetic material and what the acceptable forms of poetry were. This is no longer the case. The new poetry must be written in today's language, and it must reflect changing times and shifting concerns. It must include a consideration of war, for example. (The poem was published during World War II.) It must make use of the materials that are currently available to create a representation of those who will read it.

The poem then compares the poet with other types of artist for whom performance is a major part of their artistry. These comparisons help communicate the point that poetry must be activity if it is to speak to the present. The poet becomes an actor, a musician, and a "metaphysician in the dark" in his attempt to portray the time period as it is, for those who live in it. Elements of other arts and disciplines are attributed to poetry.

The concluding lines add to the previous definition, stating that poetry must be "the finding of a satisfaction." The earlier quest is identified as a search for "what would suffice." These two words, "suffice" and "satisfaction," suggest that poetry has as its goal a kind of consolation. The suggestion looks forward to Wallace Stevens' major statement of his poetic theory, "Notes Toward a Supreme Fiction," in which he develops a substantial argument concerning poetry: "It Must Give Pleasure." In the conclusion to "Of Modern Poetry" he also offers possible subjects for poetry—"a man skating, a woman dancing, a woman/ Combing." His subjects are all actions, activities which might be considered celebrations of the present by those who feel enough at home in it to move with its movements. Flux and flow are a necessary part of "the poem of the act of the mind."

Forms and Devices

The form of the poem as a whole reflects its insistence that form not be prescribed for modern poetry. The twenty-eight lines are arranged according to no set pattern, but the suggestion of blank verse underlies the poem and gives a feeling of coherence to it. The poem is broken into sections which provide its major propositions. It is not a syllogism or formal argument, but it makes three main points. It begins by introducing the issue of modern poetry and the difference between past and present poetry. In its most extended section, it then describes the new demands made on poetry by a complicated and skeptical age. Finally, it comments on possible subjects for poetry.

The metaphors in this poem all point in the same direction; they are all attempts to describe modern poetry in such a way as to make "Of Modern Poetry" both explanation and example. Traditional poetry is described as a theater in which "the scene was set." Past poets could repeat "what was in the script": Their powers of invention were not taxed in the same way as those of poets now are. To introduce the new poetry, the poem personifies or animates poetry itself, saying that it has to "learn the speech of the place," and "think about war." Poetry is then compared with an actor who is speaking into "the delicatest ear of the mind." In turn, the actor is compared with yet another figure, a metaphysician, who is then presented as a musician. All these shifting comparisons are confusing if analyzed logically, but they serve to characterize a poetry that is itself shifting, grounded on uncertainty, and reflective of lived life rather than tradition or convention. That drama, metaphysics, music, and poetry are in some ways equivalent and that they can flow from and into one another is a part of the theme of the poem. The metaphors demonstrate what the poem explains.

That action is a necessary part of contemporary poetry is suggested by the flowing run-on lines and by the number of present participles and gerunds that appear throughout the poem, such as "passing," "twanging," "skating," and "dancing." The modern poetry that is the "poem of the act of the mind" reflects the particular actions which are contemporary life.

Themes and Meanings

"Of Modern Poetry" is one of Stevens' most frequently anthologized poems, and it may be the most commonly encountered poem from the collection that contains it, *Parts of a World*. Its popularity may be attributable in part to the relative clarity with which it presents its themes. The quest for "what will suffice" appears in other Stevens poems as well, including "Man and Bottle." The search for a fiction that will be sustaining or nourishing to human beings in their uncertain lives is Stevens' major theme. In this poem, the theme is not hidden or presented indirectly.

The poem explores what characteristics poetry must have if it is to "suffice" — that is, to be enough or to satisfy. It is the uncertainty of the time that places so many demands on poetry, because poetry, to satisfy, must not violate reality. Therefore, wartime demands poetry which confronts war issues rather than hides from them. As each age speaks its own language, so the speech of the poem must reflect and partake of the discourse of the time. Otherwise it will not satisfy. It is axiomatic in

Stevens that building a romantic world which can serve as a shelter from the un-pleasantness of reality is not the function of poetry. Some of Stevens' early critics thought of him as an escapist, an ivory-tower poet who had little contact with the real world and little interest in it. He fought such dismissal vigorously in both poetry and essay, claiming that the poet must confront reality. The work of the imagination lies in its interactions with the real, not in disguises or evasions of reality.

The presentation of what modern poetry is actually like or should be like is more complex, presented as it is in a series of metaphors of actors, musicians, and meta-physicians. The substance of poetry is its sounds; these sounds ideally have all the dimensions that they could be given by those other art forms and disciplines.

Still more subtle is the description of the response to this ideal poetry. The audi-ence is really listening "not to the play, but to itself." If the reality of the present is adequately represented in sound, the reader will find himself or herself in the poem. There will be an identification, described in the poem in terms of music that is somehow metaphysical: "The actor is/ A metaphysician in the dark, twanging/ An instrument." Poetry is thus presented as a metaphysical music that helps the mind define itself and learn of its own limits and possibilities. The identity of mind and music is a positive pleasure, consisting of "Sounds passing through sudden right-nesses, wholly/ Containing the mind."

The conclusion of the poem retreats from the intensity of the middle section as it presents some of the materials of poetry. The subject matter of poetry is far less significant than the creative act itself, suggests the poem, and only as an after-thought should poetic subjects even be mentioned. Nevertheless, the images of the three people, two women and a man, caught in their acts of living, provide appropri-ate closure. It may be true that all of Stevens' poetry is about writing poetry, but that does not make it — or this poem — narrow or exclusive. Stevens describes the cre-ative drive as a basic force that is part of what it is to be human.

Janet McCann

OLD MASTERS

Author: Zbigniew Herbert (1924-   )
Type of poem: Lyric
First published: 1983, as "Dawni mistrzowie," in *Raport z oblężonego miasta*;
collected in *Report from the Besieged City and Other Poems*, 1985

The Poem

"Old Masters" consists of thirty-five lines of free verse, divided into short verse paragraphs of two or four lines which, though irregular, often resemble stanzas. The poem is broken into two main sections, demarcated by a shift in the left margin; the first section is descriptive, while the second verges on invocation or prayer.

The title refers to the anonymous master-painters of the early Renaissance in Italy, in the eleventh or twelfth century. These artists painted scenes of religious importance and were employed by the Roman Catholic Church to depict events in the life of Christ, the miracles of saints, and well-known figures from the Bible. Many of them were themselves monks or were closely affiliated with religious orders.

The poem begins by emphasizing the anonymity of those Old Masters; they were not concerned, Zbigniew Herbert says, with signing their names to their work in order to achieve fame or notoriety in years to come. Rather, they suppressed their artistic egos, preferring to "dissolve" into the religious wonders they were depicting. As artists, they strove not for personal glory, but to portray the glory of God.

Herbert uses the Old Masters' native Italian language when he describes their paintings in order to draw himself and the reader closer, linguistically, to the textures and visions that they would have experienced. The reader hears the actual words the painters used. The pink towers "di citta sue mare," meaning "of the city above the sea," may refer either to Venice—where many of these painters lived—or to the celestial city—the New Jerusalem of Revelation—which was often depicted floating above the earth's surface. The life "della Beata Umilta" refers to Saint Humility, or Rosana, a pious abbess of the thirteenth century. That "they dissolved/ in sogno/ miracolo/ crocifissione"—into dream, miracle, and crucifixion—suggests the emerging oneness of artist and religious subject matter.

Herbert asserts that the Old Masters discovered "paradise" in their art. Their paintings are "mirrors," he suggests, in which to view the divinity in the self, but they are not "for us" in the present spiritual state of alienation, disaffection, and what he elsewhere calls "disinheritance." They can have meaning only for those who have somehow been "chosen" or sanctified.

The second section of the poem is a prayer for this sanctity, which calls upon the Old Masters as intercessors. Herbert pleads with them, as his brother artists, to help him defeat the satanic temptations of fame and pride and to rediscover the holy "Visitation" that has passed him by. This plea seems rather strange coming from the mouth of an avowed doubter and apparent agnostic, but nevertheless carries a large amount of spiritual and poetic energy.

Forms and Devices

Herbert's streamlined Polish translates extremely well into other languages, and the English here captures his clipped, telegraphic style, as well as the poetic dynamism of his finely crafted imagery. Herbert's poetry is not pretty or opulent, but strives on the whole for both visual clarity and structural balance. His work has sometimes been characterized as "antithetical"—concerned with holding opposite worldviews or contrary figures in tension in the same poem—but here one finds only a hint of such opposition, when he contrasts the perfection of the Old Masters' paintings with the present-day fallen state; rather than exploit the ironies of, or discontinuities between, past and present, Herbert chooses to try to immerse himself in the art and technology of his masters, to turn away from the present and rediscover a lost "paradise."

The tone of the poem is not antithetical, ironic, or argumentative, but pietistic; it recalls the supplications and prayers of a catholic liturgy. Herbert merely substitutes artist for saint as his divine instructor and intercessor. Accordingly, the text is characterized by anaphora, an incantatory repetition of the same words or grammatical forms at the beginning of a syntactic unit, as in "they dissolved . . . they found . . . they drowned" or "I call on you . . . I call upon you. . . ." The last four lines of the poem repeat an invocation, attempting to name the nameless, godlike painters through their various works. Indeed, the original Polish of this section further emphasizes the sense of a writer calling out in desperation to his lost gods, when the poet employs a rarely used vocative case: "Malarzu. . . ." (*Malarz* means "painter"). Herbert's anaphoric style creates an aura of beatification and divine wisdom around the subjects of the poem; one senses, through the tone of the poetry, the spiritual qualities of their paintings.

"Old Masters," as with most of Herbert's other poems, uses little or no punctuation. Herbert demarcates the ends of sentences or of grammatical units either with line breaks or with separate verse paragraphs. His lack of periods or commas does not impair the clarity of his writing. On the contrary, by eliminating unnecessary typographical clutter from his pages, he gives the reader a sense of transparency and simplicity, which, though sometimes deceptive, nevertheless invites one to participate closely in his work, just as he would "melt" into the work of the Old Masters. The reader feels no offensive rhetoric or grandiloquence in his poem.

Furthermore, when combined with his sparing use of initial capitals, this lack of punctuation gives Herbert's verse a fluidity across the frequent line breaks, and a sense of motion that plays against the innate tendency of a syntax to close off into discrete sentences, implanting a type of musical tension into his poetry. The reader hears the pull, in Herbert's work, of a pure, musical continuum against the logical order of proper grammar.

Themes and Meanings

Like many of Herbert's earlier poems, "Old Masters" expresses a profound dissatisfaction with the present state of the world and a longing for a better, more meaningful way of life. This poem, however, differs substantially from most of its companion poems in *Report from the Besieged City* in two important ways. First, "Old Masters" is more deliberately nostalgic than the other pieces in the volume. The contrast between past and present is implied more than actualized, and Herbert dwells at length on the sweetness and beauty of the Old Masters' art, into which he longs to escape. The present state of the world holds almost no interest for him, except as something to be radically changed. Second, Herbert's usual ironic complexity is almost entirely absent here; gone are the antithetical twists and layered juxtapositions that characterize the "Mr. Cogito" poems of this volume. Instead, Herbert offers the reader a surprisingly candid and direct appeal for an imaginative, sentimental return to bygone days of spiritual unity and artistic selflessness and longs for a recapitulation for a Renaissance that had run its course over six hundred years ago.

It is peculiar, as well, that the theological center of the Old Masters' work— God— goes unmentioned in the text, as if Herbert, while crying out for the values of a lost mastery, cannot bring himself to pronounce the deity's name without violating his own post-Nietzschean sense of bathos and overt sentimentality. To say "God" would be to go too far in a world where God has been declared dead. Herbert finds himself, in the poem, performing a difficult balancing act, faced, on the one hand, with a great need to combat his "hard moments of doubt" with some sort of stable value system and, on the other hand, with an inherently modern, ironic sensibility that does not trust itself enough to utter the name of God without calling its motives and position into question. As well as of a longing for the spirituality of the Old Masters, then, Herbert's prayer reminds the reader of his irreconcilable differences from them.

Kevin McNeilly

OLGA POEMS

Author: Denise Levertov (1923-   )
Type of poem: Elegy
First published: 1966, in *The Sorrow Dance*

The Poem

The 182 lines of this poem (its subtitle identifies its subject— "Olga Levertoff, 1914-1964") are divided into six major sections that range in length from fourteen to forty-seven lines. The two longest sections are further divided; section 3 has three numbered parts and section 5 has two. The poem begins with a recollection of the poet and her sister in an early domestic scene: The older sister kneels before a gas fire, undressing while her seven-year-old sister watches from her bed. The memory of Olga's physical maturity is followed by an image of Olga now: "bones and tatters of flesh in earth."

Section 2 shifts to a vision of Olga active in a political cause, wanting "to shout the world to its senses . . . to browbeat" as she reacted to the slum conditions she had seen as a child. The memory ends with Denise Levertov addressing Olga as the "Black one," a (dark-complected?) political activist whose heart was alight with the white candle of her political commitment.

The third section is divided into three glimpses of the politically committed Olga. The first returns to a time when Olga, muttering "*Everything flows*," attacks "human puppets." The poet, a child still, felt "alien" to her sister's muttered words but also felt a link between them and lines from a hymnal they both loved. Next, Olga is with her sister "in the garden . . . we thought sometimes too small for our grand destinies." Even then Olga's passion for reform was active, aroused by her "dread" of "the rolling dark/ oncoming river." Olga's "bulwarks" against it were to perform trivial chores, write verses, pick "endless arguments," and press on to "change the course of the river." Olga's "rage for order" disordered her "pilgrimage" and drove her to "hide among strangers," still determined to "rearrange all mysteries in a new light." In the third image, Olga is again the "Black one," an evil spirit, still anguished, riding fiercely ("as Tartars ride mares") through bad years. In a dream, Levertov sees Olga, "haggard and rouged," standing in a slum street. During these "pilgrim years," Levertov lost "all sense, almost" of what Olga was experiencing.

The fourth section opens in a hospital room where Olga lies ill and in pain, her "hatreds . . . burned out." Seeing her sister "afloat on a sea/ of love and pain," Levertov remembers one of Olga's favorite cadences and sees the past (Olga's, the world's) reduced to a "sick bone" except for her sister's passionate belief and political ambition.

The fifth section begins with a quotation from an old poem about lusty youth. Olga once put it to a music that pervades the poet's own life, as Olga's life has. This thought recalls the grassy place of their childhood, where Olga spun a magical tale about a tree root leading them into a nether world. Other lines from the old poem follow as she recalls their entering the world of "silent mid-Essex churches" adorned with effigies of medieval figures. The reminiscence evokes more lines from the same poem with which the section begins.

The second part of the fifth section follows Olga the year she was "most alone," revisiting "the old roads" and sights she and the poet had explored together as children. Now, Olga finds changes, still anguished. The winter's "damp still air" and frost, her poverty, the loss of her children—all reflect Olga's depressed circumstances and hint of political failure, the stage lights gone out, the "theater" empty and locked. The vision ends with an image of Olga in her room, reading books "that winter," and outdoors among the furrows and strange cries of birds, which the poet herself had once longed to embrace, only Olga was then "trudging after" her own "anguish."

The final section recalls Olga's "brown gold" eyes, which the poet has always seen while crossing the bridge over the river Roding and "by other streams in other countries." The thought brings back another moment in their childhood when Olga's passion drives her through the Ludwig van Beethoven sonatas "savagely." The poet recalls "the fear" in Olga's eyes in a photograph and wonders where the fear went as Olga passed through troubled years, what kept the "candle" lit as she journeyed. Lines suggest that Olga is last seen in an "obscure wood" with a house; from its open door, a hand beckons to Olga "in welcome."

Turning toward her own life, Levertov has seen in the "many brooks in the world . . . many questions" her own eyes want to ask of Olga's. In those eyes, the poet glimpses "some vision/ of festive goodness" behind a gaze that is "hard, or veiled, or shining" but ultimately "unknowable."

Forms and Devices

The open structure of the poem is evident in both line and stanza. Stanzaic lengths range from one to thirty-six (in section 6) lines, the most common lengths being two and three lines. Only section 2 contains stanzas of equal length—all triads—though stanzas of equal length are often grouped together throughout the first five sections, and a pattern of diminishing lengths is evident in sections 1, 3, and 4. Stanzaic patterning and length subtly pace the reader through the poet's recollections and experience, diminishing in section 1, advancing regularly through section 2, diminishing again in part 1 of section 3, and so on. The pauses within the stanzas and lines themselves counterpoint or modulate—or refine—the structure that is developing on the more general level. Clearly, the poet has shaped the lines and stanzas to keep time with her experience of her subject, to shape and ultimately to understand it.

Line length is the immediate expression of Levertov's mood as the ideas and recollections surface and form, as it were, pools of meaning, threads of understanding, and strings on which the poet plays her revelations about Olga and explores her present relationship to past lives. No predetermined pattern could accommodate this shaping force, and no other rhythms but those discovered in the making of the poem could express Levertov's experience. Even the spaces between stanzas represent more than pauses or shifts; they are leaps in Levertov's experience from one perception to another. Within the grasp of her own search for understanding, the poet lets the lines fall as they must, stopping on a natural pause— "To change,/ to change the course of the river!"— or continuing across the "abyss" created by spaces between stanzas. The result is a naturalness of rhythm and voice only occasionally intruded upon by such "poetic" devices as enjambment: "setting herself/ to sift cinders."

The more characteristic use of line ending may be seen in lines 37-38: "there was a white/ candle in your heart." There, the pause on "white" does more than rhyme would to emphasize both attitude and meaning. The poet needs fidelity to tell the truth— Olga's candle was white— but knows that a flash of color expresses a higher truth, her sister's purity of heart, set against the background of the previous line: "Black one, black one." In this way, the poet discovers the image, the placement of a word, and line rhythm that reveal her understanding. At the same time, these three lines conclude another understanding— begun at line 15, "The high pitch of/ nagging insistence," and continued through the psychological counterpointing of Olga's strident political "rage" and her younger sister's teasing —which concludes with the taunting rhythm of "Black one, black one."

Music, which was at the heart of Levertov's relationship with her sister, now helps render the poet's experience of that relationship. One element of the poem's imagery is its shape, and certainly its rhythms create more than a felt experience. If a symphony can inspire images in the minds of the audience, this poem's modulations bring to the surface of the reader's mind images that "rhyme" with, or correspond to, the ones Levertov actually provides. The very rightness of the poet's images is established by the very rightness of the poem's rhythms.

Themes and Meanings

An attempt to resolve the poet's conflicts regarding her sister informs the entire poem, perhaps is its *raison d'etre*, and certainly determines its rises and falls, its ongoing insistence, its tabulations of Olga's activities, its discords and harmonies. The poem's many breaks, stops and starts, and shifts in rhythm and mood suggest a similar array within the poet's own feelings about Olga. Without being fitful, the poet displays conflicting attitudes toward her sister. The poem opens with the poet as a child eyeing her sister undressed and already well developed. How did the child feel: suspicious— "beady-eyed in the bed"— unconcerned— "or drowsy was I? My head/ a camera"— or envious— "Her breasts/ round, round, and/ dark-nippled"?

Olga's political activities also stir conflicting feelings in the poet. As a child, she mocked Olga's social consciousness, and she has felt the sting of Olga's passionate nature, felt the alienation that came from Olga's superior knowledge and "rage for order," all the while feeling a close bond between herself and her sister— "but linked to words we loved." Pity follows Olga through her "bad years," her "pilgrim years," her hospitalization, to the end. These images of a harried, driven, "burned out" Olga are interrupted by a recollection of the sisters as they played in the sylvan setting of their childhood. This magical tour is the closest the sisters get in the poet's journey toward a synthesis of feeling and understanding, for in this brief interlude, the poet confesses, "your life winds in me."

Levertov's vision is fluid from beginning to end, as is evident in the water imagery and the many references to water, music, and cadence. Structurally, this theme is expressed in the unendingness of many of the lines—the dashes point the reader onward as the current of a river carries one toward the sea. The cascading lines and stanzas are evidence that the poet is composing her own feelings and shaping her own acknowledgment of her sister's life and influence on her. The statement *"Everything flows"* might stand as an epigraph of this elegy and an epitaph to Olga's life. The sisters were musical, the poem is saying—one was, one is. Olga's life, played out with the same passion that informed her playing Beethoven "savagely," was an endurance "in the falls and rapids of the music." The events of her life were the "arpeggios" that rang out, that were absorbed into the younger sister's poetics and played like a psychic keyboard. They compose themselves into the images—tree roots, rivers, streams, lines from poems and songs—that run through the poet's own self: "you set the words to a tune so plaintive/ it plucks its way through my life as through a wood . . . your life winds in me."

The poem seems to ask whether the myriad notes, however fluidly shaped and thematically harmonized, can coalesce in the poet's understanding. In the final section, the dominant images—water, music, lyrical consonance—are brought together in a crowd of lines that review the poet's main subject, Olga's passionate and apparently sterile politicism, and call up Olga's "brown gold" eyes and the candle. Earlier, the candle symbolizes Olga's purity and political rage; here, it is "compassion's candle." Acceptance marks the final mood—" 'a hand beckons/ in welcome.' " Yet whether Olga herself ever took the hand remains unknown. The "rolling dark/ oncoming river" flows onward, becomes the " 'selva oscura.' " Did the river engulf Olga? Did the dark wood envelop her and extinguish the candle? The answer is as mysterious as the final vision of Olga herself, her eyes hinting of "festive goodness" but hard, veiled, shining, unknowable. The final ellipsis symbolizes Levertov's failure to arrive at a conclusive understanding of her relationship to her sister—and a triumph of the two sisters' belief in the eternal flow, in which the poet has discovered an unending confluence.

Bernard E. Morris

ON A BOARD OF RASPBERRY AND PURE GOLD

Author: Osip Mandelstam (1891-1938)
Type of poem: Lyric
First published: 1964, as "Na doske malinovoi, chervonnoi," in *Sobranie sochinenii*; collected in *Selected Poems*, 1973

The Poem

"On a Board of Raspberry and Pure Gold," written by Osip Mandelstam in 1937, is a poem of sixteen lines. The Russian original, written in rhymed trochaic lines of five to seven feet and organized in a single stanza, has been translated by Clarence Brown and W. S. Merwin as a lyric of four stanzas in free blank verse, which, however, preserves a trochaic tendency. The poem offers the reader a winter landscape and the poet's reflections upon it. In fact, there is abundant testimony, from the poet's widow, Nadezhda Mandelstam, and others, that the poem presents a view of the old city of Voronezh, seen from the vicinity of 40 Kaliaev Street, the home of Natasha Shtempel', a young teacher who was virtually Mandelstam's sole confidante during much of the Mandelstams' exile to her town in 1934-1937. Situated on hills above a high riverbank, old Voronezh (much of which would be burned down under the Nazi occupation) was very picturesque; the neighborhood portrayed in the poem was one of single-story houses descending down the hillsides to the Don River— "half town half river-bank," as the poem puts it.

The poem's opening line (which is also used in lieu of a title, since Mandelstam did not provide one) presents an art medium, a board whose surface holds a painting with two dominant tones, raspberry and gold. Although the adjective translated as "pure gold" more often means "dark red," a subsequent allusion to yellow supports the translator's choice. This allusion comes as part of a catalog of the motifs of the painting, which occupies the next seven lines. Two somewhat more concrete images, "red coals" and "yellow resin" (in a more literal translation, "yellow mastic"), reinforce the initial color impressions. The yellow shade probably refers to the yellow paint so traditional for Russian exterior walls, while the "red coals" might refer either to outdoor fires, to the glow of sunlight on red tin roofs, or to the light issuing from the windows of the houses.

The next four lines are a warning to the reader, which simultaneously raises and rejects a comparison between this provincial Russian landscape and a Flemish genre scene in the manner of Pieter Bruegel's skaters. In the final four lines, the reader is further told to "cut off" the poet's "drawing," as he now calls his picture in verse. The English preserves the ambiguous meaning of the requested action: the Russian verb has the primary meaning of "to separate," but also has the idiomatic sense of "to cut off someone's speech rudely." This ambiguity is echoed in a closing simile, likening the poet's picture to a maple bough consigned to the fire. Thus, the poet's direct address to the reader may express his own will, or it may imply his gloomy prediction of how a hostile reader will react to the poem.

Forms and Devices

"On a Board of Raspberry and Pure Gold" is a highly metaphoric poem, using juxtaposition for the purpose of giving presence to what is not there in the physical scene. The first such metaphor is the scene as painting, the two-dimensional board onto whose surface the city is transposed. Next, there is a submerged but nevertheless demonstrable metaphor, picturing the cluster of houses as a horse-drawn caravan advancing to the river shore. In another animal metaphor, the children skating and sledding become a flock of cawing birds. Finally, there are the poem as drawing, and the comparison to a maple branch.

On another plane of juxtaposition, Voronezh is being implicitly likened to the Low Countries (the setting of Bruegel's landscape). Mandelstam makes this association, however, by a means that closely resembles what folklorists call negative comparison (when one is told, for example, that Vseslav the Magician, a personage in the Russian national epic, does *not* take on the form of a gray wolf, one immediately visualizes him as a shape-shifter who becomes a wolf at will). Thus, negative comparison is a technique of simultaneous denial and assertion. Once they are invoked, the Bruegelian overtones of the Voronezh scene or the (absent) children absorbed in their winter games become quite vivid.

In the Russian, the sense of the poem is reinforced by a range of versification techniques, several of which find counterparts in the Brown-Merwin translation. The original consists of two sentences of eight lines apiece. The translators preserve the first, but break up the second into three shorter sentences, each set off as a stanza, apparently to set off the logical movement and to let the variety of sentence structures substitute for the variety of rhythmic structures within a strict, binary meter in the Russian.

In the first sentence, Mandelstam uses rhythmic effects, in conjunction with rhyme and sound play, to suggest the action implied by the idea rendered as "sleigh-tracked" in the English. The entire eight lines are bound by an identical feminine rhyme, with the final unstressed vowel preceded by two *n*'s in a row. In five of the first eight lines, the final stressed syllable is preceded by a three-syllable, unstressed interval. This lets the verse line mimic the effect of a steep, slow climb up the hill, a moment's pause at the top—which Mandelstam would emphasize by pronouncing each *n* in the rhyme separately—and the rapid onset of the descent, signaled by the single, unstressed syllable at the end of the line.

The English, while it does preserve several *n* sounds, gets a similar effect by purely syntactic means. The first seven lines, all of which belong to the grammatical subject, never allow intonational or cognitive closure. We travel uphill until we finally arrive at the rapid cadence of the predicate ("was carried away") in the eighth line—a predicate that also suggests the appropriate semantic overtones of the children's sleds rushing down the hill.

Themes and Meanings

"On a Board of Raspberry and Pure Gold" is both the opening poem in the

"Third Voronezh Notebook" and the last in the long series of meditations on the Voronezh landscape that are scattered through the first two "Voronezh Notebooks." Mandelstam considered the notebooks as the three divisions of a single book— "Natasha's Book," as the Mandelstams called it, since the poems were arranged in sequence and written out in the notebooks for Natasha Shtempel', into whose safe-keeping they were put. In this lyric diary, one of the unifying themes is the poet's changing relationship to his place of exile.

Selected Poems contains a good sampling of these lyrics. Some poems treat only the despair of exile; in "Let Me Go, Release Me, Voronezh," for example, the poet creates his own etymology for the place-name, breaking it down into *voron*, "raven," the bird of evil omen, and *nozh*, "knife." More often, however, he finds positive inspiration in the fecund black earth of the region, the broad plains and wide vistas emblematic of the potential spiritual freedom Mandelstam found so lacking in Moscow.

The poetry of exile is an important mode in Russia, whose poet-exiles see their archetype in the Latin poet Ovid, banished to what is now southern Russia. One of the commonplaces of this tradition has the poet looking back from the barbarian fringes upon the metropolitan culture. In several poems written before "On a Board of Raspberry and Pure Gold," Mandelstam wills to see the Voronezh landscape within the framework of his broader cultural loyalties. The April sky, for example, becomes the region's Michelangelo; its hills and dales are said to be worthy of van Ruisdael.

At a reading in 1937, Mandelstam responded to a provocateur by redefining Acmeism—the current to which he had given his allegiance as a young poet—as a yearning for world culture. This anecdote points out the dilemma to which he is responding in "On a Board of Raspberry and Pure Gold." There are two dimensions to the problem: Must one turn one's back on a more universal cultural legacy in order to come to terms with Voronezh, that is, with perhaps the least worst chance for survival for a poet in disgrace with the regime? Even more generally, do art (here, painting and drawing) and life have any guidance to offer each other, or is art completely sundered from life, like the drawing/branch at the end of the poem? On the surface, Mandelstam's poem answers these questions in the negative, but all its energies are bent on performing the truth of the affirmative.

Charles Isenberg

ON FIRST LOOKING INTO CHAPMAN'S HOMER

Author: John Keats (1795-1821)
Type of poem: Sonnet
First published: 1816; collected in *Poems*, 1817

The Poem

"On First Looking into Chapman's Homer" is a sonnet describing the excitement experienced by the narrator upon reading a translation of Homer's *Iliad* (c. 800 B.C.) by the sixteenth century poet George Chapman. Though it is often unwise to equate the narrator of a poem with the author, in this instance it seems appropriate to assume that John Keats himself is speaking of his own sense of amazement and delight in discovering the joys of reading Homer in such a vibrant English rendition.

The focus throughout the poem is on the feelings engendered in a person when a discovery is made. The narrator expresses himself directly to the reader, attempting to find parallels to explain what it feels like to make a great discovery for oneself. To make that feeling clear, the narrator speaks of himself as a traveler who has set out to explore uncharted lands—at least, uncharted by him. He portrays himself as someone experienced in visiting exotic places ("realms of gold," in line 1) and as having seen "many goodly states and kingdoms" (line 2) among the "western islands" (line 3) that are inhabited by "bards" who pay homage to the god "Apollo" (line 4). The conscious reference to poets and to the Greek patron of poetry should suggest to readers that this is not a literal journey; instead, it is intended to represent the mental travel one undergoes when one enters the imaginative world of literature.

The narrator describes his journey around those imaginary islands, noting finally that, though he is quite a veteran of such traveling, he had never set foot on the land ruled by the revered Homer until introduced there by Chapman, who serves as a kind of herald into the epic bard's court. Through Chapman's introduction, the narrator is able to breathe in the "pure serene" (line 8)—literally, the stimulating quality of the air in that favored land, but metaphorically, the exhilarating atmosphere that Homer's poetry creates.

The results of the narrator's arrival in the land of Homer are almost overwhelming. He feels himself like a scientist who discovers a new planet or like an explorer setting foot in the new world of America and seeing the hitherto unknown sights there. He compares himself specifically to Hernando Cortés, the conqueror of Mexico: The experience of being enveloped in the land of Homer (the environment created by Homer within his epic poem) is much like that felt by Cortés and his men when they first saw the Pacific Ocean; it leaves the traveler speechless.

Forms and Devices

Keats uses the form of the Italian sonnet to express his joy at discovering the wonders of the Homeric epic as Chapman presented it in his seventeenth century English translation. Invented by the Italian poet Petrarch (1304-1374) and first made popular in English by the sixteenth century lyricists Sir Thomas Wyatt (1503-1542) and Henry Howard, Earl of Surrey (1517-1547), the Italian sonnet is divided into two parts: An eight-line quatrain usually sets forth a problem or a dilemma, and the six-line sextet offers some resolution. Keats follows this rhetorical pattern in "On First Looking into Chapman's Homer." Using the first eight lines to describe his experiences in reading poetry by comparing them to the wanderings of a traveler to many small islands, he then follows in the sextet with an analysis of the joy he felt in discovering Homer's poetry by comparing it to the feelings of elation a scientist or explorer might feel upon first encountering a strange phenomenon. Keats follows the strict rhyme scheme of the Italian sonnet, using only four rhymes for the entire poem: *abba, abba, cdcdcd.*

The dominant literary device in this poem is metaphor. Keats plays with the notion of comparison on many levels. The entire composition can be seen as an extended metaphor, in which the narrator—a reader of books—is compared to an explorer whose voyage is rewarded with a great discovery. Individual comparisons follow the lead of that general parallel. The experience of reading is described as traveling "in the realms of gold." Individual works are compared to "many western islands" which "bards in fealty to Apollo hold"—a suggestion that writers are like so many landholders who owe allegiance to a great lord (in this case, the Greek god who was the patron of the arts). Epic poetry, one form of the literary art, is described in terms of a great tract of land, "one wide expanse" (line 5), and the Greek poet Homer, whose two epics serve as models for subsequent works in the genre, is lord of that realm. Two specific comparisons are used to describe the reader's excitement at discovering Homer through Chapman's translation. First, the narrator compares himself to an astronomer ("some watcher of the skies," line 9) who notices a new planet through his telescope. Then he likens his excitement to that which must have been felt by the Europeans who traveled to the new world and first looked upon the Pacific Ocean (lines 11-14). In both cases, the poet wishes to evoke a feeling of awe at the discovery of such a magnificent natural phenomenon. Keats suggests that those same feelings are experienced by the reader who picks up a copy of Chapman's translation of Homer and begins to read.

Themes and Meanings

"On First Looking into Chapman's Homer" is intended primarily to give readers a sense of the excitement that comes from discovering for themselves the works of a great author. Concurrently—and this is a point not often stressed—Keats suggests that the delight in this discovery is often an experience dependent on circumstances beyond those over which the author himself or herself has had direct control; in this case, the narrator's experience comes from reading the Homeric epic in translation. It is important, then, to recall that it is "Chapman's Homer" that excites the narrator; the translator has had a major role in creating the experience by serving as a bridge in communicating the story through language the reader understands. The impact of the reading experience, which Keats describes metaphorically as "breath[ing] the pure serene" air in a beautiful land, comes not directly from Homer's Greek, but from Chapman's rendition of that Greek into polished English verse.

Keats wants readers to realize the impact that a great work of literature can have. There is a clear sense that the narrator has come to his reading of Homer with some anticipation— "Oft," he says, "had I been told" of the greatness of the Greek epic (line 5). Nevertheless, the experience itself far surpasses any second-hand account; hearing of something is no substitute for experiencing it oneself. The two examples in the poem's sextet are intended to convey the sense of wonderment that can come only from direct experience. Keats wants readers to understand that reading great literature can bring the same kind of excitement to them that scientific discovery and travel can engender.

On a larger scale, the poem deals with the process of discovery itself, a human activity that has excited men since the dawn of recorded history (and before, no doubt). It is important to note that "On First Looking into Chapman's Homer" is about the process of discovery that every individual goes through when having any kind of experience for the first time—no matter how many people have had the experience before. This distinction is important, for it explains what many critics have considered the great "mistake" in the final lines of the poem: the apparent misidentification of Cortés as the first European to "discover" the Pacific Ocean. Because historians usually attribute the "discovery" of the Pacific to Vasco Núñez de Balboa, some scholars have accused Keats of not knowing his history. That may be true, but it would have no bearing on the meaning of this poem. There is no suggestion in the poem that Cortés or his men (both mentioned in lines 11-12) are the first to see the Pacific; rather, the implication is that they are viewing it for the first time in their lives. Similarly, Keats is suggesting, the reader who comes upon great works of literature for the first time will experience a sense of awe and wonder at the power of literature to excite them and to make a difference in their lives.

Laurence W. Mazzeno

ON HIS MISTRESS

Author: John Donne (1572-1631)
Type of poem: Elegy
First published: 1635, in *Poems, by J. D.: With Elegies on the Authors Death*

The Poem

"On His Mistress" (sometimes called simply Elegy 18) is an elegy of fifty-six lines which comprise twenty-eight rhyming couplets. The poem's title discloses its contemplative nature, a characteristic mandated by the elegiac form. The poem is written in the first person; this highlights the personal nature of the poem, conceived by a man before he departs on a long journey to the European continent. He seems to lament leaving his love behind as he meditates on their relationship, yet the poem's intent is ultimately ambiguous.

"On His Mistress" takes as its point of departure a stressing of the seeming futility of the lovers' efforts to stay together. The narrator discloses his love's intended scheme—she would like to dress like a man and accompany him on his journey to the Continent. Surprisingly, given the poem's elegiac form and its elevated rhetoric, the narrator chides this notion; she would be easily identified because "Richly clothed apes, are called apes" (line 31). This does not seem to be the tone a lover normally adopts when writing about and to his beloved. When the narrator adds to this notion by turning to the vulgarities of the peoples of other nations, the poem shifts in tone. Gone is the elevated rhetoric of lovers; instead, the narrator and the poem adapt an aura of superiority and absurdity: The men of France are diseased, the Italians are bisexual, and the Dutch are slovenly drunks. These clichés are meant to rationalize the narrator's reasons for dissuading his love from joining him, yet they are also serious insults aimed at those from the Continent.

By the poem's conclusion, the narrator has shifted back to the sentimental mode more typical of the elegiac genre. He instructs his beloved to remember him during his absence, but this conventional plea is then usurped by the poem's strange final lines. The narrator asks his mistress to dream happiness for him (nowhere is it mentioned that she should dream happily of the two as a couple). This demonstrates the connection between lovers even while they are separated by hundreds of miles, yet it also shows the self-centered nature of the narrator. Perhaps this could be justified by the notion that their love has been a covert affair, an idea forwarded by his hope that she will tell nobody of their feelings; however, this does not excuse the apparent one-sidedness of his plea.

The poem concludes with further irony: The narrator pleads that his mistress not have any nightmares or fear for his safety. While it is human nature to comfort one's love before departing on a long journey, the "comforting" done here is presented with an odd twist. The very mention of the possibility that he may be slain, presented in the graphic terms of line 54 ("Assailed, fight, taken, stabbed, bleed, fall, and die"), can only reinforce the fears of his lover. This expression of peril is compounded in its written form, for speech may be forgotten, while written words may be forever preserved. Thus, the attempt to calm and reassure has become, instead, a seed of doubt, a worry that could grow every day while he is gone.

Forms and Devices

"On His Mistress" is an elegy, a poem which sets forth the poet's contemplations. Elegies are usually about death, but they may be concerned with another solemn or elevated theme, such as love. The elegy form, dating back to classical literature, originally signified almost any type of serious meditation by the narrator and his concerns with love, death, hostilities, or even the presentation of information. In the Renaissance, Elizabethans such as John Donne used the form for love poems; they often were composed as complaints. While the classical authors composed their works in a distinct pattern called the "elegiac stanza," the Elizabethans strayed from this rigid technique.

Donne also varies from the traditional Elizabethan structure and subject matter in his "On His Mistress"; the elegy begins typically as the narrator laments impending departure, yet this lamentation comes in ironic terms: The lovers' meeting was a "strange and fatal interview." This introduces the first idea that this will be a non-standard love poem, a point stressed by the narrator's description of the covert nature of the lovers' affair. These lovers have obviously run the gamut of emotions during their relationship in their attempts to keep their affair secret. Yet the narrator relies upon his "masculine pervasive force" (line 4) to take the matter of their departure into account. Therefore, it is not surprising that he "calmly begs" (line 7), since the manly aspect of the elegy has already been established.

Donne also relies upon the use of anaphora to distinguish the three distinct stages of Elegy 18. The repetition of "by" in the first part of the poem serves as a precursor to the inevitable departure of the two lovers, as it hints at the lovers saying good-bye. The narrator explains or rationalizes the lovers' stormy history: They met, desired, hoped, and regretted their love. This caused the pain from which the narrator is now purposefully departing. The tone then changes as the poem shifts from a revelation of their love to the external problems of their affair. Her father certainly would not approve of their relationship, so they must keep it secret. Now they must part; only they know the truth of their affair. The language in this section is powerful and elevated; their covert affair was obviously a strain on both of them. His departure will both add to this problem and reduce it; the two will not have to worry about being detected while he is away.

The second section of the poem moves to the narrator's rationale for leaving her behind — because of the vulgarities that she would face — and examines the impractical notion that she dress as a man and accompany him on the trip. The nationalistic digression disrupts the tone of the first section and lowers it; the poem's final section will again move to a loftier level.

In the final section, Donne returns to anaphora to push a point forward. The repetition of "nor" overburdens the love images suggested by the conclusion with a negative tone. By suggesting that she should dream about him (not "us") and his happiness, he has broken the union they had created. He then asks her not to worry that he be cursed and not to have a nightmare that he has been injured or killed; all this does is plant images in her mind which will cause worry after he is gone.

Themes and Meanings

While Donne's "On His Mistress" is seemingly straightforward in its meanings, there are several aspects of Donne's life that may provide more background and add to the understanding of the poem. The elegiac conventions, here somewhat altered, are usually used as a form to express the poet's love. This is accomplished in "On His Mistress" in a backhanded way. Further, the poem contains a distinct nationalistic attack on the Continent on the part of the narrator.

Donne, while in the employ of Sir Thomas Egerton, the Lord Keeper of the Great Seal, became enamored of Egerton's young niece, Ann More. In 1601, Donne and More were secretly married, much to the dismay of Egerton, who had Donne dismissed from his estate and briefly imprisoned. For the next fourteen years, Donne was somewhat blacklisted and had a terrible time finding permanent employment. He ended up living off the good graces of his friends and patrons. This incident suggests the possibility that when Donne writes of covert affairs and their implications, he does so from experience. It may also help explain the manly tone and attitude that becomes a major theme in "On His Mistress."

The poem also is notable for its prominent disconcerting attacks on other nationalities, attacks which show the increased nationalism among Englishmen in the wake of the English defeat of the Spanish Armada in 1588. Donne himself sailed with the Earl of Essex in 1596 to sack the Spanish coastal city of Cadiz; he also accompanied Sir Walter Raleigh in 1597 on an expedition to hunt Spanish treasure ships off the Azores. Given the success of these ventures, it is evident that Donne is again speaking from personal experience as he degrades the men of continental Europe; his manliness, in a sense, has been earned.

What is surprising, however, is the seemingly indignant nature with which the narrator seems to treat his beloved. He comments on the difficult nature of their relationship, scoffs at her proposal to join him on the journey, and then plants seeds of fear in her concerning his departure and the potential perils that await him. This may be explained, at least partly, by remembering the audience to which Donne directed many of his poems. He would commonly write them to be shared with his friends in the inns and alehouses of England; the men would share camaraderie while reading one another's literary works. It is not too farfetched to suggest that this may be the reason for both the nationalism and the ironic degradation of his mistress that occur in Elegy 18. Part of the enjoyment of gathering to read one another's works, or to hear them read aloud, may simply have involved the reiteration of the writers' and listeners' masculinity.

R. T. Lambdin

ON PRAYER

Author: Czesław Miłosz (1911-   )
Type of poem: Lyric
First published: 1984; as "O Modlitwie," in *Nieobjęta ziemia*; collected in
  Unattainable Earth, 1986

The Poem

"On Prayer" is a short poem, twelve lines long, written in free verse. The title suggests a meditation on the nature of the act of prayer, which immediately signals the presence of a number of potential issues: the question of God's existence, the nature of one's relationship to God, and explorations of the ideas of faith and belief.

The poet adopts a first-person voice in this short lyric, written in the form of a direct response to a problem: "how to pray to someone who is not." The first line, in effect, announces the problem by restating a question asked by an implied listener, here assumed to be the reader. Czesław Miłosz's concise poem retains the immediacy of a personal response to the query, even to the point of a brief schoolmasterly aside in line 9 to make sure readers are paying attention. Without relying on the language of doctrine, Miłosz establishes his own quietly authoritative tone.

The first line raises the question of reconciling prayer, a desire for belief, with the contemporary context of disbelief or skepticism. How does one describe the act of prayer in such circumstances, and what function can it perform? Immediately, Miłosz has focused his readers' attention on a central paradox of spiritual expression in the twentieth century.

The next four lines make up the initial stage of the speaker's response: a description of what prayer does in his experience. The act of prayer builds a "velvet bridge," establishes a connection, and this bridge elevates people in some sense, creating a new perspective on reality. The image—softness capable with sustaining strength—touches on both the ephemeral and the substantive nature of the act. Miłosz's use of the simile of a "springboard" quickly following underscores this as a point of departure—an image that highlights both the act of prayer itself and his own poetic, imaginative foray into its description. The next two lines complete the idea by providing an image of this higher perspective in the form of magically transformed landscapes. It is worthwhile to note that the viewpoint remains materially focused. The image of light, traditionally indicating illumination and greater consciousness, is linked to a suspension of time and an epiphanic vision of richness and fecundity.

Line 6, beginning the second stage of the speaker's response, provides readers with the destination of the bridge: "the shore of Reversal." The capitalization of the noun gives the name a heightened significance, investing it with the kind of abstract quality found in allegorical representations. The formal placement of the naming appropriately marks the middle of the poem and suggests a shift in direction, an alteration in the nature of the vision or a limitation of its scope. Miłosz, by highlighting the quasi-allegorical nature of the place, suggests a complication of the simple correspondence between prayer and bridge established in the first half of the poem. Reversal implies an inversion as in a mirror or turning back in direction. The onset of abstraction immediately is linked to ambiguity of interpretation, re-creating in the poem the same limitation of verification to which all belief is subject. Miłosz takes his readers to the edge of belief but refuses to push the vision into a fixed depiction of the other.

The final section of "On Prayer" begins with the speaker's admonition "Notice: I say *we*." The scope of the explanation has moved now from abstraction to a very immediate personal relevance. The effect of reversal implicates everyone, changes the focus from the singular to the plural, and moves the altered vision back into the human sphere. With this plurality comes a consciousness of corporeal existence, a compassion and empathy with "others entangled in the flesh." The poem embodies the process it describes: prayer being the individual means toward faith, hence incomplete in a generic sense, yet offering a validation of the endeavor on moral and imaginative grounds.

Forms and Devices

One of the most striking features of Miłosz's exposition on the nature of prayer is his elaboration of the image of the bridge. Miłosz's use of metonymy (the substitution of one term for another), in this case prayer and the bridge, fixes in very concrete terms an extremely intangible subject. The description admits no merely linguistic connection, but functions as an element of fact; thus, the poet maintains the materiality of the image while using it to describe an extremely abstract and metaphysical religious concept. By this means, Miłosz retains a balance between his sense of human desire (goodness) and human limitations (the existence of evil). To leave aside the material nature of humans would be to invalidate the process, to render an untrue vision.

In an early section of *Unattainable Earth*, Miłosz remarks, "The language of literature in the twentieth century has been steeped in unbelief. Making use of that language, I was able to show only a small bit of my believing temperament." His use of the concrete reality to balance the metaphysical in "On Prayer" reflects this ongoing difficulty and incorporates the thematic material of the poem into its formal presentation. The deliberate simplicity of the diction and the generally proselike syntax is another way to keep his concerns firmly grounded in this world.

Another representative element of this short lyric is the studied, balanced tone. More extended lyrics in this volume give an indication of Miłosz's tendency toward a polyphonic voice to render the rich textures and variety of experience. Even in this short lyric, however, one gets an indication of the balances created by juxtaposing images of great poetic power (the illumination, for example) and his more prosaic, earthbound, and directive tones.

Themes and Meanings

"On Prayer" is part of a sequence entitled "Consciousness" in a volume that is organized as a single sequence—a pastiche of poetry, prose reflections, quotations from various sources, and fragments of letters. Central to the volume as a whole is Miłosz's sense of the ongoing struggle, through the limitations of mind and language, between the knowledge of God's presence and the existence of evil in the world. The historical realities of the twentieth century—war, genocide, and oppression on a scale never before known—underscore, for Miłosz, the paradox of belief. As he suggests, "While respecting tradition and recognizing analogies, we must remember that we are trying to name a new experience"—that of finding a moral position compatible with the experience of the present.

Miłosz's position is reflected in his dual perspective, which brings the abstract into continual, and necessary, conjunction with quotidian reality. "On Prayer" illustrates this in a number of ways. On one level, there is the description of prayer in material terms, the embodiment of an act of faith in the language of unbelief. On another level, Miłosz presents his desire to move away from this existence, to transcend the things of this world; then he links this irrevocably with the limitations of "the shore of Reversal," an image that turns the transcendent impulse back toward humanity. In "On Prayer," one can observe this paradox in the formal construction of the poem, in the concrete and lyrical nature of the imagery, and in the argument itself. In the nature of the reversal upon which the poem hinges, one sees a desire never to leave the reality of this world behind. Explorations into the nature of one's relation to God must always, for Miłosz, involve an incorporation of the entanglements of the flesh, must reconcile the realities of the human condition with the sense of a divine order.

While "On Prayer" shares with many other Miłosz poems this sense of an epiphany, an unexpected revelation of the nature of being, it is balanced by a recognition that this vision ultimately leads back to humanity. The emphasis in line 6 on the word "is," the singular present form of the verb "to be," indicates Miłosz's acknowledgment of the human experience of individuality, the fixation with the present, and also the element of hope that being involves. Notably, the redefinition at the center of this consciousness is not imposed from without, but rather entails a recognition with one's essential nature. Giving being an anthropomorphic focus instead of an otherworldly one, Miłosz maintains his human-centered vision.

James Panabaker

ON THE DEATH OF DR. ROBERT LEVET

Author: Samuel Johnson (1709-1784)
Type of poem: Elegy
First published: 1783; collected in *The Poetical Works of Samuel Johnson*, 1785

The Poem

"On the Death of Dr. Robert Levet" is a poetic elegy that celebrates the life, while mourning the death, of Robert Levet (1705-1782), a "lay" physician who for many years lived in Samuel Johnson's London house and tended the local poor, seldom asking a fee for his services. Johnson, the eighteenth century's greatest man of letters, was a scholar, a moralist, and a poet of limited range but genuine abilities. When Levet died in 1782, Johnson was near the end of his own long life — a life that brought him the fame and success his talents merited, yet was filled with illness, poverty, and great personal disappointment. It is hardly surprising, then, to find Johnson compressing so much life and thought within a relatively few lines occasioned by the death of a poor, awkward man unknown to the "greater" world of art and letters.

Johnson's poem is divided into nine four-line stanzas. The meter is iambic tetrameter; the rhyme scheme is *abab*. Each stanza is a grammatically self-contained unit that makes a statement not only about Levet and his life, but, by extension, about humanity and the human condition in general.

At a time when poetic diction was tending more and more toward the ornate, "inane phraseology" of which William Wordsworth later complained, Johnson instead chooses a language that is simple, direct, and "common" — a language wholly appropriate to its subject. In a like manner, Johnson foregoes the kind of elaborate imagery that so many earlier elegists had employed to "elevate" their subjects. Johnson's crowning artistic achievement, completed only a few years before, was a series of biographies of English poets now known as *Lives of the Poets* (1779-1781). Among the poets Johnson treated was the great John Milton, and one can easily imagine how, following Levet's death, Johnson's thoughts would naturally turn to the lofty language and grand images of Milton's "Lycidas," thought by many to be the finest English-language elegy ever written. Levet was not what the progressive-minded eighteenth century would call a "great" man, however, and Johnson surely must have felt that a series of highly wrought, "artificial" images would be sadly unsuited to what he saw as the eloquently sincere and uncomplicated statement made by Levet's life.

Instead, Johnson turns to the kind of simple, concrete imagery that he had employed successfully in his most famous poem, "The Vanity of Human Wishes" (1749). Moving from "Hope's delusive mine" in the first stanza to "Misery's darkest caverns" in the fifth, and on to the moving scene of the breaking of life's "vital chain" in the ninth, he gives spare, solid images that function to underscore, rather than overwhelm or obscure, Levet's accomplishments.

Johnson's strategy is straightforward. Following a general statement about the human condition that is traditionally Christian in its "philosophy" (though certainly not what one would call optimistic: people are all "Condemn'd to Hope's delusive mine"—a vision of earthly reality as a kind of purgatory), he begins to lay out Levet's life and character in a way that consistently obliges readers to look beyond the particularities of his existence—a way that obliges readers to see themselves in Levet and, significantly, to ask themselves just how their lives measure up to his.

Forms and Devices

"On the Death of Dr. Robert Levet" is traditional. It is, in fact, among those poems that anyone familiar with English poetry would immediately assign to the eighteenth century—and probably to Johnson. The consistent use of adjective-noun combinations ("sudden blasts," "useful care"); the presence of several key personifications ("fainting nature," "hopeless anguish"); and the carefully balanced phrasing ("The busy day, the peaceful night," "His frame was firm, his powers were bright") all indicate Johnson's commitment to order, form, and tradition.

Yet to speak of Johnson's poem as traditional is not to devalue it. One must remember that neither the eighteenth century in general nor Johnson in particular embraced the ideas about poetic originality that are valued in the twentieth century. (In Shakespeare's day, fools or eccentrics were often called "originals.") To be original was to veer away from the common stream of life; it was, in essence, to abdicate one's primary responsibility as a writer, which was (as Johnson put it in his celebrated "Preface to The Plays of William Shakespeare") to present "human sentiments in human language." Thus, a desire to reach out to as many men and women as possible, not just to a privileged few, can be seen in Johnson's firm commitment to poetic tradition.

In practical terms, this means Johnson commits himself to rendering Levet's story as "universal" in scope as possible, in the hope that it might function for all his readers as a moral lesson—indeed, as precisely the kind of biblical parable of which Johnson was so fond. (The parable of the "single talent," referred to in line 28 and taken from the biblical account in Matthew 25:14-30, was one of Johnson's favorites. Levet's story is ultimately an illustration of "The single talent well employ'd.")

Johnson searches out the most universal, the most "human" concerns—concerns all readers are likely to have shared at some time in their lives. He speaks of life and death, of human cares and anguish, of human virtues and accomplishments, of faith, duty, and compassion, and—though the word is never mentioned—of love.

Themes and Meanings

It is not unusual for an elegist to move quickly beyond his or her subject in pursuit of grander things. In "Adonais," for example, poor John Keats is soon forgotten as Percy Bysshe Shelley takes off on an exalted tour of the universe (which turns out, essentially, and not without some irony, to be Shelley's own mind). Johnson, however, never forgets Levet. The meaning he seeks inheres in Levet, in a sense *is* Levet.

What Johnson saw so clearly in this reserved, humble, and uncouth man may puzzle readers. It certainly puzzled Johnson's friends, most of them upper-class literati who wondered, for example, what pleasure the greatest conversationalist in England could possibly find in taking morning tea — *every* morning — with a man who seldom said a word.

Answers to such questions can only involve speculation, but it is probably safe to say that Johnson — a man whose entire life can be regarded from one perspective as a continual search after spiritual truth — saw spiritual truth in Levet. Three days after Levet's death, Johnson concluded a diary entry briefly describing the funeral with these telling words: "May God have mercy on him. May he have mercy on me."

What Johnson saw — or hoped to see — in the parable of Levet's life was the possibility of God's mercy and the hope of heaven. Throughout most of his life, Johnson was plagued by what his contemporaries called melancholy and what we would describe as depression. In his darkest moments, and in spite of his strong Christian beliefs, Johnson was tortured by religious doubts, not so much about the existence of God, but doubts about his own worthiness as a beneficiary of God's mercy. His doubts compelled him to weigh continuously his own spiritual worth (his journals and diaries are full of moments of painful self-examination), but his own immense honesty stopped him short of reading the world only in terms of his own doubts. Instead, he searched the lives and experiences of others for confirmation that life not only had meaning, but was also, in a sense, a spiritual pilgrimage with an attainable goal.

Levet's humble pilgrimage through life was for Johnson a meaningful example, a kind of *Pilgrim's Progress* (1678, 1684, by John Bunyan) in miniature, that was able to bolster his faith and bring him spiritual comfort. As readers see Levet work his way day after day through the London slums ("misery's darkest caverns"), selflessly dispensing his "useful care," they see he is walking a "narrow round" that is actually an upward spiral: When death "frees" his soul, it is called home "the nearest way."

Michael Stuprich

ON THE MORNING OF CHRIST'S NATIVITY

Author: John Milton (1608-1674)
Type of poem: Meditation
First published: 1645, in *Poems of Mr. John Milton*

The Poem

"On the Morning of Christ's Nativity" was written in 1629, while John Milton was still a student at the University of Cambridge. In some ways it is clearly an "apprentice" work, in its often naïve tone, youthful idealism, and occasional quaint conceit. In other ways, however, it shows an already clear control of the poetic medium, verse structure, and overall design. Its central concerns anticipate quite remarkably those of *Paradise Lost* (1667, 1674), written some thirty years later. The poem is thus of interest not only intrinsically, but also in that it indicates the contours of Milton's imagination and his concerns at the start of his poetic career.

In the introduction, the poem is seen as a nativity offering to the infant Christ. Milton uses the conceit of running before the three wise men in order to deliver his gift first. The poem is both gift and prophetic word, joining with the angelic choir.

In the main section of the poem ("The Hymn"), which becomes the gift itself, Milton describes first the time and place of the nativity. He is determined to move away from traditional depictions, which center on mother and child, the stable, and Joseph in an intimate, enclosed scene. Instead, his imagination soars, moving into the cosmic and universal realms, adopting a bird's-eye (or an angel's-eye) view and reaching into heavenly glory. The setting is depicted in terms of the whole of nature being at peace (an ancient belief held that at the time of Christ's birth there were no wars being waged anywhere); thus, the earth is at harmony with its Creator—since the Fall, a unique occurrence.

He returns briefly to the immediate locale, to describe the shepherds and the angelic choir they hear. This is the harmony made audible. Normally the sign of creation's harmony, the music of the spheres, is inaudible to human ears; on this night, that music blends with the angelic harmony in a transforming power, which gives a promise of a restored golden age.

Before this could happen, the poet realizes, Christ must die and be raised to glory, to judge the conquered Satan and his evil agents. Already their power is broken, however; the religions of Greece and Rome, which previously may have contained shadows of the truth, lose their prophetic and priestly power. Other pagan religions, such as those condemned in the Old Testament, also lose their evil hold: Their strongholds are overthrown. Milton catalogs those pagan gods in detail, from Peor and Baalim to Moloch and Typhon. Like ghosts, the false gods must return to the underworld at the dawn of the new Sun of righteousness. In the final stanza, the poem returns to the Nativity scene; the final image is not of the Christ child and Mary, but of "Bright-harnessed Angels"—that is, angels wearing armor—sitting about the stable in battle formation.

Forms and Devices

The poem is difficult to classify generically. Although the main section is entitled "The Hymn," it is clearly not a hymn in any traditional sense: It is not addressed to God, nor has it any explicit exhortation to fellow believers. It has features of an ode; although the Nativity is never addressed as such, it does have the elevated language associated with that genre. It also contains pastoral elements. It is best seen, perhaps, as a meditation on the transfiguring power that Christ's birth had over the created world.

"The Hymn" consists of twenty-seven eight-line stanzas, rhyming *aabccbdd*, although the last two lines never work as a couplet. The stanzas are basically one-sentence units, and they already prefigure the long sentence structures of Milton's later verse. The complex metric structure seems to have been entirely of Milton's making, showing a youthful ingenuity and mastery. The *a*- and *c*-rhyming lines are trimeters; the *b*-rhyming lines are pentameters; and the final two lines consist of a tetrameter followed by a hexameter. The meter is basically iambic, but not rigidly so. There is also a very flexible use made of syntactic structures within the metric ones. Milton exploits a wide dramatic range, from the quick, soft smoothness of stanza V, to the slow elegiac lament of stanza XX, to the dissonances of stanza XXIV.

The introduction consists of four stanzas of seven lines of iambic pentameter, apart from the final line, which is hexameter; it rhymes *ababbcc*. The complete poem thus consists of 244 lines.

One of its more remarkable features is the cyclic nature of the hymn. It consists of three cycles: stanzas I-VII; VIII-XV; and XVI-XXVII. The first two cycles begin at the Nativity scene itself, then soar away into glory, reaching powerful climaxes. The final cycle works the other way round, finishing on a dismissive note as the false gods troop off to the underworld like ghosts. The final stanza then leaves readers with the sleeping infant in an effective closure. In this cyclic structure, Milton keeps close control over his imagination.

There are two predominant trains of imagery. The first is of light and darkness; from the glory of "that Light unsufferable/ And that far-beaming blaze of Majesty" (lines 8-9) to the "greater Sun" (Christ) outshining the "bright Throne, or burning Axletree" of the sun (lines 83-84). Similarly, darkness depicts first the human condition— "a darksome House of mortal Clay" (line 14)— then the underworld, where "Th'old Dragon Swinges the scaly Horror of his folded tail" (lines 168, 172), and the sites of pagan religion: "twilight shade of tangled thickets" (line 188); "left in shadows dread/ His burning Idol all of blackest hue" (lines 206-207).

The second train of imagery is of music, especially of harmony: The music of the spheres and the angelic choir both suggest triumph; the weeping and lament suggest old powers broken and passing away. The poem itself becomes its own image of integrated music. Other images are pastoral and rustic, and even sexual— nature is a fallen woman, needing snow for a covering to restore the appearance of innocence (stanza II).

Themes and Meanings

Milton's imagination is cosmic. The central two stanzas of the introduction establish this. He wants to depict the full cosmic and spiritual significance of the Incarnation. This is his prophetic calling, similar to Isaiah's (line 28). He is also a humanist, however—a lover of classical literature. There is thus a conflict posed for him as a Christian poet: What truth values can be put on classical myths and belief systems now that Christ has come to give full revelation to all men? One traditional answer was to dismiss such myths as lies and deceptions (the Augustinian solution); the other was to accept them as partial revelation, as types and foreshadowings actually pointing the way to Christ. This is the answer Milton adopts. Christ becomes the fulfillment of the nature god Pan (stanza VIII); he is the new infant Hercules strangling the snake (Satan) in his crib (stanza XXV). Thus the prophetic oracles at Delphos did utter truth, but their power is now withdrawn and put on Christ (stanza XIX). This is how Milton states his Christian humanism, and how he establishes a basis for a transformed Christian pastoral.

When it is a question of Middle Eastern mythologies, as of Phoenicia, Canaan, or Egypt, however, his condemnation is complete, since the Old Testament condemns them utterly, and as a biblical Christian he needs to do the same. The position he adopts is the same one he retained in *Paradise Lost*: The pagan gods worshiped falsely are, in fact, not lifeless idols but real spiritual forces that need binding and defeating. The transition from the treatment of one set of beliefs to the other occurs in stanza XX, the tone of which is rather poignant and ambivalent, suggesting perhaps some lingering regret that something beautiful has been lost at the same time as the sordidness of pagan ritual.

The nativity is seen, then, not as a celebration of a personal story of a virgin birth in a humble stable, but as a breaking in upon Creation by its King: a reclaiming and a moment of glory, anticipating the final glory of the Second Advent (stanza XVI). Milton collapses time here, as he does in Book III of *Paradise Lost*. Past, present, and future all exist within his incarnational language; however, he avoids any centering on the Crucifixion, which one might expect more orthodox treatment to do (later, the Puritans actually abolished Christmas as a celebration). In fact, at no point in his poetic career did Milton ever focus on Christ's death and suffering. This lacuna is already in evidence here: The appearance of Christ foreshadows not his rejected humanity and redemptive sacrifice but his appearance in final glory and judgment over the dark falsehoods of satanic forces. That is the second climax of history; this Nativity is the first.

David Barratt

ON THE MOVE

Author: Thom Gunn (1929-   )
Type of poem: Lyric
First published: 1955; collected in *The Sense of Movement*, 1957

The Poem

"On the Move" is composed in five eight-line stanzas, with the rhyme scheme *abaccddb*. The poem begins by observing the movement of birds in their natural surroundings and comparing their movement to human action. Whether driven by natural "instinct," acquired "poise," or some combination of the two, the birds seem to have some "hidden purpose" to give meaning to their motion. The "One" of the poem who observes them wonders whether his own "uncertain violence" of motion is driven by the same forces. Until now he has been bewildered equally by both the instincts of "baffled sense" and "the dull thunder of approximate words." The rest of the poem tries to make words yield their precise meaning in relation to the experience of motion.

In the second stanza, the motorcyclists are introduced. They mediate between birds and man, their movement seeming half instinctual, half pilgrimage. First the reader sees the machines on the road, then, from a distance, "the Boys," who look "Small, black, as flies" in their leather jackets and goggles. Suddenly, "the distance throws them forth" and they look and sound huge and heroic. Like knights in armor with visors, they wear impersonal goggles and "gleaming jackets trophied with dust." The observer questions their attitude of confidence, however, suggesting that goggles and jackets not only protect them from the elements but also "strap in doubt" to make themselves appear "robust."

The third stanza continues this line of thought. Their "hardiness/ Has no shape yet." They are undefined, their course unknown. Like Don Quixote following his horse's steps, the motorcyclists go "where the tires press." They are different from the birds that they "scare across a field," whose instinct gives them direction. They have only the manufactured "machine and soul," which they "imperfectly control/ To dare a future from the taken routes." Yet the will "is a part solution, after all." They are not damned because they are only "half animal" and lack "direct instinct." By joining "movement in a valueless world" one can approach one's goal, even if it is only "toward, toward."

The final stanza invokes the brevity of the interval one has to define oneself. "A minute holds them, who have come to go: The self-defined, astride the created will." Like birds and saints, the motorcyclists cannot stop in "the towns they travel through"; they must "complete their purposes," whatever they may be. Even if they do not reach the "absolute, in which to rest,/ One is always nearer by not keeping still." The worst that can happen is that "one is in motion." The physical engagement in the activity for its own sake is its own excuse.

Forms and Devices

"On the Move" can be compared to Jack Kerouac's novel *On the Road* (1957), published the same year. Both titles suggest a restless detachment from society typical of the Beat generation of the 1950's. Early versions of the poem included the dateline *"California"* and an epigraph, *"Man, you gotta Go"* (both later dropped). The epigraph's colloquial address, hip informality, imperative urgency, and capitalized verb emphasize the poem's relation to the contemporary scene.

In contrast to the urgency of the title and epigraph, the tone of the poem is meditative. The narrator is an observer, his voice detached and philosophical; it is the still voice within that asks questions in the midst of action, though the questions about the "hidden purpose" of movement are implicit.

In this poem about "the sense of movement," Thom Gunn suitably exploits the flexibility of verbs. Action words become nouns and adjectives. A "gust of birds," for example, "spurts" across a field, and there is "scuffling" and "wheeling." When the motorcyclists arrive, these images yield another set of meanings, having to do with wind resistance, acceleration, roughhousing, and tires on the tarmac. In the same way, "baffled sense" can mean that the senses are bewildered or that the forward progress of meaning is thwarted. (A baffle is also a motorcycle muffler.)

Through a series of analogies, Gunn sustains the epic simile of the motorcyclists as existential heroes on the road of life, daring "a future from the taken routes." Like gods, they control the "thunder held by calf and thigh." Like knights in lowered visor and armor, they wear goggles and "gleaming jackets trophied with the dust" as they ride "Astride the created will." Unlike the inhabitants of the towns they travel through, they are never at home. They are rebels without a cause, heroes without a purpose, except the purpose of "not keeping still."

The poet and the motorcyclist undertake a similar action. Both must balance the reckless power of their vehicle. Gunn's technical control over the machinery of traditional verse is necessary to get him to his destination, but it is also satisfying in itself. Unable to rely on "direct instinct," the poet rides "the created will" to "complete [his] purpose." On a purely technical level, this purpose is to find the "poise" of the "noise" in "the dull thunder of approximate words."

The authority of the narrator's speculations on "the sense of movement" depends upon the similarity of his action to that of the motorcyclists. Speaking from an interested objectivity, he is not speaking for an egotistical "I" but for an indefinite "One." This raises the poem from the specific and personal to the general and universal experience of thought and emotion.

Themes and Meanings

"On the Move" is a poem about how one defines oneself through actions. Driven by instinct or will, one is able to articulate one's purpose only en route, through the act itself. This is as true of the motorcyclists as it is for the poet.

"On the Move" is the opening poem of *The Sense of Movement* (1957), which Gunn said was inspired by the existentialist philosopher Jean-Paul Sartre. A major tenet of Sartre's existentialism is that one derives authentic meaning in one's lives not from any preconceived notions of what one should be, but from one's own actions. One cannot know what one is except through what one does. Because one is, as Sartre says, "condemned to be free," one must take full responsibility for one's actions and, thus, for one's existence.

Self-definition through engaged action is the ultimate existentialist act. If one could rely on instinct, as birds do, there would be no question of authenticity. Since the individual has free will, however, he or she must exercise it and take the consequences. The myth of the American motorcyclist is one of Gunn's favorite figures for the restless, searching, often inarticulate existential hero. His doubt is part of his charm. His restless motion, instinctual or willed, is, consciously or unconsciously, a creation of meaning through "movement in a valueless world."

The articulation of that meaning is no more the task of the motorcyclist than it is the task of birds. Just as the birds are the pretext for asking questions about the human activity of the motorcyclists, the motorcyclists are the pretext for the poet's articulation of the meaning of movement. More important than where they have come from, or even where they are going, is why. What drives them? What are they seeking? These questions are only rhetorical for all but the poet, whose authentic action is to capture "the dull thunder of approximate words." Like the motorcyclist, the poet "strap[s] in doubt — by hiding it" behind a confident pose so as to appear "robust," even though he "almost hear[s] a meaning in [his] noise." This is not hypocrisy, however, because the pose is a necessary protection, like goggles and jacket; it is not an end in itself, but the gear that gets him to his destination.

One of the paradoxes of the poem is that the motorcyclists, who pretend to be individualists, run in packs. They are always referred to as "they." They think of themselves as unconventional, yet they are locked into a uniform and a posture. They think they act on instinct, yet they travel "the taken routes." They are "the Boys," who "almost hear a meaning in their noise" — but not quite. Their group "impersonality" is in strict contrast to the "One" of the poem, who is able to interpret their motion precisely because he stands apart from their group mentality and outside their action. The poet may identify with them, but he must also articulate his difference from them. "Exact conclusion of their hardiness/ Has no shape" until the poet makes it. "They burst away," but "One is always nearer by not keeping still." The ambiguity of the poem's last line suggests that the motorcyclists may or may not create what they are looking for, while the poet, in the action of the poem, has.

Richard Collins

ON THE WOUNDS OF OUR CRUCIFIED LORD

Author: Richard Crashaw (c. 1612-1649)
Type of poem: Meditation
First published: 1646, in *Steps to the Temple*

The Poem

"On the Wounds of Our Crucified Lord" is a twenty-line poem divided into five stanzas of four lines each. The meter is predominantly iambic tetrameter, and the rhyme scheme is *abab*. Richard Crashaw's title suggests that the narrator is viewing a painting or a sculpture depicting Christ either on the cross or at the moment when his body has been lowered from the cross, a standard subject of Renaissance artists. Such images were often placed in alcoves or recesses in churches as objects for meditation; it is such a meditative process that the poem traces.

The narrator of the poem begins with an apostrophe, or direct address of an inanimate object. As his eyes scan the painting or sculpture, they focus on the bleeding wounds of Jesus caused by the nails pounded through his hands and feet at Crucifixion and by the torture of the crown of thorns and the spear wounds inflicted while he was on the cross. The sight of the wounds moves the speaker, especially in their paradoxical appearance of life ("wakefull wounds") on a corpse.

At first, he simply exclaims over their horror; then, he tries to find a suitable descriptive analogy for their existence. The comparisons he uses involve, appropriately, body parts: mouths and eyes. The rest of the poem draws out an elaborate comparison of wounds/mouths/eyes that, because it is strange, farfetched, and extended throughout the poem until its resolution in the final stanza, might be called a Metaphysical conceit. The last line of the first stanza indicates how involved each watcher becomes in the spectacle of the crucifixion. Even though the wounds are in actuality neither mouths nor eyes, the community of observers, which includes all humankind, must apply the transformative metaphorical process to a sight too horrible to bear realistically.

The second stanza continues the metaphysical conceit by interpreting both images. Now, the body of humanity is implicated in observing and feeling and reading the spectacle along with the narrator. He addresses them, accepting and then expanding on both metaphorical readings of the wounds. Behold, he cajoles them, a wound that appears to be a mouth. The ragged edges of the wound transform it once again, from a mouth to a rose. Roses are standard symbols and metaphors, especially in love poems, yet here the comparison is scandalous, almost perverse. That God should sacrifice his son so that humans may find poetry is too extravagant a cost. Similarly, those who perceive the wounds as eyes find the tears (the blood of Christ, which will ultimately save humankind) to be wasteful weeping: the ultimate loss.

In the third stanza, the narrator projects himself out of his time and place to imagine others, the worshipful, who have similarly meditated before the image. Moving from the horror of the real wounds to the scandal of the metaphors that transform them, he now finds a redemption of the pain in the salvation that the wounds ultimately bring. Ironically, the steadfast worshipers have offered their kisses and their tears to the image, in empathy for the suffering that they perceive there. In the same way that Christ's wounds (as eyes and mouths) offered up the saving blood for humanity, so do the tears and kisses (from the eyes and mouths) of the worshipers redeem the poem and its metaphors from horror and scandal. There is a reciprocal relationship between Christ and his flock that hinges on metaphor and is revealed here, fittingly, in the center of the poem.

The imagination of the narrator begins to run wild in stanza 4. As he stares at the image of the foot, which has received the kisses and tears of the devout, he visualizes the wounds again as mouths and eyes, almost as if they had been placed there by the worshipful. This image may indicate the guilt of all humankind, which entailed the sacrifice of Christ. The mouths and eyes of the foot will repay the devotion of the worshipers with its own gems.

The last stanza reveals the victory of the poem, involving both the theme and the poetic figures. This victory is heightened by the altered meter of the lines: Here, the second and fourth lines are in trimeter rather than tetrameter, a foot short of what the reader has been led to expect. A tear may resemble a pearl and a drop of blood may resemble a ruby—human faith is the less-valuable form of homage (human tears, or pearls), which Christ exchanges for the more-valuable gem (his blood, or rubies) that grants forgiveness, salvation, and eternal life to those who believe.

Forms and Devices

The poem's technique is difficult to separate from the actual meanings and impact of the poem because they are so skillfully intertwined. The poem contains a baroque excess of emotion and an intense concentration on the two major tropes: mouths and eyes. Because the poet employs only these two figures, he must extend their comparisons and interrelate them. The simultaneous concentration and expansion, along with the ultimate resolution of paradoxes within the poem, renders the center of the poem a metaphysical conceit.

The comparison of wounds to mouths and eyes is not a typical one. It contains within it many suggestions that relate to the theme; for example, during Communion mouths accept the wine and wafer, which are the symbolic blood and body of Christ. The act of Communion re-creates and both laments and celebrates the sacrifice of Christ for the sins of humankind, which actually, in the poem, brings the worshipers to the time and the scene of the Crucifixion. It is kept constantly alive by human belief and devoutness and by its continued power to save.

The poem works toward a reconciliation of the oppositions inherent in the metaphysical conceit. The eyes that offer the tears (pearls) for Christ's suffering will be rewarded with the blood (rubies) of salvation. The major principle is one of exchange, yet the use of the image of a contract is not sacrilegious. Typically, God lends life to people with an implicit contract, which they then must fulfill by giving good account of that life on Judgment Day. This poem suggests the miracle of the

God-human relationship: If humans give a good account, then they will receive the ultimate exchange—eternal life for temporal life, perfection, and a release from a fallen world given over to sin.

The contemporary reader must avoid modern preconceptions regarding taste in poetic language. The comic effect of a meter of iambic tetrameter rather than pentameter, which is usually reserved for serious subject matter, combines with an excess of explicitness for what seems a sordid focus that makes the reader want to laugh or to avoid such a poem. Crashaw, however, uses such excess and relentless focus to render the miracle of salvation more strongly.

Themes and Meanings

The poem reveals two miracles simultaneously: that of eternal life and that of the transformation of the profane into the sacred. For ordinary people to understand what God offers through the sacrifice of His son, they must work with what they know, which are things of this world. The poem shows how even the most minute of earthly details reveal God's plan. It focuses more narrowly as it progresses, from the statue or painting to the wounds to the fluids emanating from the wounds. Such a complete immersion into earthly details emphasizes Crashaw's view of the glory of creation and redemption. Similarly, the humor and bathos of the poem are balanced by the miracle of salvation.

If the poem offers a direct lesson, it is that of Crashaw's belief that the devout believers in Christianity will without doubt receive their just rewards. The poem makes the reader think of the little miracles that happen daily in life and suggests that they are purposeful reflections in miniature of the great, ultimate miracle of life after death. The poet mimics God's plan by working within a similar scope. The word "poet" means "maker," and each poem is a replica of the world, a cosmos of the poet's own fashioning.

Sandra K. Fischer

ONCE

Author: Alice Walker (1944-   )
Type of poem: Narrative
First published: 1968, in *Once: Poems*

The Poem

"Once" is a poem consisting of fourteen numbered sections in free verse. The sections range from fifteen to forty-one lines, each presenting one image or short narrative from Alice Walker's work in the 1960's with the American Civil Rights movement. Together, the sections add up, like the pieces in a stained-glass window, to a complete picture.

"Once" opens with Walker in a Southern jail. Her companion points out the irony of the pretty lawn and flowers outside the jail, while Walker dryly comments on the irony that "Someone in America/ is being/ protected/ [from me]." This ironic tone informs most of the poem. At this point, the reader knows only that someone, assumed to be Walker (although no name or gender is specified), is in jail in the South. There is no reason given and no mention of when this happened.

In the next two sections, hints of the Civil Rights movement and the 1960's begin to emerge. The speaker appears carrying a sign as she runs through Atlanta's streets, and there are daily arrests. The fact that there is a "nigger" in the company of "white folks" is observed. By the end of the fourth section, the setting for the poem is clear. As soon as the reader becomes aware that this poem is about the Civil Rights movement, it is time to contemplate the title, "Once." Does Walker intend to conjure up the atmosphere of a fairy tale, to say that this happened "once upon a time" in a land long ago and far away, or does she want to emphasize that this movement is only one fight for justice among many? The answer is that she intends both meanings.

The reader is introduced to Walker's associates as the poem unfolds: the white friend who has been shunned by her family for her activism (section 4); Peter, a Jewish worker in the movement who is killed at seventeen (section 6); the arrogant black man with a smart mouth (section 2); the woman who smiles at little ironies (section 1). Introduced in the poem as well are an assortment of bigoted white Southerners: the absurdly "liberal" white woman and the stripper, who insist they are not prejudiced (sections 10 and 12); the driver who hits a young black girl with his truck and makes it seem to be her fault (section 13); the "understanding cops." The Southern blacks presented in "Once" tend to be powerless in one manner or another. They are poor and hungry (section 8); arrested (section 11); struck down (section 13). The term "nigger" is used throughout the poem, spoken both by "liberals" and by bigots.

The anecdotes are presented simply, with no interpretation. Many lines are direct quotations. Walker expects the reader to notice the ironies, to feel anger or sadness, based on the facts alone. Because most of the characters, including many speakers, are identified only by gender, race, or type, each image becomes more universal: These terrible moments are typical; they could have happened to many people, in many lands, at many times. Yet the poem ends on a hopeful note. The final scene finds a young black girl waving an American flag—timid, but just daring enough to celebrate the freedom that someday may be hers.

Forms and Devices

"Once" is written in very short lines that combine to form generally straightforward sentences. Often, a numbered section will contain only one sentence, as section 14, which closes the poem does: "then there was/ the/ picture of/ the/ bleak-eyed/ little black/ girl/ waving the/ american/ flag/ holding it/ gingerly/ with/ the very/ *tips*/ of her/ fingers." Some commentators have wondered whether, in fact, this is poetry at all. Clearly, this poem is neither as substantial nor as sophisticated as those in Walker's later collection, *Revolutionary Petunias and Other Poems* (1973). There is much to recommend "Once," though, and its simplicity is essential to its beauty and power.

One effect of the very short lines is that they force the reader to slow down, to notice each element in the stanza. A child holding a flag is a common enough sight—so common that people tend not even to see it. Walker presents simple images in a simple style, but alters the typography so that the reader is forced to notice, to ponder. Thus, "american" is spelled with a lowercase letter and set off in a line by itself. The reader cannot help but pause over that line, stopped for a moment by the lowercase *a*. By forcing the reader to pause, Walker emphasizes the word so that the irony (this integration battle is going on in America) is not lost in hasty or careless reading. Walker creates similar effects, drawing attention to particular words and phrases, by using italics ("*tips*/ of her/ fingers"), dashes, and eye-catching alignment on the page. The short lines also help bring out sound effects that might otherwise be missed. In the stanza quoted above, the assonance of "bleak-eyed/ little black" is heightened by the way in which the words are arranged on the page; the sound effect calls attention to those two essential characteristics of the girl.

Walker does not use many common poetic devices, such as rhyme, meter, metaphor, or simile, which create a heightened but artificial language for poetry. "Once" and the other poems in this collection are written in a very straightforward style—the language that people actually use when they speak. The occasional obscenity is intended not to shock but simply to be realistic. If the words sound harsh, it is because the reality of racial hatred is harsh.

Walker does not use much figurative language in her poetry either. She does not say, "This is like that"; she says, "This *is*." By presenting images simply and honestly, Walker forces the reader to look.

Themes and Meanings

"Once" deals with Walker's own involvement in the Civil Rights Movement in the South during the 1960's. The collection of poems in which it appears, *Once: Poems*, was published in 1968, the year of Martin Luther King, Jr.'s assassination. In the collection, "Once" is followed by six more poems dealing with civil rights. This poem, informed by a strong black consciousness and a somewhat youthful didacticism, shows universally bigoted and inhuman white Southerners confronted by witty and courageous black and white activists from the North. Each numbered section is another image or event Walker remembers from her own experience: She appears in ten of the fourteen sections, if only to say "I remember."

The effect of Walker continually putting herself in the scene is to make it clear that the horrors she presents are true: She can verify that they are true because she was there. For young readers, this is especially important because they do not remember what went on in this country during the days of segregation and struggle. Walker is concerned not only with her own experiences. Although she writes about what she has seen or heard herself, she avoids making this a poem about particular people or events. Only one person, activist Dick Gregory, is precisely identified, and one of the poet's friends, Peter, is identified by first name only.

The rest of the people in the poem are identified by type or by their relationship to the poet: "my friend," "a Negro cook," "a little black girl," "the blond amply boobed babe." In fact, the speaker of the poem need not be the poet at all. The "I" could be any of hundreds of black "nice girl[s] like her" who participated in the Civil Rights movement. Walker's purpose in all this is to help readers experience another time and place. By not specifying the details too much, she leaves ample room for readers to use their own imagination to supply the details—the names, faces, feelings—that will make it real for them.

Once the reader is dwelling firmly in that time and place—the American South in the 1960's—Walker hopes that he or she will begin to realize why the Civil Rights movement had to happen, what the anger and frustration was all about, and what the dream was like. She does not tell readers what to think about each scene—she simply places them in it. There is little sense here that the activists believe they are winning the fight or that victories are what matter. There are tales of arrests and confrontations, but no scenes of voters registering or walls tumbling down. Instead, the poems focus on the humanity of the activists and the bigots.

For all its vignettes of hatred and conflict, "Once" ends on a hopeful note. The picture of the young black girl timidly waving the flag stands for all the dreams of all the activists. Although the girl is "bleak-eyed," although she holds the flag "gingerly," she is a symbol that appears again and again in Walker's work—she is the hope for the future.

Cynthia A. Bily

ONE BONE TO ANOTHER

Author: Vasko Popa (1922-1991)
Type of poem: Poetic sequence
First published: 1956, as "Kost kosti," in *Nepočin-polje*; collected in *Selected Poems*, 1969

The Poem

"One Bone to Another" is a cycle of seven short poems. The title of the cycle establishes the mood and alludes to the personae of the poems, a pair of bones that engage in an intimate dialogue about the human condition in their subterranean *mise-en-scène*. The titles of the individual poems indicate the setting and order of the events in the cycle. These events are depicted as occurring in the immediate present; and the bones express their reactions to them in the first-person plural or first-person singular. As the events unfold, each poem marks a shift in the mood of the bones, from smug independence and delight after being freed from their prison of flesh, to terror and helplessness at the realization that they must submit to the forces of human fate, and finally to bewilderment and despair when confronted with the inevitable transience of human existence.

The first poem, "Na početku" ("At the Beginning"), expresses the bones' relief and newfound sense of independence after freeing themselves from the "flesh": "Now we will do what we will." In the second poem, "Posle početka" ("After the Beginning"), the bones gleefully begin to ponder the possibilities of their new existence; they will "make music," and if any hungry dogs should come along, they plan to trick them: "Then we'll stick in their throats/ And have fun." This delight in the prospect of mischief turns to a delight in each other in the charmingly romantic mood of the third poem, "Na suncu" ("In the Sun"), as they sunbathe naked and declare their love for each other. In the fourth poem, "Pod zemljom" ("Underground"), having concluded that "Muscle of darkness muscle of flesh" are "the same thing," the personae contemplate what they will do about it. They decide to call together "all the bones of all times"; they will all "bake in the sun" and "grow pure," and so they will become "eternal beings of bone" who wander about as they please.

This sense of independence is abruptly arrested in the fifth poem, "Na mesečini" ("In the Moonlight") when, bewildered, the bones begin to realize that they are slowly being covered in flesh and filled with marrow, "As if everything were beginning again/ With a more horrible beginning." Their bewilderment turns to despair in the sixth poem, "Pred kraj" ("Before the End"), as they attempt to find a means of escaping the inevitable: "Where shall we go nowhere." This despair is tinged with resignation and defeat in the seventh and final poem in the cycle, "Na kraju" ("At the End"), in which both bones express the fear that they have been swallowed by each other, and that now they can no longer see or hear or be sure of anything. The sense of freedom that preceded has vanished: "All is an ugly dream of dust."

Forms and Devices

The cyclic form is a hallmark of Vasko Popa's poetry. It enables the poet to maintain a free philosophical inquiry and thus promotes his artistic objective: the distillation of truth. As Ted Hughes writes in his introduction to *Selected Poems* (1969), "Each cycle creates the terms of a universe, which [Popa] then explores, more or less methodically, with the terms." A central theme is presented, and the poems within the cycle explore various facets of that theme (although the number of poems varies, Popa evidences a partiality for the number seven). This circular mode of inquiry enables the poet to meditate on the theme from a number of imaginative angles so that all of its cosmic conditions and possibilities are revealed. The result is disclosure of the cosmic drama, and this phenomenon is reinforced by the way the cyclic form mimics the nature of the cosmic structure: While each poem can stand alone, its meaning is always amplified in the context of its relationships to the other poems in the cycle.

The terse, economic style evinced in this cycle is a second regular feature of Popa's poetry. In Popa's case, however, reductionism is more than simply a poetic style; rather, it functions as a technical device which, like the cyclic form, promotes his philosophical and artistic aims. Typically, Popa's poems are forty to fifty words in length; they run ten to fifteen lines, with three to five words per line. They are arranged in somewhat uneven stanzas of single lines, couplets, tercets, and, more rarely, quatrains. Thus the compression is visual as well as verbal. This compression also contributes to the strong rhythm of his poetry; the meter is irregular but distinct. The majority of Popa's poems are written in the present tense, which amplifies the terseness and intensity. His syntax is highly compressed and frequently ambiguous, the lexicon is lean and concrete, the diction inordinately concise, and the neologisms are frequent. He uses a minimum of connecting particles and transition words, and punctuation is altogether absent. By adhering to this economical style, Popa is able to sustain the distillation process even as he develops a theme.

The functions of these features, however, are not mutually exclusive. While the cyclic form promotes a revealing, comprehensive inquiry by containing the thematic aspects in workable segments, it also implicitly participates in their reduction and consequent distillation. Conversely, just as reductionism exposes and reinforces the multifarious cosmic relationships inherent in the poem, it contributes to the development and enrichment of the theme. The versatility of these features, then, enhances the collective effect. Thus, the structure itself participates in the philosophical development and becomes an essential part of the meaning of the poem.

While Popa's linguistic code may seem austere, it finds a lively counterbalance in his humor, as illustrated in "One Bone to Another." Popa's wry, ironic humor is most closely related to the irrational humor of folklore. This kind of humor is distinguished by its functionality: It is understood that the folktale, or the riddle, is a kind of verbal play which attempts to account for reality by temporarily suspending the limitations of "the real world." It is a product of instinct rather than of intellect. It is humanistic and tends to suggest rather than define, it comments without judging, and it opens rather than closes the circle. This humorous tendency is most dominant in Popa's first three poetic collections— *Kora* (1953; *Bark*, 1978) *Nepočin-polje* (1956; *Unrest-Field*, 1978), and *Sporedno nebo* (1968; *Secondary Heaven*, 1978)— in which it is manifested in the delightfully unselfconscious activities of the archetypal beings, such as the "bone couple" in the present cycle, who inhabit the primordial environment of Popa's poetic world.

Popa's folkloric orientation is apparent in his imagery as well. For example, while at first glance, an image such as "The backbone of a streak of lightning" seems to reflect the kind of incongruous juxtaposition of unlike objects which is the touchstone of surrealist texts, it is in fact typical of the kinds of anomalies which regularly occur in Yugoslav folklore. Moreover, such images, though rich in dramatic associations, are often tempered— just as in folklore— by a playful, childlike tone. The humorous escapades of the personae in "One Bone to Another," for example, make readers forget that they are eavesdropping on a conversation between two bones about the wonders and frailties of the human condition.

Themes and Meanings

The central theme of "One Bone to Another" is as old as poetry itself: the apparent futility of human existence. Popa's approach to this problem is unique, however, in that he examines it in cosmic terms. He does not speak for the world; rather, it speaks through him, and his ability to see things from its point of view is remarkable. He becomes the vehicle of communication for those other mysterious worlds that exist undetected and interact in the ongoing drama of cosmic life.

A second, more subtle theme that Popa touches on here is the place and function of the psychic realm in daily life. In "Underground," the fourth poem in the cycle, Popa writes, "Muscle of darkness muscle of flesh/ It comes to the same thing." This seems to indicate that conscious life— that is, the life of the "flesh" — tends to blind people, to keep them in "darkness" about the true nature of existence. Further, it implies that the meaning which people seek to fulfill their lives can be found only by awareness and investigation of the subconscious world of the psyche, for it is the true foundation of being. Conscious life, with all of its demands, tends to obscure inner, psychic life, so that, inevitably, a person is "swallowed" by it. This preoccupation with the psychic plane and the need to maintain contact with it is a recurring theme in much of Popa's work. As Charles Simić remarks in the introduction to his translation of Popa's *The Little Box* (1970), Popa seeks to penetrate "the truth that lies behind the forms and conventions."

This cycle reflects another level of meaning. It must be remembered that this text was written during the post-World War II period and, like so much of Popa's early work, reflects the anguish and turmoil of the time. The tone of frustration and despair that characterizes the poems parallels the emotional climate of postwar Europe. The goals to which the personae aspire— freedom, understanding, and ultimately, survival— mirror those of many Europeans of that era. In addition, the personae exhibit characteristics which would appear to optimize the possibility of achieving those goals. They are tough, alert and cynical—admirable qualities in any period, but essential in order to overcome the tragic, tumultuous aftermath of the war.

If there is an ultimate message in Popa's poetry, it is that if one wants to understand and preserve humankind, one must attend to the cosmos of which it is an integral part. One must listen to the cosmos as Popa does and try to see things from its perspective, for only by maintaining contact with it can one understand one's place in it. One's inner psychic life is the instrument through which one can make that contact; it is the "telephone" which enables participation in the collective cosmic conversation.

Maria Budisavljević-Oparnica

THE ONE DAY

Author: Donald Hall (1928-   )
Type of poem: Poetic sequence
First published: 1988

The Poem

The One Day is a book-length poem of sixty-three pages divided into three major sections: "Shrubs Burnt Away," "Four Classic Texts: Prophecy, Pastoral, History, Eclogue," and "To Build a House."

Donald Hall bases *The One Day* on the "house of consciousness" — the idea that one mind might express many contradictory voices and different points of view. Its tripartite organization roughly corresponds to French moral essayist Michel Eyquem de Montaigne's *Essais* (1580, 1588, 1595; *The Essays*, 1603) traditionally held to exhibit three stages of human development: Stoicism giving way to philosophical skepticism and concluding in a moderate Epicureanism. Such an outline, however, fails to account for Hall's powerful statements about love, preparation for death, building a house as metaphor for living, and the emergence of self-knowledge and social order. Like James Joyce's novel *Ulysses* (1922), *The One Day* explores the thoughts of the poet over the course of a single day. As a poetic sequence, Hall's work invites comparisons to Robert Lowell's *Notebook 1967-1968* (1969) or John Berryman's *77 Dream Songs* (1964).

The poem begins with aphorisms or concise statements of principles taken from Montaigne ("Each man bears the entire form of man's estate"), from Picasso ("Every human being is a colony"), and most significantly from Abbé Michel de Bourdeille: "There are other voices, within my own skull I daresay. A woman speaks clearly from time to time; I do not know her name." The first and third sections of *The One Day* are spoken by a male farmer who "speaks" in roman typeface and a female sculptor who speaks in italics. A general consciousness narrates from an objective point of view. The three voices quote others, and Hall freely intermingles their narratives, speculations, and poetic effusions; sometimes two stories develop simultaneously, conflicting, supporting, and commenting indirectly on each other. Multiplicity and imaginative richness inform the poem from beginning to end, giving the book a dreamlike and intuitive ferocity.

In section 1, "Shrubs Burnt Away," the reader learns that the male struggles with his middle-aged complacency and looks forward to the only major event left for him: death. He thinks about his father, the values his father attempted to teach his son, his marital distress, lovemaking without emotion, and his memories of World War II. The male introduces other "colonists" of his mind, such as a homosexual actor, a retired man watering his lawn, a drunk who died after he fell from a parking structure, and a boy who read the complete works of Edgar Allan Poe. The poet states that the colonists enjoy building this house in his mind because it alleviates some of the stress of impotent, idle feelings that plague him.

The female voice tells of discovering creative talent as a girl sculpting dough in her mother's kitchen; her father's sudden death, however, subverts her artistic yearnings. Her mother then becomes an alcoholic and her sister suffers from nervous breakdowns and requires constant hospitalization. A cycle of failure and mental instability seems destined to repeat itself in the lifetime of this woman. Later, in section 3, she suffers from nervous breakdowns and drug addiction herself. The male and female speakers approach death with different backgrounds, but they are united in the search for peaceful self-acceptance, meaningful relationships, and satisfying work.

Section 2, "Four Classic Texts," develops the poetic modes of prophecy, pastoral, history, and eclogue. New characters emerge: Elzira, Abraham, Marc, Phyllis, Senex (who is related to Roman Stoic philosopher Lucius Seneca), and Juvenis (who is related to classical Roman satirist Juvenal). This section attempts to reject modern material culture and work toward restoration of the whole human being: soul, family, and society. Hall says that many borrowings in this section come from classical Roman poet Vergil, Amos and Isaiah in the Old Testament, Roman historian Titus Livy, an anonymous German soldier in World War I, and stories from *The Boston Globe*.

Hall shows how these four timeless themes apply to today's fragmented world, often juxtaposing ancient history with modern idiom taken from kitchen and bedroom. Through a chaos of competing ideas, Hall forges an evocative statement about returning to a peaceful state of mind through the therapeutic art of building. Hall attempts to reverse the damages done by a modern, disassociated consciousness by looking through the eyes of ancient poets.

Section 3, "To Build a House," returns to the male and female speakers. This concluding section focuses on praise, artistic renewal, celebration, and the purifying work of farming. It resolves the conflicts of earlier sections in a passionate, triumphant declaration of order. The male and his wife concentrate on restoring an old orchard, logging, gathering maple syrup, and enjoying the pleasures of this paradise of work. Their lovemaking once again becomes an act of celebration of the spirit. Together they build their house, carefully manage their land, and look toward the end of the day. Both male and female voices desire to approach death in a house wrought of their own hands, sheltered from fragmentation and violence.

The female speaker finds a renewed ability to work at her craft of sculpture, seizing each hour to chisel away at alabaster. The female looks back on her troubled past of failed relationships, psychiatric treatment including electroshock therapy, and drug addiction. She realizes that a singleness of mind is the most prized goal in her life. Through a fresh commitment to her art, she finds old grudges against her father and mother disappearing. She can now sleep without disturbing dreams, enjoy the company of old friends, and spend meaningful time with her children. Both male and female realize that their final determination to build a house means they want to leave this world as happy, fulfilled, whole people who enjoy the support of family and friends.

Forms and Devices

In its conception, *The One Day* resembles a sonnet sequence, wherein a poet writes a series of concise poems linked to one another and dealing with a single, unified theme. In addition to the contemporary poetic sequences by Lowell and Berryman, Hall may be looking back to Dante Gabriel Rossetti's "The House of Life," a sonnet sequence published in 1881 that explores the poet's love for his dead wife and records events in their life together.

Donald Hall's skill with poetic structure is evident in *The One Day*'s use of free-verse lines varying in length from ten to fourteen syllables, arranged in ten-line stanzas. Sections 1 and 3 have approximately the same number of stanzas, just as the four subheadings of section 2 are equally balanced. Hall says that the surface of the poem should appear smooth, but that — like an enormous electronic device — if one looks behind the smooth exterior, one sees a byzantine array of wires, tubes, and transistors. The organization is so precise that the reader may view each stanza as an independent lyric; however, the book is best appreciated through close attention to its uniform metaphors.

Five metaphors run through the poem, by which Hall illustrates the many pitfalls and conflicts each person must face over a lifetime. First, the dominant metaphor of the house of consciousness and building one's own home allows Hall to introduce the two main voices. The original title of the book, *Building the House of Dying*, shows that Hall looked at the work of building as necessary preparation for death; people cannot die without first leaving something of value behind, be it farmhouse or sculpture.

Second, one day in a person's life becomes a microcosm or mirror of an entire life. During one day, the male and female speakers look back to their past, living their lives over again. Thus Hall develops the concept — which also interested William Wordsworth in his poem "Lines Composed a Few Miles Above Tintern Abbey" — that a person constructs reality by the process of thinking and remembering. The poem follows Hall's thought processes as he seeks to understand his life, although much of the narrative material is pure fiction.

Third, Hall uses the metaphor of the bed as a universe. All thoughts about self, family, society, love, and death take place on this piece of furniture common to all homes. The bed both unites and divides, reflecting life's larger struggles in why people make love: for the satisfaction of lust, for companionship, for procreation, and for communication. The bed becomes another mirror of the soul in *The One Day*. In fact, one might imagine the whole "action" of the poem taking place as the poet reflects in a reclined position on his bed.

Fourth, the poem makes frequent references to airplanes. The male remembers the stories of Wrong-Way Corrigan, Amelia Earhart, Will Rogers, and a Pomona fireman, who all disappeared flying various kinds of aircraft. The female recalls with vivid clarity the stub-winged pylon racers of her youth, daredevil pilots, and tragic commercial airline crashes. The theme of flying as an escape from necessary work on Earth becomes linked to pilots who attempt to build their houses in the sky.

Finally, Hall uses the metaphor of work as a restorative activity. Humanity will save itself only if men and women can find meaningful commitment to work that nourishes the soul.

Although *The One Day* contains strong unifying themes, the subdivisions of section 2 can also be approached as independent poetic genres. "Prophecy" is the poet's inspired declaration of divine will and prediction of future catastrophes. Isaiah prophesies that obstinate nations such as Babylon and Egypt will suffer from flames and plagues of God's wrath because they refuse to worship in the proper way. Similarly, the poet of *The One Day* states that he will strike down false buildings and reject materialistic values because they corrupt the human will.

"Pastoral" is a dialogue between Marc and Phyllis. Traditionally a poet uses this mode for a treatment of shepherds and rustic life, sometimes in the form of a discussion about the virtues of country living. Hall looks back to Vergil, who made his pastorals a vehicle for social comment, and uses this dialogue to describe the emptiness felt by many contemporary married couples. Hall's characters are firmly located in modern suburbia; they lament the stultifying order, sense of restraint, and dishonesty of middle-class American ways. The husband feels incapable of the most basic emotion or defensive action. The wife feels claustrophobic in her perfect home entertaining perfect friends for a game of bridge.

"History" takes up the character of president-emperor Senex and explains the nature of his rule through ancient, medieval, and modern times. Hall brings into question the idea of recorded history. If history books tell of enslavement, executions, trench warfare, and tyranny, humankind needs to reject history in order to restore the human mind.

The last subsection, "Eclogue," returns to the pastoral formula of the love-lay, in which a shepherd sings a song of courtship. In Hall's case, this song concerns renewed love relations and the building of a new history. In order to build the future properly, the poet must concentrate on the restitution of mothers, fathers, and faithful sexual relations. Greed and dishonesty must be replaced by self-respect and the enjoyment of real labors.

Themes and Meanings

Donald Hall wrote the various sections in *The One Day* over seventeen years, but it seems to be one continuous, energetic utterance. This unity of mind and purpose drives the book toward its inevitable conclusion: Hall's statement about ecstatic renewal and the resolution of past conflicts. It is a poem about the cycle of life and about how, in declining years, one attempts evaluations about beginnings and endings. Hall's most important summary statement comes near the end of the book: "We are one cell perpetually/ dying and being born, led by a single day that presides/ over our passage through the thirty thousand days/ from highchair past work and love to suffering death."

Hall emphasizes the need to build a house in one's mind—to come to an understanding of the various conflicting voices and disappointments that life offers. The poem concerns a search for order both within and without. People need to deal with sorrow and suffering on the way to building the shelter of personal acceptance. Building this house of understanding also involves social order, because once one has established shelter, one can relate fully to others and feel that life has meaning, mostly achieved through work. The poem is both spiritual and temporal because Hall discusses the failures of marriage, family, and career. The tone of expansiveness and resolution puts an optimistic ending on this sophisticated, elegant book. The poet has been able to follow the advice of his father, who told him to do only what he wanted to do.

Hall challenges the reader to search personal and social history as he has done to listen to the otherwise silenced voices inside. In order to survive, according to Hall, one most construct a house, a place of solace that gives one the room to interpret and evaluate experience. The metaphor of building necessarily involves human understanding.

People cannot merely shuffle passively through life without attempting to grapple with a fundamental question: For whom did they live their lives? At times, *The One Day* stretches the reader's ability to grasp the main point because of the stream-of-consciousness technique and complex allusions to history, literature, and religion. Sometimes Hall is prone to the dropping of names only casually related to his theme; however, his desire for a reevaluation and reordering of American society leaves the reader in a state of awe, knowing that he is absolutely right. Society and individuals must resist entropy, the natural tendency of things to go from a state of organization into decay. Man and woman must each build a house and find satisfying work to which a life is committed.

Looking back through history, one can see how often violence and tyranny caused people to die without ever having a feeling of home or emotional shelter. At ninety years old, when the female speaker goes to the White House to accept a presidential medal for her art, she realizes that this late-won public fame means almost nothing. The real work of building the internal house of self-acceptance and order has already been done.

If people spend adequate time preparing for death, life does not have to be characterized only by fragmentation and melancholia. The male surveys his farm and reflects on taking Communion, looking toward Christ's ascension as another pattern for the renewal in his life. Hall's plea is for the living not to allow life to defeat them but to fight back by building a house, making art, working an apple farm, and loving each other with final determination. In the end, the poem celebrates, restores, and prophesies leaving this world in a happy frame of mind.

Jonathan L. Thorndike

OPEN CASKET

Author: Sandra McPherson (1943-   )
Type of poem: Lyric
First published: 1978, in *The Year of Our Birth*

The Poem

"Open Casket" is a free-verse poem in which the poet describes and moves through various California landscapes. The identity of the speaker is muted, and the personal pronoun Sandra McPherson uses is the plural "we," which de-emphasizes the individual in the scene and focuses the reader's attention on the landscape itself.

Although the title suggests a funeral at which there is an "open casket" viewing of the deceased, the poem itself seems to go off in a different direction, depicting vacation entertainments, rural landscapes seen from a bus, a field trip for schoolchildren, and other diversions. The school trip, in particular, suggests that the sights in the poem are seen from the viewpoint of a child.

The tone of voice in the poem is calm and understated, conveying a cool sweetness that contrasts ironically with other statements about the poor, going "back where we belong," or overpopulation, "Certainly too many people."

The first stanza begins with the sort of recommendation one might find in a travel brochure, describing as it does a ride in a "glass-bottomed boat," a tourist attraction in Monterey Bay near the town of Pacific Grove, on the California coast. The onlooker marvels at how clearly she can view the sea anemones and other underwater life. Presumably, this boat trip takes place on a vacation excursion.

The following, indented stanzas turn by association to other trips, or perhaps to other parts of this same one: riding a bus "between Santa Barbara and San Jose" or going to the state capital in Sacramento on a school trip to see the "gold and white capitol." She speaks of reading "the Gospel of John/ in a little red pocket version" on the bus, perhaps a child's edition or perhaps the sort of missionary publication one might find distributed in a bus station or some other public place. She also thinks of crowds of children being brought to the capital, where they learn about the state; its state flower, the golden poppy; and its mountains.

Although the speaker does not seem to have been dealing with death or a funeral, at this point the crowds of children and the Gospel of John, which deals with the life, death, and resurrection of Christ ("the friend who comes back"), make her think generally about the fact that each person will live "beyond another" and will thus have to deal with the meaning of death.

The poem moves to images of dry riverbeds seen from the bus between San Jose and Sacramento. The speaker's vision of "colored pencils" seems oddly out of place "in the grass" and "Thin wildflowers," as if the pencils had been dropped or left by someone interrupted while sketching, evidently a personal recollection that connects with the wild poppies.

These images lead into ellipses, and then, as if her attention turns back to the present from uncompleted thoughts of other times, she returns once more to the description of what it is like to look into the tidal pools and waters of the bay. The last stanza, like the first, deals with the boat trip and the image of sea life underwater. The first and last stanzas bracket the rest of the poem, which seems to be a series of memory associations in which the poet connects the present experience with thoughts of childhood, religion, beauty, and death.

Forms and Devices

McPherson uses indentation and stanza breaks to provide structure for her free-verse poem. The first and last stanzas serve as a frame for the others, but otherwise the poem is very open in form. Although the reader can occasionally hear rhymes, such as "brine" and "design," they are rare and almost incidental.

Strong visual images are very important in the poem. The poet describes things vividly and accurately in a few words, and as she does so, her observations and descriptions evoke layers of association and meaning. Although her images become metaphorical by association, McPherson's descriptions are also strongly physical. The world she describes is very concrete and real, and the connections she makes between objects and events follow channels of physical experience. In "Open Casket," the boat trip evokes feelings of peacefulness and awe and the sense of looking into another world, but the boat itself is a real object in a real world. It is associated visually with the funeral casket by the boat's shape, the flowerlike sea anenomes, and other images. An interesting poem to compare and contrast with "Open Casket" is Emily Dickinson's poem numbered 712, which depicts death as an endless carriage ride. In Dickinson's poem, the dreamlike ride evokes feelings of depression, anxiety, and resignation associated with death, but the carriage ride itself, unlike McPherson's boat ride, is imaginary.

Other important images in the poem also work visually. The bean fields seen through the bus window and the purplish blue display of amethysts in the jeweler's window are like the underwater sights seen through the window of the glass-bottomed boat, momentary glimpses of another world. These images suggest how the mind works in trying to understand and absorb things. Together, these images of looking from one world into another take the reader into the experience in a dramatic and evocative way and provoke insight by their coincidences and parallels.

The tone that McPherson uses to achieve this effect is one of wise innocence, although she uses a somewhat impersonal point of view in the poem. There is never an "I" speaking, with her "we" referring perhaps to family members or to other schoolchildren. This plural pronoun brings the reader into the experience and also emphasizes the somewhat-passive feeling of the child as onlooker, part of a crowd, always being transported by one means or another, watching and remembering it all.

Themes and Meanings

The title of the poem gives the reader a hint that the poem deals with death and associated thoughts about an afterlife. It would be difficult to determine more about what gave her the ideas for the poem, but McPherson herself has explained that the poem was in part the result of her childhood experience of attending the "open casket" funeral of her grandfather. In an essay, McPherson says, "I was twelve; it was my first and only open casket funeral. Seeing down into death, I thought, was like being in the glass-bottomed boat I took also as a child in Monterey Bay."

Yet, she does not make the funeral the focus of the poem. Rather, the poem deals with other examples of seeing into some other dimension. With the aid of the glass-bottomed boat, which the reader is advised to take, one sees into an orderly and harmonious world, akin to heaven, were the reader actually able to see it.

From this harmonious vision, however, the reader is forced to return to the world of poverty and labor, heat and dust. Wanting something more, "we read the depot literature/ of miraculous healing." Only the jeweler's window, containing expensive and unattainable objects, precious bluish violet stones, reminds the reader of that vision of heaven in the sea.

The fact that San Jose and Santa Barbara are named for saints and that Sacramento means sacred or having to do with the sacraments reinforces the idea that the poem concerns itself with religion, particularly questions about death and resurrection and the mysteries of an afterlife.

Water is typically a symbol of life and the sacrament of baptism. Water appears here as the medium through which one looks into another world, the underwater world. Where people struggle to make a living in the bean fields, the surrounding hills are "hard dust." The riverbeds of the landscape are dry with "White salts and rusts and mires/ where the rivers used to be. . . ." This dry world lacks the perfection of the underwater world, which exists in "water-oiled harmony," that is, in a state of grace.

It is difficult to tell why McPherson evokes the image of colored pencils except as one more version of the image of looking down into something where colors and forms attract the eye. Perhaps the scene is part of the lesson on the state flower and the mountains, perhaps it is some other time when she tried to capture the beauty she saw in nature by sketching wildflowers.

In any case, whatever the shortcomings of the world, there is always Monterey Bay and the glass-bottomed boat to provide a vision of eternal life and beauty. McPherson has said that the word "vacation" in the last line made her think of the body vacated by the living person. The soul or spirit of the person whose body is being viewed is literally on vacation, that is, gone. Yet, the word "vacation" also suggests something happy and entertaining, a welcome relief from the everyday world of work. Looking into the underwater world and at the life there is like looking into a paradise where it is always "summer and/ vacation." The poem ends with a sense of hopefulness, as if the trip in the glass-bottomed boat has provided insight and spiritual relief.

Barbara Drake

OPEN HOUSE

Author: Theodore Roethke (1908-1963)
Type of poem: Lyric
First published: 1941, in *Open House*

The Poem

"Open House" is the title poem of Theodore Roethke's first volume of poetry. Friend and fellow poet Stanley Kunitz proposed the book title before Roethke actually had written the poem. Then, upon completing the poem, Roethke placed it at the front of the manuscript, suggesting that both the poem and its theme were to serve as an introductory promise for the poet's first work as well as for his entire career.

"Open House" is a terse, lyric definition of the speaker's poetics and, simultaneously, of his methods for the discovery of the self, indicating that for Roethke, these are one and the same. The title resonates with meaning. Upon first opening the book, the reader is welcomed into the poet's world, a place invented by the poet out of his search for self-knowledge and truth. Thus, the reader comes to the open house on a similar search, seeking to learn from the poet by following his lead in a parallel spiritual quest. The conceit is saved from mere cleverness by the poem's forthright tone and its concluding dark discovery.

In the first stanza, the poet establishes the connection between his self and the self's labor of love, his poetry. Although his art is natural, it is so difficult that it is painful. His secrets do not speak; they "cry aloud." They are expressed without the use of a corporeal voice ("I have no need for tongue"), since the poet's expression is all spiritual. Any reader may enter the poet's life, as his "heart keeps open house" and his "doors are widely swung." His love, poetry, is "an epic of the eyes." That love is simple, without "disguise," plainly visible on the page.

In the middle stanza, Roethke shows an awareness that his self-revelatory communication is a mystical and universal act. Saying that his "truths are all foreknown," he acknowledges a personal clairvoyance, as though he has meditated on the self many times. Such prior knowledge is made humble by welcoming public inspection of his house. Nor is he the first poet to discover the kinds of "truths" poetry offers.

At the very center of the poem, Roethke declares, "I'm naked to the bone,/ With nakedness my shield." It is a lovely pair of lines, affirming that the poet's open vulnerability is his strength and protection. As the fulcrum of the poem's advancing mystery, the second stanza is less descriptive, and more prophetic, than the first. It begins the poem's assertion that such personal mystery is not without serious psychic danger. For example, what in the first stanza had been a "cry," in the second develops into "anguish."

The third stanza continues the progression of the mystic journey into the self. Nearing what seems to be the deepest recesses of the house, there is a shift away from the personal control that was evidenced in the first two stanzas. In the first stanza the poet refers to himself with the personal pronouns "I" or "my" five times; in the second, six times; but in the third stanza he refers to himself only twice, and these two referents are used as brakes after the poet's journey has taken him near the white-hot center, where violent creativity reigns. Significantly, in the last stanza Roethke uses definite articles where one might expect pronouns. He writes: "The anger will endure,/ The deed will speak the truth." He is prevented from writing "My anger," "My deed," and "my truth" at this point in the poem specifically because he no longer seems in control of his own feeling ("anger") or his own action ("deed"). The journey through his own house, the self, has taken him inward to a place of universal mystery, a deep room of dangerous creativity.

Finally, for the good of his poetry the poet must retreat from his own psychic center. He must "stop" the journey. If he does not, the creative "anger" and "Rage" that the poet discovers within himself will ultimately consume him, reducing his "clearest cry," his poetry, to a state of uncontrolled "witless agony."

Forms and Devices

"Open House" is a brief poem of eighteen lines, composed in three sextains, or six-line stanzas. The English language gets the word "stanza" from the Italian, meaning "room," so that in this "house" there are three "rooms." In each stanza, the rhyme scheme unites an alternating rhymed quatrain with a final rhymed couplet (*ababcc, dedeff, ghghii*).

The rhymed quatrains in each stanza create a sense of tension and release, as if there were a rise in pitch followed by a corresponding drop, which is then further enhanced by the finality of the rhymed couplets. Two slant rhymes appear: the first in lines 1 and 3 of the first stanza ("aloud"/"house") and the second in lines 2 and 4 of the third stanza ("truth"/"mouth").

Every line scans into a regular iambic trimeter. As a result, the poem swings with a perfect cadence, which, in the beginning of the poem, seems light and airy, but which becomes frighteningly ironic in light of the "anger," "rage," and "agony" of the poem's conclusion.

One of the interesting developments in "Open House" is how Roethke uses sentence contructions to present his theme. The poem is initiated with two brief sentences, each of which is one line long. Then he moves through the remainder of the first stanza and completely through the second in sentences of two lines, the paired lines singing like voice and echo. Finally, the cadence of the third stanza is slowed as Roethke stretches two sentences through three lines apiece. Consequently, the poem begins much more lightly cadenced than it ends. It is as if the reader's ear is at first attuned to a quick point-counterpoint rhythm that is later replaced with a more lethargic beat. The overall rhythmic effect is thus in keeping with the poem's movement from light to dark.

Themes and Meanings

As critic Peter Balakian notes in his book *Theodore Roethke's Far Fields* (1989), the phrase "To keep open house with one's heart" is philosopher Friedrich Nietzsche's. Balakian explains that maintaining an open house "is fundamental to Roethke's essential way of knowing reality and measuring truth. The title proclaims the need to search the self for the truth."

"Open House" is a poem about the poetic process of self-discovery, a theme common in the Romantic tradition. As the first poem in Roethke's first volume, it stands as a declaration of Roethke's allegiance to Romanticism, which stretches back to William Blake. One might even note that the poem's spare language, simple diction, and strict rhythms are indebted to Blake's *Songs of Innocence* (1789) and *Songs of Experience* (1794) Furthermore, in its originating metaphor, "Open House" is very similar to Robert Browning's poem "House," which begins:

> Shall I sonnet-sing you about myself?
> Do I live in a house you would like to see?
> Is it scant of gear, has it store of pelf?
> "Unlock my heart with a sonnet-key?"

Like Blake and other Romantics (especially William Wordsworth, Walt Whitman, and William Butler Yeats), Roethke believed that poetry is a mystic art quite contrary to, and more trustworthy than, reason. As "Open House" shows, however, the pursuit of self-knowledge through poetry can be dangerous and painful.

The poem might be easier to grasp if it were not so violent and oracular. The final stanza is clearly the most troublesome, particularly as the diction is more abstract, imitating the "strict and pure" language of high emotion. As the poem momentarily shifts to the future tense, the anger that "will endure" beyond the poem is as essential to Roethke's creative imagination as are notions of eternal reverie for other poets. Roethke only approaches rage at the end of the poem, as if pure creativity is like fire—life-enhancing or all-consuming, depending upon one's distance.

The poet must "stop the lying mouth" when the heat of creative rage "warps" his poetry to "witless agony." The word "witless" is especially well-chosen. Whereas its common meaning includes "stupid" or "foolish," to be without "wit" is also to be unable to perceive the metaphoric connections between words and the things, ideas, and feelings they stand for—a state, for any poet, that must indeed be close to "agony." In other words, the poem asserts the need to explore the open house of the self until that point where the exploration becomes self-defeating.

"Open House," as a journey to the center, is archetypal. Its theme is not Roethke's alone, nor is it a theme from which Roethke ever moves away entirely. For example, the first line of the title poem in Roethke's last volume of poems, *The Far Field* (1964), reads: "I dream of journeys repeatedly." Another poem in that book is entitled "Journey to the Interior."

William Hoagland

OREAD

Author: H. D. (Hilda Doolittle, 1886-1961)
Type of poem: Lyric
First published: 1916, in *Sea Garden*

The Poem

"Oread" is a six-line poem. In Greek mythology, an oread is a wood nymph. By giving the poem this title, H. D. (Hilda Doolittle) frames it as an address by the wood nymph to the sea. Although there is no "I," the poem's first-person point of view is further suggested by many of the descriptive words themselves. For example, the second line orders the sea to "whirl your pointed pines" and the third line repeats the image with "splash your great pines." Clearly, the ocean has waves, not pines, yet the waves could be referred to as trees if the oread was speaking and transposed the objects with which she is familiar onto something different. Similarly, the last line uses the image "pools of fir"; again, the reader has the sense of the oread addressing the sea through her frame of reference.

Through this action of speaking, the poem creates a picture of the wood nymph standing on the rocks, addressing the sea. What is important, though, is that the oread is not speaking in singular terms; for example, line 4 states "on our rocks" rather than "on my rocks." This plural form is not only consistent with the first person point of view (that is, it is "our rocks" rather than "their rocks"), but also adds another visual element to the poem. Although it is only one oread speaking, the plural possessive implies either many oreads or many trees. Either way, the picture created is one of thick forests and jagged coastlines, the oread standing on the rocks, the sea pounding below her, the salt spray splashing her. This is a picture of elemental nature.

Adding to this elemental picture is the fact that the verbs are all declarative in form: "whirl," "splash," "hurl," and "cover." It would be more accurate to say that the oread is invoking, not asking, the sea to perform these functions. That invocation adds to the poem's elemental nature.

Finally, this image is one of enormous unleashed energy, an impression that is further developed by the poem's brevity. Because it is so short, every word carries an importance that it might not carry in a longer poem. Not only are the actions in the poem dramatic, but the length of the poem itself suggests that everything extraneous has been stripped away, exposing the core of the experience. The reader is left with this immediacy.

Forms and Devices

H. D. is well-known for her use of ancient Greek imagery. Many critics have suggested that this imagery is a metaphor through which the poet discusses other issues of either emotional or political import. Therefore, the images of trees and water, and by extension, the entire landscape, can be seen as metaphorical. Since the poem lends itself so heavily to an imagistic reading, the entire poem can be read as metaphor.

This sense of the poem—and the poetic landscape—as metaphor is suggested by the metamorphosis that the images undergo. When one approaches the poem, he or she has an image of trees as a category and an image of ocean as a category; those two categories are clearly separate. By the second line, however, when the oread invokes the sea to "whirl your pointed pines," the poem is beginning to blur those seemingly distinct categories. If one wants to maintain that trees and ocean are still separate, it is possible to say that the sound of waves crashing onto the rocks is similar to the sound of wind whipping the trees, or that the image of a wave rising has a similar shape to that of a tree. What is clear, though, is that the poem is, at the least, making connections between objects that are normally seen as having none.

In lines 2 and 3, even if the oread sees the waves as pine trees, the reader still sees waves and pine trees as separate. In line 5, however, the oread directs the sea to "hurl your green over us." Green is the color of pine trees, but it can also be the color of the sea; these two categories, thus, are moving closer together. This combining of categories culminates in line 6, where the oread names the water "pools of fir." This image can refer either to the frothy texture of the water or to the liquid texture of the motion of trees. Either way, what were separate at the beginning of the poem are, despite the poem's brevity, much less separate by the poem's end.

This blurring of categories gives the trees and water a metaphorical quality. Clearly, this is no ordinary landscape, for in the day-to-day world objects may be similar, but they do not take on qualities of each other. Furthermore, in the day-to-day world, it is difficult to see how trees and water are at all similar; any coastline, for example, clearly delineates where water begins and earth ends. The poet, though, is weaving a very different world, and seems to be pushing the reader to look beyond the surface of things into a landscape where objects that are normally distinct take on similar attributes, or even become each other.

The title also works on a metaphorical level to suggest a look into another world—or, at least, another way of looking at this one. Because the poem is in the first person, it would seem as if the reader is merely viewing everything through the oread's eyes. If this were so, however, there would be no need for the poet to shift the boundaries between objects from the poem's beginning through to the end; the oread's view of those objects would remain the same throughout. The fact that the categories do shift suggests that the oread herself is merely a metaphorical distancing device through which the poet can lay claim to her deeper vision.

Themes and Meanings

"Oread" is a poem through which H. D. calls into question traditional constructs that she sees as being inherently bipolar and unequal. The poet accomplishes this questioning by establishing several dualities, and then blurring the basis by which those dualities are established. By the end of the poem, the reader is in a world where traditional ways of seeing and thinking have begun to break down.

Clearly, one duality is that of trees and ocean—or, perhaps, land and water. Yet as already seen, that duality, which was distinct at the beginning of the poem, is much less distinct by the poem's end. Another duality is between passive and active; this distinction also becomes rather murky. The oread can be seen as passive and the sea as active, for the sea is crashing onto the oread. The oread can also be seen as active, for she is the one invoking the sea to do that crashing. Yet is she really? Is the sea crashing because the oread has invoked it to do so, or is the sea crashing because that is what it does, and the oread is merely attempting somehow to personify an action that would happen anyway? It becomes difficult to tell which party is being active and which is being passive.

A third duality established is between violence and nonviolence. Although much of what the oread is addressing to the sea is fairly violent both in its declarative form and in the specific actions invoked ("whirl," "splash," or "hurl"), the poem ends on a nonviolent gesture ("cover us with your pools of fir"). Is this that moment of quiet eddying after the waves have crashed, or is it that what seems violent through most of the poem is not as violent as one would think?

The poem clearly does not answer these questions but only raises them. This seems to be the poet's intent: to question the basis on which bipolar thinking is established. H. D. herself was a strong feminist; this poem was written early in the twentieth century, before women even had the right to vote. Much scientific and medical research at that time was done with the intent of proving the natural superiority of men to women. Traditional thinking had set up a very clear category of polar opposites—male and female—with men having social power and women having almost none.

In the poem, the poet is questioning both a society that subordinated women, and by further extension, the entire concept of bipolar thinking, which she sees as a social construct that is inherently unequal. Through the blurring of traditionally distinct categories, H. D. is suggesting a different way of viewing the world, one in which traditional, bipolar thinking falls away and a more egalitarian and fluid world emerges.

Robert Kaplan

OUT IN THE OPEN

Author: Tomas Tranströmer (1931-   )
Type of poem: Lyric
First published: 1966, as "I det fria," in *Klanger och spåar*; collected in *Tomas Tranströmer: Selected Poems, 1954-1986*, 1987

The Poem

"Out in the Open" has thirty-three lines divided into three sections of uneven length. The poem takes place out in the open air, away from town and the town's evil; the poet attempts to bring things normally hidden out in the open. Each of these readings is problematic, partially because of the poem's fragmented nature.

The second and third sections are written in the first person, but the first section has only an implied first-person narrator. In all three sections, there is no distinction between the speaker and Tomas Tranströmer; one must assume that he, following the norms of the lyric poem, is the "I" in this poem.

The poem begins with a fragment, as if a stage direction were being given in a play: "Late autumn labyrinth." The idea of a labyrinth is appropriate for this poem because of the mystery in it as a whole and because of the abrupt and sometimes baffling changes in direction that take place especially between sections. This first section of the poem follows a thin narrative: Someone waits at the edge of the woods, then decides to enter the woods, and then leaves. While in the woods, he hears a few sounds, notices the mushrooms "have shriveled up," and decides to get out and find his landmarks again before it gets dark. The scene is somewhat frightening, mainly because of the associations the reader might have with woods and darkness; the reader has no idea, however, why the person is in the woods or why exactly he needs to find his landmarks again. The section is evocative and startling in its metaphors, but it is certainly also opaque.

Section 2 begins with a statement that seems to connect logically the first two sections: "A letter from America drove me out again, started me walking." Perhaps our questions from section 1 are being resolved here. Tranströmer, however, does not provide instant gratification; he continues in the labyrinth. The letter from America drives him out not during late autumn but on a June night, and he walks not in the woods but "in the empty suburban streets." This section also shifts from the private, solitary thoughts that surfaced as he walked in nature to larger public themes as he walks among the new buildings with America on his mind.

This section addresses the presence of evil in the world. In America, according to Tranströmer, "evil and good actually have faces," but in Sweden— "with us" — things are more complicated. Tranströmer does know that those "who run . . . errands for" death "rule from glass offices" and "mill about in the bright sun." The section ends not with an evil bang but with a transforming and momentarily saving image. Tranströmer, the seer, sees a building's window become a "mirrorlike lake with no waves" that reflects the night sky and the trees. Caught up in his vision,

Tranströmer reflects, "Violence seemed unreal/ for a few moments." That closing line shows how briefly the moment of epiphany lasted.

The third section begins with an image that seems to come out of Alfred Hitchcock's film *North by Northwest* (1959). Readers turn from the dusk and night of sections 1 and 2 and face a burning sun. A plane comes out of nowhere in the poem and places its cruciform shadow on a man "poking at something" in a field. The poem then abandons the man and the plane and cuts, in a cinematic fashion, to the picture of a "cross hanging in the cool church vaults." The cross, in Tranströmer's eyes, resembles a "snapshot of something/ moving at tremendous speed." The poem, which also jumps and moves "at tremendous speed," does not end with any final statement that might wrap up the poem's meaning. It ends where it began, in a labyrinth of images.

Forms and Devices

Metaphors are often used by poets to give unity to a poem, especially one that stays away from the other more conventional unifying forces like rhyme scheme or narrative structure. Tranströmer is no exception. The woods that the speaker enters in section one are described as "silent abandoned houses this time of year." When the speaker leaves the woods to find landmarks, he looks for a "house on the other side of the lake." He enters the house of the woods and leaves the woods to find a house. The metaphorical description of the house is both intriguing and odd. It is a "reddish square intense as a bouillon cube." The description helps the reader see the house, and serves as a link to section 2 when the "newborn" suburban blocks are "cool as blueprints." Readers leave the woods for the suburbs, the red of the rusty machine and the "reddish square" of the house for the metaphorical blueprints, and they abandon that "intense" bouillon cube-shaped house for the "cool" blocks of suburbia. The inversions and playful reshaping help keep the poem centered.

Another pattern emerges when the images associated with the city and the woods are compared. In the woods the near silence becomes mechanized. The few sounds the poet hears are compared to a person moving twigs "with pincers" or an "iron hinge . . . whining feebly inside a thick trunk." The same type of reversal takes place in the city: The constructed world becomes naturalized when the building windows are transformed into a "mirrorlike lake with no waves." These transformations do not seem to have thematic importance; they serve as structural aids only.

The most conventional figurative language in the poem comes in the second section when death is personified. As in so many other descriptions of death by both writers and painters, the abstraction becomes concrete: Death is a "he" who has people "run . . . errands for him." The conventionality of the image matches the simplicity of the concept: Evil seems external to Tranströmer. The bad people, death's right-hand men and women "rule from glass offices" and "mill about in the bright sun." The good person—Tranströmer—stands outside the offices or in nature and walks around at night. It does not seem as if the poet implicates himself in the world's evil or its violence. He stands apart, the pure visionary.

Themes and Meanings

Any poem that has thirty-three lines divided into three sections and that begins with a man journeying through woods, nearly lost, and ends with the image of a cross must be, at least for an instant, compared with Dante's *The Divine Comedy* (c. 1320). Dante's epic, divided into three parts, with two of those parts divided into thirty-three cantos, begins with Dante lost in a dark forest and ends with a vision of God. Despite the similarities, the comparison is interesting mostly because of the differences between the two works. Tranströmer's poem is a modern journey through the hell of human violence and evil, but no hope is offered at the end. The cross of the plane's shadow or the cross in the "cool church vaults" might perhaps serve as a symbol of suffering, but there is certainly no hope of that suffering having any purpose. For Christians, the cross represents both suffering and hope, but Tranströmer's use of the image seems stripped of nearly all transcendent meaning. In the center of the cross made by the airplane's shadow lies no savior, but some nameless man "sitting in the field poking at something"; and the cross in the church appears to be not only empty, but Tranströmer also turns it into something else, something stripped of value, "a split-second snapshot of something/ moving at tremendous speed." The camera eye and the speed of technology replace the formerly stable icon of Christianity.

What seems to be offered in the poem to replace the redemptive quality of the cross is the power of the poet's own imagination. Tranströmer is admired widely and has been translated by a number of poets because of the power in his lyrical voice. He banishes the normal hinges of a poem and creates a fresh vision that benefits from surprising metaphors and innovative transitions. Tranströmer, however, recognizes that all of his verbal pyrotechnics really end up not affecting the world in the least. His image of death's errands being run by office workers is horrifying; but equally horrifying is the idea that poetry does nothing to stop the devastation. A stunning image might make violence seem "unreal/ for a few moments," but the perception is false. Tranströmer admits that violence is real, suffering is always present, and poetry, like the speaker in the first section, can enter nature or a sheltered realm, but it also must return eventually to the central facts of life. As W. H. Auden once said, "Poetry makes nothing happen," but Tranströmer might counter this by saying poetry lifts the reader, for an instant, from the realm of dull logic and violence to the pleasures of images "moving at tremendous speed" and metaphors operating with the logic of dreams.

Kevin Boyle

OUT OF THE CRADLE ENDLESSLY ROCKING

Author: Walt Whitman (1819-1892)
Type of poem: Narrative
First published: 1859, as "A Child's Reminiscence"; as "A World Out of the Sea," in *Leaves of Grass*, 1860; as "Out of the Cradle Endlessly Rocking," in *Leaves of Grass*, 1871

The Poem

"Out of the Cradle Endlessly Rocking" is a poem about memory—about the ways in which an adult poet remembers and understands his childhood, and the ways in which his childhood prepared him for his adult poetic life. Like other British and American Romantic poets, Walt Whitman was interested in this relationship between the formative years of youth and the creative years of adulthood. Thus, Whitman wrote this poem, which is similar to British poet William Wordsworth's "Lines: Composed a Few Miles Above Tintern Abbey" and American poet Henry Wadsworth Longfellow's "My Lost Youth."

The opening stanzas begin with the setting, describing the past, specifically, the past in Long Island (referred to by the Indian name "Paumanok") and the memory of the "bareheaded, barefoot" child—a popular theme of nineteenth century British and American artists. A musical motif, which continues throughout the poem, is introduced in the image of a bird whose singing enchants the narrator, reminding him of his past.

This memory, enlivened by the notion of song, is emphasized through an italicized stanza in which a pair of birds sings joyous songs, introducing two important ideas: the enlivening quality of music, and the power of the individual aria, which, in fact, is the kind of lyric this poem actually is.

The poem proceeds by announcing the death of the female bird, and the subsequent italicized arias move from a reference to waiting—"I wait and I wait till you blow my mate to me"—to despair: "We two together no more." Despite this "aria sinking," all else continues, and the boy poet realizes that he will be a poetic bard, a solitary bird, and a solitary singer.

The end of the poem focuses upon this image of the "solitary me"—the solitary poet—hearing the sea sing to him of death. Death, however, is not a terminal point. Instead, death is incorporated into life, just as the "old crone rocking the cradle" suggests that the entrance into life is similarly an introduction to death, which, in turn, prefaces more life. The cycle of life and death, important in all of Whitman's poems, is thus emphasized in the conclusion of this poem. The elder poet remembers his youth; the old crone rocks the cradle; and the sea whispers to the aging poet of past, present, and future.

Forms and Devices

"Out of the Cradle Endlessly Rocking" is notable for its use of free verse and imagery. Like the King James Version of the Bible, in which free verse is frequently found, "Out of the Cradle Endlessly Rocking" relies upon the irregular rhythm of phrases, images, and lines rather than the conventional use of meter. Thus, in the first three lines of the poem, the emphasis is not upon feet or syllabic count, as it might be in other, more conventional forms of poetry, but rather upon the rhythm and repetition within the lines themselves:

> Out of the cradle endlessly rocking,
> Out of the mocking-bird's throat, the musical shuttle,
> Out of the Ninth-month midnight.

Whitman's use of imagery is similar to his reliance upon free verse in that the technique permeates, subtly yet pervasively, the entire poem. One such image is the rocking cradle, referred to in the title, in the first line, and then in the final lines of the poem, connecting all parts of this lyric by its reference to movement, to change, to the cycles of life.

Another image is that of the singing bird, introduced in the opening lines as "the bird that chanted" to the poet and used throughout the poem, culminating in the final lines, in which the song of the bird, as remembered from the poet's youth, is both recalled and transformed into the adult bard's song, sung to him by the sea and, in turn, metamorphosed into the poem itself.

Still another image is that of the youthful poet, described in traditional yet Whitmanesque terms as "alone, bareheaded, barefoot" in the first stanza of the poem. This image is recalled throughout the poem; the adult bard refers to his reminiscence of himself "with bare feet, a child, the wind wafting in my hair" in the middle section of the poem, and in the final stanzas understands that he will never again be that youth, that "peaceful child." The image of the singing bird that learns to sing alone (and as a mature voice) is a parallel to this image of the youth become adult, the boy become bard.

Another image that should be noted is that of the sea, reminder of both life's constancy and its changes. Like the bird that can transcend the death of its mate, and like the youth who can survive the change from boyhood to adulthood, the sea is represented in this poem as a body that answers the poet and that whispers to him. Its answer and whisper is the same — death — but it means more than simply death in that monosyllabic answer and whisper. It means death that ushers in life, that rocks a cradle of life and death.

Themes and Meanings

Walt Whitman was passionately in love with opera, and this passion is revealed in "Out of the Cradle Endlessly Rocking," with its reliance upon operatic techniques and references, in particular, the aria. Still another connection to the operatic form is the suggestion that apparent tragedy is cause for music, for hope, for a belief in the transcending power of life.

The first stanza of Whitman's poem ends with a line referring to the narrator's singing "a reminiscence." The reminiscence, in this case, is life that yields to death, which, in turn, ushers in new life. The arias sung by the birds present this cyclic view of life, as do the commentaries by the bard himself. It is not coincidental that the sea is critical in this remembering process and is the final image of the poem, for the sea is the image par excellence of change, of tides coming and going, of life continuing, despite storms and deaths, of songs sung by two that become arias sung by one. What comes out of a cradle endlessly rocking, in Whitman's view, is essentially life, then death, then more and endless life. The cycle, not the specific parts of the circle, is what finally counts.

Marjorie Smelstor

OVID IN THE THIRD REICH

Author: Geoffrey Hill (1932-   )
Type of poem: Dramatic monologue
First published: 1968, in *King Log*

The Poem

"Ovid in the Third Reich" is a short poem in two quatrains (four-line stanzas) of accentual verse; that is, the line is governed by the number of stressed, or accented, syllables. It is a dramatic monologue in which the poet speaks in the persona of the ancient Roman poet, Ovid. The title, however, places him in the Third Reich of Adolf Hitler's Germany, instead of the first years of the Roman Empire under the Emperor Augustus. It is clear from the title that Geoffrey Hill intends a parallel to be drawn between the two periods. They compare very clearly in several ways: First, both states were totalitarian; in both states there was such a thing as correct thinking; and deviation from general opinion was frowned upon and thought subversive in both. Second, both rulers tended to be puritanical in their habits and tastes. Women were expected to be mothers, cooks, and keepers of the state faith. Third, the expression of art, literature, and the free spirit essential to them were severely curbed to accommodate the purposes of the state. The question arises as to what a poet such as Ovid can and should do under a vicious, stultifying, and brutal dictatorship.

For the epigraph, Hill selects one of Ovid's own lines, from the *Amores* (c. 20 B.C.). Although variously translated, and ambiguous in itself, the meaning relevant to "Ovid in the Third Reich" can be paraphrased: He who refuses to accept himself as guilty is not guilty. Only those who are well-known (who have played a part in the affair?) must, of necessity, profess their guilt. Whereas the Roman poet historically was banished from his beloved city, Ovid in the Third Reich accepts a self-imposed banishment rather than take part in the madness about him. Both suffer fearfully. The Roman is exiled to the farther shores of the Black Sea to live his days among barbarous folk, as he complains in one of his poems; Ovid in the Third Reich is forced by banishment to endure limitations, is deprived of the life of the city, the joy of companions, and the freedom to love and create.

This Ovid is reduced to the essentials in his life: "I love my work and my children." As a poet, he bears witness to the terrible time. He has learned one thing, as he says, that the vicious are as tormented as the damned. Strangely, though, they are part of the divine plan. In the world of the contraries, they make the harmony of the world; if man does not see and hear the dissonant, he cannot know the vibrancy of concord and the good and love. As dire as the days may be, he knows himself to be part of the "love-choir," in which, as a poet, he will always sing.

Forms and Devices

There is an impression of completeness in Geoffrey Hill's "Ovid in the Third Reich" that comes from the perfect unity of the subject and the poetic devices he employs, namely, the poem's diction, its rhythm, and its form—three essentials in the craft of poetry.

In the first stanza, the fear and trauma of events has reduced the poet—usually of an expansive nature—to sentences that reveal little emotion and lines that are short and declarative: "God/ Is distant, difficult." A lack of coherent thought is apparent as he moves erratically from subject to subject, as if his emotion has been dammed at its source.

The diction, too, is denotative and literal, which suggests a tautness and a matter-of-factness, as though, like God, the poet would distance himself from the scene. All sensitivity to shades of meaning and feeling has been stripped from the poet's vocabulary, leaving him with only the most general and simplest words to describe the complexity of his impressions. "Things happen," he tersely comments. Exactly what things, the poet perhaps dare not or cannot say. This uncommunicative tone is overwhelmed, finally, by the last two lines of the first stanza. Sentences that have been of the simplest construction (subject, verb, direct object), with monosyllabic words, suddenly expand to accommodate "Innocence is no earthly weapon" under the impact of his reflections. Not for the first time have the "ancient troughs" run with the blood of the innocent, revealing the darker side of man's nature. Primitive rituals demanded blood sacrifice then, and the cultism of the Nazis demands it now, as only an extension of that barbarity into the twentieth century.

With this insight, the diction begins to expand, and the trip-hammer rhythms of the first stanza become less strident and insistent. The strict regular blows of the spondee in "I have learned one thing: not to look down" gives way to a gentler rhythm. The form itself opens like a floodgate, as if liberated by the recognition that the events he has witnessed "Harmonize strangely." This frees him for even greater speculation.

The poet alludes, finally, to the "sphere," a metaphor for the universe, recalling the ancient Pythagorean cosmology, in which the contraries of the world are met in the music of the spheres, and all seeming disharmony is reconciled in accordance with the laws of nature. The poet, however, presents the idea in a Christian context, in which the contraries of good and evil are alluded to in an image from Dante's *The Divine Comedy* (c. 1320). The damned, embodying the evil in human nature, are still part of the greater design of God and must be accepted—if not with charity, at least with forbearance. Man is free to choose his own path. The damned are their own hell.

Themes and Meanings

"Ovid in the Third Reich" prompts two questions in particular. What is a good man is to do when faced with such consummate evil? What is a poet to do?

The major philosophical basis of the poem is the belief that the world of nature is an eternal battleground on which good and evil, love and hate, and tyranny and freedom are in ceaseless conflict. Since there is nothing new under the sun, as the author of Ecclesiastes asserts, the drama of history will be repeated over and over.

Man confronts evil in many ways: He may choose direct action, thereby courting martyrdom. He may, on the contrary, retreat into the comfortable ease of the accepted views of the state, accepted by the mass of men; in this case, by his very passivity he gives his assent to the evil.

Customarily, and from earliest times, the role of the poet has been clearly understood and honored. He is, first, a historian recording the events of society. "Things happen," Ovid in the Third Reich avers. The poet, furthermore, must cultivate a clear perception and objectivity in order that he should be neither a propagandist nor an apologist; in effect, he must keep his distance, very like a god. He must also, finally, come to terms with his own emotional response. He must fully acknowledge the concentration camps, as others have acknowledged the "ancient troughs of blood." In an intuitive leap from experience, the poet comes to a philosophical or spiritual knowledge which satisfies or at least consoles. In "Ovid in the Third Reich," the consolation comes from the recognition that, in the biblical phrase, "one must render unto Caesar the things that are Caesar's and unto God, the things that are God's." Man cannot judge. Thus, the poet tries to wrestle with the age-old Christian problem: How can God be omnipotent and all good? If He is omnipotent, then He purposely allows evil to flourish; if all good, then He must be limited, for an all-good, omnipotent God would prevent the evil of the world. It is the individual who tips the balance, not nations, which are a construct of man. In this final representation, Hill confirms the meaning of the epilogue. As a poet, he knows — as did Ovid in the first century — that no tyranny, oppressive and limiting as it may be, can destroy man's thought and feelings, for the mind is a very private place. The individual, if he has not intentionally violated the laws of man, nature, and God, cannot be guilty. He is still part of the "love-choir."

Maureen W. Mills

OZYMANDIAS

Author: Percy Bysshe Shelley (1792-1822)
Type of poem: Sonnet
First published: 1818; collected in *Rosalind and Helen*, 1819

The Poem

"Ozymandias" is a sonnet composed by the Romantic poet Percy Bysshe Shelley and named for its subject, with the Greek name of the Egyptian king Ramses II, who died in 1234 B.C. The poem follows the traditional structure of the fourteen-line Italian sonnet, featuring an opening octave or set of eight lines that presents a conflict or dilemma, followed by a sestet or set of six lines that offers some resolution or commentary upon the proposition introduced in the octave.

The poem is conventionally written in iambic pentameter (that is, ten syllables per line of coupled unstressed then stressed sounds), so the poem's subject matter is framed both by the structure and meter constraints chosen by the poet.

The first-person narrator of "Ozymandias" introduces a conversation he has chanced to have with a "traveller from an antique land" in line 1. The reader knows neither the identity of the traveler nor the circumstances wherein the poet has encountered the traveler but may assume he is a source of information about a strange and unfamiliar world.

The remaining thirteen lines of the poem quote verbatim the tale that the traveler has borne from his trek into the desert. The intrepid explorer has encountered "Two vast and trunkless legs of stone," the vestiges of a statue in disrepair whose head lay as a "shattered visage" nearby. Despite its broken state, the "frown," the "wrinkled lip" and "sneer of cold command" of the statue's face bespeak its sculptor's skill in capturing the vanity and self-importance of its subject.

The traveler remarks that the artist has "well those passions read which yet survive" — that is, those indications of the subject's character, indelibly "stamped on . . . lifeless things": "the hand that mocked them, and the heart that fed."

The octave thus confronts the reader in its first movement with an ironic portrait of an ancient monarch whose fame and stature have been immortalized in a static gaze that connotes paradoxically both celebrity and dissolution. In the revelatory sestet which follows, the poet posits, through the testimony of the traveler, the fate of vainglorious men. On the pedestal, he finds written the great man's empty boast: "My name is Ozymandias, King of Kings,/ Look on my Works, ye Mighty, and despair!"

Yet "Nothing beside remains" but ruin, a "colossal Wreck, boundless and bare" against the lonely landscape of sand and cruel, penetrating sunlight. A double irony is at work; neither the great man nor the work of the artist remains in credible shape to challenge or delight the imagination of those who would encounter it. King and artisan, mover and maker, share the same destiny. The poem ends with the reader/observer's gaze fixed upon this pathetic legacy, contemplating his own mortality.

Forms and Devices

The Italian sonnet presents the poet with the challenge of using an utterly familiar form in an innovative or provocative way. The chief variables within this form involve rhyme scheme. The traditional Italian sonnet features an *abba, abba, cde, cde* rhyme scheme, each letter representing a different end rhyme that is repeated in pattern.

In "Ozymandias," Shelley chooses to forgo the conventional scheme and employs a more eccentric *abab, acdc, ece, fef* pattern that creates the immediate effect of a woven tapestry of sound and rhythm that helps to underscore the poem's essential irony. As the reader's expectations are unmet, the very syntax forced by the unusual rhyme of the poem creates tension that matches that of the theme.

Critics have long noted the "Chinese box" frame in which the story of Ozymandias has come to the poet and thus, indirectly, to the reader. Each line of the poem, from first to last, reveals successively one more layer of the narrative's essential irony.

One learns first something of the poet's conversation with the mysterious traveler "from an antique land." The poet, in turn, reports but one tidbit of that conversation, "Who said — ," in the very words of the traveler. Laboriously, the speaker then moves through each wave of recognition and interpretation of what he has encountered, climaxing with the presentation of Ozymandias' inscription.

Shelley's sonnet is remarkable for its spare and stark imagery. The poet is determined to re-create the barren desert landscape, the poetic counterpoint to the morbid and deserved fate of Ozymandias, the pompous fool. To do so requires that he carefully circumscribe his choice of descriptors to connote neither grandeur nor panoramic vista, but rather singular loneliness and constrained, fragmented solitude. Hence such modifiers as "trunkless," "Half-sunk," "shattered," "decay," and "wreck" serve his purpose well.

Consequently, the compression of the sonnet form, the unconventional rhyme scheme, the point of view chosen for reader entry, and the carefully wrought diction of the poem achieve the effect the poet was seeking. Amid vast stretches of unbroken sameness, the traveler — followed by the poet, then the reader — comes upon a bleak personage whose severed limbs and head first shock and dismay, then elicit reluctant mockery for the egotism of its subject.

Themes and Meanings

"Ozymandias" is at first glance a sonnet about the transitory nature of life and its pretensions of fame and fortune. The decaying, ancient statue bears witness to the fact that the pursuit of power and glory for their own sakes are not only fleeting, but they are also illusory, unworthy ambitions even within the lifetime of their seekers.

The nineteenth century was filled with "discoveries" of ancient landscapes, built upon a historiography of "great men," who were to elicit the attention and admiration of a generation of scholars and writers. Shelley choose, however, to poke holes in the "great man" theory of history, questioning its validity and its rationality.

The poem also works on another level, however—as a candid, poignant confession by the artist that his work is also ephemeral, and that as style, manner, and fashion change, so do reputation and honor. Such a confessional spirit was particularly appropriate for Shelley and other Romantics, that clan of "rebel spirits"— among them William Blake, George Gorden, Lord Byron, John Keats, Samuel Taylor Coleridge, and William Wordsworth.

This new generation of poets flaunted tradition, inventing their own vocabularies, subject matters, poetic form, and generally laboring to raise the poet's consciousness of his own imagination to an unprecedented level. "Ozymandias" exemplifies both in theme and in execution these "rebellious" notions.

Often, the poet himself was the topic and focus of his poetry, rather than the grander themes of man and God, or the courtship of ladies and gentlemen. Audiences for the first time were confronted with the artist's "personality," and not only his work. Autobiography, not history, was to become the focal point of literary endeavor—and literary criticism.

The Romantics revitalized the craft of poetry in the nineteenth century, rescuing it from the narrow constraints of "classicism" built upon elevated language, artificial form, and exaggerated dependence on tradition. The price paid for this departure was the risk of alienating themselves from public taste and private virtue. The Romantics, Shelley chief among them, constructed their own "traditions" in various manifestos about the components, meaning, and social utility of poetry, even offering advice about how their poetry should be interpreted.

More than that, Shelley, in works such as *Prometheus Unbound* (1820) and *A Defence of Poetry* (1840), attempted to create a public persona for the poet as an arbiter of morality, genius, and political order. Thus, the Romantic, as exemplified in Shelley himself, was peculiarly subject to the rather pretentious self-promotion of his vocation—not unlike the wizened Ozymandias of his sonnet.

The ancient king's narcissism, his relentless declarations of immortality and supreme might, serve as warning also to the artist whose folly may lead him to similar vanity. Read this way, "Ozymandias" is a sober exhortation to poets and politicians alike to foster realistic assessments of their influence and worth; the disposition to make truth serve the selfish ends of vainglorious men is a theme of history Shelley discerned well in his own time and attempted to expose in his poetry. In that regard, "Ozymandias" remains a powerful antidote to artistic pretensions and political hypocrisy.

Bruce L. Edwards

THE PANGOLIN

Author: Marianne Moore (1887-1972)
Type of poem: Ode
First published: 1936, in *The Pangolin and Other Verse*

The Poem

"The Pangolin" is a long, unrhymed, syllabic poem of ninety-eight lines in nine stanzas; eight stanzas have eleven lines and one has ten. The title refers to the class of animals known commonly as anteaters.

In the first half of the poem, Moore offers a rich and intense description of the anteater. She is fascinated by the armor plate, comparing the scaly covering to the layers of an artichoke with its tough, spiny leaves that protect a delicate and delectable inner meat. She focuses attention on the animal's nocturnal habits, its night feeding, its walking on the edges of its hands to save its claws for digging. Nevertheless, for all its outer toughness, the anteater avoids fights; when threatened, it can wind itself around trees and curl up into a hard ball to protect itself against its enemies.

As day breaks, the pangolin withdraws into its nest of rocks, which it closes with earth from inside to shut out the light. In the third stanza, Moore pauses briefly to observe that both humans and pangolins have a splendor, an excellence, but in humans those qualities coexist with an innate vileness.

Returning to the anteater in stanza 4, Moore comments on the animal's courage, manifested in a struggle with the dread driver ant, notorious for its warlike ferocity. Protected by its armor, the anteater attacks with both tongue and tail, an instrument of great power. If not threatened, the anteater will climb down from a tree; otherwise it will drop and walk away unhurt.

In stanza 5, Moore switches direction. Although she begins with a rich description of the anteater's multipurpose tail, she introduces a new term that applies to this body part: "graceful." Moore finds this grace in the anteater's movements at night. She comments that the animal's movements are not made graceful by virtue of its condition in life—it has not had to deal with "adversities" and "conversities."

In stanza 6, Moore turns to a direct examination of grace. Yet instead of providing a definition of "grace," she compounds the issue by raising a question of its nature, proposing various ways of looking at the meaning. Appearing to return to the subject of pangolins in stanza 7, she veers off into a consideration of the moral nature of humankind. In the inquiry, humans come up lacking.

This comparison is continued in stanza 8, where Moore declares that humans, the writing masters of the world, do not like comparisons that are denigrating. Nevertheless, humans have the capacity of humor that helps alleviate the struggle of existence. Moreover, humans have the qualities of "everlasting vigor," the "power to grow," though they also have the power to create fear and anxiety.

In the final stanza, Moore considers humans as a species of mammal—fearful, limited, and dependent on the sun, the light of day, for completing their enterprises and rejuvenating their souls.

Forms and Devices

"The Pangolin" appears to be a sprawling, formless unrhymed poem with widely varying line lengths, irregular meter, and little or no stanza pattern. Indeed, the poem does not appear to resemble traditional poetry. This impression, however, is part of its method and its charm. As a radical modernist poet, Moore utilizes a variety of visual, typological, auditory, and stylistic devices to give the appearance that her poem does not conform to traditional expectations regarding the look, sound, and content of poetry. A more critical look at the poem quickly dispels this impression, however; the apparent formlessness gives way to highly formal and traditional elements.

The largest element of form is the nine stanzas that are identified only by the two line spaces separating them. Otherwise, the stanzas flow into one another, as the last lines of each run into the next stanza. Each stanza has eleven lines (with one exception, the fifth stanza has ten lines) that follow an almost regular pattern of line lengths, measured by syllable count.

The dominant pattern of line lengths is established in the first stanza (9-14-9-17-12-11-15-8-5-9-9). Although this pattern is not exactly adhered to, Moore tries to stick closely to it from stanza to stanza. Thus, in stanza 2, the pattern is 9-15-8-16-13-12-13-8-4-10-10. She takes similar liberties throughout the remaining stanzas, perhaps because it was impossible to do otherwise in order to use the words she wanted, or because she preferred to introduce variety.

Another element of the poem's form is its music. Moore makes exquisite use of the musical devices of assonance, alliteration, and consonance. These devices of sound substitute for the more rhythmical pattern of standard meter and end rhyme, and they create a pattern of sound that is full of wit, whimsy, and surprise. The first line of the poem employs all three of these musical devices. The *a* in "another" "armored," "animal," and "scale" all combine to form an assonant pattern of vowel sounds that is supplemented by the alliteration of *n*, *m*, and *r* sounds and the consonantal sound of *l* in the same words. The accumulation of these sounds creates a sense of the whimsical treatment of the subject. The pattern also helps bind the words one to another, and each to the larger structure of meaning. Such elements appear throughout the poem and contribute to the rich pattern of sound and meaning.

Moore also uses a technique of incongruous associations of images, much like the English Metaphysical poets of the seventeenth century, who developed with great power the "conceit," a device that telescoped images of widely different associations to create a startling and witty perception of reality. Such images appear in line 4, where Moore compares the pangolin to an artichoke, or in line 6, where she compares the pangolin to Leonardo da Vinci, who, as both artist and engineer, created a drawing of an armored vehicle. In the third stanza, Moore describes the pangolin in terms of the grace of the wrought-iron vine designed in 1290 by the famous smith named Thomas—from the town of Leighton Buzzard—for the tomb of Eleanor of Castile.

Themes and Meanings

"The Pangolin" is a manifestation of Moore's passion for observation and rendering what the Germans called the *ding an sich* ("the thing in itself"). She turned her keen eye to the pangolin for the purpose of creating a real anteater in an imaginary world. Above all, her aim is to provide the reader with such a rich and powerful description of this creature that it will become a living imaginary presence. Her training in biology and in the methods of science are put to excellent use, as stanza by stanza the pangolin takes on a more substantial existence.

The poet's frame of reference for bringing this creature to life is not rooted in biology alone, but rather in human culture. In the initial stanzas where Moore details the major characteristics of the pangolin, she makes three references to give the pangolin added dimension: In stanza 1, she refers to da Vinci; in stanza 3, to Thomas (the medieval smith); and in stanza 4, to the modern Spanish sculptor, Pablo Gargallo y Catalán.

These cultural references are part of a structure of meaning that evolves within the poem. Not content to rest with observation of the pangolin, Moore takes the reader on an imaginative flight into the consideration of the moral condition of humans. This transition occurs in the final four stanzas, in which the pangolin falls into the background and human behavior becomes Moore's focus.

In stanza 6, she begins with the question of "grace." Following her logic is no simple matter, but it appears that she asks why—given the fact that grace promises eternal salvation—those who developed the idea would confuse it with lesser meaning, such as a "kindly manner," the period in which to repay debts, the cure for sins, or the stone mullions that are part of the architecture of a church ceiling?

Her answer is no answer, but an image of the "sail boat," "the first machine," followed by the image of pangolins that also move quietly and are "models of exactness." These images are clues to the poetic and moral sensibility toward which this poem evolves. Poems can be "models of exactness," and the enterprise of the poet can be to create such models. Such activity has high moral value for Moore, who seems to subscribe to the Romantic idea that poetry has a high moral purpose.

Life, on the other hand, is far from exact—it is messy and confusing. In the next two stanzas, Moore presents an ambivalent view of humans, whom she sees as destructive of the natural world, but nevertheless industrious, and paradoxically, unemotional and emotional. Torn between these perceptions of humankind, she allows that among animals only "*one* has a sense of humor," which to her is clearly a mitigating factor, a saving grace in humans, whom she otherwise castigates for their failings.

In the final paragraph, Moore's attention shifts clearly from pangolin to human. Implicitly contrasting humans to the nocturnal pangolins, she presents humans as creatures—mammals—who inhabit the light and for whom the sun provides a constant source of renewal and strength. Despite her reservations, she concludes with a celebration of human existence.

Richard Damashek

THE PANTHER

Author: Rainer Maria Rilke (1875-1926)
Type of poem: Meditation
First published: 1907, as "Der Panther," in *Neue Gedichte*; collected in
  Translations from the Poetry of Rainer Maria Rilke, 1938

The Poem

"The Panther" is a brief poem of twelve lines divided into three quatrains, each following the rhyme scheme *abab*. The title indicates the object of the poet's meditations.

From 1905 to 1906, the German poet Rainer Maria Rilke worked as secretary to the French sculptor Auguste Rodin. After studying a small bronze of a tiger sculpted by Rodin, Rilke visited the Jardin des Plantes in Paris to observe a captive panther. Conventionally, a panther suggests feral violence; however, the poem overturns such expectations. The reader's experience of the predatory creature climaxes in what critic Siegfried Mandel calls "the psychological terror of absolute inward stillness."

The first quatrain describes the captive animal's vision as having grown weary, so that all he perceives are blurs, or things without definition or significance. Such deterioration is a symptom of the animal's imprisonment. The bars that surround him multiply in his sight to a thousand; he can only glimpse fragmentary images of what lies beyond. His universe is thus rendered monotonous and meaningless.

The second quatrain reinforces this sense of futility by conveying the circularity of the panther's movement. His incessant pacing also suggests that the imprisoned animal harbors reserves of force and rebellion. The intensity of this contained energy is implied by the suppleness and massiveness of the animal's tread. The image the poet creates is of a coiled wire; the creature's awesome stride is restricted to a circle whose size and scope is "miniature." The focus on this "dance of strength" shifts at the quatrain's end to the circle's immobile center, the site of a "powerful" yet "benumbed" will.

The panther's vision also dominates the third quatrain, though this time the reader observes not from the outside but from the inside. The immobility that closes the previous quatrain extends now to the animal's "tense, quiet limbs" and climaxes with the death of the image that slips through his randomly open eyes. This image searches out the heart, or the center, where it is annihilated. The imprisoned consciousness has lost its power or will to grasp the reality beyond it.

Forms and Devices

Rilke's association with Rodin, as well as the painter Paul Cézanne, led him to develop what the poet called *Dinggedichte*, or "thing poems." Rilke considered "The Panther," an early example of this type, one of his favorite poems, because it had shown him "the way to artistic integrity."

Rilke strove to make his poems self-contained and compact with meaning, like works of visual art. Like a painter or sculptor, Rilke crafted concrete forms and perspective by means of what Mandel terms "the illusion of movement." The panther's concentric pacing gives it volume and dimension, as well as animating the poem with tension and balance and ultimately drawing the reader inward. Contrast ("soft pace" and "supple massive stride") and repetition ("pace," "stride," "dance") create patterns of motion, which, like ocean waves, produce a visual surface. It is this surface that reflects the poet's inner mood, as waves mirror the tide.

According to the poet W. H. Auden, Rilke was "almost the first poet since the seventeenth century to find a fresh solution" to the problem of "how to express abstract ideas in concrete terms." Auden wrote that Rilke thought with "physical" symbols, that he imagined the human "in terms of the non-human, of what he calls Things (*Dinge*)." The panther's repetitive motion and mechanical, cameralike registering of images emphasize his "thingness." Rilke reinforces the poem's effect of concreteness with his choice of plain, simple vocabulary. He rejects erudite and florid language in favor of unassuming speech. Complexity is achieved by the poem's imagery.

To ensure concentration of thought and feeling, Rilke develops the image of the caged panther into an extended metaphor. This device also produces the symmetry and self-sufficiency of visual art. Much of the richness attributed to Rilke's poetry derives from the coherence of his imagery. In addition, critics have commented on how Rilke's interplay of meter and rhyme create a subtle music, whose rhythm and internal balance help draw the reader into the poem's self-contained world.

Themes and Meanings

The philosopher Martin Heidegger claimed that his own work had been an attempt to articulate in philosophical language what Rilke had confronted symbolically in his poems. Heidegger's existentialist philosophy defined the human condition as "being exposed to nothingness." "Rilke's captive Panther," states critic Erich Heller, is a "Zoological relation of [Vincent] Van Gogh's Sunflowers, those rapacious 'things' that draw the whole world into their dark centers." Rilke wrote about nothingness in a strangely compelling, almost erotic way. The panther he evokes as a symbol of deadening loss attracts the reader with a horrifying magnetism.

Rilke, like William Blake, rarely lapsed into sentimentality about nature's primal chaos. At the same time, he yielded to its mysteries, unflinchingly following to their heart of darkness. In such sympathetic contemplation, he discovered a transcendence achieved through the imagination, which enabled him to overcome his despair at the spiritual bankruptcy modern life afforded him. For Rilke, the intensity of poetic vision provided him entry into the realm of the spiritual and the eternal.

Rilke's poetry reveals a man sensitive to the dualities of existence, creatively seeking to unify experience. Critics have noted in his work the complementary themes of lament and praise. In "The Panther," for example, even as he grieves over the animal's captivity, Rilke extols the power and elegance of its gait.

The poet presents the caged panther as a figure of tragedy, invoking terror and pity. Trapped by the exigencies of time and space and matter, it is emblematic of the terror of contingency. The captive animal attains transcendence, paradoxically, once it is captured in the poem, an eternally existing object of the poet's imagination.

Amy Adelstein

PARISIAN DREAM

Author: Charles Baudelaire (1821-1867)
Type of poem: Lyric
First published: 1861, as "Reve parisien," in *Les Fleurs du mal*, second edition; collected in *Flowers of Evil*, 1963

The Poem

"Parisian Dream" is divided into two parts, the first consisting of thirteen quatrains, the second of two. The eight-syllable lines rhyme in a simple, alternating *abab* pattern. Composed in 1860, this poem was included in the second edition of *Flowers of Evil* in the section "Tableaux parisiens" ("Parisian Tableaux"). The title announces a dream, qualified by the location "Paris," the loved and hated city to which Charles Baudelaire devoted much of his verse and in which he lived most of his creative life.

Part 1 recounts a dream remembered on awakening. A first person narrator speaks in the past tense, recalling a terrible but fascinating landscape from which he succeeded in banishing the irregular forms of plants. As a painter proud of his genius, he savored the intoxicating monotony of metal, marble, and water. Not a "natural" landscape, but one determined by architecture, it is an infinite palace, a "Babel" tower reaching to the heavens, where water is present in cascades falling into golden basins, crystal curtains falling along metal walls. Instead of trees, there are columns surrounding pools where gigantic naiads mirror themselves. Sheets of water between colored piers extend to the bounds of the universe. Great rivers pour from the skies into diamond abysses. An air of magic and myth hangs over the landscape; naiads are drawn from classical myth, the Babel tower from the Bible, the Ganges river personification from India.

The narrator calls himself an "architect" and his world a fairyland; he shaped his world with his own will and tamed an ocean to pass through a jeweled tunnel. Even the color black took on rainbow lightness, and light was crystallized to hold liquid. There was no sun, no exterior source of light—all illumination originated within the miraculous constructions themselves. There was no sound—"All for the eye, nothing for the ears." The words, "A silence of eternity," end the first section and the description of the dream universe.

In the two stanzas of part 2, the poet returns to reality, opening flame-filled eyes on the shack in which the real man must live. Where he was exalted in dream, he is now horrified, his soul full of worries. There is sound in the waking world: A clock strikes noon, and the sky casts shadows on a sad, sleepy world.

Forms and Devices

"Parisian Dream" is extremely clear and simple in form. Its eight-syllable verses move along quickly. They are neither cut nor run on, and the regular rhyme scheme is equally smooth. The first person narrator enters the poem in the first stanza and remains consistent throughout the poem. There are no ambiguities in time; the description of the dream world is entirely in the imperfect tense, which implies a continued or habitual action in the past. Thus, the dream world exists in a past time with no hard and fast boundaries, yet clearly distinct from the waking world of the second section, which is marked by use of two past tense verbs, "I saw . . . and felt." The imperfect tense is also used for the clock and the sky of the outer world, the habitual limits of everyday existence.

In its vocabulary and images, "Parisian Dream" appeals to the visual world, first as a painting, then as architecture. It is a "tableau," a picture, and the elements it evokes are water, gold and metal, precious stones, and crystal and marble, all agents which reflect or prismatically divide light. The color qualities of light are important. Not only is there blue water between green and rose-colored piers, but black is polished, light, rainbow colored. Baudelaire, a lover of pictorial art, uses words to produce a visual illusion. In the waking world of part 2, the sky sends shadows, not light, on the world and the return of sound, in the stroke of noon, is harsh and funereal.

Many terms are borrowed from architecture, an art of pure form, and from its materials and its constructions: staircases, arcades, basins, colonnades, and piers. These constructions are preferred to natural growth; vegetable irregularity is banished and colonnades replace rows of trees. The eye meets the regular swoops and curves of arcades and basins rather than unformed mountains or living beings. Water is architectural form in motion as well as an agent of light; cascades, cataracts, pools, sheets, and ice are all sculpted and tamed by the poet-architect. Unlike "real" water, it is purely, eerily silent.

Within the context of images of light and architectural form, the use of a vocabulary of magic and miracle is striking. Parallel with the objective world of the technical arts is the world of myth, dream, and emotion. The "monotony" of metal, marble, and water is "intoxicating." Naiads are beside the colonnades and pools, waves are magical, and rivers become the divine Ganges. The vision is qualified as a "miracle," "fairyland," "prodigy," and "moving marvel." The use of the first person narrator ensures emotional involvement in a dream world from which life and its irregularities are banished. The use of magical, emotional vocabulary ensures the complication of the mineral landscape with the qualities of human feeling.

Themes and Meanings

Baudelaire's collection of poems, *Flowers of Evil*, explores the dissonance between poetic sensitivity and the realities of life, both in people and in nature. The poet constructs many ideal landscapes, among them the erotic paradise of "Invitation to the Voyage" and the rooftop idyll of "Landscape." Where his visions may include living beings and combine delights of all the senses, "Parisian Dream" is austere and exclusive, lifeless, sunless, soundless.

There is no movement in the dreamscape except water in fountains, rivers, waves, oceans, and cataracts. This water is present in both liquid and crystal states, but not in foggy or obscure forms. There are no "misty skies" or "moist suns," as in "The Invitation to the Voyage." All edges are clear. The eternal rush of water duplicates the effect of stillness; cataracts fall like curtains, unendingly hung on metal walls.

Although the moving waters of the first twelve stanzas are described uniquely in visual terms, it is a shock to realize that they are all soundless, so strong is the habit of associating water in any form with some kind of characteristic sound. The poet announces this silence as a "terrible novelty." Ultimately, the reader hears only the murmur of words as they fall in their pattern of rhythm and rhyme.

It is equally unsettling that the light that flashes from the surfaces of the dream-scape is not sunlight but a "personal fire" from within. Unlike sunlight, this inward illumination casts no shadows. It is all brilliance without darkness. Even black is polished light in rainbow hues, not absence of light. The poet strives to reach a world so intensely personal that, although infinite and eternal, it is wholly controlled and internal. When he returns to the waking world, his eyes are still "full of flame," his own personal fire.

The suppression of the sun is an escape from time and mortality. The return to the waking world, with its harsh noontime shadows, is deathly. "The Clock," the last poem of the "Spleen and Ideal" section of *Flowers of Evil*, develops the theme of the tick of a clock as perpetual *memento mori* or reminder of mortality. In "The Sun," the second of the "Parisian Tableaux," the sun is "cruel" but also a "nourishing father" who "like a poet" descends into the life of cities and ennobles the vilest things. "Parisian Dream" attributes the creative power and illuminating beauty of the sun to the poet, liberated by the magic of sleep from death and shadow.

The world of the dream is also liberated from organic life, "irregular vegetable nature." The sonnet "Beauty," found in the "Spleen et idéal" ("Spleen and Ideal") section of *Flowers of Evil*, evokes the "dream of stone," where timeless, static beauty is given a voice and describes her relation to poets. The love she inspires is "eternal and mute as matter." This "beauty" never laughs or cries but hates movement, an essential quality of life, because it "displaces lines." Here, as in "Parisian Dream," the poet dreams of a mineral world where life is banished and eternal light shines from within the great mirror eyes of beauty itself.

"Parisian Dream" is built upon an essential paradox. In it, the poet plays with his own negation, affirming his power to create a world in which his own poetry is invalid. The poet works with sound, yet his dream world is silent. The dream precedes the poem. Waking, suffering the shock of return to poverty, sound, and time, is the only means by which the poet can capture his dream and fit his vision to a verbal architecture.

Anne W. Sienkewicz

PARISIAN NOCTURNE

Author: Paul Verlaine (1844-1896)
Type of poem: Lyric
First published: 1866, as "Nocturne parisien," in *Poèmes saturniens*; collected in
  Poems, 1961

The Poem

"Parisian Nocturne" is a poem of 106 lines, divided into seven stanzas of unequal
lengths. The title suggests a musical composition, perhaps a peaceful evocation of
Paris by night. Instead, however, one finds a macabre reflection on the winding
progress of the river Seine. This is the thirty-sixth and longest in a collection of forty
poems ostensibly written under the influence of the planet Saturn. In keeping with
the coldly pessimistic title of the collection, "Parisian Nocturne" describes only
negative aspects of the river.

   The poem addresses the Seine (a rhetorical device called apostrophe). The first
stanza (of six lines) serves as a brief introduction, in which the author calls upon the
cold, corpse-laden river to continue its flow through Paris while equally icy thoughts
of the poet flow into the lines which follow.

   In the second, twenty-eight-line stanza, Paul Verlaine describes a catalog of
rivers, all of which possess graceful, musical, or majestic attributes. These rivers
include the Guadalquivir, a chief river in Spain, the Pactolus in Asia Minor, the
Bosporus strait, the Rhine, the French rivers Lignon and Adour, the Nile, the Mississippi, the Euphrates, and, finally, the mysterious, exotic Ganges. Several elements of
the descriptions recall interests of the Romantic movement, which had preceded the
era in which Verlaine lived.

   The third stanza, of twenty lines, contrasts the squalor of the Seine and Paris to
the rivers described in the preceding stanza. The author gradually evokes the night
by describing sunset, the disappearance of swallows and emergence of bats, along
with the emergence of dreamers from "dens in slums." He invites the reader to
experience the hush of evening but also to see it as a time of illicit love and crime.

   In the fourth stanza, of twenty-two lines, Verlaine describes the sudden discordant
music of an organ grinder. This is a surprising nocturne, "desperate" and "shrill."
Verlaine also describes the thoughts evoked in listeners such as himself. Readers are
moved to tears, because the music is a reminder of the longing for harmony. Sight
mingles with sound in a poignant, self-created synthesis of fulfillment.

   In the shorter fifth stanza (of twelve lines), however, the music dies; "dull" night
descends; by gaslight the river becomes "blacker than velvet masks"; happy
thoughts are dispelled in "panic flight" and the persona of the poem is alone with
"Seine, Paris and Night."

   The next-to-last stanza (of fourteen lines) addresses these three as doom-laden,
like the mysterious writing on the wall at Belshazzar's feast in the book of Daniel,
and as "ghastly ghouls." The poet asks by which means it is better for "wretched

man" to die: by darkness, drowning, or in the arms of Paris itself. In any case, humans are all offerings to the river, a mighty "Worm."

The final stanza (of four lines) continues the idea of the ancient river-serpent, flowing indifferently through the town, carrying "cargos of wood, coal and corpses," a much-admired formulation. "Parisian Nocturne" is a despairing poem, conveying the feeling of the helplessness of the individual in the face of implacable forces, represented by the city and the Seine.

Forms and Devices

"Parisian Nocturne" is written in the traditional French poetic units of Alexandrine couplets, with alternating masculine and feminine endings. The Alexandrine line, consisting of twelve syllables, most typically with a caesura, or pause, after the sixth syllable, is not only the most classical unit of French versification but also an apt choice for a poem of this length and narrative weight.

"Parisian Nocturne" is thought to be Verlaine's earliest extant poem, written not only while he was at school but actually in the classroom, according to his lifelong friend, Edmond Lepelletier, who kept the much-corrected original until Verlaine prepared the first volume of his poetry. It is understandable that a young poet would use the dominant French verse form. Furthermore, Verlaine was enthused at that time by the Parnassian group of French poets, for whom emotional detachment and formal excellence were positive values.

The complex French rhyme system classifies ends of words according to how many elements in them are identical. The most desirable rhyme is designated as "rich." "Parisian Nocturne" is full of "rich" rhymes. These, too, correspond to the expectation for formal excellence typical of the author's time. More detailed formal aspects of this poem could be considered, such as the use of enjambment, rhetorical devices, vowel choice for sonority, in imitation of the rolling river, and the use of exclamation points to punctuate the surprising turns of the narrative. These are pertinent aspects in considering the poem's effect in French, but translation cannot duplicate them.

The dominant metaphorical qualities of this "tone poem" are those connected to exoticism, music, and death, all attributed to rivers, some also to the sounds of the city. In his use of image, even of resonant phraseology, Verlaine is frankly derivative. For example, the first line in French, "Roule, roule ton flot indolent, morne Seine," is reminiscent of the line in George Gordon, Lord Byron's *Childe Harold's Pilgrimage* (1812-1818, 1819), "Roll on, thou deep and dark-blue Ocean, roll!" (noted by Jacques Henry Bornecque, in *Les poèmes saturniens de Paul Verlaine*, 1952). The evocation of the world's rivers, too, is replete with borrowings from Victor Hugo, Théophile Gautier, François-Auguste-René de Chateaubriand, and others.

Adjectives such as "icy" and "putrid," metaphors such as "Worm" and "serpent," as well as the reiteration of the word "corpses" serve to create a sense of despair in the reader. This feeling is reinforced by the adding of discordant music, which symbolizes modern life in the crowded city. The piling up of disparate images and negative similes to a crescendo in succeeding verses is a further musical effect. The last four lines imitate the river itself, because the use of repetition, where the second and third lines flow into the last line, carries the reader, as the words describe, to unity with the river, where he or she becomes one of the cargo items with which the poem so callously ends.

Themes and Meanings

"Parisian Nocturne" is an impressionistic poetic journey through the city of Paris and, by extension, through life, to its inevitable conclusion in anonymous death. The river serves to remind the poet of unpleasant verities concerning the life of each person as well as life in Verlaine's century and in this particular European city.

The poem has a paradoxical sense of concrete times of day, such as afternoon and evening, in identifiable parts of Paris, such as the Pont de la Cité and Notre-Dame (stanza 3), while it also universalizes these experiences to encompass the times and places of each reader's individual life.

The discordant song of the organ grinder, heard at night, although it would not be appreciated by a real musician, such as the composer Gioacchino Antonio Rossini (stanza 4), serves the poet again as a summarizing device. He describes the evocation of each person's dearest hope for harmony and for the benediction "of setting suns," which symbolize a happy ending to one's life. In the dream state, the reader or poet is capable of creating a beautiful "mingling" of visual and auditory impressions with inner recollection to make a positive whole, one that would transform death into a fulfillment.

The poet destroys, however, the synesthesia and the dream called forth, as in the Romantic period, by sensory stimulation, even if it is the discordant, populist, gypsy stimulus of street music. This process is analogous to the rejection of the Romantic worldview by the nineteenth century, where realism soon passed over into a naturalism emphasizing the ugly aspects of human experience.

Verlaine ends the poem (in the last three stanzas) with loneliness, fear, lack of consolation, and intimations of suicide. The fact that he mentions the implications of the Bible and shows Orestes without his consoling sister, serves to remind the reader of the dual heritage, Greek and biblical, of Western culture. That heritage, the poem implies, is negated by the awful reality of the soulless material world, represented here by the city and the river.

The last four lines give a dull, hopeless impression. The double use of the word "agèd," particularly, takes the reader to a world outside historical time, the world after Eden, lost because of the treacherous "serpent," which still snatches people back from Paradise, as reality snatches them from the dream of harmony, and deposits them, lifeless and unredeemed, among the flotsam carried by forces they cannot overcome.

"Parisian Nocturne" is a dramatic first poem for Verlaine, whose sensibility Clive Scott describes as "a floating sensibility, operating in the ill-defined space between sentiment and sensation, between self-surrender and anxious interrogation of the physical world" (*The Riches of Rhyme: Studies in French Verse*, 1988). In "Parisian Nocturne," Verlaine used the experience of the modern city-dweller to describe the wretchedness of the human condition.

Erlis Glass

A PART OF SPEECH

Author: Joseph Brodsky (1940-   )
Type of poem: Poetic sequence
First published: 1977, as "Chast' rechi," in *Chast' rechi: Stikhotvoreniya
1972-1976*; collected in *A Part of Speech*, 1980

The Poem

Joseph Brodsky's sequence comprises fifteen sections, each twelve lines in length
(with the single exception of section three, which is sixteen lines). The sections are
written in accordance with formal metrics and employ a variety of rhyme schemes
and sound patterns to underscore the thematic concerns. Alternating between a first-
person singular and a more impersonal, omniscient voice, the individual poems create a collage of perspectives around the central themes of time, exile, and alienation.

The title, "A Part of Speech," indicates two of the sequence's primary concerns.
One is the sense of an incomplete and fragmented vision arising from the condition
of displacement, loss and alienation; the second concern relates directly to the notion of language as a continuum and the poet's sense of his partial voice, of the
difficulties inherent in speech and expression under these conditions.

The first section introduces the speaker's biographical situation and its relation to
poetic expression. The section becomes an "ars poetica," an explanation of his poetics, and an invocation to the muse, tying the nature of his temporal and spatial
condition to language and creativity itself. Of particular interest is the stress on
sound—the importance of articulation (voice) and the emphasis placed on reception
(hearing), the two components necessary for successful speech and poetry.

Section 2 begins the process of elaboration, picking up on the initial geographic
and climatic references. Here, the effects of the climate, the power of bitter cold to
destroy and the desire it engenders for warmth and inclusion, become analogies for
the speaker's psychological and political situation. Brodsky is mapping the condition of a psyche at odds with its environment, grappling with the displacements of
time and space, and using the structures of the language itself to embody this reality.

The next section provides a more extreme example, linking exile and loss to linguistic indeterminacies and mental instability. Here, language cannot fix meanings
and memory cannot reconstruct or revive a lost reality. The fourth section develops
on this idea of indeterminacy and presents an exploration of the fallibility of observation. This examination of how reality is shaped by the observer plays on the concept of altered perspectives by introducing images of distorted vision, of reading and
misreading.

Section 5 shifts the focus back toward the poet-seer, illustrating how he recognizes (re-thinks, or re-formulates) images of nature, finding in their naturally determined situations parallels for historical and political determinisms. By doing so, he
is moving outside these temporal spheres and shaping experience in accordance with
his muse—language.

The next section provides another perspective on consciousness with its illustration of recollection. A glimpse of dawn stimulates memories of a childhood classroom, boredom and ennui—of an early alienation. Section 7 is constructed around the opposite trait: forgetfulness. In this poem, the speaker re-creates memories of a northern village to replace the emptiness of a lost love.

The eighth section expands the theme of memory by relating a prosperous postwar Munich and the realities of its immediate past. The images of present material comfort and sensual enjoyment are ironically undercut by resonances from the imperial and Fascist past. The poet is indicting the failure of memory to protect man from tyrannies. The association of this forgetfulness with summer, a time of freedom and pleasure, creates an ironic perspective on the complacencies of the West—an image reiterated in the final poem of the sequence.

The next two sections shift toward a more pastoral vision, where the poet links the natural images of order and continuity. In both instances this entails the recognition of balances and limitations—in section 9, between time and space, and in section 10, between the forces of life and death. Under these strictures, in the context of an eternal present, connection with the Other seems possible.

Sections 11 and 12 continue this exploration of natural imagery in relation to the role of the artist. Both postulate the idea of completion, the added dimension of language. Section 11, by drawing on Immanuel Kant's notion of synthetic judgment, suggests a potential for meaning and a hope of futurity. The poet, in the following section, comes to embody this synthesis by assuming a hybrid form, that of the centaur.

The last three sections of "A Part of Speech" draw together elements of the speaker's alienated condition, the potential offered by vision and language, and a warning about the dangers of freedom. Against the silence of repression, the erosion of meaning and the assault upon language, Brodsky sets the poet's part: "his spoken part . . . a part of speech." The last poems function as warnings against the seductions of freedom, the assault upon memory and the dulling of vision inherent in the endless summer days of the West.

Forms and Devices

One of the most striking features of Brodsky's work is his unstinting allegiance to formalism. He understands traditional metrics to be one of the greatest challenges for a poet, the discipline of creating a vibrant, unpredictable expression within the strictures of strict metrical forms. Commenting on the formal verse of Anna Akhmatova, a Russian poet he very much admires, Brodsky suggests she avoided the comic or redundant echo of the metrics by a "collage-like diversification of the content." The meter, set against this wealth of seemingly unrelated material, acts as a "common denominator" binding them together, becoming a part of the act of speech, the means of articulation. His emulation of this practice can be observed even in the translated version of "A Part of Speech," in how the rhyme scheme works in tandem with the emotional or intellectual flow of the verses, how the qualities of assonance and alliteration highlight or comment on the material. As he suggests in the first section, his verse was formed by the "zinc-gray breakers that always marched on/ in twos. Hence all rhymes, hence that wan flat voice/ that ripples between them." This respect for the lineage and traditions of poetry permeates all of Brodsky's poetics, both in terms of his use of formal metrics and in his intertextual references—for example, the use of elements from Nikolai Gogol's story "Diary of a Madman" in section 3, or an oblique reference to Robert Lowell at the beginning of section 10.

A more specific example of Brodsky's attention to form can be found in a brief examination of section three. Here, the poet employs a variety of devices to delineate the psychological turmoil of the speaker; whether it is the passionate anguish of the lover, the despair of the exile, or the complexities of an artist's relation to his muse. Aside from its deviation from the standard lengths of the sections, this is also the only poem to adopt an epistolary form, playing on the associations of letter-writing with direct personal address. But these expectations are undercut by an onslaught of indeterminacies: the place is nowhere, the addressee is irrelevant, and the date uncertain. The lack of punctuation, coupled with the complicated clausal structure of the syntax, gives this poem a sense of breathlessness and creates a stream-of-consciousness effect that fits perfectly with the subject matter of passion, loss, and madness. A further accent to the heightened emotion of the speaker is the progressively stronger nature of the rhymes, becoming more pronounced as the tension of the poem builds. The cloistered, confined perspective of the speaker finds its mirror image in the bracketing of individual lines by repetition, assonance and alliteration. The sound quality of the verse is extremely important to Brodsky, remarking as he has that "sound . . . is the seat of time in the poem, a background against which its content acquires a stereoscopic quality." The immediacy of the connection between subject and self, the image of the double so central to the poem, is reflected in these echoes, in the very textures of the verse. Throughout the sequence Brodsky brings the metrical voice of the poetry into play.

Themes and Meanings

"A Part of Speech" re-creates the condition of a fragmented consciousness, of loss and alienation, by exploring the mind grappling with apparently irreconcilable aspects of time and space. The lightning shifts between past and present, memory and projection, here and nowhere, compress a universe of possibility into the sequence. At the same time, the strong undercurrents of the forms and meters suggest the healing potential of the poetic vision and the myriad resources of language. What he hopes to reflect is his sense of "the graspable degree of arbitrariness" in the relation of language and experience. Two main elements that Brodsky brings together are the psychological condition of exile, reflected in feelings of loss, anger, displacement and isolation, and the exile's relation to language and expression, how language itself forms and informs the nature of his condition.

One of the central concerns of the sequence is its ability to convey the sense of a mind searching for a firm vantage from which to view experience. As he remarks in the opening essay of *Less Than One: Selected Essays* (1986), relating the act of memory and writing: "Memory . . . directs our movements, including migration. . . . [T]here is something clearly atavistic in the very process of recollection, if only because such a process never is linear. . . . [I]t coils, recoils, digresses to all sides . . . so should one's narrative." In keeping with this, the movements of "A Part of Speech" are forward and back in time, unsettled and shifting between the present, the recent past, millennia and the future; similarly, the spatial dimension of the individual poems keeps changing, some set in extremely confined areas, others covering great sweeps of space in a few lines. The sequence, although read in a consecutive fashion, builds on a non-linear process that captures in language the speaker's attempt to "manage the meaninglessness of existence . . . to domesticate the reprehensible infinity by inhabiting it with familiar shadows."

One way Brodsky accentuates the nature of the fragmented experience is his construction of the sequence itself. Each section is geared to providing a part of experience, one element connected through language with the others, remaining independent yet creating resonances. For example, the image of the North in section 2 introduces ideas of inclusion and exclusion, of an isolating wasteland, and of a stifling or burial. Later poems return to these images to elaborate or provide another context for them. Section 6, for example, picks up the winter image and links it to the suffocating dreariness of a school classroom. Section 7 translates the wasteland into a remembrance of rural poverty and isolation. Section 8 and the last poem reverse the winter image to summer and redefine the wasteland in the context of political and material freedoms. The onset of time, the limitations of mind, memory and language, all contribute to this sense of unavoidable fragmentation. As he remarks in section 14: "What gets left of a man amounts/ to a part. To his spoken part. To a part of speech." The method of the sequence is to gather together diverse parts and, using the synthetic and associative processes of the poetic imagination, fashion that part of speech.

James Panabaker

PASSAGE TO INDIA

Author: Walt Whitman (1819-1892)
Type of poem: Lyric
First published: 1871, in *Passage to India*; collected in *Leaves of Grass*, 1876

The Poem

"Passage to India" was first published in 1871 as the title piece in a book of seventy-five poems (twenty-three of them new) that were subsequently incorporated into the 1876 edition of *Leaves of Grass* as a separately paginated supplement. Slightly revised, the poem became an integral part of *Leaves of Grass* in 1881 despite Walt Whitman's having conceived "Passage to India" as well as the poems he planned to add to it as marking a new and quite different direction. *Leaves of Grass*, he contended, was the song of "the Body and Existence"; "Passage to India" was to be the song of "the unseen Soul," as the "ardent and fully appointed Personality" that had been the subject of the earlier collection entered "the sphere of the restless gravitation of Spiritual Law." The decision to incorporate the later intention into the earlier work reflects Whitman's willingness to expand, revise, and even reshape *Leaves of Grass* over the years. That decision also reflects, for all the overt optimism of "Passage to India," the poet's dissatisfaction as the United States, the nation that he believed was itself the greatest poem, failed to live up to his expectations and failed as well to accept him as "affectionately" as he had accepted it. (Any lingering hopes he still had to make *Passage to India* the successor to and equal of *Leaves of Grass* were put to rest by the stroke and partial paralysis he suffered in 1873.)

In its final form, "Passage to India" is a 255-line poem in nine sections, parts of which Whitman conceived as separate, shorter works. This "song," or "chant," of "free speculations and ideal escapades" begins by pointing to three recent engineering feats: the laying of the transatlantic telegraph cable in 1866, the joining of the Union Pacific and Central Pacific to form the country's first transcontinental railway in May, 1869, and the opening of the Suez Canal in November of the same year. Whitman envisions these technological achievements propelling humankind not only ahead into the future but back as well—linking the West with the East, the modern with the ancient, America (and Europe) with India and all that it represented. Whitman sees in the myths and fables of India the very origins of that spiritual quest of which the above achievements are only the most recent manifestations. More than scientific feats, they serve as metaphoric means. As those technological achievements connect the world materially, Whitman's poem connects the world spiritually. The sights seen from the deck of a ship passing through the Suez Canal or from the window of a railway car crossing the American West (lines 43-47, 48-64) please but do not completely satisfy. More than an ordinary observer or traveler, the poem's narrator adopts a wide perspective, unfettered by either time or space. "Resuming all," he becomes engineer, explorer, and time traveler, moving back to Adam and Eve, then ahead through the course of history, paying special homage to the "gigantic, visionary" Columbus, "chief historian" on history's vast panoramic stage.

The passage to India (which Columbus sought and which the narrator now resumes) becomes the voyage of the "repressless soul" to "primal thought," to "reason's early paradise." The speaker's desire to circumnavigate the now metaphorical globe in an effort to return to this Transcendental utopia of intuitive wisdom and poetic creation takes on added urgency in the poem's eighth section. Saying farewell to the weepers, doubters, and deprecators, the narrator sails off over the seas of Time, Space, and Death to a "Thou transcendent,/ Nameless," a human as well as divine "other" that is also the narrator's "actual Me."

At the very thought of this "Thou," — at the very thought of God, Nature, Time, Space, and Death — the "I" shrinks to insignificance, only to grow (like the hero of an American tall tale) as vast as Space itself. The "gigantic, visionary" figure of the poet-explorer-savior (Whitman-Columbus-Christ) emerges only to depart, "bound where mariner has not yet dared to go," to the unmapped shores of the oldest, most impenetrable "enigmas."

Forms and Devices

Much of the cohesiveness and intelligibility of "Passage to India" derives from Whitman's elaboration of the conceit introduced in the poem's title: that of passage or voyage. The poem's greatness stems from a less obvious and more potent source. This is Whitman's artfully artless style. More spoken than written, it is a style at once intense yet diffuse, expansive yet elliptical. Drawing everything into its democratic embrace, it nevertheless tends to blur every "each" into a nearly indistinguishable "all" and seeks to convince the reader by virtue of a logic beyond or perhaps prior to reason. At once ahead of its time and primitive, it sends its "ceaseless" and "repressless" (though "varied") message via an elaborate system of rhetorical devices.

Whitman's style is orphic in form and ecstatic in effect. Parenthetical asides and purely rhetorical questions play their parts; more important are the frequent, urgent exclamations and the apostrophizing of everything from architects, engineers, and explorers to generalized facts, abstract truth, the year itself, the planet Earth ("Rondure"), unspecified "enigmas," and a "Comrade perfect" who may be friend, lover, God, or all three. The repeated apostrophizing is one of several factors that contribute to the poem's cumulative power. The repetition of individual words is another: In section 3, for example, the word "I" is used twenty-one times in only twenty-seven lines. There is also the breathless rush of Whitman's long pseudo-sentences rife with commas and syntactically parallel constructions, including the frequent use of participles to create the odd blending of motion and stasis that is one of the hallmarks of Whitman's Transcendental, oral-oraculor style. Insistent in tone and repetitive in structure, "Passage to India" achieves a nearly liturgical intensity which, like the world it describes, has its own "hidden prophetic intention."

Themes and Meanings

"There is more of me, the essential ultimate me, in ['Passage to India']," Whitman explained to his friend and follower, Horace Traubel, "than in any of the [other] poems. There is no philosophy, consistent or inconsistent, in that poem . . . but the burden of it is evolution . . . the unfolding of cosmic purposes." In addition to underscoring the value the poet himself placed on the poem, Whitman's comment establishes the poles within which the poem operates: the cosmic and the personal.

"Spurning the known" and giving himself over to "unloos'd dreams," the poet (or, more accurately, an anonymous but nevertheless autobiographical narrative "I") attempts to make the "voiceless earth" speak in order to clarify ("eclaircise") God's "inscrutable purpose." As Transcendentalist and as cosmic evolutionist, Whitman takes as his aim something more than Puritan poet John Milton's efforts "to justify the ways of God to men" in the seventeenth century Christian epic *Paradise Lost* (1667, 1674). Neither God's apologist nor His amanuensis, the Whitmanic persona is God's alter ego and democratic equal. His self-appointed task is not so much to justify God's ways as to explore them and to engineer the overcoming of doubt and death through the mystical fusion of time and space, self and other.

Against the poem's great outpouring of cosmic energy and optimistic expectancy runs a strong undercurrent of frustration and disillusionment (or at least disappointment). Because he too has felt—indeed continues to feel—the weight of this "mocking life" and the hunger of the "unsatisfied soul," Whitman longs to give shape and direction to the "restless explorations" of all men and women of all ages as they "grope" their way through life, grappling with their sense of separation from "nature." Not content to play the poet's usual role, Whitman plays the parts of explorer and engineer, prophet and savior (Moses leading others to the Promised Land that he himself could not enter and Christ saving others by sacrificing himself). Above all, Whitman projects himself ahead by looking back to Columbus, praised here as much for the neglect he suffered as for the country he discovered.

An entry in Whitman's notebook on the poem's "spinal idea" helps clarify Columbus' role in "Passage to India": "That the divine efforts of heroes, and their ideas, faithfully lived up to will finally prevail, and be accomplished however long deferred." Having already waited sixteen years for America to accept its own Transcendental role (as envisioned in the 1855 edition of *Leaves of Grass*) and to acknowledge the author as its bard, Whitman seems to have grown doubtful regarding the outcome. In "Prayer of Columbus," published three years later, after Whitman had suffered a stroke, the title figure, now depicted longing for death, is unsure whether his dream of future fame and vindication is the vision of a prophet or the raving of a madman. A similar though clearly more muted self-doubt propels "Passage to India" away from the pains and disappointments Whitman actually suffered and toward cosmic evolution, universal brotherhood, and a "Comrade perfect" who patiently waits, listens, and understands—the poem's ideal reader, or perhaps only its idealized, self-projecting author.

Robert A. Morace

THE PASSIONATE SHEPHERD TO HIS LOVE

Author: Christopher Marlowe (1564-1593)
Type of poem: Lyric
First published: 1599, in *The Passionate Pilgrim*

The Poem

"The Passionate Shepherd to His Love" is a love poem that contains six quatrains of rhyming couplets in iambic tetrameter. In marked contrast to Christopher Marlowe's plays about heroes and kings, this lyric poem purports to be the words of a shepherd speaking to his beloved. Its simple, musical language and fanciful imagery create an idyll of innocent love. The version of the poem that was printed in 1599 contained four stanzas attributed to William Shakespeare; the poem was printed again in 1600, in *Englands Helicon*, with only the six stanzas attributed to Marlowe.

In this poem, the shepherd persona speaks to his beloved, evoking "all the pleasures" of a peaceful, springtime nature. He promises her the delights of nature and his courtly attention. The first quatrain is the invitation to "Come live with me and be my love." Next, the speaker describes the pleasant natural setting in which he plans that they will live. Their life will be one of leisure; they will "sit upon the rocks," watch the shepherds, and listen to the birds.

The shepherd does not refer to the cold winter, when herding sheep becomes difficult. He does not suggest that his work requires effort or that he may need to go off into the hills away from his beloved to herd his flock. Instead, he imagines their life together as a game enjoyed in an eternal spring. He promises to make clothes and furnishings for his beloved from nature's abundant harvest: wool gowns from the sheep, beds and caps of flowers, dresses embroidered with leaves. Even the other shepherds seem to be there only to entertain the beloved, to "dance and sing/ for thy delight." The poem ends by summing up the "delights" of the pastoral idyll and repeating the opening invitation.

Forms and Devices

Marlowe was a university-educated dramatist who might have rivaled William Shakespeare had he lived longer. His plays probed the tangled passions of heroism, ambition, and power. He led an active theatrical life and frequented taverns: Indeed, he met his death at the age of twenty-nine in a tavern brawl. Yet he chose to write this poem in a shepherd's voice, using a pastoral convention that was frequently employed by Elizabethan poets. The pastoral tradition of courtly love poetry idealized the beloved and ennobled the lovers, using idyllic country settings and featuring shepherds as models of natural, unspoiled virtue.

The poem's images are all drawn from the kind, springtime nature of the pastoral tradition and from music. This imagery creates a gentle fantasy of eternal spring. The poem appeals to almost all the senses — sight, sound, smell, and touch — as the speaker tells his love that they will watch "shepherds feed their flocks" and listen to birds singing madrigals (polyphonic melodies). He promises to make beds of roses, and clothing of flowers and wool for his beloved. Images of "shallow rivers," "melodious birds," "roses," "pretty lambs," and "ivy buds" evoke a nature that is pure, simple, blooming, and kind to innocent creatures.

To complement the pastoral imagery, the poem blends alliteration, rhythm, rhyme, and other sound patterns to create a songlike lyric. The labial *l* sound is repeated in words such as "live," "love," "all," "hills," "shallow," "flocks," "falls," and "myrtle." The sibilant *s* recurs in "Seeing the shepherds feed their flocks," in "shallow rivers," "roses," "sing," and "swains." The *m* sound appears in "mountain," "melodious," "madrigals," "myrtle," "lambs," and "amber." This combination of sounds creates a soft, harmonious, gentle tone.

The poem is written in regular four-line stanzas with rhyming couplets. Most of the rhyming words are words of one syllable, and most of the lines are end stopped, thus emphasizing the rhyming words and the rhythm of the poem. The rhymes include such appealing words as "love" (repeated three times), "roses," "flocks," "fields," "sing," and "morning." There are frequent internal rhymes and partial rhymes in words such as lambs/amber, may/swains, seeing/feed, and finest/lined. The meter is iambic tetrameter with little variation. All these factors—short, regular lines, repeated simple rhymes, frequent internal rhymes and partial rhymes, and alliterative patterns—turn the poem into a song, with a melodious appeal that echoes the music of nature that it describes; the poem has been set to music by several different composers.

Themes and Meanings

Marlowe's "The Passionate Shepherd to His Love" is a celebration of youth, innocence, love, and poetry. The poem participates in an ongoing tradition of lyrical love poetry. It casts the lovers as shepherds and shepherdesses who are at home in a beneficent natural setting. According to the conventions of pastoral poetry (which began with the Greek poet Theocritus in the third century B.C.), shepherds are uncorrupted and attuned to the world of nature. Such pastoral poems are the work of urban poets who idealize the simplicity, harmony, and peace of the shepherd's life.

This idealized vision has often been subjected to satire. Sir Walter Raleigh, a contemporary of Marlowe, wrote "The Nymph's Reply to the Passionate Shepherd," in which the young woman replies somewhat cynically. The third stanza reads:

> Thy gown, thy shoes, thy beds of roses,
> Thy cap, thy kirtle, and thy posies;
> Soon break, soon wither, soon forgotten,
> In folly ripe, in reason rotten.

Three centuries later, in 1935, responding to the economic devastation of the Depression, C. Day Lewis wrote, "Come, live with me and be my love":

Care on thy maiden brow shall put
A wreath of wrinkles, and thy foot
Be shod with pain: not silken dress
But toil shall tire thy loveliness.

The many parodies of "The Passionate Shepherd to His Love" render a kind of tribute to its enduring vitality and power.

Marlowe's poem is an outstanding example of the pastoral lyric tradition. It succeeds because of its musical quality, its direct, conversational language, and its freshness of imagery and tone. It continues to be widely anthologized.

Karen F. Stein

IL PENSEROSO

Author: John Milton (1608-1674)
Type of poem: Pastoral
First published: 1645, in *Poems of Mr. John Milton*

The Poem

The poem stands as the companion piece to "L'Allegro," using the same non-stanzaic tetrameter form; at 176 lines, it is twenty-four lines longer than its companion. The title, meaning "the thinker" or "the contemplative man," suggests its opposition to its companion piece. The poem expresses the joys of the solitary man walking abroad during the evening, sitting studying at night in the midst of quiet woodlands, or finding pleasure in tragic and heroic literature and in mystic churches.

The poem's opening rejects mirth as delusion and triviality. Instead, the poet welcomes the goddess Melancholy. He gives her a more original and much older genealogy than that given to Euphrosyne in "L'Allegro," seeing her as daughter of the pre-Olympian deity Hestia (John Milton uses the Roman form of Vesta), goddess of sacred and domestic fire, whom he makes wife and daughter of Saturn. Hesiod had made her the eternally virgin daughter of Chronos and Rhea; Milton transfers her virginity to her daughter. As at her conception, Melancholy remains associated with evening and "secret shades." Her traditional blackness is, paradoxically, her intense brightness and is as beautiful as that of Cassiopeia, the Ethiopian queen who was transformed into a constellation.

He invites her to come to him, together with Peace and Quiet, rather vague personifications, and especially with "the cherub Contemplation," in a silence broken only by the nightingale's song. None of the country's sounds or society is for him; he would prefer to wander solitary in the moonlight through woods and meadows or walk near the seashore. If the weather is inclement, he would happily study through the night. His chosen reading is either ancient volumes of hermetic (or secret) wisdom, Greek and more recent tragedy, or epic poetry. He mentions Geoffrey Chaucer, Torquato Tasso, and Edmund Spenser in particular. Unlike the persona of "L'Allegro," he is not interested in seeing the drama live: He wants it to inspire him imaginatively, to transport him as if Orpheus himself were to sing to him.

Eventually he sees the morning come, and—unlike the morning of the companion piece—it conforms to his mood: It is cloudy, with blustery showers. If the sun breaks through, he would prefer to walk in the forest, listening to the murmuring of the streams, perhaps falling asleep on their banks. On waking, he wishes to hear the mysterious music of the nature spirits of the woodland. Finally, as he looks forward in his life, he would like to retire to "the studious Cloysters pale" of a college or church and be overwhelmed with the beauty of the ritual and the music of the organ. Eventually, through such study and perception of beauty, he would wish to become a prophetic figure. If Melancholy can give all this to him, he will follow her.

Forms and Devices

Most readers will read this poem after reading "L'Allegro." Attention is thus focused necessarily on the two poems' parallel structures and on the differences to be found at each level. Clearly, one of the parallel structures is the opening: ten lines of alternating iambic trimeter and pentameter. In rejecting Mirth, he sets up a parody figure, just as in "L'Allegro" a parody figure of Melancholy is set up only to be mocked and rejected.

The verse form also uses a parallel structure, with rhyming couplets of iambic tetrameter; however, the rhythm of the poem is completely different. In the difference, one may see a clear indication of the young Milton's very mature poetic technique and control (already seen in the even earlier "On the Morning of Christ's Nativity"). The rhythmic differences are established by a slightly longer line; by more clustering of stressed syllables and consonants, as in "Thy rapt soul sitting in thine eyes"; and by a preference for long vowel sounds, especially those with a darker coloring. Apart from these differences, the overall sense and tone determine the rhythm. Milton has taken a verse form which, in couplets especially, can sound very trivial, and given it a solemn and stately movement that becomes almost trancelike toward the end.

At the level of content, the structures reverse those of "L'Allegro." That poem goes from morning until late evening, this from the late evening until morning. The invocation to the goddess, together with her companions, closely parallels the other poem, although Milton expands this section considerably. He seems much more interested in the figure of Melancholy than in that of Euphrosyne. The nightingale's song is evoked rather than the lark's; the moon, rather than the sun, is "riding neer her highest noon"; and instead of the "Towers and Battlements" of the idyllic landscape, he prefers "some high lonely Towr" as a place of study. Types of literature are contrasted, as are types of music; the story of Orpheus is noble, a source of tragic beauty that moves one to tears. The morning must not be "trickt and frounc't" for good hunting weather but should suit his melancholy. References continue throughout to shade — as "comly Cloud," "twilight groves," "close covert," and "hide" — in language that John Keats was later to make his own.

The final twenty lines, however, go beyond the structure of "L'Allegro," as the speaker sees himself listening to the church service. The poem expands toward its conclusion and finishes with the climactic "To something like Prophetic strain." The poet's real engagement with his subject matter is perhaps sensed here; the earlier desire for the unfolding worlds of philosophy becomes a total sensory and spiritual experience of rapture to "bring all heav'n before mine eyes."

Themes and Meanings

Any attempt to understand "L'Allegro" and "Il Penseroso" as a pair does not exhaust the readings that "Il Penseroso" is able to generate in itself. This is largely attributable to the thematic complexity surrounding the idea of melancholy, a complexity not found in discussing mirth. Renaissance literature was profoundly interested in the subject: *The Anatomy of Melancholy* (1621) by Robert Burton had recently been published; William Shakespeare's *Hamlet* (1602) and *Timon of Athens* (c. 1607-1608) are both dramatic studies in the subject, as were many Jacobean plays. The melancholic person was seen ambiguously as a killjoy (in comedy), a depressive, and a scholar, and as having a source of wisdom denied to others. The interest in melancholy was partly an extension of medieval psychology and physiology, based on the notion of the humors, but it partly arose from a cultural mood of confusion and insecurity.

Modern readers are tempted to read into the poem the Romantic delineation of melancholy, expressed by such poets as Samuel Taylor Coleridge, Keats, and Alfred, Lord Tennyson. Keats's version seems the closest to that of "Il Penseroso," with its depiction of moonlit night, woods, streams, cloud, shade, and visions of the sublime. Thus, the poem could be read (somewhat anachronistically) as a Romantic mood poem: searching for intensity of experience, reaching beyond normative states of consciousness into ecstasy or sublimity, and thus grasping truths and revelation not available otherwise. Yet "mood" seems too weak a word here (although it would do for "L'Allegro"); one is driven to a deeper reading that, while retaining such Romantic elements, does so by virtue of its Neoplatonism.

The "spirit of Plato" is invoked in line 89 to unfold the regions forsaken by the soul in its descent into the human body at birth. The "extasies" aroused by the organ music can be seen as a parallel attempt to reach back into this Platonic state of original perfection. The hermetic wisdom to which he refers can be loosely linked to Neoplatonic philosophy. The tower that he mentions is a Neoplatonic symbol of the soul seeking divine wisdom—a symbol that the Irish poet William Butler Yeats was later to use literally. Renaissance literature in England, as elsewhere, tended to embrace Plato as part of its rejection of medieval Aristotelianism. John Milton's poetry, like Andrew Marvell's, is explicitly Platonic at times, especially in the masque *Comus* (1637). It is this tradition that Romanticism continued.

The way of melancholy is thus the only way possible to reach that higher and older wisdom denied most humans, for it is the way of contemplation. The genealogy of Melancholy also suggests this: It is a much more ancient genealogy than that given to Mirth, who must content herself with a post-Olympian birth. Saturn is the presiding star for the melancholic. Saturn is the oldest divinity, predating Zeus and the Olympians, and thus he enshrines the most ancient knowledge—a point that Keats struggled to make in *Hyperion* (1820). Thus the poet, in choosing melancholy, chooses to be the poet-philosopher of Platonic tradition and, even more powerfully, the poet-prophet, a role (already envisaged in "On the Morning of Christ's Nativity") which would give Milton's religious faith full expression.

David Barratt

THE PERFUME

Author: John Donne (1572-1631)
Type of poem: Dramatic monologue
First published: 1633, in *Poems by J. D.: With Elegies on the Authors Death*

The Poem

Although designated an elegy in its original title, "The Perfume" is really better considered a seventy-two-line Renaissance imitation of a classical form. John Donne called it an elegy because he composed it in closed couplets, consecutive lines of end-stopped iambic pentameter, a verse pattern that roughly corresponds to the Latin *elegia*. He used the same pattern for his satires, but unlike those, this is addressed to a particular lover, as a commentary on their relationship: The two lovers are being separated by the girl's parents, and this poem is written after the two had been caught together.

The poem is in two parts: The first part details the lovers' attempts to avoid the parents' vigilance; the second investigates the properties of perfume, the agent that gave them away. The speaker begins by complaining that ever since their detection, her father has blamed him for all her escapades. Still, despite the father's close supervision and his threats (even to cast her out of the will), they usually have been successful in their deceit. They even have managed to escape the scrutiny of her mother, ancient in the lore of female wiles. The girl's parents bribed her brothers and sisters to spy on them, but to no avail. The couple also managed to elude the serving man who was commissioned to shadow her. One thing alone betrayed them: They were smelled out by the perfume he was wearing.

To be betrayed by a fragrance was ironic and unjust. Had it been an evil odor, her father never would have noticed it, assuming that it was merely his feet or breath. Just as everyone becomes suspicious of things not native to his or her environment, though, so her father immediately detected something that smelled good. Notwithstanding all his precautions with all other possible giveaways, the lover forgot the one thing that would at once proceed from and be traced back to him.

The speaker proceeds to revile perfume. Compounded of the excretions of plants and animals, it is, like cosmetics, used to disguise the real physical state of the user. Prostitutes concealed infections with it and thus spread them through the population. When men used it, they ran the risk of being labeled effeminate. It was treasured only by courtiers and placeseekers, those who dealt primarily with the insubstantial and the apparent rather than the real. The use of perfume as incense and burnt offerings offers little evidence of intrinsic excellence; the gods simply are flattered by the act of sacrifice.

Furthermore, all perfumes are blended, suggesting that the individual ingredients, taken separately, are offensive. How can a health-giving whole be made out of unwholesome parts, though? Even if one concedes that perfumes are intrinsically good, they vanish, so that they are not good for long. The speaker offers to donate all of his perfumes as embalming fluids for her father—and then suddenly realizes that there is hope of his death, for in noticing a scent he is giving signs of erratic behavior, perhaps a sign of impending collapse.

Forms and Devices

The principal device used by Donne in this poem is the Metaphysical conceit, a kind of forced metaphor joining two terms by exploiting an otherwise obscure relationship that turns out unexpectedly to be illuminating, often on different levels of meaning. In many of his poems, Donne uses this technique to fuse widely separated orders of experience, for example, by linking the sacred with the profane. Here he simply is demonstrating wit, the kind of intellectual and imaginative agility highly prized in fashionable Elizabethan-Jacobean circles. On the simplest level, it is merely clever wordplay, the kind reflected in puns; but with Donne, it is usually much more sophisticated, involving irony, multiple ambiguity, and paradox.

This device first appears in "The Perfume" when the writer refers to his lover's father as "hydroptique," referring simultaneously to bloated, swollen, dropsical; unsatisfied, like an unsaturated sponge; alcoholic; and suspicious, not easily satisfied. The first and third meanings then are reinforced by his "glazed eyes," which glare "as though he came to kill a Cockatrice." This is a fabulous monster with a death-dealing glance; supposedly the glazed eyes will like a mirror reflect the deadly look back to its source. In a similar vein, her mother is described as "immortal" because she spends so much time in bed that she might as well be dead, but resolutely refuses to die. She also proves immortal in her encyclopedic knowledge of female deviousness, which she tests by "sorceries" that suggest she really is a witch.

Donne also uses more conventional devices, especially through the central part of the poem. A significant one is hyperbole, not usually considered part of Donne's repertoire. Hyperbole appears in "the grim eight-foot-high iron-bound serving-man," who appears to be the Colossus of Rhodes to the less formidable suitor, but who will not really be the worst punishment of hell. Donne also employs synesthesia, or the representation of one sense by another: The traitorous "loud" perfume "cryed" at the father's nose; and the "opprest" shoes—because they both are walked on and muffled—are rendered "dumbe and speechlesse." He even anticipates modern marketing strategy and twentieth century taste in coining the phrase "bitter sweet."

Donne returns to more complex figures, especially paradox, toward the end of the poem. The perfume, for example, has at once "fled unto him, and staid with me." Deceived by it into confusing the sweet-smelling with the wholesome, the "seely Amorous"—where "seely" means simultaneously silly, innocent, and gullible—finds death where he should find life; he "suckes his death/ by drawing in a leprous harlots breath." At court, "things that seem, exceed substantiall"—appearance, pretense, and gesture count more than competent performance.

A series of paradoxes ends the poem. The gods accepted burnt offerings simply because they were offerings; they were indifferent to smells, as gods should be.

Perfumes defy logic: A combination of independently offensive scents should not be sweet smelling. Their cost exceeds the value of the benefit they provide. Finally, the lover voices a paradoxical hope: Perhaps the perfume that undid him will be the agent of the father's death.

Themes and Meanings

The dramatic situation Donne chooses here, that of young lovers separated by protective parents, is easy for most readers to identify with, as are the emotions of the male persona. The young lovers embody the urge to generation, fertility, and the hope of the future. Opposed to them is the old-fashioned, obsolete, repressive world of the parents, dedicated to maintaining order and controlling the rate of change. Since parents basically attempt to preserve the past and prevent change, they furiously work to keep things the way they are. Looking only ahead, the lovers in no way can see through their parents' eyes. In fact, the parents become foreign, alien, even monstrous.

This accounts for the hostility of tone and the distorted characterization of the parents: the hydroptique father and immortal mother. Yet it is far short of being rancorous. In fact, the focus on witty phrasing and verbal dexterity mutes the hostility, diverting it toward playfulness. This competition between generations is far from final or deadly. Although it is waged with intensity and urgency on both sides, some of the apparent seriousness merely is assumed.

The recognition that humor tempers intensity is the central focus of the poem. Nothing is quite as it seems here. The contest is only semiserious. When the lover teases about the old lady's refusal to die, or when he breaks off the poem at the end with the abrupt "What? Will hee die?," he actually is not contemplating their death. He is merely voicing the lover's final consolation: The old man and woman cannot live forever. Yet those deaths are in the background of the action; in fact, they create much of the tension in this situation because he will die. The older generation must give way, if only at death. Normally, and more beneficially, it occurs earlier. Furthermore, easing the transition benefits both generations, hence the function of humor here. Humor lubricates transitions.

At the core of the poem, the lover declares his commitment to his mistress, despite the temporary setback of his discovery and ejection. By rallying her spirits and expressing his antagonism, he indicates his intention to stay the course, regardless of the opposition he must overcome. He is confirming the pact they have made already. His humor also cements and reinforces his decision. He shows his recognition that he occupies the favored position. He can afford to wait, and thus he can afford to make fun. In this poem, Donne makes splendid fun.

James Livingston

PETER QUINCE AT THE CLAVIER

Author: Wallace Stevens (1879-1955)
Type of poem: Lyric
First published: 1915; collected in *Harmonium*, 1923

The Poem

"Peter Quince at the Clavier" is made up of four lyrics of differing formal properties, and through them one senses that the poem has "movements," as a musical
composition often does. As in a sonata, the distinct parts involve changes of mood,
tempo, and emphasis. This is one of the best-loved and most often recited poems of
Wallace Stevens' long career, perhaps because it handles, both playfully and seriously, ideas about art that are as suggestive as John Keats's famous "Beauty is truth,
truth beauty—that is all/ Ye know on earth, and all ye need to know."

In William Shakespeare's *A Midsummer Night's Dream* (c. 1595-1596), Peter
Quince is a comic character—an over-achieving, self-conscious, aspiring director of
the stage who brings his unskilled actors into the woods to rehearse a short play for
the Duke and Duchess' impending nuptials. In Stevens' poem, the "Peter Quince"
speaker is a serious thinker on the relationship between music and feeling, beauty
and desire. To make his point, Quince ventures into an unusual account of Susanna
and the elders, a story of beauty and lust in the Old Testament Apocrypha. In the
apocryphal account, Susanna fails to be seduced by court officials who spy upon her
bathing; in their outrage, they try her as an adultress and she is put to death. In
Stevens' account, the violence is only suggested. He places the emphasis on music
and beauty. The speaker, in an unusual way, associates himself with the elders. Like
those who lusted for Susanna, he says, he sits "here in this room, desiring you"—
his beloved in part I.

In part II, the reader is taken into Susanna's point of view by a free-verse song in
which Susanna, bathing, hears music and senses a unity in everything around her.
Only the last two lines of her song hint at the cruel authority about to destroy her
complete accord. In the five tightly rhymed couplets of part III, the poem shifts to
the point of view of Susanna's weak-willed attendants, who arrive too late to help
their mistress. By the time they respond, she has already been accused by the noble-
men. Susanna is abandoned to her fate.

The last part (IV) takes a tremendous jump from the elliptical nature of the
Susanna narrative to the deeply reflective and almost philosophical tone of the ending. The sixteen lines of this self-contained poem are rhymed and have the tight,
rhymed argument and reasoned logic of a sonnet. The difficulty in the argument has
somewhat to do with a conundrum: Beauty is momentary in our minds, while in the
physical body it is immortal. One would have expected the poet to say just the
opposite—that beauty is immortal in the mind and merely fleeting in the flesh.
Thus, the poem carries the burden of explaining how flesh and immortality are not
at odds as is normally thought. The poet explains it four times until one accepts the

subtle truth of the argument. Bodies do die, but other bodies take their place; evenings die but produce a succession of evenings; gardens and maidens die, only to set up an eternity of gardens and maidens, and one maiden celebrates the whole. The last six lines argue, in difficult but lyrical language, that Susanna's music lives in the "you" — the beloved mentioned at the beginning of the poem — and lives in Peter Quince's musical attempt to consecrate Susanna by retelling her story. Some consider these last six lines among the most gorgeous in the English language; they place Stevens in the company of Sappho, Shakespeare, and Keats.

Forms and Devices

References to music abound in the poem. Some musical references are stated obviously, and others lie embedded in puns. On the narrative level, the word "music" is repeated four times in the first six lines of the poem, in which a speaker is seated at a keyboard. Other direct musical references ("melody," "chords," "choral," and "play," as in play upon a violin) combine with a host of musical instruments — clavier, viol, basses, cymbals, horns, and tambourines. These references are further compounded by "strains," "pizzicati," "pulse," "springs," "winds," "breath," "refrain," "flowings," and even "scrapings" (as of a violin badly bowed). The poet says outright that "thinking of your blue-shadowed silk/ Is music."

A reader's awareness of all these compounded references, however, does not make the poem easier to understand. In fact, awareness can add to the complication and bewilderment readers feel when they try to make sense of it. The poem's opening narrative takes place in a parlor, where a lover is making love at the keyboard. Immediately, the poem jumps to a mythic time (part II) in which a woman is made love to by bawdy, red-eyed elders (later, "white elders"). The poem seems to guide readers to a reconciliation of these two opposing images. Such reconciliation is not found in the immediacy of a story line or in the argument at the end. Stevens elsewhere stated his beliefs in "new ways of knowing." On the simplest level, this poem requires that readers find in its formal elements, involving associations of words and narratives, a new way of knowing an old story that, in the Apocrypha at least, seems to be about lust and treachery. Formally, one is presented with a way of knowing Susanna's story by the juxtaposition of a modern lover (presumably young) with those ancient thin-blooded, lecherous old men. He seems to hint that he is somewhat like these old men in the tale. His puns help him explain himself.

All lovers feel the "strain" of love, whether they feel it in a genteel way (as a strain of music) or in a more physical way — the strain in copulation and sexual performance. Lust in the old is less of a physical strain than the act itself is; lust for the young is more of a musical strain, and love-making is easier. Stevens was a master of serious puns. His pun on "strain" allows readers to suppose (in III) that the old men may have tried and failed at rape; they resorted to accusations when their own desire failed. The "uplifted flame" of passion reveals only the shame of lust, not the act itself. When the simpering attendants flee the scene, their tambourines make no music, only noise. Without true feeling there can be no music. When readers understand this, Peter's first puzzling statement (in I) becomes much clearer: Music is not sound; music is feeling.

Susanna herself (in II) seems to intuit what Peter knows without speaking a word on her own behalf. A repeated subject/verb refrain forms a kind of scaffolding for section II: "Susanna lay./ She searched// And found// She sighed,// . . . she stood// She walked . . .// She turned." Balancing these subject/verb constructions are the less active and more tentatively worded lyrical phrases—the quavering of a different sensibility in Susanna's reality—the music felt beyond sound. She is counterpart to male certainty and forced entry—the crashing cymbals and roaring horns. These cymbals and horns are the noise of desire that can be heard if Susanna's complement of music is overridden.

Stevens takes a phrase such as "touch of springs" in Susanna's section (II) and replays it in part IV as "touched the bawdy strings." Stevens relies on the reader hearing from phrase to phrase the various plays in his puns and associations and repetitions. This is part of the tremendous formal pleasure of the poem; every reading turns up more and more sound.

Themes and Meanings

The salient themes and meanings of the poem seem to be in the unraveling of "Beauty is momentary in the mind" but immortal in the flesh. One way to read this puzzle is to put the young poet together with the lecherous old man, much as one might prefer to keep them apart—the one loving, the other violent toward his object of desire. In such minds (young poet/old lecher), Susanna (the beauty) is only able to last momentarily, since these individual minds die away. Susanna is independent. First, her flesh lives on in other flesh. Susanna, as a beauty in body and soul, survives people's weaknesses—moral and physical. Second, her flesh is immortal in the whole scheme of nature and of change. One knows evenings both in their multiple and in their individual returns. There is no way for one to know an evening without knowing constant change from day to evening, nor is there any way to forget. Susanna lives in the perception of beauty always with people in the flesh. Her body dies, but that dying is only an escape from desire's pitiful scrapings. When the speaker says that after all this time Susanna is still remembered, readers must remember that the "now" of the poem is at the beginning, when Peter Quince plays "in this room" to his Susanna and tries, by placing his fingers on the keys, to connect the two beauties and thus participate in a constant music, a "constant" (or immortal) sacrament of praise.

Beverly Coyle

PHILHELLENE

Author: Constantine P. Cavafy (Kōnstantionos Petrou Kabaphēs, 1863-1933)
Type of poem: Dramatic monologue
First published: 1912, as "Philhellene"; in *Poiēmata*, 1935; collected in *The Poems of C. P. Cavafy*, 1951

The Poem

"Philhellene," which means "a lover of things Greek," is a short dramatic monologue spoken by a king of one of the puppet monarchies on the edge of the Roman empire in western Asia. "Beyond the Zagros" (mountains that straddle the border between Iraq and Iran), this imaginary kingdom is far from the center of what the king regards as civilization. The time is not specified, although one can assume that it is sometime in or after the first century A.D. The king is addressing either his coin designer or one of his courtiers, a man named Sithaspes, about the design on a planned coin. The poem is in (in the original Greek) a very loose iambic meter, with line lengths usually from eleven to fourteen syllables; such a varied pattern allows the speaker to seem informal and colloquial, but the language is still highly controlled.

The king commands his listener to be careful with the design. Above all, it must be in good taste—that is, Greek. For example, the "diadem" on the coin must "be rather narrow." Otherwise, it would be too extreme, opposed to the classical Greek ideal of "the middle way." Indeed, the king adds, almost sneeringly, in an attempt to establish his own Greekness, that the bad taste, the excessiveness, of the neighboring Parthians, at that time a real antagonist of the Romans, does not please him.

The very vehemence of his words reveal the king's insecurities. He goes on to say that the "inscription" must be in Greek, not the native language of the kingdom, and it must be restrained, "nothing hyperbolic, nothing pompous," especially because that might also be a political error, since the Roman proconsul could perhaps misread it and report to Rome. At the same moment, the king, trying to hang on to his dignity, says, "It should be, however, honorable."

For the reverse side of the coin, the king wants something carefully artistic, perhaps "a handsome young disk-thrower." With that, though, the poem comes to the real concern of the king—how to make the world know that he is truly civilized. "Above all," he says to Sithaspes, make sure that after the words "King" and "Savior" on the coin there be added the term "Philhellene." Above all, he is a lover of things Greek—especially the restrained taste of the Greeks—and so indeed is a kind of Greek himself.

As in most dramatic monologues, there are implied reactions by the listener, and here the king must see some hint of a smile on Sithaspes' face, for he says: "Don't make your jokes, your remarks about 'Where are the Greeks?' and 'Where is the Greek culture here beyond the Zagros Mountains, beyond Phraata?'" (Phraata was the summer capital of the Parthian empire.) On he goes, suggesting that they have a right to be considered somehow Greek: "People who are far more barbarian than we write such things [on their coins], therefore we will also write them." Moreover, occasional sophists, versifiers, and other such "wiseacres" from Syria come here. Therefore, "we are not non-Greek, I think," he concludes.

Forms and Devices

Constantine Cavafy, especially in the poems he regarded as his real poems, avoided language that was flowery, hyperbolic, or expressive of self. Indeed, one could say that his choice of the dramatic monologue as a common device was an attempt to control the language so that it did not become excessive.

One finds few figures of speech in Cavafy's poetry—especially in this poem— no striking similes or metaphors, no obvious images used as symbols. Even rhymes are rare, if not accidental, here, although he does make use of them elsewhere.

The whole purpose of the poem, at least on the surface, is to create the character of the king, not to be a personal expression of the poet. The poem is not presented as a beautiful object in itself, although in its very restraint it does achieve a kind of beauty. The poem's language must be simple, within limits, in order to make its effect. Indeed, the essence of Cavafy's poetry is not in external elaboration or ornamentation, but in a precise control of tone and structure, elements that shift subtly, letting the reader know much more than the speaker says.

Therefore, the king is direct, seeming simply to give orders. He is revealing himself, however, revealing what he regards as beautiful and wise but also aspects of his own ego that perhaps he does not know himself. For example, when he describes the front of the coin, where his *own* profile will be, he immediately warns Sithaspes about being careful with the inscription, so that the Romans who are the real power will not be offended. In the next line, however, he turns to the design of the coin's back and once more emphasizes the beautiful—the figure of the discus thrower. Then he returns to his own insecurities, his knowledge that he is not really Greek. It is with this insecurity that the poem ends. Indeed, the last line, with its poignant negatives, emphasizes this: "So we are not un-Greek, I think."

Themes and Meanings

To read Cavafy, one must know how he viewed himself. He once said that he had two abilities: to write poetry and to write history. The history that he used allowed him to objectify the world he lived in and was of interest in itself, for it was the history of Greek civilization. After Alexander the Great's conquests in Asia, despite the collapse of his empire, there were for many years small and large Greek-ruled states as far away from Greece as the borders of India; political power was also cultural power. Greek culture did not, however, die with the loss of political power.

The history that Cavafy uses is largely the history of the Hellenistic world after the end of Greek independence. Even before the Romans conquered the eastern part of the Mediterranean, however, the prestige of Greek civilization had a powerful effect on the Empire. After the conquest, the high culture of that eastern half of the

Mediterranean was Greek, and everywhere Greek culture was regarded as the epitome of cultural achievement. Although in one sense Cavafy is satirizing the philhellene king, in another he is in agreement with him. They both love the Greek language and Greek culture; these things give meaning to their lives.

For Cavafy, history is not simply the recounting of events or the examination of an underlying economic or social substructure. Indeed, one of the reasons for Cavafy's use of the dramatic monologue was that it served his idea that it is the "dramatic" in history that matters. He admired historians who wrote history as drama, since drama is lived, not merely experienced intellectually.

"Philhellene" is not merely a poem about history. The king is also an aspect of Cavafy himself. Therefore, despite its appearance of objectivity, one must admit that the poem is an expression of the poet. The poem is, in essence, the examination of an insecure soul who is seeking some sort of dignity and identity in being part of a greater civilization, not merely a king without power. It is, in short, an examination of a kind of alienation. Cavafy, who was a homosexual, was a Greek who was born in Alexandria, Egypt; he was an outsider in both his sexual orientation and his nationality.

In a sense, the king's idea of the work of art expresses the aesthetic belief of Cavafy that a work of art is to be judged by the quality of its workmanship. The king wishes for a thing of beauty, which is perhaps a way of overcoming his sense of being outside. There is one more connection between Cavafy and the king: Cavafy was a man who believed in the life of the body—in pleasure—both artistic and physical. The king's insistence upon the discus-thrower figure for the back of the coin suggests something about his idea of living—that it be pleasurable, and not only to the eye.

Cavafy remarked that his talents were those of a poet and a historian, but one must note that "poet" comes first. Cavafy was first a man of letters, an artist; second, a historian; and, finally, an outsider.

L. L. Lee

PHONEMICS

Author: Jack Spicer (1925-1965)
Type of poem: Lyric
First published: 1965, in *Language*

The Poem

"Phonemics" is in serial form; it consists of six related poems, varying in length between eleven and twenty lines. The title alludes to the study of language sounds, and it helps bring to the foreground the materiality of language in this poem as in other works of Jack Spicer.

Spicer was a professional linguist, and "Phonemics" is one of seven such serial poems in a 1965 book entitled *Language*. The book jacket of *Language* consists of the title page from an issue of a linguistics journal of the same name, an issue that contains Spicer's sole professional publication. Obviously, the poet wanted to remind his readers that poems, whatever their sentiments, consist of language, that the words one uses govern the way one thinks, and that the ways that one's culture provides for putting words together delineate the boundaries of what it is possible to "say" with words.

It would be misleading to term this a first-person poem, for three of the six sections do not contain the word "I." The form of address is rather that of a lecturer who is being objective concerning a situation. That said, however, it should be noted that the voice remains thoroughly idiosyncratic, completely identifiable as Spicer's idiolect, so that even though the first-person pronoun, in either subjective or objective case, seldom occurs, the presence of a single speaker can be felt throughout—the presence, as the poet and critic Ron Silliman has remarked, of a felt absence.

"Phonemics," in common with much other poetry by Spicer, examines, poetically rather than academically, the matter of distance—its role in communication, the ways in which speaking or writing causes it to be felt and discerned between would-be communicants. "The lips/ Are never quite as far away as when you kiss," he writes, offering a paradox that can exemplify this condition. The double role that lips play—kissing and speaking—in human interaction also informs the following lines from the ensuing section:

> Tough lips that cannot quite make the sounds of love
> The language
> Has so misshaped them.

For Spicer, the struggle to be authentic involves a deep mistrust, if not a downright rejection, of any language that convention assigns to various duties. Those clichés predict behavior, whereas love requires freshness, the use of inventive and playful language, spontaneity—the kind of use that this poem embodies, with an irregularity which is that of life and not the predictable pattern of death.

People are always looking for shortcuts, Spicer implies, but true love has a course that is not only rough but also lengthy:

> On the tele-phone (distant sound) you sounded no distant than
>   if you were talking to me in San Francisco on the telephone
>   or in a bar or in a room. Long
> Distance calls. They break sound
> Into electrical impulses and put it back again. Like the long
>   telesexual route to the brain or the even longer teleerotic
>   route to the heart. The numbers dialed badly, the
>   connection faint.

It might not be too much of an exaggeration or a simplification to say of Spicer that he wrote antipoetry and was against love—love, at least, as commonly lived (and voiced) by those around him. It should be added, however, that he took those positions for what he perceived to be the good of poetry and of love.

Forms and Devices

The free-verse sections—poems in their own right, really, which make up the poem "Phonemics"—are united by a number of qualities found throughout. In the first place, their sentence structure is unorthodox: Many of the sentences are actually sentence fragments; phrases are left dangling, unattended by the normal considerations of verb or subject; there is considerable underpunctuation and heavy reliance upon ellipses; quotations are interpolated without attribution; words are broken into their phonemic parts with total disregard for customary procedures. All these violations are deliberate and serve again to highlight the language; the awkwardness and out-of-the-ordinary quality they lend to the writing are calculated to remind the reader that language has a primary, privileged role in one's thinking about reality, and indeed in the creation of that reality.

These sentences and sentence ruins often comment upon one another, so that the progression through a Spicer poem is less linear than crablike or sideways. Take, for example, the following passage:

> Wake up one warm morning. See the sea in the distance.
> Die Ferne, water
> Because mainly it is not land. A hot day too
> The shreads of fog have already vaporized
> Have gone back where they came from. There may be a whale
>   in this ocean.
> Empty fragments, like the shards of pots found in some
>   Mesopotamian expedition. Found but not put together. The
>   unstable
> Universe has distance but not much else.
> No one's weather or room to breathe in.

This, the second section of "Phonemics" in its entirety, illustrates a number of the devices referred to above. Intrusion of the scholarly sounding "Die Ferne," German for "distance" may also occur to the poet because it contains the English word "far" half-hidden in it; Spicer interrupts what had been promising to be a bland beginning—just the kind of "poetic" language he abhorred, with the heavy alliteration of the first sentence, the platitudinous rhyming of "sea" and "see"—with a pedantic-sounding footnote, which he follows with a second academic pun, "main," another word for sea, half-buried in "mainly." The poem then loops back to further landscape evocation, quite accurately characterizing the conditions of that portion of Northern California in which Spicer lived, and quite neutral in tone—although the lack of punctuation at the end of lines 3 and 4 sends a characteristic signal, as does the apparent afterthought qualifying the fog, a phrase more often applied to unwanted visitors. The speculative assertion that ensues concerning the possible whale leads only to a sentence apparently summarizing the poem thus far, although it might, at the same time, refer to the poet's feelings about the depicted scene.

While "Found but not put together" lacks explicit signs of value, there is a suggestion in the context of "Phonemics" and *Language* that it is a good thing to leave such shards "as is" and not to try to force or contrive unity, not to glue things back together. The poem itself partakes of this condition of shards incompletely welded to one another. It does so, Spicer implies, because reality is also shardlike rather than unified, and because the poem owes a debt to reality, if only by creating what one calls the real out of our words.

Themes and Meanings

Baseball provided Spicer with many figures of speech. "The poet," he wrote, "thinks he is the pitcher. But actually he is the catcher." People may think they initiate what, in actuality, they only participate in. The ego-strong poet (or person) thinks he is deciding the course of his poem (or his life); in reality language, or life itself, is dictating the course of things, and one can only attend. The poet, Spicer said elsewhere, is a radio, receiving first, and only then transmitting. What he or she receives are messages from all over, messages that are simply "in the air," and which the poet sits down to sort out whenever he or she writes. While this procedure has affinities with the automatic writing practiced by André Breton and other Surrealists, Spicer did not believe in accepting wholesale whatever was delivered; he believed that one still had to discern between false and true senders and messages.

In "Phonemics," one sees Spicer's beliefs embodied in two ways: in the very form of the poem, with its sudden gaps (as though another transmitting station had broken in on one's radio), its many puns (as though two stations were transmitting and being received simultaneously), and its indecipherable passages (as though heavy static interfered with a message); and in the semantic content, with its warnings of an unreliable, uncommandable, ungovernable universe, its reiterated cautions about distance, and its passages concerning the double role of language as creator and betrayer of human intentions. In "Phonemics," the dynamics and mechanics of language use are constantly being brought to the foreground, and people are forever appearing to be embedded in these dynamics and mechanics of language, rather than being language's lords and masters.

David Bromige

PIANO

Author: D. H. Lawrence (1885-1930)
Type of poem: Lyric
First published: 1918, in *New Poems*

The Poem

"Piano" is a lyric poem reflecting the thoughts and feelings of a single speaker as he listens at dusk to a woman singing a song that brings back childhood memories of sitting at his mother's feet while she played the piano. It is a short poem of twelve lines divided into three quatrains, rhymed *aabb*. The poem contains vivid images, and specific and concrete details provide a clear embodiment of his memory.

In the first stanza, a woman is singing softly to the speaker. The song takes him in memory back to his childhood, where he sees a child sitting under the piano, surrounded by the sounds of music and pressing "the small poised feet of a mother who smiles as she sings." The scene is one of homely comfort and ease, of childlike innocence, of intimacy and peace.

In the second stanza, the speaker realizes that he is being sentimentally nostalgic. Yet in spite of himself, the power of memory sweeps him back into the familiar scene of a Sunday evening at home, with the cold and storms of winter kept outside. Inside, his mother is singing and playing the piano in the cozy parlor, leading the family in the singing of hymns. It is crucial that the speaker does not give in easily to his emotion; it is "in spite of myself," he says, that "the insidious mastery of song/ Betrays me back" (lines 5-6). The diction clearly shows that the speaker, now an adult, realizes the gap between his childhood perceptions, which are idealized and romanticized, and those that he has as a mature adult.

In stanza 3, the reader discovers that he is no longer listening to the current singer and the current piano; he is so overcome by his memories that he weeps like a child for the past. Again, he struggles against this retreat into the past before he finally succumbs. He recognizes that what he sees is nostalgic and sentimental, the "glamor of childish days" (line 11) — deliberately not "childlike" days — that reduces him from being a man to being a child once again, and he weeps like a child for the past.

D. H. Lawrence in this poem does a convincing job of seeing from a child's perspective, while juxtaposing it with the point of view of an adult. Though the *abab* rhyme scheme is perhaps a strained choice for this theme, and though the diction is somewhat trite, especially in the second stanza, the concrete detail and clearly visual images reproduce effectively the experience of an adult who knows that his own childhood eyes cast an aura of illusory beauty over that time. Stanza 2 is weakened for some readers by lines 7 and 8: Lawrence's word choice here, "the old Sunday evenings at home, with winter outside/ And hymns in the cozy parlor, the tinkling piano our guide," seems too ordinary to carry the burden of nostalgia created by the speaker's memory earlier in the poem. There is, however, enough detail in the first and third stanzas to keep the poem as whole from becoming blurry or sentimental.

Forms and Devices

Lawrence centers much of his writing, both poetic and fictional, on the creation and development of a central metaphor. In "Piano," it is the image, with all of its associations, at least in Western European Christian culture, of Sunday evenings at home with one's family. No matter that most people's experiences were seldom so peaceful and harmonious—Lawrence's certainly were not either. It is the idea of a cozy and warm parlor on a cold winter's evening, with a family gathered around a piano singing hymns and enjoying one another's company, that is the important factor. The setting and the music combine to invoke the myth of the ideal family at home: warm, loving, reverent, and peaceful. Lawrence effectively juxtaposes this with the singer and the piano in the speaker's present, a speaker who is about to "burst into clamor" (line 9), accompanying a piano which is reaching a crescendo with a "great black" apassionato. Notice that it is the present experience which is large, dark, and noisy; the speaker's remembered experience is small, warm and "tingling" (line 3).

The ironic tone in the poem, and the clear ironic distance between the poetic voice and his memories of childhood, are central to the poem's success. Without them the tone might become maudlin, but with them one sees and experiences the clear disjunction between a child's and an adult's eye—between a child's perspective that all is well in the world and the adult's knowledge, after the fact, that this was not really the case.

Lawrence's poetic forms and devices, then, echo and reinforce the ironic gap between the original experience of the child, now transformed through the power of memory and imagination, and the current experience of the adult, which acts as trigger and catalyst for his descent into his own past.

Themes and Meanings

"Piano" is a poem about the power of memory and about the often disillusioning disjunction between the remembered experience of childhood and the realities of adult life. The poem is nostalgic without being sentimental; that is, it captures the power of one's experiences as a child without ignoring the facts that one's adult memories are selective and one's perceptions and perspective as a child are severely limited by lack of experience, ignorance, and innocence. Lawrence does, however, provide adequate reason for the intense feeling, and he supports it with concrete, physical detail about the piano and the child's mother.

The theme in "Piano" is a common one in much of Lawrence's writing, from short stories such as "The Rocking-Horse Winner" to novels such as *Sons and Lovers* (1913). How do adults make their peace with the memories they have of their childhoods, and how do they separate memories of actual experience from imagined and invented moments? The speaker in this poem knows that his memory casts a romanticized and sentimentalized glow over the actual events that occurred, yet the power of the past, and his deep need to recapture a similar sense of the peace and protection he felt as a child, overwhelm his rational mind. In Lawrence's world, the power of emotion is almost always too potent for the power of thought; what one feels intrudes on one's thinking, even at times one does not wish it to.

It is important in the poem that the speaker believes that the singer is singing to him, for this reflects the egocentric world that is captured in his childhood memory. This is an experience with which most readers will identify; one can remember times when one believed that some piece of art, music, or literature was created or delivered especially for oneself, and perhaps times when a parent seemed to belong to oneself alone. It is even more important that the speaker (and his audience) recognizes the ironic gap between what he wished (and perhaps believed) were the case, and what the case was in fact. This tension between the heart's desires and the mind's qualifications, between hope and experience, create a necessary if paradoxical balance in the poem. It seems as if D. H. Lawrence is suggesting finally that one should listen more to one's deeply feeling heart than to one's perhaps overly analytical mind; yet the tension between the two is for him an essential part of being human.

Clark Mayo

PICTURE BRIDE

Author: Cathy Song (1955-   )
Type of poem: Meditation
First published: 1980; collected in *Picture Bride*, 1983

The Poem

"Picture Bride" is the title poem of Korean-American writer Cathy Song's first book, one that earned the Yale Series of Younger Poets Prize in 1982 for its Hawaii-born author. It is a meditative poem in thirty-four lines of free verse.

To present-day Euramerican readers, the title may conjure up the vision of a stereotypically picture-perfect bride decked out with veil, lace, and train. If so, this vision would contrast ironically with the historical Asian-American reality of the term. The title refers to a matchmaking practice common among many Asians who immigrated to the United States during the late nineteenth and early twentieth centuries. As part of this practice, intermediaries and family members arranged a marriage between an Asian immigrant man in the United States and an Asian woman in Asia. Usually, the only contact between the bride and the bridegroom during the courtship, if it can be called such, was an exchange of letters and photographs—hence the term "picture bride." Often, the wedding was solemnized by proxy in Asia, after which the bride proceeded to the New World to meet her groom in the flesh and to consummate the marriage.

The picture bride of Song's poem is the grandmother of the poem's speaker. The grandmother is the object of meditation for her granddaughter, a persona who closely resembles the author in age, gender, and ethnic background (Song's father and mother are of Korean and Chinese ancestry, respectively). The speaker of the poem is thus a third-generation Asian-American woman, a twenty-four-year-old who imaginatively projects herself into the thoughts and feelings that the now-matriarch of her family must have had when she first crossed the Pacific Ocean to establish a family with a "stranger" (line 26) she had never met, in an unfamiliar new land.

The speaker marvels at the notion that her grandmother was only twenty-three years old, a year younger than the speaker herself, when she left her family in southern Korea to assume her destiny in the United States. She wonders how her grandmother must have felt as she left the familial protection of her ancestral hearth and her native city, the port of Pusan, to set sail for the distant Hawaiian Islands, a place she had learned about only a short time before. She also wonders how her grandmother regarded the husband whom she had never met. All her grandmother knew was that he was a Korean immigrant laborer thirteen years her senior who worked for the Waialau Sugar Mill. The speaker is curious about how her grandmother felt and acted when this stranger took her from the dock to their new home, where she had to undress for the sudden intimacy of their nuptial bed.

Throughout, the poem maintains a tone of admiration for the grandmother's up-

bringing and strength of character, which armed her with the acceptance and fortitude to undergo the shock of marrying a stranger chosen for her by other people. In
different ways, her grandmother's act is as extraordinary to the speaker as it was
strange to the grandmother. The grandmother's performance is seen as a paradoxically self-denying yet self-defining act; it is this act that bears fruit by giving life to
her more freely choosing granddaughter, who now pays tribute to her grandparent.
The grandmother's act is also one that originates within a cultural and historical
context vastly different from that of the speaker. Mingled with admiration, the
poem's tone also suggests that the speaker herself would shrink from an act as demanding and self-denying as her grandmother's. However much the speaker may
admire her grandmother, to whom she is connected by family, ethnicity, and gender,
the two women are estranged by the gaps of generations, socialization, and implicit
notions of individual freedom of choice — the grandmother's generation and culture
socialized her to disregard her individual prerogatives, whereas the granddaughter's
viewpoint has been shaped by her upbringing as an American woman of the late
twentieth century.

Forms and Devices

To consider this poem as a meditation, it might be useful to note that meditation is
a serious, imaginative, and time-honored practice advocated by several religions.
Usually, the purpose of a religious meditation (such as that encouraged by Saint
Ignatius of Loyola) is to bring the meditator into closer understanding and communion with a sacred text, a divine mystery, or a moment in a saint's life. For example,
one purpose of a Christian meditator could be to think and imagine oneself as being
present during a crucial moment of Christ's life, such as the Crucifixion — in such a
sense is John Donne's seventeenth century metaphysical poem "Good Friday, 1613.
Riding Westward" a meditation.

The object of meditation in Song's poem, however, is a secular rather than a
religious one, although the grandmother is, nevertheless, highly esteemed and even
revered. It is common in several Asian cultures for ancestors to be regarded in a
worshipful manner. One could then read the poem as a meditation in which the
speaker thinks and imagines herself into the situation of her revered grandmother at
a crucial moment in the latter's life, thereby achieving an understanding and communion with her.

That the speaker chooses to honor a female ancestor in her meditation rather than
a male one seems natural, given the speaker's sex. Within an Asian context, however, it could be considered a rather unusual choice, for within the highly patriarchal
Asian hierarchy the place of honor and reverence would normally be accorded to the
male ancestor: the grandfather. Song's meditator, however, salutes the matriarchal
figure of her family and devalues the grandfather into a "stranger." This choice by
Song may thus be read as a feminist one.

The poem makes extensive use of contrasts in situations and imagery. Some of the
more noticeable situational contrasts are those between the speaker and the matri-

arch: the younger freer generation and the older more-constrained generation, the turn-of-the-century Asian and the modern American, the bride and her husband, the long-familiar and the suddenly strange. These contrasting situations serve to highlight the matriarch's strength of character and the speaker's sense of wonder.

The poem's imagery creates immediacy and lends it a dramatic quality; it also furthers the impact of the poem's situational contrasts. For example, the bittersweet quality of the grandmother's experience is reflected in the sensory contrast between the implied sweetness of the sugar "cane stalks" (line 22) and the bitterness of the "burning . . . cane" after the harvest (line 34—a line that was added in the 1983 version of the poem). There is the dramatic imagist contrast between the bride's disciplined self-control as she "politely untie[s]/ the silk bow of her jacket" to undress (lines 29 and 30) and a thirsting passion implied by "her tent-shaped dress/ filling with the dry wind" (lines 31 and 32). Most striking perhaps is the contrast between the dark of the night and the light of the lantern (lines 16 to 21), which suggests a parallel between the grandmother's risky journey from Asia to the United States and the moths' risking death in "migrating" from their natural habitat of the dark "cane stalks" toward the artificial light of the lantern.

Themes and Meanings

"Picture Bride" is about immigration, generational differences, women, and individuality. By imaginatively recovering her grandmother's experiences, Song reconstructs the experiences of an entire subgroup of Asian-American immigrants: the Korean Americans and the Japanese Americans. Picture brides were uncommon among Chinese Americans because American immigration laws were enforced between 1882 and 1945 to exclude Chinese women from American shores; however, female subjects of the militarily powerful Japanese empire, which included Korea, were grudgingly allowed to migrate to the United States. (A knowledgeable account of the Asian-American experience of immigration is to be found in Ronald Takaki's 1989 book *Strangers from a Different Shore*.) Although Song's poem focuses on the psychological and emotional impact of immigration on a single individual, it also hints at the economic hard times facing these Asian immigrants as well as the cultural reservoirs of endurance that enabled them to survive such an alienating experience.

The poem juxtaposes an American woman of the twentieth century and an Asian woman of two generations earlier. Their assumptions about what it means to be a woman and their assumptions about self-fulfillment are worlds apart—so far apart as to provoke a wondering near-incomprehension from the younger woman. The woman of the past generation was schooled to negate her individual prerogatives, to allow others to determine her destiny, and to accede without argument to male authority. The modern woman is hard put to understand this attitude, and by implication she would assert her individuality, control her destiny, and abhor submission to arbitrary male authority.

The contrastive structure of the poem tempts the modern reader to an evaluation of the grandmother's experience of immigration and notions of individuality. One may well wonder how much of one was positive, how much of the other negative. Perhaps an answer lies in the key image of the photograph of the bride. After all, a photograph is a developed picture that is the bright positive print of a dark negative film. Print and film, dark and light, positive and negative—their contrasting existences are inextricable in the same way that the final sum of human experience is.

C. L. Chua

PIED BEAUTY

Author: Gerard Manley Hopkins (1844-1889)
Type of poem: Sonnet
First published: 1918, in *Poems of Gerard Manley Hopkins, Now First Published, with Notes by Robert Bridges*

The Poem

"Pied Beauty" is a rhymed "curtal" (shortened) sonnet divided into two stanzas, consisting of three full tercets and a truncated fourth. The title refers to the variegated beauty of the world that first may appear ugly or chaotic. Though "pied" suggests at least two tones or colors, it also suggests a blotched or botched effect, as when in an earlier era, a printer spilled a galley of set type, creating a printer's "pie."

Though traditional sonnets are fourteen lines, Gerard Manley Hopkins, in his experiments with poetic form, line, and meter, altered the shape of the sonnet. In the case of "Pied Beauty," he "curtailed" or shortened the sonnet's traditional fourteen lines to eleven; in some other cases, he lengthened the form and wrote sonnets "with codas," or tails.

The poem celebrates God for the beauty in a varied creation. Hopkins, a devout Jesuit priest, isolates a number of instances of this "pied" or dappled beauty in the first stanza (lines 1-6). He finds it in two-toned skies as well as on cows, on spotted trout, and on the wings of birds. He also sees variety and unity in the contrasts between all these life-forms, for he sees echoes of plants on fish— "rose-moles . . . upon trout," echoes of the dying embers of fires in the chestnuts falling from the tree.

In fact, the first stanza catalogs God's infinite variety in creation in instances that symbolize all life as well as inanimate forms, from the heavens to the seas, from plants to animals, from animals finally even to humans. The fifth line observes the pied quality of the landscape as humans have altered it. The landscape is a pied checkerboard with pens for animals (such as sheepfolds), plowed fields, and those fields lying unplowed (fallow). The human pied effect on land is then juxtaposed against the variety of human mercantile activity or trades.

As in most sonnets, the second part or stanza generalizes, summarizes, or abstracts from the particular details observed by the poet in the first part. Therefore, the next three lines (lines 7-9) point out the general patterns of contrast. The word "counter" suggests this contrariness: The beauty of God's creation grows out of oppositions. Many of the adjectives— such as "fickle"—Hopkins uses to describe the pied beauty may seem in themselves unappealing or ugly. "Fickle" usually connotes unpredictability, disloyalty, perhaps even immorality. In the context of a vast creation, however, these strange, pied qualities are amalgamated to the overall beauty. The ninth line itself reiterates this effect of balanced and beautiful contrast in a series of paired oppositions. Having described the pied beauty of the Creation in the first nine lines, or first three tercets, Hopkins turns to the Creator or "father" (God) in the last two lines and concludes by directing the reader to "Praise him."

Forms and Devices

Characteristic of Hopkins is his use of a variety of intricate sound devices, each heightened or altered in some untraditional way. Hopkins' idiosyncratic and innovative techniques perhaps explain why the majority of his poems were published only in the first decades of the twentieth century, nearly thirty years after his death. "Pied Beauty" consists of patterns of such idiosyncracy in its alliteration, assonance, neologism, archaism, end rhyme, and rhythm. All these patterns interconnect and contrast with one another so that the poem itself is an example of "pied" beauty, or mixed elements.

Thus the alliterative *g* sounds of the first line ("Glory . . . God") give way to the *l* sound, which echoes in "dappled," "couple," "colour," "moles," and "stipple," interconnecting the patterns of the first three lines with the entire first stanza. The alliterative pattern of sounds connects the "couple-colour" of the sky to the skin of the "cow." The *c* sounds are thus "pied" or combined in contrast with the *l* sounds.

At first glance, a word such as "rose-moles" seems both odd and hard to pronounce because the assonance of the *o* sounds contrasts with the following consonants of *s* and *l*. It is a near rhyme or off-rhyme that occasionally turns a Hopkins lyric into a near tongue twister. Even a sympathetic reader may wonder what a rose-mole is, for it is indeed one of Hopkins' neologisms (or invented words) to describe the colored pattern of a trout's skin. It is not surprising that in the same line he employs the archaism "brinded" to described a pied pattern of grey flecks or streaks on a cow's hide. Also, normal associations with rose, usually an image of perfection or beauty, contrast radically with traditional associations with mole, usually seen as a beauty defect or unpleasant growth. Yet the phrase, the sound, the very unusualness of the concept suggest the exciting variety of a universe constantly changing and contrasting.

In addition, the structure of the poem is itself an example of pied beauty, since the expected patterns established by the rhyme schemes of the first six lines (*abcabc*) are broken in the next five (*dbcdc*). The poem's tercet pattern ends abruptly in a line and a half (lines 10 and 11) instead of three full lines. This last shift marks the radical difference between God's creation and God. Hopkins thus dramatically reminds one that God, unlike the dappled things, is powerful and unchanging and has a beauty of oneness or integrity. He also simultaneously shows one that the relation of God (unchanging) to his Creation (fickle, changing) is itself an example of pied or mixed, contrasting beauty.

The abrupt ending also forces the last two words ("Praise him") to bear enormous weight; because of the established pentameter rhythm of the preceding lines, they enjoy the supposed five-beat stress typical of that pattern. This makes those two words both momentous and simultaneously humble, like a quiet prayer.

The stunted end is what makes this a "curtal" or curtailed sonnet. One misses the patterned, traditional beauty of a fourteen-line sonnet but finds instead another beauty in an odd form Hopkins created particularly for this occasion.

Themes and Meanings

In Hopkins' poetry it is virtually impossible to separate device and form from meaning since he is constantly at work molding lines, words, and sounds to create an intricate pattern, making one feel that the poem one is reading is nearly a synesthetic version of the aspect of creation or theology on which he is commenting. Thus this analysis of theme may seem somewhat repetitive of comment on forms and devices. In effect, that is part of the point of the poem.

"Pied Beauty" is essentially a list reminding us again and again, in a variety of ways, that the visible universe and human creation is varied and beautiful even in its ugliness and contrast, and all is a hymn of praise to God the Creator. In this list, Hopkins isolates details that reveal his perceptiveness as a poet and that invite the reader to see the world and word anew and more carefully. Thus the strategy of the poem's first part is that of enumerating unique details conveyed in unusual words, such as "stipple" or "brinded." Each detail is like the brush stroke of a great painter, and for Hopkins, God is the careful painter mixing and matching, putting all into a whole. Though individual details are striking, unusual, unique, or even initially ugly, the overall effect is one of massive pattern, reiterated by the echo of the word "all" at the end of one stanza and beginning of the next.

God's Creation is beautiful because the seeming variety and contrast conceals a principle of unity that links all living things to one another and to God — sky to earth, fish to cow, the dying embers of a fire to the fall of a chestnut from a tree. Though most of the first examples come from nature, and even the first human examples of pied beauty are from agriculture, Hopkins finds beauty also in mercantile work — in all the trades, often despised by other religious writers for being nonspiritual, and even in the equipment used in trade. Perhaps one can also see that the "tackle" used to catch the trout is as beautiful as the trout itself — and beautiful by contrast.

In Hopkins' vision, God is the creator of beauty, traditionally the father, the divine spark. He is "past change" in that he is eternal, omniscient, a fixed and absolute entity. He encompasses the variegated creation simply as mention of him both begins and ends the poem.

Hopkins remarks upon this beauty, announces it, embodies it in the intricate interwoven complexity of his words, but he does not purport to understand it. The mystery of how the variegation occurs and how or why it is beautiful is announced in the very conversational, almost nonpoetic "who knows how?" — a rhetorical question of amazing power and honesty.

"Pied Beauty" is an ironic paean to God for not creating a perfect universe, but for creating one that is beautiful because of apparent imperfection. The odd locutions and abrupt stuntedness of the poem itself embody the pied quality Hopkins discerns in the external world.

Jonathan L. Price

PIKE

Author: Ted Hughes (1930-   )
Type of poem: Narrative/meditation
First published: 1960, in *Lupercal*

The Poem

"Pike" is written in free verse and consists of forty-four lines divided into eleven stanzas. The title focuses immediate attention on the creature under scrutiny and on the natural world, which informs most of Ted Hughes's work. The poem can be divided into three sections or perspectives.

The first section, stanzas 1 and 2, sets the scene, depicting the voracious, ruthless nature of this fish and establishing its green water world. In these first stanzas, Hughes maintains an objective narrative perspective in which the fish and its environment occupy the center of attention.

The next section, the third through seventh stanzas, begins a consideration of the predatory nature of the pike and describes it as it moves through a green, gold, shadowy habitat. No sounds disturb the quiet of the fish's waiting expectation beneath the water's surface. In stanzas 3 and 4, Hughes graphically describes the fish's "jaws' hooked clamp and fangs" and makes the reader sense the pike's ruthless nature as it lurks silently waiting in the weeds for its prey. In stanzas 5 and 6, he heightens this vision by describing what happened when he kept three small pike captive in an aquarium: The ruthless fish preyed upon one another until only one remained, "with a sag belly and the grin it was born with." Hughes juxtaposes a second scene of the pike as unstoppable predator by concluding this section with the image of two dead, six-pound, two-foot-long pikes lying on a river bank, one jammed down the gullet of the other. Even in death these fish are portrayed as grimly determined.

The final section, stanzas 8 through 11, brings the narrator into direct contact with this coldly grim predator. Here Hughes describes the evening encounter he had while casting for pike on an ancient, quiet monastery pond. Set in the waning twilight, this section recapitulates the skulking, waiting nature of the submarine predator and makes the reader experience the fear that the pike engenders, even in the man standing safely on the bank — afraid to fish for what he imagines to be monstrous pike, yet unable not to.

The last stanza of "Pike" concludes with an image of the silent fish slowly surfacing to consider the fisherman who has dared disturb its nighttime lair with his puny flycasting. It is clear from Hughes's choice of detail that this world, both pond and bank, belongs to the menacing pike and that the narrator violates the fish's domain at his peril.

Forms and Devices

The conversational tone of "Pike" serves as an effective device for Hughes to heighten the tension and impact of the poem's violence. Hughes's choice of language is simple, with few polysyllabic words; his phrases are stark, almost bare — without the frills that people seem to need in order to escape from the brutal realities of living. Such simplicity allows Hughes to make "Pike" a highly visual poem; his descriptions evoke sharp images for the reader in which the fish becomes tangible. One can see the water, see the weeds, and sense the presence of the pike as it blends in, waiting to lunge at its unsuspecting quarry. The descriptions are rhythmic, lulling the reader and allowing the final stanzas to take on additional sinister import.

Hughes skillfully juxtaposes the natural with the human world, pairing the images of the fish floating patiently in its natural element with those of an artificial world that imprisons the creature for the cruel or whimsical purposes of the human that has captured it. Because Hughes contrasts what he regards as naturally appropriate, such as the pike's very existence, which he describes as "A life subdued to its instrument," with the next section in which the pike eat one another in the tank, the poet is able to call into question the behavior of the people who captured the fish in the first place.

By focusing on the expression of the pike — as a grinning set of hungry, vicelike jaws — Hughes increases the uneasiness that many people feel when they must witness the raw hunger and power of natural impulse. Repeatedly, in each section of "Pike," Hughes draws his readers' attention to the fish's mouth: a grin, open and waiting in the weeds, smiling with a full belly — still determined in death, locked around the body of its kin. Because the fish is depicted as lurking, shadowed, and mysterious, the choice of the word "grin" to describe its expression is jarring and disconcerting. Nothing about the pike, which Hughes clearly respects and even admires, makes this image one with which the reader will be comfortable.

Finally, Hughes leaves the reader with the impression that the fisherman, not the pike, is the real intruder, perhaps even the only source of true violence in the natural world. By doing so, the poet invites the reader to examine his or her attitudes about the natural world, about who or what has the "right" to behave in a particular way. It is the narrator, not the pike, who feels fear; the pike, on the other hand, rises to the surface prepared to stare down this intruder.

Themes and Meanings

As in most of his poetry, in "Pike" Ted Hughes uses the natural world to its fullest advantage as a stage where humans are only one species among many and are clearly not as powerful as they would like to believe. Hughes's poetry dwells on the innate violence in the natural world and on instinctive predatory behavior; yet, because this behavior is presented in such a manner as to seem uncontrived and natural, Hughes seems to view it as appropriate. Nature as depicted in a poem such a "Pike" shares the perspective of other British poets such as Alfred, Lord Tennyson, who described nature as "red in tooth and claw" (*In Memoriam A. H. H.*, 1850). These writers — Hughes included — attempt to reconcile what at first appears to be a horrible violence in nature. Their concern reflects a conflict that has troubled people since Charles Darwin's theory of evolution offered an explanation for human development that appeared to omit the hand of God. Perhaps humans are no different from a creature such as the pike, driven by impulse and appetite in a universe that follows no moral law but eat or be eaten.

Hughes clearly views the pike as a creature that belongs in its water world, an animal that exemplifies survival of the fittest. The fish is a part of, rather than apart from, the natural world in which it feeds. The pike shares the colors of the water, the weeds, the pond bottom, and the shadows; it is in harmony with and a necessary part of this world, but it is a type of creature—like the shark—that many will view as unwholesome because of its very drive to survive. Hughes clearly believes that the pike belongs where it is and has a "right" to behave as it does, no matter the violence, for it follows a naturally preordained path, instincts that drive it even when the fish is only a three-inch fry: Pike are "Killers from the egg." Those who find the fish's appetite and killer instinct unsettling do not see the world as Hughes does; to them, killing to survive is repugnant. Hughes, on the other hand, expresses subtle admiration for the one pike out of three that remained alive in his aquarium prison, having outlived—and eaten—its kin.

If anything, it is the narrator of the poem, the voice that emerges in the last half of the poem, who is out of place in this natural world. This person has not only removed young fish from their natural habitat and imprisoned them in a glass cage but also invaded the pike's sanctuary to fish for creatures that have outsmarted fishermen for generations, pike that Hughes describes as "too immense to stir." Gradually the narrator is overcome by fear; the violence that the pike direct at their prey seems to be turned toward him as the fish rises slowly to the surface of the bottomless pond to regard the man who foolishly thinks he will catch the natural killer. By his use of a monastery as the site of this particular pond, Hughes implies that the violent, hungry pike has a divine right to live where it does and, by extension, to behave in the way that it does. By equating the pike with the legendary nature of the monastery pond, he makes it a creature of myth like the dragon: powerful, haughty, and impervious to human needs. It is the narrator, not the fish, who must learn a lesson—that pike behavior is "good" and that nature exists for nature's sake, not for man's.

Melissa E. Barth

PITY THIS BUSY MONSTER,MANUNKIND

Author: E. E. Cummings (1894-1962)
Type of poem: Sonnet
First published: 1944, in *1x1*

The Poem

E. E. Cummings' brief lyric "pity this busy monster,manunkind" is a fourteen-line poem and is thus a sonnet, at least in Cummings' deliberately broad definition of that poetic form. Though the punctuation (and certainly the capitalization) is unconventional, the poem clearly breaks into four sentences. This grammatical division is not reinforced by the line or stanza breaks, however; stanzas vary from one to four lines and begin in mid-sentence. In many respects, the poem is typical of Cummings: It presents some of his favorite poetic devices and themes.

The opening sentence urges the reader not to pity the "busy monster" of humanity, or, rather, in Cummings' invented term, "manunkind." The next sentence describes progress as a disease of which humanity is the victim unawares. Then the poet asserts the distinction between natural and artificial: "A world of made/ is not a world of born." The reader is thus invited to pity, instead of humankind, the defenseless things of the organic world — from trees to stars — which are, presumably, victims of the increasing artificiality of progress. The disease metaphor is invoked again in the concluding sentence of the poem where doctors declare the modern world to be a "hopeless case" and invite the reader to join them in the "hell of a good universe next door." The force of the concluding line is ironic; the reader knows that there is no alternative universe to which one can escape.

Cummings' poem, like so many of his lyrics, is an eloquent protest against what he saw as dehumanizing trends of contemporary culture. Its eloquence resides not in complex argument or traditional poetic elevation, but in the value-laden wordplay that strives to expose the myths of modern society as life-denying. Thus humankind is rendered as a self-important monster, spreading incurable disease and worshiping false gods ("electrons deify one razorblade/ into a mountainrange"). The term "monster" calls to mind the frightening perversion of the natural; the conglomeration of innocent and natural individual beings forms a whole ("this busy monster") that is neither innocent nor natural. Cummings' humor and playfulness, however, keep the poem from becoming a tract or a tirade. Amused irony tempers his righteous indignation.

Forms and Devices

Readers are struck first by Cummings' unorthodox use of lowercase letters. Indeed, he even signed his poems "e. e. cummings." His avoidance of initial capital letters takes one step further the modernist tendency to capitalize only the first words of sentences, not the first word of each poetic line. In this poem, Cummings does use initial capital letters for new sentences, except in the title and first line. In any case, his unconventional punctuation (including the absence of spaces after commas and semicolons) reflects essentially the same tendencies throughout his career. First, the typographical idiosyncrasies call attention to the poem as the product of the typewriter, a machine-age self-consciousness apparent (through different means) in the poetry of William Carlos Williams and Marianne Moore as well. In addition, the typographical unconventionality asserts a larger unconventionality of values that the poet wishes to reflect in the poem. "I oppose the staid and traditional" is what Cummings' poems seem to say by their very look on the page.

Similarly, Cummings invents his own comic compound words—in this poem as in many others. These compounds assert a desire for linguistic freedom and a willingness to play with forms of contemporary rhetoric: from advertising lingo to political neologisms to scientific coinages. A phrase such as "hypermagical/ ultraomnipotence" mocks the pretensions of science to magic and religion in form as well as content. The prefixes "hyper-" and "ultra-" parody the typical exaggeration of advertisements and reinforce the poet's deflation of pretension. Cummings' reliance on coined compounds is apparent in the following lines: "lenses extend/ unwish through curving wherewhen till unwish/ returns on its unself." Here, context helps clarify a potentially baffling line. "Unwish" suggests the social tendency to bring about negative change: Even though no one wishes for the decline in the quality of life, progress may bring it about in the future's here and now (the "wherewhen") because the nameless force of change (the "unself") has a self-perpetuating power. Cummings' point is advanced as much by the playful absurdity of the language itself as by this sort of analytical paraphrase.

The most dramatic use of a compound coinage occurs in the opening lines that form the poem's title. "Manunkind" clearly puns on the lack of kindness in mankind considered as a whole. The force of the opening command, however, is intensified by the poetic syntax that moves the damning negative, "not," not only to the final position in the sentence but also to the next line and stanza. What first appears as a call to pity humanity is deflated by the strategically placed "not."

Traditionally, a sonnet is defined as a fourteen-line poem in iambic pentameter with a regular rhyme scheme. By that definition, this poem is not strictly a sonnet. Cummings, however, was drawn to the brief controlled utterance of the sonnet form throughout his career, and he wrote hundreds of fourteen-line lyrics. "Pity this busy monster,manunkind," however, is carefully structured. Though the meter is rarely strictly iambic, each line is ten syllables long. There is no clear rhyme scheme, but some decidedly slant rhymes connect words ending lines (hypermagical/hell, unwish/this, know/go). Cummings' use of the sonnet form reflects the idiosyncratic mix of conventionality and rebellion characteristic of his verse. Cummings is attracted to the controlled form of the sonnet—both in the overall length of the poem and in the discipline given to line lengths. At the same time, the deliberate resistance of iambic meter and rhyme shows that Cummings is not interested in the metrical balance of the sonnet form or its tendency to divide the lyric into sections of an argument (as in three quatrains and a couplet or an octet and a sestet).

Themes and Meanings

Cummings' poetry is essentially a poetry of oppositions, and this poem dramatizes two of the most important of those oppositions: the individual against the collective, and the organic or natural against the artificial. Cummings deplored the
trends in modern society toward the conquest of the natural environment by the
manmade and synthetic and toward the destruction of the individual by the mass.
The busy monster of "manunkind" is pictured as a society frenetically engaged in
subverting the natural ("poor stones and stars") in the name of progress. This progress that supposedly advances the good of the collective, however, ignores the vitality of the individual and thus fails miserably. Such is the motivation behind the
incipient metaphors of the body politic pictured as terminal patient: "your victim
(death and life safely beyond)/ plays with the bigness of his littleness." Society has
moved "beyond" life and death because, in treating the mass, the individual has
been dehumanized (an experience Cummings witnessed in both world wars).

This metaphor continues in the glib talk of the experts— the doctors— that concludes the poem. The body politic, stripped of the individual and the organic, becomes "a hopeless case." Faced with the reality of death, the technology-driven
doctors seek, in imperialist fashion, to find new territories to conquer, and they set
off for the universe "next door." The final invitation— "let's go"— works in two
ways. First, it forms the ironic conclusion of the progress worshipers faced with the
corpse of a society: They go off into the optimistic utopia of tomorrow that will
prove to be (as "utopia" suggests) nowhere. The poet is also a doctor of sorts here,
diagnosing the ills of society, and his invitation to move to another universe may be a
serious call to reimagine the world through poetic sensibility. If people follow the
poet's advice and save their pity for the natural world and learn to cherish it, then
their future might indeed promise a "hell of a good universe." Such is the faith that
Cummings extolls throughout his poetry.

Christopher Ames

THE PLACE FOR NO STORY

Author: Robinson Jeffers (1887-1962)
Type of poem: Lyric meditation
First published: 1932, in *Thurso's Landing and Other Poems*

The Poem

"The Place for No Story" is a short free-verse lyric of twelve lines varying in length from ten to two words. Despite its brevity, the poem is one of Robinson Jeffers' most important, expressing succinctly and in concentrated form a major theme of his poetry: the supremacy of unconscious nature over the human social worlds of culture and civilization. In this poem, Jeffers returns to the majestic coastal California landscape of his long narrative poems but without the tragic passions of their human characters. That is the significance of the poem's title; in this lyric, the rocky California coast which provides setting for most of Jeffers' narrative poems and for the actions of his human characters is now treated as a subject in its own right.

In both *Thurso's Landing and Other Poems* (1932) and *The Selected Poetry of Robinson Jeffers* (1938), "The Place for No Story" immediately follows the long title narrative of *Thurso's Landing*, an especially sanguine story of infidelity, insanity and murder. This positioning suggests that "The Place for No Story" is to be understood as a kind of palinode, a poem of apology or recantation, offered by Jeffers as a partial corrective for the fury and violence of his narrative.

The poem begins, as many of Jeffers' poems do, with the place name of a real site along the California coast—in this case, Sovranes Creek, south of Monterey. Jeffers believed that poetry should conform to physical realities, and he expressed a reverence for the spiritual significance of specific places that recalls in its intensity the pagan worship of local deities (genius loci) in sacred groves and streams. Jeffers intends his lyric to be the evocation of the spiritual significance of this specific place.

The poem's speaker, whom it is reasonable to accept as the poet himself, immediately begins a description of the estuary landscape where Sovranes Creek meets the sea. The poet first describes the area's treeless upland pastures with their thin covering of soil stretched above granite bedrock. The striations and contours of this underlying rock are likened to flame, a simile suggesting their volcanic and molten origin. From these upland pastures, the poet draws one's attention westward to the cliffscarp and the ocean below, where a plunging surf appears as a line of "long white violence" bordering an enormous gray expanse of open sea fading to the horizon. From there, one's gaze is lifted upward to a dark mountain slope dotted near its summit with a distant herd of grazing cattle and, above all, the sky itself, overcast and "haunted with hawks." The description of hawks as haunting the sky may suggest that in the heavy cloud cover they can be heard but not seen or that they are riding rising thermals of warm air in arcs so high as to be only dimly visible. This descriptive passage conveys a sense of tremendous distance and isolation.

At this point, the speaker of the poem declares simply that "This place is the noblest thing I have ever seen." The poet's curious ascription of a human quality, nobility, to an aggregate of inanimate and animal phenomena composing a landscape is immediately reinforced by the claim that any "human presence" in this wild scene would only detract from its nobility, its "lonely self-watchful passion." The descriptive adjective "lonely" in this final line expresses a normal human response to a landscape of this kind. This response had been suspended in the descriptive passage opening the poem. Now that a subjective word is used, the reader is surprised to learn that "lonely" is meant as praise for the conditions making this landscape's nobility possible: the absence of man. The landscape's loneliness, at first neutrally described by the poet, is now embraced and contrasted, implicitly and negatively, with the social world of man and human-centered concerns.

Forms and Devices

A distinguishing aspect of Jeffers' poetic style is his extensive use of a form of personification called the "pathetic fallacy," which is the ascription of human characteristics and emotions to material things such as trees, water, and rocks. This kind of personification, especially characteristic of Romantic poets, is evident in "The Place for No Story." Jeffers describes the ocean surf as "violent" and credits the landscape with both "nobility" and a form of consciousness which makes possible its "self-watchful passion."

For many poets, this form of personification is only a convention, a bit of poetic license not to be taken seriously. For Jeffers, however, and for his Romantic predecessors such as William Wordsworth, this use of the pathetic fallacy is seriously meant. Like the Romantics, Jeffers was something of a pantheist—one who believes that consciousness, even a divine consciousness, is distributed throughout the whole of nature. Jeffers describes the landscape of the Sovranes estuary as "noble" because for him it is, in a real sense, alive and aware. Jeffers bases this belief upon a combination of mysticism and science, arguing that since all things are composed of the same material (atomic) constituents, they must all share a fundamentally common nature. This aspect of Jeffers' poetic vision, sometimes called panpsychism, is likely to seem most strange to a reader unfamiliar with the philosophical backgrounds of his work.

In addition to the use of personification, Jeffers incorporates two important symbols common to his poetry: the rock and the hawk. They represent the fierce integrity of nonhuman nature; both are embodiments of impassive and impersonal forces dividing between them the animate world of focused energy and the inanimate world of stolid calm. Elsewhere in his poetry, Jeffers frequently contrasts man, with his anxiety and doubt-ridden consciousness, unfavorably with the unitary strength and simplicity of the rock and hawk. The consciousness of nature, the pantheistic sentience of things, is symbolized for Jeffers in the bird and stone. Nature's consciousness, which they share, is whole, while the human consciousness is divided. Rock and hawk in harmony with natural forces possess an organic completeness, a "nobility," that men lack. In "The Place for No Story," mankind is only significant by his absence; neither the soaring hawk nor the ocean beaten stone need him; they are sufficient in themselves.

Themes and Meanings

Late in his career, Jeffers suggested that many of his poems were expressions of a philosophical outlook that he provocatively called Inhumanism. Jeffers defined the basic tenets of this creed in various ways, but its essence is simple: Man has exaggerated his importance in the scale of natural creation and now invites disaster. Only if man recovers a sense of his insignificance in the face of transhuman nature can he regain balance and dignity. As it is, man is self-absorbed and self-obsessed, cutting himself off from the strength of natural order in favor of artificial powers derived from technology and bureaucratic organization. Jeffers owed something of his philosophical outlook to the pessimistic German philosopher Oswald Spengler (1880-1936), who argued that civilizations grow old and decadent as part of an inalterable historical process resembling the biological processes of birth, aging, and death. According to Spengler, symptoms of this coming social decay in Western civilization included the rise of metropolitan cities, mass production, and rampant population growth—all of which Jeffers notes and deplores in his poetry.

In the face of this coming collapse of civilization, Jeffers suggests that the best way to retain courage and integrity is to look away from man and toward nature. The speaker of "The Place for No Story" does exactly this; he gazes into the "self-watchful passion" of a landscape empty of human turbulence and strife. If it contains violence, it is only the great cyclical violence of crashing waves and the balancing "nobility" of isolation and endurance.

Jeffers is, as many of his critics recognize, a moralizing poet, a man with a message. Didactic poetry of the kind favored by Jeffers, which seeks to instruct or admonish its readers with forthright statement and a lofty, prophetic tone, lost favor among the ironical poets of the modern and postmodern era. Jeffers, once lionized, is now seldom read. For some readers, the poet's verses are little more than misanthropic rant filled with irrational hatred of democracy and rational progress. For others, a fiercely loyal minority, the verses are prophetic visions of man's current predicament, and Jeffers himself is a voice crying in the wilderness.

Whitney Hoth

PLANETARIUM

Author: Adrienne Rich (1929-   )
Type of poem: Lyric
First published: 1971, in *The Will to Change*

The Poem

"Planetarium" is a forty-five-line poem in free verse that was prompted by a visit to a planetarium during which Adrienne Rich read about the work of astronomer Caroline Herschel (1750-1848). Herschel had worked with her brother William, the discoverer of Uranus, and later worked on her own. The poem is in "free" verse only in that its groupings of lines and phrases are irregular; they are actually carefully arranged to emphasize the progression of observations and thoughts that make up the poem.

The opening lines refer to the constellations, their shapes identified since ancient times with mythological beings; among them is "a monster in the shape of a woman." Then Rich moves to a real woman, Caroline Herschel, and quotes from a description of her working with scientific instruments; Herschel, she notes, discovered eight comets. In seven words, Rich deftly points out a kinship among Herschel, herself, and all women: "She whom the moon ruled/ like us." In a description that sounds like a metaphor but is based on the fact that astronomers often observed from cages that were raised high in the air within the observatory to allow them to see through the telescope, Herschel is seen "levitating into the night sky" and "riding" the lenses.

Rich links the mythological women in the heavens with all women; all are serving "penance," and it is implied that the penance is being demanded by the men who created the myths and named the constellations. Another quotation appears, this one of astronomer Tycho Brahe speaking of his own observations. Brahe, in 1573, discovered the "NOVA," the "new star" in Cassiopeia (actually a star that, in the final stage of its existence, had expanded to thousands of times its original size). Rich relates the nova to women ("us"), the life exploding outward from them.

The poem then shifts subtly in tone, as the speaker (presumably Rich herself) gradually moves into the foreground, leading to the forceful declaration of personal vision that concludes the poem. "What we see, we see," Rich states, then, crucially, "and seeing is changing." She sees a paradox of power and delicacy; she sees a joining of the cosmic and the minuscule (and the inanimate and the animate). Light can destroy a mountain yet not hurt a person; the pulsar and her own heartbeat combine in her body.

Line 34 stands alone in the poem, and it acts as both a pronouncement of strength ("I stand") and a pause before the final section—eleven lines that run together, broken only by brief pauses within the lines. In the final section, Rich attempts to define herself anew, apart from history and old mythologies. She is a deep galactic cloud; she stands in the path of signals, an "untranslatable language." Discarding the ancient celestial monster/woman of line 2, she declares herself "an instrument in the shape of a woman." That is, she is a writer, a creator of "images," trying to make sense of her own observations and experiences; moreover, since "seeing is changing," she is reconstructing—as she realizes she must—the way she views herself and the world.

Forms and Devices

The groupings of lines in "Planetarium" are too irregular to be called stanzas; they are clusters of lines grouped according to separate thoughts, observations, and quotations. The fact that the words "An eye" have a line to themselves, for example, hints at the importance of vision (and re-vision) in the poem. The poem is dated 1968 (Rich regularly puts the year of composition at the end of her poems), and a number of poems dated 1968 in *Leaflets* (1969) and *The Will to Change* use structures similar to that of "Planetarium" The poems also have spaces within the lines that add to the fragmentation of the thoughts being expressed. The reader senses hesitations, directions being pondered, options being weighed:

> Galaxies of women, there
> doing penance for impetuousness
> ribs chilled
> in those spaces   of the mind.

The density of the poem's closing group of eleven lines presents a rush of thoughts, with occasional pauses in midline that seem to be pauses for breath as well as momentary breaks in the sudden forward movement of connected ideas. The density also reflects the content, mirroring Rich's depiction of herself as an "involuted" galactic cloud through which it has taken light fifteen years to travel.

In many of her poems of the late 1960's, Rich combines the cosmic and the personal; the words that unite the two can often be applied to astronomy, physics, and communication. In "Planetarium," one finds impulses of light, a "radio impulse" from Taurus, "signals," and "pulsations." In "The Demon Lover" (1966), in a figure similar to the one in "Planetarium" that unites heart and pulsar, a "nebula/ opens in space, unseen,/ your heart utters its great beats/ in solitude." Immediately preceding "The Demon Lover" in *Leaflets* is a Rich translation of a Gerrit Achterberg poem named for the Dwingelo observatory in Holland: "signals" are coming from constellations, "the void" whispers in the radio telescope, and "the singing of your nerves is gathered." In "Implosions," Rich offers the "word" of her pulse and asks the person she addresses to "Send out your signals."

Astronomy for Rich is, in one sense, a metaphor for the search for truth—particularly for the attempt to discover a new truth. The night sky, with its constellations (in the poem "Orion" and the "Dwingelo" translation as well as here), contains both the old myths and the potential for overturning those myths. The fact that astronomy involves studying pulses and signals also unites it with both the physical body and communication—and therefore with language, the instrument of the poet.

Themes and Meanings

Through its allusions to mythology, anecdotes from the history of astronomy, and final personal declaration, "Planetarium" depicts a moment of awakening consciousness. Rich states, in metaphorical terms, that she is at last seeing things clearly and is consequently taking a stand.

During the late 1960's, Rich was struggling to learn truths about herself and about the traditional female roles—wife and mother—that she had filled in the 1950's and early 1960's. In those earlier years, she experienced intense feelings of anger, conflict, and failure that she sought—desperately sought, she says—to understand. The "mad webs of Uranisborg" in "Planetarium" echo the "dark webs" (as she herself put it) that she groped among in those years.

Beginning with references to the women shaped like monsters that inhabit the sky—representing the distorted identities that men have given to women who refuse to fit into prescribed social roles—the poem moves to its closing declaration of independence both from those limited roles and from the old wrong-headed perceptions of those who refuse those roles. The power to change things begins with awareness. Astronomy, concerned with "observing" the sky—with vision—here embodies the struggle for that awareness. Rich frequently speaks of "instruments," of objects that can assist in the struggle to gain knowledge or freedom; sometimes, as here, the instrument and the person become one.

In a 1971 essay entitled "When We Dead Awaken: Writing as Re-Vision," Rich discusses the necessity for women to view society and history in new ways. "Re-vision," she says, is "an act of survival" that can enable women to refuse to participate in the "self-destructiveness of male-dominated society." She also notes the power of language in this process: "Writing is re-naming." Because seeing anew and writing anew are part of the same process, "Planetarium" concludes with the image of the woman being bombarded with "untranslatable" signals and pulsations that she must translate "for the relief of the body/ and the reconstruction of the mind."

In the 1965 poem, "Orion," Rich gazes at that constellation, first remembering how she thought of it as a child (her "cast-iron Viking"), then seeing it in the present as her "fierce half-brother" who "burns" like a defiant pirate. In "When We Dead Awaken," she writes that Orion represented the active part of herself; that is, she saw two alternatives, the female (various types of love) and the male (creative egotism), and saw no way of combining the two. In retrospect, she sees those as false alternatives. Rich calls "Planetarium," written three years later, a companion poem to "Orion." In the later poem, she says, "at last the woman in the poem and the woman writing the poem become the same person."

Howard McCrea

A POEM BEGINNING WITH A LINE BY PINDAR

Author: Robert Duncan (1919-1988)
Type of poem: Ode
First published: 1958; collected in *The Opening of the Field*, 1960

The Poem

This is an "open" poem drafted according to new writing principles developed in the mid-twentieth century, aimed at breaking up the repetitive structures of argument and discourse in so-called closed or conventional poetry. Content of various sorts flows into the poem constantly, demanding close attention to the winding course of its plot. The advantage of openness is the unpredictability of outcome that keeps the reader guessing at each new turn in the poem. This mode of suspense depends on the poet's ability to synthesize all that is introduced into the argument.

The ode, ancient or modern, is a form in which a poet takes up the theme of death and allows the mind to wander over many experiences before responding. The Romantic ode explores the emotions aroused by reaching middle life, as in William Wordsworth's "Ode: Intimations of Immortality," and Samuel Taylor Coleridge's "Frost at Midnight." Robert Duncan is thinking in particular of John Keats's "Ode on a Grecian Urn," with its theme of eternal innocence and desire set against the ravages of time. Duncan approaches the subject of aging similarly, regarding the innocence and desire of various lovers from his vantage point at a corrupt, degraded moment of history: "Only a few posts of the good remain."

The poem opens with a "misreading" of a line from an ode by the Greek poet Pindar (522?-443 B.C.), known for his sensuous lyricism. In the Pindar line, one hears a light foot with a lover's expectancy, but Duncan misreads the line as "the light foot hears." This error generates a new line of thought which the poet then follows through four numbered sections, each organized around the premise that what is meant by love is the mind's longing to flesh itself in a material form, or for the body to embrace the immortal ideal with its aging flesh. Mind and body are the ultimate lovers whose passion is never satisfied, and which art celebrates in the guise of male and female figures.

Duncan considers various depictions of classic lovers; after Pindar, he turns to Francisco Goya's portrait of Cupid and Psyche, which he interprets as "carnal fate that sends the soul wailing." Soul and mind are interchangeable terms; carnal fate is the eventual death of the body. Part II begins by noting that the gods prevent aging in these lovers; they are principles, or archetypes, more than figures representing actual life. Psyche, whose name stands for mind (as in psychology) "is preserved." Mind is eternal, its powers passing from one generation to the next, while the body lives, dies, and is buried. Hence, the "old poets" have died but their minds live on in texts.

Duncan shifts from ancient poets to American presidents, sarcastically referred to as the "*Thundermakers*," the opposite of poets in their self-interest, their violent political goals. The succession stretches back from Dwight D. Eisenhower, in his second term of office as the poem is being written, to Andrew Johnson, Abraham Lincoln's vice-president, who came to power after Lincoln's assassination in 1865. Duncan is thinking of Walt Whitman's lament for Lincoln in his poem "When Lilacs Last in the Dooryard Bloom'd," in which the themes of love and death emerge.

The mind knows mainly despair in its life as spirit; it witnesses death in all its forms, Duncan says in part III. This brings Ezra Pound to mind, who wrote *The Pisan Cantos* (1948) at the close of World War II and lamented the death of all his friends in Europe. He, too, writes of profound despair at the breaking up of a cherished ideal. Part IV returns to the footfall, now equated with the presence of any image in the mind waking it to the world around it. Other ill-fated lovers are introduced—Jason and Medea who turn against each other over the "golden fleece," and Orpheus and Eurydice, separated by the underworld. The poem closes on the image of sacred mountains where spirit is enshrined in nature, the religious form of expressing the mind's yearning to embrace the physical world.

Forms and Devices

Duncan tells the reader in his prose note in part IV that Pindar's art is "mosaic," composed of small units of language instead of being a "statue," composed of one material in a single form. This is an apt description of the ode in general, made of smaller thoughts joined by perceptual links to form a larger recognition. Duncan's poem shifts back and forth between pithy lyrics rich in metaphor to longer, digressive passages in which he lists items under a general heading, as with the American presidents who form a monotonous tradition of warriors linking periods of war.

Duncan was a careful student of sacred literature, and he copied many of its devices into his poems. Among liturgical techniques is the chant, with its repetitive syntax, which Duncan reproduces here to create a sense of magic and incantation and to remind readers of one of his poetic sources, the poetry of Walt Whitman, which also used repetitive phrasing throughout *Leaves of Grass* (1855). Repetition is found in prayer, lamentation, spells, children's songs, even states of madness, and thus leads to the threshold of the inner realm of dreams and spirits. Set against this tendency is the more prosaic language of political diatribe against the presidential line, with its strident tempo and anger.

Notable are the indented passages emphasizing the lilting rhythm of song, or used to "map" the process of ideation as Duncan struggles to clarify his understanding of love. In other passages, the language is compressed to gnomic density as Duncan reworks ancient myths. In part III, dedicated to the experimental poet Charles Olson, Duncan imitates Olson's method of spacing out lines and letting paragraphs loosely sprawl; the language here forms complex echoes as it recalls not only Olson but also his mentor, Pound, as it quotes directly from passages of *The Pisan Cantos*. Here, too, style advances argument; drawing on the words of other poets is a merging of spirits (minds) as all despair over the fate of Eros and the body.

Themes and Meanings

Duncan's poetry is a modern extension of Romantic themes—the love of beauty, the meaning of death, the sacred function of the poet, the role of vision in imagination. In this poem, Duncan explores the historic preoccupation with representing love. His interest in the subject is principally to grasp how this archetype of lovers yearning to possess one another in countless works of poetry, painting, and sculpture contains a deeper truth about the painful divisions lying within human nature. The poet is struck by the fact that the fable of unrequited or sundered passion stretches across the length of Western culture down to his own time. His allusions cite Pindar's poem from fifth century Greece, Goya's painting in the eighteenth century, Keats's ode in the early nineteenth century, Whitman's lament for Lincoln in the 1860's, and Rainer Maria Rilke's love poetry at the beginning of the twentieth century.

Duncan's view of poetry and the arts is that they express the same truths in a tradition not unlike that of the prophets of the Old Testament, as a heritage of sacred wisdom passed from one mind to another through the ages. Love lies at the heart of sacred wisdom: It expresses the irreconcilable relation between body and soul, divine and mortal beings, between the pure idea and the vagaries of nature, the image in the mind and the erratic powers of the artist to express it. Despair is thus the true voice of art, since vision can never be fully captured in language.

The presidential succession in the United States comes into the argument as a representation of the part of society that turns its back on vision. This is the materialistic dross of society, with its refusal to reach for the divine or the ineffable. Love is an ennobling form of despair, an elevated suffering in which the divine order of things is partially revealed.

The poem closes as it opened, with Duncan reading Pindar at his desk, having digressed into his own response to a line misread; it ends with the light of dawn spreading around him at the end of this meditation. The final three lines present the reader with the image of children turning in a circle, Duncan's metaphor of innocence prior to the divisive knowledge of adults. The dawn reminds him of youth, the beginning of life. The children's rhythmic turning in a game is both with and against time as they sing songs, uttering truths that will outlive them.

Paul Christensen

POEM ON HIS BIRTHDAY

Author: Dylan Thomas (1914-1953)
Type of poem: Lyric
First published: 1952, in *In Country Sleep*

The Poem

"Poem on His Birthday" is composed of twelve stanzas of nine lines each. It was written to mark Dylan Thomas' thirty-fifth birthday, and is the fourth and last of Thomas' birthday poems. In the first four stanzas, the poet looks out at the real and imagined scene from his house overlooking the bay on his thirty-fifth birthday. As he gazes at the river and sea illumined by an October sun, he "celebrates" but also "spurns" his birthday, likening the passage of his life to "driftwood."

The first stanzas abound with images of sea birds and fish—cormorants, flounders, gulls, curlews, eels, and herons—as they instinctively go about their appointed tasks. The poet is acutely conscious that the scene he observes, apparently so full of industrious life, is in truth a steady passage toward death. He realizes that all nature is a vast killing field: "Finches fly/ In the claw tracks of hawks." He applies this insight to his own life. In his inner ear he can hear bells tolling, not only in celebration but also in anticipation of his own death. Yet, although the natural scene is filled with the omens of death, it is also holy. The herons, with which each of the first three stanzas closes, are "steeple stemmed" and "bless."

Stanzas 5 to 7 switch from the natural scene to the landscape of the poet's own mind and his anticipation of a rejuvenated life after death. Once again he hears the tolling of thirty-five bells, one for each year of his age, but each bell is a reminder of death and loss. He imagines the terror of death and sees a flash of flame; then divine love "unbolts the dark," and he inherits a more joyous life "lost/ In the unknown, famous light of great/ and fabulous, dear God." This is not a conventional Christian heaven. The poet imagines his soul wandering with the spirits of all the sea creatures and birds that inhabited the "horseshoe bay," every one of them now a priest of God.

In stanza 8, the poet returns to the present, realizing that the liberating experience of death is a long way away. As long as he is alive, he must pray with the living. He knows that death is inherent in all things, and ultimately, all things will return to God. This awareness leads him, in stanza 9, to plead that he may be allowed, in his middle age, to mourn "the voyage to ruin [he] must run," but with full realization of the holiness of the process.

In the final three stanzas, the poet puts his anguish aside and exultantly celebrates his life. His five senses are undergirded by a spiritual sense that propels him through the world of "spun slime" to his "nimbus bell cool kingdom come." The closer he moves to death, the more holy the entire creation appears, and the more wholeheartedly he is able to praise it. Angels bestride every human soul, and this is a consoling thought for the poet as he "sail[s] out to die."

Forms and Devices

Throughout the poem, the most conspicuous poetic device is alliteration. "Bent bay," "birthday bell," "finches fly," "seizing sky," "dolphins dive," "boulders bleed," "midlife mourn," "secret selves," and "black base bones" are only some of the many examples. Less immediately noticeable is the assonance in such phrases as "mustardseed sun" and "driftwood thirty-fifth wind turned age." Sometimes Thomas combines alliteration with assonance, as with "tumbledown tongue," "This sandgrain day in the bent bay's grave," "livelong river's robe" and "Herons, steeple stemmed, bless." These devices, when combined with subtle variations in rhythm that occur throughout, give the poem a charming, incantatory quality, especially when read aloud, that works quite independently of the poem's meaning.

"Poem on His Birthday" is one of the last poems Thomas wrote; like most of his later poems, it is much less dense than his early work. It gives an impression of spaciousness and openness, unlike the taut intensity of many of the early poems. The result is greater lucidity and less obscurity. Some of Thomas' characteristic tricks with language can still be observed, however; he forms compounds to create new expressions, such as "cloud quaking," "wind turned," "tide daubing," and "steeple stemmed" (although Thomas does not hyphenate them). He creates expressions with more than one meaning, often employing an unusual syntax in the process, as in "I hear the bouncing hills/ Grow larked," "larked" being a way of saying "full of larks" but also implying a playful frolic (a lark), which reinforces the sense of triumph and exultation in the last stanza. Sometimes Thomas will surprise his reader by substituting an unexpected word, as in "the dew larks sing/ Taller this thunderclap spring," where "taller" replaces the expected "louder" and appeals to a different sense. The technique can also be seen in the synaesthetic line "The louder the sun blooms."

The image of the sea voyage toward death, derived in part perhaps from D. H. Lawrence's poem "The Ship of Death," underlies the poem. The sea is the sea of life, the all-embracing ocean from which life emerges and to which it returns. This image pattern is first suggested in stanza 1, in which the poet compares his life to a piece of driftwood. It can be sensed in the next two stanzas in the poet's observation of sea creatures and comes to the foreground in the references to shipwreck in stanzas 3 and 5. After going underground, it emerges again much more explicitly in stanza 9, in which the poet mourns "the voyage to ruin [he] must run." The image then dominates the remainder of the poem, culminating in the vision of the poet sailing out on a turbulent sea to die, accompanied by angels.

Themes and Meanings

While he was writing the poem, Thomas made a manuscript summary of the meaning he was trying to convey:

Now exactly half of his three score and ten years is gone . . . he looks back at his times: his loves, his hates, all he has seen, and sees the logical progress of death in every thing he has seen & done. His death lurks for him, and for all, in the next lunatic war, and still singing, still praising the radiant earth, still loving, though remotely, the animal creation also gladly pursuing their inevitable & grievous ends, he goes towards his. Why should he praise God, and the beauty of the world as he moves to horrible death? He does not like the deep zero dark and the nearer he gets to it, *the louder he sings, the higher the salmon leaps, the shriller the birds carol.*

The idea that every breath of life is also a movement toward death and that human-kind is intimately involved in the same processes that operate throughout the natural world is not a new thought for Thomas. He stated it in an early poem, "The Force That Through the Green Fuse Drives the Flower," and repeated it many times over. In "Poem on His Birthday," however, he draws a distinction. The creatures of the animal kingdom are all "Doing what they are told"; as they "Work at their ways to death," they have no self-consciousness and therefore suffer no mental anguish, un-like the poet, toiling at the "the hewn coils of his trade" in full awareness of what awaits him. Seen in this light, the poem is a successful struggle by the poet, who carries the burden of mortality, toward a heroic affirmation of the sacramental na-ture of the universe.

From the outset, the poet attempts to read the deeper realities in the natural scene. He watches as the "herons, steeple stemmed, bless," a phrase which builds on the religious connotations discernible in the phrase "Herons spire and spear" in stanza 1 ("spire" suggesting the spire of a church in addition to its primary meaning of "to rise upward"). When Thomas writes of herons, he draws on symbolic mean-ings that he has established in earlier poems. In another birthday poem, "Poem in October," he refers to the "heron/ Priested shore," and in "Over Sir John's Hill," the heron is also a central image of the holiness to be found in nature.

The poet's affirmation of life even in the face of death becomes even more impres-sive when it is realized that he has no firm intellectual basis for his faith. Although he possesses a vague sense of the divine realm as a *coincidentia oppositorium*—a harmony between the light and dark elements in creation—the stanzas which de-scribe the heaven that awaits all creatures, human and nonhuman, are full of contra-dictions and uncertainties. God is described as "fabulous" and "unborn"; the latter may mean "eternal," but it could equally mean "not present." The priestlike souls are "gulled," which suggests that they may be fooled, and the "cloud quaking peace" that envelops them does not sound very peaceful.

The doubts and ambiguities make the poet's ringing celebration of life in the final stanzas even more impressive. It does not seem to matter that this is an emotional rather than a carefully reasoned response. The poet has come to feel that his life is more than the piece of driftwood he described in the first stanza. He realizes that he is aflame with divine love and that this unites him in spiritual communion with every other human soul in its perilous, seaborn pilgrimage.

Bryan Aubrey

POEM WITHOUT A HERO

Author: Anna Akhmatova (Anna Andreyevna Gorenko, 1889-1966)
Type of poem: Meditation
First published: 1960, as *Poema bez geroya;* collected in *Requiem and Poem Without a Hero*, 1976

The Poem

Poem Without a Hero is subtitled "A Triptych." Each of the three parts consists of a series of lyrics which together amount to about 750 lines. The poem was composed over a period from 1940 to 1962, in three Russian cities (Leningrad, Tashkent, and Moscow). The poet continually came back to the poem, revising and changing her work under conditions of war, personal danger, sickness, and severe government censorship during the darkest of the Stalinist years. The complicated fate of the poem—fragmentary, frequently revised, and with a complex and fugitive publication history—is a mirror of the unsettled circumstances of its composition. Indeed, in her foreword Anna Akhmatova herself reports that she had been advised by readers to make her poem "clearer." She replies, "This I decline to do. It [*Poem Without a Hero*] contains no third, seventh, or twenty-ninth thoughts. I shall neither explain nor change anything. What is written is written."

Poem Without a Hero is Anna Akhmatova's protracted meditation on the fate of St. Petersburg/Leningrad, her beloved adopted city, a fate that is intricately bound up with the fate of herself and of those she loves and remembers. Many of the details of the life she shared with her compatriots are obscure to those not intimately familiar with that long vanished world, but the poet turns those intimate details into parables with which the contemporary reader of an English translation can identify.

The poem as a whole contrasts the creativity, youth, and passion of St. Petersburg (the city of Alexander Pushkin and many other Russian artists and poets) with the war-torn suffering of post-revolutionary Leningrad. The renamed "Leningrad" is a site of the silencing of poetry and of poets; it is the place where many of the heirs of the earlier cultural heritage, as well as the visionary promise of the Revolution, have been arrested and executed by the state. Although the poem has no "hero" in the conventional sense, the city itself, in both its romantic and its tragic incarnations (particularly as these qualities are embodied in the friends Akhmatova knew as a young woman), is the sustaining image of the heroic.

In the dedicatory poems that precede the first part of the poem proper, the unhappy love affair between two of Akhmatova's friends—a young officer named Vasevolod Knyazev and a beautiful dancer named Olga Glebova-Sudeikina—becomes the background for Akhmatova's exploration of her youthful aspirations at the St. Petersburg hangout for young artists named the Roving Dog. Akhmatova's focus of attention is on the consequences that follow from the fact that the dragoon's love for the lovely dancer was not returned. When he discovered her entertaining a rival, the officer shot himself and died outside her door. The death this young man chooses becomes entwined with the political, unchosen deaths of many of Akhmatova's associates, including her husband and the poet Osip Mandelstam, both of whom perish in the hands of the state police.

The dedication and foreword, however, were written long after the crystallizing event that triggered the poem. One learns about that event in the first part, entitled "Nineteen Thirteen": On New Year's Eve, 1940, Akhmatova is packing to flee to the relative safety of Tashkent just as the German army is about to begin the siege of Leningrad. She is "visited by shadows from the year 1913, disguised as mummers." At first she wishes to repel the masqueraders: "You're wrong:/ This isn't the Doge's Palace./ It's next door." The revelers insist, however, and the poet ultimately welcomes them, saying, "It's you I celebrate."

The guests are more than costumed celebrants. They are the dramatization of the literary, spiritual, and personal experience that is now practically gone. They are Faust, Don Juan, John the Baptist, Dorian Gray, figures from Greek mythology and Russian folklore, Hamlet, the Man in the Iron Mask, and the Prince of Darkness. Being able to see the past so clearly (she compares its vividness to Francisco de Goya's painting) is more upsetting than consoling. She asks, "But by what necromancy/ Am I living and they dead?" The black art of communicating with the dead (necromancy) is less potent than the art of the poet, and she exercises her greater power when she writes that "As in the past the future is maturing,/ So the past is rotting in the future—/ A terrible carnival of dead leaves."

The first part of the triptych ends with the poet back in the terrible present of 1941. Akhmatova, speaking through the poem, claims the right to be the "ancient Conscience" who lives to remember and speak of the death of the young lover. The persistence and power of the poem is validated in the emphatic capitalized words that conclude the first part: "WHAT IF, SUDDENLY, THE THEME ESCAPES/ AND HAMMERS ON THE WINDOW WITH ITS FISTS."

Part 2, subtitled "Obverse," is set in the same house in Leningrad on January 5, 1941. Akhmatova's editor is displeased with her work: "It's got to be simpler!/ You read, and when you've finished/ You still don't know who's in love/ With whom and why . . . who's/ Author and who's hero." It may well be that these questions and others of the same sort that follow from the editor's mouth are the very ones a contemporary reader might ask. Akhmatova's ironic strategy is to allow the reader to hear the banal words from a contemptible Soviet party functionary. She is able to imply a critique not only of those who censor art from a political perspective but also of those who expect it to be nothing more than ordinary transparent communication.

The ongoing meditation of the section is broken into numbered stanzas. At stanza 10, Akhmatova includes several lines of ellipses. At stanza 12 there is only blank space. Following Alexander Pushkin, Akhmatova includes these absences to indicate the poetry that could not be written, the life that could not be lived in the historical turmoil of the Soviet Union. Unlike the "heroic" figures of English Romantic poets, Akhmatova cannot transcend history. She alludes to Percy Bysshe

Shelley "dead on the shore" while Lord Byron "held the brand [which was Shelley's incombustible heart], and/ All the world's skylarks shattered/ The dome beneath eternity." These lines refer to Shelley's "Ode to a Skylark" and to "Adonais," his elegy on the death of his young fellow poet John Keats. Akhmatova here conflates two powerful confirmations in English of the poetic imagination against the ravages of suffering and death. She does not possess, she says, "that English muse . . . I have no ancestry." She refers to the thoughts of T. S. Eliot in *Four Quartets* (1943), spoken from a London under the threat of German invasion. Akhmatova endeavors both to connect with such an endangered traditional and personal past and to assert her specific and historic uniqueness.

"Epilogue" is part 3 of the poem, its final element. Akhmatova speaks from the point of view of, and on behalf of, the many exiles from the city of Leningrad. She is in Tashkent, but others who suffer exile, from New York to Siberia, feel with her that the "Bitter air of exile/ is like poisoned wine." Leningrad itself is nearly abandoned and the "witness of all in the world,/ at dawn or twilight" is an old maple that both inhabits the external world and looks into the room where Akhmatova began the poem some time before the devastation. The maple not only sees but bears auditory witness. It is neither the "first nor the last dark/ Auditor of bright madness." The sound it hears was the "red planet . . . streaking/ Through my still unbroken roof." The red planet is Mars, named for the god of war, and represents the ideological "redness" of Soviet repression. The maple tree outside Akhmatova's house registers both the foreign invasion by the Nazi army and the brutal domestic destruction of life and art by the Soviets. More significant than either its witnessing and auditing, its seeing and hearing the historical crisis, is the fact that the maple endures.

In the early part of the poem Akhmatova is "doubled" by the dancer Olga in her romantic entanglement with art and love. In this last part of the poem Akhmatova is doubled by an unnamed inhabitant of the gulag "In the dense taiga's heart." That the prisoner is nameless does not mean that he or she is depersonalized for the poet. On the contrary, the vivid personalities enduring terror and death in the subarctic forests, reduced to "a pile of camp-dust," are individuals—her former husband, her son, and her friends, especially the poet Mandelstam. Her memory of these people is so intense that she virtually becomes them. She writes that as her "double goes to interrogation,/ With the two thugs sent by the Noseless Slut" the sound she hears answering the thugs is "The sound of my own voice."

As the poem comes to an end, and as the poetic doubling that had begun as the romantic entanglements of youth ("Love, betrayal and passion") is completed in the tragic entanglements of the historical present, "Where there's no end to weeping/ The still fraternal graves," Akhmatova is able to say, "my city is shrouded but standing." The reader of "Poem Without a Hero" is left with the image of Akhmatova herself, looking down on the panoramic landscape of Russia from the window of the airplane that brings her back from exile to her city: "Knowing the calendar/ Of vengeance, having wrung her/ Hands, her dry eyes lowered, Russia/ Walked before me towards the east."

Forms and Devices

The conditions of censorship, betrayal, and imprisonment under which Akhmatova wrote and rewrote *Poem Without a Hero* are tangibly present in the form and technique of the poem. Critics point out her use of the characteristic Russian device known as *tainopis*, or secret writing: When a poet could not be named or quoted for reasons of censorship or discretion, lines from an officially permitted poet would be used instead as an ironic or secret reference to what the state had declared to be forbidden. Akhmatova said that this practice of *tainopis* enforced a subtlety on her poetry that would not otherwise have been possible.

The English-speaking reader of the Russian *Poem Without a Hero* is struck with the abundant presence—through direct quotation, indirect influence, and subtle allusion—of Romantic and modernist English poetry. Byron, Shelley, and Keats—the most conspicuously present—can be freely quoted and alluded to. Their association with freedom and the value of the individual is not seen to be threatening, although the work of contemporary Russian writers such as Mandelstam or Boris Pasternak would be. T. S. Eliot can express his sense of despair and recovery at the bombing and destruction of London when his counterparts (Akhmatova and her circle) in the Soviet Union could not do so in reacting to the siege of Leningrad.

Akhmatova employs "secret writing" not only in regard to English poets. Even classical Russian and other European poets and artists are enlisted in this subversive truth telling. Pushkin can speak of his sense of the endangerment of the city of St. Petersburg when Akhmatova cannot. Akhmatova can present Wolfgang Amadeus Mozart referring in *Don Giovanni* to the cruel and literally petrifying force of the Stalin-like "Commandatore" when no one in Soviet Russia would be allowed to make the same presentation. Russian-speaking readers of Akhmatova's poem must feel that *Poem Without a Hero* is a sanctuary of the forbidden heritage and treasures of Russian literature.

Themes and Meanings

The overarching theme of *Poem Without a Hero* is introduced in the frivolous harlequin and masquerade of the opening section and brought to conclusion in the ghostly prisoner-double of the poet in the last section. Put simply, the theme is that of the enduring personal power of poetry (especially Russian poetry) itself. This is a *Poem Without a Hero* in the usual sense—the hero is poetry itself. The anonymous brutality of Fascism and Communism operating in the name of the collective good are only a mockery of the true community, one that endures in the land, the people, and the language of which the poet is the steward.

The stewardship of the poet, her reverent salvaging of the poetry and culture of the past, is her memory. Her memory is the sanctuary that protects and preserves the living consciousness of her race; *Poem Without a Hero* is a record of that consciousness. The symmetry between Akhmatova's personal memory and the poem is established very early, when she describes the "absent Companionship" with which she will "hallow/ The coming forty-first year." This companionship takes the form of the mummers who invade her room as she packs for her evacuation from the city, as well as being seen as traces of the lost past. The sense of absent companionship is the ghostly presence of the dead, the preserving companionship of those who can live only in the imagination of the poet.

As the Russian critic Viktor Zhirmunsky observes, "the poet is both hero and author of the poem, contemporary and guilty along with the people of her generation but at the same time a judge pronouncing a verdict over them." In attempting to fathom the meaning of this intricate poem, the reader can keep in mind the ways that Akhmatova is committed to being at once a commentator on and an impresario of her life. She is determined to live deeply in the historical reality in which she finds herself. *Poem Without a Hero* attempts to mirror in every ambiguous and terrifying detail the events of the first forty or so years of the twentieth century. The meaning for which it strives is the meaning of the time during which it was written and which it reflects. To experience the poem is to experience the devastation of meaning itself in completely personal and at the same time completely historic terms.

Sharon Bassett

THE POEMS OF DOCTOR ZHIVAGO

Author: Boris Pasternak (1890-1960)
Type of poem: Poetic sequence
First published: 1957, in *Doktor Zhivago*; collected in *Doctor Zhivago*, 1958, and
The Poems of Doctor Zhivago, 1965

The Poems

The Poems of Doctor Zhivago is a collection of twenty-five poems that Boris Pasternak appended to his novel *Doctor Zhivago* (1958). Some were published individually in various publications; others appeared for the first time when the novel was published in Italian in 1957, in many other languages (including English) in 1958, and in the first Russian edition in Paris in 1959. The significance of the title lies in Pasternak's insistence on the authorship of Yuri Zhivago, the protagonist of the novel (Pasternak had good reason for this insistence). The poems are not simply appended to the novel without being connected to it. Their most important characteristic is the fact that they correspond to the novel closely and therefore must be considered an organic part of it. In fact, in the original volume, the poems are designated as the final, seventeenth, chapter of the novel.

One-half of the poems are told in the first person, that of Yuri Zhivago. One-fourth are in the form of a third person, often Christ, and an equal number are descriptions by an omniscient observer.

The opening poem of the collection, "Hamlet," is perhaps Pasternak's best-known poem. It can also serve as an introduction or prologue to the rest of the collection. The main reason for invoking Hamlet is his famous soliloquy in which he muses about his dilemmas and his indecision in solving them. Pasternak's Hamlet finds himself in a similar situation except that he is addressing Pasternak's own predicaments, time, and place. In this sense, "Hamlet" is the most autobiographical of the poems.

The collection follows a pattern of seasons, not chronologically within the novel but harmonically, starting with spring, the most natural symbol of a beginning. The first of the five poems of the spring cycle, "March," depicts the hustle and bustle of annual renewal, ending with the metaphor of a pile of manure, a source of the nutrients that are necessary for new life. "Holy Week" moves from renewal to resurrection, the foundation of Christianity. As it wakes up and rejuvenates everything, spring also awakens love feelings in the young man ("White Night"). "Bad Roads in Spring" recalls Zhivago's abduction by the partisans on his way home. The last poem in this cycle, "Explanation," refers to the three women of Zhivago's life— Tonya, Lara, and Marina—and the different appeals that they hold for him. As love is awakened, the light tone of the poem corresponds to the awakened sensuality in life and nature.

The summer cycle is short (only three poems), as is the Russian summer. "Summer in Town," "Wind," and "Hopbines" all picture the ripening stillness of the summer, sometimes interrupted by storms, while the two lovers, Zhivago and Lara, blissfully share their love amid the intoxicating fragrance of the summer idyll.

That idyllic atmosphere carries over into the autumn cycle, which consists of five poems. Many of these poems are connected in some way with Lara. The first, "False [Indian] Summer," exudes the contentment of family life amid the homey winter preparations from the bountiful harvest. This time, the woman in the poem is Tonya, Zhivago's wife. "Wedding" expresses earthy joys and affirmation of life in the fullest sense, but it also represents symbolically the spiritual wedding of Lara and Zhivago. In a highly lyrical fashion, "Autumn" depicts their happiness under the cloud of impending disaster, which makes their love even more fateful and passionate. At the same time, Yuri laments the departure of his wife, whom he still professes to love. "Fairy Tales" is the linchpin of the entire collection. It portrays a fearless knight who slays a dragon and saves a maiden—a reference to Yuri and Lara. The final poem in the autumn cycle, "August," bemoans their final parting at "this predestined hour," ending "years of timelessness."

The winter cycle also has five poems. The opening poem, "Winter Night," refers to the moment when Zhivago saw in a window a candle which had been lit by Lara. He had not met her yet, and the moment exemplifies the theme of predestined coincidence that runs through the novel. The next two poems, "Parting" and "Encounter," deal with Lara's departure from Zhivago and his pining for her, as he is unable to "draw a line" between her and him.

The remaining poems in the collection deal with the life, death, and resurrection of Christ as they influence Zhivago's life. "Star of the Nativity" celebrates the birth of the Child (Lara and Zhivago's?) in all its splendor, renewing Yuri's hopes after Lara's departure. The atmosphere of gloom that threatens to return in the city poem "Dawn" is relieved by the poet's rediscovered faith in God and by his identification with every human being and creature in nature. The poem seems to refer to the last years of Zhivago's life.

In the last six poems, Zhivago returns once again to spring. The second spring cycle points to life's new beginnings, as if to underscore the certainty that there is no end, only renewal. References to Christ continue. Through an episode in Christ's life, "Miracle" broaches a problem of artistic sterility and the need for God's patience and faith in the talented. "Earth" is related to "Dawn," except it takes place in the spring and shows the poet communing with friends, which is reminiscent of the early days of Christ and his disciples. The final four poems deal with the last days of Christ. "Evil Days" depicts Christ's thoughts and reminiscences as he was being betrayed and condemned. The two poems of "Magdalene" and "Garden of Gethsemane" are self-explanatory. In all these references to Christ, Zhivago sees parallels with his own destiny in his final days.

Forms and Devices

The Poems of Doctor Zhivago are of different forms and length. They are almost equally divided among trochaic and iambic meters, while only one is in anapest.

The stanzas are mostly rhymed quatrains, but some show varying lines.

Metaphors and images are the most important and powerful devices that Pasternak uses in these poems. Furthermore, metaphors are often used together with images, which tends to strengthen the impact of the metaphors. With the metaphor of Hamlet in the introductory poem, as Zhivago seems to reflect Pasternak's views and sentiments and Hamlet's thoughts parallel those of Zhivago, it can be assumed that Hamlet speaks for the author as well. While translating William Shakespeare's *Hamlet* (c. 1600-1601), Pasternak noted that the play is not a drama of weakness but of duty and self-denial. Accordingly, "Hamlet" emphasizes those two traits of Zhivago's character. Hamlet's lament "I stand alone" implies that Zhivago is weak. Yet, Zhivago often shows a surprising strength of character. Thus, just as Hamlet is a victim of his sense of duty and sacrifice, often too weak to defy fate and at times unable or unwilling to act toward the solution of his dilemma, so is Zhivago a victim of the events and forces that he cannot control. The depth of Zhivago's precarious position is seen in the image of thousands of binoculars staring at him in the murky night. He is ready to admit defeat because someone else has set the order of the acts and "nothing can avert the final curtain's fall." The only thing left for him to do is to beg the Father to remove the cup from him. Herein lies the answer to his prayers. For, by frequently using the metaphor of Jesus Christ as the only salvation, Zhivago steels himself enough to strengthen his sense of duty and sacrifice, thus transforming himself from a weakling into a strong man.

Another set of metaphors is connected with the perennial change of seasons that symbolizes the endless passage of life to death and death to life. There are numerous images reinforcing the seasonal changes of humanity and nature and their constant rejuvenation. Spring is "that corn-fed, husky milkmaid," and the pile of manure— the source of fertility— "is pungent with ozone" ("March"). During the summer, linden trees "have a glum look about them/ Because they haven't slept themselves out" ("Summer in Town"). In the autumn, Yuri's woman sheds her garments as a grove sheds its leaves ("Autumn").

"Fairy Tales" is a metaphor containing the central theme of the novel, that of the knight saving a maiden from a dragon. Although the knight is anonymous, it is not hard to see in him the legendary Saint George slaying the dragon. A variation of the name "George" in Russian is "Yuri." From the plot of the novel, one can easily see Yuri saving Lara from her demon Komarovsky, thus affirming his love for her and the sense of duty and sacrifice proclaimed in "Hamlet."

Lara is also referred to metaphorically. She is the symbol of beauty and freedom, standing for Russia itself. Zhivago dreams about her as if "she had been cast up from the depths/ By a high wave of destiny." In the Orthodox mythology, Larisa (Lara) stands for a seabird or a sea gull. Lara is thus a force in nature, rather than merely a woman.

Many metaphors are connected directly with Christ. One depicts Christ's encounter with a fig tree full of leaves but barren of fruit which is destroyed by God for its uselessness. The poet likens this situation to artistic sterility and pleads with God for patience ("Miracle"). Another metaphor relates to Mary Magdalene, in a clear reference to Lara. Both women are sinful, yet they play consoling roles: Magdalene washes Christ's feet on the eve of his death, and Lara offers Yuri the true love that he craves. Finally, in "Garden of Gethsemane" Zhivago sees similarities between his troubles with his "Judas" and "Pharisees" with those of Christ. Yet, as Christ did, Zhivago will live again (the meaning of the name "Zhivago").

One of the strongest devices of Pasternak's artistry is imagery. His image of the nightingale that enthralls with its singing but also heralds approaching danger with its frantic song ("Bad Roads in Spring") is a beautiful one. Another striking image is that of a candle burning in a window, which seems to fascinate Yuri even though he knows nothing of its origin ("Winter Night"). A flickering light in the dark winter night adds an aura of mysticism. It also points to predestination at work because Lara, the woman who had lit the candle, will become the woman of his life.

Themes and Meanings

The Poems of Doctor Zhivago have several meanings that parallel closely those of the novel proper. In fact, almost all the poems can be traced to events in the novel. Questions arise, however, as to whether these poems are necessary and whether they provide something that the novel does not. The poems are not concerned with the plot, and they do not refer openly to the characters of the novel. What they do provide is additional emphasis on important aspects of the novel. Moreover, they offer a deeper insight into the psyche of Yuri Zhivago in a condensed poetic form.

The central theme of *Doctor Zhivago* is the struggle of a Russian intellectual to preserve his individuality amid revolutionary changes and to fulfill his artistic destiny in service to truth, goodness, and beauty. By representing a window into Zhivago's soul, the poems allow the reader to follow his heroic struggle to preserve his self, which eventually leads to a triumph of individualism over collectivism.

Another important theme of the novel is the idea of the immortality of the human spirit, and the poems express this idea much more effectively than the prose. As well-constructed, compact works of art, they celebrate a constant renewal of life through the regular change of seasons, thus crystallizing the triumph of life over death.

The novel shows that humans are spiritual beings in a constant struggle with forces attempting to rob them of their spirituality. By displaying a deeply felt, although somewhat unconventional, religiosity and communion with Christ in some of the best poems in the collection, Zhivago's spirituality triumphs over the materialism that is rampant around him.

Individuality, immortality, and spirituality are unthinkable without personal freedom. Zhivago fights to preserve at all costs his freedom and the freedom of those he loves, thus bringing about a triumph of freedom over slavery, as best illustrated in "Fairy Tales."

Finally, the novel is basically a love story in several variations. Zhivago's love for the three women, each in his own way, coupled with his love for his fellow human beings and for the wonders of nature, is demonstrated in the poems. Some of the poems can be considered apotheoses of love—both pure and down-to-earth love.

The novel tells of Zhivago's life and mission but also of his poetic talent. Yet, there is little tangible evidence in the novel of his poetic achievements. The poems bolster Pasternak's assertion that Zhivago is a great poet, which gives the character added importance and his life deeper fulfillment.

In the last analysis, both the novel and the poems belong to their creator, Boris Pasternak, and they enhance his already well-established stature, not only in Russian letters but also in world literature. As one of his last works which, more than anything else, garnered for him the Nobel Prize in Literature, *Doctor Zhivago* and *The Poems of Doctor Zhivago* occupy a special place in Pasternak's opus.

Vasa D. Mihailovich

POETRY

Author: Marianne Moore (1887-1972)
Type of poem: Lyric
First published: 1921, in *Poems*

The Poem

Marianne Moore's "Poetry," one of her earliest lyrics, is written in free verse. It is so subtle in its arrangement on the page as to seem almost fragmentary, a quality frequently found among Imagist poets of the early twentieth century. The Imagist movement, by which she was much influenced, proposed in their manifesto to discard the shopworn and hackneyed diction of the previous generation. They intended to free poetry from the strictures of metrical patterns so as to approximate more closely the rhythms of colloquial speech.

Moore begins her poem with an astonishing confession for a poet: She says about poetry that "I, too, dislike it." The assumption is that most people do not like poetry simply because it has ceased to reflect the world they know or the speech they use. She hints slyly that the writing of poetry is only fiddling, thus voicing the frustration of many poets who take pains in the search for the *mot juste*, the "right word," to express their feelings, impressions, and ideas.

Having nothing but "contempt" for "all of this fiddle," and questioning the value of the whole process, she can still maintain that poetry is valid, but only insofar as it is "genuine." As long as a poem is a mirror of reality and is exact in its detail, as opposed to presenting idealized preconceptions, there is much to be said for poetry. Moore would insist on the real "hands that can grasp," as opposed to the lily-white and delicate hand of the idealized woman. Similarly, she would prefer the "hair that can rise" to the silken tresses so much admired by the Victorians.

Moore counsels her reader and other poets to look clearly and steadily at the object or subject; when they do, she notes, they will see a most "unpoetic" scene of "wild horses taking a roll," or perhaps an "immovable critic twitching his skin like a horse that feels a flea." By looking at things anew, one finds a much more substantial body of subject matter to be explored. The poet and the reader are not confined, then, to the traditional themes of poetry which have become tiresome with overuse; nor are they confined in their treatment of such subjects. In effect, there are as many subjects as there are things in the world, all of which are equally fit and proper for poetry. Moore would not even exclude the most banal of "business documents" or the most boring "school-books" as too prosaic for consideration.

She concludes by insisting that "all . . . phenomena are important" and speculates as to why, in the "imaginary" constructs of the mind, such as a garden, poets cannot present to the reader a real "toad." In all of its ugliness and with all of its curious features, she implies that the toad may be much more interesting than the prince. If "you" are interested in the honest and "genuine" toad, and in that which shows you, in all its rawness, the material of the physical world, and if, furthermore, you are not offended by his intrusion into the garden, then "you are interested in poetry."

Forms and Devices

Certainly one of the most notable aspects of "Poetry" is the sense of liberation of thought and expression that the free-verse form allows. The natural, colloquial diction, almost intimate and companionable, encourages trust as Moore leads the reader into territories in which the familiar is viewed in an uncommon way, and the unfamiliar (that is, to the topography of poetry), is viewed with all the precision of a scientist's eye.

Her own surprise at the riches that her careful observation brings to her is conveyed by her images, which are vigorous in detail, and her sound devices, which are traditional though barely perceptible in the context of her free-verse.

She is particularly skillful in her use of the internal rhyme. Rhyme, as used in "Hands that can grasp, eyes/ that can dilate, hair that can rise," holds together the poetic line internally, although it scarcely presents a familiar poetic image. She uses a half-rhyme as well on several occasions, most notably when she observes that we "do not admire what/ we cannot understand: the bat" ("what" is half-rhymed with "bat"). Far from being accidental, the half-rhyme indicates how tenuous the relationship of man to bats is.

She links much of her world of nature in a curious and exciting way by this use of sound. Images of another sort appear which, although strange and startling in themselves, are given an added vividness by the sound used in describing them. The "elephants pushing," for example, fairly imitates the lumbering visual image of the beasts. Although she has a fondness for such imagery, the ridiculous in human behavior does not escape her attention. Moore declares that although all these phenomena are important, a "distinction" must be made; humorously, she envisions a situation in which ponderous and solemn ideas are promulgated and "dragged into prominence by half poets" — perhaps, half-baked ideas by "half poets." The alliteration and explosive consonants emphasize their self-importance.

Frequently, too, her humor is displayed in her juxtaposition of images. Although she provides no verbal link of comparison, it is clear that the "wild horse taking a roll," and the "critic twitching his skin like a horse that feels a flea" bear more than a passing resemblance; both suffer from a minor aggravation of a perpetual itch.

In "Poetry" the animal world provides the source of much of Moore's imagery, and its appearance is a disquieting departure from the more frequent traditional views of animals, where the wildest might be a tiger, hand-painted by the poet himself. Moore's are very real creatures in a very real world.

Themes and Meanings

The main theme of "Poetry" is simply what poetry is, what a suitable subject is, and what approach should be taken by both the poet and the reader.

It is clear that Moore has some difficulty, as do most readers, in defining poetry.

She comes as close as she can to a definition through the negative. It is easier, in this case, to define the subject by realizing what it is not, and by eliminating those characteristics, to understand it.

Poetry is not intended to be informational. In effect, the purpose is not to disseminate knowledge as "business documents" are so intended; although, as Moore observes, they cannot be totally excluded as part of the raw material of experience. Nor is poetry intended to inspire with a "high-sounding interpretation" of experience, thus abstracting it to fit a mold of thought. Poetry is not intended, furthermore, to teach like the "immovable critic." It may do so, but that is not its essential purpose. Above all, poetry is not intended for simple self-aggrandizement on the part of the poet, with all its attendant "insolence and triviality."

What, then, is poetry? Moore insists, above all, that poetry must be "genuine" for both the poet and the reader. The response of both must not be colored by preconceptions or learned responses. The ideas and emotions cannot be, she believes, "so derivative as to become unintelligible," because "we do not admire what we cannot understand." Moore also demands that the subject be firmly grounded in reality, that the images, sounds, and rhythms mirror life as people know it, in all its "rawness." By "rawness" the poet means both the data of life and the recognition that life is not ideal, that there is much ugliness but that poetry is certainly no sermon to proclaim high moral values.

The raw material—that is, the data—should find its way into an artistic structure which is the poet's own particular "garden" of impressions, of feelings, of ideas absorbed in a given time and place—that is, the "imaginary garden" which is created by the art of poetry. It must be honest, and it must be "genuine."

When Marianne Moore edited a subsequent collection of her work (*Collected Poems*, 1951), she ruthlessly deleted from "Poetry" all but the first three lines. One can only speculate as to the rationale for her doing so. Perhaps she believed that she had violated her own dictum by teaching in "Poetry."

Maureen W. Mills

POLITICAL POEM

Author: Amiri Baraka (LeRoi Jones, 1934-   )
Type of poem: Meditation
First published: 1964, in *The Dead Lecturer*

The Poem

"Political Poem" is a fairly short poem of twenty-eight lines, divided into three stanzas, written in free verse. Despite the title, it is no more political than most of Amiri Baraka's poems; rather, it is a poem about the politics in American poetry.

The first six-line stanza is by far the most easily accessible. It is a short meditation on the effects of luxury on thought. Basically, Baraka is saying that luxury is a way of avoiding thought. Living in luxury is like living under a heavy tarpaulin, protected from information and ideas. In such sheltered conditions, theories can thrive easily, because they do not have to contend with unpleasant ideas or with facts which might contradict the theory.

Although there is no explicit first-person identity in the first stanza, there is no reason to think that the speaker is anyone other than Baraka himself. In the second stanza, though, a first-person narrator appears. The stanza begins with the opening of a parenthesis that never closes. This seems to be a way of signaling that the poetic voice is about to shift, and in fact, the first word of the stanza is "I," indicating that a definite persona is now speaking. The speaker says that he has not seen the earth for years, and now associates dirt with society; the implication is that he is cut off not only from the earth but also from people. He goes on living as a natural man, but he knows that this cut-off existence is unnatural.

When a second parenthesis opens, it seems to be the same speaker still. The parenthesis shows how the small interruptions of answering a phone and getting a sandwich prevent him from even following through on the thoughts he has been pursuing. More important, however, his poem has been undone by his "station," as one of the people living in too much luxury. When the parenthesis closes, he ruminates on the mistake that people such as he make by trying to fill their lives with an unclear ideal of love.

The third stanza begins with the thought that the speaker's poetry is also undone by "the logic of any specific death"—meaning that any individual death can have more power than any poem. Then another parenthesis begins, which also remains open. The speaker refers to "Old gentlemen/ who still follow fires," perhaps meaning professors and critics of art and poetry. They ask the poet, "Who are you? What are you/ saying?" In their eyes, "you" are "Something to be dealt with." Their rules and guidelines of art and poetry are poisonous; they say "No, No,/ you cannot feel," unlike the poetry of the Beat generation, with which Baraka was associated, which values emotion highly. The "fast suicide" of the last line, similar to the message of the "old gentlemen," is the suicide of renouncing feeling.

Forms and Devices

Amiri Baraka was greatly influenced by the Surrealist movement of the early part of the twentieth century, particularly by the Dadaist movement which flourished in France in the 1910's and 1920's. Surrealism in general was a movement in all the arts that disdained conventional forms. The Surrealists tried to create images directly from the unconscious mind, without putting them into any conventional framework. The Dadaists took this one step further, and tried deliberately to subvert conventional forms in art.

Baraka was not trying to write Dadaist or Surrealist poetry in "Political Poem," but the influence of these movements can be seen in, among other things, his unconventional grammar and punctuation. He used such devices as opening two parentheses that he never closes, and he wrote much of the poem in a series of sentence fragments. The use of fragments demands that the reader find the connection between the individual images for himself or herself; the reader must re-create the associations that Baraka saw.

Much of the meaning of this poem is created by its images, and each image may suggest several meanings. For example, when near the end of the first stanza he talks about theories thriving "under heavy tarpaulins," the reader might picture these tarpaulins as covering the clearly negative "open market/ of least information" of lines 3 and 4. When taken together with the opening of the next stanza, however, in which the speaker talks of being cut off from the earth, dirt, and seeds, a reader might get the sense that theories are like mushrooms, which grow in dark enclosed spaces, while ideas are seeds, which need the fertile "dirt" of society to take root. Both interpretations are suggested. Similarly, there are many possible interpretations of an image such as "The darkness of love,/ in whose sweating memory all error is forced." It refers not only to the dark and unclear ideal of love but also to two people making love in the dark.

To appreciate Baraka's poems fully, one must read or hear them read aloud; "Political Poem" is no exception. Baraka works closely with the sounds and rhythms of his poem. A simple phrase such as "Gettin up/ from the desk to secure a turkey sandwich" begins with almost waltzlike rhythm, which is broken at the end. This rhythm has a light, singsong quality to it that is noticeably missing from the lines immediately before and after the parenthetical material from the lines immediately before and after the parenthetical material in the middle of the second stanza, and it sets up a similarly singsong quality in the next lines, "the poem undone/ undone by my station, by my station." Although the speaker here is lamenting that his poem is "undone," the music seems to suggest that the interruption from his weighty meditations comes as a relief—indicating that the relief he feels is the real problem.

Themes and Meanings

"Political Poem" is a cautionary statement about the danger of separating poetry from real-world society and politics, but also about the danger of putting it at the service of political beliefs that are out of touch with society. Although it would be a mistake to identify the first-person speaker of the poem with Baraka himself, it would also be a mistake to miss such things as the reference to Newark, where Baraka lived when he wrote this poem. The speaker who declares, "I have not seen the earth for years," seems to be a version of Baraka—that is, the poet he would be if he did *not* write poetry that actively engaged the political issues of his day.

As such, because this poet is trying to write a type of poetry that can only thrive "under heavy tarpaulins," his poem is easily interrupted—by a phone call, by a turkey sandwich, and by the "bad words of Newark." The real world undoes his poetry.

In the course of his ruminations on this dilemma, however, this poet's position evolves. He realizes the futility of trying to create poetry in isolation from the world and cannot help but see his efforts in a wider context of trying to fill the breech of "this/ crumbling century" with "the darkness of love." Yet this position—of trying to create a bridge of love with his poems—is insufficient and is "undone by the logic of any specific death." More must go into the poetry; anger as well as love has a place in poetry, because there are some things which must be rejected.

When, in the third stanza, a parenthesis opens (it will remain open), it marks the completion of the change of the persona that was presented in the second stanza. That is, the speaker who was presented as the type of poet Baraka would be if he avoided political themes in his poetry has been transformed into the poet that Baraka was at the time he wrote this. This is the poet who knows that theories are worthless without ideas and that reason cannot replace feeling in either politics or poetry.

The second stanza concerns itself specifically with the creation of a poem, but a second meaning emerges if the reader understands that Baraka is also addressing the dangers of formulating political theories while out of touch with society. When a theory of politics tries to substitute sterile reason for feeling, it becomes politically as noxious as the poem that makes this substitution. For either a poetically or politically inspired person, this substitution is suicidal to the cause. Another point the poem makes, then, is that poetry should not serve the reasons of politics, but that good poetry is nurtured by the same ground from which healthy politics grow.

Thomas J. Cassidy

POPPIES IN JULY

Author: Sylvia Plath (1932-1963)
Type of poem: Lyric
First published: 1965, in *Ariel*

The Poem

"Poppies in July" is a short poem written in free verse. Its fifteen lines are divided into eight stanzas. The first seven stanzas are couplets, and the eighth consists of a single line. The title presents an image of natural life at its most intense — at the height of summer. It evokes a pastoral landscape and suggests happiness, if not joy or passion. The title is ironic, however, because the poem is not a hymn to nature but a hallucinatory projection of the landscape of the speaker's mind and emotions.

Sylvia Plath begins the poem innocently, even playfully, as the speaker addresses the poppies, calling them "little poppies." The tone changes immediately, however, as the poppies become "little hell flames," and the speaker asks if they do no harm. She can see them flickering, but when she puts her hands into the imagined flames, "nothing burns." She feels exhausted from watching the poppies, but she imagines that their "wrinkly and clear red" petals are like "the skin of a mouth." This introduces an erotic element into the poem, but it is followed by an image of violence — "A mouth just bloodied." Immediately, another change occurs, as the poppies become "little bloody skirts." This shocking image marks the exact center of the poem.

Aside from the obvious implications of bloody skirts, another meaning is suggested by the fact that "skirt" is a slang term for a woman, and in England, where Plath was living, "bloody" is a curse, a profanity. Combined with the word "marry," which occurs later in the poem, these details suggest that the speaker is responding to her husband's marital infidelity. In anger, she has bloodied his mouth, and her invocation of "hell flames" indicates that she would like to see the adulterers punished for their sin against her. The speaker feels like she is in hell. As thoughts of the situation surface in her consciousness, she turns away from images based on the color, shape, and texture of the poppy, to images based on its smell and the drugs that are extracted from it.

The poppies smell like "fumes" to her. In a derangement of her senses, she confuses smell with touch and says she cannot touch them, as she could not touch the earlier "flames." She asks the poppies where their opiates are and thinks of "nauseous capsules." She thinks she could achieve relief if she could "bleed, or sleep," but an emotional wound does not bleed, and her state of mind will not let her sleep. An alternative is to "marry a hurt like that," but she cannot accept or tolerate the situation. She wants the "liquors" of the poppy to "seep" to her in what she calls "this glass capsule." She feels separated from reality; this is why she cannot touch anything. She wants the liquors to be "colorless," with everything suggested by the color of poppies to be refined away.

Forms and Devices

The couplet form traditionally exemplifies order, balance, harmony, and reason. Each line exhibits the same grammatical and metrical structures. Each couplet forms a complete unit of meaning, and often the lines rhyme. Plath draws on this tradition by writing the poem in couplets, but she violates the form by writing free-verse lines. Her couplets represent the speaker's effort to control her thoughts and feelings, which are expressed in the lines of free verse. The length, rhythm, and grammar of these lines vary with the ebb and flow of the speaker's emotions. For example, the longest line in the poem evokes the image— "the skin of a mouth"— which precipitates the speaker's anger in the next couplet, which in turn refers to the bloodied mouth and bloody skirts. This is the shortest couplet in the poem, each line having only five syllables. It concentrates and releases the speaker's anger, like the blow of a fist.

The free-verse couplets also facilitate the presentation of the images of the poem. These follow one another according to the speaker's associational process in a logic of emotion, rather than the couplet's usual logic of reason. The images advance leap by leap, each suggesting the next by a shared characteristic, such as color, shape, or texture, in a series that is increasingly disturbing. Plath transforms the images, one into another, in a manner characteristic of motion pictures, in which one image dissolves as another forms to take its place. The poppies fade into flames; the petals dissolve and the skin of a mouth replaces them. This technique contributes to the hallucinatory quality of the poem.

The poem exhibits instances of parallel grammatical and metrical structures, but the parallels do not usually appear together. The word "little" prefaces the images of poppies and flames in the first line, then is repeated in the eighth line in a phrase which is parallel to the first two— "little bloody skirts." When the three images prefaced by the word "little" are considered together, they form a complex of associations— poppies, flames, skirts— suggesting sexual passion. The first image of a mouth is in the sixth line and the second is in the eighth line, but the third does not occur until the twelfth line, where the speaker thinks she could achieve relief if her mouth could "marry a hurt like that." The hurt refers back to the mouth bloodied in the seventh stanza. Likewise, the phrase "nauseous capsule" finds its parallel in "this glass capsule."

Many other examples of parallelism occur in the poem. It is as if a poem written in traditional couplets has exploded, and the speaker is trying to put the parts back together. This effectively expresses what has happened to the speaker's marriage. A couplet is a pair of lines. The one-line stanza that ends the poem may signify the separation of the speaker from her marital partner, perhaps through loss of consciousness or even death.

Themes and Meanings

The term "Confessional" has been applied to the poetry of Sylvia Plath. It refers to a poem in which the poet speaks in her own person, not as the impersonal poet or through a persona. Subjects and themes of confessional poetry are usually intensely personal, often disturbing, experiences and emotions. "Poppies in July" has sources in Plath's life, and its meaning is strongly implied by its place in a sequence of poems Plath wrote during a three-month-period in the summer of 1962: "The Other," "Words heard, by accident, over the phone," "Poppies in July," "Burning the Letters," and "For a Fatherless Son." Sylvia Plath committed suicide on February 11, 1963, by inhaling fumes from her gas stove.

In her autobiographical novel, *The Bell Jar* (1963) published just before her death under the pseudonym Victoria Lucas, Plath depicts the schizophrenic episode that preceded her first suicide attempt, when she was twenty. Esther Greenwood, the heroine, imagines that a great bell jar has descended around her, enclosing her in an invisible and colorless barrier between herself and the world. She attempts to kill herself by taking sleeping pills. The bell jar parallels the "glass capsule" of "Poppies in July."

Although the poem reflects events in Plath's life, it transcends purely personal experience and stands on its own, communicating its meaning without the need for references to outside sources. The poet speaks not only for herself but for all who have experienced the mental and emotional torment accompanying the infidelity of a partner in marriage.

The speaker of the poem is alienated from life, represented by the blood-red poppies. When she transforms the image of the bloody mouth into the vaginal mouth implied by "bloody skirts," she expresses an emotion close to revulsion for all of the blood of female experience—menstruation, loss of virginity, giving birth. The image may also suggest rape; Plath hemorrhaged as the result of a date rape when she was a student at Smith College. When the poppies become flames, they represent sexual passion, which the speaker's husband did not control and which she cannot feel. The alienation expressed through these images causes her to desire the oblivion represented by the opiates that can be derived from the poppy, "dulling" her senses and "stilling" her mind.

Most of the poems collected in *Ariel*, including a companion poem to "Poppies in July"—"Poppies in October"—were composed after "Poppies in July." In the companion poem, poppies are a "love gift/ Utterly unasked for," representing the exhilaration of life. Poetry itself, for Plath, is "the blood jet," as she expressed it in "Kindness." "This glass capsule" from "Poppies in July" can also represent the poem, as well as imply the detachment necessary for the poet to create art out of life.

James Green

PORTRAIT OF A LADY

Author: T. S. Eliot (1888-1965)
Type of poem: Dramatic monologue
First published: 1915; collected in *Prufrock and Other Observations*, 1917

The Poem

The title of the poem is drawn from two sources: Henry James's novel *The Portrait of a Lady* (1881) and Ezra Pound's poem "Portrait D'une Femme" (1912). The lady in question in this poem and in Pound's is based upon Adeleine Moffatt, who lived in Boston and invited T. S. Eliot and other selected undergraduates to tea and conversation. She was described in Conrad Aiken's fictionalized autobiography, *Ushant: An Essay* (1952), as "the *précieuse ridicule* to end all preciosity, serving tea so exquisitely among her bric-a-brac."

The epigraph is taken from Christopher Marlowe's play *The Jew of Malta* (published 1633) and is important for setting a mood of betrayal, though, by comparison, the persona in Eliot's poem appears to be much less culpable than the character in Marlowe's play. This character, Barabas, accuses himself of certain lesser crimes in order to disguise his poisoning of a convent of nuns.

The poem, in three sections of approximately forty lines each, follows for a year the relationship between the male persona and the lady. In free verse, the young man (clearly much younger than the lady) quotes his hostess, at least as he remembers her words, and offers his highly judgmental, apparently detached, introspective reaction.

In the first section, situated in midwinter, the two are returning from a concert of Frédéric Chopin's piano music. In this very brief space, the lady refers to friendship five times. Friendship seems a bit of a letdown, though, since the young man has begun his account by describing the room as looking like Juliet's tomb. This allusion to the romantic double-suicide that concludes William Shakespeare's *Romeo and Juliet* (c. 1595-1596), like the violent and repulsive epigraph from Marlowe, makes this harping upon "friendship" seem unattractively bland. The young man's response is proud rejection of the lady's interest—though he says nothing of the sort to her. The section ends with his escape from her parlor to the male habitat of a bar, where he can remain untouched by her emotions and, in conversation, can dissect her with his comrades.

The second section is set in spring, but the only thing blooming (apart from the mention of lilacs) appears to be the young man's increasing discomfort in the lady's presence. The lady recognizes in the lilacs an example of the fleeting beauty of youth and alludes to her earlier life and to her present comparative old age and fragility. She describes the young man as embodying, like the lilacs, the perfection, beauty, and strength of burgeoning life, to which, she confesses, she can add little. The last stanza of this section offers the youth's embarrassed reaction to the lady's observations and his confused reflection upon this embarrassment. Why, he wonders, should this woman's problems upset him more than the tragedies he reads about in the newspaper—and why should he still be upset when a particular melody or the fragrance of flowers reminds him of her?

The third section takes place in autumn, a time of dying. The young man's emotional discomfort in visiting the lady is now felt in his whole body—it is as though he is walking, perhaps like an animal, on his hands and knees when he mounts the stairs. The two discuss his going away on a permanent basis to Europe, and she recognizes that he has remained as distant emotionally as he soon will be physically. Her clear insight forces the youth to even greater attempts at deception: He does not want to lose "control" of the situation by letting her understand how disturbed he is. In the last stanza, he imagines her death and frames the questions that will plague him even after she is gone.

Forms and Devices

Eliot claimed that the form of expression in this poem and in much of his early writing drew upon the conversational style of later Elizabethan drama and upon the French Symbolist, Jules Laforgue. The latter's influence on him is evident especially in "Portrait of a Lady," which marks the development in Eliot's style from that of a romantic to a postromantic. There is in the diction and tone of the language, in other words, a sense of greater detachment and irony, a tentativeness and a general sense of disillusionment.

Rhyme is scattered throughout the verses, and the rhythm is frequently close to iambic pentameter, but both rhyme and rhythm follow no set pattern. Instead, they are used to establish a languid and even haltingly self-conscious tone, close enough to ordinary speech to convey the scene and characters convincingly, but musical enough to render these few chosen moments of memory as special and unusually significant in the mind of the persona.

Music is, in fact, the principal metaphor in the poem, representing the fluid movement of emotions between the older woman and the younger man. Beginning with a reference to a Chopin prelude, identified with the lady, the poem is interrupted by the "false note" of the young man's own prelude, beating in his head in rebellious counterpoint. As the relationship fails to develop and harmonize, the jarring music from the two players leads inevitably to a "dying fall" and an early, disastrous collapse of their concert. In the concluding stanza of the first section, for example, the movement from the delicacy of violins, through the harshness of cornets and drums and on to the dubious "music" of clocks in watchtowers, demonstrates the young man's insistence on getting away from the highly strung world of the lady's tea parties and back to his pedestrian world of beer and pretzels. Along with an emphasis on music, the poem makes insistent reference to the passage of time, with careful allusion to the specific season in each section, as well as an indication of various timepieces.

Themes and Meanings

This early poem already sounds themes that were to obsess Eliot throughout his career, reaching its fullest expression in his late *Four Quartets* (1943). The passage of time, its effects on the body and human emotions, the individual's consequent search for some sense of permanence, history, and personal significance—all are present even in an early poem such as "Portrait of a Lady." One sees their expression principally in the older woman's quiet but somewhat desperate attempt to craft a meaningful relationship with this younger man, finding in his relative youth the energy and hope that seem to be slipping from her grasp.

The poem, however, seems finally to focus attention not on the lady but on the youth. The reader is made quite aware that the woman is being viewed through the youth's rather haughty eyes, and one gradually recognizes the speaker's own discomfort not only with the lady's "advances" but also with his own timorous retreats. He is resentful of her attempt to treat him as an equal, as simply one who, were it not for their arbitrary differences in age, shares personal needs and fears.

Ultimately, his retreat from the woman is not a sexual rejection. To the extent that there may be a sexual overtone to their "friendship," it suggests simply another manifestation of the limitations placed on the human condition by time: a literal embodiment of the yearning for completion that continues on even into physical frailty. As perverse and sad as it may appear to the younger man, readers who are observing both characters with a more objective eye may be able to view the woman's ongoing interest in the relationship itself as far more positive than the younger man's paralysis. It is not until the concluding stanza of the poem that the young man allows himself consciously to ponder his own advancing years, when he too will face the loneliness and regret that seem so important in the life of the woman. Where, he wonders, will his air of superiority have taken him by then?

Like the James novel to which Eliot's title refers, this poem is about incompletion, attenuation, and half-sentences left hanging in midair. It is a poem of "what-ifs": What if these two characters had been the same age? What if he had been more forthcoming, either in rejecting the woman outright or in revealing to her his own fears about mortality and individual isolation? What if, in later life, he were to learn of her death and become plagued by his youthful lack of response to another human being's obvious pain? Like a melancholy musical prelude that is suddenly interrupted, the questions remain.

John C. Hawley

A POSTCARD FROM THE VOLCANO

Author: Wallace Stevens (1879-1955)
Type of poem: Elegy
First published: 1935, in *Ideas of Order*

The Poem

"A Postcard from the Volcano" is a short elegy written in three-line verses of unrhymed tetrameter. The title image captures the theme and perspective of the poem. It suggests a small or compressed message from something big and violent, conveying a loss that is too huge for the tiny means chosen for the communication.

The poem is written from a first-person plural viewpoint. The speaker projects into the future, referring to another generation ("children") looking back at the present one. There appears to be a significant gap between what they will see and what currently exists. One senses the inadequacy of the small "postcard" to express proper feelings of loss, or death.

The first half of the elegy, assuming the perspective of a future generation, expands on what they are missing—it is a loss that comes with the absence of firsthand experience. Hence, the poet employs images that betray action ("foxes"), sensual involvement ("smell" of grapes ripening), and feeling as a way of seeing. Yet all imply death ("breathing frost"), since they will be lost in the future.

At the center of the message there is a significant shift of tense—a transitional sentence connects yet separates the two generations. Now the poet uses images of distance ("spring clouds" beyond a "mansion-house") to illustrate a "literate despair." In abstract terms, he seems to make a judgment on language itself as a "limited" vehicle to convey meaning across time and space. It may be a comment on poetry itself as subject of the elegy.

In the last half, the poem picks up again the subject of the future children. The focus continues to be on language, spoken and written, as a means of knowing ("Children,/ . . . Will speak our speech . . ./ will say"). The present generation appears symbolically as "the mansion" that the children can never completely know or understand any more than people can understand an erupting volcano from afar.

The conclusion of the poem adds another dimension. The children not only see (that is, know, understand, and appreciate) the mansion (the past) in a limited way, but also actually change it in the process of knowing. Here the poet introduces colors (white and gold) associated with the imagination—or, as in Wallace Stevens' "The Man with the Blue Guitar," the imagination's action on the external world. The mansion is "peaked" and "smeared"—in a way, destroyed—indicating a new or double sense of loss.

The final note of "A Postcard from the Volcano," however, indicates more than loss. The poem is also a tribute to the power of the imagination to change things creatively. In the end, the reader sees three worlds. One is the current generation's— "what we felt/ At what we saw." This world, however, is "A tatter of shadows" (an outworn scarecrow) to the second world—the children's. The third is a brighter, "opulent" world that the children have redone in their own image.

Forms and Devices

This poem is in itself a kind of "postcard from a volcano." Stevens uses a short piece of writing (the poem) to convey a wealth of feeling and thought (the volcano) to the reader. As a poet, he senses all the limitations of such an effort, yet he attempts it. He uses the language of poetry—such as colorful images, different kinds of rhythms, repetition, and finally alliteration—to send his message.

The key image used to convey loss is the rural Southern setting—the "mansion-house" over which hang "spring clouds" "Beyond . . . the windy sky." The poet connects two generations, separate and removed. The house is a mansion, suggesting a bygone aristocracy, and it is "shuttered"—protective of its mysterious, inner sanctum. Indeed, it becomes symbolic of a prior tradition, or old ways of thinking and acting—what "we felt/ At what we saw" and "said of it."

Children are active in their way, yet within the rural scene connecting them to tradition. If the older order sees itself as "quick as foxes" (referring to an old Southern sport), the children are now "weaving budded aureoles," not recognizing the foxes whose "bones" they are "picking up." Indeed, there are "walls" between the "look of things" and "what we felt/ At what we saw"—between appearance and reality.

Into the rural scene the poet then injects the changing seasons—images and rhythms which capture the loss that comes with time and are natural to the country. Children pick up the bones in the spring, but what they do not reflect upon is the autumn. That is when the grapes are most ripe, alive, and pungent, although they are also "breathing frost." Life and death are coextensive in the country, something that may be lost on the children, but not on the poet—or on "us," the readers.

To enhance further his rural changing scene, with its traditional ways, the poet employs changing rhythms. The poem starts out briskly, emphasizing vivacious country life, as the enjambment (run-on lines) of the first stanza captures the action of the foxes. Then the pace slows; the sentences are shorter and broken with clauses, as the poet becomes more reflective, even approaching "despair." The fragmentation of the lines also matches the sense of loss—both between generations and in the poet's inability to communicate fully.

As the poem moves toward a conclusion, the tempo again changes, this time reaching a steady but mounting crescendo. The rhythm underpins the new theme of confidence (will) as the children take the words of the older generation (tradition) and re-create them ("speak our speech"). The word "will" is repeated twice, giving new and definite direction to their action. Now "never know" and "seems as if" disappear as the poet generates new hope and confidence with a steadily mounting pace, forceful repetition of key words, and the bright, colorful images—"white" and "gold"—of the last lines.

Themes and Meanings

If in "The Man with the Blue Guitar" Stevens examines the relation between the poet and the present world, in "A Postcard from the Volcano" he adds the dimension of time—the relation between future and present generations. In the former poem, he speaks of a "nothingness" that results when a person imagines the world, as if smell and taste are lost in imagining a baked pie. The latter adds the further gap of time, and therefore a double loss, when children try to experience, or imagine, the life of past generations.

At the center of this poem is a "literate despair"—the inability of words (written or oral) to convey the total (contextual) meaning of another time or place. This gives one cause to mourn, and for this reason the poet, along with the children looking back at the present, "Cries out" in frustration. Yet there is more to this elegy than loss.

The poem is rooted in irony. Death and life are closely connected in this piece. The "bones" of the foxes are juxtaposed with foxes that are "quick" (alive). The dying of the grapes ("breathing frost") is directly associated with life at its height, having made "sharp air sharper by their smell." Autumn can only give birth to spring.

It is the spring that most excites or "springs anew" for Stevens. For the older generation (the "we" of the poem), the "mansion's look," once articulated, "became/ A part of what it is." These people, too, are imaginative. The mansion got its being from their view, perspective, and feelings, not necessarily from any essential being apart from them. Though this will be lost on their children, that loss will generate new life or imaginings. Death and life are coextensive, part of the natural flow of things. Stevens is above all a poet of the present, not of romantic or theistic systems.

The last part of the elegy, therefore, is ironically a celebration of life. The children may "never know" what "we," their forebears, meant when they "speak our speech"; tradition is never fully understood, and that is tragic. Yet, all things considered, it does not really matter. The house may seem "dirty," bathed in "shadows," its walls "blank" (meaningless), the whole thing "gutted." These things imply death, but they also represent a point of view that is necessary to regeneration. Out of this dark, empty shell, the children make the most of their old house (their ancestors) by re-creating it imaginatively.

The poem's final phrases, like "spirit storming," are important, for they suggest vivacious internal action, an ironic contrast to the "gutted" and "blank" house. "Smeared" is also double-edged; it may mean disfigured, but here it suggests something totally covered with life—"the gold of the opulent sun." This is Stevens' final message, that life follows death and that the best instrument for creating the highest type of life is the human mind, as full of potential ("opulent") as the sun itself.

The "volcano," therefore, need not be limited to the past, and this is the final irony. The poem becomes a tribute to the future generations that the poet initially seems to criticize. Ultimately, it is the children who are not afraid to imagine—

to feel deeply, explode verbally, and spew emotion in controlled blasts. That is also the job of the poet in all generations, and to fulfill that end Wallace Stevens sends his postcard.

Thomas Matchie

A PRAYER FOR MY DAUGHTER

Author: William Butler Yeats (1865-1939)
Type of poem: Lyric
First published: 1919; collected in *Michael Robartes and the Dancer*, 1921

The Poem

Anne Butler Yeats, the poet's first child, was born on February 26, 1919, only a month after William Butler Yeats completed "The Second Coming," his apocalyptic vision of violence and anarchy. Four months later, he composed "A Prayer for My Daughter," in which he expanded his belief that a return to tradition and ceremony remained the single means of avoiding the earlier poem's "blood-dimmed tide" now "loosed upon the world." Yeats prays that his daughter may cultivate self-regard and independence and that she may marry into a home that respects ritual and ceremony. Only in these ways, he believes, can she find the innocence and peace to transcend the impending cataclysm of physical and spiritual chaos that he had foreseen in "The Second Coming."

"Things fall apart; the centre cannot hold;/ Mere anarchy is loosed upon the world," he had written in "The Second Coming," prophesying the rise of Fascism in Europe and recalling the bloodshed of both the Russian Revolution (1917) and the Irish Easter Rebellion (1916). These powerful images refer as well to the emotional, psychological, and spiritual disintegration that accompanies international and social crisis. If Yeats's vision of the violent and lawless modern world had prompted "The Second Coming," it was the possibility of transcending such a world that prompted "A Prayer for My Daughter"; the two poems can be read as companion pieces.

It is well acknowledged that the bulk of Yeats's great work drew upon the events of his life. "A Prayer for My Daughter" is one of his most exquisite personal poems, for here Yeats prays that his daughter may shun those very qualities that characterized the woman he loved throughout most of his life. Maud Gonne, whom he had met when he was twenty-two, and whom he wooed unsuccessfully for nearly thirty years, was both an actress and political activist. Yeats not only shared some of Maud's political and professional interests but also, because of his unabating love for her, wrote a body of love (and political) poems about the exaltation and dejection incumbent upon wooing "a proud woman not kindred of his soul" ("A Dialogue of Self and Soul").

Yet if Yeats celebrated Maud's beauty and nationalistic fervor, he also immortalized her unhappiness and single-mindedness—those personal qualities that ultimately destroyed Maud and many others who had similarly fought for Irish freedom in the early years of the twentieth century. It was only in 1917, and at the age of fifty-two, that Yeats turned to another woman, Georgie Hyde-Lees, and married. Georgie was a woman of decidedly less beauty and flair than Maud, but she was also a woman who, as one sees in "A Prayer for My Daughter," was worthy of celebration. Her "charm" finally "made [him] wise," as did her virtuous "glad kindness." Georgie, it would appear, embodied those qualities of generosity and self-sufficiency that he hoped to see perpetuated in their daughter.

The first two of the poem's ten stanzas describe the violence of the outer world. "Once more," he begins, "the storm is howling," and nothing can stop the "screaming" wind that threatens to level nature (the woods and haystacks) and civilization (the roofs and his tower). He listens to the howling "sea-wind scream," along with the storm in the "elms above the flooded streams." He then imagines "in excited reverie" that his daughter has grown to adulthood. The prayer begins in the following, third stanza: "May she be granted . . . ." First, he would have her granted physical beauty — but not Maud's excessive beauty, for this not only makes men "distraught," but, more important, leads its possessor to vanity and indifference to others. Overly beautiful women ignore the cultivation of natural kindness and thus lose the capability of recognizing and retaining true friendship.

Of her various personal virtues, he would have her cultivate ("learn") "courtesy." Yeats suggests that kindness and generosity breed trust and affection between people. Yeats would also wish his daughter a life of stability and deep-rootedness — that is, a quiet life away from noisy thoroughfares — an immersion in a world that is distant from intellectual, political, financial, or emotional struggle. Planted in such an environment, she might cultivate her own personal worth and, most important, her soul. Contact with the soul would give her a sense of self-measure, pleasure, and ultimate peace; she might thus transcend the chaotic external world and achieve a kind of existential triumph. She would realize that the soul's "own sweet will is Heaven's will." Many of Yeats's later poems repeat this notion that self-mastery is humankind's greatest achievement (when the "soul clap[s] its hands and sing[s]/ and louder sing[s]," as he expresses it in "Sailing to Byzantium"). This alone provides a means of transcending external contingency.

Forms and Devices

After first reestablishing the mood of "The Second Coming," Yeats builds a series of images that contrast the virtues he would wish for his daughter and a set of specifics associated with Maud. He sets "custom" and "ceremony" against "hatred" and arrogance," and "radical innocence" against "murderous innocence." So too he opposes the "horn of plenty" and an "old bellows full of angry wind"; the "flourishing hidden tree" and "the wares/ Peddled in the thoroughfares"; the "linnet [firmly planted on] the leaf" and the screaming "sea-wind," along with "flooded stream"; and "magnanimities of sound" and "scowl[s] [from] every windy quarter."

In using the traditional image of the cornucopia, an emblem of bounty or fecundity, he says of Maud Gonne that although he has "seen the loveliest woman born/ Out of the mouth of Plenty's horn," she, like Helen of Troy and Venus, was overly beautiful ("chosen") and vain, and she lacked the necessary qualities to choose an appropriate man to love. ("Helen," although "chosen," also "found life flat and dull," and in preferring Paris to Menelaus, later "had much trouble from a fool.") Similarly, Venus, the "great Queen" who "rose out of the spray," who might also have chosen any man, selected the bandy-legged Vulcan for her husband. The erratic and eccentric behavior of such "chosen" women inevitably leads to their own undoing: "It's certain that fine women eat/ A crazy salad with their meat/ Whereby the Horn of Plenty is undone."

In wishing that his daughter live a life filled with tradition and that she have deep roots, he proceeds to another traditional image, the tree—in fact, the laurel tree, usually associated with victory. Yeats would want his child to entertain only magnanimous and beautiful thoughts, and he would have her "dispense" them "round" like the melodies of the linnet bird. The opposite kind of behavior, one filled with intellectual hatred, neither sustains itself nor soothes the tribulations of the external world. Again expanding images from "The Second Coming," he continues: "Assault and battery of the wind/ Can never tear the linnet from the leaf." Although people might "scowl" at her and "every windy quarter howl," she could remain "happy still."

Finally, Yeats would have a bridegroom bring his daughter to a traditional home, "where all's accustomed [and] ceremonious," rather than to a life in the "thoroughfares," for, as he explains in a rhetorical question, how can one be free to cultivate the virtues of selfhood and soul if she must worry about concrete matters of survival: "How but in custom and in ceremony/ Are innocence and [true] beauty born?"

Having thus far explained his two abstractions ("ceremony" and "custom"), and having established the metaphoric possibilities of the cornucopia and tree, he concludes the poem by connecting his images in a summary statement: "Ceremony's a name for the rich horn,/ And custom for the spreading laurel tree."

Themes and Meanings

"A Prayer for My Daughter" is concerned with surviving the chaos of the modern world—the separation of reason from passion, or the surrender of reason to one's own violence or the anarchy of the external world. The ascendancy of irrationality or animal instinct over reason and culture is vividly expressed in the widely quoted image of "The Second Coming" where "Turning and turning in the widening gyre/ The falcon cannot hear the falconer."

Yeats thus far in his career had celebrated the mighty Irish heroes of both legend and the historical past and present—those courageous men and women who sacrificed themselves for their ideals. Now, however, the poet expresses a certain ambivalence toward those heroes. He understands that in the necessary sacrifice for a cause, one may surrender "heart" ("Too long a sacrifice/ Can make a stone of the heart," he wrote in "Easter 1916"). In fact, any single-minded commitment—to political, social, or intellectual causes, even to beauty—may become obsessive and negate one's more important personal and humane concerns. "A Prayer for My Daughter" proposes the means of rescuing the self, heart, and soul—true beauty—from a world of growing disorder and increasing human misery.

Lois Gordon

PRELUDES

Author: T. S. Eliot (1888-1965)
Type of poem: Lyric
First published: 1915; collected in *Prufrock and Other Observations*, 1917

The Poem

"Preludes" is a lyric poem in free verse, divided into four numbered parts of thirteen, ten, fifteen, and sixteen lines. These sections were written at different times during T. S. Eliot's years of undergraduate and graduate studies at Harvard University and in Europe.

The title is appropriate if it suggests a type of short musical composition in an improvisational or free style. Since some of the images in this very early poem anticipate the barren, rubble-filled atmosphere of *The Waste Land* (1922) and other poems, it could be considered a "prelude" to Eliot's later works. The title may also be viewed as an ironic one, such as "The Love Song of J. Alfred Prufrock" and "Rhapsody on a Windy Night," because it creates expectations about the poem's contents that are not fulfilled. Although the first three sections or preludes move from evening to morning, the fourth returns to the evening hours without suggesting that anything in the poem is a preliminary to a more important or enlightening action or event.

The point of view shifts from an objective description of a city street on a "gusty" winter evening in prelude I to a more emotional first-person response to this scene in the middle of IV. The "you" in preludes I and IV could refer to the reader or to anyone who has walked the city streets. The scene moves from the dirty streets to dingy rooms at the end of II, with the transition introduced by the formal observation, "One thinks." A woman in such a room is addressed as "you" in III, which describes her actions and thoughts as she wakes up. Prelude IV contains three separate parts, beginning with a third-person description of a man's soul in relation to the street scene, followed by a more lyrical, subjective thought expressed in the first person. The closing lines use imperatives and second-person pronouns to direct the listener's or reader's responses, as the poem ends with an uncouth gesture, laughter, and a bleak image of "ancient women" in the "vacant lots" that were introduced in prelude I.

With this shifting and uncertain point of view, it is impossible to define a persona speaking in the poem. One catches glimpses of an inner life—of someone's familiarity with a woman and her thoughts—and discovers some tender feelings in prelude IV. Most of the poem, however, reflects Eliot's efforts to avoid the subjectivity of nineteenth century Romanticism in favor of a more objective technique using concrete images to create a mood and represent emotions.

The images in "Preludes" are more unified than those in most of Eliot's other poems because they all come from the city streets and all suggest the tedium and emptiness of modern urban life. Although this urban scene has been associated with

St. Louis, Boston, and Paris—all cities Eliot knew as a young man—he selected images that would represent any modern city. One of Eliot's earliest poems showing his fascination with the squalid life of the slums, "Preludes" also reveals the influence of the French writer Charles-Louis Philippe. Two of his novels of Parisian life supplied images that Eliot adapted in "Preludes" and "Rhapsody on a Windy Night," including the details of the woman with sordid thoughts and "soiled hands" rising from bed in prelude III.

Forms and Devices

Although the line lengths and meters of "Preludes" are more uniform than those of many of Eliot's other poems, its forms show him experimenting with irregular and fragmented structures. The first two lines begin in iambic tetrameter, like the "Sweeney" poems and several other early poems, but the third line, with only three syllables, creates an abrupt interruption in the rhythm; there is frequent variation from the eight-syllable iambic line through the rest of the poem.

Rhymes are interspersed irregularly in each prelude. They often link parts of related images, such as "wraps" and "scraps," or "stamps" and "lamps" in prelude I, or "shutters" and "gutters" in III. Prelude II has the most regular rhyme scheme (*abcadefdef*), with the three rhymes in the last six lines connecting the two sentences that make up this section and marking the transition from the street to shabby "furnished rooms."

The syntax of the poem also mixes the regular and the irregular; its structures reinforce the perception that modern life is both fragmented and monotonous. The regular syntax and meter of the first two lines are followed by two fragments emphasizing the time—the end of the day. Next begins the first of many sentences and phrases starting with "and," several of them fragments, which contribute to the impression that this poem is an accumulation of images with connections and implications that are not always explained logically. Prelude III is one long sentence that contains sequences of parallel clauses beginning with "you" and "and." These repetitions of ordinary structures create a monotonous effect that emphasizes the tedious routines of daily life as the woman's morning actions are narrated.

Prelude IV contains the most irregular and confusing syntax. Its first section can be read as a series of noun phrases, but the relationships among them are uncertain. Is the soul, besides being "stretched tight across the skies," somehow "trampled by insistent feet" as well as by the fingers, newspapers, and eyes in the following phrases? Does "the conscience" refer to the eyes of the previous phrase, or is it also part of the image of "his soul"?

The relationship between these irregular forms and the images they contain shows Eliot's connections with the English and American Imagist poets in the first two decades of the twentieth century. Imagists used concentrated, concrete images, conveyed in simple and precise language, with no restrictions on the choice of subjects for their poems. As the fragments and the ambiguous syntax of prelude IV demonstrate, they were most concerned with conveying each image directly to the reader as it occurs to the mind. Gertrude Patterson observes that in doing so, the poet "will not take time to 'translate' it into the expository prose sentence with the normal grammatical rules of syntax" (*T. S. Eliot: Poems in the Making*, 1971).

Also influenced by the French Symbolist poets, especially Jules Laforgue, Eliot went beyond Imagism by constructing more elaborate sequences of vivid images that represent intense emotions and moods, demonstrating that physical sensations and thought are inseparable. Throughout "Preludes," the concrete images from the streets and glimpses of human actions, presented in plain language, become increasingly suggestive of some deeper significance; their associations with abstractions such as consciousness and conscience become more prominent in each prelude. The complex and ironic meanings of the poem are embodied in the connotations and symbolism of these images.

Themes and Meanings

Several critics have called preludes I and II Imagist poems. Their concentrated images of wet and dirty streets create a dreary atmosphere that permeates the explorations of mind and soul later in the poem. Prelude I consists entirely of physical sensations and actions, including the vivid image of wasted energy in its only metaphor, "the burnt-out ends of smoky days" (similar to the "butt-ends of my days" found in "The Love Song of J. Alfred Prufrock"). Symbols and themes introduced in I continue throughout this poem and many of Eliot's later works: the passage of time; smoke, wind and rain; the broken, decayed, and discarded objects and grime in the street; domestic smells that become stale by morning; and glimpses of the routine actions of city dwellers.

Isolation and depersonalization are themes represented by the scarce, fragmentary, and anonymous human images in this urban setting. The "lonely cab-horse" waits for someone while rain and wind sweep across vacant lots. "The lighting of the lamps" suggests a human action in nearly deserted streets, but it is expressed only as a fragment floating at the end of prelude I. Feet are the only specific human detail in I, "street" and "feet" being prominently repeated words in all four preludes. "Insistent feet" trampling muddy streets represent the crowds beginning and ending the "masquerades" of their work day, while the hands "raising dingy shades/ In a thousand furnished rooms" are reminders of the cramped and anonymous masses in the city.

The passive woman in prelude III is shown physically only through gestures involving her artificially curled hair and her soiled hands and feet. In IV, fingers stuffing pipes, eyes "assured of certain certainties," and a mouth engaged in derisive gestures mock human ignorance and futility. The brief moment of compassion inspired by these fragmentary images takes the vague form of "some infinitely gentle/ Infinitely suffering thing" rather than a definite vision of human romance or tragedy.

The images of "yellow soles" at the end of III and "his soul" in the first line of IV provide an ironic juxtaposition of the sordid and the spiritual, an apparent movement from the shabby and sensual to the profound. Yet since in Eliot's view no experience could be separated from the physical, the thoughts and soul of a woman or a man in this setting are "constituted" in relation to images from the street. Their "vision" of the world is limited to understanding the life around them, where morning light brings only the resumption of meaningless routines until night "blackens" the street again. The "I" who yearns for deeper significance also fears, like Prufrock, that his gentler feelings will be ridiculed by his listeners, so he ends by reducing the revolving of worlds to the image of "ancient women/ Gathering fuel in vacant lots."

Tina Hanlon